P9-DCH-515
Vol. 2 of 2

THE WORLD OF PSYCHOLOGY

THE WORLD
OF
PSYCHOLOGY

Edited with Introductions by

G. B. LEVITAS

II

IDENTITY AND MOTIVATION

George Braziller New York

Published simultaneously in Canada by Ambassador Books, Ltd., Toronto

For information, address the publisher,
George Braziller, Inc.
One Park Avenue, New York 10016

Library of Congress Catalog Card Number:
62-18229

First Printing March, 1963
Second Printing September, 1963
Third Printing April, 1964
Fourth Printing May, 1965

Printed in the United States of America

CONTENTS

VOLUME II

BOOK THREE IDENTITY AND MOTIVATION

I. The Pawn of Fate 3

PLATO—*Timaeus* 5
RENÉ DESCARTES—*Discourse on Method* 8
IVAN PAVLOV—*Conditioned Reflexes* 19
SIGMUND FREUD—*Determinism—Chance—and Superstitious Beliefs* 32
EDMUND BERGLER and GÉZA RÓHEIM—*Psychology of Time Perception* 62
VOLTAIRE—*Candide* 75
OLIVER GOLDSMITH—*Asem: An Eastern Tale* 85
FRANZ KAFKA—*The Hunter Gracchus* 90
FRANZ KAFKA—*A Little Fable* 95
EUGENE ZAMIATIN—*We* 95
W. B. YEATS—*Sailing to Byzantium* 123

II. The Master of Fate 124

CICERO—*The Moral Duties of Mankind* 126
G. W. LEIBNIZ—*New Essays Concerning Human Understanding* 128
FRIEDRICH NIETZSCHE—*Beyond Good and Evil* 132
MAURICE VAISBERG—*An Existential View of a Man Suffering from Chronic Schizophrenia* 141
JEAN-PAUL SARTRE—*Intimacy* 154
NATHANIEL HAWTHORNE—*The Birthmark* 179

III. The Power-Seeker and the Security-Seeker 194

Alfred Adler—*Individual Psychology* 195
Martha Wolfenstein—*Two Types of Jewish Mothers* 207
Aldous Huxley—*The Claxtons* 225
Rudyard Kipling—*The Man Who Would Be King* 248

IV. The Guilt-Ridden 277

St. Augustine—*The Confessions* 278
Theodor Reik—*Myth and Guilt* 284
Ernest Jones—*The Death of Hamlet's Father* 298
Philip Roth—*Eli, the Fanatic* 302

V. The Alienated 335

Margaret Mead—*Art and Reality* 337
Mason Griff—*The Commercial Artist* 339
Dollard, Doob, Miller, Mowrer, and Sears—*Criminality* 364
Jean-Paul Sartre—*Childhood of a Leader* 390
Allen Ginsberg—*Howl (for Carl Solomon)* 407
Robert Louis Stevenson—*A Lodging for the Night* 414
Henry James—*The Figure in the Carpet* 430

VI. The Religious Man 461

St. Augustine—*The Vision at Ostia* 462
St. John of the Cross—*Advice to the Religious* 464
C. G. Jung—*Psychology and Religion* 469
Miguel de Unamuno—*Saint Manuel Bueno, Martyr* 493

VII. The Whole Man 522

John Stuart Mill—*Individuality* 523
A. H. Maslow—*Self-Actualizing People* 527
Ralph Waldo Emerson—*Ode Inscribed to W. H. Channing* 556
Robert Browning—*Rabbi Ben Ezra* 559
C. E. Montague—*Action* 564

BOOK THREE

IDENTITY AND MOTIVATION

The manner in which man identifies himself as a person and develops his personality is as much a product of his basic drives or motives, and of the incorporation of the mores of his society, as it is a result of his perceptual capabilities and his emotional makeup. Whether he considers himself to be driven by unknown forces, or rationally capable of overcoming them; whether he is oriented toward security or freedom; driven by guilt or the need for power, man can be seen, finally, not as an isolated phenomenon but as a carrier of culture and an innovator of culture; a group product and still, very much, an individual.

I

THE PAWN OF FATE

Belief in the predetermination of life has a long history. A constellation of gods set an orderly pattern for the Greeks; Yahweh ruled the ancient Hebrews. Today the idea of predetermination is conditioned by religious, mechanical, psychological or nihilistic forces. We have moved from platonic fatalism through the mechanism of Descartes, to the Pavlovian nightmare of the conditioned reflex, and the Freudian specter of psychic determination.

Kafka's tales, in which life and death are subject to the caprice of chance provide a reflection of the Schopenhauerian-Freudian concept of will and instinct. Both Schopenhauer and Freud viewed man as psychically determined. Schopenhauer called the life force "the will." Freud named the same life force "instinct." Both of them recognized in addition a striving toward death. Man thus was conceived as within time and subject to will or instinct; or outside time as an ascetic or a corpse. Indeed, Kafka's resolution of the conflict between life and death is to present us with a living corpse—a man who is in time, and yet out of it. Yeats's solution lies in art. For art represents "life in death and death in life." Art embodies the sensual imagery of the will in an unchanging, eternal form. Obliteration of the ego is possible through the distancing of art—and it is both welcomed and feared by Yeats in "Sailing to Byzantium."

Implied in both these fictional works is a concept of time as explained by Róheim and Bergler in which the search for immortality or timelessness may be equated with the search for the meaning of life and with the attempt to re-create for ourselves the world of infancy, the time of endless pleasure and gratification, the time in which we had no sense of time, no sense of self, no sense of ego. Timelessness may therefore be seen to comprise death as well as immortality and involves us in a paradoxical search for death and life in the same place.

Less complex than these—but equally frightening—are the

rationalist theories of fatalism. Voltaire's "Candide," Goldsmith's "Asem," Zamiatin's "We," all exhibit an understructure of belief in man as a psychically determined animal. The Pavlovian conception of man as a series of conditioned reflexes allows rationalism to win out over instinct—but victorious rationalism brings on the same kind of annihilation of the personality. The nightmare of "We" is thus more than an extrapolation of ultimate societal forms: it is the prophecy of death to the personality as we know it —but death achieved through reason rather than instinct. Like "Brave New World" and "1984," but predating both of these, "We" is the story of a cold, loveless, scientifically determined society. It is the story of man as machine, man without love, without hope, without time and ultimately, without ego.

PLATO / Timaeus*

THERE IS a corresponding enquiry concerning the mode of treatment by which the mind and the body are to be preserved, about which it is meet and right that I should say a word in turn, for it is more our duty to speak of the good than of the evil. Everything that is good is fair, and the fair is not without proportion, and the animal which is to be fair must have due proportion. Now we perceive lesser symmetries or proportions and reason about them, but of the highest and greatest we take no heed; for there is no proportion or disproportion more productive of health and disease, and virtue and vice, than that between soul and body. This however we do not perceive, nor do we reflect that when a weak or small frame is the vehicle of a great and mighty soul, or conversely, when a little soul is encased in a large body, then the whole animal is not fair, for it lacks the most important of all symmetries; but the due proportion of mind and body is the fairest and loveliest of all sights to him who has the seeing eye. Just as a body which has a leg too long, or which is unsymmetrical in some other respect, is an unpleasant sight, and also, when doing its share of work, is much distressed and makes convulsive efforts, and often stumbles through awkwardness, and is the cause of infinite evil to its own self—in like manner we should conceive of the double nature which we call the living being; and when in this compound there is an impassioned soul more powerful than the body, that soul, I say, convulses and fills with disorders the whole inner nature of man; and when eager in the pursuit of some sort of learning or study, causes wasting; or again, when teaching or disputing in private or in public, and strifes and controversies arise, inflames and dissolves the composite frame of man and introduces rheums; and the nature of this phenomenon is not understood by most professors of medicine, who ascribe it to the opposite of the real cause. And once more, when a body large and too strong for the soul is united to a small and weak intelligence, then inasmuch as there are two desires natural to man,—one of food for the sake of the body, and one of wisdom for the sake of the diviner part of us—then, I say, the motions of the stronger, getting the better and increasing their own power, but making the soul dull, and stupid, and forgetful, engender ignorance, which is the greatest of diseases. There is one protection against both kinds of disproportion:—that we should not move the body without the soul or the soul without the body, and thus they will be on their guard against

* Plato, *Timaeus* 87-90 (tr. Jowett).

each other, and be healthy and well balanced. And therefore the mathematician or any one else whose thoughts are much absorbed in some intellectual pursuit, must allow his body also to have due exercise, and practise gymnastic; and he who is careful to fashion the body, should in turn impart to the soul its proper motions, and should cultivate music and all philosophy, if he would deserve to be called truly fair and truly good. And the separate parts should be treated in the same manner, in imitation of the pattern of the universe; for as the body is heated and also cooled within by the elements which enter into it, and is again dried up and moistened by external things, and experiences these and like affections from both kinds of motions, the result is that the body if given up to motion when in a state of quiescence is overmastered and perishes; but if any one, in imitation of that which we call the foster-mother and nurse of the universe, will not allow the body ever to be inactive, but is always producing motions and agitations through its whole extent, which form the natural defence against other motions both internal and external, and by moderate exercise reduces to order according to their affinities the particles and affections which are wandering about the body, as we have already said when speaking of the universe, he will not allow enemy placed by the side of enemy to stir up wars and disorders in the body, but he will place friend by the side of friend, so as to create health. Now of all motions that is the best which is produced in a thing by itself, for it is most akin to the motion of thought and of the universe; but that motion which is caused by others is not so good, and worst of all is that which moves the body, when at rest, in parts only and by some external agency. Wherefore of all modes of purifying and re-uniting the body the best is gymnastic; the next best is a surging motion, as in sailing or any other mode of conveyance which is not fatiguing; the third sort of motion may be of use in a case of extreme necessity, but in any other will be adopted by no man of sense: I mean the purgative treatment of physicians; for diseases unless they are very dangerous should not be irritated by medicines, since every form of disease is in a manner akin to the living being, whose complex frame has an appointed term of life. Nor not the whole race only, but each individual—barring inevitable accidents—comes into the world having a fixed span, and the triangles in us are originally framed with power to last for a certain time, beyond which no man can prolong his life. And this holds also of the constitution of diseases; if any one regardless of the appointed time tries to subdue them by medicine, he only aggravates and multiplies them. Wherefore we ought always to manage them by regimen, as far as man can spare the time, and not provoke a disagreeable enemy by medicines.

Enough of the composite animal, and of the body which is a part of him, and of the manner in which a man may train and be trained by himself so as to live most according to reason: and we must above and before all provide that the element which is to train him shall be the fairest and best adapted to that purpose. A minute discussion of this subject would be a serious task; but if, as before, I am to give only an outline, the subject may not unfitly be summed up as follows.

I have often remarked that there are three kinds of soul located within us, having each of them motions, and I must now repeat in the fewest words possible, that one part, if remaining inactive and ceasing from its natural motion, must necessarily become very weak, but that which is trained and exercised, very strong. Wherefore we should take care that the movements of the different parts of the soul should be in due proportion.

And we should consider that God gave the sovereign part of the human soul to be the divinity of each one, being that part which, as we say, dwells at the top of the body, and inasmuch as we are a plant not of an earthly but of a heavenly growth, raises us from earth to our kindred who are in heaven. And in this we say truly; for the divine power suspended the head and root of us from that place where the generation of the soul first began and thus made the whole body upright. When a man is always occupied with the cravings of desire and ambition, and is eagerly striving to satisfy them, all his thoughts must be mortal, and, as far as it is possible altogether to become such, he must be mortal every whit, because he has cherished his mortal part. But he who has been earnest in the love of knowledge and of true wisdom, and has exercised his intellect more than any other part of him, must have thoughts immortal and divine, if he attain truth, and in so far as human nature is capable of sharing in immortality, he must altogether be immortal; and since he is ever cherishing the divine power, and has the divinity within him in perfect order, he will be perfectly happy. Now there is only one way of taking care of things, and this is to give to each the food and motion which are natural to it; and the motions which are naturally akin to the divine principle within us are the thoughts and revolutions of the universe. These each man should follow, and correct the courses of the head which were corrupted at our birth, and by learning the harmonies and revolutions of the universe, should assimilate the thinking being to the thought, renewing his original nature, and having assimilated them should attain to that perfect life which the gods have set before mankind, both for the present and the future.

RENÉ DESCARTES/Discourse on Method

I WOULD here willingly have proceeded to exhibit the whole chain of truths which I deduced from these primary; but as with a view to this it would have been necessary now to treat of many questions in dispute among the learned, with whom I do not wish to be embroiled, I believe that it will be better for me to refrain from this exposition, and only mention in general what these truths are, that the more judicious may be able to determine whether a more special account of them would conduce to the public advantage. I have ever remained firm in my original resolution to suppose no other principle than that of which I have recently availed myself in demonstrating the existence of God and of the soul, and to accept as true nothing that did not appear to me more clear and certain than the demonstrations of the geometers had formerly appeared; and yet I venture to state that not only have I found means to satisfy myself in a short time on all the principal difficulties which are usually treated of in Philosophy, but I have also observed in all that exists or takes place in the world: and farther, by considering the concatenation of these laws, it appears to me that I have discovered many truths more useful and more important than all I had before learned, or even had expected to learn.

But because I have essayed to expound the chief of these discoveries in a Treatise which certain considerations prevent me from publishing, I cannot make the results known more conveniently than by here giving a summary of the contents of this Treatise. It was my design to comprise in it all that, before I set myself to write it, I thought I knew of the nature of material objects. But like the painters who, finding themselves unable to represent equally well on a plain surface all the different faces of a solid body, select one of the chief, on which alone they make the light fall, and throwing the rest into the shade, allow them to appear only in so far as they can be seen while looking at the principal one; so, fearing lest I should not be able to comprise in my discourse all that was in my mind, I resolved to expound singly, though at considerable length, my opinions regarding light; then to take the opportunity of adding something on the sun and the fixed stars, since light almost wholly proceeds from them; on the heavens, since they transmit it; on the planets, comets, and earth, since they reflect it; and particularly on all the bodies that are upon the earth, since they are either coloured, or transparent, or luminous; and finally on man, since he is the spectator of these objects. Further, to enable me to cast this variety of subjects somewhat into the shade, and to express my judgment regarding them with greater freedom, without being necessitated to adopt or refute the opinions of the learned, I resolved to leave all the people here to their disputes, and to speak only of what would happen in a new world if God were now to create somewhere in the imaginary spaces matter sufficient to compose one, and were to agitate variously and confusedly the different parts of this matter, so that there resulted a chaos as disordered as the poets ever feigned, and after that did nothing more than lend his ordinary concurrence to nature, and allow her to act in accordance with the laws which he had established. On this supposition, I, in the first place described this matter, and essayed to represent it in such a manner that to my mind there can be nothing clearer and more intelligible, except what has been recently said regarding God and the soul; for I even expressly supposed that it possessed none of those forms or qualities which are so debated in the Schools, nor in general anything the knowledge of which is not so natural to our minds that no one can so much as imagine himself ignorant of it. Besides, I have pointed out what are the laws of nature; and, with no other principle upon which to found my reasonings except the infinite perfection of God, I endeavoured to demonstrate all those about which there could be any room for doubt, and to prove that they are such, that even if God had created more worlds, there could have been none in which these laws were not observed. Thereafter, I showed how the greatest part of the matter of this chaos must, in accordance with these laws, dispose and arrange itself in such a way as to present the appearance of heavens; how in the meantime some of its parts must compose an earth and some planets and comets, and others a sun and fixed stars. And, making a digression at this stage on the subject of light, I expounded at considerable length what the nature of that light must be which is found in the sun and the stars, and how thence in an instant of time it traverses the immense spaces of the heavens, and how from the planets and comets it is reflected towards the earth. To this I likewise added much respecting the substance, the situation, the motions, and all the different qualities of these heavens and stars; so that I thought I had said enough respecting them to show that there is nothing observable in the heavens or stars of our system that must not, or at least may not, appear precisely alike in those of the system which I described. I came next to speak of the earth in particular, and to show how, even though I had expressly supposed that God had given no weight to the matter of which it is composed, this should not prevent all its parts from tending exactly to its centre; how with water and air on its surface, the disposition of the heavens and heavenly bodies, more especially of the moon, must cause a flow and ebb, like in all its circumstances to that observed in our seas, as also a certain current both of water and air from east to west, such as is likewise observed between the tropics; how the mountains, seas, fountains, and rivers might naturally be formed in it, and the metals produced in the mines, and the plants, grow in the fields; and in general, how all the bodies which are commonly denominated mixed or composite might be generated: and, among other things in the discoveries alluded to, inasmuch as besides the stars, I know nothing except fire which produces light, I spared no pains to set forth all that pertains to its nature,—the manner of its production and support, and to explain how heat is sometimes found without light, and light without heat; to show how it can induce various colours upon different bodies and other diverse qualities; how it reduces some to a liquid state and hardens others; how it can consume almost all bodies, or convert them into ashes and smoke; and finally, how from these ashes, by the mere intensity of its action, it forms glass: for as this transmutation of ashes into glass appeared to me as wonderful as any other in nature, I took a special pleasure in describing it.

I was not, however, disposed, from these circumstances, to conclude that this world had been created in the manner I described; for it is much more likely that God made it at the first such as it was to be. But this is certain, and an opinion commonly received among theologians, that the action by which he now sustains it is the same with that by which he originally created it; so that even although he had from the beginning given it no other form than that of chaos, provided only he had established certain laws of nature, and had lent it his concurrence to enable it to act as it is wont to do, it may be believed, without discredit to the miracle of creation, that, in this way alone, things purely material might, in course of time, have become such as we observe them at present; and their nature is much more easily conceived when they are beheld coming in this manner gradually into existence, than when they are only considered as produced at once in a finished and perfect state.

From the description of inanimate bodies and plants, I passed to animals, and particularly to man. But since I had not as yet sufficient knowledge to enable me to treat of these in the same manner as of the rest, that is to say, by deducing effects from their causes, and by showing from what elements and in what manner Nature must produce them, I remained satisfied with the supposition that God formed the body of man wholly like to one of ours, as well in the external shape of the members as in the internal conformation of the organs, of the same matter with that I had described, and at first placed in it no Rational Soul, nor any other principle, in room of the Vegetative or Sensitive Soul, beyond kindling in the heart one of those fires without light, such as I had already described, and which I thought was not different from the heat in hay that has been heaped together before it is dry, or that which causes fermentation in new wines before they are run clear of the fruit. For, when I examined the kind of functions which might, as consequences of this supposition, exist in this body, I found precisely all those which may exist in us independently of all power of thinking, and consequently without being in any measure owing to the soul; in other words, to that part of us which is distinct from the body, and of which it has been said above that the nature distinctively consists in thinking,—functions in which the animals void of Reason may be said wholly to resemble us; but among which I could not discover any of those that, as dependent on thought alone, belong to us as men, while, on the other hand, I did afterwards discover these as soon as I supposed God to have created a Rational Soul, and to have annexed it to this body in a particular manner which I described.

But, in order to show how I there handled this matter, I mean here to give the explication of the motion of the heart and arteries, which, as the first and most general motion observed in animals, will afford the means of readily determining what should be thought of all the rest. And that there may be less difficulty in understanding what I am about to say on this subject, I advise those who are not versed in Anatomy, before they commence the perusal of these observations, to take the trouble of getting dissected in their presence the heart of some large animal possessed of lungs, (for this is throughout sufficiently like the human), and to have shewn to them its two ventricles or cavities: in the first place, that in the right side, with which correspond two very ample tubes, viz., the hollow vein, *(vena cava,)* which is the principal receptacle of the blood, and the trunk of the tree, as it were, of which all the other veins in the body are branches; and the arterial vein, *(vena arteriosa,)* inappropriately so denominated, since it is in truth only an artery, which, taking its rise in the heart, is divided, after passing out from it, into many branches which presently disperse themselves all over the lungs; in the second place, the cavity in the left side, with which correspond in the same manner two canals in size equal to or larger than the preceding, viz., the venous artery, *(arteria venosa,)* likewise inappropriately thus designated, because it is simply a vein which comes from the lungs, where it is divided into many branches, interlaced with those of the arterial vein, and those of the tube called the windpipe, through which the air we breathe enters; and the great artery which, issuing from the heart, sends its branches all over the body. I should wish also that such persons were carefully shewn the eleven pellicles which, like so many small valves, open and shut the four orifices that are in these two cavities, viz., three at the entrance of the hollow vein, where they are disposed in such a maner as by no means to prevent the blood which it contains from flowing into the right ventricle of the heart, and yet exactly to prevent its flowing out; three at the entrance to the arterial vein, which, arranged in a manner exactly the opposite of the former, readily permit the blood contained in this cavity to pass into the lungs from returning to this cavity; and, in like manner, two others at the mouth of the venous artery, which allow the blood from the lungs to flow into the left cavity of the heart, but preclude its return; and three at the mouth of the great artery, which suffer the blood to flow from the heart, but prevent its reflux. Nor do we need to seek any other reason for the number of these pellicles beyond this that the orifice of the venous artery being of an oval shape from the nature of its situation, can be adequately closed with two, whereas the others being round are more conveniently closed with three. Besides, I wish such persons to observe that the grand artery and the arterial vein are of much harder and firmer texture than the venous artery and the hollow vein; and that the two last expand before entering the heart, and there form, as it were, two pouches denominated the auricles of the heart, which are composed of a substance similar to that of the heart itself; and that there is always more warmth in the heart than in any other part of the body; and, finally, that this heat is capable of causing any drop of blood that passes into the cavities rapidly to expand and dilate, just as all liquors do when allowed to fall drop by drop into a highly heated vessel.

For, after these things, it is not necessary for me to say anything more with a view to explain the motion of the heart, except that when its cavities are not full of blood, into these the blood of necessity flows,—from the hollow vein into the right, and from the venous artery into the left; because these two vessels are always full of blood, and their orifices, which are turned towards the heart, cannot then be closed. But as soon as two drops of blood have thus passed, one into each of the cavities, these drops which cannot but be very large, because the orifices through which they pass are wide, and the vessels from which they come full of blood, are immediately rarefied, and dilated by the heat they meet with. In this way they cause the whole heart to expand, and at the same time press home and shut the five small valves that are at the entrances of the two vessels from which they flow, and thus prevent any more blood from coming down into the heart, and becoming more and more rarefied, they push open the six small valves that are in the orifices of the other two vessels, through which they pass out, causing in this way all the branches of the arterial vein and of the grand artery to expand almost simultaneously with the heart—which immediately thereafter begins to contract, as do also the arteries, because the blood that has entered them has cooled, and the six small valves close, and the five of the hollow vein and of the venous artery open anew and allow a passage to other two drops of blood, which cause the heart and the arteries again to expand as before. And, because the blood which thus enters into the heart passes through these two pouches called auricles, it hence happens that their motion is the contrary of that of the heart, and that when it expands they contract. But lest those who are ignorant of the force of mathematical demonstrations, and who are not accustomed to distinguish true reasons from mere verisimilitudes, should venture, without examination, to deny what has been said, I wish it to be considered that the motion which I have now explained follows as necessarily from the very arrangement of the parts, which may be observed in the heart by the eye alone, and from the heat which may be felt with the fingers, and from the nature of the blood as learned from experience, as does the motion of a clock from the power, the situation, and shape of its counterweights and wheels.

But if it be asked how it happens that the blood in the veins, flowing in this way continually into the heart, is not exhausted, and why the arteries do not become too full, since all the blood which passes through the heart flows into them, I need only mention in reply what has been written by a physician[1] of England, who has the honour of having broken the ice on this subject, and of having been the first to teach that there are many small passages at the extremities of the arteries, through which the blood received by them from the heart passes into the small branches of the veins, whence it again returns to the heart; so that its course amounts precisely to a perpetual circulation. Of this we have abundant proof in the ordinary experience of surgeons, who by binding the arm with a tie of moderate straitness above the part where they open the vein, cause the blood to flow more copiously than it would have done without any ligature; whereas quite the contrary would happen were they to bind it below; that is, between the hand and the opening, or were to make the ligature above the opening very tight. For it is manifest that the tie, moderately straitened, while adequate to hinder the blood already in the arm from returning towards the heart by the veins, cannot on that account prevent new blood from coming forward through the

[1] Harvey—Lat. Tr.

arteries, because these are situated below the veins, and their coverings, from their greater consistency, are more difficult to compress; and also that the blood which comes from the heart tends to pass through them to the hand with greater force than it does to return from the hand to the heart through the veins. And since the latter current escapes from the arm by the opening made in one of the veins, there must of necessity be certain passages below the ligature, that is, towards the extremities of the arm, through which it can come thither from the arteries. This physician likewise abundantly establishes what he has advanced respecting the motion of the blood, from the existence of certain pellicles, so disposed in various places along the course of the veins, in the manner of small valves, as not to permit the blood to pass from the middle of the body towards the extremities, but only to return from the extremities to the heart; and farther, from experience which shows that all the blood which is in the body may flow out of it in a very short time through a single artery that has been cut, even although this had been closely tied in the immediate neighbourhood of the heart, and cut between the heart and the ligature, so as to prevent the supposition that the blood flowing out of it could come from any other quarter than the heart.

But there are many other circumstances which evince that what I have alleged is the true cause of the motion of the blood: thus, in the first place, the difference that is observed between the blood which flows from the veins, and that from the arteries, can only arise from this, that being rarefied, and, as it were, distilled by passing through the heart, it is thinner, and more vivid, and warmer immediately after leaving the heart, in other words, when in the arteries, than it was a short time before passing into either, in other words, when it was in the veins; and if attention be given, it will be found that this difference is very marked only in the neighbourhood of the heart; and is not so evident in parts more remote from it. In the next place, the consistency of the coats of which the arterial vein and the great artery are composed, sufficiently shows that the blood is impelled against them with more force than against the veins. And why should the left cavity of the heart and the great artery be wider and larger than the right cavity and the arterial vein, were it not that the blood of the venous artery, having only been in the lungs after it has passed through the heart, is thinner and rarefies more readily, and in a higher degree, than the blood which proceeds immediately from the hollow vein? And what can physicians conjecture from feeling the pulse unless they know that according as the blood changes its nature it can be rarefied by the warmth of the heart, in a higher or lower degree, and more or less quickly than before? And if it be inquired how this heat is communicated to the other members, must it not be admitted that this is effected by means of the blood, which, passing through the heart, is there heated anew, and thence diffused over all the body? Whence it happens, that if the blood be withdrawn from any part, the heat is likewise withdrawn by the same means; and although the heart were as hot as glowing iron, it would not be capable of warming the feet and hands as at present, unless it continually sent thither new blood. We likewise perceive from this, that the true use of respiration is to bring sufficient fresh air into the lungs, to cause the blood which flows into them from the right ventricle of the heart, where it has been rarefied and, as it were, changed into vapours, to become thick, and to convert it anew into blood, before it flows into the left cavity, without which process it would be unfit for the nourishment of the fire that is there. This receives confirmation from the circumstance, that it is observed of animals destitute of lungs that they have also but one cavity in the heart, and that in children who cannot use them while in the womb, there is a hole through which the blood flows from the hollow vein into the left cavity of the heart, and a tube through which it passes from the arterial vein into the grand artery without passing through the lung. In the next place, how could digestion be carried on in the stomach unless the heart communicated heat to it through the arteries, and along with this certain of the more fluid parts of the blood, which assist in the dissolution of the food that has been taken in? Is not also the operation which converts the juice of food into blood easily comprehended, when it is considered that it is distilled by passing and repassing through the heart perhaps more than one or two hundred times in a day? And what more need be adduced to explain nutrition, and the production of the different humours of the body, beyond saying, that the force with which the blood, in being rarefied, passes from the heart towards the extremities of the arteries, causes certain of its parts to remain in the members at which they arrive, and there occupy the place of some others expelled by them; and that according to the situation, shape, or smallness of the pores with which they meet, some rather than others flow into certain parts, in the same way that some sieves are observed to act, which, by being variously perforated, serve to separate different species of grain? And, in the last place, what above all is here worthy of observation, is the generation of the animal spirits, which are like a very subtle wind or rather a very pure and vivid flame which, continually ascending in great abundance from the heart to the brain, thence penetrates through the nerves into the muscles, and gives motion to all the members; so that to account for other parts of the blood which, as most agitated and penetrating, are the fittest to compose these spirits, proceeding towards the brain, it is not necessary to suppose any other cause, than simply, that the arteries which carry them thither proceed from the heart in the most direct lines, and that, according to the rules of Mechanics, which are the same with those of Nature, when many objects tend at once to the same point where there is not sufficient room for all, (as is the case with the parts of the blood which flow forth from the left cavity of the heart and tend towards the brain,) the weaker and less agitated parts must necessarily be driven aside from that point by the stronger which alone in this way reach it.

I had expounded all these matters with sufficient minuteness in the Treatise which I formerly thought of publishing. And after these, I had shewn what must be the fabric of the nerves and the muscles of the human body to give the animal spirits contained in it the power to move the members, as when we see heads shortly after they have been struck off still move and bite the earth, although no longer animated; what changes must take place in the brain to produce walking, sleep, and dreams, how light, sounds, odours, tastes, heat, and all the other qualities of external objects impress it with different ideas by means of the senses; how hunger, thirst, and the other internal affections can likewise impress upon it divers ideas; what must be understood by the common sense (*senus communis*) in which these ideas are received, by the memory which retains them, by the fantasy which can change them in various ways, and out of them compose new ideas, and which, by the same means, distributing the animal spirits through the muscles, can cause the members of such a body to move in as many different ways, and in a manner as suited, whether to the objects that are presented to its senses or to its internal affections, as can take place in our own case apart from the guidance of the will. Nor will this appear at all strange to those who are acquainted with the variety of movements performed by the different automata, or moving machines fabricated by human industry, and that with help of but few pieces compared with the great multitude of bones, muscles, nerves, arteries, veins, and other parts that are found in the body of each animal. Such persons will look upon this body as a machine made by the hands of God, which is incomparably better arranged, and adequate to movements more admirable than is any machine of human invention. And here I specially stayed to show that, were there such machines exactly resembling in organs and outward form an ape or any other irrational animal, we could have no means of knowing that they were in any respects of a different nature from these animals; but if there were machines bearing the image of our bodies, and capable of imitating our actions as far as it is morally possible, there would still remain two most certain tests whereby to know that they were not therefore really men. Of these the first is that they could never use words or other signs arranged in such a manner as is competent to us in order to declare our thoughts to others; for we may easily conceive a machine to be so constructed that it emits vocables, and even that it emits some correspondent to the action upon it of external objects which cause a change in its organs; for example, if touched in a particular place it may demand what we wish to say to it; if in another it may cry out that it is hurt, and such like; but not that it should arrange them variously so as appositely to reply to what is said in its presence, as men of the lowest grade of intellect can do. The second test is, that although such machines might execute many things with equal or perhaps greater perfection than any of us, they would, without doubt, fail in certain others from which it could be discovered that they did not act from knowledge, but solely from the disposition of their organs: for while Reason is an universal instrument that is alike available on every occasion, these organs, on the contrary, need a particular arrangement for each particular action; whence it must be morally impossible that there should exist in any machine a diversity of organs sufficient to enable it to act in all the occurrences of life, in the way in which our reason enables us to act. Again, by means of these two tests we may likewise know the difference between men and brutes. For it is highly deserving of remark, that there are no men so dull and stupid, not even idiots, as to be incapable of joining together different words, and thereby constructing a declaration by which to make their thoughts understood; and that on the other hand, there is no other animal, however perfect or happily circumstanced, which can do the like. Nor does this inability arise from want of organs: for we observe that magpies and parrots can utter words like ourselves, and are yet unable to speak as we do, that is, so as to show that they understand what they say; in place of which men born deaf and dumb, and thus not less, but rather more than the brutes, destitute of the organs which others use in speaking, are in the habit of spontaneously inventing certain signs by which they discover their thoughts to those who, being usually in their company, have leisure to learn their language. And this proves not only that the brutes have less Reason than man, but that they have none at all: for we see that very little is required to enable a person to speak; and since a certain inequality of capacity is observable among animals of the same species, as well as among men, and since some are more capable of being instructed than others, it is incredible that the most perfect ape or parrot of its species, should not in this be equal to the most stupid infant of its kind, or at least to one that was crack-brained, unless the souls of brutes were of a nature wholly different from ours. And we ought not to confound speech with the natural movements which indicate the passions, and can be imitated by machines as well as manifested by animals; nor must it be thought with certain of the ancients, that the brutes speak, although we do not understand their language. For if such were the case, since they are endowed with many organs analogous to ours, they could as easily communicate their thoughts to us as to their fellows. It is also very worthy of remark that, though there are many animals which manifest more industry than we in certain of their actions, the same animals are yet observed to show none at all in many others: so that the circumstance that they do better than we does not prove that they are endowed with mind, for it would thence follow that they possessed greater Reason than any of us, and could surpass us in all things; on the contrary, it rather proves that they are destitute of Reason, and that it is Nature which acts in them according to the disposition of their organs: thus it is seen, that a clock composed only of wheels and weights can number the hours and measure time more exactly than we with all our skill.

I had after this described the Reasonable Soul, and shewn that it could by no means be educed from the power of matter, as the other things of which I had spoken, but that it must be expressly created; and that it is not sufficient that it be lodged in the human body exactly like a pilot in a ship, unless perhaps to move its members, but that it is necessary for it to be joined and united more closely to the body, in order to have sensations and appetites similar to ours, and thus constitute a real man. I have entered, in conclusion, upon the subject of the soul at considerable length, because it is of the greatest moment: for after the error of those who deny the existence of God, an error which I think I have already sufficiently refuted, there is none that is more powerful in leading feeble minds astray from the straight path of virtue than the supposition that the soul of the brutes is of the same nature with our own; and consequently that after this life we have nothing to hope for or fear, more than flies and ants; in place of which, when we know how far they differ we must better comprehend the reasons which establish that the soul is of a nature wholly independent of the body, and that consequently it is not liable to die with the latter; and finally, because no other causes are observed capable of destroying it, we are naturally led thence to judge that it is immortal.

IVAN PAVLOV / Conditioned Reflexes

The development of the objective method in investigating the physiological activities of the cerebral hemispheres.

THE CEREBRAL hemispheres stand out as the crowning achievement in the nervous development of the animal kingdom. These structures in the higher animals are of considerable dimensions and exceedingly complex, being made up in man of millions upon millions of cells—centres or foci of nervous activity—varying in size, shape and arrangement, and connected with each other by countless branchings from their individual processes. Such complexity of structure naturally suggests a like complexity of function, which in fact is obvious in the higher animal and in man. Consider the dog, which has been for so many countless ages the servant of man. Think how he may be trained to perform various duties, watching, hunting, etc. We know that this complex behaviour of the animal, undoubtedly involving the highest nervous activity, is mainly associated with the cerebral hemispheres. If we remove the hemispheres in the dog [Goltz[1] and others[2]], the animal becomes not only incapable of performing these duties but also incapable even of looking after itself. It becomes in fact a helpless invalid, and cannot long survive unless it be carefully tended.

In man also the highest nervous activity is dependent upon the structural and functional integrity of the cerebral hemispheres. As soon as these structures become damaged and their functions impaired in any way, so man also becomes an invalid. He can no longer proceed with his normal duties, but has to be kept out of the working world of his fellow men.

In astounding contrast with the unbounded activity of the cerebral hemispheres stands the meagre content of present-day physiological knowledge concerning them. Up to the year 1870, in fact, there was no physiology of the hemispheres; they seemed to be out of reach of the physiologist. In that year the common physiological methods of stimulation and extirpation were first applied to them [Fritsch and Hitzig[3]]. It was found by these workers that stimulation of certain parts of the cortex of the hemispheres (motor cortex) regularly evoked contractions in definite groups of skeletal muscles: extirpation of these parts of the cortex led to

[1] F. Goltz, "Der Hund ohne Grosshirn," Pflüger's *Archiv,* V. li. p. 570, 1892.

[2] M. Rothmann, "Der Hund ohne Grosshirn." *Neurologisches Centralblatt,* V. xxviii. p. 1045, 1909.

[3] Fritsch und E. Hitzig, "Ueber die elektrische Erregbarkeit des Grosshirns." *Archiv für (Anatomie und) Physiologie,* p. 300, 1870.

disturbances in the normal functioning of the same groups of muscles. Shortly afterwards it was demonstrated [Ferrier,[4] H. Munk[5]] that other areas of the cortex which do not evoke any motor activity in response to stimulation are also functionally differentiated. Extirpation of these areas leads to definite defects in the nervous activity associated with certain receptor organs, such as the retina of the eye, the organ of Corti, and the sensory nerve-endings in the skin. Searching investigations have been made, and still are being made, by numerous workers on this question of localization of function in the cortex. Our knowledge has been increased in precision and filled out in detail, especially as regards the motor area, and has even found useful application in medicine. These investigations, however, did not proceed fundamentally beyond the position established by Fritsch and Hitzig. The important question of the physiological mechanism of the whole higher and complex behaviour of the animal which is—as Goltz showed—dependent upon the cerebral hemispheres, was not touched in any of these investigations and formed no part of the current physiological knowledge.

When therefore we ask the questions: What do those facts which have up to the present been at the disposal of the physiologist explain with regard to the behaviour of the higher animals? What general scheme of the highest nervous activity can they give? or what general rules governing this activity can they help us to formulate?—the modern physiologist finds himself at a loss and can give no satisfactory reply. The problem of the mechanism of this complex structure which is so rich in function has got hidden away in a corner, and this unlimited field, so fertile in possibilities for research, has never been adequately explored.

The reason for this is quite simple and clear. These nervous activities have never been regarded from the same point of view as those of other organs, or even other parts of the central nervous system. The activities of the hemispheres have been talked about as some kind of special psychical activity, whose working we feel and apprehend in ourselves, and by analogy suppose to exist in animals. This is an anomaly which has placed the physiologist in an extremely difficult position. On the one hand it would seem that the study of the activities of the cerebral hemispheres, as of the activities of any other part of the organism, should be within the compass of physiology, but on the other hand it happens to have been annexed to the special field of another science—psychology.

What attitude then should the physiologist adopt? Perhaps

[4] D. Ferrier, *Functions of the Brain,* London, 1876.

[5] H. Munk, *Ueber die Functionen der Grosshirnrinde,* Berlin, 1890 and 1909.

he should first of all study the methods of this science of psychology, and only afterwards hope to study the physiological mechanism of the hemispheres? This involves a serious difficulty. It is logical that in its analysis of the various activities of living matter physiology should base itself on the more advanced and more exact sciences—physics and chemistry. But if we attempt an approach from this science of psychology to the problem confronting us we shall be building our superstructure on a science which has no claim to exactness as compared even with physiology. In fact it is still open to discussion whether psychology is a natural science, or whether it can be regarded as a science at all.

It is not possible here for me to enter deeply into this question, but I will stay to give one fact which strikes me very forcibly, viz. that even the advocates of psychology do not look upon their science as being in any sense exact. The eminent American psychologist, William James, has in recent years referred to psychology not as a science but as a *hope* of science. Another striking illustration is provided by Wundt, the celebrated philosopher and psychologist, founder of the so-called experimental method in psychology and himself formerly a physiologist. Just before the War (1913), on the occasion of a discussion in Germany as to the advisability of making separate Chairs of Philosophy and Psychology, Wundt opposed the separation, one of his arguments being the impossibility of fixing a common examination schedule in psychology, since every professor had his own special ideas as to what psychology really was. Such testimony seems to show clearly that psychology cannot yet claim the status of an exact science.

If this be the case there is no need for the physiologist to have recourse to psychology. It would be more natural that experimental investigation of the physiological activities of the hemispheres should lay a solid foundation for a future true science of psychology; such a course is more likely to lead to the advancement of this branch of natural science.

The physiologist must thus take his own path, where a trail has already been blazed for him. Three hundred years ago Descartes evolved the idea of the reflex. Starting from the assumption that animals behaved simply as machines, he regarded every activity of the organism as a *necessary* reaction to some external stimulus, the connection between the stimulus and the response being made through a definite nervous path: and this connection, he stated, was the fundamental purpose of the nervous structures in the animal body. This was the basis on which the study of the nervous system was firmly established. In the eighteenth, nineteenth and twentieth centuries the conception of the reflex was used to the full by physiologists. Working at first only on the lower parts of the central nervous system, they came gradually to study more highly developed parts, until quite recently Magnus,[6] continuing the classical investigations of Sherrington[7] upon the spinal reflexes, has succeeded in demonstrating the reflex nature of all the elementary motor activities of the animal organism. Descartes' conception of the reflex was constantly and fruitfully applied in these studies, but its application has stopped short of the cerebral cortex.

It may be hoped that some of the more complex activities of the body, which are made up by a grouping together of the elementary locomotor activities, and which enter into the states referred to in psychological phraseology as "playfulness," "fear," "anger," and so forth, will soon be demonstrated as reflex activities of the subcortical parts of the brain. A bold attempt to apply the idea of the reflex to the activities of the hemispheres was made by the Russian physiologist, I. M. Sechenov, on the basis of the knowledge available in his day of the physiology of the central nervous system. In a pamphlet entitled "Reflexes of the Brain," published in Russian in 1863, he attempted to represent the activities of the cerebral hemispheres as reflex—that is to say, as *determined.* Thoughts he regarded as reflexes in which the effector path was inhibited, while great outbursts of passion he regarded as exaggerated reflexes with a wide irradiation of excitation. A similar attempt was made more recently by Ch. Richet,[8] who introduced the conception of the psychic reflex, in which the response following on a given stimulus is supposed to be determined by the association of this stimulus with the traces left in the hemispheres by past stimuli. And generally speaking, recent physiology shows a tendency to regard the highest activities of the hemispheres as an association of the new excitations at any given time with traces left by old ones (associative memory, training, education by experience).

All this, however, was mere conjecture. The time was ripe for a transition to the experimental analysis of the subject—an analysis which must be as objective as the analysis in any other branch of natural science. An impetus was given to this transition by the rapidly developing science of comparative physiology, which itself sprang up as a direct result of the Theory of Evolution. In dealing with the lower members of the animal kingdom physiologists were, of necessity, compelled to reject anthropomorphic preconceptions, and to direct all their effort towards the elucidation of the connections between the external stimulus and

[6] R. Magnus, *Koerperstellung,* Berlin, 1924.

[7] C. S. Sherrington, *The Integrative Action of the Nervous System,* London, 1906.

[8] Ch. Richet, *Réflexes Psychiques. Réflexes Conditionels. Automatisme Mental.* Pavlov's *Jubilee Volume,* Petrograd, 1925.

the resulting response, whether locomotor or other reaction. This led to the development of Loeb's doctrine of Animal Tropisms;[9] to the introduction of a new objective terminology to describe animal reactions [Beer, Bethe and Uexkull[10]]; and finally, it led to the investigation by zoologists, using purely objective methods, of the behaviour of the lower members of the animal kingdom in response to external stimuli—as for example in the classical researches of Jennings.[11]

Under the influence of these new tendencies in biology, which appealed to the practical bent of the American mind, the American School of Psychologists—already interested in the comparative study of psychology—evinced a disposition to subject the highest nervous activities of animals to experimental analysis under various specially devised conditions. We may fairly regard the treatise by Thorndyke, *The Animal Intelligence* (1898),[12] as the starting point for systematic investigations of this kind. In these investigations the animal was kept in a box, and food was placed outside the box so that it was visible to the animal. In order to get the food the animal had to open a door, which was fastened by various suitable contrivances in the different experiments. Tables and charts were made showing how quickly and in what manner the animal solved the problems set it. The whole process was understood as being the formation of an association between the visual and tactile stimuli on the one hand and the locomotor apparatus on the other. This method, with its modifications, was subsequently applied by numerous authors to the study of questions relating to the associative ability of various animals.

At about the same time as Thorndyke was engaged on this work, I myself (being then quite ignorant of his researches) was also led to the objective study of the hemispheres, by the following circumstance: In the course of a detailed investigation into the activities of the digestive glands I had to inquire into the so-called psychic secretion of some of the glands, a task which I attempted in conjunction with a collaborator. As a result of this investigation an unqualified conviction of the futility of subjective methods of inquiry was firmly stamped upon my mind. It became clear that the only satisfactory solution of the problem lay in an experimental investigation by strictly objective methods. For this purpose I started to record all the external stimuli falling on the animal at the time its reflex reaction was manifested (in this

[9] J. Loeb, *Studies in General Physiology,* Chicago, 1905.
[10] Beer, Bethe und Uexküll, "Vorschläge zu einer objectivirenden Nomenklatur in der Physiologie des Nervensystems," *Biologisches Centralblatt,* V. xix, p. 517, 1899.
[11] H. S. Jennings, *The Behavior of Lower Organisms,* New York, 1906.
[12] E. L. Thorndyke, *The Animal Intelligence. An Experimental Study of the Associative Process in Animals,* New York, 1898.

particular case the secretion of saliva), at the same time recording all changes in the reaction of the animal.

This was the beginning of these investigations, which have gone on now for twenty-five years—years in which numerous fellow-workers on whom I now look back with tender affection have united with mine in this work their hearts and hands. We have of course passed through many stages, and only gradually has the subject been opened up and the difficulties overcome. At first only a few scattered facts were available, but to-day sufficient material has been gathered together to warrant an attempt to present it in a more or less systematized form. At the present time I am in a position to present you with a physiological interpretation of the activities of the cerebral hemispheres which is, at any rate, more in keeping with the structural and functional complexity of this organ than is the collection of fragmentary, though very important, facts which up to the present have represented all the knowledge of this subject. Work on the lines of purely objective investigation into the highest nervous activities has been conducted in the main in the laboratories under my control, and over a hundred collaborators have taken part. Work on somewhat similar lines to ours has been done by the American psychologists. Up to the present, however, there has been the one essential point of difference between the American School and ourselves. Being psychologists, their mode of experimentation, in spite of the fact that they are studying these activities on their external aspect, is mostly psychological—at any rate so far as the arrangement of problems and their analysis and the formulation of results are concerned. Therefore—with the exception of a small group of "behaviourists"—their work cannot be regarded as purely physiological in character. We, having started from physiology, continue to adhere strictly to the physiological point of view, investigating and systematizing the whole subject by physiological methods alone. As regards other physiological laboratories a few only have directed their attention to this subject, and that recently; nor have their investigations extended beyond the limits of a preliminary inquiry.

I shall now turn to the description of our material, first giving as a preliminary an account of the general conception of the reflex, of specific physiological reflexes, and of the so-called "instincts." Our starting point has been Descartes' idea of the nervous reflex. This is a genuine scientific conception, since it implies necessity. It may be summed up as follows: An external or internal stimulus falls on some one or other nervous receptor and gives rise to a nervous impulse; this nervous impulse is transmitted along nerve fibres to the central nervous system, and here, on account of existing nervous connections, it gives rise to a fresh impulse which passes along outgoing nerve fibres to the active organ, where it excites a special activity of the cellular structures. Thus a stimulus appears to be connected of necessity with a definite response, as cause with effect. It seems obvious that the whole activity of the organism should conform to definite laws. If the animal were not in exact correspondence with its environment it would, sooner or later, cease to exist. To give a biological example: if, instead of being attracted to food, the animal were repelled by it, or if instead of running from fire the animal threw itself into the fire, then it would quickly perish. The animal must respond to changes in the environment in such a manner that its responsive activity is directed towards the preservation of its existence. This conclusion holds also if we consider the living organism in terms of physical and chemical science. Every material system can exist as an entity only so long as its internal forces, attraction, cohesion, etc., balance the external forces acting upon it. This is true for an ordinary stone just as much as for the most complex chemical substances; and its truth should be recognized also for the animal organism. Being a definite circumscribed material system, it can only continue to exist so long as it is in continuous equilibrium with the forces external to it: so soon as this equilibrium is seriously disturbed the organism will cease to exist as the entity it was. Reflexes are the elemental units in the mechanism of perpetual equilibration. Physiologists have studied and are studying at the present time these numerous machine-like, inevitable reactions of the organism—reflexes existing from the very birth of the animal, and due therefore to the inherent organization of the nervous system.

Reflexes, like the driving-belts of machines of human design, may be of two kinds—positive and negative, excitatory and inhibitory. Although the investigation of these reflexes by physiologists has been going on now for a long time, it is as yet not nearly finished. Fresh reflexes are continually being discovered. We are ignorant of the properties of those receptor organs for which the effective stimulus arises inside the organism, and the internal reflexes themselves remain a field unexplored. The paths by which nervous impulses are conducted in the central nervous system are for the most part little known, or not ascertained at all. The mechanism of inhibitions confined within the central nervous system remains quite obscure: we know something only of those inhibitory reflexes which manifest themselves along the inhibitory efferent nerves. Furthermore, the combination and interaction of different reflexes are as yet insufficiently understood. Nevertheless physiologists are succeeding more and more in unravelling the mechanism of these machine-like activities of the organism, and may reasonably be expected to elucidate and control it in the end.

To those reflexes which have long been the subject of physiological investigation, and which concern chiefly the activities of separate organs and tissues, there should be added another group of inborn reflexes. These also take place in the nervous system, and they are the inevitable reactions to perfectly definite stimuli. They have to do with reactions of the organism as a whole, and comprise that general behaviour of the animal which has been termed "instinctive." Since complete agreement as regards the essential affinity of these reactions to the reflex has not yet been attained, we must discuss this question more fully. We owe to the English philosopher, Herbert Spencer, the suggestion that instinctive reactions are reflexes. Ample evidence was later advanced by zoologists, physiologists, and students of comparative psychology in support of this. I propose here to bring together the various arguments in favour of this view. Between the simplest reflex and the instinct we can find numerous stages of transition, and among these we are puzzled to find any line of demarcation. To exemplify this we may take the newly hatched chick. This little creature reacts by pecking to any stimulus that catches the eye, whether it be a real object or only a stain in the surface it is walking upon. In what way shall we say that this differs from the inclining of the head, the closing of the lids, when something flicks past its eyes? We should call this last a defensive reflex, but the first has been termed a feeding instinct: although in pecking nothing but an inclination of the head and a movement of the beak occurs.

It has also been maintained that instincts are more complex than reflexes. There are, however, exceedingly complex reflexes which nobody would term instincts. We may take vomiting as an example. This is very complex and involves the co-ordination of a large number of muscles (both striped and plain) spread over a large area and usually employed in quite different functions of the organism. It involves also a secretory activity on the part of certain glands which is usually evoked for a quite different purpose.

Again, it has been assumed that the long train of actions involved in certain instinctive activities affords a distinctive point of contrast with the reflex, which is regarded as always being built on a simple scale. By way of example we may take the building of a nest, or of dwellings in general, by animals. A chain of incidents is linked together: material is gathered and carried to the site chosen; there it is built up and strengthened. To look upon this as reflex we must assume that one reflex initiates the next following—or, in other words, we must regard it as a chain-reflex. But this linking up of activities is not peculiar to instincts alone. We are familiar with numerous reflexes which most certainly fuse into chains. Thus, for example, if we stimulate an afferent nerve, *e.g.* the sciatic nerve, a reflex rise of blood pressure occurs; the high pressure in the left ventricle of the heart, and first part of the aorta, serves as the effective stimulus to a second reflex, this time a depressor reflex which has a moderating influence on the first. Again, we may take one of the chain reflexes recently established by Magnus. A cat, even when deprived of its cerebral hemispheres, will in most cases land on its feet when thrown from a height. How is this managed? When the position of the otolithic organ in space is altered a definite reflex is evoked which brings about a contraction of the muscles in the neck, restoring the animal's head to the normal position. This is the first reflex. With the righting of the head a fresh reflex is evoked, and certain muscles of the trunk and limbs are brought into play, restoring the animal to the standing posture. This is the second reflex.

Some, again, object to the identification of instincts with reflexes on this ground: instincts, they say, frequently depend upon the internal state of an organism. For instance, a bird only builds its nest in the mating season. Or, to take a simpler case, when an animal is satiated with eating, then food has no longer any attraction and the animal leaves off eating. Again, the same is true of the sexual impulse. This depends on the age of the organism, and on the state of the reproductive glands; and a considerable influence is exerted by hormones (the products of the glands of internal secretion). But this dependence cannot be claimed as a peculiar property of "instincts." The intensity of any reflex, indeed its very presence, is dependent on the irritability of the centres, which in turn depends constantly on the physical and chemical properties of the blood (automatic stimulation of centres) and on the interaction of reflexes.

Last of all, it is sometimes held that whereas reflexes determine only the activities of single organs and tissues, instincts involve the activity of the organism as a whole. We now know, however, from the recent investigations of Magnus and de Kleijn, that standing, walking and the maintenance of postural balance in general, are all nothing but reflexes.

It follows from all this that instincts and reflexes are alike the inevitable responses of the organism to internal and external stimuli, and therefore we have no need to call by them by two different terms. Reflex has the better claim of the two, in that it has been used from the very beginning with a strictly scientific connotation.

The aggregate of reflexes constitutes the foundation of the

nervous activities both of men and of animals. It is therefore of great importance to study in detail all the fundamental reflexes of the organism. Up to the present, unfortunately, this is far from being accomplished, especially, as I have mentioned before, in the case of those reflexes which have been known vaguely as "instincts." Our knowledge of these latter is very limited and fragmentary. Their classification under such headings as "alimentary," "defensive," "sexual," "parental" and "social" instincts, is thoroughly inadequate. Under each of these heads is assembled often a large number of individual reflexes. Some of these are quite unidentified; some are confused with others; and many are still only partially appreciated. I can demonstrate from my own experience to what extent the subject remains inchoate and full of gaps. In the course of the researches which I shall presently explain, we were completely at a loss on one occasion to find any cause for the peculiar behaviour of an animal. It was evidently a very tractable dog, which soon became very friendly with us. We started off with a very simple experiment. The dog was placed in a stand with loose loops round its legs, but so as to be quite comfortable and free to move a pace or two. Nothing more was done except to present the animal repeatedly with food at intervals of some minutes. It stood quietly enough at first, and ate quite readily, but as time went on it became excited and struggled to get out of the stand, scratching at the floor, gnawing the supports, and so on. This ceaseless muscular exertion was accompanied by breathlessness and continuous salivation, which persisted at every experiment during several weeks, the animal getting worse and worse until it was no longer fitted for our researches. For a long time we remained puzzled over the unusual behaviour of this animal. We tried out experimentally numerous possible interpretations, but though we had had long experience with a great number of dogs in our laboratories we could not work out a satisfactory solution of this strange behaviour, until it occurred to us at last that it might be the expression of a special *freedom reflex,* and that the dog simply could not remain quiet when it was constrained in the stand. This reflex was overcome by setting off another against it—the reflex for food. We began to give the dog the whole of its food in the stand. At first the animal ate but little, and lost considerably in weight, but gradually it got to eat more, until at last the whole ration was consumed. At the same time the animal grew quieter during the course of the experiments: the freedom reflex was being inhibited. It is clear that the freedom reflex is one of the most important reflexes, or, if we use a more general term, reactions, of living beings. This reflex has even yet to find its final recognition. In James's writings it is not even enumerated among the special human "instincts." But it is clear that if the animal were not provided with a reflex of protest against boundaries set to its freedom, the smallest obstacle in its path would interfere with the proper fulfilment of its natural functions. Some animals as we all know have this freedom reflex to such a degree that when placed in captivity they refuse all food, sicken and die.

As another example of a reflex which is very much neglected we may refer to what may be called the *investigatory reflex*. I call it the "What-is-it?" reflex. It is this reflex which brings about the immediate response in man and animals to the slightest changes in the world around them, so that they immediately orientate their appropriate receptor organ in accordance with the perceptible quality in the agent bringing about the change, making full investigation of it. The biological significance of this reflex is obvious. If the animal were not provided with such a reflex its life would hang at every moment by a thread. In man this reflex has been greatly developed with far-reaching results, being represented in its highest form by inquisitiveness—the parent of that scientific method through which we may hope one day to come to a true orientation in knowledge of the world around us.

Still less has been done towards the elucidation of the class of negative or inhibitory reflexes (instincts) which are often evoked by any strong stimulus, or even by weak stimuli, if unusual. Animal hypnotism, so-called, belongs to this category.

As the fundamental nervous reactions both of men and of animals are inborn in the form of definite reflexes, I must again emphasize how important it is to compile a complete list comprising all these reflexes with their adequate classification. For, as will be shown later on, all the remaining nervous functions of the animal organism are based upon these reflexes. Now, although the possession of such reflexes as those just described constitutes the fundamental condition for the natural survival of the animal, they are not in themselves sufficient to ensure a prolonged, stable and normal existence. This can be shown in dogs in which the cerebral hemispheres have been removed. Leaving out of account the internal reflexes, such a dog still retains the fundamental external reflexes. It is attracted by food; it is repelled by nocuous stimuli; it exhibits the investigatory reflex, raising its head and pricking up its ears to sound. In addition it exhibits the freedom reflex, offering a powerful resistance to any restraint. Nevertheless it is wholly incapable of looking after itself, and if left to itself will very soon die. Evidently something important is missing in its present nervous make-up. What nervous activities can it have lost? It is easily seen that, in this dog, the number of stimuli evoking reflex reaction is considerably diminished; those remaining are of an elemental, generalized nature, and act at a very short range. Consequently the dynamic equilibrium between the inner forces of the animal system and the external forces in its environment has become elemental as compared with the exquisite adaptability of the normal animal, and the simpler balance is obviously inadequate to life.

Let us return now to the simplest reflex from which our investigations started. If food or some rejectable substance finds its way into the mouth, a secretion of saliva is produced. The purpose of this secretion is in the case of food to alter it chemically, in the case of a rejectable substance to dilute and wash it out of the mouth. This is an example of a reflex due to the physical and chemical properties of a substance when it comes into contact with the mucous membrane of the mouth and tongue. But, in addition to this, a similar reflex secretion is evoked when these substances are placed at a distance from the dog and the receptor organs affected are only those of smell and sight. Even the vessel from which the food has been given is sufficient to evoke an alimentary reflex complete in all its details; and, further, the secretion may be provoked even by the sight of the person who brought the vessel, or by the sound of his footsteps. All these innumerable stimuli falling upon the several finely discriminating distance receptors lose their power for ever as soon as the hemispheres are taken from the animal, and those only which have a direct effect on mouth and tongue still retain their power. The great advantage to the organism of a capacity to react to the former stimuli is evident, for it is in virtue of their action that food finding its way into the mouth immediately encounters plenty of moistening saliva, and rejectable substances, often nocuous to the mucous membrane, find a layer of protective saliva already in the mouth which rapidly dilutes and washes them out. Even greater is their importance when they evoke the motor component of the complex reflex of nutrition, *i.e.* when they act as stimuli to the reflex of seeking food.

Here is another example—the reflex of self-defence. The strong carnivorous animal preys on weaker animals, and these if they waited to defend themselves until the teeth of the foe were in their flesh would speedily be exterminated. The case takes on a different aspect when the defence reflex is called into play by the sights and sounds of the enemy's approach. Then the prey has a chance to save itself by hiding or by flight.

How can we describe, in general, this difference in the dynamic balance of life between the normal and the decorticated animal? What is the general mechanism and law of this distinction? It is pretty evident that under natural conditions the normal animal must respond not only to stimuli which themselves bring immediate benefit or harm, but also to other physical or chemical agencies—waves of sound, light, and the like—which in themselves only *signal* the approach of these stimuli; though it is not the sight and sound of the breast of prey which is in itself harmful to the smaller animal, but its teeth and claws.

Now although the *signalling stimuli* do play a part in those comparatively simple reflexes we have given as examples, yet this is not the most important point. The essential feature of the highest activity of the central nervous system, with which we are concerned and which in the higher animals most probably belongs entirely to the hemispheres, consists not in the fact that innumerable signalling stimuli do initiate reflex reactions in the animal, but in the fact that under different conditions these same stimuli may initiate quite different reflex reactions; and conversely the same reaction may be initiated by different stimuli.

In the above-mentioned example of the salivary reflex, the signal at one time is one particular vessel, at another time another; under certain conditions one man, under different conditions another—strictly depending upon which vessel had been used in feeding and which man had brought the vessel and given food to the dog. This evidently makes the machine-like responsive activities of the organism still more precise, and adds to its qualities of yet higher perfection. So infinitely complex, so continuously in flux, are the conditions in the world around, that that complex animal system which is itself in living flux, and that system only, has a chance to establish dynamic equilibrium with the environment. Thus we see that the fundamental and the most general function of the hemispheres is that of reacting to signals presented by innumerable stimuli of interchangeable signification.

SIGMUND FREUD / Determinism—Chance—And Superstitious Beliefs*

Points of View

As THE general result of the preceding separate discussions, we must put down the following principle: *Certain inadequacies of our psychic functions—whose common character will soon be more definitely determined—and certain performances which are apparently unintentional prove to be well motivated when subjected to psychoanalytic investigation, and are determined through the consciousness of unknown motives.*

In order to belong to the class of phenomena which can thus be explained, a faulty psychic action must satisfy the following conditions:

(a) It must not exceed a certain measure, which is firmly established through our estimation, and is designated by the expression "within normal limits."

(b) It must evince the character of the momentary and temporary disturbance. The same action must have been previously performed more correctly or we must always rely on ourselves to perform it more correctly; if we are corrected by others, we must immediately recognize the truth of the correction and the incorrectness of our psychic action.

(c) If we at all perceive a faulty action, we must not perceive in ourselves any motivation of the same, but must attempt to explain it through "inattention" or attribute it to an "accident."

Thus, there remain in this group the cases of forgetting, the errors, the lapses in speaking, reading, writing, the erroneously carried-out actions and the so-called chance actions. The explanations of these very definite psychic processes are connected with a series of observations which may in part arouse further interest.

I. By assuming that a part of our psychic function is unexplainable through purposive ideas, we ignore the realms of determinism in our mental life. Here, as in still other spheres, determinism reaches farther than we suppose. In the year 1900, I read an essay published in the *Zeit* written by the literary historian R. M. Meyer, in which he maintains and illustrates by examples, that it is impossible to compose nonsense intentionally and arbitrarily. For some time, I have been aware that it is impossible to

*Reprinted from *The Basic Writings of Sigmund Freud,* translated and edited by Dr. A. A. Brill, copyright 1938 by Random House, Inc. Copyright renewed 1965 by Gioia Bernheim and Edmund Brill. Reprinted by permission.

think of a number, or even of a name, of one's own free will. If one investigates this seeming voluntary formation, let us say, of a number of many digits uttered in unrestrained mirth, it always proves to be so strictly determined that the determination seems impossible. I will now briefly discuss an example of an "arbitrarily chosen" first name, and then exhaustively analyze an analogous example of a "thoughtlessly uttered" number.

While preparing the history of one of my patients for publication, I considered what first name I should give her in the article. There seemed to be a wide choice; of course, certain names were at once excluded by me, in the first place the real name, then the names of members of my family to which I would have objected, also some female names having an especially peculiar pronunciation. But, excluding these, there should have been no need of being puzzled about such a name. It would be thought, and I myself supposed, that a whole multitude of feminine names would be placed at my disposal. Instead of this, only one sprang up, no other besides it; it was the name Dora.

I inquired as to its determination: "Who else is called Dora?" I wished to reject the next idea as incredulous; it occurred to me that the nurse of my sister's children was named Dora. But I possess so much self-control, or practice, in analysis, if you like, that I held firmly to the idea and proceeded. Then a slight incident of the previous evening soon flashed through my mind which brought the looked-for determinant. On my sister's dining room table, I noticed a letter bearing the address, "Miss Rosa W." Astonished, I asked whose name this was, and was informed that the right name of the supposed Dora was really Rosa, and that on accepting the position, she had to lay aside her name because Rosa would also refer to my sister. I said pityingly; "Poor people! They cannot even retain their own names!" I now recall that on hearing this, I became quiet for a moment and began to think of all sorts of serious matters which merged into obscurity, but which I could now easily bring into my consciousness. Thus, when I sought a name for a person *who could not retain her own name,* no other except "Dora" occurred to me. The exclusiveness here is based, moreover, on firmer internal associations, for in the history of my patient, it was a stranger in the house, the governess, who exerted a decisive influence on the course of the treatment.

This slight incident found its unexpected continuation many years later. While discussing in a lecture the long since published history of the girl called Dora, it occurred to me that one of my two women pupils had the very name Dora, which I was obliged to utter so often in the different associations of the case. I turned to the young student whom I knew personally with the apology that I had really not thought that she bore the same name, and that I was ready to substitute it in my lecture by another name.

I was now confronted with the task of rapidly choosing another name, and reflected that I must not now choose the first name of the other woman student, and so set a poor example to the class, who were already quite conversant with psychoanalysis. I was therefore well pleased when the name "Erna" occurred to me as the substitute for Dora, and Erna I used in the discourse. After the lecture, I asked myself whence the name "Erna" could possibly have originated and had to laugh as I observed that the feared possibility in the choice of the substitutive name had come to pass, in part at least. The other lady's family name was Lucerna, of which Erna was a part.

In a letter to a friend, I informed him that I had finished reading the proof sheets of *The Interpretation of Dreams,* and that I did not intend to make any further changes in it, "even if it contained 2,467 mistakes." I immediately attempted to explain to myself the number and added this little analysis as a postscript to the letter. It will be best to quote it now as I wrote it when I caught myself in this transaction:

"I will add hastily another contribution to the *Psychopathology of Everyday Life.* You will find in the letter the number 2,467 as a jocose and arbitrary estimation of the number of errors that may be found in the dream-book. I meant to write: no matter how large the number might be, and this one presented itself. But there is nothing arbitrary or undetermined in the psychic life. You will therefore rightly suppose that the unconscious hastened to determine the number which was liberated by consciousness. Just previous to this, I had read in the paper that General E. M. had been retired as Inspector-General of Ordnance. You must know that I am interested in this man. While I was serving as military medical student, he, then a colonel, once came into the hospital and said to the physician: 'You must make me well in eight days, as I have some work to do for which the Emperor is waiting.'

"At that time, I decided to follow this man's career, and just think, today (1899) he is at the end of it—Inspector-General of Ordnance and already retired. I wished to figure out in what time he had covered this road, and assumed that I had seen him in the hospital in 1882. That would make 17 years. I related this to my wife, and she remarked, 'Then you, too, should be retired.' And I protested, 'The Lord forbid!' After this conversation, I seated myself at the table to write to you. The previous train of thought continued, and for good reason. The figuring was incorrect; I had a definite recollection of the circumstances in my mind. I had celebrated my coming of age, my *24th* birthday, in the military prison (for being absent without permission). Therefore, I must have seen him in 1880, which makes it 19 years ago. You then have the number 24 in 2,467! Now take the number that represents my age, 43, and add 24 years to it and you get *67*! That is, to the question whether I wished to retire, I had expressed the wish to work 24 years more. Obviously, I am annoyed that in the interval during which I followed Colonel M., I have not accomplished much myself, and still there is a sort of triumph in the fact that he is already finished, while I still have all before me. Thus we may justly say that not even the unintentionally thrown-out number 2,467 lacks its determination from the unconscious."

Since this first example of the interpretation of an apparently arbitrary choice of a number, I have repeated a similar test with the same result; but most cases are of such intimate content that they do not lend themselves to report.

It is for this reason that I shall not hesitate to add here a very interesting analysis of a "chance number" which Dr. Alfred Adler (Vienna) received from a "perfectly healthy" man.[1] Adler wrote to me: "Last night, I devoted myself to the *Psychopathology of Everyday Life,* and I would have read it all through, had I not been hindered by a remarkable coincidence. When I read that every number that we apparently conjure up quite arbitrarily in our consciousness has a definite meaning, I decided to test it. The number 1,734 occurred to my mind. The following associations then came up: 1,734÷17=102; 102÷17=6. I then separated the number into 17 and 34. I am 34 years old. I believe that I once told you that I consider 34 the last year of youth, and for this reason, I felt miserable on my last birthday. The end of my 17th year was the beginning of a very nice and interesting period of my development. I divide my life into periods of 17 years. What do the divisions signify? The number 102 recalls the fact that volume 102 of the Reclam Universal Library is Kotzebue's play *Menschenhass und Reue* (Human Hatred and Repentance).

"My present psychic state is 'human hatred and repentance.' Number 6 of the U. L. (I know a great many numbers by heart) is Mullner's *Schuld* (Fault). I am constantly annoyed at the thought that it is through my own fault that I have not become what I could have been with my abilities.

"I then asked myself, 'What is Number 17 of the U. L.?' But I could not recall it. But as I positively knew it before, I assumed that I wished to forget this number. All reflection was in vain. I wished to continue with my reading, but I read only mechanically without understanding a word, for I was annoyed by

[1] Alfred Adler, "Drei Psychoanalysen von Zahlen einfällen und obsedierender Zahlen," *Psych. Neur Wochenschr.*, No. 28, 1905.

the number 17. I extinguished the light and continued my search. It finally came to me that number 17 must be a play by Shakespeare. But which one? I thought of Hero and Leander. Apparently, a stupid attempt of my will to distract me. I finally arose and consulted the catalogue of the U. L. Number 17 was *Macbeth*! To my surprise, I had to discover that I knew nothing of the play, despite the fact that it did not interest me any less than any other Shakespearean drama. I only thought of: murder, Lady Macbeth, witches, 'nice is ugly,' and that I found Schiller's version of *Macbeth* very nice. Undoubtedly, I also wished to forget the play. Then it occurred to me that 17 and 34 may be divided by 17 and result in 1 and 2. Numbers 1 and 2 of the U. L. is Goethe's *Faust*. Formerly, I found much of Faust in me."

We must regret that the discretion of the physician did not allow us to see the significance of ideas. Adler remarked that the man did not succeed in the synthesis of his analysis. His associations would hardly be worth reporting unless their continuation would bring out something that would give us the key to the understanding of the number 1,734 and the whole series of ideas.

To quote further: "To be sure, this morning I had an experience which speaks much for the correctness of the Freudian conception. My wife, whom I awakened through my getting up at night, asked me what I wanted with the catalogue of the U. L. I told her the story. She found it all pettifogging but—very interesting. *Macbeth,* which caused me so much trouble, she simply passed over. She said that nothing came to her mind when she thought of a number. I answered, 'Let us try it. She named the number 117. To this I immediately replied: '17 refers to what I just told you; furthermore, I told you yesterday that if a wife is in the 82nd year and the husband is in the 35th year, it must be a gross misunderstanding.' For the last few days, I have been teasing my wife by maintaining that she was a little old mother of 82 years. 82+35 =117."

The man who did not know how to determine his own number at once found the solution when his wife named a number which was apparently arbitrarily chosen. As a matter of fact, the woman understood very well from which complex the number of her husband originated, and chose her own number from the same complex, which was surely common to both as it dealt in his case with their relative ages. Now, we can find it easy to interpret the number that occurred to the man. As Dr. Adler indicates, it expressed a repressed wish of the husband which, fully developed, would read: "For a man of 34 years as I am, only a woman of 17 would be suitable."

Lest one should think too lightly of such "playing," I will

add that I was recently informed by Dr. Adler that a year after the publication of this analysis, the man was divorced from his wife.[2]

Adler gives a similar explanation for the origin of obsessive numbers. Also the choice of so-called "favorite numbers" is not without relation to the life of the person concerned, and does not lack a certain psychologic interest. A gentleman who evinced a particular partiality for the numbers 17 and 19 could specify, after brief reflection, that at the age of 17, he attained the greatly longed-for academic freedom by having been admitted to the university, that at 19, he made his first long journey, and shortly thereafter, made his first scientific discovery. But the fixation of this preference followed later, after two questionable affairs, when the same numbers were invested with importance in his "love-life."

Indeed, even those numbers which we use in a particular connection extremely often and with apparent arbitrariness can be traced by analysis to an unexpected meaning. Thus, one day, it struck one of my patients that he was particularly fond of saying, "I have already told you this from 17 to 36 times." And he asked himself whether there was any motive for it. It soon occurred to him that he was born on the 27th day of the month, and that his younger brother was born on the 26th day of another month, and he had grounds for complaint that Fate had robbed him of so many of the benefits of life only to bestow them on his younger brother. Thus he represented this partiality of Fate by deducting 10 from the date of his birth and adding it to the date of his brother's birthday. "I am the elder and yet am so 'cut short.' "

I shall tarry a little longer at the analysis of chance numbers, for I know of no other individual observation which would so readily demonstrate the existence of highly organized thinking processes, of which consciousness has no knowledge. Moreover, there is no better example of analysis in which the suggestion of the position, a frequent accusation, is so distinctly out of consideration. I shall therefore report the analysis or a chance number of one of my patients (with his consent), to which I will only add that he is the youngest of many children and that he lost his beloved father in his young years.

While in a particularly happy mood, he let the number 426,718 come to his mind, and put to himself the question, "Well, what does it bring to your mind?" First came a joke he had heard: "If your catarrh of the nose is treated by a doctor, it lasts 42 days, if it is not treated, it lasts—6 weeks." This corresponds to the first

[2] As an explanation of *Macbeth,* number 17 of the U. L., I was informed by Dr. Adler that in his seventeenth year, this man had joined an anarchistic society whose aim was regicide. Probably this is why he forgot the content of the play *Macbeth.* The same person invented at that time a secret code in which numbers were substituted by letters.

digit of the number ($42=6\times7$). During the blocking that followed this first solution, I called his attention to the fact that the number of six digits selected by him contains all the first numbers except 3 and 5. He at once found the continuation of the solution:

"We were altogether 7 children, I was the youngest. Number 3 in the order of the children corresponds to my sister A., and 5 to my brother L.; both of them were my enemies. As a child, I used to pray to the Lord every night that He should take out of my life these two tormenting spirits. It seems to me that I have fulfilled for myself this wish: '3' and '5', the *evil* brother and the hated sister, are omitted."

"If the number stands for your sisters and brothers, what significance is there to 18 at the end? You were altogether only 7."

"I often thought if my father had lived longer, I should not have been the youngest child. If one more would have come, we should have been 8, and there would have been a younger child, toward whom I could have played the role of the older one."

With this, the number was explained, but we still wished to find the connection between the first part of the interpretation and the part following it. This came very readily from the condition required for the last digits—if the father had lived longer. $42=6\times7$ signifies the ridicule directed against the doctors who could not help the father, and in this way, expresses the wish for the continued existence of the father. The whole number really corresponds to the fulfillment of his two wishes in reference to his family circle—namely, that both the evil brother and sister should die and that another little child should follow him. Or, briefly expressed: *If only these two had died in place of my father!*[3]

Another analysis of numbers I take from Jones.[4] A gentleman of his acquaintance let the number 986 come to his mind, and defied him to connect it to anything of special interest in his mind. "Six years ago, on the hottest day he could remember, he had seen a joke in an evening newspaper, which stated that the thermometer had stood at 986° F., evidently an exaggeration of 98.6° F. We were at the time seated in front of a very hot fire, from which he had just drawn back, and he remarked, probably quite correctly, that the heat had aroused his dormant memory. However, I was curious to know why this memory had persisted with such vividness as to be so readily brought out, for with some people, it surely would have been forgotten beyond recall, unless it had become associated with some other mental experience of more significance.

[3] For the sake of simplicity, I have omitted some of the not less suitable thoughts of the patient.

[4] *Loc. cit.*, p. 36.

He told me that on reading the joke, he had laughed uproariously, and that on many subsequent occasions, he had recalled it with great relish. As the joke was obviously of an exceedingly tenuous nature, this strengthened my expectation that more lay behind. His next thought was the general reflection that the conception of heat had always greatly impressed him, that heat was the most important thing in the universe, the source of all life, and so on. This remarkable attitude of a quite prosaic young man certainly needed some explanation, so I asked him to continue his free associations. The next thought was of a factory stack which he could see from his bedroom window. He often stood of an evening watching the flame and smoke issuing out of it, and reflecting on this deplorable waste of energy. Heat, flame, the source of life, the waste of vital energy issuing from an upright, hollow tube—it was not hard to divine from such associations that the ideas of heat and fire were unconsciously linked in his mind with the idea of love, as is so frequent in symbolic thinking, and that there was a strong masturbation complex present, a conclusion that he presently confirmed."

Those who wish to get a good impression of the way the material of numbers becomes elaborated in the unconscious thinking, I refer to two papers by Jung[5] and Jones.[6]

In personal analysis of this kind, two things were especially striking. First, the absolute somnambulistic certainty with which I attacked the unknown objective point, merging into a mathematical train of thought, which later suddenly extended to the looked-for number, and the rapidity with which the entire subsequent work was performed. Secondly, the fact that the numbers were always at the disposal of my unconscious mind, when as a matter of fact, I am a poor mathematician and find it very difficult to consciously recall years, house numbers and the like. Moreover, in these unconscious mental operations with figures, I found a tendency to superstition, the origin of which had long remained unknown to me.

It will not surprise us to find that not only numbers, but also mental occurrences of different kinds of words regularly prove on analytic investigation to be well determined.

Brill relates, "While working on the English edition of this book, I was obsessed one morning with the strange word '*Cardillac.*' Busily intent on my work, I refused at first to pay attention to it, but, as is usually the case, I simply could not do anything else. '*Cardillac*' was constantly in my mind. Realizing that my refusal to recognize it was only a resistance, I decided to analyze it.

[5] "Ein Beitrag zur Kenntnis des Zahlentraumes," *Zentralb. f. Psychoanalyse,* i. 12.
[6] "Unconscious Manipulation of Numbers" (*ibid.,* ii. 5, 1912).

The following associations occurred to me: *Cardillac, cardiac, carrefour, Cadillac.*

"*Cardiac*" recalled cardalgia—heartache—a medical friend who had recently told me confidentially that he feared that he had some attacks of pain in the region of his heart. Knowing him so well, I at once rejected his theory, and told him that his attacks were of a neurotic character, and that his other apparent physical ailments were also only the expression of his neurosis.

"I might add that just before telling me of his heart trouble, he spoke of a business matter of vital interest to him which had suddenly come to naught. Being a man of unbounded ambitions, he was very depressed because of late he had suffered many reverses. His neurotic conflicts, however, had become manifest a few months before this misfortune, soon after his father's death had left a big business on his hands. As the business could be continued only under his management, he was unable to decide whether to enter into commercial life or continue his chosen career. His great ambition was to become a successful physician, and although he had practised medicine successfully for many years, he was not altogether satisfied with the financial fluctuations of his professional income. On the other hand, his father's business promised him an assured, though limited, return. In brief, he was 'at a crossing and did not know which way to turn.'

"I then recalled the word *carrefour,* which is the French for 'crossing,' and it occurred to me that while working in a hospital in Paris, I lived near the 'Carrefour St. Lazare.' And now I could understand what relation all these associations had for me.

"When I resolved to leave the state hospital, I made the decision, first, because I desired to get married, and secondly, because I wished to enter private practice. This brought up a new problem. Although my State hospital service was an absolute success, judging by promotions and so on, I felt like a great many others in the same situation, namely, that my training was ill suited for private practice. To specialize in mental work was a daring undertaking for one without money and social connections. I also felt that the best I could do for patients, should they ever come my way, would be to commit them to one of the hospitals, as I had little confidence in the home treatment then in vogue. In spite of the substantial advances in mental work, the specialist was almost helpless when confronted with the average case of insanity. This was partially due to the fact that such cases were brought to him only after they had fully developed the psychosis when hospital treatment was imperative. Of the great army of milder mental disturbances, the so-called border-line cases, which make up the bulk of clinic and private practice, I knew very little. Such patients were only rarely seen in the state hospital, and what I knew concerning the treatment of neurasthenia, hysteria and psychasthenia hardly held out more hope for a successful private practice.

"It was in this state of mind that I came to Paris, where I hoped to learn enough about the psychoneuroses to enable me to continue my specialty in private practice, with a feeling that I could do something for my patients. What I saw in the Paris hospitals, however, did not help to change my state of mind. I was, therefore, seriously thinking of giving up my mental work for some other specialty. As can be seen, I was confronted with a situation similar to the one of my medical friend. I, too, was at a 'crossing' and did not know which way to turn. However, my suspense was soon ended. One day, I received a letter from my friend, Professor Peterson, who originally introduced me to the State hospital service, in which he urged me not to give up psychiatry and suggested that I visit the psychiatric clinic of Zurich.

"But what does *Cadillac* mean? Cadillac is the name of a hotel and of an automobile. A few days before, in a country place, my medical friend and I had been trying to hire an automobile, but there was none to be had. We both expressed the wish to own an automobile—again an unrealized ambition. I also recalled that the 'Carrefour St. Lazare' always impressed me as being one of the busiest thoroughfares in Paris. It was always congested with automobiles. Cadillac also recalled that only a few days ago, on the way to my clinic, I noticed a large sign over a building which announced that on a certain day, 'this building was to be occupied by the Cadillac,' etc. This at first made me think of the Cadillac Hotel, but on second sight, I noticed that it referred to the Cadillac motor-car. There was a sudden obstruction here for a few moments. The word Cadillac reappeared and by sound association the word *catalogue* occurred to me. This word brought back a very mortifying occurrence of recent origin, the motive of which was again blighted ambition.

"When one wishes to report any auto-analysis, he must be prepared to lay bare many intimate affairs of his own life. Anyone reading carefully Professor Freud's works cannot fail to become fully acquainted with him and his family life. I have often been asked by persons who claimed to have read and studied Freud's works such questions as 'How old is Freud?' 'Is Freud married?' 'How many children has he?' etc. Such questions can only be asked by those who have not read Freud's works, or by very careless and superficial readers. All these questions and many more intimate ones are answered in Freud's works. Auto-analyses are autobiographies *par excellence;* but whereas the autobiographer may for definite reasons consciously and unconsciously hide many facts of his life, the auto-analyst not only tells the truth consciously, but perforce brings to light his whole intimate personality. It is for these reasons that one finds it very unpleasant to report his own auto-analyses. However, as we often report our patient's unconscious productions, it is but fair that we should now and then sacrifice ourselves on the altar of publicity. This is my apology for having thrust some of my personal affairs on the reader, and for being obliged to continue a little longer in the same strain.

"Before digressing with the last remarks, I mentioned that the word *Cadillac* brought the word association *catalogue*. This association brought back another important epoch in my life with which Professor Peterson was connected. When I was informed by the secretary of the faculty that I was appointed chief of clinic of the department of psychiatry, I was exceedingly pleased to be so honored. It was the realization of an ambition which I dared entertain only in special euphoric states and, a compensation for the many unmerited criticisms from those who were blindly and unreasonably opposing my work as an expositer of Freud. Thereafter, I called on the stenographer of the faculty and spoke to her about a correction to be made in my name as it was printed in the catalogue. For some unknown reason (perhaps racial prejudice) this stenographer, a maiden lady, must have taken a dislike to me. For about three years I repeatedly requested her to have this correction made, but she paid no attention to me; she always promised to attend to it, but the mistake remained uncorrected.

"This time, I again reminded her of this correction, and also called her attention to the fact that as I had been appointed chief of clinic, I was especially anxious to have my name correctly printed in the catalogue. She apologized for her remissness and assured me that everything would be corrected as I requested, but on receiving the new catalogue, I found that while the correction had been made in my name, I was not listed as chief of clinic. When I spoke to her about it, she seemed puzzled; she said that she had no idea that I had been appointed chief of clinic. She had to consult the minutes of the faculty, written by herself, before she was convinced of it.[7] She was naturally very apologetic and said that she would at once write to the superintendent of the clinic to inform him of my appointment. I gained nothing by her regrets and apologies; the catalogue was already published and I was not listed as chief of clinic.

"Thus, the obsessive neologism *cardillac,* a condensation of *cardiac, Cadillac* and *catalogue,* contained some of the most important events of my medical career. When I was almost at the end

[7] This is another excellent example showing how a conscious intention was powerless to counteract an unconscious resistance.

of this analysis, I suddenly recalled a dream containing this neologism, cardillac, in which my wish was realized. My name appeared in its rightful place in the catalogue. The person who showed it to me in the dream was Professor Peterson. It was when I was at the first 'crossing' after I had graduated from the medical college that Professor Peterson advised me to enter the State hospital service. About five years later, when I was at the second crossing—the state of indecision described above—it was again Professor Peterson who directed me to the clinic of psychiatry at Zurich, where through Bleuler and Jung, I became acquainted with Professor Freud and his works, and it was also through the kind recommendation of Dr. Peterson that I was elevated to position of chief of clinic."

I am indebted to Dr. Hitschman for the solution of another case in which a line of poetry repeatedly obtruded itself on the mind in a certain place without showing any trace of its origin and relation.

Related by the jurist E.: "Six years ago, I travelled from Biarritz to San Sebastian. The railroad crosses over the Bidassao —a river which here forms the boundary between France and Spain. On the bridge one has a splendid view, on the one side of the broad valley and the Pyrenees and on the other of the sea. It was a beautiful, bright summer day; everything was filled with sun and light. I was on a vacation and pleased with my trip to Spain. Suddenly, the following words came to me: *'But the soul is already free, floating on a sea of light.'*

"At that time, I was trying to remember whence these lines came, but I could not remember; judging by the rhythm, the words must be a part of some poem, which, however, entirely escaped my memory. Later, when the verse repeatedly came to my mind, I asked many people about it without receiving any information.

"Last year, I crossed the same bridge on my return journey from Spain. It was a very dark night and it rained. I looked through the window to ascertain whether we had already reached the frontier station and noticed that we were on the Bidassao bridge. Immediately the above-cited verse returned to my memory and again I could not recall its origin.

"At home, many months later, I found Uhland's poems. I opened the volume and my glance fell upon the verse: *'But the soul is already free, floating on a sea of light,'* which were the concluding lines of the poem entitled 'The Pilgrim.' I read the poem and dimly recalled that I had known it many years ago. The scene of action is in Spain, and this seemed to me to be the only relation between the quoted verse and the place on the railroad journey described by me. I was only half satisfied with my discovery and mechanically continued to turn the pages of the book. On turning the next page, I found a poem, the title of which was *'Bidassao Bridge.'*

"I may add that the contents of this poem seemed even stranger to me than that of the first, and that its first verse read:

" 'On the Bidassao bridge stands a saint grey with age, he blesses to the right the Spanish mountain, to the left he blesses the French land.' "

II. This understanding of the determination of apparently arbitrarily selected names, numbers, and words may perhaps contribute to the solution of another problem. As is known, many persons argue against the assumption of an absolute psychic determinism by referring to an intense feeling of conviction that there is a free will. This feeling of conviction exists, but is not incompatible with the belief in determinism. Like all normal feelings, it must be justified by something. But, so far as I can observe, it does not manifest itself in weighty and important decisions; on these occasions, one has much more the feeling of a psychic compulsion and gladly falls back upon it. (Compare Luther's "Here I stand, I cannot do anything else.")

On the other hand, it is in trivial and indifferent decisions that one feels sure that he could just as easily have acted differently, that he acted of his own free will, and without any motives. From our analyses we therefore need not contest the right of the feeling of conviction that there is a free will. If we distinguish conscious from unconscious motivation, we are then informed by the feeling of conviction that the conscious motivation does not extend over all our motor resolutions. *Minima non curat praetor.* What is thus left free from the one side receives its motive from the other side, from the unconscious, and the determinism in the psychic realm is thus carried out uninterruptedly.[8]

III. Athough conscious thought must be altogether ignorant of the motivation of the faulty actions described above, yet it would be desirable to discover a psychologic proof of its existence; indeed, reasons obtained through a deeper knowledge of the un-

[8] These conceptions of strict determinism in seemingly arbitrary actions have already borne rich fruit for psychology—perhaps also for the administration of justice. Bleuler and Jung have in this way made intelligible the reaction in the so-called association experiments, wherein the test person answers to a given word with one occurring to him (stimulus-word reaction), while the time elapsing between the stimulus-word and answer is measured (reaction-time). Jung has shown in his *Diagnostische Assoziationsstudien,* 1906, what fine reagents for psychic occurrences we possess in this association-experiment. Three students of criminology, H. Gross, of Prague, and Wertheimer and Klein, have developed from these experiments a technique for the diagnosis of facts (*Tatbestands-Diagnostik*) in criminal cases, the examination of which is now tested by psychologists and jurists.

conscious make it probable that such proofs are to be discovered somewhere. As a matter of fact, phenomena can be demonstrated in two spheres which seem to correspond to an unconscious and hence, to a displaced knowledge of these motives.

(a) It is a striking and generally recognized feature in the behavior of paranoiacs, that they attach the greatest significance to trivial details in the behavior of others. Details which are usually overlooked by others they interpret and utilize as the basis of far-reaching conclusions. For example, the last paranoiac seen by me concluded that there was a general understanding among people of his environment, because at his departure from the railway station, they made a certain motion with one hand. Another noticed how people walked on the street, how they brandished their walking-sticks, and the like.[9]

The category of the accidental, requiring no motivation, which the normal person lets pass as a part of his own psychic functions and faulty actions, is thus rejected by the paranoiac in his application to the psychic manifestations of others. All that he observes in others is full of meaning; all is explainable. But how does he come to look at it in this manner? Probably here, as in so many other cases, he projects into the mental life of others what exists in his own unconscious activity. Many things obtrude themselves on consciousness in paranoia, which in normal and neurotic persons can only be demonstrated through psychoanalysis as existing in their unconscious.[10] In a certain sense, the paranoiac behavior is justified; he perceives something that escapes the normal person; he sees clearer than one of normal intellectual capacity, but his knowledge becomes worthless when he imputes to others the state of affairs he thus recognizes. I hope that I shall not be expected to justify every paranoiac interpretation. But the point which we grant to paranoia in this conception of chance actions will facilitate for us the psychologic understanding of the conviction which the paranoiac attaches to all these interpretations. *There is certainly some truth to it;* even our errors of judgment, which are not designated as morbid, acquire their feeling of conviction in the same way. This feeling is justified for a certain part of the erroneous train of thought or for the source of its origin, and we shall later extend to it the remaining relationships.

(b) The phenomena of superstition furnish another indi-

[9] Proceeding from other points of view, this interpretation of trivial and accidental acts by the patient has been designated as "delusions of reference."

[10] For example, the phantasies of the hysterical regarding sexual and cruel abuse which are made conscious by analysis often correspond in every detail with the complaints of persecuted paranoiacs. It is remarkable, but not altogether unexpected that we also meet the identical content as reality in the contrivances of perverts for the gratification of their desires.

cation of the unconscious motivation in chance and faulty actions. I will make myself clear through the discussion of a simple experience which gave me the starting-point to these reflections.

Having returned from my vacation, my thoughts immediately turned to the patients with whom I was to occupy myself in the beginning of my year's work. My first visit was to a very old woman (see above) for whom I had twice daily performed the same professional services for many years. Owing to this monotony, unconscious thoughts have often found expression on the way to the patient and during my occupation with her. She was over ninety years old; it was therefore pertinent to ask oneself at the beginning of each year how much longer she was likely to live.

On the day of which I speak, I was in a hurry and took a carriage to her house. Every coachman at the cabstand near my house knew the old woman's address, as each of them had often driven me there. This day, it happened that the driver did not stop in front of her house, but before one of the same number in a nearby and really similar-looking parallel street. I noticed the mistake and reproached the coachman, who apologized for it.

Is it of any significance when I am taken to a house where the old woman is not to be found? Certainly not to me; but were I *superstitious,* I should see an omen in this incident, a hint of fate that this would be the last year for the old woman. A great many omens which have been preserved by history have been founded on no better symbolism. Of course, I explain the incident as an accident without further meaning.

The case would have been entirely different had I come on foot and, "absorbed in thought" or "through distraction," I had gone to the house in the parallel street instead of the correct one. I would not explain that as an accident, but as an action with unconscious intent requiring interpretation. My explanation of this "lapse in walking" would probably be that I expected that the time would soon come when I should no longer meet the old woman.

I therefore differ from a superstitious person in the following manner:

I do not believe that an occurrence in which my mental life takes no part can teach me anything hidden concerning the future shaping of reality; but I do believe that an unintentional manifestation of my own mental activity surely contains something concealed which belongs only to my mental life—that is, I believe in outer (real) chance, but not in inner (psychic) accidents. With the superstitious person, the case is reversed: he knows nothing of the motive of his chance and faulty actions; be believes in the existence of psychic contingencies; he is therefore inclined to attribute meaning to external chance, which manifests itself in actual occurrence, and to see in the accident a means of expression for something hidden outside of him. There are two differences between me and the superstitious person: first, he projects the motive to the outside, while I look for it in myself; second, he explains the accident by an event which I trace to a thought. What he considers hidden corresponds to the unconscious with me, and the compulsion not to let chance pass as chance, but to explain it as common to both of us.

Thus, I admit that this conscious ignorance and unconscious knowledge of the motivation of psychic accidentalness is one of the psychic roots of superstition. *Because* the superstitious person knows nothing of the motivation of his own accidental actions, and because the fact of this motivation strives for a place in his recognition, he is compelled to dispose of them by displacing them into the outer world. If such a connection exists, it can hardly be limited to this single case. As a matter of fact, I believe that a large portion of the mythological conception of the world which reaches far into the most modern religions, *is nothing but psychology projected to the outer world.* The dim perception (the endo-psychic perception, as it were) of psychic factors and relations[11] of the unconscious was taken as a model in the construction of a *transcendental reality,* which is destined to be changed again by science into *psychology of the unconscious.*

It is difficult to express it in other terms; the analogy to paranoia must here come to our aid. We venture to explain in this way the myths of paradise and the fall of man, of God, of good and evil, of immortality and the like—that is, to transform *metaphysics* into *meta-psychology.* The gap between the paranoiac's displacement and that of superstition is narrower than appears at first sight. When human beings began to think, they were obviously compelled to explain the outer world in an anthropomorphic sense by a multitude of personalities in their own image; the accidents which they explained superstitiously were thus actions and expressions of persons. In that regard, they behaved just like paranoiacs, who draw conclusions from insignificant signs which others give them, and like all normal persons, who justly take the unintentional actions of their fellow-beings as a basis for the estimation of their characters. Only in our modern, philosophical, but by no means finished views of life does superstition seem so much out of place: in the view of life of prescientific times and nations, it was justified and consistent.

The Roman who gave up an important undertaking because he sighted an ill-omened flock of birds was relatively right; his

[11] Which naturally has nothing of the character of perception.

action was consistent with his principles. But if he withdrew from an undertaking because he had stumbled on his threshold (*un Romain retournerait*), he was absolutely superior even to us unbelievers. He was a better psychologist than we are striving to become. For his stumbling could demonstrate to him the existence of a doubt, an internal counter-current, the force of which could weaken the power of his intention at the moment of its execution. For only by concentrating all psychic forces on the desired aim can one be assured of perfect success. How does Schiller's Tell, who hesitated so long to shoot the apple from his son's head, answer the bailiff's question, why he had provided himself with a second arrow?

"With the second arrow I would have pierced you, had I struck my dear child—and truly, I should not have failed to reach you."

IV. Whoever has had the opportunity of studying the concealed feelings of persons by means of psychoanalysis can also tell something new concerning the quality of unconscious motives, which express themselves in superstition. Nervous persons afflicted with compulsive thinking and compulsive states, who are often very intelligent, show very plainly that superstition originates from repressed hostile and cruel impulses. The greater part of superstition signifies fear of impending evil, and he who has frequently wished evil to others, but because of a good bringing-up, has repressed the same into the unconscious, will be particularly apt to expect punishment for such unconscious evil in the form of a misfortune threatening him from without.

If we concede that we have by no means exhausted the psychology of superstition in these remarks, we must, on the other hand, at least touch upon the question whether real roots of superstition should be altogether denied, whether there are really no omens, prophetic dreams, telepathic experiences, manifestations of supernatural forces and the like. I am now far from willing to repudiate without anything further all these phenomena, concerning which we possess so many minute observations even from men of intellectual prominence, and which should certainly form a basis for further investigation. We may even hope that some of these observations will be explained by our present knowledge of the unconscious psychic processes without necessitating radical changes in our present aspect. If still other phenomena, as, for example, those maintained by the spiritualists, should be proven, we should then consider the modification of our "laws" as demanded by the new experience, without becoming confused in regard to the relation of things of this world.

In the sphere of these analyses, I can only answer the questions here proposed subjectively—that is, in accordance with my personal experience. I am sorry to confess that I belong to that class of unworthy individuals before whom the spirits cease their activities and the supernatural disappears, so that I have never been in position to experience anything personally that would stimulate belief in the miraculous. Like everybody else, I have had forebodings and experienced misfortunes; but the two evaded each other, so that nothing followed the foreboding, and the misfortune struck me unannounced. When as a young man, I lived alone in a strange city, I frequently heard my name suddenly pronounced by an unmistakable, dear voice, and I then made a note of the exact moment of the hallucination in order to inquire carefully of those at home what had occurred at that time. There was nothing to it. On the other hand, I later worked among my patients calmly and without foreboding while my child almost bled to death. Nor have I ever been able to recognize as unreal phenomena any of the forebodings reported to me by my patients.

The belief in prophetic dreams numbers many adherents, because it can be supported by the fact that some things really so happen in the future as they were previously foretold by the wish of the dream.[12] But in this, there is little to be wondered at, as many far-reaching deviations may be regularly demonstrated between a dream and the fulfillment which the credulity of the dreamer prefers to neglect.

A nice example, one which may be justly called prophetic, was once brought to me for exhaustive analysis by an intelligent and truth-loving patient. She related that she once dreamed that she had met a former friend and family physician in front of a certain store in a certain street, and next morning when she went downtown, she actually met him at the placed named in the dream. I may observe that the significance of this wonderful coincidence was not proven to be due to any subsequent event—that is, it could not be justified through future occurrences. Careful examination definitely established the fact that there was no proof that the woman recalled the dream in the morning following the night of the dream—that is, before the walk and before the meeting. She could offer no objection when this state of affairs was presented in a manner that robbed this episode of everything miraculous, leaving only an interesting psychologic problem. One morning, she had walked through this very street, had met her old family physician before that certain store, and on seeing him, received the conviction that during the preceding night, she had dreamed of this meeting at this place. The analysis then showed with great probability how she came to this conviction, to which, in accordance

[12] Cf. Freud, *Traum und Telepathie* (Dream and Telepathy), G. S., Bd. III.

with the general rule, we cannot deny a certain right to credence. A meeting at a definite place following a previous expectation really describes the fact of a *rendezvous*. The old family physician awakened her memory of old times, when meetings with a *third person,* also a friend of the physician, were of marked significance to her. Since that time, she had continued her relations with this gentleman, and the day before the mentioned dream, she had waited for him in vain. If I could report in greater detail the circumstances here before us, I could easily show that the illusion of the prophetic dream at the sight of the friend of former times is perchance equivalent to the following speech: "Ah, doctor, you now remind me of bygone times, when I never had to wait in vain for N. when we had arranged a meeting."

I have observed in myself a simple and easily explained example, which is probably a good model for similar occurrences of those familiar "remarkable coincidences" wherein we meet a person of whom we were just thinking. During a walk through the inner city a few days after the title of "Professor" was bestowed on me, which carried with it a great deal of prestige even in monarchical cities, my thoughts suddenly turned to a childish revenge-phantasy against a certain married couple. Some months previous, this couple had called me to see their little daughter, who suffered from an interesting compulsive manifestation following the appearance of a dream. I took a great interest in the case, the genesis of which I believed I could surmise, but the parents were unfavorable to my treatment and gave me to understand that they thought of applying to a foreign authority who treated by hypnotism. I now fancied to myself that after the failure of this treatment, the parents begged me to take the patient under my care, saying that they now had full confidence in me, etc. But I answered: "Now that I have become a professor, you have confidence in me. The title has made no change in my ability; if you could not use me when I was instructor, you can get along without me now that I am a professor." At this point, my phantasy was interrupted by a loud "Good evening, Professor!" and as I looked up, there was the same couple on whom I had just taken this imaginary vengeance.

The next reflection destroyed all semblance of the miraculous. I was walking towards this couple on a straight, almost deserted street; glancing up hastily at a distance of perhaps twenty steps from me, I had seen and realized their stately personalities; but this perception, following the model of a negative hallucination, was set aside by certain emotionally accentuated motives and then asserted itself spontaneously as an emerging phantasy.

A similar experience is related by Brill, which also throws some light on the nature of telepathy.

"While engrossed in conversation during our customary Sunday evening dinner at one of the large New York restaurants, I suddenly stopped and irrelevantly remarked to my wife, 'I wonder how Dr. R is doing in Pittsburgh.' She looked at me much astonished and said: 'Why, that is exactly what I have been thinking for the last few seconds! Either you have transferred this thought to me or I have transferred it to you. How can you otherwise explain this strange phenomenon?' I had to admit that I could offer no solution. Our conversation throughout the dinner showed not the remotest association to Dr. R., nor, so far as our memories went, had we heard or spoken of him for some time. Being a skeptic, I refused to admit that there was anything mysterious about it, although inwardly I felt quite uncertain. To be frank, I was somewhat mystified.

"But we did not remain very long in this state of mind, for on looking toward the cloak-room, we were surprised to see Dr. R. Closer inspection, however, showed our mistake, but we were struck by the remarkable resemblance of this stranger to Dr. R. From the position of the cloak-room, we were forced to conclude that this stranger had passed our table. Absorbed in our conversation, we had not noticed him consciously, but the visual image had stirred up the association of his double, Dr. R. That we should both have experienced the same thought is also quite natural. The last that we had heard from Dr. R. was that he had taken up private practice in Pittsburgh, and, being aware of the vicissitudes that beset the beginner in private practice, it was quite natural that we should wonder how he was getting along.

"What promised to be a supernatural manifestation was thus easily explained on a normal basis; but had we not noticed the stranger before he left the restaurant, it would have been impossible to exclude the mysterious. I venture to say that such simple mechanisms are at the basis of the most complicated telepathic manifestations; at least, that has been my experience in all those cases that were accessible to investigation."

To the category of the wonderful and uncanny, we may also add that strange feeling we perceive in certain moments and situations when it seems as if we had already had exactly the same experience, or had previously found ourselves in the same situation. Yet we are never successful in our efforts to recall clearly those former experiences and situations. I know that I follow only the loose colloquial expression when I designate that which stimulates us in such moments as a "feeling." We undoubtedly deal with a judgment, and, indeed, with a judgment of cognition; but these cases, nevertheless, have a character peculiar to themselves, and besides, we must not ignore the fact that we never recall what we are seeking.

I do not know whether this phenomenon of *Déjà vu* (having already seen this or that) was ever seriously offered as a proof of a former psychic existence of the individual; but it is certain that psychologists have taken an interest in it, and have attempted to solve the riddle in a multitude of speculative ways. None of the proposed tentative explanations seems right to me, because none takes account of anything but the accompanying manifestations and the conditions favoring the phenomenon. Those psychic processes which, according to my observation, are alone responsible for the explanation of the *Déjà vu* phenomenon—namely, the unconscious phantasies—are generally neglected by the psychologist even today.

I believe that it is wrong to designate the feeling of having experienced something before as an illusion. On the contrary, in such moments, something is really touched that we have already experienced, only we cannot consciously recall the latter because it never was conscious. In the latter, the feeling of *Déjà vu* corresponds to the memory of an unconscious phantasy. There are unconscious phantasies (or day-dreams) just as there are similar conscious creations, which everyone knows from personal experience.

I realize that the object is worthy of most minute study, but I will here give the analysis of only one case of *Déjà vu* in which the feeling was characterized by particular intensity and persistence. A woman of thirty-seven years asserted that she most distinctly remembered that at the age of twelve and a half, she paid her first visit to some school friends in the country, and as she entered the garden, she immediately had the feeling of having been there before. This feeling was repeated as she went through the living rooms, so that she believed she knew beforehand how big the next room was, what views one could have on looking out of it, etc. But the belief that this feeling of recognition might have its source in a previous visit to the house and garden, perhaps a visit paid in earliest childhood, was absolutely excluded and disproved by statements from her parents. The woman who related this sought no psychologic explanation, but saw in the appearance of this feeling a prophetic reference to the importance which these friends later assumed in her emotional life. On taking into consideration, however, the circumstance under which this phenomenon presented itself to her, we found the way to another conception.

When she decided on visiting her schoolmates, she knew that these girls had an only brother who was then seriously ill. In the course of the visit, she actually saw him. She found him looking very badly and thought to herself that he would soon die. But it happened that her own only brother had had a serious attack of diphtheria some months before, and during his illness, she had lived for weeks with relatives far from her parental home. She believed that her brother was taking part in this visit to the country, imagined even that this was his first long journey since his illness; still, her memory was remarkably indistinct in regard to these points, whereas all other details, and particularly the dress which she wore that day, remained most clearly before her eyes.

To the initiated, it will not be difficult to conclude from these indications that the expectation of her brother's death had played a great part in the girl's mind at that time, and that either it never became conscious or it was more energetically repressed after the favorable issue of the illness. Under other circumstances, she would have been compelled to wear another dress—namely, mourning clothes. She found the analogous situation in her friends' home; their only brother was in danger of an early death, an event that really came to pass in a short time. She might have consciously remembered that she had lived through a similar situation a few months previous, but instead of recalling what was inhibited through repression, she transferred the memory feeling to the locality, to the garden and the house and merged it into the *fausse reconnaissance,* namely, that she had already seen everything exactly as it was.

From the fact of the repression, we may conclude that the former expectation of the death of her brother was not far from evincing the character of a wish-phantasy. She would then have become the only child. In her later neurosis, she suffered in the most intense manner from the fear of losing her parents, behind which the analysis disclosed, as usual, the unconscious wish of the same content.

My own experience of *Déjà vu* I can trace in a similar manner to the emotional constellation of the moment. It may be expressed as follows: "That would be another occasion for awakening certain phantasies (unconscious and unknown) which were formed in me at one time or another as a wish to improve my situation."

Dr. Ferenczi, to whom this edition is indebted for so many contributions, wrote to me concerning this: "I have been convinced, from my experience as well as that of others, that the inexplicable feeling of familiarity can be referred to unconscious phantasies of which we are unconsciously reminded in an actual situation. With one of my patients, the process was apparently different, but in reality it was quite analogous. This feeling returned to him very often, but showed itself regularly as originating in a forgotten (repressed) portion of a dream of the preceding night. Thus it appears that the *Déjà vu* can originate not only from day-dreams but also from night dreams."

In 1915, I described another phenomenon which resembles much the *Déjà vu*. It is the *Déjà raconté* feeling, the illusion that something has already been related during the psychoanalytic treatment, which is especially interesting. The patient asserts with all subjective signs of certainty, that he previously related this definite episode. The physician, however, is sure of the contrary and, as a rule, can convince the patient of it. The explanation of this interesting phenomenon is undoubtedly based on the fact that the patient had the impulse and intention of imparting this memory, but failed to execute it, and that he now puts the memory of the first resolution as a substitute for the second feeling.

V. Recently, when I had occasion to recite to a colleague of a philosophical turn of mind some examples of name-forgetting with their analyses, he hastened to reply: "That is all very well, but with me the forgetting of a name proceeds in a different manner." Evidently, one cannot dismiss this question as simply as that; I do not believe that my colleague had ever thought of an analysis for the forgetting of a name, nor could he say how the process differed in him. But his remark, nevertheless, touches upon a problem which many would be inclined to place in the foreground. Does the solution given for faulty and chance actions apply in general or only in particular cases, and if only in the latter, what are the conditions under which it may also be employed in the explanation of the other phenomena?

In answer to this question, my experiences leave me in the lurch. I can only urge against considering the demonstrated connections as rare, for as often as I have made the test in myself and with my patients, it was always definitely demonstrated exactly as in the examples reported, or there were at least good reasons to assume this. One should not be surprised, however, when one does not succeed every time in finding the concealed meaning of the symptomatic action, as the amount of inner resistances ranging themselves against the solution must be considered a deciding factor. Also, it is not always possible to explain every individual dream of oneself or of patients. To substantiate the general validity of the theory, it is enough if one can penetrate only a certain distance into the hidden associations. The dream which proves refractory when the solution is attempted on the following day can often be robbed of its secret a week or a month later, when the psychic factors combating one another have been reduced as a consequence of a real change that has meanwhile taken place. The same applies to the solution of faulty and symptomatic actions. It would, therefore, be wrong to affirm of all cases which resist analysis that they are caused by another psychic mechanism than that here revealed; such assumption requires more than negative proofs; moreover, the readiness to believe in a different explanation of faulty and symptomatic actions, which probably exists universally in all normal persons, does not prove anything; it is obviously an expression of the same psychic forces which produced the secret, which therefore strives to protect and struggle against its elucidation.

On the other hand, we must not overlook the fact that the repressed thoughts and feelings are not independent in attaining expression in symptomatic and faulty actions. The technical possibility for such an adjustment of the innervations must be furnished independently of them, and this is then gladly utilized by the intention of the repressed material to come to conscious expression. In the case of linguistic faulty actions, an attempt has been made by philosophers and philologists to verify through minute observations what structural and functional relations enter into the service of such intention. If in the determinations of faulty and symptomatic actions, we separate the unconscious motive from its co-active physiological and psychophysical relations, the question remains whether there are still other factors within normal limits which, like the unconscious motive, or a substitute for it, can produce faulty and symptomatic actions on the path of these relations. It is not my task to answer this question.

To be sure, it is not my intention to exaggerate still more the differences, large as they are, between the psychoanalytic and the current concepts of faulty actions. I prefer to give cases in which these differences are not so marked. In the simplest and least striking examples of lapses in talking and writing, wherein perhaps only words are fused or words and letters omitted, there is no very complicated interpretation. Psychoanalytically, it can only be asserted, that in these cases one sees some disturbance of the intention, but one cannot say whence it originated and what its purpose is. It really produces nothing except a manifestation of its presence. In the same cases, one also observes that the faulty actions become effective through the undisputed favorable influences of sound relations and mediate psychological associations. But scientifically, it is only fair to demand that we judge such rudimentary cases of lapses in speech or writing by the more marked expressions, the investigations of which result in unequivocal explanations of the causation of faulty actions.

VI. Since the discussion of speech-blunders, we have been content to demonstrate that faulty actions have a concealed motive, and through the aid of psychoanalysis, we have traced our way to the knowledge of their motivation. The general nature and the peculiarities of the psychic factors brought to expression in these faulty actions, we have hitherto left almost without consideration; at any rate, we have not attempted to define them more accurately or to examine into their lawfulness. Nor will we now attempt a thorough elucidation of the subject, as the first steps have already taught us that it is more feasible to enter this structure from another side.[13] Here, we can put before ourselves certain questions which I will cite in their order. (1) What are the content and origin of the thoughts and feelings which show themselves through faulty and chance actions? (2) What are the conditions which force a thought or a feeling to make use of these occurrences as a means of expression and place it in a position to do so? (3) Can constant and definite associations be demonstrated between the manner of the faulty action and the qualities brought to expression through it?

I shall begin by bringing together some material for answering the last question. In the discussion of the examples of speech-blunders, we found it necessary to go beyond the contents of the intended speech, and we had to seek the cause of the speech disturbance outside the intention. The latter was quite clear in a series of cases, and was known to the consciousness of the speaker. In the example that seemed most simple and transparent, it was a similar sounding but different conception of the same thought, which disturbed its expression without anyone being able to say why the one succumbed and the other came to the surface (Meringer and Mayers' *Contaminations*).

In a second group of cases, one conception succumbed to a motive which did not, however, prove strong enough to cause complete submersion. The conception which was withheld was clearly presented to consciousness.

Only of the third group can we affirm unreservedly that the disturbing thought differed from the one intended, and it is obvious that it may establish an essential distinction. The disturbing thought is either connected with the disturbed one through a thought association (disturbance through inner contradiction), or it is substantially strange to it, and just the disturbed word is connected with the disturbing thought through a surprising outer association, which is frequently unconscious.

In the examples which I have given from my psychoanalyses, the entire speech is either under the influence of thoughts which have become active simultaneously, or under absolutely

[13] This work should be considered popular. Through an accumulation of many examples, it wishes to pave the way for the necessary assumption of unconscious, yet effective, psychic processes. It wishes to avoid all theoretical discussions concerning the nature of this unconscious.

unconscious thoughts which betray themselves either through the disturbance itself, or which evince an indirect influence by making it possible for the individual parts of the unconsciously intended speech to disturb one another. The retained or unconscious thoughts from which the disturbances in speech emanate are of most varied origin. A general survey does not reveal any definite direction.

Comparative examinations of examples of mistakes in reading and writing lead to the same conclusions. Isolated cases, as in speech-blunders, seem to owe their origin to an unmotivated work of condensation (*e.g.*, the *Apel*). But we should like to know whether special conditions must not be fulfilled in order that such condensation, which is considered regular in dream-work and faulty in our waking thoughts, should take place. No information concerning this can be obtained from the examples themselves. But I would refuse to draw the conclusion from this, that there are no such conditions, as, for instance, the relaxation of conscious attention; for I have learned elsewhere that automatic actions are especially characterized by correctness and reliability. I would rather emphasize the fact that here, as so frequently in biology, it is the normal relations, or those approaching the normal, that are less favorable objects for investigation than the pathological. What remains obscure in the explanation of these most simple disturbances will, according to my expectation, be made clear through the explanation of more serious disturbances.

Also, mistakes in reading and writing do not lack examples in which more remote and more complicated motivation can be recognized.

There is no doubt that the disturbances of the speech functions occur more easily and make less demand on the disturbing forces than other psychic acts.

But one is on different ground when it comes to the examination of forgetting in the literal sense—*i.e.*, the forgetting of past experiences. (To distinguish this forgetting from the others, we designate *sensu strictiori* the forgetting of proper names and foreign words, as in Chapters I and II, as "slips"; and the forgetting of resolutions as "omissions.") The principal conditions of the normal process in forgetting are unknown.[14] We are also reminded

[14] I can perhaps give the following outline concerning the mechanism of actual forgetting. The memory material succumbs in general to two influences, condensation and distortion. Distortion is the work of the tendencies dominating the psychic life and directs itself above all against the affective remnants of memory traces which maintain a more resistive attitude towards condensation. The traces which have grown indifferent, merge into a process of condensation without opposition; in addition, it may be observed that tendencies of distortion also feed on the indifferent material, because they have not been gratified where they wished to manifest themselves. As these processes of condensation and distortion continue for long periods,

of the fact that not all is forgotten which we believe to be. Our explanation deals here only with those cases in which the forgetting arouses our astonishment, in so far as it infringes upon the rule that the unimportant is forgotten, while the important matter is guarded by memory. Analysis of these examples of forgetting, which seems to demand a special explanation, shows that the motive of forgetting is always an unwillingness to recall something which may evoke painful feelings. We come to the conjecture that this motive universally strives for expression in psychic life, but is inhibited through other and contrary forces from regularly manifesting itself. The extent and significance of this dislike to recall painful impressions seems worthy of the most painstaking psychologic investigation. The question as to what special conditions render possible the universally resistant forgetting in individual cases cannot be solved from this further connection.

A different factor steps into the foreground in the forgetting of resolutions; the supposed conflict resulting in the repression of the painful memory becomes tangible, and in the analysis of the examples, one regularly recognizes a counter-will which opposes but does not put an end to the resolution. As in previously discussed faulty acts, we here also recognize two types of the psychic process: the counter-will either turns directly against the resolution (in intentions of some consequence) or it is substantially foreign to the resolution itself and establishes its connection with it through an outer association (in almost indifferent resolutions).

The same conflict governs the phenomena of erroneously carried-out actions. The impulse which manifests itself in the disturbances of the action is frequently a counter-impulse. Still oftener, it is altogether a strange impulse which only utilizes the opportunity to express itself through a disturbance in the execution of the action. The cases in which the disturbance is the result of an inner contradiction are the most significant ones, and also deal with the more important activities.

The inner conflict in the chance or symptomatic actions then withdraws into the background. Those motor expressions,

during which all fresh experiences act upon the transformation of the memory content, it is our belief that it is time that makes memory uncertain and indistinct. It is quite probable that in forgetting, there can really be no quesion of a direct function of time. From the repressed memory traces, it can be verified that they suffer no changes even in the longest periods. The unconscious, at all events, knows no time limit. The most important, as well as the most peculiar character of psychic fixation consists in the fact that all impressions are, on the one hand, retained in the same form as they were received, and also in the forms that they have assumed in their further development. This state of affairs cannot be elucidated by any comparison from any other sphere. By virtue of this theory, every former state of the memory content may thus be restored, even though all original relations have long been replaced by newer ones.

which are least thought of, or are entirely overlooked by consciousness, serve as the expression of numerous unconscious or restrained feelings. For the most part, they represent symbolically wishes and phantasies.

The first question (as to the origin of the thoughts and emotions which find expression in faulty actions) we can answer by saying that in a series of cases, the origin of the disturbing thoughts can be readily traced to repressed emotions of the psychic life. Even in healthy persons, egotistic, jealous and hostile feelings and impulses, burdened by the pressure of moral education, often utilize the path of faulty actions to express in some way their undeniably existing force which is not recognized by the higher psychic instances. Allowing these faulty and chance actions to continue, corresponds, in great part, to a comfortable toleration of the unmoral. The manifold sexual currents play no insignificant part in these repressed feelings. That they appear so seldom in the thoughts revealed by the analyses of my examples, is simply a matter of coincidence. As I have undertaken the analyses of numerous examples from my own psychic life, the selection was partial from the first, and aimed at the exclusion of sexual matters. At other times, it seemed that the disturbing thoughts originated from the most harmless objection and consideration.

We have now reached the answer to the second question—that is, what psychologic conditions are responsible for the fact that a thought must seek expression, not in its complete form, but, as it were, in parasitic form, as a modification and disturbance of another. From the most striking examples of faulty actions, it is quite obvious that this determinant should be sought in a relation to conscious capacity, or in the more or less firmly pronounced character of "repression." But an examination of this series of examples shows that this character consists of many indistinct elements. The tendency to overlook something because it is wearisome, or the reflection that the concerned thought does not really belong to the intended matter, seems to play the same rôle as motives for the reflection of a thought (which later depends for expression on the disturbance of another), as the moral condemnation of a rebellious emotional feeling, or as the origin of absolutely unconscious trains of thought. An insight into the general nature of the condition of faulty and chance actions cannot be gained in this way.

However, this investigation gives us one single significant fact; the more harmless the motivation of the faulty act, the less obnoxious and hence, the less incapable of consciousness, the thought to which it gives expression is; the easier also becomes the solution of the phenomenon after we have turned our attention toward it. The simplest cases of speech-blunders are immediately noticed and spontaneously corrected. Where one deals with motivation through actually repressed feelings, the solution requires a painstaking analysis, which may sometimes strike against difficulties or turn out unsuccessful.

One is therefore justified in taking the result of this last investigation as an indication of the fact that the satisfactory explanation of the psychological conditions of faulty and chance actions is to be acquired in another way and from another source. The indulgent reader can, therefore, see in these discussions the demonstration of the surfaces of fracture in which this theme was quite artificially evolved from a broader connection.

VII. Just a few words to indicate the direction of this broader connection. The mechanism of the faulty and chance actions, as we have learned to know it through the application of analysis, shows in the most essential points an agreement with the mechanism of dream formation, which I have discussed in the chapter "The Dream Work" of my book on the interpretation of dreams. Here, as there, one finds condensation and compromise formation ("contaminations"); in addition, the situation is much the same, since unconscious thoughts find expression as modifications of other thoughts in unusual ways and through outer associations. The incongruities, absurdities and errors in the dream content, by virtue of which the dream is scarcely recognized as a psychic function, originate in the same way—to be sure, through freer usage of the existing material—as the common error of our every-day life; *here, as there, the appearance of the incorrect function is explained through the peculiar interference of two or more correct functions.*

An important conclusion can be drawn from this combination: the peculiar mode of operation, whose most striking function we recognize in the dream content, should not be attributed only to the sleeping state of the psychic life, when we possess abundant proof of its activity during the waking state in faulty actions. The same connection also forbids us from assuming that these psychic processes which impress us as abnormal and strange, are determined by deep-seated decay of psychic activity or by morbid state of function.[15]

The correct understanding of this strange psychic work, which allows the faulty actions to originate like the dream pictures, will only be possible after we have discovered that the psychoneurotic symptoms, particularly the psychic formations of hysteria and compulsion neurosis, repeat in their mechanisms all

[15] Cf. here *The Interpretation of Dreams* (p. 540, this volume), p. 559. Macmillan, New York; and Allen & Unwin, London.

the essential features of this mode of operation. The continuation of our investigation would therefore have to begin at this point.

There is still another special interest for us in considering the faulty, chance and symptomatic actions in the light of this last analogy. If we compare them to the function of the psychoneuroses and the neurotic symptoms, two frequently recurring statements gain in sense and support—namely, that the border-line between the nervous, normal and abnormal states is indistinct, and that we are all slightly nervous. Regardless of all medical experience, one may construe various types of such barely suggested nervousness, the *formes frustes* of the neuroses. There may be cases in which only a few symptoms appear, or they may manifest themselves rarely or in mild forms; the extenuation may be transferred to the number, intensity, or to the temporal outbreak of the morbid manifestation. It may also happen that just this type, which forms the most frequent transition between health and disease, may never be discovered. The transition type, whose morbid manifestations come in the form of faulty and symptomatic actions, is characterized by the fact that the symptoms are transformed to the least important psychic activities, while everything that can lay claim to a higher psychic value, remains free from disturbance. When the symptoms are disposed of in a reverse manner—that is, when they appear in the most important individual and social activities in a manner to disturb the functions of nourishment and sexual relations, professional and social life—such disposition is found in the severe cases of neuroses, and is perhaps more characteristic of the latter than the multiformity or vividness of the morbid manifestations.

But the common character of the mildest, as well as the severest cases, to which the faulty and chance actions contribute, lies *in the ability to refer the phenomena to unwelcome, repressed, psychic material, which, though pushed away from consciousness, is nevertheless not robbed of all capacity to express itself.*

EDMUND BERGLER & GEZA ROHEIM / Psychology of Time Perception

Clinical Observations

THE MOST important contribution to the psychology of time perception is Freud's discovery that the unconscious is timeless.[1] Classical proof is the evidence of dreams in which split seconds are felt as eternities, years are disregarded, chronology is scrambled or reversed.

No direct connection has been traced between infantile omnipotence and time perception although Freud stated that in the unconscious everybody considers himself to be immortal.[2] In fairy tales, daydreams, myths, and children's play, the element of time is freely disregarded.

Hanns Sachs has observed that the infant probably first learns appreciation of time during intervals between nursing.

In clinical analysis one finds that the child which persists in the neurotic personality of the adult still clings to the omnipotent fantasy of an existence free of the painful realities implicit in the progression of time.

An intelligent business woman sought analysis because of the bizarre phobia that a lion would attack her from behind in the dark. She could not remain alone at home evenings and was fearful of going out. 'Don't tell me, please,' she begged, 'there are no lions running around in apartments of a modern city. I know my fears are stupid and irrational.' She expressed preference for a treatment hour directly after her noon meal: 'I suffer from an old stomach disorder and have cramps after every meal. I have been advised to rest an hour after every meal. Since I have to lie on a couch for analysis, I thought to save time I could combine my midday rest with analysis.' Her 'organic' stomach troubles, she answered a little impatiently, were peculiar cramps in her bowels after eating. Rest relieved distressing flatulence after which she felt 'like a newborn.'

Analysis disclosed her fear of being attacked by a lion to

[1] Other contributions to this topic: Hollós, Isván: *Über das Zeitgefühl.* Int. Ztschr. f. Psa., VIII, 1922, pp. 421-439; Spielrein, Sabina; *Die Zeit im unterschwelligen Seelenleben.* Imago, IX, 1923, pp. 300-317. Hárnik, J.: *Die triebhaft-affektiven Momente im Zeitgefühl.* Imago, XI, 1925, pp. 32-57. Winterstein, Alfred: *Dürer's Melancholie.* Imago, XV, 1929, p. 195. Schilder, Paul: *Psychopathologie der Zeit.* Imago, XXI, 1935, pp. 261-278.

[2] Freud: *Reflections on War and Death.* New York: Moffat, Yard & Co., 1918.

be an œdipal rape fantasy. At the age of three she was taken by her father, a herculean man, to the zoo where she admired the lions. 'He is nearly as big as you are,' she told her flattered father. She wanted to feed the lions from her lunch box but was warned by her father that this would be dangerous. The substitution of lion for father was easily established. An attack from behind corresponded to her infantile fantasy that the anus was the female sexual organ. Darkness was associated with a primal scene. So far this is a commonplace anxiety hysteria. More interesting was the psychogenesis of her gastrointestinal symptoms. Eating proved to be a thinly disguised sexual fantasy. Each meal was an oral impregnation. The orally conceived baby developed in the bowels, and following labor pains (cramps) was delivered per anum (flatulence). It was psychologically quite appropriate that she then felt 'like a newborn.' This hysterical materialization of a typical childish fantasy of oral conception, intestinal pregnancy and anal birth was consummated in one hour, three times a day. In addition to the complete disregard of the realities of time, other evidences of infantile omnipotence were the multitude of 'children' she gave birth to in fantasy, the magical gratification of her unconscious incestuous strivings, and the perpetuation of her alimentary fantasy of sex.

A patient suffering from writer's cramp remembered that in early childhood he kept himself awake from sexual curiosity about his parents. His father died when the patient was four. He remembered that his father came home, ate dinner, went to bed, his mother urinated, his father put out the light, and then recollection faded. In the morning his mother awoke the boy who started immediately to investigate her face. 'What are you looking for?' the mother asked laughingly. 'Scars,' was the boy's laconic reply. In the child's sadistic misconception of parental coitus the 'wounds' inflicted on his mother healed overnight.

The study of alcoholic addicts repeatedly revealed, when they were asked specifically without leading questions, that they felt, when urinating in states of intoxication, they could 'urinate indefinitely'. Some reported they had a peculiar feeling of power when urinating, the expression of sadistic fantasies of omnipotence.[3]

A married woman of fifty, analyzed for her inability to

[3] *Cf.* Bergler, Edmund: *Zur Problematik des 'oralen' Pessimisten.* Imago, XX, 1934, pp. 330-376; also: Bergler, Edmund: *Contributions to the Psychogenesis of Alcohol Addiction.* Quarterly J. of Studies on Alcohol, Dec. 1944. The connection between urethral eroticism and infantile omnipotence was first stressed by Abraham, Karl: *Zur narzisstischen Bewertung der Exkretionsvor-gänge in Traum und Neurose.* In *Klinische Beiträge zur Psychoanalyse.* Vienna, 1921; and Róheim, Géza: *Das Selbst.* Imago, VII, 1921, p. 17.

react realistically toward time and money, arrived regularly half an hour late for her analytical appointment and always tried to prove that the analyst had cheated her of two or three minutes at the end. If the analyst left the room during the hour she regularly altered the clock to gain a few minutes to which she always confessed. Always late for appointments, she became anxious whenever she saw a bank and refused in her work to submit expense accounts. She talked in a high-pitched voice like a little girl and walked like a child. Of course, she was constantly begging cigarettes or food. She believed in ghosts, fairies, magic carpets, fortunetellers, telepathy, thought-waves and 'hunches'. She had severe anxieties that analysis might deprive her of these 'oddities', her greatest pleasures in life. Time and reality represented to her her frustrating mother against whom she was, with the aid of her supernatural powers (infantile omnipotence), continuously in revolt.

A psychotic man (hebephrenic) of thirty years, verbalized freely a personal myth replete with magic and with data bearing on temporal relationships.[4] On a theme of oral frustration, he said: 'All this trouble about the food and the bugs and about losing the wall and about things closing in upon me[5] is the same trouble as the sundial. People thought that kind of funny, too. I was trying to make it stand straight at twelve o'clock and to stop the sun while hurrying in the sky. There was a girl, she thought it was about her and that I was trying to catch her. . . . It was the same thing about the Fourth of July. People had lost the Fourth of July. It did not come when it ought to have come and many people died of hunger in consequence. I was examined but it was found that I had got the right date.' This was proved when he showed what he had eaten on the first, the second, the third and fourth.

These sentences clearly state 'there is something wrong with time' which has to do with hunger and a defense of himself. '*Others* had some trouble, and *others* suffered from hunger' is the refrain; then he declares that when it was discovered he was not wrong about the date, and that he had eaten something (or everything), he was President of the United States. To test whether 'time and tide wait for no man', he tried (mentally) to reach out for a ship at sea. 'This was noon and I was taking my food too seriously. . . . This was in the year 1894 but people had lost part of the time; they thought it was 1849. . . .' He would not trust the watch that was in the house but he could 'trust the sundial because

[4] Róheim, Géza: *The Psychology of Magic.* (in preparation) will include a detailed interpretation of the psychopathology of this patient studied by the author for eighteen months.

[5] This theme is always related in connection with stories about his birth.

that was like a drinking fountain'. Once he said 'ten o'clock' and as the word came out of his teeth it was lost, so he went to see where ten o'clock was, and then he had trouble with the sundial again. He lost track of time from believing it was breakfast time when really it was dinner time. At first the loss was only eight or nine years but soon it amounted to a hundred years, all because somebody was hungry; some people thought he was hungry. He kept track of time by keeping track of ships; also by the sun, but then he would look at a line made by the sun, or at railroads, because clocks were not reliable. Food can make you lose time and lose yourself. Losing his job and losing time are the same thing and both are identical with the food trouble. Once when he was for seven or eight years in a place like this (State Hospital), somebody asked him what time it was. It was noon and he was eating his noon meal, but he was fooling and said it was breakfast time the next day. Then the whole trouble was started by somebody eating the soup that he was eating but eating it in the opposite direction. He could not discover what mistake he had made—perhaps with the food. He used to travel about with a man whose name was Teethy. He was eating a beef stew 'and it was full of bugs but not real bugs, you know'. Whenever he moved the sundial, he tried to move the sun from its course. 'They' did not like that; it was as if he had eaten the stew and accidentally splashed it on someone else. Something was wrong with time; he was not born at the time people said he was born; consequently he tried to remove the sun from the sky.

Like Joshua and Maui this patient was trying to prevent time from passing. He states quite literally that this loss of time is caused by someone's hunger which is his way of saying he had to wait too long for his food and the time passed very slowly. In his fantasies of magical omnipotence this painful experience is transformed into a great victory: time passes very quickly and it is he who prevents the sun from progressing too rapidly. In eating his dinner at breakfast time, or at dinner in saying it is breakfast time the next day, he is always ahead of time; a complete denial of having to wait for his food. He was indeed 'taking his food too seriously'.

Every conscious or latent fantasy of infantile omnipotence disturbs the normal perception of time. These feelings of omnipotence are abundant in dreams and fantasies, evident in games and during coitus. Seriously questioned about their estimate of the duration of sexual intercourse, most individuals and patients first parry with the joke that they do not carry a watch at such times, and are then vague and indefinite. Frustration being absent during coitus, there is no perception of time. It is assumed that the reality principle is based on the intrusion of a certain modicum of frustration.

Infantile omnipotence and time perception are mutual contradictions. Omnipotence is in unalloyed accord with the pleasure principle; perception of time is a function of the reality principle. Infantile omnipotence is a product of the child's 'autarchic fantasy'[6] which negates everything not in agreement with its omnipotence. This fiction is shattered gradually by the infant's gradual realization of its complete dependence on the mother.[7]

Interestingly enough, the oral 'autarchic fantasy' can be utilized—even after it has been partially corrected by reality—to negate the anxiety of being separated from the mother which is gradually overcome by the transition from passivity to activity. Activity resolves the necessity of waiting for gratification of one's needs. The cathexis is withdrawn from the object and invested in the ego.[8]

Being punctual, doing things at given times, are duties imposed on the child which become incorporated in its superego, in many instances not without rebellion. A schizoid writer did everything at unconventional times. He worked during the night, slept during the daytime, had his dinner at three A.M. and so on. This was an exaggerated repetitive compulsion to defy parentally imposed schedules for specific tasks. In the manner of reversal, the element of infantile omnipotence is apparent.

A grandmother visiting her grandchild, age five, brought her a cake. The child, pleased, said, 'A birthday cake, and we are going to have a birthday party!' The grandmother objected, 'We can't do that, you know, because your birthday is the fifteenth of October.' The child retorted angrily, 'I can have a birthday cake, and a birthday, and a birthday party every day if I want to!'

There are patients whose narcissism is so intense that the end of each analytic appointment is perceived as being 'thrown out'. The patient understands *logically* the limitation of his time, that the next patient is waiting, and the end of the appointment no personal offense. *Affectively,* however, he reacts differently. With unerring accuracy and without looking at his watch, he gets up from the couch announcing that the time is up. Careful experi-

[6] Jekels, Ludwig and Bergler, Edmund: *Übertragung und Liebe.* Imago, XX, 1934, pp. 5-32.

[7] For details see Ferenczi, Sándor: *Stages in the Development of the Sense of Reality.* In *Contributions to Psychoanalysis.* Boston: Richard G. Badger, 1916. For an up-to-date summary of clinical investigations on childlike omnipotence: Bergler, Edmund: *Thirty Some Years After Ferenczi's 'Stages in the Development of the Sense of Reality'.* Psa. Rev., XXXII, 1945, No. 2.

[8] *Cf.* Freud's 'unconscious repetition compulsion' which comprises also *active* repetition of *passive* experiences. *Beyond the Pleasure Principle.* New York: Boni & Liveright, 1922.

ment to exclude covert glancing at a watch or clock, or the sounds announcing the arrival of a succeeding patient by postponing that appointment, makes no difference. With the regularity of a clock these patients correctly, subjectively measure the interval of time in the service of their narcissistic defense: they end the appointment, not the analyst and thus 'save face'. It is, of course, a common observation that many individuals keep accurate account of time while asleep, awakening without external stimulus at regular intervals to feed a baby, or on rare occasions awakening similarly at an unaccustomed hour to make ready for a journey.

The ultimate relationship between time and weaning is shown in the following dream of a woman patient, age twenty-five, with phobias, whose husband was expected shortly to be discharged from the army.

> 'My mother tells me at a lunch counter that my cousin Betty is being analyzed by you and I am jealous . . . The clock has stopped. Betty is helping me to dress. I am rushing to be on time for my appointment with you. The runners are down my hose. . . . I don't know the name of the place where you live. I rush with Betty and get into a bus. There are two buses waiting. The bus becomes a taxi. Betty disappears. I pay the driver with *centavos*. . . . You appear on a porch. First you look like my father; then you become my stepmother, Kitty. There are children around and one of them is shooting. I told Betty before she disappeared that we would meet again at the luncheon counter.'

The association to the unknown name of the place is Utopia. *Centavos* is five, the age she was when her brother was born. She reacts to her husband as a sibling-rival as she does to her cousin Betty. Betty in this dream is equated with her brother in the past and her husband in the present. The birth of her brother was for her a severe oral disappointment and frustration. The clock stops to prevent her husband (brother) from returning (being born). Her husband's presence is a threat to her analysis. Stopping the clock simultaneously cancels the birth of her brother: she never had been nor will be separated from the luncheon counter (mother-analyst) in a timeless Utopia. The little boy who shoots with a toy gun proves to be herself. The hostility is directed towards Kitty, her father's second wife, whom she can kill, and, in Utopia, have her father in accordance with her unresolved œdipal demands. She is back in her infancy, the clock has stopped, time is abolished.

The part of the unconscious personality which watches over time perception is the unconscious part of the ego, under the influence of the superego.

Much confusion is introduced into the problem if one

studies proverbs, adages and the like as a guide to what libidinous stage of development time perception is attached because these expressions lead, and mislead, to every stage. From 'time runs short' and 'time which devours everything' (Plutarch)—one might conclude that urethral and oral elements are exclusively involved. Anal elements may be erroneously deduced from expressions like 'pressed for time', 'saving time', 'wasting time' and the like. These are all secondary to feelings of infantile omnipotence attached to every erogenous zone, and have nothing to do with time perception *per se*.

With the development of the superego and the yielding of fantasies of omnipotence to the encroachment of reality, the child finds out that it is, after all, under the 'command of the clock'.[9] From reasonable punctuality this may progress under the stimulus of an excessive superego to the grotesque extremes of self-torture seen in obsessional neuroses.

In summary: time perception is an artefact built in the unconscious ego after partial mastering of blows against the 'autarchic fiction'. Therefore time and duty are associated. In every endeavor in which childlike omnipotence is fantasied, normal perception of time is disturbed.[10]

Timelessness in Fantasy and Folklore

The pleasure principle and timelessness are linked together, as are time and the reality principle. In Fairyland, Elysium, The Happy Otherworld, there exists what we all seek in this world: eternal youth.

The Irish story of the Voyage of Bran preserved in manuscripts ranging from the twelfth to the sixteenth century tells us how Bran went to the Land of the Hereafter and how he returned.

One day Bran, Son of Febal, heard music and such was its sweetness that he fell asleep. When he awoke (i.e. in his dream) he saw a beautiful woman with a branch of an apple tree. He followed her over the sea and came to the Land of Women and Eternal Youth. Welcomed there by the Chief of Women, 'The woman throws the ball of thread to Bran which clave to his palm.

[9] Being unpunctual has many different determinants, among them, aggression, self-punishment, reparation for childhood disappointments by letting other people wait. An example of punctuality in the service of the superego is the legend cultivated over sixty years for the benefit of Austrian school children that the Emperor Franz Joseph got up every day at six, was sitting at his desk at six thirty, and that he always arrived on the dot for every official function.

[10] Some connections of time perception with impatience and with feelings of uncanniness have been incorporated in other studies. *Cf.* Bergler, Edmund: *Psychoanalysis of the Ability to Wait and of Impatience.* Psa. Rev., XXVI, 1939, pp. 11-32, and *Psychoanalysis of the Uncanny.* Int. J. Psa., XV, 1934, pp. 215-244.

The thread of the ball was in the woman's hands and she pulled the coracle towards the port. Thereupon they went into a large house in which there was a bed for every couple. The food that was put on the dish vanished not from them. It seemed a year to them that they were there—it chanced to be many years.'[11] (The mythological themes of 'inexhaustible food' and of 'eternal youth' are practically interchangeable.) But homesickness seizes Bran and his fellow voyagers. They return and as soon as they touch the earth of Ireland they become a heap of ashes. Many hundreds of years have passed in what seemed a short time to them.[12]

In the *Echtra Connla* (Adventures of Connla) the woman from the *sid* (fairy mound) is in love with Connla of the Ruddy Hair. She invites him to the Land of Eternal Youth where she leaves him. 'So she departed and left to Connla an apple, and this was his sole sustenance for a month and yet nothing was diminished of it'.[13]

Oisin describes the Land of Youth in the following verses:

> 'Abundant there are honey and wine
> And aught else the eye has beheld.
> Fleeting time shall not bend thee
> Death nor Decay shalt thou see.'

Again we find the golden apple in the hand of the damsel.[14] When Cuchulinn goes to the fairy mansion

> 'There is a vat there of merry mead
> A-distributing into the household.
> Still it remains, constant the custom
> So that it is ever full, ever and always.'[15]

In Mælduin's Voyage, 'for forty nights each of the three apples sufficed them and the apples took care of hunger and thirst alike'.[16] The apple of immortality is the mother's breast. In current European folklore we find the same story elements.

In a story of Northeastern Bohemia, a poor woman held her infant with one arm and picked strawberries in the forest with the other. She was thinking of her hard work and poverty when a cave opened suddenly; it was full of gold coins and treasures. She rushed in to get the treasure and when she ran out again she had forgotten the child and the cave was closed. She cried and implored the fairy of the hill to return the infant. But it was all in vain.

[11] Meyer, K. and Nutt, A.: *The Voyage of Bran, Son of Febal.* (Grimm Library, No. 4.) London: David Nutt, 1895, I, p. 30.
[12] *Ibid.*, I, p. 32.
[13] *Ibid.*, I, p. 145.
[14] *Ibid.*, I, p. 150.
[15] *Ibid.*, I, p. 155.
[16] *Ibid.*, I, p. 169.

Next year at the same time when the strawberries were ripe she went again to pick them. Behold, the cave was open and there was the child just as she had left it, playing with an apple, held in its hand. The happy mother pressed the infant to her *breast,* and at home the child told her that the golden apple was the fairy woman's gift, and henceforth the presence of the apple in the cottage protected them from all want and poverty.[17]

A mother cannot be continuously with her children. A short period of separation may seem an eternity to the child which feels abandoned. The 'gold' (fæces) is the 'anal magic' of the child during periods of separation. The fairy mother of the child's fantasy is one from whom the child is never separated. The child is in continuous possession of the apple[18] which in all folklore is unmistakably the breast.

At Szöreg and Ó'Szent Iván, if a child smiles and looks at its own nails, it is playing with the golden apple. So long as it does not touch a cat it is playing with the golden apple. The apple is the one the Virgin Mary gave to the infant Jesus. The milk of the mother, used for curative or magical purposes, is called Milk of the Virgin Mary,[19] linking the Virgin Mary's apple and the mother's breast. The apples of the Hesperides, probably also that of the Garden of Eden,[20] and those of Iduna and the Norse gods are such apples of immortality.[21] Teleut and other heroes lose all track of time while they are feasting.[22]

In these myths, the food (breast) eaten by the protagonists makes them immortal. Immortality is lost whenever they eat in the world of reality.[23] The hero returns home from fairyland; he is aged but does not know it. No sooner has he eaten food offered to him by mortals than he falls dead.[24] This is not a change, but a persistence of the same theme in another form: the hero has achieved the lasting immortality of the dead, liberated from time and frustration.

[17] Kühnau, R.: *Schlesische Sagen.* Leipzig. Teubner, 1911, III, p. 669.

[18] In Kühnau's collection we find several of these legends. *Cf.* the one quoted by Hartland, E. S.: *The Science of Fairy Tales.* London: Walter Scott, 1891, p. 176, quoting Grohmann: *Sagen aus Böhmen,* 1883, pp. 29, 289, 296, 298, and Müller: *Siebenbürgische Sagen.* 1885, p. 83.

[19] Kálmány, L.: *Boldogasszony, ösvallásunk istenasszonya. (Boldogasszony, a Goddess of Hungarian Paganism.)* Budapest: Magyar Tudományos Akademia, 1885, pp. 22, 23. On the apple see further Róheim. Géza: *Aphrodite, or the Woman With a Penis* This QUARTERLY, XIV 1945, pp. 386-387.

[20] *Cf.* Róheim, Géza: *The Garden of Eden.* Psa. Rev., XXVII, 1940, p. 180.

[21] Meyer, R. M.: *Altgermanische Religionsgeschichte.* Leipzig: Quelle und Meyer, 1910, p. 386. The fairy takes an apple from her bosom and uses it to revive the dead hero. Krauss, F. S.: *Slavische Volksforschungen.* Leipzig: W. Heims, 1908, p. 374.

[22] Radloff, W.: *Proben der Volksliteratur der Türkischen Stämme Süd Sibiriens.* St. Petersburg: Kais. Akad. d. Wiss., 1886, I, p. 95.

[23] Hartland, E. S.: *Op. cit.,* p. 189.

[24] Rhys, John: *Celtic Folklore.* Oxford: Clarendon Press, 1901, I, p. 155.

Whatever the form, the period during which time stops is always one of pleasurable activity. A man hears enchanting music which lures him to the Otherworld. He has been dancing with the fairies a little while and awakens to discover he has been away for years, and when he is drawn out of the enchantment, he molders away.[25]

Alice's Adventures in Wonderland provide perhaps the clearest illustration of the victory of oral magic over time. To cite only one striking incident, the Mad Hatter's tea party, it will be recalled that the March Hare and the Mad Hatter were always having tea because, time having stopped, it was always six o'clock.

> 'If you knew time as well as I do,' said the Hatter, 'you wouldn't talk about wasting *it*. It's him.'
>
> 'I don't know what you mean', said Alice. 'Of course you don't', the Hatter said, tossing his head contemptuously. 'I dare say you have never spoken to Time.'
>
> 'Perhaps not', Alice cautiously replied, 'but I know I have to beat time when I learn music'.
>
> 'Ah, that accounts for it', said the Hatter. 'He won't stand beating. Now if you only kept on good terms with him, he'd do almost anything you liked with the clock. For instance, suppose it were nine o'clock in the morning, just time to begin lessons: you'd only have to whisper a hint to Time and round goes the clock in a twinkling! Half past one, time for dinner!'

The Alice who 'beats' Time is the impatient infant waiting for oral gratification and experiencing both aggression and reality at the same time. Being on good terms with Time ensures continuous oral gratification, time for dinner. Trouble had started when the Mad Hatter, who was singing about a 'tea tray in the sky', was 'murdering time'; whereupon the Queen (frustrating mother) said, 'Off with his head'. Here we have a literal statement of the sequence: time-suspense-hunger-child's aggression directed against the mother and the mother's retaliation against the child. Time and oral frustration are combined associatively when the Mad Hatter mends his watch with the very best butter, and when gloomily he dips it into his cup of tea. The Dormouse, who has overcome time not by eating but by sleeping, when he wakes up eventually, tells a story about people who lived in a treacle well.

Time in Primitive and Advanced Cultures

There can be no doubt about the fact that there are differences in the way primitive races, European peasants, country squires, and city dwellers behave in their reactions to time.

[25] Hartland, E. S.: *Op. cit.*, pp. 161-165.

At the bottom end of the scale, the relationship of the stone age people of Central Australia to time seems practically nil from our point of view. Whether something happens now or several months later does not matter very much. They have nothing like planning for the future, no means of producing or of storing food. They are never worried that they will have to go without food. They have a word for day, for month and for the year, but no calendar. Their attitudes towards numbers and quantities are parallel phenomena. Enumeration ends with four. Any number that exceeds four is 'a big mob'. They readily exchange one object for another, and have no definite quantitative system of values.

A previous interpretation of these facts[26] relating them to the absence of anal character formation is partly correct only as it refers to cleanliness. The relative absence of anxiety about time is certainly correlated with the fact that they have very permissive and good mothers; however, that their religion and ritual contains denials of time strongly suggests a substratum of anxiety even in this primitive society. The gods or ancestors of these tribes are the 'eternal ones of the dream'. Every human being has an immortal double who lives eternally in the totemic case (womb) and who is identical with the mythical father or ancestor who eternally 'procreates' his sons by throwing a symbolic penis (*tjurunga*) at the women. These eternal ancestors are represented ritualistically by the old men of the tribe who during the ritual are believed literally to become the ancestors whom they represent. The representation of these 'eternal' beings is a countermeasure against separation anxiety (primary frustration).[27]

By contrast, on Normanby Island, an agricultural community, the life of the natives revolves around the idea of food, especially the yam. They have an agricultural calendar with lunar months named chiefly in accordance with phases of agricultural work. Their sense of time is, as one would expect, stronger. They prepare for food distribution ceremonies within a certain period, and they store food to last them for a certain period. The mothers are hostile to the children, each child being really unwanted.

The obsessional overevaluation of time appears in our culture in part as a striving to achieve mastery over infantile disappointments. Prominent anal determinants ('Time is money') derive from that important phase of the infantile fantasy of omnipotence associated with the sense of power in yielding or withholding the content of the rectum. The measurement of work and

[26] Róheim, Géza: *Psychoanalysis of Primitive Cultural Types.* Int. J. Psa., XIII, 1932, p. 84.

[27] *Cf.* Róheim, Géza: *The Eternal Ones of the Dream.* New York: International Universities Press, 1945, p. 149.

of compensation for it stems from a gradual molding of social reality by the autonomous magic of the human body.

The nuclear element in the calendar is the moon. The interlunium is a period of anxiety, and the reappearance of the moon an occasion for rejoicing. At the new moon the natives of Normanby Island clap their hands on their half open lips intermittently producing the sound u-u-u. They repeat, 'My prey, big, come up!' to ensure success in hunting, and in the hope of growing as fat as the moon. In the neighboring Ferguson Islands it is the children who watch for the new moon rising to greet its appearance with a loud u-u-u, beating their mouths with their fingers.[28] Among the Nandi when children see the new moon they spit at it and say, 'Welcome moon! If thou eatest anything may it choke thee. If I eat anything may it do me good.'[29] When a Masai sees the new moon he throws a twig at it and says, 'Give me long life; give me strength.' When a pregnant woman sees the new moon she milks some milk into a small gourd which she covers with green grass and then pours it in the direction of the moon saying, 'Moon, give my child safety'.

In these and many other instances, the moon represents the maternal object with the emphasis on object-loss in the interlunium and rejoicing with lip-play and references to food when the moon reappears. The attitude towards the disappearing and reappearing mother symbol is ambivalent. Its disappearance, for example, is ascribed to its being eaten by a demon, the demon of the eclipse representing the child. The Masai and other Northeast African tribes reckon the month from the days during which the moon is invisible,[30] the nights of greatest anxiety.

The classical home of the calendar is Babylonia. The Babylonian calendar of Hammurabi marked the seventh, fourteenth, twenty-first and twenty-eighth days—which divide the lunar phases—as days of evil.[31] A change in the moon causes anxiety. In all these regulations, however, the moon is less a maternal object than a symbol of the king. Very frequently the moon represents something with which the male identifies in his relationship to the female. Identification and object relationship originally converge in a dual unity. The regulations for the seventh day read: 'An evil day. The shepherd of great peoples

[28] Jenness, I. and Ballantyne, H.: *The Northern d'Entre-Castreaux.* Oxford: Clarendon Press, 1920, p. 160.

[29] Hollis, A. C.: *The Nandi, Their Language and Folklore.* Oxford: Clarendon Press, 1909, pp. 122, 123.

[30] Hirschberg, W.: *Die Zeitrechnung der Masai und verwandter Völker.* Ztschr. f. Ethnologie, LXV, 1933, p. 244.

[31] Webster, H.: *Rest Days.* New York: The Macmillan Co., 1916, pp. 223-225.

(king) shall not eat flesh cooked upon the coals, or bread of the oven. The garment of his body he shall not change, he shall not put on clean garments.' The nineteenth day would seem to have been particularly taboo, for then the king was not supposed to eat anything touched by fire. Although the taboo extends to other aspects of life as well there seems to be special emphasis on food and fire as with the Hebrew Sabbath.[32] The *shabattum* in Babylonia was the full moon and, according to Jastrow, was the equivalent of *um nukh libbi* which was a standard expression for appeasing the anger of the deity. *Shabattum* is therefore a day of propitiation.[33] It is not quite clear whether, as Jastrow implies, the gods cease their anger, or whether the human beings refrain from provoking the anger of the gods.

In Babylonian calendars certain days are called *nubattu,* a term signifying rest, pause, especially, a 'god's connubial rest with his consort goddess'. The observance of such days prohibited attending to important diplomatic missions or setting out on a journey. 'It is quite possible that *shabattum* and *nubattum* are from the same root.'[34] The day would seem unconsciously to signify the opposite of rest—the *coniunctio* of the parents—and activity taboo because of the anxiety associated with the primal scene. In ancient Athens the new moon was the marriage of the sun and the moon.[35] If time signifies separation from the mother to the nursing infant, the primal scene is especially charged with such painful significance.

Anthropological data confirm the interpretations of clinical observation. The passage of time symbolizes the period of separation. Observation of the phases of the moon and other phenomena are based on this anxiety. Timelessness is the fantasy in which mother and child are endlessly united. The calendar is an ultimate materialization of separation anxiety.

[32] *Ibid.*

[33] Jastrow, M.: *The Original Character of the Hebrew Sabbath.* Amer. J. of Theology, II, 1898, pp. 316, 351.

[34] Johns, C. H. C.: Encyclopædia Britannica (Eleventh Edition), Vol. XXIII, p. 961. The last days of the month are the days of ravishment of the moon god, when the moon descends into the lower world. Langdon, S.: *Babylonian Menologies and the Semitic Calendar.* London: The British Academy, 1935, pp. 81-82.

[35] Roscher, W. H.: *Über Selene und Verwandtes.* Leipzig: Teubner, 1890, p. 77.

VOLTAIRE / Candide

How Candide Was Brought Up in a Fine Castle and How He Was Expelled From Thence

THERE LIVED in Westphalia, in the castle of my Lord the Baron of Thunder-ten-tronckh, a young man, on whom nature had bestowed the most agreeable manners. His face was the index to his mind. He had an upright heart, with an easy frankness; which, I believe, was the reason he got the name of *Candide*. He was suspected, by the old servants of the family, to be the son of my Lord the Baron's sister, by a very honest gentleman of the neighborhood, whom the young lady declined to marry, because he could only produce seventy-one armorial quarterings; the rest of his genealogical tree having been destroyed through the injuries of time.

The Baron was one of the most powerful lords in Westphalia; his castle had both a gate and windows; and his great hall was even adorned with tapestry. The dogs of his outer yard composed his hunting pack upon occasion, his grooms were his huntsmen, and the vicar of the parish was his chief almoner. He was called My Lord by everybody, and everyone laughed when he told his stories.

My Lady the Baroness, who weighed about three hundred and fifty pounds, attracted, by that means, very great attention, and did the honors of the house with a dignity that rendered her still more respectable. Her daughter Cunegonde, aged about seventeen years, was of a ruddy complexion, fresh, plump, and well calculated to excite the passions. The Baron's son appeared to be in every respect worthy of his father. The preceptor, Pangloss, was the oracle of the house, and little Candide listened to his lectures with all the simplicity that was suitable to his age and character.

Pangloss taught metaphysico-theologo-cosmolonigology. He proved most admirably, that there could not be an effect without a cause; that, in this best of possible worlds, my Lord the Baron's castle was the most magnificent of castles, and my Lady the best of Baronesses that possibly could be.

"It is demonstrable," said he, "that things cannot be otherwise than they are: for all things having been made for some end, they must necessarily be for the best end. Observe well, that the nose has been made for carrying spectacles; therefore we have spectacles. The legs are visibly designed for stockings, and therefore we have stockings. Stones have been formed to be hewn, and make castles; therefore my Lord has a very fine castle; the greatest baron of the province ought to be the best accommodated. Swine were made to be eaten; therefore we eat pork all the year round: consequently, those who have merely asserted that all is good, have said a very foolish thing; they should have said all is the best possible."

Candide listened attentively, and believed implicitly; for he thought Miss Cunegonde extremely handsome, though he never had the courage to tell her so. He concluded, that next to the good fortune of being Baron of Thunder-ten-tronckh, the second degree of happiness was that of being Miss Cunegonde, the third to see her every day, and the fourth to listen to the teachings of Master Pangloss, the greatest philosopher of the province, and consequently of the whole world.

One day Cunegonde having taken a walk in the environs of the castle, in a little wood, which they called a park, espied Doctor Pangloss giving a lesson in experimental philosophy to her mother's chambermaid; a little brown wench, very handsome, and very docile. As Miss Cunegonde had a strong inclination for the sciences, she observed, without making any noise, the reiterated experiments that were going on before her eyes; she saw very clearly the sufficient reason of the Doctor, the effects and the causes; and she returned greatly flurried, quite pensive, and full of desire to be learned; imagining that she might be a sufficient reason for young Candide, who also, might be the same to her.

On her return to the castle, she met Candide, and blushed; Candide also blushed; she wished him good morrow with a faltering voice, and Candide answered her, hardly knowing what he said. The next day, after dinner, as they arose from table, Cunegonde and Candide happened to get behind the screen. Cunegonde dropped her handkerchief, and Candide picked it up; she, not thinking any harm, took hold of his hand; and the young man, not thinking any harm neither, kissed the hand of the young lady, with an eagerness, a sensibility, and grace, very particular; their lips met, their eyes sparkled, their knees trembled, their hands strayed.—The Baron of Thunder-ten-tronckh happening to pass close by the screen, and observing this cause and effect, thrust Candide out of the castle, with lusty kicks. Cunegonde fell into a swoon and as soon as she came to herself, was heartily cuffed on the ears by my Lady the Baroness. Thus all was thrown into confusion in the finest and most agreeable castle possible.

What Became of Candide Among the Bulgarians

Candide being expelled the terrestrial paradise, rambled a long while without knowing where, weeping, and lifting up his eyes to heaven, and sometimes turning them towards the finest of castles, which contained the handsomest of baronesses. He laid himself down, without his supper, in the open fields, between two furrows, while the snow fell in great flakes. Candide, almost frozen to death, crawled next morning to the neighboring village, which was called Waldber-ghoff-trarbk-dikdorff. Having no money, and almost dying with hunger and fatigue, he stopped in a dejected posture before the gate of an inn. Two men, dressed in blue, observing him in such a situation, "Brother," says one of them to the other, "there is a young fellow well built, and of a proper height." They accosted Candide, and invited him very civilly to dinner.

"Gentlemen," replied Candide, with an agreeable modesty, "you do me much honor, but I have no money to pay my shot."

"O sir," said one of the blues, "persons of your appearance and merit never pay anything; are you not five feet five inches high?"

"Yes, gentlemen, that is my height," returned he, making a bow.

"Come, sir, sit down at table; we will not only treat you, but we will never let such a man as you want money; men are made to assist one another."

"You are in the right," said Candide; "that is what Pangloss always told me, and I see plainly that everything is for the best."

They entreated him to take a few crowns, which he accepted, and would have given them his note; but they refused it, and sat down to table.

"Do not you tenderly love—?"

"O yes," replied he, "I tenderly love Miss Cunegonde."

"No," said one of the gentlemen; "we ask you if you do tenderly love the King of the Bulgarians?"

"Not at all," said he, "for I never saw him."

"How! he is the most charming of kings, and you must drink his health."

"O, with all my heart, gentlemen," and drinks.

"That is enough," said they to him; "you are now the bulwark, the support, the defender, the hero of the Bulgarians; your fortune is made, and you are certain of glory." Instantly they put him in irons, and carried him to the regiment. They made him turn to the right, to the left, draw the rammer, return the rammer, present, fire, step double; and they gave him thirty blows with a cudgel. The next day, he performed his exercise not quite so badly, and received but twenty blows; the third day the blows were restricted to ten, and he was looked upon by his fellow-soldiers, as a kind of prodigy.

Candide, quite stupefied, could not well conceive how he had become a hero. One fine Spring day he took it into his head to walk out, going straight forward, imagining that the human, as well as the animal species, were entitled to make whatever use they pleased of their limbs. He had not travelled two leagues, when four other heroes, six feet high, came up to him, bound him, and put him into a dungeon. He is asked by a Court-martial, whether he chooses to be whipped six and thirty times through the whole regiment, or receive at once twelve bullets through the forehead? He in vain argued that the will is free, and that he chose neither the one nor the other; he was obliged to make a choice; he therefore resolved, in virtue of God's gift called *free-will,* to run the gauntlet six and thirty times. He underwent this discipline twice. The regiment being composed of two thousand men, he received four thousand lashes, which laid open all his muscles and nerves, from the nape of the neck to the back. As they were proceeding to a third course, Candide, being quite spent, begged as a favor that they would be so kind as to shoot him; he obtained his request; they hoodwinked him, and made him kneel; the King of the Bulgarians passing by, inquired into the crime of the delinquent; and as this prince was a person of great penetration, he discovered from what he heard of Candide, that he was a young metaphysician, entirely ignorant of the things of this world; and he granted him his pardon, with a clemency which will be extolled in all histories, and throughout all ages. An experienced surgeon cured Candide in three weeks, with emollients prescribed by no less a master than Dioscorides. His skin had already begun to grow again, and he was able to walk, when the King of the Bulgarians gave battle to the King of the Abares. . . .

Tempest, Shipwreck, Earthquake and What Became of Dr. Pangloss, Candide and James the Anabaptist

One half of the passengers being weakened, and ready to breathe their last, with the inconceivable anguish which the rolling of the ship conveyed through the nerves and all the humors of the body, which were quite disordered, were not capable of being alarmed at the danger they were in. The other half uttered cries and made prayers; the sails were rent, the masts broken, and the ship became leaky. Every one worked that was able, nobody cared for any thing, and no order was kept. The Anabaptist contributed his assistance to work the ship. As he was upon deck, a furious sailor rudely struck him, and laid him sprawling on the planks; but with the blow he gave him, he himself was so violently jolted, that he tumbled overboard with his head foremost, and remained suspended by a piece of a broken mast. Honest James ran to his assistance, and helped him on deck again; but in the attempt, he fell into the sea, in the sight of the sailor, who suffered him to perish, without deigning to look upon him. Candide drew near and saw his benefactor, one moment emerging, and the next swallowed up for ever. He was just going to throw himself into the sea after him, when the philosopher Pangloss hindered him, by demonstrating to him, that the road to Lisbon had been made on purpose for this Anabaptist to be drowned in. While he was proving this, *a priori,* the vessel foundered, and all perished except Pangloss, Candide, and the brutal sailor, who drowned the virtuous Anabaptist. The villain luckily swam ashore, whither Pangloss and Candide were carried on a plank.

When they had recovered themselves a little, they walked towards Lisbon. They had some money left, with which they hoped to save themselves from hunger, after having escaped from the storm.

Scarce had they set foot in the city, bewailing the death of their benefactor, when they perceived the earth to tremble under their feet, and saw the sea swell in the harbor, and dash to pieces the ships that were at anchor. The whirling flames and ashes covered the streets and public places, the houses tottered, and their roofs fell to the foundations, and the foundations were scattered; thirty thousand inhabitants of all ages and sexes were crushed to death in the ruins. The sailor, whistling and swearing, said, "There is some booty to be got here." "What can be the sufficient reason of this phenomenon?" said Pangloss. "This is certainly the last day of the world," cried Candide. The sailor ran quickly into the midst of the ruins, encountered death to find money, found it, laid hold of it, got drunk, and having slept himself sober, purchased the favors of the first willing girl he met with, among the ruins of the demolished houses, and in the midst of the dying and the dead. While he was thus engaged, Pangloss pulled him by the sleeve; "My friend," said he, "this is not right; you trespass against universal reason, you choose your time badly." "Brains and blood!" answered the other; "I am a sailor, and was born at Batavia; you have mistaken your man, this time, with your universal reason."

Some pieces of stone having wounded Candide, he lay sprawling in the street, and covered with rubbish. "Alas!" said he to Pangloss, "get me a little wine and oil; I am dying." "This trembling of the earth is no new thing," answered Pangloss. "The City of Lima, in America, experienced the same concussions last year; the same cause has the same effects; there is certainly a train of sulphur under the earth, from Lima to Lisbon." "Nothing is more probable," said Candide; "but, for God's sake, a little oil and wine." "How probable?" replied the philosopher; "I maintain that the thing is demonstrable." Candide lost all sense, and Pangloss brought him a little water from a neighboring fountain.

The day following, having found some provisions, in rummaging through the rubbish, they recruited their strength a little. Afterwards, they employed themselves like others, in administering relief to the inhabitants that had escaped from death. Some citizens that had been relieved by them, gave them as good a dinner as could be expected amidst such a disaster. It is true that the repast was mournful, and the guests watered their bread with their tears. But Pangloss consoled them by the assurance that things could not be otherwise; "For," said he, "all this must necessarily be for the best. As this volcano is at Lisbon, it could not be elsewhere; as it is impossible that things should not be what they are, as all is good."

A little man clad in black, who belonged to the inquisition, and sat at his side, took him up very politely, and said: "It seems, sir, you do not believe in original sin; for if all is for the best, then there has been neither fall nor punishment."

"I most humbly ask your excellency's pardon," answered Pangloss, still more politely; "for the fall of man and the curse necessarily entered into the best of worlds possible." "Then, sir, you do not believe there is liberty," said the inquisitor. "Your Excellency will excuse me," said Pangloss; "liberty can consist with absolute necessity; for it was necessary we should be free; because, in short, the determinate will—"

Pangloss was in the middle of his proposition, when the inquisitor made a signal with his head to the tall armed footman in a cloak, who waited upon him, to bring him a glass of port wine.

How a Fine Inquisition Was Celebrated to Prevent Earthquakes, and How Candide Was Whipped

After the earthquake, which had destroyed three-fourths of Lisbon, the sages of the country could not find any means more effectual to prevent a total destruction, than to give the people a splendid inquisition. It had been decided by the university of Coimbra, that the spectacle of some persons burnt to death by a slow fire, with great ceremony, was an infallible antidote for earthquakes.

In consequence of this resolution, they had seized a Biscayan, convicted of having married his god-mother, and two Portuguese, who, in eating a pullet, had stripped off the lard. After dinner, they came and secured Dr. Pangloss, and his disciple Candide; the one for having spoke too freely, and the other for having heard with an air of approbation. They were both conducted to separate apartments, extremely damp, and never incommoded with the sun. Eight days after, they were both clothed with a gown and had their heads—adorned with paper crowns. Candide's crown and gown were painted with inverted flames, and with devils that had neither tails nor claws; but Pangloss' devils had claws and tails, and the flames were pointed upwards. Being thus dressed, they marched in procession, and heard a very pathetic speech followed by fine music on a squeaking organ. Candide was whipped on the back in cadence, while they were singing; the Biscayan, and the two men who would not eat lard, were burnt; and Pangloss, though it was contrary to custom, was hanged. The same day, the earth shook anew, with a most dreadful noise.

Candide, affrighted, interdicted, astonished, all bloody, all panting, said to himself: "If this is the best of possible worlds, what then are the rest? Supposing I had not been whipped now, I have been so, among the Bulgarians; but, Oh, my dear Pangloss; thou greatest of philosophers, that it should be my fate to see thee hanged without knowing for what! Oh! my dear Anabaptist! thou best of men, that it should be thy fate to be drowned in the harbor! Oh! Miss Cunegonde! the jewel of ladies, that it should be thy fate to have been outraged and slain!"

He returned, with difficulty, supporting himself, after being lectured, whipped, absolved, and blessed, when an old woman accosted him, and said: "Child, take courage, and follow me." . . .

Conclusion

Candide had no great desire, at the bottom of his heart, to marry Cunegonde. But the extreme impertinence of the Baron determined him to conclude the match, and Cunegonde pressed it so earnestly, that he could not retract. He advised with Pangloss, Martin, and the trusty Cacambo. Pangloss drew up an excellent memoir, in which he proved, that the Baron had no right over his sister, and that she might, according to all the laws of the empire, espouse Candide with her left hand. Martin was for throwing the Baron into the sea: Cacambo was of opinion that it would be best to send him back again to the Levant captain, and make him work at the galleys. This advice was thought good; the old woman approved it, and nothing was said to his sister about it. The scheme was put in execution for a little money, and so they had the pleasure of punishing the pride of a German Baron.

It is natural to imagine that Candide, after so many disasters, married to his sweetheart, living with the philosopher Pangloss, the philosopher Martin, the discreet Cacambo, and the old woman, and especially as he had brought so many diamonds from the country of the ancient Incas, must live the most agreeable life of any man in the whole world. But he had been so cheated by the Jews, that he had nothing left but the small farm; and his wife, growing still more ugly, turned peevish and insupportable. The old woman was very infirm, and worse humored than Cunegonde herself. Cacambo, who worked in the garden, and went to Constantinople to sell its productions, was worn out with labor, and cursed his fate. Pangloss was ready to despair, because he did not shine at the head of some university in Germany. As for Martin, as he was firmly persuaded that all was equally bad throughout, he bore things with patience. Candide, Martin, and Pangloss, disputed sometimes about metaphysics and ethics. They often saw passing under the windows of the farm-house boats full of effendis, bashaws, and cadis, who were going into banishment to Lemnos, Mitylene, and Erzerum. They observed that other cadis, other bashaws, and other effendis, succeeded in the posts of those who were exiled, only to be banished themselves in turn. They saw heads nicely impaled, to be presented to the Sublime Porte. These spectacles increased the number of their disputations; and when they were not disputing, their *ennui* was so tiresome that the old woman would often say to them, "I want to know which is the worst;—to be ravished an hundred times by Negro pirates, to run the gauntlet among the Bulgarians, to be whipped and hanged, to be dissected, to row in the galleys; in a word, to have suffered all the miseries we have undergone, or to stay here, without doing anything?" "That is a great question," said Candide.

This discourse gave rise to new reflections, and Martin concluded upon the whole, that mankind were born to live either in the distractions of inquietude, or in the lethargy of disgust. Candide did not agree with that opinion, but remained in a state of suspense. Pangloss confessed, that he had always suffered dreadfully; but having once maintained that all things went wonderfully well, he still kept firm to his hypothesis, though it was quite opposed to his real feelings.

What contributed to confirm Martin in his shocking principles, to make Candide stagger more than ever, and to embarrass Pangloss, was, that one day they saw Paquetta and Girofflee, who were in the greatest distress, at their farm. They had quickly squandered away their three thousand piastres, had parted, were reconciled, quarrelled again, had been confined in prison, had made their escape, and Girofflee had at length turned Turk. Paquetta continued her trade wherever she went, but made nothing by it. "I could easily foresee," said Martin to Candide, "that your presents would soon be squandered away, and would render them more miserable. You and Cacambo have spent millions of piastres, and are not a bit happier than Girofflee and Paquetta." "Ha! ha!" said Pangloss to Paquetta, "has Providence then brought you amongst us again, my poor child? Know, then, that you have cost me the tip of my nose, one eye, and one of my ears, as you see. What a world this is!" This new adventure set them to philosophizing more than ever.

There lived in the neighborhood a very famous dervise, who passed for the greatest philosopher in Turkey. They went to consult him. Pangloss was chosen speaker, and said to him, "Master, we are come to desire you would tell us, why so strange an animal as man was created."

"What's that to you?" said the dervise; "is it any business of thine?" "But, my reverend father," said Candide, "there is a horrible amount of evil in the world." "What signifies," said the dervise, "whether there be good or evil? When his Sublime Highness sends a vessel to Egypt, does it trouble him, whether the mice on board are at their ease or not?" "What would you have one do then?" said Pangloss. "Hold your tongue," said the dervise. "I promised myself the pleasure," said Pangloss, "of reasoning with you upon effects and causes, the best of possible worlds, the origin of evil, the nature of the soul, and the pre-established harmony." —The dervise, at these words, shut the door in their faces.

During this conference, news was brought that two viziers and a mufti were strangled at Constantinople, and a great many of their friends impaled. This catastrophe made a great noise for several hours. Pangloss, Candide, and Martin, on their way back to the little farm, met a good-looking old man, taking the air at his door, under an arbor of orange trees. Pangloss, who had as much curiosity as philosophy, asked him the name of the mufti who was lately strangled. "I know nothing at all about it," said the good man; "and what's more, I never knew the name of a single mufti, or a single vizier, in my life. I am an entire stranger to the story you mention: and presume that, generally speaking, they who trouble their heads with state affairs, sometimes die shocking deaths, not without deserving it. But I never trouble my head about what is doing at Constantinople; I content myself with sending my fruits thither, the produce of my garden, which I cultivate with my own hands!" Having said these words, he introduced the strangers into his house. His two daughters and two sons served them with several kinds of sherbet, which they made themselves, besides caymac, enriched with the peels of candied citrons, oranges, lemons, ananas, pistachio nuts, and Mocoa coffee, unadulterated with the bad coffee of Batavia and the isles. After which the two daughters of this good Mussulman perfumed the beards of Candide, Pangloss, and Martin.

"You must certainly," said Candide to the Turk, "have a very large and very opulent estate!" "I have only twenty acres," said the Turk; "which I, with my children, cultivate. Labor keeps us free from three of the greatest evils; tiresomeness, vice, and want."

As Candide returned to his farm, he made deep reflections on the discourse of the Turk. Said he to Pangloss and Martin, "The condition of this good old man seems to me preferable to that of the six kings with whom we had the honor to sup." "The grandeurs of royalty," said Pangloss, "are very precarious, in the opinion of all philosophers. For, in short, Eglon, king of the Moabites, was assassinated by Ehud; Absalom was hung by the hair of his head, and pierced through with three darts; King Nadab, the son of Jeroboam, was killed by Baasha; King Elah by Zimri; Ahaziah by Jehu; Athaliah by Jehoiadah; the kings Joachim, Jechonias, and Zedekias, were carried into captivity. You know the fates of Crœsus, Astyages, Darius, Dionysius of Syracuse, Pyrrhus, Perseus, Hannibal, Jugurtha, Ariovistus, Cæsar, Pompey, Nero, Otho, Vitellius, Domitian, Richard II., Edward II., Henry VI., Richard III., Mary Stuart, Charles I. of England, the three Henrys of France, and the Emperor Henry IV. You know—" "I know very well," said Candide, "that we ought to look after our garden," "You are in the right," said Pangloss, "for when man was placed in the garden of Eden, he was placed there, *ut operatur cum,* to cultivate it; which proves that mankind are not created to be idle." "Let us work," said Martin, "without disputing; it is the only way to render life supportable."

All their little society entered into this laudable design, according to their different abilities. Their little piece of ground produced a plentiful crop. Cunegonde was indeed very homely, but she became an excellent pastry cook. Paquetta worked at embroidery, and the old woman took care of the linen. There was no idle person in the company, not excepting even Girofflee; he made a very good carpenter, and became a very honest man.

As to Pangloss, he evidently had a lurking consciousness that his theory required unceasing exertions, and all his ingenuity, to sustain it. Yet he stuck to it to the last; his thinking and talking faculties could hardly be diverted from it for a moment. He seized every occasion to say to Candide, "All the events in this best of possible worlds are admirably connected. If a single link in the great chain were omitted, the harmony of the entire universe would be destroyed. If you had not been expelled from that beautiful castle, with those cruel kicks, for your love to Miss Cunegonde; if you had not been imprisoned by the inquisition; if you had not travelled over a great portion of America on foot; if you had not plunged your sword through the baron; if you had not lost all the sheep you brought from that fine country, Eldorado, together with the riches with which they were laden, you would not be here to-day, eating preserved citrons, and pistachio nuts."

"That's very well said, and may all be true," said Candide; "but let's cultivate our garden."

OLIVER GOLDSMITH / Asem: An Eastern Tale

WHERE TAURIS lifts its head above the storm, and presents nothing to the sight of the distant traveller but a prospect of nodding rocks, falling torrents, and all the variety of tremendous nature; on the bleak bosom of this frightful mountain, secluded from society, and detesting the ways of men, lived Asem the Man-Hater.

Asem had spent his youth with men, had shared in their amusements, and had been taught to love his fellow-creatures with the most ardent affection; but, from the tenderness of his disposition, he exhausted all his fortune in relieving the wants of the distressed. The petitioner never sued in vain; the weary traveller never passed his door; he only desisted from doing good when he had no longer the power of relieving.

For a fortune thus spent in benevolence he expected a grateful return from those he had formerly relieved, and made his application with confidence of redress: the ungrateful world soon grew weary of his importunity; for pity is but a short-lived passion. He soon, therefore, began to view mankind in a very different light from that in which he had before beheld them: he perceived a thousand vices he had never before suspected to exist; wherever he turned, ingratitude, dissimulation, and treachery, contributed to increase his detestation of them. Resolved, therefore, to continue no longer in a world which he hated, and which repaid his detestation with contempt, he retired to this region of sterility, in order to brood over his resentment in solitude, and converse with the only honest heart he knew—namely, with his own.

A cave was his only shelter from the inclemency of the weather; fruits, gathered with difficulty from the mountain's side, his only food; and his drink was fetched, with danger and toil, from the headlong torrent. In this manner he lived, sequestered from society, passing the hours in meditation, and sometimes exulting that he was able to live independent of his fellow-creatures.

At the foot of the mountain an extensive lake displayed its glassy bosom, reflecting on its broad surface the impending horrors of the mountain. To this capacious mirror he would sometimes descend, and, reclining on its steep banks, cast an eager look on the smooth expanse that lay before him. "How beautiful," he often cried, "is Nature! how lovely even in her wildest scenes! How finely contrasted is the level plain that lies beneath me with yon awful pile that hides its tremendous head in clouds! But the beauty of these scenes is no way comparable with their utility; hence an hundred rivers are supplied, which distribute health and verdure to the various countries through which they flow. Every part of the universe is beautiful, just, and wise; but man, vile man, is a solecism in nature, the only monster in the creation. Tempests and whirlwinds have their use; but vicious, ungrateful man is a blot in the fair page of universal beauty. Why was I born of that detested species, whose vices are almost a reproach to the wisdom of the divine Creator? Were men entirely free from vice, all would be uniformity, harmony, and order. A world of moral rectitude should be the result of a perfect moral agent. Why, why then, O Alla! must I be thus confined in darkness, doubt, and despair?"

Just as he uttered the word despair, he was going to plunge into the lake beneath him, at once to satisfy his doubts, and put a period to his anxiety, when he perceived a most majestic being walking on the surface of the water, and approaching the bank on which he stood. So unexpected an object at once checked his purpose; he stopped, contemplated, and fancied he saw something awful and divine in his aspect.

"Son of Adam," cried the Genius, "stop thy rash purpose; the Father of the Faithful has seen thy justice, thy integrity, thy miseries, and hath sent me to afford and administer relief. Give me thine hand, and follow without trembling wherever I shall lead: in me behold the Genius of Conviction, kept by the great Prophet, to turn from their errors those who go astray, not from curiosity, but a rectitude of intention. Follow me and be wise."

Asem immediately descended upon the lake, and his guide conducted him along the surface of the water, till, coming near the centre of the lake, they both began to sink; the waters closed over their heads; they descended several hundred fathoms, till

Asem, just ready to give up his life as inevitably lost, found himself, with his celestial guide, in another world, at the bottom of the waters, where human foot had never trod before. His astonishment was beyond description, when he saw a sun like that he had left, a serene sky over his head, and blooming verdure under his feet.

"I plainly perceive your amazement," said the Genius; "but suspend it for a while. This world was formed by Alla, at the request, and under the inspection, of our great Prophet, who once entertained the same doubts which filled your mind when I found you, and from the consequence of which you were so lately rescued. The rational inhabitants of this world are formed agreeable to your own ideas; they are absolutely without vice. In other respects it resembles your earth, but differs from it in being wholly inhabited by men who never do wrong. If you find this world more agreeable than that you so lately left, you have free permission to spend the remainder of your days in it; but permit me for some time to attend you, that I may silence your doubts, and make you better acquainted with your company and your new habitation."

"A world without vice! Rational beings without immorality!" cried Asem, in a rapture; "I thank thee, O Alla! who hast at length heard my petitions: this, this indeed will produce happiness, ecstasy, and ease. Oh, for an immortality, to spend it among men who are incapable of ingratitude, injustice, fraud, violence, and a thousand other crimes that render society miserable!"

"Cease thine exclamations," replied the Genius. "Look around thee: reflect on every object and action before us, and communicate to me the result of thine observations. Lead wherever you think proper, I shall be your attendant and instructor." Asem and his companion travelled on in silence for some time, the former being entirely lost in astonishment; but at last recovering his former serenity, he could not help observing, that the face of the country bore a near resemblance to that he had left, except that this subterranean world still seemed to retain its primeval wildness.

"Here," cried Asem, "I perceive animals of prey and others that seem only designed for their subsistence; it is the very same in the world over our heads. But had I been permitted to instruct our Prophet, I would have removed this defect, and formed no voracious or destructive animals, which only prey on the other parts of the creation."—"Your tenderness for inferior animals is, I find, remarkable," said the Genius, smiling. "But, with regard to meaner creatures, this world exactly resembles the other, and, indeed, for obvious reasons; for the earth can support a more considerable number of animals by their thus becoming food for each other, than if they had lived entirely on her vegetable productions.

So that animals of different natures thus formed, instead of lessening their multitude, subsist in the greatest number possible. But let us hasten on to the inhabited country before us, and see what that offers for instruction."

They soon gained the utmost verge of the forest, and entered the country inhabited by men without vice; and Asem anticipated in idea the rational delight he hoped to experience in such an innocent society. But they had scarcely left the confines of the wood, when they beheld one of the inhabitants flying with hasty steps, and terror in his countenance, from an army of squirrels, that closely pursued him. "Heavens!" cried Asem, "why does he fly? What can he fear from animals so contemptible?" He had scarcely spoken, when he perceived two dogs pursuing another of the human species, who with equal terror and haste attempted to avoid them. "This," cried Asem to his guide, "is truly surprising; nor can I conceive the reason for so strange an action."—"Every species of animals," replied the Genius, "has of late grown very powerful in this country; for the inhabitants, at first, thinking it unjust to use either fraud or force in destroying them, they have insensibly increased, and now frequently ravage their harmless frontiers."—"But they should have been destroyed," cried Asem; "you see the consequence of such neglect."—"Where is, then, that tenderness you so lately expressed for subordinate animals?" replied the Genius, smiling; "you seem to have forgot that branch of justice."—"I must acknowledge my mistake," returned Asem; "I am now convinced that we must be guilty of tyranny and injustice to the brute creation, if we would enjoy the world ourselves. But let us no longer observe the duty of man to these irrational creatures, but survey their connections with one another."

As they walked farther up the country, the more he was surprised to see no vestiges of handsome houses, no cities, nor any mark of elegant design. His conductor, perceiving his surprise, observed, that the inhabitants of this new world were perfectly content with their ancient simplicity; each had a house, which, though homely, was sufficient to lodge his little family; they were too good to build houses, which could only increase their own pride, and the envy of the spectator: what they built was for convenience, and not for show. "At least, then," said Asem, "they have neither architects, painters, nor statuaries, in their society; but these are idle arts, and may be spared. However, before I spend much more time here, you should have my thanks for introducing me into the society of some of their wisest men: there is scarce any pleasure to me equal to a refined conversation; there is nothing of which I am so much enamoured as wisdom."—"Wisdom!" replied his instructor; "how ridiculous! We have no wisdom here, for we have no occasion for it; true wisdom is only a knowledge of our own duty, and the duty of others to us; but of what use is such wisdom here? each intuitively performs what is right in himself, and expects the same from others. If by wisdom you should mean vain curiosity and empty speculation, as such pleasures have their origin in vanity, luxury, or avarice, we are too good to pursue them."—"All this may be right," says Asem: "but methinks I observe a solitary disposition prevail among the people; each family keeps separately within their own precincts, without society, or without intercourse."—"That indeed, is true," replied the other; "here is no established society, nor should there be any; all societies are made either through fear or friendship: the people we are among are too good to fear each other; and there are no motives to private friendship, where all are equally meritorious."—"Well, then," said the sceptic, "as I am to spend my time here, if I am to have neither the polite arts, nor wisdom, nor friendship, in such a world, I should be glad at least of an easy companion, who may tell me his thoughts, and to whom I may communicate mine."—"And to what purpose should either do this?" says the Genius: "flattery or curiosity are vicious motives, and never allowed of here; and wisdom is out of the question."

"Still, however," said Asem, "the inhabitants must be happy; each is contented with his own possessions, nor avariciously endeavours to heap up more than is necessary for his own subsistence; each has therefore leisure for pitying those that stand in need of his compassion." He had scarce spoken, when his ears were assaulted with the lamentations of a wretch who sat by the way-side, and in the most deplorable distress seemed gently to murmur at his own misery. Asem immediately ran to his relief, and found him in the last stage of a consumption. "Strange," cried the son of Adam, "that men who are free from vice should thus suffer so much misery without relief!"—"Be not surprised," said the wretch who was dying: "would it not be the utmost injustice for beings who have only just sufficient to support themselves, and are content with a bare subsistence, to take it from their own mouths to put it into mine? They never are possessed of a single meal more than is necessary, and what is barely necessary cannot be dispensed with."—"They should have been supplied with more than is necessary," cried Asem—"and yet I contradict my own opinion but a moment before—all is doubt, perplexity, and confusion. Even the want of ingratitude is no virtue here, since they never received a favour. They have, however, another excellence yet behind; the love of their country is still, I hope, one of their darling virtues."—"Peace, Asem," replied the Guardian, with a countenance not less severe than beautiful; "nor forfeit all thy pretensions to wisdom: the same selfish motives by which we prefer our own interests to that of others, induce us to regard our country preferably to that of another. Nothing less than universal benevolence is free from vice, and that you see is practised here."—"Strange!" cries the disappointed pilgrim, in an agony of distress; "what sort of a world am I now introduced to? There is scarce a single virtue, but that of temperance, which they practise: and in that they are no way superior to the very brute creation. There is scarce an amusement which they enjoy; fortitude, liberality, friendship, wisdom, conversation, and love of country, all are virtues entirely unknown here: thus it seems that to be unacquainted with vice is not to know virtue. Take me, O my Genius, back to that very world which I have despised: a world which has Alla for its contriver is much more wisely formed than that which has been projected by Mahomet. Ingratitude, contempt, and hatred, I can now suffer, for perhaps I have deserved them. When I arraigned the wisdom of Providence, I only showed my own ignorance; henceforth let me keep from vice myself, and pity it in others."

He had scarce ended, when the Genius, assuming an air of terrible complacency, called all his thunders around him, and vanished in a whirlwind. Asem, astonished at the terror of the scene, looked for his imaginary world; when, casting his eyes around, he perceived himself in the very situation, and in the very place, where he first began to repine and despair; his right foot had been just advanced to take the fatal plunge, nor had it been yet withdrawn; so instantly did Providence strike the series of truths just imprinted on his soul. He now departed from the water-side in tranquillity; and leaving his horrid mansion, travelled to Segestan, his native city, where he diligently applied himself to commerce, and put in practice that wisdom he had learned in solitude. The frugality of a few years soon produced opulence; the number of his domestics increased; his friends came to him from every part of the city; nor did he receive them with disdain; and a youth of misery was concluded with an old age of elegance, affluence, and ease.

FRANZ KAFKA/The Hunter Gracchus

Two boys were sitting on the harbour wall playing with dice. A man was reading a newspaper on the steps of the monument, resting in the shadow of a hero who was flourishing his sword on high. A girl was filling her bucket at the fountain. A fruit-seller was lying beside his scales, staring out to sea. Through the vacant window and door openings of a café one could see two men quite at the back drinking their wine. The proprietor was sitting at a table in front and dozing. A bark was silently making for the little harbour, as if borne by invisible means over the water. A man in a blue blouse climbed ashore and drew the rope through a ring. Behind the boatman two other men in dark coats with silver buttons carried a bier, on which, beneath a great flower-patterned tasselled silk cloth, a man was apparently lying.

Nobody on the quay troubled about the newcomers; even when they lowered the bier to wait for the boatman, who was still occupied with his rope, nobody went nearer, nobody asked them a question, nobody accorded them an inquisitive glance.

The pilot was still further detained by a woman who, a child at her breast, now appeared with loosened hair on the deck of the boat. Then he advanced and indicated a yellowish two-storeyed house that rose abruptly on the left beside the sea; the bearers took up their burden and bore it to the low but gracefully pillared door. A little boy opened a window just in time to see the party vanishing into the house, then hastily shut the window again. The door too was now shut; it was of black oak, and very strongly made. A flock of doves which had been flying round the belfry alighted in the street before the house. As if their food were stored within, they assembled in front of the door. One of them flew up to the first storey and pecked at the window-pane. They were bright-hued, well-tended, beautiful birds. The woman on the boat flung grain to them in a wide sweep; they ate it up and flew across to the woman.

A man in a top hat tied with a band of crêpe now descended one of the narrow and very steep lanes that led to the harbour. He glanced round vigilantly, everything seemed to displease him, his mouth twisted at the sight of some offal in a corner. Fruit skins were lying on the steps of the monument; he swept them off in passing with his stick. He rapped at the house door, at the same time taking his top hat from his head with his black-gloved hand. The door was opened at once, and some fifty little boys appeared in two rows in the long entry-hall, and bowed to him.

The boatman descended the stairs, greeted the gentleman in black, conducted him up to the first storey, led him round the bright and elegant loggia which encircled the courtyard, and both of them entered, while the boys pressed after them at a respectful distance, a cool spacious room looking towards the back, from whose window no habitation, but only a bare, blackish grey rocky wall was to be seen. The bearers were busied in setting up and lighting several long candles at the head of the bier, yet these did not give light, but only scared away the shadows which had been immobile till then, and made them flicker over the walls. The cloth covering the bier had been thrown back. Lying on it was a man with wildly matted hair, who looked somewhat like a hunter. He lay without motion and, it seemed, without breathing, his eyes closed; yet only his trappings indicated that this man was probably dead.

The gentleman stepped up to the bier, laid his hand on the brow of the man lying upon it, then kneeled down and prayed. The boatman made a sign to the bearers to leave the room; they went out, drove away the boys who had gathered outside, and shut the door. But even that did not seem to satisfy the gentleman, he glanced at the boatman; the boatman understood, and vanished through a side door into the next room. At once the man on the bier opened his eyes, turned his face painfully towards the gentleman, and said: "Who are you?" Without any mark of surprise the gentleman rose from his kneeling posture and answered: "The Burgomaster of Riva."

The man on the bier nodded, indicated a chair with a feeble movement of his arm, and said, after the Burgomaster had accepted his invitation: "I knew that, of course, Burgomaster, but in the first moments of returning consciousness I always forget, everything goes round before my eyes, and it is best to ask about anything even if I know. You too probably know that I am the hunter Gracchus."

"Certainly," said the Burgomaster. "Your arrival was announced to me during the night. We had been asleep for a good while. Then towards midnight my wife cried: 'Salvatore'—that's my name—'look at that dove at the window.' It was really a dove, but as big as a cock. It flew over me and said in my ear: 'To-morrow the dead hunter Gracchus is coming; receive him in the name of the city.' "

The hunter nodded and licked his lips with the tip of his tongue: "Yes, the doves flew here before me. But do you believe, Burgomaster, that I shall remain in Riva?"

"I cannot say that yet," replied the Burgomaster. "Are you dead?"

"Yes," said the hunter, "as you see. Many years ago, yes, it must be a great many years ago, I fell from a precipice in the Black Forest—that is in Germany—when I was hunting a chamois. Since then I have been dead."

"But you are alive too," said the Burgomaster.

"In a certain sense," said the hunter, "in a certain sense I am alive too. My death ship lost its way; a wrong turn of the wheel, a moment's absence of mind on the pilot's part, a longing to turn aside towards my lovely native country, I cannot tell what it was; I only know this, that I remained on earth and that ever since my ship has sailed earthly waters. So I, who asked for nothing better than to live among my mountains, travel after my death through all the lands of the earth."

"And you have no part in the other world?" asked the Burgomaster, knitting his brow.

"I am for ever," replied the hunter, "on the great stair that leads up to it. On that infinitely wide and spacious stair I clamber about, sometimes up, sometimes down, sometimes on the right, sometimes on the left, always in motion. The hunter has been turned into a butterfly. Do not laugh."

"I am not laughing," said the Burgomaster in self-defence.

"That is very good of you," said the hunter. "I am always in motion. But when I make a supreme flight and see the gate actually shining before me I awaken presently on my old ship, still stranded forlornly in some earthly sea or other. The fundamental error of my one-time death grins at me as I lie in my cabin. Julia, the wife of the pilot, knocks at the door and brings me on my bier the morning drink of the land whose coasts we chance to be passing. I lie on a wooden pallet, I wear—it cannot be a pleasure to look at me—a filthy winding sheet, my hair and beard, black tinged with grey, have grown together inextricably, my limbs are covered with a great flower-patterned woman's shawl with long fringes. A sacramental candle stands at my head and lights me. On the wall opposite me is a little picture, evidently of a Bushman who is aiming his spear at me and taking cover as best he can behind a beautifully painted shield. On shipboard one is often a prey to stupid imaginations, but that is the stupidest of them all. Otherwise my wooden case is quite empty. Through a hole in the side wall come in the warm airs of the southern night, and I hear the water slapping against the old boat.

"I have lain here ever since the time when, as the hunter Gracchus living in the Black Forest, I followed a chamois and fell from a precipice. Everything happened in good order. I pursued, I fell, bled to death in a ravine, died, and this ship should have conveyed me to the next world. I can still remember how gladly I stretched myself out on this pallet for the first time. Never did the mountains listen to such songs from me as these shadowy walls did then.

"I had been glad to live and I was glad to die. Before I stepped aboard, I joyfully flung away my wretched load of ammunition, my knapsack, my hunting rifle that I had always been proud to carry, and I slipped into my winding sheet like a girl into her marriage dress. I lay and waited. Then came the mishap."

"A terrible fate," said the Burgomaster, raising his hand defensively. "And you bear no blame for it?"

"None," said the hunter. "I was a hunter; was there any sin in that? I followed my calling as a hunter in the Black Forest, where there were still wolves in those days. I lay in ambush, shot, hit my mark, flayed the skins from my victims: was there any sin in that? My labours were blessed. 'The great hunter of the Black Forest' was the name I was given. Was there any sin in that?"

"I am not called upon to decide that," said the Burgomaster, "but to me also there seems to be no sin in such things. But, then whose is the guilt?"

"The boatman's," said the hunter. "Nobody will read what I say here, no one will come to help me; even if all the people were commanded to help me, every door and window would remain shut, everybody would take to bed and draw the bedclothes over his head, the whole earth would become an inn for the night. And there is sense in that, for nobody knows of me, and if anyone knew he would not know where I could be found, and if he knew where I could be found, he would not know how to deal with me, he would not know how to help me. The thought of helping me is an illness that has to be cured by taking to one's bed.

"I know that, and so I do not shout to summon help, even though at moments—when I lose control over myself, as I have done just now, for instance—I think seriously of it. But to drive out such thoughts I need only look round me and verify where I am, and—I can safely assert—have been for hundreds of years."

"Extraordinary," said the Burgomaster, "extraordinary.—And now do you think of staying here in Riva with us?"

"I think not," said the hunter with a smile, and, to excuse himself, he laid his hand on the Burgomaster's knee. "I am here, more than that I do not know, further than that I cannot go. My ship has no rudder, and it is driven by the wind that blows in the undermost regions of death."

FRANZ KAFKA / A Little Fable

"ALAS," said the mouse, "the world is growing smaller every day. At the beginning it was so big that I was afraid, I kept running and running, and I was glad when at last I saw walls far away to the right and left, but these long walls have narrowed so quickly that I am in the last chamber already, and there in the corner stands the trap that I must run into." "You only need to change your direction," said the cat, and ate it up.

EUGENE ZAMIATIN / We

Ballet
Square Harmony
X

SPRING. From behind the Green Wall, from some unknown plains the wind brings to us the yellow honeyed pollen of flowers. One's lips are dry from this sweet dust. Every moment one passes one's tongue over them. Probably all women whom I meet in the street (and certainly men also) have sweet lips today. This somewhat disturbs my logical thinking. But the sky! The sky is blue. Its limpidness is not marred by a single cloud. (How primitive was the taste of the ancients, since their poets were always inspired by these senseless, formless, stupidly rushing accumulations of vapor!) I love, I am sure it will not be an error if I say *we* love, only such a sky—a sterile, faultless sky. On such days the whole universe seems to be moulded of the same eternal glass, like the Green Wall, and like all our buildings. On such days one sees their wonderful equations, hitherto unknown. One sees these equations in everything, even in the most ordinary, everyday things.

Here is an example: this morning I was on the dock where the *Integral* is being built, and I saw the lathes; blindly, with abandon, the balls of the regulators were rotating; the cranks were swinging from side to side with a glimmer; the working beam proudly swung its shoulder; and the mechanical chisels were dancing to the melody of unheard tarantellas. I suddenly perceived all the music, all the beauty, of this colossal, this mechanical ballet, illuminated by light blue rays of sunshine. Then the thought came: why beautiful? Why is the dance beautiful? Answer: because it is an *unfree* movement. Because the deep meaning of the dance is contained in its absolute, ecstatic submission, in the ideal *non-freedom*. If it is true that our ancestors would abandon themselves in dancing at the most inspired moments of their lives (religious mysteries, military parades), then it means only one thing: the instinct of non-freedom has been characteristic of human nature from ancient times, and we in our life of today, we are only consciously—

I was interrupted. The switchboard clicked. I raised my eyes—O-90, of course! In half a minute she will be here to take me for the walk.

Dear O-! She always seems to me to look like her name, O-. She is approximately ten centimeters shorter than the required Maternal Norm. Therefore she appears round all over; the rose-colored O of her lips is open to meet every word of mine. She has a round soft dimple on her wrist. Children have such dimples. As she came in, the logical flywheel was still buzzing in my head, and following its inertia, I began to tell her about my new formula which embraced the machines and the dancers and all of us.

"Wonderful, isn't it?" I asked.

"Yes, wonderful . . . Spring!" she replied, with a rosy smile.

You see? Spring! She talks about Spring! Females! . . . I became silent.

We were down in the street. The avenue was crowded. On days when the weather is so beautiful, the afternoon personal hour is usually the hour of the supplementary walk. As always, the big Musical Tower was playing the March of the United State with all its pipes. The Numbers, hundreds, thousands of Numbers in light blue unifs (probably a derivative of the ancient uniform) with golden badges on the chest—the State number of each one, male or female—the Numbers were walking slowly, four abreast, exaltedly keeping step. I, we four, were but one of the innumerable waves of a powerful torrent: to my left, O-90 (if one of my long-haired ancestors were writing this a thousand years ago he would probably call her by that funny word, *mine*); to my right, two unknown Numbers, a she-Number and a he-Number.

Blue sky, tiny baby suns in each one of our badges; our faces are unclouded by the insanity of thoughts. Rays. . . . Do you picture it? Everything seems to be made of a kind of smiling, a ray-like matter. And the brass measures: Tra-ta-ta-tam . . . Tra-ta-ta-tam . . . Stamping on the brassy steps that sparkle in the sun, with every step you rise higher and higher into the dizzy blue heights. . . . Then, as this morning on the dock, again I saw, as if for the first time in my life, the impeccably straight streets, the glistening glass of the pavement, the divine parallelepipeds of the transparent dwellings, the square harmony of the grayish-blue rows of Numbers. And it seemed to me that not past generations, but I myself, had won a victory over the old god and the old life, that I myself had created all this. I felt like a tower: I was afraid to move my elbow, lest the walls, the cupola, and the machines should fall to pieces.

Then without warning—a jump through centuries: I remembered (apparently through an association by contrast) a picture in the museum, a picture of an avenue of the twentieth century, a thundering, many-colored confusion of men, wheels, animals, billboards, trees, colors, and birds. . . . They say all this once actually existed!

It seemed to me so incredible, so absurd, that I lost control of myself and laughed aloud. A laugh, as if an echo of mine, reached my ear from the right. I turned. I saw white, very white, sharp teeth, and an unfamiliar female face.

"I beg your pardon," she said, "but you looked about you like an inspired mythological god on the seventh day of creation. You look as though you are sure that I, too, was created by you, by no one but you. It is very flattering."

All this without a smile, even with a certain degree of respect (she may know that I am the builder of the *Integral*). In her eyes, nevertheless, and on her brows, there was a strange irritating X, and I was unable to grasp it, to find an arithmetical expression for it. Somehow I was confused; with a somewhat hazy mind, I tried logically to explain my laughter.

"It was absolutely clear that this contrast, this impassable abyss, between the things of today and of years ago—"

"But why impassable?" (What bright, sharp teeth!) "One might throw a bridge over that abyss. Please imagine: a drum battalion, rows—all this existed before and consequently—"

"Oh, yes, it is clear," I exclaimed.

It was a remarkable intersection of thoughts. She said almost in the same words the things I had written down before the walk! Do you understand? Even the thoughts! It is because nobody is *one*, but *one of*. We are all so much alike—

"Are you sure?" I noticed her brows that rose to the temples in an acute angle—like the sharp corners of an X. Again I was confused, casting a glance to the right, then to the left. To my right—she, slender, abrupt, resistantly flexible like a whip, I-330 (I saw her number now). To my left, O—, totally different, all made of circles with a childlike dimple on her wrist; and at the very end of our row, an unknown he-Number, double-curved like the letter S. We were all so different from one another. . . .

The one to my right, I-330, apparently caught the confusion in my eye, for she said with a sigh, "Yes, alas!"

I don't deny that this exclamation was quite in place, but again there was something in her face or in her voice . . .

With an abruptness unusual for me, I said, "Why, 'alas'? Science is developing and if not now, then within fifty or one hundred years—"

"Even the noses will—"

"Yes, noses!" This time I almost shouted, "Since there is

still a reason, no matter what, for envy. . . . Since my nose is button-like and someone else's is—"

"Well, your nose is rather classic, as they would have said in ancient days, although your hands— No, no, show me your hands!"

I hate to have anyone look at my hands; they are covered with long hair—a stupid atavism. I stretched out my hand and said as indifferently as I could, "Apelike."

She glanced at my hand, then at my face.

"No, a very curious harmony."

She weighed me with her eyes as though with scales. The little horns again appeared at the corners of her brows.

"He is registered in my name," exclaimed O-90 with a rosy smile.

I made a grimace. Strictly speaking, she was out of order. This dear O-, how shall I say it? The speed of her tongue is not correctly calculated; the speed per second of her tongue should be slightly less than the speed per second of her thoughts—at any rate not the reverse.

At the end of the avenue the big bell of the Accumulating Tower resounded seventeen. The personal hour was at an end. I-330 was leaving us with that S-like he-Number. He has such a respectable, and I noticed then, such a familiar, face. I must have met him somewhere, but where I could not remember. Upon leaving me I-330 said with the same X-like smile:

"Drop in day after tomorrow at auditorium 112."

I shrugged my shoulders: "If I am assigned to the auditorium you just named—"

She, with a peculiar, incomprehensible certainty: "You will be."

The woman had a disagreeable effect upon me, like an irrational component of an equation which you cannot eliminate. I was glad to remain alone with dear O-, at least for a short while. Hand in hand with her, I passed four lines of avenues; at the next corner she went to the right, I to the left. O- timidly raised her round blue crystalline eyes.

"I would like so much to come to you today and pull down the curtains, especially today, right now. . . ."

How funny she is. But what could I say to her? She was with me only yesterday and she knows as well as I that our next sexual day is day after tomorrow. It is merely another case in which her thoughts are too far ahead. It sometimes happens that the spark comes too early to the motor.

At parting I kissed her twice—no, I shall be exact, three times, on her wonderful blue eyes, such clear, unclouded eyes. . . .

I Do Not Believe
Tractors
A Little Human Splinter

Do you believe that *you will die?* Oh, yes, "Man is mortal; I am a man; consequently . . ." No, not that; I know that; you know it. But I ask: Has it ever happened that you *actually believed* it? Believed definitely, believed not with your reason but with your *body,* that you actually felt that someday those fingers which now hold this page will become yellow, icy? . . .

No, of course you cannot believe this. That is why you haven't jumped from the tenth floor to the pavement before now; that is why you eat, turn over these pages, shave, smile, write.

This very thing, yes, exactly this is alive in me today. I know that that small black hand on the clock will slide down here toward midnight, then it will again start to ascend, and it will cross some last border and the improbable tomorrow will have arrived. I *know* it, but somehow I do not *believe* it—or perhaps I think that twenty-four hours are twenty-four years. So I am still able to act, to hurry, to answer questions, to climb the rope ladder to the *Integral.* I am still able to feel how the *Integral* shakes the surface of the water and I still understand that I must grasp the railing, and I am still able to feel the cold glass in my hand. I see the transparent, living cranes, bending their long necks, carefully feeding the *Integral* with the terrible explosive food which the motors need. I still see below on the river the blue veins and knots of water swollen by the wind. . . . Yet all this seems very distant from me, foreign, flat, like a draft on a sheet of paper. And it seems to me strange, when the flat draft-like face of the Second Builder suddenly asks:

"Well, then. How much fuel for the motors shall we load on? If we count on three, or say three and a half hours . . ."

I see before me, over a draft, my hand with the counter and the logarithmic dial at the figure 15.

"Fifteen tons. But you'd better take . . . yes, better take a thousand."

I said that because I *know* that tomorrow . . . I noticed that my hands and the dial began to tremble.

"A thousand! What do you need such a lot for? That would last a week! No, more than a week!"

"Well, nobody knows . . ."

I do know. . . .

The wind whistled, the air seemed to be stuffed to the limit with something invisible. I had difficulty in breathing, difficulty in walking, and with difficulty, slowly but without stopping for a second, the hand of the Accumulating Tower was crawling, at the end of the avenue. The peak of the Tower reached into the very clouds—dull, blue, groaning in a subdued way, sucking electricity from the clouds. The tubes of the Musical Tower resounded.

As always—four abreast. But the rows did not seem as firm as usual; they were swinging, bending more and more, perhaps because of the wind. There! They seemed to stumble upon something at the corner; they drew back and stopped, congealed, a close mass, a clot, breathing rapidly; at once all of them stretched their necks like geese.

"Look! No, look, look—there, quick!"

"*They?* Are those *they?*"

"Ah, never! Never! I'd rather put my head straight into the Machine. . . ."

"Silence! Are you crazy?"

On the corner, the doors of the auditorium were ajar, and a wide column of about fifty people—the word "people" is not the right one. These were heavy-wheeled automatons seemingly bound in iron and moved by an invisible mechanism. Not people, but a sort of human-like tractor. Over their heads, floating in the air —a white banner with a golden sun embroidered on it, and the rays of the sun: "We are the first! We have already been operated upon! Follow us, all of you!"

Slowly, unhesitatingly they moved through the crowd, and it was clear that if they had had in their way a wall, a tree, a house, they would have moved on just as unhesitatingly through the wall, the tree, the house. In the middle of the avenue they fused and stretched out into a chain, arm in arm, their faces turned toward us. And we, a human clot, tense, the hair pricking our heads, we waited. Our necks were stretched out goose fashion. Clouds. The wind whistled. Suddenly the wings of the chain from right and left bent quickly around us, and faster, faster, like a heavy engine descending a hill, they closed the ring and pulled us toward the yawning doors and inside. . . .

Somebody's piercing cry: "They are driving us in! Run!"

Everybody ran. Close to the wall there was still an open, living gate of human beings. Everybody dashed through it, heads forward. Their heads became sharp wedges, and with their ribs, shoulders, hips . . . Like a stream of water compressed in a fire hose they spurted out in the form of a fan, and all around me stamping feet, raised arms, unifs. . . . The double curved S- with his transparent wing ears appeared for a moment close before my eyes; he disappeared as suddenly; I was alone among arms and legs appearing for a second and disappearing. I was running. . . .

I dashed to the entrance of a house to stop to catch my breath, my back close to the door—and suddenly, like a splinter borne by the wind, a human being was thrown toward me.

"All the while I . . . I have been following you. I do not want . . . do you see? I do not want . . . I am ready to . . ."

Small round hands on my sleeves, round dark blue eyes —it was O-90. She just slipped along my body like a unif which, its hanger broken, slips along the wall to fall upon the floor. Like a little bundle she crumpled below me on the cold doorstep, and I stood over her, stroking her head, her face. My hands were wet. I felt as if I were very big and she very small, a small part of myself. I felt something quite different from what I feel toward I-330. I think the ancients must have had similar feelings toward their private children.

Below, filtering through her hands with which she was covering her face, a voice came to me:

"Every night I . . . I cannot! If they cure me . . . Every night I sit in the darkness alone and think of *him,* and of what he will look like when I . . . If I am cured I would have nothing to live with—do you understand me? You must . . . you must . . ."

An absurd feeling, yet it was there; I really must! Absurd, because this "duty" of mine was nothing but another crime. Absurd, because white and black cannot be one, duty and crime cannot coincide. Or perhaps there is no black and white in life, but everything depends upon the first logical premise? If the premise is that I unlawfully gave her a child . . .

"It's all right, but don't, only don't . . ." I said, "Of course I understand. . . . I must take you to I-330, as I once offered to, so that she . . ."

"Yes." (This in a low voice, without uncovering her face.)

I helped her rise. Silently we went along the darkening street, each busy with his own thoughts, or perhaps with the same thought. . . . We walked between silent, leaden houses, through the tense, whipping branches of the wind. . . .

All at once, through the whistling of the wind, I heard, as if splashing through ditches, the familiar footsteps coming from some unseen point. At the corner I turned around, and among the clouds, flying upside down in the dim glass reflection of the pavement, I saw S-. Instantly my arms became foreign, swinging out of time, and I began to tell O-90 in a low voice that tomorrow, yes, tomorrow, was the day of the first flight of the *Integral,* and that it was to be something that had never happened before in all history, great, miraculous.

"Think of it! For the first time in life to find myself outside the limits of our city and see—who knows what is beyond the Green Wall?"

O-90 looked at me extremely surprised, her blue eyes trying to penetrate mine; she looked at my senselessly swinging arms. But I did not let her say a word—I kept talking, talking. . . . And within me, apart from what I was saying and audible only to myself, a thought was feverishly buzzing and knocking. "Impossible! You must somehow . . . you must not lead *him* to I-330!"

Instead of turning to the right I turned to the left. The bridge submissively bent its back in a slavish way to all three of us, to me, to O-, to him behind. Lights were falling from the houses across the water, falling and breaking into thousands of sparks which danced feverishly, sprayed with the mad white foam of the water. Somewhere not far away the wind was moaning like the tensely stretched string of a double bass. And through this bass, behind us, all the while . . .

The house where I live. At the entrance O- stopped and began:

"No! You promised, did you not, that . . ."

I did not let her finish. Hastily I pushed her through the entrance and we found ourselves in the lobby. At the controller's desk the familiar, hanging, excitedly quivering cheeks—a group of Numbers around. They were quarreling about something, heads bending over the banisters on the second floor; they were running downstairs one by one. But about that later. I drew O-90 at once into the opposite, unoccupied corner and sat down with my back to the wall. I saw a dark, large-headed shadow gliding back and forth over the sidewalk. I took out my notebook. O-90 in her chair was sinking slowly, as if she were evaporating from under her unif, as if her body were thawing, as if only her empty unif were left, and empty eyes taking one into the blue emptiness. In a tired voice:

"Why did you bring me here? You lied to me."

"No, not so loud! Look here! Do you see? Through the wall?"

"Yes, I see a shadow."

"He is always following me . . . I cannot . . . Do you understand? I cannot, therefore . . . I am going to write a few words to I-330. You take the note and go alone. I know he will remain here."

Her body began again to take form and to move beneath the unif; on her face a faint sunrise, dawn. I put the note between her cold fingers, pressed her hand firmly, and for the last time looked into her blue eyes.

"Good-by. Perhaps someday . . ." She freed her hand. Bending over slightly, she slowly moved away, made two steps, turned around quickly, and again we were side by side. Her lips were moving; with her lips and with her eyes she repeated some inaudible word. What an unbearable smile! What suffering!

Then the bent-over human splinter went to the door; a bent-over little shadow beyond the wall; without turning around she went on faster, still faster. . . .

I went to U-'s desk. With emotion filling her indignant gills, she said to me:

"They have all gone crazy! He, for instance, is trying to assure me that he himself saw a naked man covered with hair near the Ancient House . . ."

A voice from the group of empty raised heads:

"Yes. I repeat it, yes."

"Well, what do you think of that? Oh, what a delirium!" The word "delirium" came out of her mouth so full of conviction, so unbending, that I asked myself: "Perhaps it really was nothing but delirium, all that has been going on around me lately." I glanced at my hairy hand, and I remembered: "There are, undoubtedly, some drops of that blood of the sun and woods in you. That is why perhaps you . . ." No, fortunately it was not delirium; or no, *un*fortunately it was not delirium.

This Without a Synopsis, Hastily, the Last

The day.

Quick, to the newspaper! Perhaps there . . . I read the paper with my eyes (exactly; my eyes now are like a pen, or like a counting machine which you hold and feel in your hands like a tool, something foreign, an instrument). In the newspaper, on the first page, in large print:

THE ENEMIES OF HAPPINESS ARE AWAKE! HOLD TO YOUR HAPPINESS WITH BOTH HANDS. TOMORROW ALL WORK WILL STOP AND ALL NUMBERS ARE TO COME TO BE OPERATED UPON. THOSE WHO FAIL TO COME WILL BE SUBMITTED TO THE MACHINE OF THE WELL-DOER.

Tomorrow! How can there be, how can there be any tomorrow?

Following my daily habit, I stretched out my arm (instrument!) to the bookshelf to put today's paper with the rest within a cover ornamented with gold. While doing this: "What for? What does it matter? Never again shall I . . . Within this cover, never . . ." And out of my hands, down to the floor it fell.

I stood looking all around, over all my room; hastily I was taking away, feverishly putting into some unseen valise, everything I regretted leaving here: my desk, my books, my chair. Upon that chair I-330 had sat that day; I was below on the floor . . . My bed . . . Then for a minute or two I stood and waited for some miracle to happen; perhaps the telephone would ring, perhaps she would say that . . . But no, no miracle . . .

I am leaving, going into the unknown. These are my last lines. Farewell you, my unknown beloved ones, with whom I have lived through so many pages, before whom I have bared my diseased soul, my whole self to the last broken little screw, to the last cracked spring . . . I am going . . .

The Forgiven Ones
A Sunny Night
A Radio-Valkyrie

Oh, if only I had actually broken myself to pieces! If only I had actually found myself with her in some place beyond the Wall, among beasts showing their yellow tusks. If only I had never actually returned here! It would be a thousand, a million times easier! But now—what? Now to go and choke that—! But would it help? No, no, no! Take yourself in hand, D-503! Set into yourself the firm hub of logic; at least for a short while weigh heavily with all your might on the lever and, like the ancient slave, turn the millstones of syllogisms until you have written down and understood everything that happened. . . .

When I boarded the *Integral,* everyone was already there and in his place; all the cells of the gigantic hive were filled. Through the decks of glass—tiny, antlike people below, at the telegraph, dynamo, transformers, altimeters, ventilators, indicators, motor, pumps, tubes. . . . In the saloon people were sitting over tables and instruments, probably those commissioned by the Scientific Bureau; near them the Second Builder and his two aides. All three had their heads down between their shoulders like turtles, their faces gray, autumnal, rayless.

"Well?" I asked.

"Well, somewhat uncanny," one of them replied, smiling a gray, rayless smile. "Perhaps we shall have to land in some unknown place. And, generally speaking, nobody knows . . ."

I could hardly bear to look at them, when in an hour or so I was to throw them out with my own hands, to cast them out from the cozy figures of our Table of Hours, to tear them away forever from the mother's breast of the United State. They reminded me of the tragic figures of "The Three Forgiven Ones"—a story known to all of our school children. It tells about three Numbers, who by way of experiment were exempted for a whole month from any work.[1] "Go wherever you will, do what you will," they were told. The unhappy three spent their whole time wandering around their usual place of work and gazing within with hungry eyes. They would stop on the plazas and busy themselves for hours repeating the motions which they had been used to making during certain hours of the day; it became a bodily necessity for them to do so. They would saw and plane the air; with unseen sledge hammers they would bang upon unseen stakes. Finally, on the tenth day, they could bear it no longer; they took one another by the hand, entered the river, and to the accompaniment of the March they waded deeper and deeper until the water ended their sufferings forever.

I repeat, it was hard for me to look at them, and I was anxious to leave them.

"I just want to take a glance into the engine room, and then off!" I said.

They were asking me questions: "What voltage should be used for the initial spark, how much ballast water was needed in the tank aft?" As if a phonograph were somewhere within me, I was giving quick and precise answers, but I, my inner self, was busy with my own thoughts.

In the narrow passage gray unifs were passing, gray faces, and, for a second, one face with its hair low over the forehead, eyes gazing from deep beneath it—it was *that same man*. I understood: *they* had come, and there was no escape from it for me; only minutes remained, a few dozen minutes. . . . An infinitesimal, molecular quiver of my whole body. This quivering did not stop to the very end—it was as if an enormous motor had been placed under the very foundation of my body, which was so light that the walls, partitions, cables, beams, lights—everything was quivering. . . .

[1] **It happened long ago, in the third century A. T. (After the Tables).**

I did not yet know whether *she* was there. But I had no time . . . They were calling me: quick! To the commander's bridge; time to go . . . where?

Gray, rayless faces. Below in the water—tense blue veins. Heavy, cast-iron patches of sky. It was so difficult to lift my cast-iron hand and take up the receiver of the commander's telephone! . . . "Up! Forty-five degrees!"

A heavy explosion—a jerk—a rabid, greenish-white mountain of water aft—the deck beneath my feet began to move, soft as rubber; and everything below, my whole life, forever . . . For a second, falling deeper and deeper into a sort of funnel, becoming more and more compressed—the icy-blue relief map of the City, the round bubbles of cupolas, the lonely leaden finger of the Accumulating Tower. . . . Then, instantaneously, a cotton curtain of cloud . . . We pierced it, and there was the sun and the blue sky! Seconds, minutes, miles—the blue was hardening, fast filling with darkness; like drops of cold, silver sweat the stars appeared. . . .

A sad, unbearably bright, black, starry, sunny night. . . . As if one had become deaf, one still saw that the pipes were roaring, but one only *saw;* dead silence all about. The sun was mute. It was natural, of course. One might have expected it; we were beyond the terrestrial atmosphere. The transition was so quick, so sudden, that everyone became timid and silent. Yet I . . . I thought I felt easier under that fantastic, mute sun. I had bounded over the inevitable border, having left my body somewhere there below, and I was soaring bodiless to a new world, where everything was to be different, upside down.

"Keep the same course!" I shouted into the engine room, or perhaps it was not I but a phonograph in me, and the same machine that I was, with a mechanical, hinge-like movement, handed the commander's trumpet to the Second Builder. Permeated by that most delicate, molecular quiver known only to me, I ran down the companionway, to seek . . .

The door of the saloon. . . . An hour later it was to latch and lock itself. . . . At the door stood an unfamiliar Number. He was small, with a face like a hundred or a thousand others which are usually lost in a crowd, but his arms were exceptionally long —they reached down to his knees, as if they had been taken by mistake from another set of human organs and fastened to his shoulders.

The long arm stretched out and barred the way.

"Where do you want to go?"

It was obvious that he was not aware that I knew everything. All right! Perhaps it had to be that way. From above him, in a deliberately significant tone, I said:

"I am the Builder of the *Integral,* and I am directing the test flight. Do you understand?"

The arm drew away.

The saloon. Heads covered with bristles, gray iron bristles, and yellow heads, and bald, ripe heads were bent over the instruments and maps. Swiftly, with a glance, I gathered them in with my eyes; off I ran, back down the long passage, then through the hatch into the engine room. It was hot there from the red tubes, overheated by the explosions: a constant roar—the levers were dancing their desperate, drunken dance, moving ceaselessly with a barely noticeable quiver; the arrows on the dials . . . There! At last! Near the tachometer, a notebook in his hand, was that man with the low forehead.

"Listen," I shouted straight into his ear (because of the roar). "Is she here? Where is she?"

"She? There, at the radio."

I dashed over. There were three of them, all with receiving helmets on. And she seemed a head taller than usual, wingy, sparkling, flying like an ancient Valkyrie; the bluish sparks from the radio seemed to emanate from her—from her also that ethereal, lightning-like odor of ozone.

"Someone—well, you, for instance," I said to her, panting from having run, "I must send a message down to earth, to the docks. Come, I shall dictate it to you."

Close to the apparatus there was a small, box-like cabin. We sat at the table side by side. I found her hand and pressed it hard.

"Well, what is going to happen?"

"I don't know. Do you realize how wonderful it is? To fly without knowing where . . . no matter where? It will soon be twelve o'clock and nobody knows what . . . And when night . . . Where shall you and I be tonight? Perhaps somewhere on the grass, on dry leaves . . ."

Blue sparks emanated from her, and the odor of lightning, and the vibration within me became more and more frequent.

"Write down," I said loudly, panting (from having run). "Time: eleven-twenty; speed, 5,800 . . ."

"Last night she came to me with your note. I know . . . I know everything; don't talk. . . . But the child is yours. I sent her over; she is already beyond the Wall. She will live. . . ."

I was back on the commander's bridge, back in the delirious night with its black starry sky and its dazzling sun. The hands of the clock on the table were slowly moving from minute to minute. Everything was permeated by a thin, hardly perceptible quivering (only I noticed it). For some reason a thought passed through my head: it would be better if all this took place not here but somewhere below, nearer to earth.

"Stop!" I commanded.

We kept moving by inertia, but more and more slowly. Now the *Integral* was caught for a second by an imperceptible little hair, for a second it hung motionless, then the little hair broke and the *Integral,* like a stone, dashed downward with increasing speed. That way minutes, tens of minutes passed in silence. My pulse was audible; the hand of the clock before my eyes came closer and closer to twelve. It was clear to me that I was a stone, I-330 the earth, and the stone was under irresistible compulsion to fall downward, to strike the earth and break into small particles. What if . . .? Already the hard, blue smoke of clouds appeared below. . . . What if . . .? But the phonograph within me, with a hinge-like motion and precision, took the telephone and commanded: "Low speed!" The stone ceased falling. Now only the four lower tubes were growling, two ahead and two aft, only enough to hold the *Integral* motionless; and the *Integral,* only slightly trembling, stopped in the air as if anchored, about one kilometer from the earth.

Everybody came out on deck (it was shortly before twelve, before the sounding of the dinner gong) and leaned over the glass railing; hastily, in huge gulps, they devoured the unknown world which lay below, beyond the Green Wall. Amber, blue, green, the autumnal woods, prairies, a lake. At the edge of a little blue saucer some lone yellow debris, a threatening, dried-out yellow finger—it must have been the tower of an ancient "church" saved by a miracle. . . .

"Look, there! Look! There to the right!"

There—over the green desert—a brown blot was rapidly moving. I held a telescope in my hands and automatically I brought it to my eyes: the grass reaching their chests, a herd of brown horses was galloping, and on their backs—*they,* black, white, and dark . . .

Behind me:

"I assure you, I saw a face!"

"Go away! Tell it to someone else!"

"Well, look for yourself! Here is the telescope."

They had already disappeared. Endless green desert—and in that desert, dominating it completely and dominating me, and everybody, the piercing vibrations of the gong; dinnertime, one minute to twelve.

For a second the little world around me became incoherent,

dispersed. Someone's brass badge fell to the floor. It mattered little. Soon it was under my heel. A voice: "And I tell you, it was a face!" A black square, the open door of the main saloon. White teeth pressed together, smiling . . . And at that moment, when the clock began slowly to strike, holding its breath between beats, and when the front rows began to move toward the dining saloon, the rectangle of the door was suddenly crossed by the two familiar, unnaturally long arms.

"STOP!"

Someone's fingers sank piercing into my palm. It was I-330. She was beside me.

"Who is it? Do you know him?"

"Is he not? . . . Is he not? . . ."

He was already lifted upon somebody's shoulders. Above a hundred other faces, his face like hundreds, like thousands of other faces, yet unique among them all. . . .

"In the name of the Guardians! You, to whom I talk, *they* hear me, every one of them hears me. I talk to you: *we know!* We don't know your numbers yet, but we know everything else. The *Integral* shall not be yours! The test flight will be carried out to the end and you, you will not dare to make another move! You, with your own hands, will help to go on with the test and afterward . . . well, I have finished!"

Silence. The glass plates under my feet seemed soft, cotton-like. My feet, too—soft, cotton-like. Beside me—she with a dead-white smile, angry blue sparks. Through her teeth to me:

"Ah! It is your work! You did your 'duty'! Well . . ." She tore her hand from mine; the Valkyrie helmet with indignant wings was soon to be seen some distance in front of me. I was alone, torpid, silent. Like everyone else I followed into the dining saloon.

But it was not I, not I! I told nobody, save these white, mute pages . . . I cried this to her within me, inaudibly, desperately, loudly. She was across the table, directly opposite me, and not once did she even touch me with her gaze. Beside her someone's ripe, yellow, bald head. I heard (it was I-330's voice):

" 'Nobility' of character! But my dear professor, even a superficial etymological analysis of the word shows that it is a superstition, a remnant of the ancient feudal epoch. We . . ."

I felt I was growing pale, and that they would soon notice it. But the phonograph within me performed the prescribed fifty chewing movements for every bite. I locked myself into myself as though into an opaque house; I threw up a heap of rocks before my door and lowered the window blinds. . . .

Afterward, the telephone of the commander was again in

my hands, and again we made the flight through the clouds with icy, supreme anxiety into the icy, starry, sunny night. Minutes, hours passed. . . . Apparently all that time the motor of logic within me was working feverishly at full speed. For suddenly somewhere, at a distant point of the dark blue space, I saw my desk, and the gill-like cheeks of U- bent over it, and the forgotten pages of my records! It became clear to me; nobody but her . . . everything was clear to me!

If only I could reach the radio room soon . . . wing-like helmets, the odor of blue lightning . . . I remember telling her something in a low voice, and I remember how she looked *through* me, and how her voice seemed to come from a distance:

"I am busy. I am receiving a message from below. You may dictate yours to her."

The small, box-like little cabin . . . I thought for a second and then dictated in a firm voice:

"Time fourteen-forty. Going down. Motors stopped. The end of all."

The commander's bridge. The machine heart of the *Integral* stopped; we were falling; my heart could not catch up and would remain behind and rise higher and higher into my throat. . . . Clouds. . . . And then a distant green spot—everything green, more and more distinct, running like a storm toward us. "Soon the end."

The porcelain-like distorted white face of the Second Builder! It was he who struck me with all his strength; I hurt my head on something; and through the approaching darkness, I heard while falling:

"Full speed—aft!"

A brusque jolt upward. . . .

In a Ring
A Carrot
A Murder

I did not sleep all night. But one thought the whole night . . . As a result of yesterday's mishap my head is tightly bandaged —it seems to me not a bandage but a ring, a pitiless ring of glass iron, riveted about my head. And I am busy with the same thought, always the same thought in my riveted circle: to kill U-. To kill U- and then go to *her* and say: "Now do you believe?"

What is most disquieting is that to kill is dirty, primitive. To break her head with something—the thought of it gives me a peculiar sensation of something disgustingly sweet in my mouth, and I am unable to swallow my saliva; I am always spitting into my handkerchief, yet my mouth feels dry.

I had in my closet a heavy piston rod which had cracked during the casting, and which I had brought home in order to find out with a microscope the cause of the cracking. I made my manuscript into a tube (let her read me to the last letter!), pushed the broken piston into that tube, and went downstairs. The stairway seemed endless, the steps disgustingly slippery, liquid. I had to wipe moisture from off my mouth very frequently. Downstairs . . . my heart dropped. I took the piston out and went to the controller's table. But she was not there; instead, an empty, icy desk with ink blots. And then I remembered that today all work had stopped; everyone was to go to be operated on. There was no need for her to stay here. There was nobody to be registered. . . .

The street. It was windy. The sky seemed to be composed of soaring panels of cast iron. And exactly as it had seemed for one moment yesterday, the whole world was broken up into separate, sharp, independent fragments, and each of these fragments was falling at full speed; each would stop for a second, hang before me in the air, and disappear without a trace. It was as if the precise, black letters on this page should suddenly move apart and begin to jump hither and thither in fright, so that there was not a word on the page, only nonsensical "ap," "jum," "wor." The crowd seemed just as nonsensical, dispersed (not in rows), going forward, backward, diagonally, transversely. . . .

Then nobody. For a second, suddenly stopping in my mad dashing, I saw on the second floor, in the glass cage of a room hanging in the air, a man and a woman—a kiss; she, standing with her whole body bent backward, brokenly: "This is for the last time, forever. . . ."

At a corner a thorny, moving bush of heads. Above the heads separate, floating in the air, a banner: "Down with the machines! Down with the Operation!" And, distinct from my own self, I thought: "Is it possible that each one of us bears such a pain, that it can be removed only with his heart? . . . That something must be done to each one, before he . . ." For a second everything disappeared for me from the world, except my beast-like hand with the heavy, cast-iron package it held. . . .

A boy appeared. He was running, a shadow under his lower lip. The lower lip turned out like the cuff of a rolled-up sleeve. His face was distorted; he wept loudly; he was running away from someone. The stamping of feet was heard behind him. . . .

The boy reminded me: "U- must be in school. I must hurry!" I ran to the nearest opening of the Underground Railway. At the entrance someone passed me and said, "Not running. No trains today . . . there!" I descended. A sort of general delirium was reigning. The glitter of cut-crystal suns; the platform packed closely with heads. An empty, torpid train.

In the silence—a voice. I could not see her but I knew, I knew that intense, living, flexible, whip-like, flogging voice! I felt there that sharp triangle of brows drawn to the temples. . . .

"Let me! Let me reach her! I must! . . ."

Someone's tentacles caught my arm, my shoulders. I was nailed. In the silence I heard:

"No. Go up to them. There they will cure you; there they will overfeed you with that leavened happiness. Satiated, you will slumber peacefully, organized, keeping time, and snoring sweetly. Is it possible that you do not hear yet that great symphony of snoring? Foolish people! Don't you realize that they want to liberate you from these gnawing, worm-like, torturing question marks? And you remain standing here and listening to me? Quick! Up! To the Great Operation! What is your concern, if I remain here alone? What does it matter to you if I want to struggle, hopelessly struggle? So much the better! What does it matter to you that I do not want others to desire for me? I want to desire for myself. If I desire the impossible . . ."

Another voice, slow, heavy:

"Ah, the impossible! Which means to run after your stupid fancies; those fancies would whirl from under your very noses like a tail. No, we shall catch that tail, and then . . ."

"And then—swallow it and fall snoring; a new tail will become necessary. They say the ancients had a certain animal which they called 'ass.' In order to make it go forward they would attach a carrot to a bow held in front of its nose, so that it could not reach it. . . . If it had caught and swallowed it . . ."

The tentacles suddenly let me go; I threw myself toward the place she was speaking from; but at that very moment everything was brought down in confusion. Shouts from behind: "They are coming here! Coming here!" The lights twinkled and went out—someone had cut the cable—and everything was like a lava of cries, groaning, heads, fingers. . . .

I do not know how long we were rolled about that way in the underground tube. I only remember that underneath my feet steps were felt, dusk appeared, becoming brighter and brighter, and again we were in the street, dispersing fan wise in different directions.

Again I was alone. Wind. Gray, low twilight crawling over my head. In the damp glass of the sidewalk, somewhere very deep, there were light, topsy-turvy walls and figures moving along, feet upward. And that terribly heavy package in my hands pulled me down into that depth, to the bottom.

At the desk again. U- was not yet there; her room was dark and empty. I went up to my room and turned on the light. My temples, tightly bound by the iron ring, were pulsating. I paced and paced, always in the same circle: my table, the white package on the table, the bed, my table, the white package on the table . . . In the room to my left the curtains were lowered. To my right, the knotty bald head bent over a book, the enormous, parabolic forehead. Wrinkles on the forehead like a series of yellow, illegible lines. At times our eyes met, and then I felt that those lines were about me.

. . . It happened at twenty one o'clock exactly. U- came in on her own initiative. I remember that my breathing was so loud that I could hear it, and that I wanted to breathe less noisily but was unable to.

She sat down and arranged the fold of her unif on her knees. The pinkish-brown gills were waving.

"Oh, dear, is it true that you are wounded? I just learned about it, and at once I ran . . ."

The piston was before me on the table. I jumped up, breathing even louder. She heard, and stopped halfway through a word and rose. Already I had located the place on her head; something disgustingly sweet was in my mouth. . . . My handkerchief! I could not find it. I spat on the floor.

The fellow with the yellow, fixed wrinkles which think of me! He must not see. It would be even more disgusting if he could . . . I pressed the button (I had no right to, but who cared about rights at that moment?). The curtains fell.

Evidently she felt and understood what was coming, for she rushed to the door. But I was quicker than she, and I locked the door with the key, breathing loudly and not for a second taking my eyes from that place on her head. . . .

"You . . . you are mad! How dare you . . ." She moved backward toward the bed, put her trembling hands between her knees. . . . Like a tense spring, holding her firmly with my gaze, I slowly stretched out my arm toward the table (only one arm could move), and I snatched the piston.

"I implore you! One day—only one day! Tomorrow I shall go and attend to the formalities . . ."

What was she talking about? I swung my arm . . . And I consider I killed her. Yes, you my unknown readers, you have the right to call me murderer. I know that I should have dealt the blow on her head had she not screamed:

"For . . . for the sake . . . I agree. . . . I . . . one moment

. . ." With trembling hands she tore off her unif—a large, yellow, drooping body, she fell upon the bed. . . .

Then I understood; she thought that I pulled the curtains . . . in order to . . . that I wanted . . .

This was so unexpected and so stupid that I burst out laughing. Immediately the tense spring within me broke, and my hand weakened, and the piston fell to the floor.

Here I learned from personal experience that laughter is the most terrible of weapons; you can kill anything with laughter, even murder. I sat at my table and laughed desperately; I saw no way out of that absurd situation. I don't know what would have been the end if things had run their natural course, but suddenly a new factor in the arithmetical chain: the telephone rang.

I hurried, grasped the receiver. Perhaps she . . . I heard an unfamiliar voice:

"Wait a minute."

Annoying, infinite buzzing. Heavy steps from afar, nearer and louder like cast iron, and . . .

"D-503? The Well-Doer speaking. Come at once to me."

Ding! He hung up the receiver. Ding! like a key in a keyhole.

U- was still in bed, eyes closed, gills apart in the form of a smile. I picked up her clothes, threw them on her, and said through clenched teeth:

"Well. Quick! Quick!"

She raised her body on her elbow, her breasts hanging down to one side, eyes round. She became a figure of wax.

"What?"

"Get dressed, that is what!"

Face distorted, she firmly snatched her clothes and said in a flat voice, "Turn away . . ."

I turned away, pressed my forehead against the glass. Light, figures, sparks were trembling in the black, wet mirror. . . . No, all this was I, myself—within me. . . . What did HE call me for? Is it possible that HE knows already about her, about me, about everything?

U-, already dressed, was at the door. I make a step toward her and pressed her hand as hard as though I hoped to squeeze out of it, drop by drop, what I needed.

"Listen . . . Her name, you know whom I am talking of, did you report her name? No? Tell the truth, I must . . . I don't care what happens, but tell the truth!"

"No."

"No? But why not, since you . . ."

Her lower lip turned out like the lip of that boy and her face . . . tears were running down her cheeks.

"Because I . . . I was afraid that if I did you might . . . you would stop lov—Oh, I cannot, I could not!"

I understood. It was the truth. Absurd, ridiculous, human truth. I opened the door.

Empty Pages
The Christian God
About My Mother

It is very strange that a kind of empty white page should be left in my hand. How I walked there, how I waited (I remember I had to wait), I know nothing about it; I remember not a sound, not a face, not a gesture, as if all communicating wires between me and the world were cut.

When I came to, I found myself standing before Him. I was afraid to raise my eyes; I saw only the enormous cast-iron hands upon His knees. Those hands weighed upon Him, bending His knees with their weight. He was slowly moving His fingers. His face was somewhere above, as if in fog. And, only because His voice came to my ears from such a height, it did not roar like thunder, it did not deafen me but appeared to be an ordinary, human voice.

"Then you, too, you, the Builder of the *Integral!* You, whose lot it was to become the greatest of all *conquistadores!* You, whose name was to have been at the head of a glorious new chapter in the history of the United State! You . . ."

Blood ran to my head, to my cheeks—and here again a white page; only the pulsation in my temples and the heavy voice from above; but I remember not a word. Only when He became silent, I came to and noticed how His hand moved heavily like a thousand pounds, and crawled slowly—His finger threatened me.

"Well? Why are you silent? Is it true, or not? Executioner? So!"

"So," I repeated submissively. And then I heard clearly every one of His words.

"Well, then? Do you think I am afraid of the Word? Did you ever try to take off its shell and look into its inner meaning? I shall tell you. . . . Remember a blue hill, a crowd, a cross? Some up on the hill, sprinkled with blood, are busy nailing a body to the cross; others below, sprinkled with tears, are gazing upward. Does it not occur to you that the part which those above must play is the more difficult, the more important part? If it were not for them, how could that magnificent tragedy ever have been staged? True, they were hissed by the dark crowd, but for that the author of the tragedy, God, should have remunerated them the more liberally, should He not? And the most clement, Christian God himself, who burned all the infidels on a slow fire, is He not an executioner? Was the number of those burned by the Christians less than the number of burned Christians? Yet (you must understand this!), yet this God was for centuries glorified as the God of love! Absurd? Oh, no. Just the contrary. It is instead a testament to the imperishable wisdom of man, written in blood. Even at the time when he still was wild and hairy, man knew that real, algebraic love for humanity must inevitably be inhuman, and that the inevitable mark of truth is cruelty—just as the inevitable mark of fire is its property of causing the sensation of burning. Could you show me a fire that would not hurt? Well, now prove your point! Proceed! Argue!"

How could I argue? How could I argue when those thoughts were once mine, though I was never able to dress them in such a splendid, tempered armor? I remained silent.

"If your silence is intended to mean that you agree with me, then let us talk as adults do after the children have gone to bed; let us talk to the logical end. I ask: what was it that man from his diaper age dreamed of, tormented himself for, prayed for? He longed for that day when someone would tell him what happiness is, and then would chain him to it. What else are we doing now? The ancient dream about a paradise . . . Remember: there in paradise they know no desires any more, no pity, no love; there they are all—blessed. An operation has been performed upon their center of fancy; that is why they are blessed, angels, servants of God. . . . And now, at the very moment when we have caught up with that dream, when we hold it like this" (He clenched his hand so hard, that if he had held a stone in it sap would have run out!). ". . . At the moment when all that was left for us was to adorn our prize and distribute it among all in equal pieces, at that very moment you, you . . ."

The cast-iron roar was suddenly broken off. I was as red as a piece of iron on an anvil under the moulding sledge hammer. The hammer seemed to have stopped for a second, hanging in the air, and I waited, waited . . . until suddenly:

"How old are you?"

"Thirty-two."

"Just double the age, and as simple as at sixteen! Listen.

Is it possible that it really never occurred to you that *they* (we do not yet know their names, but I am certain you will disclose them to us), that *they* were interested in you only as the Builder of the *Integral?* Only in order to be able, through the use of you—"

"Don't! Don't!" I cried. But it was like protecting yourself with your hands and crying to a bullet: you may still be hearing your own "don't," but meanwhile the bullet has burned you through, and writhing with pain you are prostrated on the ground.

Yes, yes: the Builder of the *Integral* . . . Yes, yes. . . . At once there came back to me the angry face of U- with twitching, brick-red gills, on that morning when both of them . . .

I remember now, clearly, how I raised my eyes and laughed. A Socrates-like, bald-headed man was sitting before me; and small drops of sweat dotted the bald surface of his head.

How simple, how magnificently trivial everything was! How simple . . . almost to the point of being ridiculous! Laughter was choking me and bursting forth in puffs; I covered my mouth with my hand and rushed wildly out. . . .

Steps. Wind. Damp, leaping fragments of lights and faces . . . And while running: "No! Only to see her! To see her once more!"

Here again an empty white page. All I remember is feet: not people, just feet, hundreds of feet, confusedly stamping feet, falling from somewhere in the pavement, a heavy rain of feet . . . And some cheerful, daring voice, and a shout that was probably for me: "Hey, hey! Come here! Come along with us!"

Afterward—a deserted square heavily overloaded with tense wind. In the middle of the square a dim, heavy, threatening mass—the Machine of the Well-Doer. And a seemingly unexpected image arose within me in response to the sight of the Machine: a snow-white pillow, and on the pillow a head thrown back, and half-closed eyes, and a sharp, sweet line of teeth . . . All this seemed so absurdly, so terribly connected with the Machine. I know *how* this connection has come about, but I do not yet want to see it nor to say it aloud—I don't want to! I don't!

I closed my eyes and sat down on the steps which led upward to the Machine. I must have been running hard, for my face was wet. From somewhere far away cries were coming. But nobody heard them; nobody heard me crying: "Save me from it—save me!"

If only I had a mother as the ancients had—my mother, *mine*, for whom I should be not the Builder of the *Integral*, and not D-530, not a molecule of the United State, but merely a living human piece, a piece of herself, a trampled, smothered, cast-off piece . . . And though I were driving the nails into the cross, or being nailed to it (perhaps it is the same), she would hear what no one else could hear, her old, grown-together, wrinkled lips. . . .

Infusorian
Doomsday
Her Room

This morning while we were in the refectory my neighbor to my left whispered to me in a frightened tone:

"But why don't you eat? Don't you see, they are looking at you!"

I had to pluck up all my strength to show a smile. I felt it—like a crack in my face; I smiled, and the borders of the crack drew apart wider and wider; it was quite painful.

And then: no sooner had I lifted the small cube of paste upon my fork, than the fork jerked from my hand and tinkled against the plate. And at once the tables, the walls, the plates, even the air, trembled and rang; outside, too, an enormous, iron, round roar reaching the sky—floating over heads and houses, it died away in the distance in small, hardly perceptible circles like those upon water.

I saw faces instantaneously grow faded and bleached; I saw mouths filled with food suddenly motionless, and forks hanging in air. Then everything became confused, jumped off the centuries-old tracks; everybody jumped up from his place (without singing the Hymn!) and confusedly, in disorder, hastily finishing chewing, choking, grasping one another. . . . They were asking: "What? What happened? What? . . ." And the disorderly fragments of the Machine, which was once perfect and great, fell down in all directions—down the elevators, down the stairs. . . . Stamping of feet . . . Pieces of words like pieces of torn letters carried by the wind. . . .

The same outpour from the neighboring houses. A minute later the avenue seemed like a drop of water seen under a microscope: the infusoria locked up in the transparent, glass-like drop of water were tossing around, from side to side, up and down.

"Ah!" Someone's triumphant voice. I saw the back of a neck, and a finger pointing to the sky. I remember very distinctly a yellowish-pinkish nail, and under the nail a crescent crawling out as if from under the horizon. The finger was like a compass; all eyes were raised to the sky.

There, running away from invisible pursuit, masses of cloud were rushing upon each other; colored by the clouds, the aeros of the Guardians were floating with their tube-like antennae. And farther to the west—something like . . . At first nobody could understand what it was, even I, who knew (unfortunately) more than the others. It was like a great hive of black aeros swarming somewhere at an extraordinary height—they looked like hardly noticeable, swiftly moving points . . . Near and nearer . . . Hoarse, guttural sounds began to reach the earth, and finally we saw *birds* just over our heads! They filled the sky with their sharp, black, descending triangles. The furious wind drove them down, and they began to land on the cupolas, on the roofs, poles, and balconies.

"Ah—ah!" and the triumphant back of the neck turned; again I saw that man with the protruding forehead, but it seemed that the name, so to speak, was all that was left of him: he seemed to have crawled out from under his forehead, and on his face, around the eyes and lips, bunches of rays were growing. Through the noise of the wind and the wings and the cawing he cried to me:

"Do you realize? Do you realize! They have blown up the Wall! The Wall has been blown up! Do you *understand?*"

Somewhere in the background figures with their heads drawn in were hastily rushing by and into the houses. In the middle of the pavements was a mass of those who had already been operated upon; they moved toward the west . . .

. . . Hairy bunches of rays around the lips and eyes . . . I grasped his hands:

"Tell me. Where is she? Where is I-330? There? Beyond the Wall, or . . . ? I must . . . Do you hear me? At once . . . I cannot . . ."

"Here!" he shouted in a happy, drunken voice, showing strong yellow teeth, "here in town, and she is acting! Oh, we are doing great work!"

Who are those "we"? Who am I?

There were about fifty around him. Like him, they seemed to have crawled out from under their foreheads. They were loud, cheerful, strong-toothed, swallowing the stormy wind. With their simple not at all terrible-looking electrocutors (where did they get them?), they started to the west, toward the operated ones, encircling them, keeping parallel to avenue Forty-eight . . .

Stumbling against the tightly drawn ropes woven by the wind, I was running to her. What for? I did not know. I was stumbling . . . Empty streets . . . The city seemed foreign, wild, filled with the ceaseless, triumphant hubbub of the birds. It seemed like the end of the world, *Doomsday*.

Through the glass of the walls in quite a few houses (this cut into my mind), I saw male and female Numbers in shameless embraces—without curtains lowered, without pink checks, in the middle of the day! . . .

The house—her house; the door ajar. The lobby, the control desk, all were empty. The elevator had stopped in the middle of its shaft. I ran panting up the endless stairs. The corridor. Like the spokes of a wheel figures on the doors dashed past my eyes: 320, 326, 330—I-330! Through the glass wall I could see everything in her room upside down, confused, creased: the table overturned, its legs in the air like a beast; the bed absurdly placed away from the wall, obliquely; strewn over the floor—fallen, trodden petals of pink checks.

I bent over and picked up one, two, three of them; all bore the name D-503. I was on all of them, drops of myself, of my molten, poured-out self. And that was all—that was left . . .

Somehow I felt they should not lie there on the floor and be trodden upon. I gathered a handful of them, put them on the table, and carefully smoothed them out, glanced at them, and . . . laughed aloud! I never knew it before but now I know—and you, too, know—that laughter may be of different colors. Laughter is but a distant echo of an explosion within us; it may be the echo of a holiday—red, blue, and golden fireworks—or at times it may represent pieces of human flesh exploded into the air. . . .

I noticed an unfamiliar name on some of the pink checks. I do not remember the figures but I do remember the letter—F. I brushed the stubs from the table to the floor, stepped on them, on myself, stamped on them with my heels—and went out . . .

In the corridor I sat on the window sill in front of her door and waited long and stupidly. An old man appeared. His face was like a pierced, empty bladder with folds; from beneath the puncture something transparent was still slowly dripping. Slowly, vaguely, I realized—tears. And only when the old man was quite far off I came to and exclaimed:

"Please . . . listen. . . . Do you know . . . Number I-330?"

The old man turned around, waved his hand in despair, and stumbled farther away. . . .

I returned home at dusk. On the west side the sky was twitching every second in a pale blue, electric convulsion; a subdued, heavy roar could be heard from that direction. The roofs were covered with black, charred sticks—birds.

I lay down; and instantly, like a heavy beast, sleep came and stifled me. . . .

I Don't Know What Title—Perhaps the Whole Synopsis May Be Called a Castoff Cigarette Butt

I awoke. A bright glare painful to look at. I half-closed my eyes. My head seemed filled with some caustic blue smoke. Everything was enveloped in fog, and through the fog:

"But I did not turn on the light . . . then how is it . . ."

I jumped up. At the table, leaning her chin on her hand and smiling, sat I-330, looking at me.

She was at the very table at which I am now writing. Those ten or fifteen minutes are already well behind me, cruelly twisted into a very firm spring. Yet it seems to me that the door closed after her only a second ago, and that I could still overtake her and grasp her hand, and that she might laugh out and say . . .

I-330 was at the table. I rushed toward her.

"You? You! I have been . . . I saw your room. . . . I thought you . . ." But midway I hurt myself upon the sharp, motionless spears of her eyelashes, and I stopped. I remembered: she had looked at me in the same way before, in the *Integral*. I felt I had to tell her everything in one split second, and in such a way that she would surely believe, or she would never . . .

"Listen, I-330, I must . . . I must . . . everything! No, no, one moment—let me have a glass of water first."

My mouth was as dry as if it were lined with blotting paper. I poured a glass of water but I couldn't . . . I put the glass back upon the table, and with both hands firmly grasped the carafe.

Now I noticed that the blue smoke came from a cigarette. She brought the cigarette to her lips, and eagerly drew in and swallowed the smoke as I did water; then she said:

"Don't. Be silent. Don't you see it matters very little? I came, anyway. They are waiting for me below. . . . Do you want these minutes, which are our last . . . ?"

Abruptly she threw the cigarette on the floor and bent backward, over the side of the chair, to reach the button in the wall (it was quite difficult to do), and I remember how the chair swayed slightly, how two of its legs were lifted. Then the curtains fell.

She came close to me and embraced me. Her knees, through her dress, were like a slow, gentle, warm, enveloping, and permeating poison . . .

Suddenly (it happens at times) you plunge into sweet, warm sleep—when all at once, as if something pricks you, you tremble and your eyes are again widely open. So it was now;

there on the floor in her room were the pink checks stamped with traces of footsteps, some of them bore the letter F- and some figures . . . Plus and minus fused within my mind into one lump . . . I could not say even now what sort of feeling it was, but I crushed her so that she cried out with pain . . .

One more minute out of those ten or fifteen; her head thrown back, lying on the bright white pillow, her eyes half-closed, a sharp, sweet line of teeth . . . And all this reminded me in an irresistible, absurd, torturing way about something forbidden, something not permissible at that moment. More tenderly, more cruelly, I pressed her to myself, brighter grew the blue traces of my fingers . . .

She said, without opening her eyes (I noticed this), "They say you went to see the Well-Doer yesterday; is it true?"

"Yes."

Then her eyes opened widely and with delight I looked at her and saw that her face grew quickly paler and paler, that it effaced itself, disappearing—only the eyes remained.

I told her everything. Only for some reason, why I don't know (no, that's not true, I know the reason), I was silent about one thing: His assertion at the end that they needed me only in order . . .

Like the image on a photographic plate in a developing fluid, her face gradually reappeared: the cheeks, the white line of teeth, the lips. She stood up and went to the mirror door of the closet. My mouth was dry again. I poured water but it was revolting to drink it; I put the glass back on the table and asked:

"Did you come to see me because you wanted to inquire . . . ?"

A sharp, mocking triangle of brows drawn to the temples looked at me from the mirror. She turned around to say something, but said nothing.

It was not necessary; I knew.

To bid her good-by, I moved my foreign limbs, struck the chair with them. It fell upside down, dead, like the table in her room. Her lips were cold . . . just as cold was once the floor, here, near my bed . . .

When she left I sat down on the floor, bent over the cigarette butt . . .

I cannot write any more—I no longer want to!

W. B. YEATS / Sailing to Byzantium

THAT IS no country for old men. The young
In one another's arms, birds in the trees,
—Those dying generations—at their song,
The salmon-falls, the mackerel-crowded seas,
Fish, flesh, or fowl, commend all summer long
Whatever is begotten, born, and dies.
Caught in that sensual music all neglect
Monuments of unaging intellect.

An aged man is but a paltry thing,
A tattered coat upon a stick, unless
Soul clap its hands and sing, and louder sing
For every tatter in its mortal dress,
Nor is there singing school but studying
Monuments of its own magnificence;
And therefore I have sailed the seas and come
To the holy city of Byzantium.

O sages standing in God's holy fire
As in the gold mosaic of a wall,
Come from the holy fire, perne in a gyre,
And be the singing-masters of my soul.
Consume my heart away; sick with desire
And fastened to a dying animal
It knows not what it is; and gather me
Into the artifice of eternity.

Once out of nature I shall never take
My bodily form from any natural thing,
But such a form as Grecian goldsmiths make
Of hammered gold and gold enameling
To keep a drowsy Emperor awake;
Or set upon a golden bough to sing
To lords and ladies of Byzantium
Of what is past, or passing, or to come.

II

THE MASTER OF FATE

It was almost inevitable that since the Greeks gave us fatalism, the Romans in their turn should have developed rationalism. The Stoic philosophy of the Greeks reached its highest form in the writings and practice of the Romans. The Stoic ideal contains elements of fatalism, but is characterized principally by the belief that control of one's self and one's world can be achieved through intellect. Stoic psychology—rooted in common sense—supports the rational ability of man to overcome his physical and psychic environment. Like Leibniz, the Stoics saw man as the source of all his acts and assumed that each man had a moral responsibility for what he did. Today's existentialist thinkers have molded this idea into a philosophy of action: life is being, acting and doing. Life is dependent upon individual willingness to make a choice and then take the responsibility for it.

Existentialism seems often to be a philosophy of despair. And it is frequently difficult to differentiate between the freely chosen death of the existentialist and the deterministic renunciation of the fatalist. The difference lies solely in the existential affirmation of the human being as the master of, at least, his own life on earth.

The schizophrenic in Vaisberg's case history appears at first glance to be a victim of fate. He is a "frail flower." Nothing in his past can be found to which one can attribute his disease. No psychic determinism has been at work here, but a more profound fatalism: the man is what he is because he was made that way. Yet within his fractured psyche, life has gasped to the surface and he has made a choice: he will subject himself to the narrow confines of orthodox religious belief and thereby escape his schizophrenia. It seems like a heartbreaking resolution for a brilliant man. But, says Vaisberg, who are we to judge? He has found the solution, his own solution, to the existential problem. Like Sartre's wracked heroes, or Hawthorne's seeker after perfect beauty, he is now the master of the situation and no longer its victim. The existentialist may choose death—but if he wants annihilation, then the choice reaffirms him as a human being. Life seems bleak for the existentialist as for the fatalist only because most of us are not able to realize the psychic liberation of choice, which is, after all, proof that though we may well be something less than divine, we are something more than animal.

CICERO/The Moral Duties of Mankind

ALL QUESTIONS concerning duty are of two sorts. The first relates to the final good; the second consists of those rules which are to regulate the practice of life in all its relations. Examples of the former are as follows:—Whether all duties are perfect in themselves? Whether one duty is of more importance than another? together with other questions of the same nature. Now the rules for moral duties relate, indeed, to the final good; but it is not so perceptible that they do, because they seem chiefly to refer to the regulation of ordinary life, and of them we are to treat in this book. . . .

The distinguishing property of man is to search for and to follow after truth. Therefore, when relaxed from our necessary cares and concerns, we then covet to see, to hear, and to learn somewhat; and we esteem knowledge of things either obscure or wonderful to be the indispensable means of living happily. From this we understand that truth, simplicity, and candor, are most agreeable to the nature of mankind. To this passion for discovering truth is added a desire to direct; for a mind well formed by nature is unwilling to obey any man but him who lays down rules and instructions to it, or who, for the general advantage, exercises equitable and lawful government. From this proceeds loftiness of mind and contempt for worldly interests.

Neither is it a mean privilege of nature and reason that man is the only animal who is sensible of order, of decency, and of propriety, both in acting and speaking. In like manner, no other creature perceives the beauty, the gracefulness, and the harmony of parts, in those objects which are discerned by the sight. An analogous perception to which nature and reason convey from the sight to the mind; and consider that beauty, regularity, and order in counsels and actions should be still more preserved. She is cautious not to do aught that is indecent or effeminate, or to act or think wantonly in any of our deliberations or deeds. The effect and result of all this produces that *honestum* which we are now in search of; that virtue which is honorable even without being ennobled; and of which we may truly say that even were it praised by none it would be commendable in itself. . . .

Now every human action ought to be free from precipitancy and negligence, nor indeed ought we to do anything for which we cannot give a justifiable reason. This indeed almost amounts to a definition of duty. Now we must manage so as to keep the appetites subservient to reason that they may neither outstrip it nor fall behind through sloth and cowardice. Let them be ever composed and free from all perturbation of spirit; and thus entire consistency and moderation will display themselves. For those appetites that are too vagrant and rampant as it were, either through desire or aversion, are not sufficiently under the command of reason; such, I say, undoubtedly transgress bounds and moderation. For they abandon and disclaim that subordination to reason, to which by the law of nature they are subjected, and thereby not only the mind but the body is thrown into disturbance. Let any one observe the very looks of men who are in a rage, and those who are agitated by desire or fear, or who exult in an excess of joy; all whose countenances, voices, motions, and attitudes are changed.

But to return to my description of duty. From these particulars we learn that all our appetites ought to be awake so that we do nothing in a rash, random, thoughtless, and inconsiderate manner. For nature has not formed us to sport and merriment, but rather to seriousness and studies that are important and sublime. Sport and merriment are not always disallowable; but we are to use them as we do sleep and other kinds of repose, when we have despatched our weighty and important affairs. Nay, our very manner of joking should be neither wanton nor indecent, but genteel and good-humored. For as we indulge boys not in an unlimited licence of sport, but only in that which is not inconsistent with virtuous conduct, so in our very jokes there should appear some gleam of a virtuous nature.

The manner of joking is reduceable under two denominations;—one that is ill-bred, insolent, profligate, and obscene; another that is elegant, polite, witty, and good-humored. We have abundance of this last, not only in our Plautus, and the authors of the old Greek comedy, but in the writings of the Socratic philosophers. Many collections have likewise been made of various writers, of humorous sayings, such as that made by Cato, and called his Apopthegms. The distinction, therefore, between a genteel and an ill-mannered joke is a very ready one. The former, if seasonably made, and when the attention is relaxed, is worthy of a virtuous man; the other, if it exhibit immorality in its subject or obscenity in the expression, is unworthy even of a man. There is likewise a certain limit to be observed, even in our amusements, that we do not give up everything to amusement and that, after being elevated by pleasure, we do not sink into some immorality. Our Campus Martius, and the sport of hunting, supply creditable examples of amusement.

G. W. LEIBNIZ/New Essays Concerning Human Understanding

Philalethes. So long as man has the power to think or to refrain from thinking, to move or not to move according to the preference or choice of his own mind, so long he is *free.*

Theophilus. The term *freedom* is very ambiguous. There is freedom of right and of fact. As regards that of *right* a slave is not at all free, a subject is not wholly free, but a poor man is as free as a rich man. Freedom of *fact* consists either in the power *to will as one ought,* or in the power to do what one wills. It is of the *freedom to do* of which you speak, and it has its degrees and varieties. *Generally* he who has the most means is the freest to do what he wills: but *in particular* freedom is understood of the use of things which are ordinarily in our power, and above all, of the free use of our body. Thus the prison and the diseases which prevent us from giving to our body and our limbs the motion we wish and which we can ordinarily give them detract from our freedom: thus a prisoner is not at all free, and a paralytic has no free use of his limbs. *Freedom of will* is furthermore understood in two different senses. The first is when it is opposed to the imperfection or the slavery of the spirit, which is a coaction or constraint, but internal like that arising from the passions. The other sense has place when freedom is opposed to necessity. In the first sense the Stoics said that the wise man alone is free; and in fact the spirit is not at all free when it is filled with a great passion, for one cannot then will as he should, that is to say, with the deliberation which is requisite. Thus God alone is perfectly free, and created spirits are so, only to the extent that they are superior to their passions. And this freedom concerns properly our understanding. But the freedom of spirit, opposed to necessity, concerns the naked will, and in so far as it is distinguished from the understanding. This is what is called *free-will* (*franc arbitre*) and it consists in this, that we will that the strongest reasons or impressions which the understanding presents to the will do not prevent the act of the will from being contingent, and do not give it an absolute, and, so to speak, metaphysical necessity. And it is in this sense that I am accustomed to say that the understanding can determine the will, according to the prevalence of perceptions and reasons, in a manner which, even where it is certain and infallible, inclines without compelling.

Ph. A man awake is no more at liberty to think or not to think, than he is at liberty to prevent or not to prevent his body from touching any other body. But to transfer his thoughts from one idea to another is often within his determination. And in that case he is as much at liberty as regards his ideas, as he is as regards the bodies upon which he rests, being able to transfer himself from one to the other as the fancy arises. There are, however, ideas, which, like certain (bodily) movements, are so fixed in the mind, that, in certain circumstances, you cannot avoid them whatever effort you make. A man upon the rack is not at liberty to put aside the idea of pain, and sometimes a violent passion acts upon our mind as the most violent wind acts upon our body.

Th. There is order and connection in ideas, as there is in (bodily) movements, for the one corresponds perfectly to the other, although the determination in the movements be unconscious and free, or with choice in the thinking being whom good and evil cause to incline without forcing him. For the soul, while representing bodies, preserves its (own) perfections, and although dependent upon the body (in seizing the good) in the voluntary acts, it is independent and makes the body depend upon itself in others. But this *dependence* is only *metaphysical,* and consists in the considerations which God has for the one while ruling the other, or rather for both, according to the original perfections of each; whilst *physical dependence* would consist in an immediate influence, which the one would receive from the other on which it depends. For the rest, there come to us involuntary thoughts, partly from outside by means of objects which strike our senses, and partly from within by reason of the impressions (often insensible) which remain from preceding perceptions whose action continues and which mingle with those which appear for the first time. As regards these we are passive, and even when we wake up, *images* (under which designation I include not only the representations of figures, but also those of sounds and other sensible qualities) come to us, as in dreams, without being called. The German language calls them *fliegende Gedanken,* that is, flying thoughts (*pensées volantes*), which are not within our control, and among which there are sometimes many absurdities which raise scruples in good people, and furnish exercise to casuists and directors of consciences. It is as in the magic lantern, which makes figures appear upon the wall according as something within is turned. But our mind, perceiving some image which recurs to it, may say: stop there, and, so to speak, arrest it. Moreover, the mind enters, as seems good to itself, into certain *trains of thought,* which lead it on to others. But this is true only when internal or external impressions do not at all prevail. It is true that in this thing men differ very much, both according to their temperament and according as they have exercised their control, so that one can master impressions where another lets them go.

Ph. In my opinion the question should not be, whether the will is free,—that is to speak in a very improper manner,—but whether the *man is free.* That granted, I say that so long as any one can by the direction or choice of his mind prefer the existence of an action to its non-existence, and the contrary, *i.e.* can make it exist or not exist according as he wills, so long he is *free.* And we can scarcely say how we could possibly conceive a being freer than so far as he is able to do what he wills. So that man seems to be as free in reference to those actions which depend upon this power he finds in himself, as it is possible for freedom to make him, if I may so express myself.

Th. When we reason about the freedom of the will or upon free-will (*franc arbitre*), we do not ask if man can do what he wills, but if there is enough independence in his will itself. We do not ask if he has free limbs or elbow-room, but if he has a free spirit, and in what it consists. In this respect one intelligence might be freer than another, and the supreme intelligence will exist in perfect freedom of which creatures are not at all capable. . . .

Ph. I am also for this intelligent determination of the will by what is in the perception and the understanding. To will and do conformably to the final result of a sincere examination is rather a perfection than a defect of our nature. And this so far from being a suppression or an abridgement of freedom, is its greatest perfection and advantage. And the more we are prevented from determining ourselves in this way, the nearer we are to misery and slavery. In fact, if you suppose in the mind a perfect and absolute *indifference* which cannot be determined by the final judgment which it makes of good or evil, you put it in a very imperfect state.

Th. All this is very much to my taste, and shows that the mind has not entire and direct power always to stop its desires, else it would never be determined, whatever examination it might make, and whatever good reasons or efficacious sentiments it might make, and it would always remain irresolute and fluctuate eternally between fear and hope. It must, then, after all, be determined, and thus it could itself oppose only *indirectly* its desires, by itself preparing in advance the arms which fight them in time of need; as I have just explained.

Ph. But a man is at liberty to lift his hand to his head or to let it lie quiet. He is perfectly indifferent regarding either of these acts, and it would be an imperfection in him if he lacked that power.

Th. To speak accurately, one is never indifferent regarding two alternatives, whatever they may propose; for example, turning to the right or left, putting the right foot forward (as was necessary in the case of Trimalchio) or the left; for we do the one or the other without thinking of it, and this is an indication that a *concurrence* of internal dispositions and external impressions (although insensible) determines us to the side that we take. But the *prevalence* is very small, and in case of need it is as if we were indifferent in this respect, since the least sensible subject which presents itself to us is capable of determining us without difficulty to one rather than to the other; and although there is a little trouble in lifting the arm to raise the hand to the head, it is so small that we overcome it without difficulty; otherwise, I admit it would be a great imperfection if man were less indifferent, and if he were wanting in power to determine easily to raise or not to raise his arm.

Ph. But it would be as great an imperfection if he had the same indifference on all occasions, as when he would defend his head or his eyes from a blow, by which he saw he was about to be struck. That is to say, it were as easy for him to stop this movement as others of which we have just spoken, and in which he is almost indifferent; for that would make its influence insufficiently strong and prompt in time of need. Thus determination is useful to us, and, indeed, very often necessary; for if we were less determined on every sort of occasion, and as it were insensible to reasons drawn from the perception of good or evil, we would be without effective choice. And if we were determined by something else than the final result, which we have formed in our own mind according as we have judged a certain action good or evil, we should not be free.

Th. Nothing is truer, and those who seek another freedom know not what they ask. . . .

Ph. To be determined by the reason to the best, is to be the freest. Who would wish to be foolish for the reason that a fool is less determined by wise reflections than a man of good sense? If freedom consists in throwing off the yoke of reason, fools and madmen will be the only free men; but I do not believe that for love of such freedom any one would wish to be a fool, save he who is one already.

Th. There are people to-day who consider it clever to declaim against reason, and to treat it as an inconvenient pedant. I see little books, discourses about nothing, which make great pretentions, and I sometimes see verses even too beautiful to be employed in such false thoughts. In fact, if those who mock at reason spoke in earnest, it would be a new kind of extravagance unknown to past centuries. To speak against reason is to speak against truth; for reason is a concatenation of truths. It is to speak against one's self, against one's good, since the principal point of reason consists in knowing the truth and following the good.

FRIEDRICH NIETZSCHE / Beyond Good and Evil

To REFRAIN mutually from injury, from violence, from exploitation, and put one's will on a par with that of others: this may result in a certain rough sense in good conduct among individuals when the necessary conditions are given (namely, the actual similarity of the individuals in amount of force and degree of worth, and their co-relation within one organisation). As soon, however, as one wished to take the principle more generally, and if possible even as the *fundamental principle of society,* it would immediately disclose what it really is—namely, a Will to the *denial* of life, a principle of dissolution and decay. Here one must think profoundly to the very basis and resist all sentimental weakness; life itself is *essentially* appropriation, injury, conquest of the strange and weak, suppression, severity, obtrusion of peculiar forms, incorporation, and at the least, putting it mildest, exploitation;—but why should one for ever use precisely these words on which for ages a disparaging purpose has been stamped? Even the organisation within which, as was previously supposed, the individuals treat each other as equal—it takes place in every healthy aristocracy—must itself, if it be a living and not a dying organisation, do all that towards other bodies, which the individuals within it refrain from doing to each other: it will have to be the incarnated Will to Power, it will endeavour to grow, to gain ground, attract to itself and acquire ascendency—not owing to any morality or immorality, but because it *lives,* and because life *is* precisely Will to Power. On no point, however, is the ordinary consciousness of Europeans more unwilling to be corrected than on this matter; people now rave everywhere, even under the guise of science, about coming conditions of society in which "the exploiting character" is to be absent:—that sounds to my ears as if they promised to invent a mode of life which should refrain from all organic functions. "Exploitation" does not belong to a depraved, or imperfect and primitive society: it belongs to the *nature* of the living being as a primary organic function; it is a consequence of the intrinsic Will to Power, which is precisely the Will to Life.—Granting that as a theory this is a novelty—as a reality it is the *fundamental fact* of all history: let us be so far honest towards ourselves!

In a tour through the many finer and coarser moralities which have hitherto prevailed or still prevail on the earth, I found certain traits recurring regularly together, and connected with one another, until finally two primary types revealed themselves to me, and a radical distinction was brought to light. There is *master-morality* and *slave-morality*;—I would at once add, however, that in all higher and mixed civilisations, there are also attempts at the reconciliation of the two moralities; but one finds still oftener the confusion and mutual misunderstanding of them, indeed, sometimes their close juxtaposition—even in the same man, within one soul. The distinctions of moral values have either originated in a ruling caste, pleasantly conscious of being different from the ruled—or among the ruled class, the slaves and dependents of all sorts. In the first case, when it is the rulers who determine the conception "good," it is the exalted, proud disposition which is regarded as the distinguishing feature, and that which determines the order of rank. The noble type of man separates from himself the beings in whom the opposite of this exalted, proud disposition displays itself: he despises them. Let it at once be noted that in this first kind of morality the antithesis "good" and "bad" means practically the same as "noble" and "despicable";—the antithesis "good" and *"evil"* is of a different origin. The cowardly, the timid, the insignificant, and those thinking merely of narrow utility are despised; moreover, also, the distrustful, with their constrained glances, the self-abasing, the dog-like kind of men who let themselves be abused, the mendicant flatterers, and above all the liars:—it is a fundamental belief of all aristocrats that the common people are untruthful. "We truthful ones"—the nobility in ancient Greece called themselves. It is obvious that everywhere the designations of moral value were at first applied to *men*, and were only derivatively and at a later period applied to *actions*; it is a gross mistake, therefore, when historians of morals start questions like, "Why have sympathetic actions been praised?" The noble type of man regards *himself* as a determiner of values; he does not require to be approved of; he passes the judgment: "What is injurious to me is injurious in itself"; he knows that it is he himself only who confers honor on things; he is a *creator* of *values*. He honors whatever he recognises in himself: such morality is self-glorification. In the foreground there is the feeling of plenitude, of power, which seeks to overflow, the happiness of high tension, the consciousness of a wealth which would fain give and bestow:

—the noble man also helps the unfortunate, but not—or scarcely —out of pity, but rather from an impulse generated by the superabundance of power. The noble man honors in himself the powerful one, him also who has power over himself, who knows how to speak and how to keep silence, who takes pleasure in subjecting himself to severity and hardness, and has reverence for all that is severe and hard. "Wotan placed a hard heart in my breast," says an old Scandinavian Saga: it is thus rightly expressed from the soul of a proud Viking. Such a type of man is even proud of *not* being made for sympathy; the hero of the Saga therefore adds warningly: "He who has not a hard heart when young, will never have one." The noble and brave who think thus are the furthest removed from the morality which sees precisely in sympathy, or in acting for the good of others, or in *désintéressement,* the characteristic of the moral; faith in oneself, pride in oneself, a radical enmity and irony towards "selflessness," belong as definitely to noble morality, as do a careless scorn and precaution in presence of sympathy and the "warm heart."—It is the powerful who *know* how to honour, it is their art, their domain for invention. The profound reverence for age and for tradition—all law rests on this double reverence,— the belief and prejudice in favor of ancestors and unfavourable to newcomers, is typical in the morality of the powerful; and if, reversely, men of "modern ideas" believe almost instinctively in "progress" and the "future," and are more and more lacking in respect for old age, the ignoble origin of these "ideas" has complacently betrayed itself thereby. A morality of the ruling class, however, is more especially foreign and irritating to present-day taste in the sternness of its principle that one has duties only to one's equals; that one may act towards beings of a lower rank, towards all that is foreign, just as seems good to one, or "as the heart desires," and in any case "beyond good and evil": it is here that sympathy and similar sentiments can have a place. The ability and obligation to exercise prolonged gratitude and prolonged revenge—both only within the circle of equals,—artfulness in retaliation, *raffinement* of the idea in friendship, a certain necessity to have enemies (as outlets for the emotions of envy, quarrelsomeness, arrogance—in fact, in order to be a good *friend*): all these are typical characteristics of the noble morality, which, as has been pointed out, is not the morality of "modern ideas," and is therefore at present difficult to realise, and also to unearth and disclose. —It is otherwise with the second type of morality, *slave-morality.* Supposing that the abused, the oppressed, the suffering, the unemancipated, the weary, and those uncertain of themselves, should moralise, what will be the common element in their moral estimates? Probably a pessimistic suspicion with regard to the entire situation of man will find expression, prepare a condemnation of man, together with his situation. The slave has an unfavorable eye for the virtues of the powerful; he has a scepticism and distrust, a *refinement* of distrust of everything "good" that is there honored—he would fain persuade himself that the very happiness there is not genuine. On the other hand, *those* qualities which serve to alleviate the existence of sufferers are brought into prominence and flooded with light; it is here that sympathy, the kind, helping, hand, the warm heart, patience, diligence, humility, and friendliness attain to honour; for here these are the most useful qualities, and almost the only means of supporting the burden of existence. Slave-morality is essentially the morality of utility. Here is the seat of the origin of the famous antithesis "good" and "evil":—power and dangerousness are assumed to reside in the evil, a certain dreadfulness, subtlety, and strength, which do not admit of being despised. According to slave-morality, therefore, the "evil" man arouses fear; according to master-morality, it is precisely the "good" man who arouses fear and seeks to arouse it, while the bad man is regarded as the despicable being. The contrast attains its maximum when, in accordance with the logical consequences of slave-morality, a shade of depreciation—it may be slight and well-intentioned—at last attaches itself to the "good" man of this morality; because, according to the servile mode of thought, the good man must in any case be the *safe* man: he is good-natured, easily deceived, perhaps a little stupid, *un bonhomme*. Everywhere that slave-morality gains the ascendency, language shows a tendency to approximate the significations of the words "good" and "stupid."—At last fundamental difference: the desire for *freedom,* the instinct for happiness and the refinements of the feeling of liberty belong as necessarily to slave-morals and morality, as artifice and enthusiasm in reverence and devotion are the regular symptoms of an aristocratic mode of thinking and estimating.—Hence we can understand without further detail why love *as a passion*—it is our European specialty—must absolutely be of noble origin; as is well known, its invention is due to the Provencal poet-cavaliers, those brilliant, ingenious men of the *"gai saber,"* to whom Europe owes so much, and almost owes itself. . . .

At the risk of displeasing innocent ears, I submit that egoism belongs to the essence of a noble soul, I mean the unalterable belief that to a being such as "we," other beings must naturally be in subjection, and have to sacrifice themselves. The noble soul accepts the fact of his egoism without question, and also without consciousness of harshness, constraint, or arbitrariness therein, but rather as something that may have its basis in the primary law of things:—if he sought a designation for it he would say: "It is justice itself." He acknowledges under certain circumstances, which made him hesitate at first, that there are other equally privileged ones; as soon as he has settled this question of rank, he moves among those equals and equally privileged ones with the same assurance, as regards modesty and delicate respect, which he enjoys in intercourse with himself—in accordance with an innate heavenly mechanism which all the stars understand. It is an *additional* instance of his egoism, this artfulness and self-limitation in intercourse with his equals—every star is a similar egoist; he honours *himself* in them, and in the rights which he concedes to them, he has no doubt that the exchange of honours and rights, as the *essence* of all intercourse, belongs also to the natural condition of things. The noble soul gives as he takes, prompted by the passionate and sensitive instinct of requital, which is at the root of his nature. The notion of "favour" has, *inter pares,* neither significance nor good repute; there may be a sublime way of letting gifts as it were light upon one from above, and of drinking them thirstily like dew-drops; but for those arts and displays the noble soul has no aptitude. His egoism hinders him here: in general, he looks "aloft" unwillingly—he looks either *forward,* horizontally and deliberately, or downwards—*he knows that he is on a height.*

"One can only truly esteem him who does not *look out for* himself."—Goethe to Rath Schlosser.

The Chinese have a proverb which mothers even teach their children: *"Siao-sin"* (*"make thy heart small"*). This is the essentially fundamental tendency in latter-day civilisations. I have no doubt that an ancient Greek, also, would first of all remark the self-dwarfing in us Europeans of today—in this respect alone we should immediately be "distasteful" to him.

What, after all, is ignobleness?—Words are vocal symbols for ideas; ideas, however, are more or less definite mental symbols for frequently returning and concurring sensations, for groups of sensations. It is not sufficient to use the same words in order to understand one another: we must also employ the same words for the same kind of internal experiences, we must in the end have experiences *in common.* On this account the people of one nation understand one another better than those belonging to different nations, even when they use the same language; or rather, when people have lived long together under similar conditions (of climate, soil, danger, requirement, toil) there *originates* therefrom an entity that "understands itself"—namely, a nation. In all souls a like number of frequently recurring experiences have gained the upper hand over those occurring more rarely: about these matters people understand one another rapidly and always more rapidly—the history of language is the history of a process of abbreviation; on the basis of this quick comprehension people always unite closer and closer. The greater the danger, the greater is the need of agreeing quickly and readily about what is necessary; not to misunderstand one another is danger—that is what cannot at all be dispensed with in intercourse. Also in all loves and friendships one has the experience that nothing of the kind continues when the discovery has been made that in using the same words, one of the two parties has feelings, thoughts, intuitions, wishes, or fears different from those of the other. (The fear of the "eternal misunderstanding": that is the good genius which so often keeps persons of different sexes from too hasty attachments, to which sense and heart prompt them—and *not* some Schopenhauerian "genius of the species"!) Whichever groups of sensations within a soul awaken most readily, begin to speak, and give the word of command—these decide as to the general order of rank of its values, and determine ultimately its list of desirable things. A man's estimates of value betray something of the *structure* of his soul, and wherein it sees its conditions of life, its intrinsic needs. Supposing now that necessity has from all time drawn together only such men as could express similar requirements and similar experiences by similar symbols, it results on the whole that the easy communicability of need, which implies ultimately the undergoing only of average and *common* experiences, must have been the most potent of all the forces which have hitherto operated upon mankind. The more similar, the more ordinary people, have always had and are still having the advantage; the more select, more refined, more unique, and difficulty comprehensible, are liable to stand alone; they succumb to accidents in their isolation, and seldom propagate themselves. One must appeal to immense opposing forces in order to thwart this natural, all-too-natural *progressus* in simile, the evolution of man to the similar, the ordinary, the average, the gregarious—to the ignoble!—

The more a psychologist—a born, an unavoidable psychologist and soul-diviner—turns his attention to the more select cases and individuals, the greater is his danger of being suffocated by sympathy: he *needs* sternness and cheerfulness more than any other man. For the corruption, the ruination of higher men, of the more unusually constituted souls, is in fact, the rule: it is dreadful to have such a rule always before one's eyes. The manifold torment of the psychologist who has discovered this ruination, who discovers once, and then discovers *almost* repeatedly throughout all history, this universal inner "desperateness" of higher men, this eternal "too late!" in every sense—may perhaps one day be the cause of his turning with bitterness against his own lot, and of his making an attempt at self destruction—of his "going to ruin" himself. One may perceive in almost every psychologist a tell-tale inclination for delightful intercourse with commonplace and well-ordered men: the fact is thereby disclosed that he always requires healing, that he needs a sort of flight and forgetfulness, away from what his insight and incisiveness—from what his "business"—has laid upon his conscience. The fear of his memory is peculiar to him. He is easily silenced by the judgment of others; he hears with unmoved countenance how people honour, admire, love, and glorify, where he has *perceived*—or he even conceals his silence by expressly assenting to some plausible opinion. Perhaps the paradox of his situation becomes so dreadful that precisely where he has learned great *sympathy,* together with *great contempt,* the multitude, the educated, and the visionaries, have on their part learned great reverence—reverence for "great men" and marvellous animals, for the sake of whom one blesses and honours the fatherland, the earth, the dignity of mankind, and one's own self, to whom one points the young, and in view of whom one educates them. And who knows but in all great instances hitherto just the same happened; that the multitude worshipped a God, and that the "God" was only a poor sacrificial animal! *Success* has always been the greatest liar—and the "work" itself is a success; the great statesman, the conqueror, the discoverer, are disguised in their creations until they are unrecognisable; the "work" of the artist, of the philosopher, only invents him who has created it, is *reputed* to have created it; the "great men," as they are reverenced, are poor little fictions composed afterwards; in the world of historical values spurious coinage *prevails.* Those great poets, for example, such as Byron, Musset, Poe, Leopardi, Kleist, Gogol (I do not venture to mention much greater names, but I have them in my mind), as they now appear, and were perhaps obliged to be: men of the moment, enthusiastic, sensuous, and childish, light-minded and impulsive in their trust and distrust; with souls in which usually some flaw has to be concealed; often taking revenge with their works for an internal defilement, often seeking forgetfulness in their soaring from a too true memory, often lost in the mud and almost in love with it, until they become like the Will-o'-the-Wisps around the swamps, and *pretend to be* stars—the people then call them idealists,—often struggling with protracted disgust, with an ever-reappearing phantom of disbelief, which makes them cold, and obliges them to languish for *gloria* and devour "faith as it is" out of the hands of intoxicated adulators:—what a *torment* these great artists are and the so-called higher men in general, to him who has once found them out! It is thus conceivable that it is just from woman—who is clairvoyant in the world of suffering, and also unfortunately eager to help and save to an extent far beyond her powers—that *they* have learned so readily those outbreaks of boundless devoted *sympathy,* which the multitude, above all the reverent multitude, do not understand, and overwhelm with prying and self-gratifying interpretations. This sympathising invariably deceives itself as to its power; woman would like to believe that love can do *everything*—it is the *superstition* peculiar to her. Alas, he who knows the heart finds out how poor, helpless, pretentious, and blundering even the best and deepest love is—he finds that it rather *destroys* than saves!—It is possible that under the holy fable and travesty of the life of Jesus there is hidden one of the most painful cases of the martyrdom of *knowledge about love:* the martyrdom of the most innocent and most craving heart, that never had enough of any human love, that *demanded* love, that demanded inexorably and frantically to be loved and nothing else, with terrible outbursts against those who refused him their love; the story of a poor soul insatiated and insatiable in love, that had to invent hell to send thither those who *would not* love him—and that at last, enlightened about human love, had to invent a God who is entire love, entire *capacity* for love—who takes pity on human love, because it is so paltry, so ignorant! He who has such sentiments, he who has such *knowledge* about love—*seeks* for death!—But why should one deal with such painful matters? Provided, of course, that one is not obliged to do so.

The intellectual haughtiness and loathing of every man who has suffered deeply—it almost determines the order of rank *how* deeply men can suffer—the chilling certainty, with which he is thoroughly imbued and coloured, that by virtue of his suffering he *knows more* than the shrewdest and wisest can ever know, that he has been familiar with, and "at home" in many distant, dreadful worlds of which "*you* know nothing"!—this silent intellectual haughtiness of the sufferer, this pride of the elect of knowledge, of the "initiated," of the almost sacrificed, finds all forms of disguise necessary to protect itself from contact with officious and sympathising hands, and in general from all that is not its equal in suffering. Profound suffering makes noble: it separates.—One of the most refined forms of disguise is Epicurism, along with a certain ostentatious boldness of taste, which takes suffering lightly, and puts itself on the defensive against all that is sorrowful and profound. They are "gay men" who make use of gaiety, because they are misunderstood on account of it—they *wish* to be misunderstood. There are "scientific minds" who make use of science, because it gives a gay appearance, and because scientificalness leads to the conclusion that a person is superficial—they *wish* to mislead to a false conclusion. There are free insolent minds which would fain conceal and deny that they are broken, proud, incurable hearts (the cynicism of Hamlet—the case of Galiani); and occasionally folly itself is the mask of an unfortunate *over-assured* knowledge.—From which it follows that it is the part of a more refined humanity to have reverence "for the mask," and not to make use of psychology and curiosity in the wrong place.

That which separates two men most profoundly is a different sense and grade of purity. What does it matter about all their honesty and reciprocal usefulness, what does it matter about all their mutual good-will: the fact still remains—they "cannot smell each other!" The highest instinct for purity places him who is affected with it in the most extraordinary and dangerous isolation, as a saint: for it is just holiness—the highest spiritualisation of the instinct in question. Any kind of cognisance of an indescribable excess in the joy of the bath, any kind of ardour or thirst which perpetually impels the soul out of night into the morning, and out of gloom, out of "affliction" into clearness, brightness, depth, and refinement:—just as much as such a tendency *distinguishes* —it is a noble tendency—it also *separates*.—The pity of the saint is pity for the filth of the human, all-too-human. And there are grades and heights where pity itself is regarded by him as impurity, as filth.

Signs of nobility: never to think of lowering our duties to the rank of duties for everybody; to be unwilling to renounce or to share our responsibilities; to count our prerogatives, and the exercise of them, among our *duties*.

A man who strives after great things, looks upon every one whom he encounters on his way either as a means of advance, or a delay and hindrance—or as a temporary resting-place. His peculiar lofty *bounty* to his fellow-men is only possible when he attains his elevation and dominates. Impatience, and the consciousness of being always condemned to comedy up to that time—for even strife is a comedy, and conceals the end, as every means does —spoil all intercourse for him; this kind of man is acquainted with solitude, and what is most poisonous in it.

The Problem of those who Wait.—Happy chances are necessary, and many incalculable elements, in order that a higher man in whom the solution of a problem is dormant may yet take action, or "break forth," as one might say—at the right moment. On an average it *does not* happen; and in all corners of the earth there are waiting ones sitting who hardly know to what extent they are waiting, and still less that they wait in vain. Occasionally, too, the waking call comes too late—the chance which gives "permission" to take action—when their best youth, and strength for action have been used up in sitting still; and how many a one, just as he "sprang up," has found with horror that his limbs are benumbed and his spirits are now too heavy! "It is too late," he has said to himself—and has become self-distrustful and henceforth for ever useless.—In the domain of genius, may not the "Raphael without hands" (taking the expression in its widest sense) perhaps not to be the exception, but the rule?—Perhaps genius is by no means so rare: but rather the five hundred *hands* which it requires in order to tyrannise over the Χαιρὸς "the right time"—in order to take chance by the forelock!

He who does not wish to see the height of a man, looks all the more sharply at what is low in him, and in the foreground —and thereby betrays himself.

In all kinds of injury and loss the lower and coarser soul is better off than the nobler soul: the dangers of the latter must be greater, the probability that it will come to grief and perish is in fact immense, considering the multiplicity of the conditions of its existence.—In a lizard a finger grows again which has been lost; not so in man.—

MAURICE VAISBERG / An Existential View of a Man Suffering from Chronic Schizophrenia

WE ARE going to relate the story of a most unhappy young man. Unhappy, though he came into the world as a gifted child with a most favorable environment. Yet this apparently fortunate young man was to suffer the intense agony of utter dread, facing the terror of the immeasurable abysses of Nothingness.

We, you and I, are going to attempt to secure some measure of understanding, albeit inadequate, utilizing several frames of reference about this boy's existence—of his sufferings, of his world view and his adaptation to the overwhelming situation.

Aside from the "normal" neurotic trends of a modern sane society (which according to Fromm and others is alienated from man's existence) there was no overt mental illness in the entire known family tree, which goes back for several generations. Members of the family had been successful business and professional people—lawyers, doctors, a psychiatrist (sic), merchants and manufacturers.

M. was not only fortunate enough to be born with a "neologistic" uranium spoon in his mouth, but he also had "plenty on the ball" in his own right. He was a handsome, precocious child, the pride of his family, his parents and especially his mother. In later years when he was ill, she could not bring herself to admit to the actuality of his psychosis. Rather, she felt that he was a genius who was stubborn and a nonconformist, and that he needed only a "good talking to." This was an interminable repetitive process with definitely negative results. These monologues occurred while he was a guest at the X Psychiatric Institute from 1955-1957. His mother was an active, rather assertive woman in her social relationships who engaged extensively in philanthropic projects, was highly intelligent, warm, outgoing with many friends, yet maintaining an adequate close relationship with her son. The mother died of carcinoma of breast with brain mestastatis in 1956 while M. was at X Psychiatric Institute. His father is a man whose function as a father has left nothing to be desired. He is kind, tolerant, affectionate and understanding, and a very close bond has always existed between him and his son. In my opinion it is scarcely necessary in this case to belabor any adverse parental influence and to build miniscules of trauma into mountains of dynamics. Rather, here, it is the concept of the "frail flower" which seems to predominate in this patient's existence and world concept.

There is one older brother of 27, a doctor who is a charming, honest and down-to-earth, stable individual. In academic affairs he was always surpassed by M.

As a child, M. had two successful operations for strabismus. All through his elementary and high school course he excelled in the academic, social, work and play areas. He did anything he undertook well and expressed a great desire to be a leader, with an abounding ambition to achieve perfection. He was an omnivorous reader in all sorts of subjects with great versatility in his selections. In 1952 at the age of eighteen he entered Columbia

University, finishing seventh in the freshman class of five hundred. He had few relationships with his contemporaries but was extolled and befriended by his professors. At this time he began to find school work boring and felt that he would rather study things in his own way than amid the turmoil of undergraduate activities. His goal at this time was to be a journalist. He went about seeking a university program that would permit him to carry out this plan. In screening tests at the University of Chicago, he showed an IQ of 166, and subsequently entered Johns Hopkins University in 1953 to major in postgraduate Romance languages. Here, once more, he had a few peer relationships but was again praised and favored by his teachers. At the end of six months he became disgruntled, feeling that his teachers had let him down. They told him that he would have to remain longer than he had intended in order to complete his studies. He then returned to live with his family in New York.

For two years previous to admission to X he had had dealings with his draft board. He earnestly desired conscientious objector status. It appears that he had been informed by a board representative that he would be granted this status. He was told that he needed a routine interview (actually a psychiatric examination) before this status could be final. The examiner found him psychotic and he was automatically placed in the 4F category rather than in the objector status. He was crushed by the "perfidy" of his fellow man—he felt he had been double-crossed.

Since 1953, at the age of nineteen M. had had a close relationship with a girl two years his junior. She was of the Jewish Orthodox faith, and in an effort to please her and her parents he became interested in orthodox tenets and attended a Jewish Theological Seminary in Brooklyn where he was thought to be bright and serious, yet bizarre. His girl friend entered psychotherapy six months after he met her and his attitude toward this was highly critical; he made many attempts to dissuade her. Two weeks before he entered X, after he had been placed in the 4F class by his draft board for psychiatric reasons, he asked the young lady to marry him and to go to India with him. Realizing by now his illogicality and disorganization, she refused, apparently crushing him into despair, according to the account of M.'s mother.

While at home in 1954, he engaged in a flurry and frenzy of numerous undertakings, including the composition of philosophical and abstract dissertations, and poetry—none of which sold. He gradually deteriorated into incoherence and confusion which were mingled with ideas of extreme religiosity. After his 4F classification he became more difficult at home, restless, insomniac, and he refused to eat. One dismal morning he wandered off from home and was picked up by the Westchester police, taken to H. and thence to X Psychiatric Institute.

Here he received the most modern type of care, including individual, highly personalized psychotherapy (with a plethora of doctor's notes). (I am also guilty of this commission, since there are 27 pages of clinical notes that I have made since his admission over 2 years ago.) He also had drugs, ECT and ICT, given without any significant improvement. His father ran out of sustaining funds and M. entered our hospital portals on January 30, 1957.

I shall never forget my first meeting with this groping, uncertain, unhappy fellow human and subsequent friend. I encountered him in the lower hallway of MR at the East door, a tall, good-looking, presentable young man who seemed rather puzzled and who was surrounded by at least six pieces of impedimenta. He expressed a marked reluctance to stay in a locked space (the door had already been bolted), and refused to walk to the supervisor's office. This impasse lasted so long that he had to be carried bodily to a chair in the office, where he sat looking exhausted and repeating over and over "He alone, the Dreaded One, shall reign after all things there have ended." He was placed in the disturbed ward. He was given 10 mg. Serpasil intramuscularly daily because of extreme agitation characterized by restlessness, laughing and crying spells, refusal to eat the non-kosher food, all the while asking for punishment, saying, "God will not forgive me, He must annul me. I must be punished according to law. The congregation will decapitate me and stone me or strangle me."

In about ten days he had quieted down somewhat and with great circumstantiality expressed marked guilt feelings over his incestuous feelings toward his mother, shame over not having joined the Army, and marked guilt over some rare heterosexual relationships. He was fearful of others, of being a homosexual, and of sexual attack by men. Religiosity was expressed in demands that the Lord guide him, command him, and show him the way. Serpasil was increased to 15 mg. daily and he began to display extreme hostility toward me as the representative of hospital authority. He secured his prayer book in Hebrew and sermonized the patients —to the point of self-exhaustion. At this time he implied that he was in communication with God verbally and visually. Many times he would sit on the floor in the Yogi position in a semi-catatonic state, stark naked. At this time he was attending group therapy, where he tried to monopolize the situation with lengthy, disorganized, abstruse, philosophico-religious and mystical dissertations. When challenged he would temporarily go into a catatonic attitude of meditation. On one occasion he stripped completely in the group and sat on the floor for over half an hour. Thorazine 100 mg. three times a day orally was added to the Serpasil, and raised till he was getting 15 mg. Serpasil with 900 mg. Thorazine per day and was completely "zombi-ized" (if I may be permitted to coin another neologism). He presented a sorry picture—shivering, teeth chattering, slow rigidity, discharging draining eyes, and drooling, at which time Serpasil was reduced to 10 mg. daily. His main and pervading theme throughout his entire hospitalization (even during these early phases) has been "I want to leave. There is nothing wrong with me. Tell me why I am here." On April first the Serpasil was stopped and Thorazine continued. During this phase he showed marked infantile dependency, asking me to cover him in bed and to turn him over, though he was quite capable of doing so himself.

By the middle of April, 1957, he was transferred to a better ward, attended occupational therapy and was active in group therapy. At this time he expressed ideas about going to live in Israel where he would join a Kibbutz, but he had his doubts about this since he had heard that it was expedient to carry rifles in such a settlement. His one overweening ambition since then has been to go to Israel to the Wailing Wall and to rebuild the Temple. This he would do despite the fact, known to him, that the Wall is entirely within the confines of Jordan's Jerusalem. When the subject of familial separation is brought up, he says, "I will take my entire family along with me."

He continued to wear old dirty clothing. The matter of shaving was, and has been, a constant bugbear and aggravation to the personnel. He rationalizes this attitude by quoting in Hebrew from the Talmud something to the effect that "no sharp instrument shall touch thine head or face."

There has always been great difficulty in giving him medication, and since he denies his illness, he feels that medication is not needed, and also, since there is no specific commandment to take medication, he feels that it is sinful to do so. He avoided most secular activities and maintained that all that was needed to sustain life was "a morsel of bread, water by measure, and kosher salt." Later, when he had to be tube-fed for a short time, he displayed a good sense of humor during one incident. I had passed a large gavage tube through the nose, and he turned and spoke to the attendant, "Dr. Vaisberg has some peculiar ideas about vitamins, calories and nourishment and he is trying to force those ideas down my throat." By July 1957 his behavior was such that he shuttled back and forth between the better ward and the disturbed one. On large doses of Thorazine he began to show regression, along with depression and marked guilt feelings, in which he stated, "I have had intercourse with three women. But I cannot marry all of them, therefore I must expiate and be put to death by the community."

Because of the suicide threat and acute depression he was placed on Marsilid. With this energizer his depression left, but he developed a toxic reaction to the medication consisting of a fall in hemoglobin, a hemorrhagic papular eruption, and edema of both legs. These symptoms cleared with discontinuance of Marsilid, and did not recur after Marsilid was resumed about six weeks later, when he again began to express suicidal ideas. At this time he began making a medieval type of cradle for his brother's expected baby. He insisted on making it by hand, completely of wood, eliminating metal, since the Temple at Jerusalem had allegedly been built without any metal. He ate sparingly and slept on the floor during this time. By October, 1957 he was working in Ward 14 (the sick ward) where his conduct was most exemplary and kind. He would tenderly help the old men, express deep sympathy for their sufferings, and often call my attention to their needs and infirmities. In this area he has always proven to be a most tender, considerate and gentle person, with great respect for old age. He also helped assiduously with the ward chores, and was well liked by the personnel. In December, 1957 his white count began to fall and Marsilid was discontinued. He again became depressed, denuditive, asking to be killed. It was during this time that I took my Florida vacation and he was sent to Building 58 and given about six electroshock treatments with considerable alleviation of the depression but with the usual post-electroshock sensorial defects. Without any medications he began to exhibit panic reactions in February, 1958, frequently having me called on an emergency basis. These episodes were helped by intravenous Sparine, and during the period of sedation he gave forth with a great deal of material stating that he had been stupid to leave home, that he had read the wrong books; and he expressed guilt feeling over his incestuous desires toward his mother. He was started on Compazine 25 mg. four times daily, and this has been the sheet-anchor for his relative behavioral stability ever since. On this he improved to the extent of becoming protestingly cooperative, attending occupational therapy and group therapy, where he tended to monopolize the session with philosophical and religious ramblings. In June, 1958 he was granted a limited honor card restricting him to the grounds of MR. His innate sense of humor came more to the fore and his brilliant intelligence began to shine out. Since then a definite pattern in regard to Compazine has become apparent.

As long as he would take it, he functioned at a fairly satisfactory plateau. But it has been impossible at times to get him to accept the medication. After several days of such rejection a typical sequence of events would follow, consisting of refusal to eat, shave and bathe, and sleeping on the floor, along with catatonic-like spells of introspection and lack of distractibility. When medication was resumed, initially by injection, he returned to his fairly well-adjusted behavioral plateau. In this latter situation he socializes well with the infirm, the older men, the doctors and some of the attendants. He also has close relationships with our rabbis, helps Rabbi S. in his office, and has frequent dissertations—difficult to stop—with them concerning the food, shaving, bathing and religious services. In this regard he has organized a Friday night meeting or "*Minion*"[1] in MR to hold prayers and to eat a special type of meal. Since March, 1959 he has had several seven-day home visits to his father and stepmother, during which time he has almost constantly attended Jewish services and had long discourses with rabbis of these congregations. His present plans, which are minimal in nature to him, consist of his attending his former Yeshiva in Brooklyn with Rabbi L., to learn there at the feet of the wise, to work his way through the school by doing menial labor in a janitorial capacity. The Rabbi has expressed his interest in the young man and also a desire to try him out on a probationary basis. However, M. also has the consuming and persistent desire to go to Israel to help rebuild the Temple.

I have drawn a schematic type of description and diagram which may help to better illustrate what I presume to call an existential analysis and/or dynamics of this boy. Of course, included in this exposition are some general tenets and concepts of existentialism as it applies to our field of psychiatry. [See figs. 1-4]

The basic existential-phenomenological situation lying at the root of emotional disturbance is *decisionlessness*. This can be considered to be the antithesis of freedom of choice which the existentialists believe to be the unique characteristic of man as compared to animals and machines. Concomitant with this freedom of choice there is a responsibility for making and following this choice, along with the propensity for making valid value-judgments (or preferences).

This situation of decisionlessness can be equated somewhat to the "ambivalence of will" of Bleuler. According to the theological existentialist, Buber, this decisionlessness is the source of evil or sin. And, by extension, we can readily infer that mental illness is an evil. (cf. Mowrer, 1959)

As a result of this decisionlessness there develops "angst," (German agony) or anguish or anxiety. In this state one does not know which way to turn. This agony or anxiety none of us can deny—we have all felt it over and over during our lives when we

[1] For a Jewish service it is necessary to have a "*Minion*" or a quorum of ten men.

were faced with the need for making a decision and were unable to make it, we have all had it to greater or lesser degree depending upon the importance and meaning of such a decision to us. Concomitant with this anxiety comes awareness of existential guilt (in contrast to cultural guilt). The existentialists hold that guilt is inherent in the human and not necessarily inculcated into the individual through society, though the latter effect is not denied as playing its part. This guilt has been divided into three kinds by Binswanger (1942) (1) guilt over failure of the level of the Eigenwelt (2) the Umwelt, and (3) the Mitwelt. The Eigenwelt is the personal internalized world, the Umwelt is the world of things, and the Mitwelt is the area of interpersonal relationships. Failure in any of these leads to a sense of inadequacy, a lack of fulfillment, or a sense of partial death (Menninger). In another frame of reference we may call this situation the inferiority complex of Adler, or the death instinct (Thanatos) with death wishes of Freud involving the concepts of conscience and punishment.

The greatest anguish, and the most fundamental agony we all have to endure is the dread or fear of death or nothingness. Nothingness seems to be a better term semantically from the existential viewpoint. This dread is universal in man, who presumably, unlike animals, knows in advance that some day he must face it. Yet so many of us, yes, all of us face nothingness with a greater or lesser dread each and every day, each and every moment. It is here where religion with the promise of an after-life offers solace and a "defense" against this anguish. Another source of relief and help is an adequate philosophy of the *meaning* of life and death. And this is not a standardized philosophy—life has a different meaning for each of us—but the important thing is to find a meaning.

The picture as painted thus far, however, is only one-sided, and presents the more somber aspect of the situation. As positive aspects of the existential concept, there is a counter force within us, which can be termed generically "the will to live." As you will note on the left side of the diagram, I have enumerated somewhat parallel concepts from different frames of reference. First there is "the will to find meaning in life" which involves the personal experiences of one's past and the hope for a future. This is the basis of Victor Frankl's logotherapy. He is the author of the recent book, "From Death Camp to Existentialism." Then we have the "will to power" of Nietzsche. This has been variously interpreted by others as (1) the desire to be the superman, and (2) the will to the realization of one's potentialities. I prefer the latter interpretation. Then we have Adler's concept of "the will to be superior" and finally Freud's "will to pleasure" (or Eros, the pleasure principle).

And now to return to the earth again and our friend, M., in an effort to concretize some of this phenomenological dissertation. As you can see from the graph, he was born into a most sunny and hopeful and relatively non-traumatic environment, endowed with great intellectual capabilities, which he displayed very soon. Possibly even before he entered college there was a gradual crumbling of his ego, which became shattered and crushed into despair after he was rejected by his fiancée. The ultimate "why" of anything is something that metaphysics tries to answer. The "how" of anything depends on the frame of reference and the truth thus can never be completely realized. We must, in most cases, be satisfied with the "what." And in this case the "what" is the conclusion that our M. was a "fragile flower" who readily succumbed to environmental influences which would scarcely have fazed many another youth. He felt that he had failed his parents, himself and his girl friend, experiencing the guilt to such an overwhelming extent, along with extreme anguish and despair, then he reached the purgatory of decisionlessness and watched with dread the cold embracing arms of nothingness reaching out to engulf him.

How to escape from this anguish, this all-pervading agony, this soul's torture, this insatiable maelstrom, mingling light with darkness, good with evil, and above all spiritual confusion? No way out? Ah, yes—there is a gleam of hope, a guiding glint in the storm. Once I loved, and my love, who is she? An orthodox Jewess. She is my salvation. I must cling to her. But how can I do so, for I am unworthy and guilty? So I will cling to that which she symbolizes—orthodoxy. Yes, that is my salvation—and yet there is more. For orthodoxy is God, the vengeful and the forgiving. And, too, orthodoxy will give me a way of life, for in this there are strict rules and commandments. From these I cannot stray.

You will forgive me for going off at this imaginative tangent, but it is no worse nor better than those into which some psychoanalysts conduct their clients' unconscious within a particular school's frame of reference. I feel that the most acceptable part of the last dissertation could be shown diagramatically by the two arms of the patient reaching up and embracing the Tablets of the Commandments. You will note that several ways "out" of this impasse are indicated. At the left is a scholastic career, next to that is a factory or office. To the right is a family and beyond that a question mark indicating miscellaneous categories. However M. (as indicated) embraces the Ten Commandments as a rigid, absolute, and inflexible basis for his life. (Fig. I)

This, then, is his inner world, his own unique concept of

the world order. You will note, then, that arrows go opposite directions in the so-called everyday world of our western culture. This would correspond to Lewin's (1935) field theory, that is, certain goals are perceived as having intrinsic meanings for the

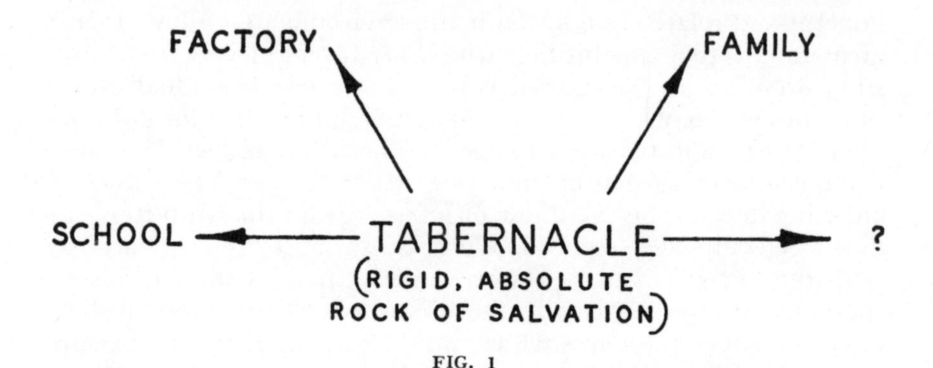

FIG. 1

individual. These values can be represented as vectors; positive vectors lead to adient responses and negative vectors lead to avoidance responses. There is a constant, though varying, flow of communication between the individual's inner world and this outer world (this outer world which some call "reality"—but which in

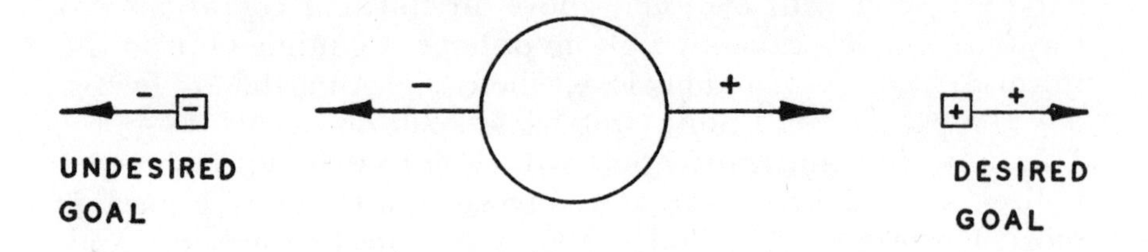

PERCEPTION OF CONFLICT-COMPROMISE
(CF. APPROACH-AVOIDANCE IN LEWIN'S TERMS)

FIG. 2

no sense can be proven from any philosophical or even scientific frame of reference). But for the sake of the discussion we shall call this the world of reality, understanding that this is the realm of everyday practical and spiritual affairs, the "koinus kosmos" or "common world" of Binswanger. In M. there can be no compromise between his inner world and the outer world and hence there is considerable discontinuity of communication, with resulting conflict in the reception and interpretation of messages. The line to the area of decisionlessness illustrates what is called feedback in communication parlance. As a result of lack of compromise with ensuing conflict and guilt there is a return to the confusional state. As an instance I may cite an outstanding example. One day M. handed me his honor card, saying, "Here, Doctor, take this, for I no longer deserve it." When I asked the reason, he continued,

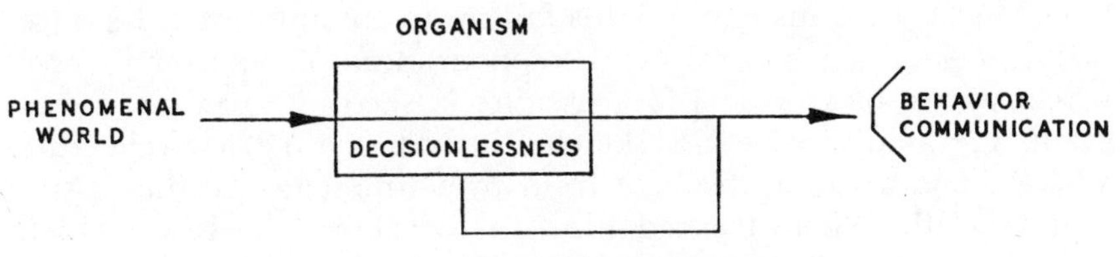

NOTE: PART OF THE SCHIZOPHRENIC EXPERIENCE IS THEN DIFFICULTY IN THE DECISION-MAKING PROCESS (SEE SCHER, 1959 A) WHICH RESULTS IN COMMUNICATION DISORDER (SEE SCHER, 1957 B)

FIG. 3

"This afternoon I was standing on the curb with both feet on the ground of MR. Suddenly I found that I had put one foot into the gutter. I do not know how it got there, but there it was. And so I have sinned and thus I must be punished."

To proceed: one might postulate a theory of communication, which infers that the greater the discontinuity of communication between the inner and outer world the greater the degree of mental disturbance as we commonly understand it. This is illustrated in the double figure to the right between the tablets and the globe. When Dr. Gosline was here he once made a very cogent observation on this subject, namely, "The unworldliness of the schizophrenic is one of his outstanding characteristics." And we have examples of this in M. I once met M. tenderly and carefully escorting a doddering, confused, deteriorated, senile man down the hall. He stopped, turned to me, and said almost ecstatically, "See, this man has the wisdom of the ages. He will be my teacher and I shall learn all from him." This is an example of the prelogical thinking which Arieti stresses in his book on schizophrenia. If this is not clear I will illustrate as follows. "Old men are very wise. This is an old man. Therefore this old man is very wise."

As a second example of this break in communication (which leads to misinterpretations) I shall cite the time when M. was making wooden playing blocks for his new nephew. These had Hebrew letters on them and he was most enthusiastic about the project. Suddenly it ceased. Asked for the reasons he frankly said that the letters might through chance spell out the name of God and that this fortuitous combination might lie face down on the ground in the hands of his nephew. And this would be the lowest form of sacrilege. How blessed he was that he had avoided the commission of this heinous sin!

As a third instance of this failure to communicate, he once had a project which involved the construction of a potter's wheel which was to be run by a foot treadle. I asked him to draw a diagram. He avidly drew the sketch illustrated. First a circle (the wheel), and at some distance from it, a line (the treadle). And that was all. When I asked him, "How about the lever which connects the two?" he replied, "No, that is not necessary, just these two here (the treadle and the wheel). Nothing else is necessary." This is also a graphic example of the associational loosenings of Bleuler. (Fig. 4)

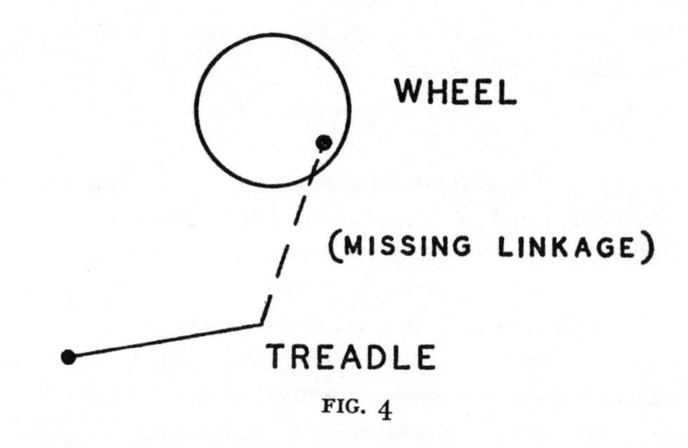

FIG. 4

In summary I might point out that the gifted M. was born a frail flower who crumbled and shattered under the "cruel blows of fate" or environmental stresses and entered into a state of decisionlessness, an agonizing despair-laden purgatory which opened downwards into the dreadful vastness of nothingness. In his effort to escape this torture and confusion he seized upon the rock (as he saw it) of salvation, of self-preservation—a rigid, inflexible, absolute system which, while a stern taskmaster, offered him complete safety from his dilemma and solace from his agony. And this was not a distant rock conjured out of dreams. It was something he had dealt with, something in his immediately preceding environment, his fiancée's religion. By one adroit maneuver he was able to keep her symbolically, to gain refuge for himself, and to keep from being shaken into the senseless atoms of disintegration. Now, we may be able to see why, in his case, it might be unwise to attempt to bring him back to what we consider our world of reality. Let us ask ourselves, "Are we then Gods that we would make him into our image?" This all means essentially that psychiatrically speaking, from the viewpoint of prognosis, we cannot very well hope to bring him further (would it be up or down?)—further than the plateau of integration and usefulness he has already reached. This is his zone of comfort and contentment. And we say, "He has no insight." Let us think some time, about the meaning of this statement that we make so glibly each day in so many cases, and try to realize its truer significance.

By describing M.'s existence phenomenologically I have attempted to communicate to you the "what" of the mystery of his existence with some more or less ineffectual efforts to delineate the "how" of his being, yet without ever hoping to know the "why" of his—and of all—existence.

References

ARIETI, S.: *Interpretation of Schizophrenia.* New York: Brunner, 1955.

BINSWANGER, L.: *Grundformen und Erkenntnis menschlichen Daseins.* Zurich: Max Niehaus Verlag, 1942.

FRANKEL, V.: *From Death Camp to Existentialism.* Boston: Beacon Press, 1959.

LEWIN, K.: *A Dynamic Theory of Personality.* New York: McGraw-Hill, 1935.

MOWRER, O.: Psychopathology and the Problem of Guilt, Confession and Expiation." *Current Trends Symposium.* Pittsburgh: University of Pittsburgh Press, 1959.

SCHER, J.: "The Decision-Making Process, Limit and Channel Setting in Schizophrenia: Communication and Structure in the Therapeutic Process." Address given at the A.P.A. Convention, Chicago, May, 1957.

——: "Indirection: A Communitive Basis for a Theory of Schizophrenia." Congress Report of the 2nd International Congress of Psychiatry, Zurich, Switzerland, September, 1957, Vol. III.

JEAN-PAUL SARTRE / Intimacy

LULU SLEPT naked because she liked to feel the sheets caressing her body and also because laundry was expensive. In the beginning Henri protested: you shouldn't go to bed naked like that, it isn't nice, it's dirty. Anyhow, he finally followed her example, though in this case it was merely laziness; he was stiff as a poker when there was company (he admired the Swiss, particularly the Genevans: he thought them high class because they were so wooden), but he was negligent in small matters, for example, he wasn't very clean, he didn't change his underwear often; when Lulu put it in the dirty laundry bag she couldn't help noticing the bottoms were yellow from rubbing between his legs. Personally, Lulu did not despise uncleanliness: it was more intimate and made such tender shadows; in the crook of the arm, for instance; she couldn't stand the English with their impersonal bodies which smelt of nothing. But she couldn't bear the negligence of her husband, because it was a way of getting himself coddled. In the morning, he was always very tender toward himself, his head full of dreams, and broad daylight, cold water, the coarse bristles of the brush made him suffer brutal injustices.

Lulu was sleeping on her back, she had thrust the great toe of her left foot into a tear in the sheet: it wasn't a tear, it was only the hem coming apart. But it annoyed her; I have to fix that tomorrow, but still she pushed against the threads so as to feel them break. Henri was not sleeping yet, but he was quiet. He often told Lulu that as soon as he closed his eyes he felt bound by tight, resistant bonds, he could not even move his little finger. A great fly caught in a spider web. Lulu loved to feel this gross, captive body against her. If he could only stay like that, paralysed, I would take care of him, clean him like a child and sometimes I'd turn him over on his stomach and give him a spanking, and other times when his mother came to see him, I'd find some reason to uncover him, I'd pull back the sheet and his mother would see him all naked. I think she'd fall flat on her face, it must be fifteen years since she'd seen him like that. Lulu passed a light hand over her husband's hip and pinched him a little in the groin. Henri muttered but did not move. Reduced to impotence, Lulu smiled; the word "impotence" always made her smile. When she still loved Henri, and when he slept, thus, she liked to imagine he had been patiently tied up by little men like the ones she had seen in a picture when she was a child and reading *Gulliver's Travels*. She often called Henri "Gulliver" and Henri liked that because it was an

English name and it made her seem educated, only he would have rather had her pronounce it with the accent. God, how they annoyed me: if he wanted someone educated all he had to do was marry Jeanne Beder, she's got breasts like hunting horns but she knows five languages. When we were still at Sceaux, on Sundays, I got so annoyed with his family I read books, any book; there was always somebody who came and watched what I was reading and his little sister asked me, "Do you understand, Lucie?" The trouble is he doesn't think I'm distinguished enough. The Swiss, yes, they're distinguished all right because his older sister married a Swiss who gave her five children and then they impress him with their mountains. I can't have a child because of my constitution, but I never thought it was distinguished, what he does, when he goes out with me, always going into the *urinoirs* and I have to look at the store windows waiting for him, what does that make me look like? and he comes out pulling at his pants and bending his legs like an old man.

Lulu took her toe out of the slit in the sheet and wiggled her feet for the pleasure of feeling herself alert next to this soft, captive flesh. She heard rumblings: a gurgling stomach, I hate it, I can never tell whether it's his stomach or mine. She closed her eyes; liquids do it, bubbling through packs of soft pipes, everybody has them, Rirette has them, I have them (I don't like to think about it, it makes my stomach hurt). He loves me, he doesn't love my bowels, if they showed him my appendix in a glass, he wouldn't recognize it, he's always feeling me, but if they put the glass in his hands he wouldn't touch it, he wouldn't think "that's hers," you ought to love all of somebody, the esophagus, the liver, the intestines. Maybe we don't love them because we aren't used to them, if we saw the way we saw our hands and arms maybe we'd love them; the starfish must love each other better than we do. They stretch out on the beach when there's sunlight and they poke out their stomachs to get the air and everybody can see them; I wonder where we could stick ours out, through the navel. She had closed her eyes and blue circles began to turn, like a carnival; yesterday I was shooting those circles with rubber arrows and letters lit up, one at every shot and they made the name of a city, he kept me from finishing Dijon with his mania for pressing himself up behind me, I hate people to touch me from behind, I'd rather not have a back, I don't like people to do things to me when I can't see them, they can grab a handful and then you don't see their hands, you can feel them going up and down but you can't tell where they're going, they look at you with all their eyes and you don't see them, he loves that; Henri would never think of it but he, all he thinks about is getting behind me and I know he does it on purpose to touch my behind because he knows I practically die of shame because I have one, when I'm ashamed it excites him but I don't want to think about him (she was afraid) I want to think about Rirette. She thought about Rirette every evening at the same time, just at the moment when Henri began to snuffle and grunt. But there was resistance to the thought and someone else came in her place, she even caught a glimpse of crisp black hair and she thought here it comes and she shuddered because you never know what's coming, if it's the face it's all right, that can still pass, but there were nights she spent without closing her eyes because of those horrible memories coming to the surface, it's terrible when you know all of a man and especially *that*. It isn't the same thing with Henri, I can imagine him from head to foot and it touches me because he's soft with flesh that's all grey except the belly and that's pink, he says when a well built man sits down, his belly makes three folds, but he has six, only he counts by twos and he doesn't want to see the others. She felt annoyed thinking about Rirette: "Lulu, you don't know what the body of a handsome man is like." It's ridiculous, naturally I know, she means a body hard as rock, with muscles, I don't like that, and I felt soft as a caterpillar when he hugged me against him; I married Henri because he was soft, because he looked like a priest. The priests are soft as women with their cassocks and it seems they wear stockings. When I was fifteen I wanted to lift up their skirts quietly and see their men's knees and their drawers, it was so funny they had something between their legs; I would have taken the skirt in one hand and slipped the other up their legs as far as you think, it's not that I like women so much but a man's thing when it's under a skirt is so soft, like a big flower. The trouble is you can never really hold it in your hands, if it would only stay quiet, but it starts moving like an animal, it gets hard, it frightens me when it's hard and sticking up in the air, it's brutal; God, how rotten love is. I loved Henri because his little thing never got hard, never raised its head, I laughed, sometimes I embarrassed him, I wasn't any more afraid of his than of a child's; in the evening I always took his soft little thing between my fingers, he blushed and turned his head away, sighing, but it didn't move, it behaved itself in my hand, I didn't squeeze it, we always stayed like that for a long time and then he went to sleep. Then I stretched out on my back and thought about priests and pure things, about women, and I stroked my stomach first, my beautiful flat stomach, then I slid my hands down and it was pleasure; the pleasure only I know how to give myself.

The crisp hair, the hair of a negro. And anguish in her throat like a ball. But she closed her eyes tightly and finally the ear of Rirette appeared, a small ear, all red and golden, looking like a sugar candy. Lulu had not as much pleasure as usual at the sight of it because she heard Rirette's voice at the same time. It was a sharp, precise voice which Lulu didn't like. "You *should* go away with Pierre, Lulu; it's the only intelligent thing to do." I like Rirette very much, but she annoys me a little when she acts important and gets carried away by what she says. The night before, at the *Coupole,* Rirette was bent over her with a reasonable and somewhat haggard look. "You *can't* stay with Henri, because you don't love him, it would be a crime." She doesn't lose a chance to say something bad about him, I don't think it's very nice, he's always been perfect with her; maybe I don't love him any more, but it isn't up to Rirette to tell me; everything looks so simple and easy to her: you love or you don't love any more: but I'm not simple. First I'm used to it here and then I do like him, he's my husband. I wanted to beat her, I always wanted to hurt her because she's fat. "It would be a crime." She raised her arms, I saw her armpit, I always like her better when she has bare arms. The armpit. It was half-open, you might have thought it was a mouth; Lulu saw purple wrinkled flesh beneath the curly hairs. Pierre calls her "Minerva the Plump," she doesn't like that at all, Lulu smiled because she thought of her little brother Robert who asked her one day when she had on nothing but her slip. "Why do you have hair under your arms?" and she answered, "It's a sickness." She liked to dress in front of her little brother because he made such funny remarks, and you wondered where he picked them up. He always felt her clothes and folded her dresses carefully, his hands were so deft: one day he'll be a great dressmaker. That's a charming business, I'll design the materials for him. It's odd for a little boy to want to be a dressmaker; if I had been a boy I would have wanted to be an explorer or an actor, but not a dressmaker; but he always was a dreamer, he doesn't talk enough, he sticks to his own ideas; I wanted to be a nun and take up collections in beautiful houses. My eyes feel all soft, all soft as flesh, I'm going to sleep. My lovely pale face under the stiff headdress. I would have looked distinguished. I would have seen hundreds of dark hallways. But the maid would have turned the light on right away; then I'd have seen family portraits, bronze statues on the tables. And closets. The woman comes with a little book and a fifty franc note "Here you are, Sister." "Thank you madame, God bless you. Until the next time." But I wouldn't have been a real nun. In the bus, sometimes, I'd have made eyes at some fellow, first he'd be dumbfounded, then he'd follow me, telling me a lot of nonsense and I'd have a policeman lock him up. I would have kept the collection money myself. What would I have bought? *Antidote.* It's silly. My eyes are getting softer, I like that, you'd think they were soaked in water and my whole body's comfortable. The beautiful green tiara with emeralds and lapis lazuli. The tiara turned and it was a horrible bull's head, but Lulu was not afraid, she said, "Birds of Cantal. Attention." A long red river dragged across arid countrysides. Lulu thought of her meat-grinder, then of hair grease.

"It would be a crime." She jumped bolt upright in the blackness, her eyes hard. They're torturing me. "You'll come to my house, I want you all for good intentions," but she who's so reasonable for other people, she ought to know I need to think it over. He said "You'll come!" making fiery eyes at me. "You'll come into my house, I want you all for myself!" His eyes terrify me when he wants to hypnotize; he kneaded my arms; when I see him with eyes like that I always think of the hair he has on his chest. You will come, I want you all for myself; how can he say things like that? I'm not a dog.

When I sat down, I smiled at him. I had changed my powder for him and I made up my eyes because he likes that, but he didn't see a thing, he doesn't look at my face, he looks at my breasts and I wish they'd dry up, just to annoy him, even though I don't have too much, they're so small. You will come to my villa in Nice. He said it was white with a marble staircase, that it looked out on the sea, and we'd live naked all day, it must be funny to go up a stairway when you're naked; I'd make him go up ahead of me so that he wouldn't look at me; or else I wouldn't be able to move a foot, I'd stay motionless, wishing with all my heart he'd go blind; anyhow, that would hardly change anything; when he's there I always think I'm naked. He took me by the arm, he looked wicked, he told me "You've got me under your skin!" and I was afraid and said, "Yes"; I want to make you happy, we'll go riding in the car, in the boat, we'll go to Italy and I'll give you everything you want. But his villa is almost unfurnished and we'd have to sleep on a mattress on the floor. He wants me to sleep in his arms and I'll smell his odor; I'd like his chest because it's brown and wide, but there's a pile of hair on it, I wish men didn't have hair, his is black and soft as moss, sometimes I stroke it and sometimes I'm horrified by it, I pull back as far as possible but he hugs me against him. He'll want me to sleep in his arms, he'll hug me in his arms and I'll smell his odor; and when it's dark we'll hear the noise of the sea and he may wake me up in the middle of the night if he wants to do it: I'll never be able to sleep peacefully except when I have my sickness because, then, he'll shut up but even so it seems there are men who do it with women then and afterwards they have blood on them, blood that isn't theirs, and there must be some on the sheets, everywhere, it's disgusting, why must we have bodies?

Lulu opened her eyes, the curtains were colored red by a light coming from the street, there was a red reflection in the mirror: Lulu loved this red light and there was an armchair which made funny shadows against the window. Henri had put his pants on the arm of the chair, and his suspenders were hanging in emptiness. I have to buy him new suspenders. Oh I don't want to, I don't want to leave. He'll kiss me all day and I'll be *his,* I'll be his pleasure, he'll look at me, he'll think, "this is my pleasure, I touched her there and there and I can do it again if it pleases me." At Port-Royal. Lulu kicked her feet in the sheets, she hated Pierre when she remembered what happened at Port-Royal. She was behind the hedge, she thought he had stayed in the car, looking at the map, and suddenly she saw him, running up behind her, he looked at her. Lulu kicked Henri. He's going to wake up. But Henri said "Humph," and didn't waken. I'd like to know a handsome young man, pure as a girl, and we wouldn't touch each other, we'd walk along the seashore and we'd hold hands, and at night we'd sleep in twin beds, we'd stay like brother and sister and talk till morning. I'd like to live with Rirette, it's so charming, women living together; she has fat, smooth shoulders; I was miserable when she was in love with Fresnel, and it worried me to think he petted her, that he passed his hands slowly over her shoulders and thighs and she sighed. I wonder what her face must look like when she's stretched out like that, all naked, under a man, feeling hands on her flesh. I wouldn't touch her for all the money in the world, I wouldn't know what to do with her, even if she wanted, even if she said, "I want it!" I wouldn't know how, but if I were invisible I'd like to be there when somebody was doing it to her and watch her face (I'd be surprised if she still looked like Minerva) and stroke her spread knees gently, her pink knees and hear her groan. Dry throated, Lulu gave a short laugh: sometimes you think about things like that. Once she pretended Pierre wanted to rape Rirette. And I helped him, I held Rirette in my arms. Yesterday. She had fire in her cheeks, we were sitting on her sofa, one against the other, her legs were pressed together, but we didn't say anything, we'll never say anything. Henri began to snore and Lulu hissed. I'm here, I can't sleep, I'm upset and he snores, the fool. If he were to take me in his arms, beg me, if he told me, "You are all mine, Lulu, I love you, don't go!" I'd make the sacrifice for him, I'd stay, yes, I'd stay with him all my life to give him pleasure.

Rirette sat on the terrace of the *Dôme* and ordered a glass of port. She felt weary and angry at Lulu:

And their port has a taste of cork, Lulu doesn't care because she drinks coffee, but still you can't drink coffee at aperitif time;

here they drink coffee all day or café-crême because they don't have a cent, God that must annoy them, I couldn't do it, I'd chuck the whole place in the customer's faces, these people don't need to keep up with anybody. I don't know why she always meets me in Montparnasse, it would be in just as close if she met me at the *Café de la Paix* or the *Pam-Pam,* and it wouldn't take me so far from my work; impossible to imagine how sad it makes me feel to see these faces all the time, as soon as I have a minute to spare, I have to come here, it's not so bad on the terrace, but inside it smells like dirty underwear and I don't like failures. Even on the terrace I feel out of place because I'm clean, it must surprise everybody that passes to see me in the middle of these people here who don't even shave and women who look like I don't know what. They must wonder "What's she doing there?" I know rich Americans sometimes come in the summer, but it seems they're stopping in England now, what with the government we've got, that's why the commerce-de-luxe isn't going so well, I sold a half less than last year at this same time, and I wonder how the others make out, because I'm the best salesgirl, Mme. Dubech told me so, I feel sorry for the little Yonnel girl, she doesn't know how to sell, she can't have made a cent commission this month, and when you're on your feet all day you like to relax a little in a nice place, with a little luxury and a little art and stylish help. You like to close your eyes and let yourself go and then you like to have nice soft music, it wouldn't cost so much to go dancing at the *Ambassadeurs* sometimes; but the waiters here are so impudent, you can tell they're used to handling a cheap crowd, except the little one with brown hair who serves me, he's nice; I think Lulu must like to be surrounded with all these failures, it would scare her to go into a chic place, fundamentally, she isn't sure of herself, it frightens her as soon as there's a man with good manners, she didn't like Louis; well, she ought to be comfortable here, some of them don't even have collars, with their shoddy appearance and their pipes and the way they look at you, they don't even try to hide it, you can see they don't have enough money to pay for a woman, but that isn't what's lacking in the neighborhood, it's disgusting; you'd think they're going to eat you and they couldn't even tell you nicely that they want you, to carry it off in a way to make you feel good.

The waiter came: "Did you want dry port, mademoiselle?"

"Yes, please."

He spoke again, looking friendly, "Nice weather we're having."

"Not too soon for it," Rirette said.

"That's right. You'd think winter wouldn't ever end."

He left and Rirette followed him with her eyes. "I like that waiter," she thought, he knows his place, he doesn't get familiar, but he always has something to say to me, a little special attention.

A thin, bent young man was watching her steadily; Rirette shrugged her shoulders and turned her back on him: When they want to make eyes at a woman they could at least change their underwear. I'll tell him that if he says anything to me. I wonder why she doesn't leave. She doesn't want to hurt Henri, I think that's too stupid: a woman doesn't have the right to spoil her life for some impotent. Rirette hated impotents, it was physical. She's got to leave, she decided, her happiness is at stake, I'll tell her she can't gamble with her happiness. Lulu, you don't have the right to gamble with your happiness. I won't say anything to her, it's finished, I told her a hundred times, you can't make people happy if they don't want to be. Rirette felt a great emptiness in her head, because she was so tired, she looked at the port, all sticky in the glass, like a liquid caramel and a voice in her repeated, "Happiness, happiness," and it was a beautifully grave and tender world. And she thought that if anybody had asked her opinion in the *Paris-Soir* contest she would have said it was the most beautiful word in the French language. Did anyone think of it? They said energy, courage, but that's because they were men, there should have been a woman, the women could find it, there should have been two prizes, one for men and one for women and the most beautiful name would have been Honor; one for the women and I'd have won, I'd have said Happiness. Happiness and Honor. I'll tell her, Lulu, you don't have the right to miss out on your happiness. Your Happiness, Lulu, your Happiness. Personally, I think Pierre is very nice, first, he's a real man, and besides, he's intelligent and that never spoils anything, he has money, he'd do anything for her. He's one of those men who knows how to smooth out life's little difficulties, that's nice for a woman; I like people who know how to command, it's a knack, but he knows how to speak to waiters and head waiters; they obey him, I call that a dominant personality. Maybe that's the thing that's most lacking in Henri. And then there's the question of health, with the father she had, she should take care, it's charming to be slender and light and never to be hungry or sleepy, to sleep four hours a night and run all over Paris all day selling material but it's silly, she ought to follow a sensible diet, not eat too much at one time, but more often and at regular hours. She'll see when they send her to the sanatorium for ten years.

She stared perplexedly at the clock over the Montparnasse intersection, it said 11:20. I don't understand Lulu, she's got a funny temperament, I could never find out whether she liked men or whether they disgusted her; still, she ought to be happy with

Pierre, that gives her a change, anyhow, from the one she had last year, from her Rabut, *Rebut* I called him. This memory amused her but she held back her smile because the thin young man was still watching her, she caught him by surprise when she turned her head. Rabut had a face dotted with blackheads and Lulu amused herself by removing them for him, pressing on the skin with her nails: It's sickening, but it's not her fault, Lulu doesn't know what a good-looking man is, I love cute men, first, their things are so pretty, their men's shirts, their shoes, their shiny ties, it may be crude, but it's so sweet, so strong, a sweet strength, it's like the smell of English tobacco and eau de cologne and their skin when they've just shaved, it isn't . . . it isn't like a woman's skin, you'd think it was cordova leather, and their strong arms close around you and you put your head on their chest, you smell their sweet strong odor of well-groomed men, they whisper sweet words to you; they have nice things, nice rough cowhide shoes, they whisper, "Darling, dearest darling" and you feel yourself fainting; Rirette thought of Louis who left her last year and her heart tightened; a man in love with himself, with a pile of little mannerisms, a ring and gold cigarette case and full of little manias . . . but they can be rough sometimes, worse than women. The best thing would be a man about forty, someone who still took care of himself, with grey hair on the sides, brushed back, very dry, with broad shoulders, athletic, but who'd know life and who'd be good because he'd suffered. Lulu is only a kid, she's lucky to have a friend like me, because Pierre's beginning to get tired and some people would take advantage of it if they were in my place; I always tell him to be patient, and when he gets a little sweet on me I act like I'm not paying attention, I begin to talk about Lulu and I always have a good word for her, but she doesn't deserve the luck she has, she doesn't realize; I want her to live alone a little the way I did when Louis went away, she'd see what it was like to go back alone to her room every evening, when you've worked all day and find the room empty and dying to put your head on a shoulder. Sometimes you wonder where you find the courage to get up the next morning and go back to work and be seductive and gay and make everybody feel good when you'd rather die than keep on with that life.

The clock struck 11:30. Rirette thought of happiness, the bluebird, the bird of happiness, the rebel bird of love. She gave a start. Lulu is half an hour late, that's usual. She'll never leave her husband, she doesn't have enough will power for that. At heart, it's mainly because of respectability that she stays with Henri: she cheats on him but so long as they call her "Madame," she doesn't think it matters. She can say anything against him she wants but you can't repeat it the next day, she'd burn up. I did everything I could and I've told her everything I had to tell her, too bad for her.

A taxi stopped in front of the *Dôme* and Lulu stepped out. She was carrying a large valise and her face was solemn.

"I left Henri," she called.

She came nearer, bent under the weight of the valise. She was smiling.

"What?" Rirette gasped, "you don't mean . . ."

"Yes," Lulu said. "Finished, I dropped him."

Rirette was still incredulous. "He knows? You told him?"

Lulu's eyes clouded. "And how!" she said.

"Well, well . . . my own little Lulu!"

Rirette did not know what to think, but in any case, she supposed Lulu needed encouragement.

"That's good news," she said. "How brave you were."

She felt like adding: you see, it wasn't so hard. But she restrained herself. Lulu let herself be admired: she had rouged her cheeks and her eyes were bright. She sat and put the valise down near her. She was wearing a grey wool coat with a leather belt, a light yellow sweater with a rolled collar. She was bareheaded. She recognized immediately the blend of guilt and amusement she was plunged in; Lulu always made that impression on her. What I like about her, Rirette thought, is her vitality.

"In two shakes," Lulu said, "I told him what I thought. He was struck dumb."

"I can't get over it," said Rirette. "But what came over you, darling? Yesterday evening I'd have bet my last franc you'd never leave him."

"It's on account of my kid brother, I don't mind him getting stuck up with me but I can't stand it when he starts on my family."

"But how did it happen?"

"Where's the waiter?" Lulu asked, stirring restlessly on the chair. "The Dôme waiters aren't ever there when you want them. Is the little brown-haired one serving us?"

"Yes," Rirette said, "did you know he's mad about me?"

"Oh? Look out for the woman in the washroom then, he's always mixed up with her. He makes passes at her but I think he just does it to see the women go into the toilets; when they come out he looks hard enough to make you blush. By the way, I've got to leave you for a minute. I have to go down and call Pierre, I'd like to see his face! If you see the waiter, order a café-crême for me: I'll be only a minute and then I'll tell you everything."

She got up, took a few steps and came back towards Rirette. "Dearest Lulu," said Rirette, taking her by the hands.

Lulu left her and stepped lightly across the terrace. Rirette watched her. I never thought she could do it. How gay she is, she thought, a little scandalized, it's good for her to walk out on her husband. If she had listened to me she'd have done it long ago. Anyhow, it's thanks to me; fundamentally, I have a lot of influence on her.

Lulu was back a few minutes later.

"Pierre was bowled over," she said, "He wanted the details but I'll give them to him later, I'm lunching with him. He says maybe we can leave tomorrow night."

"How glad I am, Lulu," Rirette said. "Tell me quickly. Did you decide last night?"

"You know, I didn't decide anything," Lulu said modestly, "it was decided all by itself." She tapped nervously on the table. "Waiter! Waiter! God, he annoys me. I'd like a café-crême."

Rirette was shocked. In Lulu's place and under circumstances as serious as this she wouldn't have lost time running after a café-crême. Lulu was charming, but it was amazing how futile she could be, like a bird.

Lulu burst out laughing. "If you'd seen Henri's face!"

"I wonder what your mother will say?" said Rirette seriously.

"My mother? She'll be en-chan-ted," Lulu said with assurance. "He was impolite with her you know, she was fed up. Always complaining because she didn't bring me up right, that I was this, I was that, that you could see I was brought up in a barn. You know, what I did was a little because of her."

"But what happened?"

"Well, he slapped Robert."

"You mean Robert was in your place?"

"Yes, just passing by this morning because mother wants to apprentice him with Gompez. I think I told you. So, he stopped in while we were eating breakfast and Henri slapped him."

"But why," Rirette asked, slightly annoyed. She hated the way Lulu told stories.

"They had an argument," Lulu said vaguely, "and the boy wouldn't let himself be insulted. He stood right up to him. 'Old asshole,' he called him, right to his face. Because Henri said he was poorly raised, naturally, that's all he can say. I thought I'd die laughing. Then Henri got up, we were eating in the kitchenette, and smacked him, I could have killed him!"

"So you left?"

"Left?" Lulu asked, amazed, "where?"

"I thought you left him then. Look, Lulu, you've got to tell me these things in order, otherwise I don't understand. Tell me," she added, suspiciously, "you really left him, that's all true?"

"Of course. I've been explaining to you for an hour."

"Good. So Henri slapped Robert. Then what?"

"Then," Lulu said, "I locked him on the balcony, it was too funny! He was still in his pajamas, tapping on the window but he didn't dare break the glass because he's as mean as dirt. If I had been in his place, I'd have broken up everything, even if I had to cut my hands to pieces. And the Texiers came in. Then he started smiling through the window acting as if it were a joke."

The waiter passed; Lulu seized his arm:

"So there you are, waiter. Would it trouble you too much to get me a café-crême?"

Rirette was annoyed and she smiled knowingly at the waiter but the waiter remained solemn and bowed with guilty obsequiousness. Rirette was a little angry at Lulu: she never knew the right tone to use on inferiors, sometimes she was too familiar, sometimes too dry and demanding.

Lulu began to laugh.

"I'm laughing because I can still see Henri in his pajamas on the balcony; he was shivering with cold. Do you know how I managed to lock him out? He was in the back of the kitchenette, Robert was crying and he was making a sermon. I opened the window and told him, 'Look Henri! There's a taxi that just knocked over the flower woman.' He came right out; he likes the flower woman because she told him she was Swiss and he thinks she's in love with him. 'Where? Where?' he kept saying. I stepped back quietly, into the room, and closed the window. Then I shouted through the glass, 'That'll teach you to be a brute to my brother.' I left him on the balcony more than an hour, he kept watching us with big round eyes, he was green with rage. I stuck my tongue out at him and gave Robert candy; after that I brought my things into the kitchenette and got dressed in front of Robert because I know Henri hates that: Robert kissed my arms and neck like a little man, he's so charming, we acted as if Henri weren't there. On top of all that, I forgot to wash."

"And Henri outside the window. It's too funny for words," Rirette said, bursting with laughter.

Lulu stopped laughing. "I'm afraid he'll catch cold," she said seriously. "You don't think when you're mad." She went on gaily, "He shook his fist at us and kept talking all the time but I didn't understand half of what he said. Then Robert left and right after that the Texiers rang and I let them in. When he saw them he was all smiles and bowing at them and I told them, 'Look at my husband, my big darling, doesn't he look like a fish in an aquarium?' The Texiers waved at him through the glass, they were a little surprised but they didn't let on."

"I can see it all," Rirette said, laughing. "Haha! Your husband on the balcony and the Texiers in the kitchenette . . ." She wanted to find the right comic and picturesque words to describe the scene to Lulu, she thought Lulu did not have a real sense of humor, but the words did not come.

"I opened the window," Lulu said, "and Henri came in. He kissed me in front of the Texiers and called me a little clown. 'Oh the little clown,' he said, 'she wanted to play a trick on me.' And I smiled and the Texiers smiled politely, everybody smiled. But when they left he hit me on the ear. Then I took a brush and hit him in the corner of the mouth with it: I split his lip."

"Poor girl," Rirette said with tenderness.

But with a gesture Lulu dismissed all compassion. She held herself straight, shaking her brown curls combatively and her eyes flashed lightning.

"Then we talked it over: I washed his mouth with a towel and then I told him I was sick of it, that I didn't love him any more and that I was leaving. He began to cry. He said he'd kill himself. But that didn't work any more: you remember, Rirette, last year, when there was all that trouble in the Rhineland, he sang the same tune every day: 'there's going to be a war, I'm going to enlist and I'll be killed and you'll be sorry, you'll regret all the sorrow you've caused me.' 'That's enough,' I told him, 'you're impotent, they wouldn't take you.' Anyhow, I calmed him down because he was talking about locking me up in the kitchenette, I swore I wouldn't leave before a month. After that he went to the office, his eyes were all red and there was a piece of cloth sticking to his lip, he didn't look too good. I did the housework, I put the lentils on the stove and packed my bag. I left him a note on the kitchen table."

"What did you write?"

"I said," Lulu said proudly, "The lentils are on the stove. Help yourself and turn off the gas. There's ham in the icebox. I'm fed up and I'm leaving. Goodbye."

They both laughed and two passers-by turned around. Rirette thought they must present a charming sight and was sorry they weren't sitting on the terrace of the *Viel* or the *Café de la Paix*. When they finished laughing, they were silent a moment and Rirette realized they had nothing more to say to each other. She was a little disappointed.

"I've got to run," Lulu said, rising; "I meet Pierre at noon. What am I going to do with my bag?"

"Leave it with me," Rirette said, "I'll check it with the woman in the lady's room. When will I see you again?"

"I'll pick you up at your place at two, I have a pile of errands to do: I didn't take half my things, Pierre's going to have to give me money."

Lulu left and Rirette called the waiter. She felt grave and sad enough for two. The waiter ran up: Rirette already noticed that he always hurried when she called him.

"That's five francs," he said. He added a little dryly, "You two were pretty gay, I could hear you laughing all the way back there."

Lulu hurt his feelings, thought Rirette, spitefully. Blushing, she said, "My friend is a little nervous this morning."

"She's very charming," the waiter said soulfully, "Thank you very much, mademoiselle."

He pocketed the six francs and went off. Rirette was a little amazed, but noon struck and she thought it was time for Henri to come back and find Lulu's note: this was a moment full of sweetness for her.

"I'd like all that to be sent *before tomorrow evening,* to the Hotel du Théatre, Rue Vandamme." Lulu told the cashier, putting on the air of a great lady. She turned to Rirette:

"It's all over. Let's go."

"What name?" the cashier asked.

"Mme. Lucienne Crispin."

Lulu threw her coat over her arm and began to run; she ran down the wide staircase of the Samaritain. Rirette followed her, almost falling several times because she didn't watch her step: she had eyes only for the slender silhouette of blue and canary yellow dancing before her! It's true, she does have an obscene body . . . Each time Rirette saw Lulu from behind or in profile, she was struck by the obscenity of her shape though she could not explain why; it was an impression. She's supple and slender, but there's something indecent about her, I don't know what. She does everything she can to display herself, that must be it. She says she's ashamed of her behind and still she wears skirts that cling to her rump. Her tail is small, yes, a lot smaller than mine, but you can see more of it. It's all around, under her thin back, it fills the skirt, you'd think it was poured in, and besides it jiggles.

Lulu turned around and they smiled at each other. Rirette thought of her friend's indiscreet body with a mixture of reprobation and languor: tight little breasts, a polished flesh, all yellow—when you touched it you'd swear it was rubber—long thighs, a long, common body with long legs: the body of a negress, Rirette thought, she looks like a negress dancing the rhumba. Near the revolving door a mirror gave Rirette the reflection of her own full body. I'm more the athletic type, she thought, taking Lulu's arm, she makes a better impression than I do when we're dressed, but naked, I'm sure I'm better than she is.

They stayed silent for a moment, then Lulu said:

"Pierre was simply charming. You've been charming too, Rirette, and I'm very grateful to both of you."

She said that with a constrained air, but Rirette paid no attention: Lulu never knew how to thank people, she was too timid.

"What a bore," Lulu said suddenly, "I have to buy a brassiere."

"Here?" Rirette asked. They were just passing a lingerie shop.

"No. But I thought of it because I saw them. I go to Fisher's for my brassieres."

"Boulevard Montparnasse?" Rirette cried. "Look out, Lulu," she went on gravely, "better not hang around the Boulevard Montparnasse, especially now: we'd run into Henri and that would be most unpleasant."

"Henri?" said Lulu, shrugging her shoulders; "Of course not. Why?"

Indignation flushed purple on Rirette's cheeks and temples.

"You're still the same, Lulu, when you don't like something, you deny it, pure and simple. You want to go to Fisher's so you insist Henri won't be on the Boulevard Montparnasse. You know very well he goes by every day at six, it's his way home. You told me that yourself: he goes up the Rue de Rennes and waits for the bus at the corner of the Boulevard Raspail."

"First, it's only five o'clock," Lulu said, "and besides, maybe he didn't go to the office: the note I wrote must have knocked him out."

"But Lulu," Rirette said suddenly, "you know there's another Fisher not far from the Opera, on the Rue du Quatre Septembre."

"Yes," Lulu said weakly, "but it's so far to go there."

"Well, I like that; so far to go. It's only two minutes from here, it's a lot closer than Montparnasse."

"I don't like their things."

Rirette thought with amusement that all the Fisher's sold the same things.

But Lulu was incomprehensibly obstinate: Henri was positively the last person on earth she would want to meet now and you'd think she was purposely throwing herself in his way.

"Well," she said indulgently, "if we meet him, we meet him, that's all. He isn't going to eat us."

Lulu insisted on going to Montparnasse on foot; she said she needed air. They followed the Rue de Seine, then the Rue de L'Odéon and the Rue de Vaugirard. Rirette praised Pierre and showed Lulu how perfect he had been under the circumstances.

"How I love Paris," Lulu said, "I'm going to miss it!"

"Oh be quiet, Lulu, when I think how lucky you are to go to Nice and then you say how much you'll miss Paris."

Lulu did not answer, she began looking right and left sadly, searching.

When they came out of Fisher's they heard six o'clock strike. Rirette took Lulu's elbow and tried to hurry her along, but Lulu stopped before Baumann the florist.

"Look at those azaleas, Rirette. If I had a nice living room I'd have them everywhere."

"I don't like potted plants," Rirette said.

She was exasperated. She turned her head toward the Rue de Rennes and sure enough, after a minute, she saw Henri's great stupid silhouette appear. He was bare-headed, and wearing a brown tweed sport coat. Rirette hated brown: "There he is, Lulu, there he is," she said hurriedly.

"Where?" Lulu asked. "Where is he?"

She was scarcely more calm than Rirette.

"Behind us, on the other side of the street. Run and don't turn around."

Lulu turned around anyhow.

"I see him," she said.

Rirette tried to drag her away, but Lulu stiffened and stared at Henri. At last she said, "I think he saw us."

She seemed frightened, suddenly yielded to Rirette and let herself be taken away quietly.

"Now for Heaven's sake, Lulu, don't turn around again," Rirette said breathlessly. "We'll turn down the first street on the right, Rue Delambre."

They walked very quickly, jostling the passersby. At times Lulu held back a little, or sometimes it was she who dragged Rirette. But they had not quite reached the corner of the Rue Delambre when Rirette saw a large brown shadow behind Lulu; she knew it was Henri and began shaking with anger. Lulu kept her eyes lowered, she looked sly and determined. She's regretting her mistake, but it's too late. Too bad for her.

They hurried on; Henri followed them without a word. They passed the Rue Delambre and kept walking in the direction of the Observatoire. Rirette heard the squeak of Henri's shoes; there was also a sort of light, regular rattle that kept time with their steps; it was his breathing (Henri always breathed heavily, but never that much; he must have run to catch up with them or else it was emotion.)

We must act as if he weren't there, Rirette thought. Pretend not to notice his existence. But she could not keep from looking out of the corner of her eye. He was white as a sheet and his eyelids were so lowered they seemed shut. Almost looks like a sleep-walker, thought Rirette with a sort of horror. Henri's lips were trembling and a little bit of pink gauze trembled on the lower lip. And the breathing—that hoarse, even breathing, now ending with a sort of nasal music. Rirette felt uncomfortable: she was not afraid of Henri, but sickness and passion always frightened her a little. After a moment, Henri put his hand out gently and took Lulu's arm. Lulu twisted her mouth as if she were going to cry and pulled it away, shuddering.

Henri went "Phew!"

Rirette had a mad desire to stop: she had a stitch in the side and her ears were ringing. But Lulu was almost running; she too looked like a sleep-walker. Rirette had the feeling that if she let go of Lulu's arm and stopped, they would both keep on running side by side, mute, pale as death, their eyes closed.

Henri began to speak. With a strange, hoarse voice he said: "Come back with me."

Lulu did not answer. Henri said again in the same toneless voice:

"You are my wife. Come back with me."

"You can see she doesn't want to go back," Rirette answered between her teeth. "Leave her alone."

He did not seem to hear her. "I am your husband," he repeated. "I want you to come back with me."

"For God's sake let her alone," Rirette said sharply, "bothering her like that won't do any good, so shut up and let her be."

"She is my wife," he said, "she belongs to me, I want her to come back with me."

He had taken Lulu's arm and this time Lulu did not shake him off.

"Go away," Rirette said.

"I won't go away, I'll follow her everywhere, I want her to come back home."

He spoke with effort. Suddenly he made a grimace which showed his teeth and shouted with all his might.

"You belong to me!"

Some people turned around, laughing. Henri shook Lulu's arm, curled back his lips and howled like an animal. Luckily an empty taxi passed. Rirette waved at it and the taxi stopped.

Henri stopped too. Lulu wanted to keep on walking but they held her firmly, each by one arm.

"You ought to know," said Rirette, pulling Lulu towards the street, "you'll never get her back with violence."

"Let her alone, let my wife alone," Henri said, pulling in the opposite direction. Lulu was limp as a bag of laundry.

"Are you getting in or not," the taxi driver called impatiently.

Rirette dropped Lulu's arm and rained blows on Henri's hand. But he did not seem to feel them. After a moment he let go and began to look at Rirette stupidly. Rirette looked at him too. She could barely collect her thoughts, an immense sickness filled her. They stayed, eye to eye, for a few seconds, both breathing heavily. Then Rirette pulled herself together, took Lulu by the waist and drew her to the taxi.

"Where to?" the driver asked.

Henri had followed. He wanted to get in with them. But Rirette pushed him back with all her strength and closed the door quickly.

"Drive, drive!" she told the chauffeur. "We'll tell you the address later."

The taxi started up and Rirette dropped to the back of the car. How vulgar it all was, she thought. She hated Lulu.

"Where do you want to go, Lulu?" she asked sweetly.

Lulu did not answer. Rirette put her arms around her and became persuasive.

"You must answer me. Do you want me to drop you off at Pierre's?"

Lulu made a movement Rirette took for acquiescence. She leaned forward. "11 Rue Messine."

When Rirette turned around again, Lulu was watching her strangely.

"What the . . ." Rirette began.

"I hate you," Lulu screamed, "I hate Pierre, I hate Henri. What do you all have against me? You're torturing me."

She stopped short and her features clouded.

"Cry," Rirette said with calm dignity, "cry, it'll do you good."

Lulu bent double and began to sob. Rirette took her in her arms and held her close. From time to time she stroked her hair. But inside she felt cold and distrustful. Lulu was calm when the cab stopped. She wiped her eyes and powdered her nose.

"Excuse me," she said gently, "it was nerves. I couldn't bear seeing him like that, it hurt me."

"He looked like an orang-outang," said Rirette, once more serene.

Lulu smiled.

"When will I see you again?" Rirette asked.

"Oh, not before tomorrow. You know Pierre can't put me up because of his mother. I'll be at the Hotel du Théatre. You could come early, around nine, if it doesn't put you out, because after that I'm going to see Mama."

She was pale and Rirette thought sadly of the terrible ease with which she could break down.

"Don't worry too much tonight," she said.

"I'm awfully tired," Lulu said, "I hope Pierre will let me go back early, but he never understands those things."

Rirette kept the taxi and was driven home. For a moment she thought she'd go to the movies but she had no heart for it. She threw her hat on a chair and took a step towards the window. But the bed attracted her, all white, all soft and moist in its shadowy hollows. To throw herself on it, to feel the caress of the pillow against her burning cheeks. I'm strong. I did everything for Lulu and now I'm all alone and no one does anything for me. She had so much pity for herself that she felt a flood of sobs mounting in her throat. They're going to go to Nice and I won't see them any more. I'm the one who made them happy but they won't think about me. And I'll stay here working eight hours a day selling artificial pearls in Burma's. When the first tears rolled down her cheeks she let herself fall softly on the bed. "Nice," she repeated, weeping bitterly, "Nice . . . in the sunlight . . . on the Riviera . . ."

"Phew!"

Black night. You'd think somebody was walking around the room: a man in slippers. He put one foot out cautiously, then the other, unable to avoid a light cracking of the floor. He stopped, there was a moment of silence, then, suddenly transported to the other end of the room, he began his aimless, idiotic walking again. Lulu was cold, the blankets were much too light. She said *Phew* aloud and the sound of her voice frightened her.

Phew! I'm sure he's looking at the sky and the stars now, he's lighting a cigarette, he's outside, he said he liked the purple color of the Paris sky. With little steps, he goes back, with little steps: he feels poetic just after he's done it, he told me, and light as a cow that's just been milked, he doesn't think any more about it—and me, I'm defiled. It doesn't surprise me that he's pure now that he left his own dirt here, in the blackness, there's a hand towel full of it and the sheet's wet in the middle of the bed, I can't stretch out my legs because I'll feel the wet on my skin, what filth and him all dry, I heard him whistle under my window when he left; he was down there dry and fresh in his fine clothes and top-coat, you must admit he knows how to dress, a woman would be proud to go out with him, he was under the window and I was naked in the blackness and I was cold and rubbed my belly with my hands because I thought I was still wet. I'll come up for a minute, he said, just to see your room. He stayed two hours and the bed creaked—this rotten little iron bed. I wonder where he found out about this hotel, he told me he spent two weeks here once, that I'd be all right here, these are funny rooms, I saw two of them, I never saw such little rooms cluttered up with furniture, cushions and couches and little tables, it stinks of love, I don't know whether he stayed here two weeks but he surely didn't stay alone; he can't have much respect for me to stick me in here. The bellboy laughed when we went up, an Algerian, I hate those people, he looked at my legs, then he went into the office, he must have thought, That's it, they're going to do it, and imagined all sorts of dirty things, they say it's terrible what they do with women down there; if they ever get hold of one she limps for the rest of her life; and all the time Pierre was bothering me I was thinking about that Algerian who was thinking about what I was doing and thinking a lot of dirtiness worse than it was. Somebody's in this room!

Lulu held her breath but the creaking stopped immediately. I have a pain between my thighs, it itches, I want to cry and it will be like that every night except tomorrow night because we'll be on the train. Lulu bit her lip and shuddered because she remembered she had groaned. It's not true, I didn't groan, I simply breathed hard a little because he's so heavy, when he's on me he takes my breath away. He said, "You're groaning, you're coming." I hate people to talk to me when I'm doing that, I wish they'd forget but he never stops saying a lot of dirty things. I didn't groan, in the first place, I can't have any pleasures, it's a fact, the doctor said so, unless I do it to myself. He won't believe it, they never want to believe it, they all said: "it's because you got off to a bad start, I'll teach you"; I let them talk, I knew what the trouble was, it's medical; but that provokes them.

Someone was coming up the stairs. Someone coming back. God, don't let him come back. He's capable of doing it if he feels like it again. It isn't him, those are heavy steps—or else—Lulu's heart jumped in her breast—if it was the Algerian, he knows I'm alone, he's going to knock on the door, I can't, I can't stand that, no, it's the floor below, it's a man going in, he's putting his key in the lock, he's taking his time, he's drunk, I wonder who lives in this hotel, it must be a fine bunch; I met a red-head this afternoon, on the stairs, she had eyes like a dope fiend. I didn't groan. Of course, he did manage to bother me with all his feeling around, he knows how; I have a horror of men who know how, I'd rather sleep with a virgin. Those hands going right to where they want, pressing a little, not too much . . . they take you for an instrument they're proud of knowing how to play. I hate people to bother me, my throat's dry, I'm afraid and I have a bad taste in my mouth and I'm humiliated because they think he dominates me, I'd like to slap Pierre when he puts on his elegant airs and says, "I've got technique." My God, to think that's life, that's why you get dressed and wash and make yourself pretty and all the books are written about that and you think about it all the time and finally that's what it is, you go to a room with somebody who half smothers you and ends up by wetting your stomach. I want to sleep. Oh, if I could only sleep a little bit, tomorrow I'll travel all night, I'll be all in. Still I'd like to be a little fresh to walk around Nice; they say it's so lovely, little Italian streets and colored clothes drying in the sun, I'll set myself up with my easel and I'll paint and the little girls will come to see what I'm doing. Rot! (she had stretched out a little and her hip touched the damp spot in the sheet) That's all he brought me here for. Nobody, nobody loves me. He walked beside me and I almost fainted and I waited for one tender word he could have said, "I love you." I wouldn't have gone back to him of course, but I'd have said something nice, we would have parted good friends, I waited and waited, he took my arm and I let him, Rirette was furious, it's not true he looked like an orang-outang but I knew she was thinking something like that, she was watching him out of the corner of her eye, nastily, it's amazing how nasty she can be, well, in spite of that, when he took my arm I didn't resist but it wasn't *me* he wanted, he wanted his wife because he married me and he's my husband; he always depreciated me, he said he was more intelligent than I and everything that happened is all his fault, he didn't need to treat me so high and mighty, I'd still be with him. I'm sure he doesn't miss me now, he isn't crying, he's raving, that's what he's doing and he's glad to have the bed all to himself so he can stretch his long legs out. I'd like to die. I'm so afraid he'll think badly of me; I couldn't explain anything to him because Rirette was between us, talking, talking, she looked hysterical. Now she's glad, she's complimenting herself on her courage, how rotten that is with Henri who's gentle as a lamb. I'll go. They can't make me leave him like a dog. She jumped out of bed and turned the switch. My stockings and slip are enough. She was in such a hurry that she did not even take the trouble to comb her hair. And the people who see me won't know I'm naked under my heavy grey coat, it comes down to my feet.

The Algerian—she stopped, her heart pounding—I'll have to wake him up to open the door. She went down on tiptoe—but the steps creaked one by one; she knocked at the office window.

"Who is it," the Algerian asked. His eyes were red and his hair tousled, he didn't look very frightening.

"Open the door for me," Lulu said dryly.

Fifteen minutes later she rang at Henri's door.

"Who's there?" Henri asked through the door.

"It's me."

He doesn't answer, he doesn't want to let me in my own home. But I'll knock on the door till he opens, he'll give in because of the neighbors. After a minute the door was half opened and Henri appeared, pale, with a pimple on his nose; he was in pajamas. He hasn't slept, Lulu thought tenderly.

"I didn't want to leave like that, I wanted to see you again."

Henri still said nothing. Lulu entered, pushing him aside a little. How stupid he is, he's always in your way, he's looking at me with round eyes with his arms hanging, he doesn't know what to do with his body. Shut up, shut up, I see you're moved and you can't speak. He made an effort to swallow his saliva and Lulu had to close the door.

"I want us to part good friends," she said.

He opened his mouth as if to speak, turned suddenly and fled. What's he doing? She dared not follow him. Is he crying? Suddenly she heard him cough: he's in the bathroom. When he came back she hung about his neck and pressed her mouth against his: he smelled of vomit. Lulu burst out sobbing.

"I'm cold," Henri said.

"Let's go to bed," she said, weeping, "I can stay till tomorrow morning."

They went to bed and Lulu was shaken with enormous sobs because she found her room and bed clean and the red glow in the window. She thought Henri would take her in his arms but he did nothing: he was sleeping stretched out full length as if someone had put a poker in the bed. He's as stiff as when he talks to a Swiss. She took his head in her two hands and stared at him. "You are pure, pure." He began to cry.

"I'm miserable," he said, "I've never been so miserable."

"I haven't either," Lulu said.

They wept for a long time. After a while she put out the light and laid her head on his shoulder. If we could stay like that forever: pure and sad as two orphans; but it isn't possible, it doesn't happen in life. Life was an enormous wave breaking on

Lulu, tearing her from the arms of Henri. Your hand, your big hand. He's proud of them because they're big, he says that descendants of old families always have big limbs. He won't take my waist in his hand any more—he tickled me a little but I was proud because he could almost make his fingers meet. It isn't true that he's impotent—he's pure, pure and a little lazy. She smiled through her tears and kissed him under the chin.

"What am I going to tell my parents?" Henri asked. "My mother'll die when she hears."

Mme. Crispin would not die, on the contrary, she would triumph. They'll talk about me, at meals, all five of them, blaming me, like people who know a lot about things but don't want to say everything because of the kid who's sixteen and she's too young to talk about certain things in front of her. She'll laugh inside herself because she knows it all, she always knows it all and she detests me. All this muck. And appearances are against me.

"Don't tell them right away," she pleaded, "tell them I'm at Nice for my health."

"They won't believe me."

She kissed Henri quickly all over his face.

"Henri, you weren't nice enough to me."

"That's true," Henri said, "I wasn't nice enough. Neither were you," he reflected, "you weren't nice enough."

"I wasn't. Ah!" Lulu said, "how miserable we are!" She cried so loudly she thought she would suffocate: soon it would be day and she would leave. You never, never do what you want, you're carried away.

"You shouldn't have felt like that," said Henri.

Lulu sighed. "I loved you a lot, Henri."

"And now you don't?"

"It isn't the same."

"Who are you leaving with?"

"People you don't know."

"How do you know people I don't know?" Henri asked angrily, "Where did you meet them?"

"Never mind, darling, my little Gulliver, you aren't going to act like a husband now?"

"You're leaving with a man," Henri said, weeping.

"Listen, Henri, I swear I'm not, I swear, men disgust me now. I'm leaving with a family, with friends of Rirette, old people. I want to live alone, they'll find a job for me; Oh Henri, if you knew how much I needed to live alone, how it all disgusts me."

"What?" Henri asked, "what disgusts you?"

"Everything!" She kissed him. "You're the only one that doesn't disgust me, darling."

She passed her hands under Henri's pajamas and caressed his whole body. He shuddered under her icy hands but he did not turn away, he said only, "I'm going to get sick."

Surely, something was broken in him.

At seven o'clock, Lulu got up, her eyes swollen with tears. She said wearily, "I have to go back there."

"Back where?"

"Hotel du Théâtre, Rue Vandamme. A rotten hotel."

"Stay with me."

"No, Henri, please, don't insist. I told you it was impossible."

The flood carries you away; that's life; we can't judge or understand, we can only let ourselves drift. Tomorrow I'll be in Nice. She went to the bathroom to wash her eyes with warm water. She put on her coat, shivering. It's like fate, I only hope I can sleep on the train tonight, or else I'll be completely knocked out when I get to Nice. I hope he got first-class tickets; that'll be the first time I ever rode first class. Everything is always like that: for years I've wanted to take a long trip first class, and the day it happens it works out so that I can't enjoy it. She was in a hurry to leave now, for these last moments had been unbearable.

"What are you going to do with that Gallois person?" she asked.

Gallois had ordered a poster from Henri, Henri had made it and now Gallois didn't want it any more.

"I don't know," Henri said.

He was crouched under the covers, only his hair and the end of his ear was visible. Slowly and softly, he said, "I'd like to sleep for a week."

"Goodbye, darling," Lulu said.

"Goodbye."

She bent over him, drawing aside the covers a little, and kissed him on the forehead. She stayed a long while on the landing without deciding to close the door of the apartment. After a moment, she turned her eyes away and pulled the knob violently. She heard a dry noise and thought she was going to faint: she had felt like that when they threw the first shovelful of dirt on her father's casket.

Henri hasn't been nice. He could have gotten up and gone as far as the door with me. I think I would have minded less if he had been the one who closed it.

"She did that!" said Rirette, with a far off look. "She did that!"

It was evening. About six Pierre had called Rirette and she had met him at the *Dôme*.

"But you," Pierre said, "weren't you supposed to see her this morning at nine?"

"I saw her."

"She didn't look strange?"

"No indeed," Rirette said, "I didn't notice anything. She was a little tired but she told me she hadn't slept after you left because she was so excited about seeing Nice and she was a little afraid of the Algerian bellboy . . . Wait . . . She even asked me if I thought you'd bought first class tickets on the train, she said it was the dream of her life to travel first class. No," Rirette decided, "I'm sure she didn't have anything like that in mind; at least not while I was there. I stayed with her for two hours and I can tell those things, I'd be surprised if I missed anything. You tell me she's very close-mouthed but I've known her for four years and I've seen her in all sorts of situations. I know Lulu through and through."

"Then the Texiers' made her mind up. It's funny . . ." He mused a few moments and suddenly began again. "I wonder who gave them Lulu's address. I picked out the hotel and she'd never heard of it before."

He toyed distractedly with Lulu's letter and Rirette was annoyed because she wanted to read it and he hadn't offered it to her.

"When did you get it?" she asked, finally.

"The letter? . . ." He handed it to her with simplicity. "Here, you can read it. She must have given it to the concierge around one o'clock."

> Dearest Darling,
>
> The Texiers came (I don't know who gave them the address) and I'm going to cause you a lot of sorrow, but I'm not going, dearest, darling Pierre; I am staying with Henri because he is too unhappy. They went to see him this morning, he didn't want to open the door and Mme. Texier said he didn't look human. They were very nice and they understood my reasons, they said all the wrong was on his side, that he was a bear but at heart he wasn't bad. She said he needed that to make him understand how much he needed me. I don't know who gave them the address, they didn't say, they must have happened to see me when I was leaving the hotel this morning with Rirette. Mme. Texier said she knew she was asking me to make an enormous sacrifice but that she knew me well enough to know that I wouldn't sneak out. I'll miss our lovely trip to Nice very much, darling, but I thought you would be less unhappy because I am still yours. I am yours with all my heart and all my body and we shall see each other as often as before. But

Henri would kill himself if he didn't have me any more. I am indispensable to him; I assure you that it doesn't amuse me to feel such a responsibility. I hope you won't make your naughty little face which frightens me so, you wouldn't want me to be sorry, would you? I am going back to Henri soon, I'm a little sick when I think that I'm going to see him in such a state but I will have the courage to name my own conditions. First, I want more freedom because I love you and I want him to leave Robert alone and not say anything bad about Mama any more, ever. Dearest, I am so sad, I wish you could be here, I want you, I press myself against you and I feel your caresses in all my body. I will be at the *Dôme* tomorrow at five.

LULU

"Poor Pierre."

Rirette took his hand.

"I'll tell you," Pierre said, "I feel sorry for her. She needed air and sunshine. But since she decided that way . . . My mother made a frightful scene," he went on, "the villa belongs to her, she didn't want me to take a woman there."

"Ah?" Rirette said, in a broken voice, "Ah? So everything's all right, then, everybody's happy!"

She dropped Pierre's hand; without knowing why she felt flooded with bitter regret.

NATHANIEL HAWTHORNE / The Birthmark

IN THE latter part of the last century there lived a man of science, an eminent proficient in every branch of natural philosophy, who not long before our story opens had made experience of a spiritual affinity more attractive than any chemical one. He had left his laboratory to the care of an assistant, cleared his fine countenance from the furnace smoke, washed the stain of acids from his fingers, and persuaded a beautiful woman to become his wife. In those days when the comparatively recent discovery of electricity and other kindred mysteries of Nature seemed to open paths into the region of miracle, it was not unusual for the love of science to rival the love of woman in its depth and absorbing energy. The higher intellect, the imagination, the spirit, and even the heart might all find their congenial aliment in pursuits which, as some of their ardent votaries believed, would ascend from one step of powerful intelligence to another, until the philosopher should lay his hand on the secret of creative force and perhaps make new worlds for himself. We know not whether Aylmer possessed this degree of faith in man's ultimate control over Nature. He had devoted himself, however, too unreservedly to scientific studies ever to be weaned from them by any second passion. His love for his young wife might prove the stronger of the two; but it could only be by intertwining itself with his love of science, and uniting the strength of the latter to his own.

Such a union accordingly took place, and was attended with truly remarkable consequences and a deeply impressive moral. One day, very soon after their marriage, Aylmer sat gazing at his wife with a trouble in his countenance that grew stronger until he spoke.

"Georgiana," said he, "has it never occurred to you that the mark upon your cheek might be removed?"

"No, indeed," said she, smiling; but perceiving the seriousness of his manner, she blushed deeply. "To tell the truth it has been so often called a charm that I was simple enough to imagine it might be so."

"Ah, upon another face perhaps it might," replied her husband; "but never on yours. No, dearest Georgiana, you came so nearly perfect from the hand of Nature that this slightest possible defect, which we hesitate whether to term a defect or a beauty, shocks me, as being the visible mark of earthly imperfection."

"Shocks you, my husband!" cried Georgiana, deeply hurt; at first reddening with momentary anger, but then bursting into tears. "Then why did you take me from my mother's side? You cannot love what shocks you!"

To explain this conversation it must be mentioned that in the centre of Georgiana's left cheek there was a singular mark, deeply interwoven, as it were, with the texture and substance of her face. In the usual state of her complexion—a healthy though delicate bloom—the mark wore a tint of deeper crimson, which imperfectly defined its shape amid the surrounding rosiness. When she blushed it gradually became more indistinct, and finally vanished amid the triumphant rush of blood that bathed the whole cheek with its brilliant glow. But if any shifting motion caused her to turn pale there was the mark again, a crimson stain upon the snow, in what Aylmer sometimes deemed an almost fearful distinctness. Its shape bore not a little similarity to the human hand, though of the smallest pygmy size. Georgiana's lovers were wont to say that some fairy at her birth hour had laid her tiny hand upon the infant's cheek, and left this impress there in token of the magic endowments that were to give her such sway over all hearts. Many a desperate swain would have risked life for the privilege of pressing his lips to the mysterious hand. It must not be concealed, however, that the impression wrought by this fairy sign manual varied exceedingly, according to the difference of temperament in the beholders. Some fastidious persons—but they were exclusively of her own sex—affirmed that the bloody hand, as they chose to call it, quite destroyed the effect of Georgiana's beauty, and rendered her countenance even hideous. But it would be as reasonable to say that one of those small blue stains which sometimes occur in the purest statuary marble would convert the Eve of Powers to a monster. Masculine observers, if the birthmark did not heighten their admiration, contented themselves with wishing it away, that the world might possess one living specimen of ideal loveliness without the semblance of a flaw. After his marriage,—for he thought little or nothing of the matter before,—Aylmer discovered that this was the case with himself.

Had she been less beautiful,—if Envy's self could have found aught else to sneer at,—he might have felt his affection heightened by the prettiness of this mimic hand, now vaguely portrayed, now lost, now stealing forth again and glimmering to and fro with every pulse of emotion that throbbed within her heart; but seeing her otherwise so perfect, he found this one defect grow more and more intolerable with every moment of their united lives. It was the fatal flaw of humanity which Nature, in one shape or another, stamps ineffaceably on all her productions, either to imply that they are temporary and finite, or that their perfection must be wrought by toil and pain. The crimson hand expressed the ineludible gripe in which mortality clutches the highest and purest of earthly mould, degrading them into kindred with the lowest, and even with the very brutes, like whom their visible frames return to dust. In this manner, selecting it as the symbol of his wife's liability to sin, sorrow, decay, and death, Aylmer's sombre imagination was not long in rendering the birthmark a frightful object, causing him more trouble and horror than ever Georgiana's beauty, whether of soul or sense, had given him delight.

At all the seasons which should have been their happiest, he invariably and without intending it, nay, in spite of a purpose to the contrary, reverted to this one disastrous topic. Trifling as it at first appeared, it so connected itself with innumerable trains of thought and modes of feeling that it became the central point of all. With the morning twilight Aylmer opened his eyes upon his wife's face and recognized the symbol of imperfection; and when they sat together at the evening hearth his eyes wandered stealthily to her cheek, and beheld, flickering with the blaze of the wood fire, the spectral hand that wrote mortality where he would fain have worshipped. Georgiana soon learned to shudder at his gaze. It needed but a glance with the peculiar expression that his face often wore to change the roses of her cheek into a deathlike paleness, amid which the crimson hand was brought strongly out, like a bass-relief of ruby on the whitest marble.

Late one night when the lights were growing dim, so as hardly to betray the stain on the poor wife's cheek, she herself, for the first time, voluntarily took up the subject.

"Do you remember, my dear Aylmer," said she, with a feeble attempt at a smile, "have you any recollection of a dream last night about this odious hand?"

"None! none whatever!" replied Aylmer, starting; but then he added, in a dry, cold tone, affected for the sake of concealing the real depth of his emotion, "I might well dream of it; for before I fell asleep it had taken a pretty firm hold of my fancy."

"And you did dream of it?" continued Georgiana, hastily; for she dreaded lest a gush of tears should interrupt what she had to say. "A terrible dream! I wonder that you can forget it. Is it possible to forget this one expression?—'It is in her heart now; we must have it out!' Reflect, my husband; for by all means I would have you recall that dream."

The mind is in a sad state when Sleep, the all-involving, cannot confine her spectres within the dim region of her sway, but suffers them to break forth, affrighting this actual life with secrets that perchance belong to a deeper one. Aylmer now remembered his dream. He had fancied himself with his servant Aminadab, attempting an operation for the removal of the birthmark; but the deeper went the knife, the deeper sank the hand, until at length its tiny grasp appeared to have caught hold of Georgiana's heart; whence, however, her husband was inexorably resolved to cut or wrench it away.

When the dream had shaped itself perfectly in his memory, Aylmer sat in his wife's presence with a guilty feeling. Truth often finds its ways to the mind close muffled in robes of sleep, and then speaks with uncompromising directness of matters in regard to which we practise an unconscious self-deception during our waking moments. Until now he had not been aware of the tyrannizing influence acquired by one idea over his mind, and of the lengths which he might find in his heart to go for the sake of giving himself peace.

"Aylmer," resumed Georgiana, solemnly, "I know not what may be the cost to both of us to rid me of this fatal birthmark. Perhaps its removal may cause cureless deformity; or it may be the stain goes as deep as life itself. Again: do we know that there is a possibility, on any terms, of unclasping the firm gripe of this little hand which was laid upon me before I came into the world?"

"Dearest Georgiana, I have spent much thought upon the subject," hastily interrupted Aylmer. "I am convinced of the perfect practicability of its removal."

"If there be the remotest possibility of it," continued Georgiana, "let the attempt be made at whatever risk. Danger is nothing to me; for life, while this hateful mark makes me the object of your horror and disgust,—life is a burden which I would fling down with joy. Either remove this dreadful hand, or take my wretched life! You have deep science. All the world bears witness of it. You have achieved great wonders. Cannot you remove this little, little mark, which I cover with the tips of two small fingers? Is this beyond your power, for the sake of your own peace, and to save your poor wife from madness?"

"Noblest, dearest, tenderest wife," cried Aylmer, rapturously, "doubt not my power. I have already given this matter the deepest thought—thought which might almost have enlightened me to create a being less perfect than yourself. Georgiana, you have led me deeper than ever into the heart of science. I feel myself fully competent to render this dear cheek as faultless as its fellow; and then, most beloved, what will be my triumph when I shall have corrected what Nature left imperfect in her fairest work! Even Pygmalion, when his sculptured woman assumed life, felt not greater ecstasy than mine will be."

"It is resolved, then," said Georgiana, faintly smiling. "And, Aylmer, spare me not, though you should find the birthmark take refuge in my heart at last."

Her husband tenderly kissed her cheek—her right cheek—not that which bore the impress of the crimson hand.

The next day Aylmer apprised his wife of a plan that he had formed whereby he might have opportunity for the intense thought and constant watchfulness which the proposed operation would require; while Georgiana, likewise, would enjoy the perfect repose essential to its success. They were to seclude themselves in the extensive apartments occupied by Aylmer as a laboratory, and where, during his toilsome youth, he had made discoveries in the elemental powers of Nature that had roused the admiration of all the learned societies in Europe. Seated calmly in this laboratory, the pale philosopher had investigated the secrets of the highest cloud region and of the profoundest mines; he had satisfied himself of the causes that kindled and kept alive the fires of the volcano; and had explained the mystery of fountains, and how it is that they gush forth, some so bright and pure, and others with such rich medicinal virtues, from the dark bosom of the earth. Here, too, at an earlier period, he had studied the wonders of the human frame, and attempted to fathom the very process by which Nature assimilates all her precious influences from earth and air, and from the spiritual world, to create and foster man, her masterpiece. The latter pursuit, however, Aylmer had long laid aside in unwilling recognition of the truth—against which all seekers sooner or later stumble—that our great creative Mother, while she amuses us with apparently working in the broadest sunshine, is yet severely careful to keep her own secrets, and, in spite of her pretended openness, shows us nothing but results. She permits us, indeed, to mar, but seldom to mend, and, like a jealous patentee, on no account to make. Now, however, Aylmer resumed these half-forgotten investigations; not, of course, with such hopes or wishes as first suggested them; but because they involved much physiological truth and lay in the path of his proposed scheme for the treatment of Georgiana.

As he led her over the threshold of the laboratory, Georgiana was cold and tremulous. Aylmer looked cheerfully into her face, with intent to reassure her, but was so startled with the intense glow of the birthmark upon the whiteness of her cheek that he could not restrain a strong convulsive shudder. His wife fainted.

"Aminadab! Aminadab!" shouted Aylmer, stamping violently on the floor.

Forthwith there issued from an inner apartment a man of low stature, but bulky frame, with shaggy hair hanging about his visage, which was grimed with the vapors of the furnace. This personage had been Aylmer's underworker during his whole scientific career, and was admirably fitted for that office by his great mechanical readiness, and the skill with which, while incapable of comprehending a single principle, he executed all the details of his master's experiments. With his vast strength, his shaggy hair, his smoky aspect, and the indescribable earthiness that incrusted him, he seemed to represent man's physical nature; while Aylmer's slender figure, and pale, intellectual face, were no less apt a type of the spiritual element.

"Throw open the door of the boudoir, Aminadab," said Aylmer, "and burn a pastil."

"Yes, master," answered Aminadab, looking intently at the lifeless form of Georgiana; and then he muttered to himself, "If she were my wife, I'd never part with that birthmark."

When Georgiana recovered consciousness she found herself breathing an atmosphere of penetrating fragrance, the gentle potency of which had recalled her from her deathlike faintness. The scene around her looked like enchantment. Aylmer had converted those smoky, dingy, sombre rooms, where he had spent his brightest years in recondite pursuits, into a series of beautiful apartments not unfit to be the secluded abode of a lovely woman. The walls were hung with gorgeous curtains, which imparted the combination of grandeur and grace that no other species of adornment can achieve; and as they fell from the ceiling to the floor, their rich and ponderous folds, concealing all angles and straight lines, appeared to shut in the scene from infinite space. For aught Georgiana knew, it might be a pavilion among the clouds. And Aylmer, excluding the sunshine, which would have interfered with his chemical processes, had supplied its place with perfumed lamps, emitting flames of various hue, but all uniting in a soft, impurpled radiance. He now knelt by his wife's side, watching her earnestly, but without alarm; for he was confident in his science, and felt that he could draw a magic circle round her within which no evil might intrude.

"Where am I? Ah, I remember," said Georgiana, faintly; and she placed her hand over her cheek to hide the terrible mark from her husband's eyes.

"Fear not, dearest!" exclaimed he. "Do not shrink from me! Believe me, Georgiana, I even rejoice in this single imperfection, since it will be such a rapture to remove it."

"Oh, spare me!" sadly replied his wife. "Pray do not look at it again. I never can forget that convulsive shudder."

In order to soothe Georgiana, and, as it were, to release her mind from the burden of actual things, Aylmer now put in practice some of the light and playful secrets which science had taught him among its profounder lore. Airy figures, absolutely bodiless ideas, and forms of unsubstantial beauty came and danced before her, imprinting their momentary footsteps on beams of light. Though she had some indistinct idea of the method of these optical phenomena, still the illusion was almost perfect enough to warrant the belief that her husband possessed sway over the spiritual world. Then again, when she felt a wish to look forth from her seclusion, immediately, as if her thoughts were answered, the procession of external existence flitted across a screen. The scenery and the figures of actual life were perfectly represented, but with that bewitching, yet indescribable difference which always makes a picture, an image, or a shadow so much more attractive than the original. When wearied of this, Aylmer bade her cast her eyes upon a vessel containing a quantity of earth. She did so, with little interest at first; but was soon startled to perceive the germ of a plant shooting upward from the soil. Then came the slender stalk; the leaves gradually unfolded themselves; and amid them was a perfect and lovely flower.

"It is magical!" cried Georgiana. "I dare not touch it."

"Nay, pluck it," answered Aylmer,—"pluck it, and inhale its brief perfume while you may. The flower will wither in a few moments and leave nothing save its brown seed vessels; but thence may be perpetuated a race as ephemeral as itself."

But Georgiana had no sooner touched the flower than the whole plant suffered a blight, its leaves turning coal-black as if by the agency of fire.

"There was too powerful a stimulus," said Aylmer, thoughtfully.

To make up for this abortive experiment, he proposed to take her portrait by a scientific process of his own invention. It was to be effected by rays of light striking upon a polished plate of metal. Georgiana assented; but, on looking at the result, was affrighted to find the features of the portrait blurred and indefinable; while the minute figure of a hand appeared where the cheek should have been. Aylmer snatched the metallic plate and threw it into a jar of corrosive acid.

Soon, however, he forgot these mortifying failures. In the intervals of study and chemical experiment he came to her flushed and exhausted, but seemed invigorated by her presence, and spoke in glowing language of the resources of his art. He gave a history of the long dynasty of the alchemists, who spent so many ages in quest of the universal solvent by which the golden principle might be elicited from all things vile and base. Aylmer appeared to believe that, by the plainest scientific logic, it was altogether within the limits of possibility to discover this long-sought medium; "but," he added, "a philosopher who should go deep enough to acquire the power would attain too lofty a wisdom to stoop to the exercise of it." Not less singular were his opinions in regard to the elixir vitæ. He more than intimated that it was at his option to concoct a liquid that should prolong life for years, perhaps interminably; but that it would produce a discord in Nature which all the world, and chiefly the quaffer of the immortal nostrum, would find cause to curse.

"Aylmer, are you in earnest?" asked Georgiana, looking at him with amazement and fear. "It is terrible to possess such power, or even to dream of possessing it."

"Oh, do not tremble, my love," said her husband. "I would not wrong either you or myself by working such inharmonious effects upon our lives; but I would have you consider how trifling, in comparison, is the skill requisite to remove this little hand."

At the mention of the birthmark, Georgiana, as usual, shrank as if a redhot iron had touched her cheek.

Again Aylmer applied himself to his labors. She could hear his voice in the distant furnace room giving directions to Aminadab, whose harsh, uncouth, misshapen tones were audible in response, more like the grunt or growl of a brute than human speech. After hours of absence, Aylmer reappeared and proposed that she should now examine his cabinet of chemical products and natural treasures of the earth. Among the former he showed her a small vial, in which, he remarked, was contained a gentle yet most powerful fragrance, capable of impregnating all the breezes that blow across a kingdom. They were of inestimable value, the contents of that little vial; and, as he said so, he threw some of the perfume into the air and filled the room with piercing and invigorating delight.

"And what is this?" asked Georgiana, pointing to a small crystal globe containing a gold-colored liquid. "It is so beautiful to the eye that I could imagine it the elixir of life."

"In one sense it is," replied Aylmer; "or, rather, the elixir of immortality. It is the most precious poison that ever was concocted in this world. By its aid I could apportion the lifetime of any mortal at whom you might point your finger. The strength of the dose would determine whether he were to linger out years, or drop dead in the midst of a breath. No king on his guarded throne could keep his life if I, in my private station, should deem that the welfare of millions justified me in depriving him of it."

"Why do you keep such a terrific drug?" inquired Georgiana in horror.

"Do not mistrust me, dearest," said her husband, smiling; "its virtuous potency is yet greater than its harmful one. But see! here is a powerful cosmetic. With a few drops of this in a vase of water, freckles may be washed away as easily as the hands are cleansed. A stronger infusion would take the blood out of the cheek, and leave the rosiest beauty a pale ghost."

"Is it with this lotion that you intend to bathe my cheek?" asked Georgiana, anxiously.

"Oh, no," hastily replied her husband; "this is merely superficial. Your case demands a remedy that shall go deeper."

In his interviews with Georgiana, Aylmer generally made minute inquiries as to her sensations and whether the confinement of the rooms and the temperature of the atmosphere agreed with her. These questions had such a particular drift that Georgiana began to conjecture that she was already subjected to certain physical influences, either breathed in with the fragrant air or taken with her food. She fancied likewise, but it might be altogether fancy, that there was a stirring up of her system—a strange, indefinite sensation creeping through her veins, and tingling, half painfully, half pleasurably, at her heart. Still, whenever she dared to look into the mirror, there she beheld herself pale as a white rose and with the crimson birthmark stamped upon her cheek. Not even Aylmer now hated it so much as she.

To dispel the tedium of the hours which her husband found it necessary to devote to the processes of combination and analysis, Georgiana turned over the volumes of his scientific library. In many dark old tomes she met with chapters full of romance and poetry. They were the works of the philosophers of the middle ages, such as Albertus Magnus, Cornelius Agrippa, Paracelsus, and the famous friar who created the prophetic Brazen Head. All these antique naturalists stood in advance of their centuries, yet were imbued with some of their credulity, and therefore were believed, and perhaps imagined themselves to have acquired from the investigation of Nature a power above Nature, and from physics a sway over the spiritual world. Hardly less curious and imaginative were the early volumes of the Transactions of the Royal Society, in which the members, knowing little of the limits of natural possibility, were continually recording wonders or proposing methods whereby wonders might be wrought.

But to Georgiana the most engrossing volume was a large folio from her husband's own hand, in which he had recorded every experiment of his scientific career, its original aim, the methods adopted for its development, and its final success or failure, with the circumstances to which either event was attributable. The book, in truth, was both the history and emblem of his ardent, ambitious, imaginative, yet practical and laborious life. He handled physical details as if there were nothing beyond them; yet spiritualized them all, and redeemed himself from materialism by his strong and eager aspiration towards the infinite. In his grasp the veriest clod of earth assumed a soul. Georgiana, as she read, reverenced Aylmer and loved him more profoundly than ever, but with a less entire dependence on his judgment than heretofore. Much as he had accomplished, she could not but observe that his most splendid successes were almost invariably failures, if compared with the ideal at which he aimed. His brightest diamonds were the merest pebbles, and felt to be so by himself, in comparison with the inestimable gems which lay hidden beyond his reach. The volume, rich with achievements that had won renown for its author, was yet as melancholy a record as ever mortal hand had penned. It was the sad confession and continual exemplification of the shortcomings of the composite man, the spirit burdened with clay and working in matter, and of the despair that assails the higher nature at finding itself so miserably thwarted by the earthly part. Perhaps every man of genius in whatever sphere might recognize the image of his own experience in Aylmer's journal.

So deeply did these reflections affect Georgiana that she

laid her face upon the open volume and burst into tears. In this situation she was found by her husband.

"It is dangerous to read in a sorcerer's books," said he, with a smile, though his countenance was uneasy and displeased. "Georgiana, there are pages in that volume which I can scarcely glance over and keep my senses. Take heed lest it prove as detrimental to you."

"It has made me worship you more than ever," said she.

"Ah, wait for this one success," rejoined he, "then worship me if you will. I shall deem myself hardly unworthy of it. But come, I have sought you for the luxury of your voice. Sing to me, dearest."

So she poured out the liquid music of her voice to quench the thirst of his spirit. He then took his leave with a boyish exuberance of gayety, assuring her that her seclusion would endure but a little longer, and that the result was already certain. Scarcely had he departed when Georgiana felt irresistibly impelled to follow him. She had forgotten to inform Aylmer of a symptom which for two or three hours past had begun to excite her attention. It was a sensation in the fatal birthmark, not painful, but which induced a restlessness throughout her system. Hastening after her husband, she intruded for the first time into the laboratory.

The first thing that struck her eye was the furnace, that hot and feverish worker, with the intense glow of its fire, which by the quantities of soot clustered above it seemed to have been burning for ages. There was a distilling apparatus in full operation. Around the room were retorts, tubes, cylinders, crucibles, and other apparatus of chemical research. An electrical machine stood ready for immediate use. The atmosphere felt oppressively close, and was tainted with gaseous odors which had been tormented forth by the processes of science. The severe and homely simplicity of the apartment, with its naked walls and brick pavement, looked strange, accustomed as Georgiana had become to the fantastic elegance of her boudoir. But what chiefly, indeed almost solely, drew her attention, was the aspect of Aylmer himself.

He was pale as death, anxious and absorbed, and hung over the furnace as if it depended upon his utmost watchfulness whether the liquid which it was distilling should be the draught of immortal happiness or misery. How different from the sanguine and joyous mien that he had assumed for Georgiana's encouragement!

"Carefully now, Aminadab; carefully, thou human machine; carefully, thou man of clay!" muttered Aylmer, more to himself than his assistant. "Now, if there be a thought too much or too little, it is all over."

"Ho! ho!" mumbled Aminadab. "Look, master! look!"

Aylmer raised his eyes hastily, and at first reddened, then grew paler than ever, on beholding Georgiana. He rushed towards her and seized her arm with a gripe that left the print of his fingers upon it.

"Why do you come hither? Have you no trust in your husband?" cried he, impetuously. "Would you throw the blight of that fatal birthmark over my labors? It is not well done. Go, prying woman, go!"

"Nay, Aylmer," said Georgiana with the firmness of which she possessed no stinted endowment, "it is not you that have a right to complain. You mistrust your wife; you have concealed the anxiety with which you watch the development of this experiment. Think not so unworthily of me, my husband. Tell me all the risk we run, and fear not that I shall shrink; for my share in it is far less than your own."

"No, no, Georgiana!" said Aylmer, impatiently; "it must not be."

"I submit," replied she calmly. "And, Aylmer, I shall quaff whatever draught you bring me; but it will be on the same principle that would induce me to take a dose of poison if offered by your hand."

"My noble wife," said Aylmer, deeply moved, "I knew not the height and depth of your nature until now. Nothing shall be concealed. Know, then, that this crimson hand, superficial as it seems, has clutched its grasp into your being with a strength of which I had no previous conception. I have already administered agents powerful enough to do aught except to change your entire physical system. Only one thing remains to be tried. If that fail us we are ruined."

"Why did you hesitate to tell me this?" asked she.

"Because, Georgiana," said Aylmer, in a low voice, "there is danger."

"Danger? There is but one danger—that this horrible stigma shall be left upon my cheek!" cried Georgiana. "Remove it, remove it, whatever be the cost, or we shall both go mad!"

"Heaven knows your words are too true," said Aylmer, sadly. "And now, dearest, return to your boudoir. In a little while all will be tested."

He conducted her back and took leave of her with a solemn tenderness which spoke far more than his words how much was now at stake. After his departure Georgiana became rapt in musings. She considered the character of Aylmer, and did it completer justice than at any previous moment. Her heart exulted, while it trembled, at his honorable love—so pure and lofty that it would accept nothing less than perfection nor miserably make itself contented with an earthlier nature than he had dreamed of. She felt how much more precious was such a sentiment than that meaner kind which would have borne with the imperfection for her sake, and have been guilty of treason to holy love by degrading its perfect idea to the level of the actual; and with her whole spirit she prayed that, for a single moment, she might satisfy his highest and deepest conception. Longer than one moment she well knew it could not be; for his spirit was ever on the march, ever ascending, and each instant required something that was beyond the scope of the instant before.

The sound of her husband's footsteps aroused her. He bore a crystal goblet containing a liquor colorless as water, but bright enough to be the draught of immortality. Aylmer was pale; but it seemed rather the consequence of a highly-wrought state of mind and tension of spirit than of fear or doubt.

"The concoction of the draught has been perfect," said he, in answer to Georgiana's look. "Unless all my science have deceived me, it cannot fail."

"Save on your account, my dearest Aylmer," observed his wife, "I might wish to put off this birthmark of mortality by relinquishing mortality itself in preference to any other mode. Life is but a sad possession to those who have attained precisely the degree of moral advancement at which I stand. Were I weaker and blinder it might be happiness. Were I stronger, it might be endured hopefully. But, being what I find myself, methinks I am of all mortals the most fit to die."

"You are fit for heaven without tasting death!" replied her husband. "But why do we speak of dying? The draught cannot fail. Behold its effect upon this plant."

On the window seat there stood a geranium diseased with yellow blotches, which had overspread all its leaves. Aylmer poured a small quantity of the liquid upon the soil in which it grew. In a little time, when the roots of the plant had taken up the moisture, the unsightly blotches began to be extinguished in a living verdure.

"There needed no proof," said Georgiana, quietly. "Give me the goblet. I joyfully stake all upon your word."

"Drink, then, thou lofty creature!" exclaimed Aylmer, with fervid admiration. "There is no taint of imperfection on thy spirit. Thy sensible frame, too, shall soon be all perfect."

She quaffed the liquid and returned the goblet to his hand.

"It is grateful," said she with a placid smile. "Methinks it is like water from a heavenly mountain; for it contains I know not what of unobtrusive fragrance and deliciousness. It allays a feverish thirst that had parched me for many days. Now, dearest, let me sleep. My earthly senses are closing over my spirit like the leaves around the heart of a rose at sunset."

She spoke the last words with a gentle reluctance, as if it required almost more energy than she could command to pronounce the faint and lingering syllables. Scarcely had they loitered through her lips ere she was lost in slumber. Aylmer sat by her side, watching her aspect with the emotions proper to a man the whole value of whose existence was involved in the process now to be tested. Mingled with this mood, however, was the philosophic investigation characteristic of the man of science. Not the minutest symptom escaped him. A heightened flush of the cheek, a slight irregularity of breath, a quiver of the eyelid, a hardly perceptible tremor through the frame,—such were the details which, as the moments passed, he wrote down in his folio volume. Intense thought had set its stamp upon every previous page of that volume, but the thoughts of years were all concentrated upon the last.

While thus employed, he failed not to gaze often at the fatal hand, and not without a shudder. Yet once, by a strange and unaccountable impulse, he pressed it with his lips. His spirit recoiled, however, in the very act; and Georgiana, out of the midst of her deep sleep, moved uneasily and murmured as if in remonstrance. Again Ayler resumed his watch. Nor was it without avail. The crimson hand, which at first had been strongly visible upon the marble paleness of Georgiana's cheek, now grew more faintly outlined. She remained not less pale than ever; but the birthmark, with every breath that came and went, lost somewhat of its former distinctness. Its presence had been awful; its departure was more awful still. Watch the stain of the rainbow fading out of the sky, and you will know how that mysterious symbol passed away.

"By Heaven! it is well-nigh gone!" said Aylmer to himself, in almost irrepressible ecstasy. "I can scarcely trace it now. Success! success! And now it is like the faintest rose color. The lightest flush of blood across her cheek would overcome it. But she is so pale!"

He drew aside the window curtain and suffered the light of natural day to fall into the room and rest upon her cheek. At the same time he heard a gross, hoarse chuckle, which he had long known as his servant Aminadab's expression of delight.

"Ah, clod! ah, earthly mass!" cried Aylmer, laughing in a sort of frenzy, "you have served me well! Matter and spirit—earth and heaven—have both done their part in this! Laugh, thing of the senses! You have earned the right to laugh."

These exclamations broke Georgiana's sleep. She slowly unclosed her eyes and gazed into the mirror which her husband had arranged for that purpose. A faint smile flitted over her lips when she recognized how barely perceptible was now that crimson hand which had once blazed forth with such disastrous brilliancy as to scare away all their happiness. But then her eyes sought Aylmer's face with a trouble and anxiety that he could by no means account for.

"My poor Aylmer!" murmured she.

"Poor? Nay, richest, happiest, most favored!" exclaimed he. "My peerless bride, it is successful! You are perfect!"

"My poor Aylmer," she repeated, with a more than human tenderness, "you have aimed loftily; you have done nobly. Do not repent that with so high and pure a feeling, you have rejected the best the earth could offer. Aylmer, dearest Aylmer, I am dying!"

Alas! it was too true! The fatal hand had grappled with the mystery of life, and was the bond by which an angelic spirit kept itself in union with a mortal frame. As the last crimson tint of the birthmark—that sole token of human imperfection—faded from her cheek, the parting breath of the now perfect woman passed into the atmosphere, and her soul, lingering a moment near her husband, took its heavenward flight. Then a hoarse, chuckling laugh was heard again! Thus ever does the gross fatality of earth exult in its invariable triumph over the immortal essence which, in this dim sphere of half development, demands the completeness of a higher state. Yet, had Aylmer reached a profounder wisdom, he need not thus have flung away the happiness which would have woven his mortal life of the selfsame texture with the celestial. The momentary circumstance was too strong for him; he failed to look beyond the shadowy scope of time, and, living once for all in eternity, to find the perfect future in the present.

III

THE POWER-SEEKER AND THE SECURITY-SEEKER

Man's search for security, like his search for pleasure, has had unexpected results: it often accomplishes the surrender of the self to neurotic or authoritarian forces. Thus, the man in search of self-aggrandizement may often achieve his goal only at the price of a ruined and battered ego. The man who attempts to wield power is often the man driven by doubts and insecurity. In fact, according to Alfred Adler, the power-seeker is the man who is attempting to compensate for his feelings of insecurity by achieving a false independence. Such a man eventually pays for his power in his self-destruction. Kipling's "Man Who Would be King" is thus exposed to us as a man with a weak ego whose lack of security leads him into a fruitless search for power.

The manner in which individuals become insecure or power-mad is not yet fully understood, even today. But Martha Wolfenstein's analysis of "Two Types of Jewish Mothers" and Aldous Huxley's "The Claxtons" provide a graphic description of the development of a specific type of neurotic personality as a result of a misplaced parental idea of authority and responsibility. Here self-effacement rather than outright conflict with the child leads to neurotic distortions of the personality.

Security, it appears, can be achieved only through the freedom of the individual to grow and develop in his own direction. Interference with the growing organism—whether it appears to be passive and self-effacing, or whether it is direct and brutal—results either in an apparently insecure personality or in its obverse, the pathological seeker after power.

ALFRED ADLER / Individual Psychology

A SURVEY of the views and theories of most psychologists indicates a peculiar limitation both in the nature of their field of investigation and in their methods of inquiry. They act as if experience and knowledge of mankind were, with conscious intent, to be excluded from our investigations and all value and importance denied to artistic and creative vision as well as to intuition itself. While the experimental psychologists collect and devise phenomena in order to determine types of reaction—that is, are concerned with the physiology of the psychical life properly speaking—other psychologists arrange all forms of expression and manifestations in old customary, or at best slightly altered, systems. By this procedure they naturally rediscover the interdependence and connection in individual expressions, implied from the very beginning in their schematic attitude toward the psyche.

Either the foregoing method is employed or an attempt is made by means of small, if possible measurable individual phenomena of a physiological nature, to construct psychical states and thought by means of an equation. The fact that all subjective thinking and subjective immersion on the part of the investigator are excluded—although in reality they dominate the very nature of these connections—is from this viewpoint regarded as an advantage.

The method employed, and the very importance it seems to possess as a preparation for the human mind, reminds us of the type of natural science completely antiquated to-day, with its rigid systems, replaced everywhere now by views that attempt to grasp living phenomena and their variations as connected wholes, biologically, philosophically, and psychologically. This is also the purpose of that movement in psychology that I have called *"comparative individual-psychology"*. By starting with the assumption of the *unity of the individual,* an attempt is made to obtain a picture of this unified personality regarded as a variant of individual life-manifestations and forms of expression. The individual traits are then compared with one another, brought into a common plane, and finally fused together to form a composite portrait that is, in turn, individualized.[1]

It may have been noticed that this method of looking upon man's psychic life is by no means either unusual or even particularly daring. This type of approach is particularly noticeable in the study of child-psychology, in spite of other lines of inquiry also

[1] William Stern has come to the same conclusions starting from a different method of approach.

used there. It is the essence and the nature above all of the work of the artist, be he painter, sculptor, musician, or particularly poet, so to present the minute traits of his creations that the observer is able to obtain from them the general principles of personality. He is thus in a position to reconstruct those very things that the artist when thinking of his *finale* had previously hidden therein. Since life in any given society, life without any of the preconceptions of science, has always been under the ban of the question "whither?", we are warranted in definitely stating that, scientific views to the contrary notwithstanding, no man has ever made a judgment about an event without endeavouring to strain toward the point which seems to bind together all the psychic manifestations of an individual; even to an *imagined goal* if necessary.

When I hurry home, I am certain to exhibit to any observer the carriage, expression, the gait, and the gestures that are to be expected of a person returning home. My reflexes indeed might be different from those anticipated, the causes might vary. The essential point to be grasped psychologically and the one which interests us exclusively and practically and psychologically more than all others, *is the path followed.*

Let me observe that if I know the goal of a person I know in a general way what will happen. I am in a position to bring into their proper order each of the successive movements made, to view them in their connections, to correct them and to make, where necessary, the required adaptations for my approximate psychological knowledge of these associations. If I am acquainted only with the causes, know only the reflexes, the reaction-times, the ability to repeat and such facts, I am aware of nothing that actually takes place in the soul of the man.

We must remember that the person under observation would not know what to do with himself were he not orientated toward some goal. As long as we are not acquainted with the objective which determines his "life-line", the whole system of his recognized reflexes, together with all their causal conditions, can give us no certainty as to his next series of movements. They might be brought into harmony with practically any psychic resultant. This deficiency is most clearly felt in association-tests. I would never expect a man suffering from some great disappointment to associate "tree" with "rope". The moment I knew his objective, however, namely suicide, then I might very well expect that particular sequence of thoughts—expect it with such certainty that I would remove knives, poison, and weapons from his immediate vicinity.

If we look at the matter more closely, we shall find the following law holding in the development of all psychic happenings:

we cannot think, feel, will, or act without the perception of some goal. For all the causalities in the world would not suffice to conquer the chaos of the future nor obviate the planlessness to which we would be bound to fall a victim. All activity would persist in the stage of uncontrolled gropings; the economy visible in our psychic life unattained; we should be unintegrated and in every aspect of our physiognomy, in every personal touch, similar to organisms of the rank of the amœba.

No one will deny that by assuming an objective for our psychic life we accommodate ourselves better to reality. This can be easily demonstrated. For its truth in individual examples, where phenomena are torn from their proper connections, no doubt exists. Only watch, from this point of view, the attempts at walking made by a small child or a woman recovering from a confinement. Naturally he who approaches this whole matter without any theory is likely to find its deeper significance escape him. Yet it is a fact that before the first step has been taken the objective of the person's movement has already been determined.

In the same way it can be demonstrated that all psychic activities are given a direction by means of a previously determined goal. All the temporary and partially visible objectives, after the short period of psychic development of childhood, are under the domination of an imagined terminal goal, of a final point felt and conceived of as definitely fixed. In other words the psychic life of man is made to fit into the fifth act like a character drawn by a good dramatist.

The conclusion thus to be drawn from the unbiased study of any personality viewed from the standpoint of individual-psychology leads us to the following important proposition: *every psychic phenomenon, if it is to give us any understanding of a person, can only be grasped and understood if regarded as a preparation for some goal.*

To what an extent this conception promotes our psychological understanding, is clearly apparent as soon as we become aware of the *multiplicity of meaning of those psychical processes that have been torn from their proper context.* Take for example the case of a man with a "bad memory". Assume that he is quite conscious of this fact and that an examination discloses an inferior capacity for the repetition of meaningless syllables. According to present usage in psychology, which we might more properly call an abuse, we would have to make the following inference: the man is suffering, from hereditary or pathological causes, from a deficient capacity for repetition. Incidentally, let me add, that in this type of investigation we generally find the inference already stated in different words in the premises. In this case *e.g.*

we have the following proposition: if a man has a bad memory, or if he only remembers a few words—then he has an inferior capacity for repetition.

The procedure in individual-psychology is completely different. After excluding the possibility of all organic causes, we would ask ourselves what is the objective of this weakness of memory? This we could only determine if we were in possession of an intimate knowledge of the whole individual, so that an understanding of one part becomes possible only after we have understood the whole. And we should probably find the following to hold true in a large number of cases: this man is attempting to prove to himself and to others that for certain reasons of a fundamental nature, that are either not to be named or have remained unconscious, *but which can most effectively be represented by poorness of memory,* he must not permit himself to perform some particular act or to come to a given decision (change of profession, studies, examination, marriage). We should then have unmasked this weakness of memory as tendencious and could understand its importance as a weapon against a contemplated undertaking. In every test of ability to repeat we should then expect to find the deficiency due to the secret life-plan of an individual. The question then to be asked is how such deficiencies or evils arise. They may be simply "arranged" by purposely underlining general psysiological weaknesses and interpreting them as personal sufferings. Others may succeed either by subjective absorption into an abnormal condition or by pre-occupation with dangerous pessimistic anticipations, in so weakening their faith in their own capacities, that their strength, attention or will-power are only partially at their disposal.

A similar observation may be made in the case of affects. To give one more example, take the case of a woman subject to outbreaks of anxiety recurring at certain intervals. As long as nothing of greater significance than this was discernible, the assumption of some hereditary degeneration, some disease of the vaso-motor system, of the vagus nerve, etc., sufficed. It is also possible that we might have regarded ourselves as having arrived at a fuller understanding of the case, if we have discovered in the previous history of the patient, some frightful experience, or traumatic condition and attributed the disease to it. As soon, however, as we examined the personality of this individual and inquired into her directive-lines we discovered an excess of will-to-power, with which anxiety as a weapon of aggression had associated itself, an anxiety which was to become operative as soon as the force of the will-power had abated and the desired resonance was absent, a situation occurring, for example, when the patient's husband left the house without her consent.

Our science demands a markedly individualizing procedure and is consequently not much given to generalizations. For general guidance I would like to propound the following rule: *as soon as the goal of a psychic movement or its life-plan has been recognized, then we are to assume that all the movements of its constituent parts will coincide with both the goal and the life-plan.*

This formulation, with some minor provisos, is to be maintained in the widest sense. It retains its value even if inverted: *the properly understood part-movements must when combined, give the picture of an integrated life-plan and final goal.* Consequently we insist that, without worrying about the *tendencies, milieu and experiences,* all psychical powers are under the control of a directive idea and all expressions of emotion, feeling, thinking, willing, acting, dreaming as well as psycho-pathological phenomena, are permeated by one unified life-plan. Let me, by a slight suggestion, prove and yet soften down these heretical propositions: more important than tendencies, objective experience and milieu is *the subjective evaluation,* an evaluation which stands furthermore in a certain, often strange, relation to realities. Out of this evaluation however, which generally results in the development of a permanent mood *of the nature of a feeling of inferiority* there arises, depending upon the unconscious technique of our thought-apparatus, an imagined goal, an attempt at a planned final compensation and a life-plan.

I have so far spoken a good deal of men who have "grasped the situation". My discussion has been as irritating as that of the theorists of the "psychology of understanding" or of the psychology of personality, who always break off just when they are about to show us what exactly it is they have understood, as for instance, Jaspers. The danger of discussing briefly this aspect of our investigations namely, *the results of individual-psychology,* is sufficiently great. To do so we should be compelled to force the dynamics of life into static words and pictures, overlook differences in order to obtain unified formulas, and have, in short, in our description to make that very mistake that in practice is strictly prohibited: of approaching the psychic life of the individual with a dry formula, as the Freudian school attempt.

This then being my assumption, I shall in the following present to you the most important results of our study of psychic life. Let me emphasize the fact that the dynamics of psychic life that I am about to describe hold equally for healthy and diseased. What distinguishes the nervous from the healthy individual is the stronger safeguarding tendency with which the former's life-plan is filled. With regard to the "positing of a goal" and the life-plan adjusted to it there are no fundamental differences.

I shall consequently speak of a general goal of man. A thorough-going study has taught us that we can best understand the manifold and diverse movements of the psyche as soon as our *most general pre-supposition,* that the psyche has as its objective the *goal of superiority,* is recognized. Great thinkers have given expression to much of this; in part everyone knows it, but in the main it is hidden in mysterious darkness and comes definitely to the front only in insanity or in ecstatic conditions. Whether a person desires to be an artist, the first in his profession, or a tyrant in his home, to hold converse with God or humiliate other people; whether he regards his suffering as the most important thing in the world to which everyone must show obeisance, whether he is chasing after unattainable ideals or old deities, over-stepping all limits and norms, at every part of his way he is guided and spurred on by his longing for superiority, the thought of his godlikeness, the belief in his special magical power. In his love he desires to experience his power over his partner. In his purely optional choice of profession the goal floating before his mind manifests itself in all sorts of exaggerated anticipations and fears, and thirsting for revenge, he experiences in suicide a triumph over all obstacles. In order to gain control over an object or over a person, he is capable of proceeding along a straight line, bravely, proudly, overbearing, obstinate, cruel; or he may on the other hand prefer, forced by experience, to resort to by-paths and circuitous routes, to gain his victory by obedience, submission, mildness and modesty. Nor have traits of character an independent existence, for they are also adjusted to the individual life-plan, really representing the most important preparations for conflict possessed by the latter.

This goal of complete superiority, with its strange appearance at times, does not come from the world of reality. Inherently we must place it under "fictions" and "imaginations". Of these Vaihinger (*The Philosophy of 'As If'*) rightly says that their importance lies in the fact that whereas in themselves without meaning, they nevertheless possess in practice the greatest importance. For our case this coincides to such an extent that we may say *that this fiction of a goal of superiority so ridiculous from the viewpoint of reality, has become the principal conditioning factor of our life as hitherto known.* It is this that teaches us to differentiate, gives us poise and security, moulds and guides our deeds and activities and forces our spirit to look ahead and to perfect itself. There is of course also an obverse side, for *this goal introduces into our life a hostile and fighting tendency,* robs us of the simplicity of our feelings and is always the cause for an estrangement from reality since it puts near to our hearts the idea of attempting to over-power reality. Whoever takes this goal of godlikeness seriously or literally, will soon be compelled to flee from real life and compromise, by seeking a life within life; if fortunate in art, but more generally in pietism, neurosis or crime.[2]

I cannot give you particulars here. A clear indication of this super-mundane goal is to be found in every individual. Sometimes this is to be gathered from a man's carriage, sometimes it is disclosed only in his demands and expectations. Occasionally one comes upon its track in obscure memories, phantasies and dreams. If purposely sought it is rarely obtained. However, every bodily or mental attitude indicates clearly its origin in a striving for power and carries within itself the ideal of a kind of perfection and infallibility. In those cases that lie on the confines of neurosis there is always to be discovered a reinforced pitting of oneself against the environment, against the dead or heroes of the past.

A test of the correctness of our interpretation can be easily made. If everyone possesses within himself an ideal of superiority, such as we find to an exaggerated degree among the nervous, then we ought to encounter phenomena whose purpose is the oppression, the minimizing and undervaluation of others. Traits of character such as intolerance, dogmatism, envy, pleasure at the misfortune of others, conceit, boastfulness, mistrust, avarice,—in short all those attitudes that are the substitutes for a struggle, force their way through to a far greater extent, in fact, than self-preservation demands.

Similarly, either simultaneously or interchangingly, depending upon the zeal and the self-confidence with which the final goal is sought, we see emerging indications of pride, emulation, courage, the attitudes of saving, bestowing and directing. A psychological investigation demands so much objectivity that a moral evaluation will not disturb the survey. In fact *the different levels of character-traits* actually neutralize our good-will and our disapproval. Finally we must remember that these hostile traits, particularly in the case of the nervous, are often so concealed that their possessor is justifiably astonished and irritated when attention is drawn to them. For example, the elder of two children can create quite an uncomfortable situation in trying to arrogate to himself through defiance and obstinacy, all authority in the family. The younger child pursues a wiser course, poses as a model of obedience and succeeds in this manner in becoming the idol of the family and in having all wishes gratified. As ambition spurs him on, all willingness to obey becomes destroyed and pathological-compulsion phenomena develop, by means of which every parental order is nullified even

[2] *Cf.* also "The Problem of Distance," in this volume.

when the parents notice that the child is making efforts to remain obedient. Thus we have an act of obedience immediately nullified by means of a compulsion-thought. We get an idea of the circuitous path taken here in order to arrive at the same objective as that of the other child.

The whole weight of the personal striving for power and superiority passes, at a very early age in the case of the child, into the form and the content of its striving, its thought being able to absorb for the time being only so much as the eternal, real and physiologically rooted *community-feeling* permits. Out of the latter are developed tenderness, love of neighbour, friendship and love, the desire for power unfolding itself in a veiled manner and seeking secretly to push its way along the path of group consciousness.

At this place let me go out of my way to endorse an old fundamental conception of all who know human nature. Every marked attitude of a man can be traced back to an origin in childhood. In the nursery are formed and prepared all of man's future attitudes. Fundamental changes are produced only by means of an exceedingly high degree of introspection or among neurotics by means of the physician's individual psychological analysis.

Let me, on the basis of another case, one which must have happened innumerable times, discuss in even greater detail the positing of goals by nervous people. A remarkably gifted man who by his amiability and refined behaviour had gained the love of a girl of high character, became engaged to her. He then forced upon her his ideal of education which made severe demands upon her. For a time she endured these unbearable orders but finally put an end to all further ordeals by breaking off relations. The man then broke down and became a prey to nervous attacks. The individual-psychological examination of the case showed that the superiority-goal in the case of this patient—as his domineering demands upon his bride indicated—had long ago pushed from his mind all thought of marriage, and that his object really was to secretly work toward a break, secretly because he did not feel himself equal to the open struggle in which he imagined marriage to consist. *This disbelief in himself* itself dated from his earliest childhood, to a time during which he, an only son, lived with an early widowed mother somewhat cut off from the world. During this period, spent in continuous family quarrels he had received the ineradicable impression, one he had never openly admitted to himself, that he was not sufficiently virile, and would never be able to cope with a woman. These psychical attitudes are comparable to a permanent inferiority-feeling and it is easily understood how they had decisively interfered in his life and compelled him to obtain prestige along other lines than those obtainable through the fulfilment of the demands of reality.

It is clear that the patient attained just what his concealed preparations for bachelordom aimed at, and what his fear of a life-partner, with the quarrels and restless relationship this implied, had awakened in him. Nor can it be denied that he took the same attitude toward both his bride and his mother, namely the wish to conquer. This attitude induced by a longing for victory has been magnificently misinterpreted by the Freudian school as the permanently incestuous condition of being enamoured of the mother. As a matter of fact this reinforced childhood-feeling of inferiority occasioned by the patient's painful relation to his mother, spurred this man on to prevent any struggle in later life with a wife by providing himself with all kinds of safeguards. Whatever it is we understand by love, in this particular case it is simply *a means to an end* and that end is the final securing of a triumph over some suitable woman. Here we have the reason for the continual tests and orders and for the cancelling of the engagement. This solution had not just "happened", but had on the contrary been artistically prepared and arranged with the old weapons of experience employed previously in the case of his mother. A defeat in marriage was out of the question because marriage was prevented.

Although we consequently realize nothing puzzling in the behaviour of this man and should recognize in his domineering attitude simply aggression *posing as love,* some words of explanation are necessary to clear up the less intelligible nervous breakdown. We are here entering upon the real domain of the psychology of neuroses. As in the nursery so here our patient has been worsted by a woman. The neurotic individual is led in such cases to strengthen his protections and to retire to a fairly great distance from danger.[3] Our patient is utilizing his break-down in order to feed an evil reminiscence, to bring up the question of guilt again, to solve it in an unfavourable sense for the woman, so that in future he may either proceed with even greater caution or take final leave of love and matrimony! This man is thirty years old now. Let us assume that he is going to carry his pain along with him for another ten or twenty years and that he is going to mourn for his lost ideal for the same length of time. He has thereby protected himself against every love-affair and permanently saved himself from new defeat.

He interprets his nervous break-down by means of old, now strengthened, weapons of experience, just as he had as a child refused to eat, sleep or to do anything and played the rôle of a dying person. His fortunes ebb and *his beloved carries all the stigma,* he himself rises superior to her in both culture and character, and lo and behold: he has attained that for which he longed,

[3] Cf. "The Problem of Distance" . . .

for he is the superior person, becomes the better man and his partner like all girls is the guilty one. Girls cannot cope with the man in him. In this manner he has consummated what as a child he had already felt, the duty of demonstrating his superiority over the female sex.

We can now understand that this nervous reaction can never be sufficiently definite or adequate. *He is to wander through the world as a living reproach against women.*[4]

Were he aware of his secret plans he would realize how ill-natured and evil-intentioned all his actions have been. However he would, in that case, not succeed in attaining his object of elevating himself above women. He would see himself just as we see him, falsifying the weights and how everything he has done has only led to a goal previously set. His success could not be described as due to "fate" nor assuredly would it represent any increased prestige. But his goal, his life-plan and his life-falsehood demand this prestige! In consequence it so "happens" that the *life-plan remains in the unconscious,* so that the patient may believe that an *implacable fate* and not a long prepared and long meditated plan for which he alone is responsible, is at work.

I cannot go into a detailed description of what I call the "distance" that the neurotic individual places between himself and the final issue, which in this case is marriage. The discussion of the manner in which he accomplishes it I must also postpone to my chapter on nervous "arrangements". I should like to point out here however that the "distance" expresses itself clearly in the "hesitating attitudes," the principles, the point of view and the life-falsehood. In its evolution neurosis and psychosis play leading rôles. The appropriation for this purpose of perversions and every type of impotence arising from the latter is quite frequent. Such a man concludes his account and reconciles himself with life by constructing one or a number of "if-clauses". "If conditions had been different. . . ."

The importance of the educational questions that arise and upon which our school lays the greatest stress (*Heilen und Bilden,* Munich, 1913) follows from what has been discussed.

From the method of presentation of the present work it is to be inferred that as in the case of a psycho-therapeutic cure, our analysis proceeds backwards; examining first the *superiority-goal,* explaining by means of it the type of *conflict-attitude*[5] adopted particularly by nervous patients and only then attempting to investigate the sources of the vital psychic mechanism. One of the bases

[4] The paranoidal trait is recognizable. Cf. "Life-lie and Responsibility in Neurosis and Psychosis" . . .

[5] The "struggle for existence," the "struggle of all against all," etc., are merely other perspectives of the same kind.

of the psychical dynamics we have already mentioned, the presumably unavoidable artistic trait of the psychical apparatus which, by means of the *artistic artifice of the creation of a fiction and the setting of a goal,* adjusts itself to and extends itself into the world of possible reality. I shall now proceed to explain briefly how the goal of godlikeness transforms the relation of the individual to his environment into hostility and how the struggle drives an individual towards a goal either along a direct path such as aggressiveness or along byways suggested by precaution. If we trace the history of this aggressive attitude back to childhood we always come upon the outstanding fact that *throughout the whole period of development, the child possesses a feeling of inferiority in its relations both to parents and the world at large.* Because of the immaturity of his organs, his uncertainty and lack of independence, because of his need for dependence upon stronger natures and his frequent and painful feeling of subordination to others, a sensation of inadequacy develops that betrays itself throughout life. This feeling of inferiority is the cause of his continual restlessness as a child, his craving for action, his playing of rôles, the pitting of his strength against that of others, his anticipatory pictures of the future and his physical as well as mental preparations. The whole potential educability of the child depends upon this feeling of insufficiency. In this way the future becomes transformed into the land that will bring him compensations. His conflict-attitude is again reflected in his feeling of inferiority; and only conflict does he regard as a compensation which will do away permanently with his present inadequate condition and will enable him to picture himself as elevated above others. Thus the child arrives at the positing of a goal, an imagined goal of superiority, whereby his poverty is transformed into wealth, his subordination into domination, his suffering into happiness and pleasure, his ignorance into omniscience and his incapacity into artistic creation. The longer and more definitely the child feels his insecurity, the more he suffers either from physical or marked mental weakness, the more he is aware of life's neglect, the higher will this goal be placed and the more faithfully will it be adhered to. He who wishes to recognize the nature of this goal, should watch a child at play, at optionally selected occupations or when phantasying about his future profession. The apparent change in these phenomena is purely external for in every new goal the child imagines a predetermined triumph. A variant of this weaving of plans, one frequently found among weakly aggressive children, among girls and sickly individuals, might be mentioned here. This consists of so misusing their frailties that they compel others to become subordinate to them. They will later on pursue the same method until their life-plan and life-falsehood have been clearly unmasked.

The attentive observer will find the nature of the *compensatory dynamics* presenting a quite extraordinary aspect as soon as he permits the sexual rôle to be relegated to one of minor importance and realizes that it is the former that is impelling the individual toward superhuman goals. In our present civilization both the girl and the youth will feel themselves forced to extraordinary exertions and manœuvres. A large number of these are admittedly of a distinctively progressive nature. To preserve this progressive nature but to ferret out those by-paths that lead us astray and cause illness, to make these harmless, that is our object and one that takes us far beyond the limits of medical art. It is to this aspect of our subject that society, child-education and folk-education may look for germs of a far-reaching kind. *For the aim of this point-of-view is to gain a reinforced sense of reality, the development of a feeling of responsibility and a substitution for latent hatred of a feeling of mutual goodwill, all of which can be gained only by the conscious evolution of a feeling for the common weal and the conscious destruction of the will-to-power.*

He who is looking for the power-phantasies of the child will find them drawn with a master hand by Dostoevsky in his novel entitled *A Raw Youth.* I found them blatantly apparent in one of my patients. In the dreams and thoughts of this individual the following wish recurred repeatedly: others should die so that he might have enough room in which to live, others should suffer privations so that he might obtain more favourable opportunities. This attitude reminds one of the inconsiderateness and heartlessness of many men who trace all evil back to the fact that there are already too many people in the world; impulses that have unquestionably made the world-war more palatable. The feeling of certainty, in fictions of this kind, has been taken over in the above-mentioned case from the basic facts of capitalistic trade, where admittedly, the better the condition of one individual the worse that of another. "I want to be a grave-digger", said a four-year-old boy to me; "I want to be the person who digs graves for others".

MARTHA WOLFENSTEIN / Two Types of Jewish Mothers

The cases reported here were observed in the Child Guidance Institute of the Jewish Board of Guardians in New York City. I saw both Mrs. L and her daughter Karen in psychotherapy once a week for two and a half years. Mrs. S was similarly in treatment with me for a period of two years. Her son Stan was treated by another therapist, whose detailed case notes were utilized for this study. I am greatly indebted to the Jewish Board of Guardians for their kind permission to use the material from these cases.

I SHOULD like to present here the picture of two mothers, one of Eastern European Jewish origin and the other of an American Jewish family. Markedly different mother-child relations appear in the two cases, which can be regarded as expressing different cultural patterns. These mothers were seen over a period of two or more years in a child-guidance clinic, where their children were also in treatment, and both were primarily concerned about quarrelsome relations with their children. It would have been ideal if these two cases could have been matched in respect to age of the mother, age and sex of the child, socio-economic status of the family, and so on, so that the cultural background would have been the main variable. Unfortunately, the clinical material which comes one's way is not so neatly arranged for research purposes. However, in assessing the culturally characteristic aspects of the two cases, I have drawn on considerable antecedent research on Eastern European Jewish culture,[1] as well as on other observations of American and Jewish mothers,[2] research on old American non-Jewish families,[3] and an analysis of American child-training literature.[4]

Mrs. S is a stout, ruddy-faced woman of fifty-one who speaks with a marked Yiddish accent. She came to this country as a young woman. Born in Russia, she was the fourth of a family of eleven, three of whom died in childhood. She had little schooling, which she regrets; her intelligence appears to be superior. She retains close ties to her family of origin, sharing a house with her older sister, who is "like a mother" to her. Her husband, also of Eastern European origin, is a workingman, whom she describes as excessively good-natured—everyone takes advantage of him—and for whom she has considerable contempt. She has three sons to whom she is intensely devoted. It is on account of her youngest son, Stan, who is fourteen, that she has come to the child-guidance clinic.

Stan has frequent violent quarrels with his mother, cursing and insulting her, after which he cries and implores her forgiveness. Mrs. S weeps when she talks about these scenes, exclaims how it hurts her, how it is killing her, speaks of her intense feelings as a mother and her life of sacrifice for her children.

Mrs. L is a slender, youthful-looking woman of thirty-four. She is second-generation American (her parents having been of Eastern European origin) and the eldest of a family of five, all of whom are living. She is a college graduate. Her family unit excludes her family of origin; she feels that involvement in the affairs of her mother, brothers, or sisters would conflict with giving proper attention to her husband and children. Her husband was born in Eastern Europe, came to this country as a boy, got his schooling here, and is also a college graduate. He is an office manager. They have two little girls. The elder, Karen, who is nine, is brought for treatment. The parents are concerned about her hostility toward her mother. Mrs. L speaks of Karen's "negativism," then reproaches herself for her "rejection" of Karen during her early years. When Mrs. L relates family upsets, she usually assumes a humorous tone as if she would like to turn it all into an amusing anecdote.

I should like to consider certain contrasting attitudes of these two mothers, first in respect to the image which the mother has of the child. Children pass through various stages of development, as, for instance the helpless infant, the school child bent on acquisition of skills, the rebellious adolescent. Cultures differ in their emphasis on one or another phase of development, taking the characteristics of the child in a particular phase as constituting his essential nature. The way in which the mother conceives her own role varies accordingly. If the image of the helpless infant predominates, the mother must feed and care for him and guard him from harm; she cannot leave him to take care of himself. This conception of the mother-child relationship may persist through all phases of the child's development. If, on the other hand, the phase or aspect of the child's life which has to do with acquisition of skills is most strongly emphasized, the mother's role is more that of an educator, and the child is encouraged to be independent from an early age.

Mrs. S continues to think of her adolescent son as a helpless infant, who cannot be trusted to do anything for himself and who, if left to his own devices, will injure himself, probably irreparably. She is constantly worried about his health: he is in danger of catching cold from not buttoning up his jacket or not wearing his scarf or sleeping with the windows open. When she cautions him about these things, he flies into a rage, yelling that he is not a baby. (Her anxieties reinforce his own adolescent fears about himself, that he may have damaged himself by masturbation. This contributes to making the mother's expressions of worry about the son's health intolerable to him.) To this mother her big athletic boy is still as fragile as an infant, just as vulnerable to the hazards of the environment, and just as dependent on the mother's vigilant care in order to survive. Similarly, when it comes to buying clothes, which he would like to do by himself, she is sure that he will be cheated if she does not go with him. When he wants to get a summer job, she is convinced that he is too young, that the only possible job for him would be one which she would arrange for him to get in her sister's store. About his studies, she again expresses mainly fears that he is damaging himself, either endangering his future prospects by not studying or ruining his health by studying too late at night.

If we attempt to relate this maternal attitude to the Eastern European Jewish background, we can see factors there which made for the fixation of the mother-child relation on the earliest infantile phase. In the traditional Jewish community the mother was not the educator of her dearly beloved sons. At about the age of three the little boy was snatched from the arms of his weeping mother and sent to school. Learning was the province of the men exclusively.[5] The time when the mother could have her son to herself, to love and care for, was when he was baby, before the world of men and of learning claimed him. For the older boy she had no comparably important role to play. Her image of the child remained complementary to her own role, which was not that of an educator but one of feeding the infant, anxiously protecting his fragile organism, aware of his helplessness, his inability to survive without her constant care.[6] One might say that just as a child tends to become fixated on a certain phase of development if it is extremely gratifying or to regress to it if a later phase is too frustrating, so similarly a mother may remain fixated to the maternal role of corresponding to that phase of the child's development which was most gratifying for her and to regress to this in the face of frustration in later phases.[7]

The Jewish religion has as a major motive the consolidation of father-son relations through the submission of the son to paternal authority. There is one god, the father, not the son or the mother deified by Christianity. The custom of the Eastern European Jewish community of separating boys from their mothers at such an early age was in the interest of inducing submission to paternal elders. Before the development of the oedipal phase, with its rebellious impulses toward the father, the boy was already subjected to the tutelage of men, the rod of the teacher, and the word of God. The separation from the mother curtailed opportunities for expression of the oedipal attachment to her. As a result, the mother knew her little boy much better in the pre-oedipal phase, when he was passive to her ministrations, than in the oedipal phase, in which boys develop more active impulses toward their mothers; and the boy on his side had more opportunity for expressing the earlier than the later strivings toward the mother.

A reality factor in the European Jewish situation which contributed to the mother's anxiety about her child was the high infant mortality rate. In Mrs. S's case, three of her siblings had died in childhood. Such experiences reinforce anxiety about the fragility and vulnerability of the infant.[8]

While Mrs. S's sons were born in this country and brought up under different conditions of life from those of her original community, it would seem that Mrs. S perpetuates the model of her own mother, from whom she learned the maternal role. This role, as the mother of babies, did not include educational functions, and even less could Mrs. S assume those in a strange country where she knows little of what her children must learn.

From Mrs. L, on the other hand, we hear: "When will Karen grow up? Why is she still so babyish?" When she feels less dissatisfied with her daughter, she reports that Karen is beginning to assume some responsibilities. Mrs. L is greatly concerned about skill and accomplishments. She complains that Karen is clumsy, that she lacks manual dexterity, and also that she is not socially adept. When Karen is nine, her mother is already thinking about her independent adult life. If Karen's relations to her family are disturbed, then she may not have good relations to the opposite sex later on. That is why Mrs. L feels that Karen should have treatment. Later Mrs. L is thinking about sending Karen away to college, though she is only at this time in the sixth grade.

The American family has been characterized by Margaret Mead as a "launching platform," the place from which the children take off for their own independent existence. The mother is not supposed to hover protectively over her little one but to speed him off on his tricycle to join his age mates. Recent American child-training literature has stressed the motor and exploratory impulses of the infant, his tendency from a very early age to get going and master his environment.[9] Mothers who study Gesell check whether their children are demonstrating the appropriate skills from month to month. The aspect of the growing child as one who acquires skills is strongly emphasized. The mother's role is to facilitate the acquisition of skills, to preside over the child's learning. In America the role of teacher is to a high degree a woman's role, both at home and in school.[10]

Mrs. L exemplifies this maternal attitude. She is troubled because her child does not show so much skill or so much independent activity as the mother expects. We do not hear from Mrs. L the anxieties about the child wearing enough sweaters or possibly catching cold and so on which so constantly haunt Mrs. S.

Another major question in respect to which maternal attitudes vary is this: How vulnerable is the mother in relation to the child? How much can the child's behavior hurt or wound her? In the case of Mrs. S, the thought is repeatedly expressed that her children can kill her. Though she sees her son Stan as a helpless and fragile baby, who needs her constant care to stay alive, she also sees him as terribly strong and powerful, capable of killing her. When he quarrels with her, she tells him that he is "aggravating" her to death. The doctor has said that, because of her high blood pressure, aggravation could kill her. She frequently tells Stan about a woman who lived across the street whose son actually aggravated her to death. On one occasion when Stan was angry at her, she went out on the porch without a coat and thought she caught cold. In his rages, he tells her to drop dead. She answers him that she will; if he is like that, what does she have to live for? Following a quarrel she often feels sick. She retires to her room and lies down. When Stan comes in and tries to mollify her, she does not speak; she acts as if she were dead.

Death wishes toward the parents, who are at the same time deeply loved, are inevitable in human childhood. And with the child's illusions of omnipotence there is the fantasy that these wishes can kill. In the S family this is not just a guilt-ridden fantasy of the child, it is even more a firm belief of the mother. By his show of anger against her, her son is attacking her very life. The quarrel itself is an act of murder.

A number of factors contribute to this maternal reaction. Mrs. S deeply represses any negative feelings of her own toward her mother and toward her children. She would never have behaved toward her mother the way her son behaves toward her. Recalling her own childhood and how the children would never have dared to answer their mother back, Mrs. S remembered how her sister, after having been punished by their mother, muttered to herself: "It should happen to me"—meaning that what she wickedly wished to the mother should fall on her own head. Hostile feelings were turned back against the self. Perpetuating her strong positive ties to her mother, Mrs. S still lives with her older sister, who is like a mother to her. In relation to her children she also denies any negative feelings; she is never aware of anything but self-sacrificing love toward them.[11] The fate of these unacknowledged hostile feelings would seem to be that they are projected onto her children. The hostility which she dared not admit toward her mother assumes terrifying proportions in her son and is directed toward her. The unadmitted negative feelings which she has toward the son are similarly projected and contribute to her belief that he will fatally damage himself.

Mrs. S is vulnerable not only to the attacks of her son against her but to his tendency to damage himself, which is equally destructive to her.[12] If by not following her admonitions he catches a cold and makes himself sick, who will suffer? She will. The two of them are inextricably bound together in life and death. Mrs. S has also told her son that if she dies, he dies. Presumably he could not survive her, either because of his helplessness or because he would die of guilt and grief.

If we look for a model of the mother-child relationship as Mrs. S experiences it, a situation in which the child is at the same time most vulnerable and most capable of killing the mother, we may find this in childbirth. It is then that the child's life is most endangered, while the child in turn causes the mother intense suffering and endangers her life. For Mrs. S every emotionally fraught scene with her son would seem to be a repetition of childbirth. We may ask what circumstances make for such a strong fixation on this experience. For a mother who is impelled to relive it in this way, we may guess that it represents a very deep gratification. In the Eastern European Jewish community the importance attached to having children was tremendous. A wife who produced no children could be divorced.[13] Mrs. S expresses the traditional pride in maternity. She frequently clasps her hands to her large bosom and exclaims: "I am a mother." However, the high value attached to being a mother does not necessarily carry with it such an intense emotional fixation on the act of birth itself.

In trying to account for this, I would propose the following hypothesis. Traditional Jewish life involved strong defenses against sexual impulses. The preponderance of rituals and avoidances hedging every act strongly suggests a compulsive character structure, profoundly impressed with the dangers of sexuality. At the same time it was recognized that complete genital abstinence was not feasible. Sexual thoughts could obtrude themselves and disturb serious occupations, particularly the ideal pursuit of the man, that of constant study. Thus the sexual act was to be performed to free the man's mind from disturbing thoughts. It seems likely that sexual relations were thus carried out as quickly as possible, to get the thing done and out of the way, that sex was brief and isolated from the rest of life. It was shameful, for instance, for a man and wife to see each other naked.[14] There can have been little erotic elaboration under such circumstances, and one may suppose that the aim of satisfying the woman was absent.

For the sexually unsatisfied wife the great genital experience was childbirth. Then she received from her son the intense and prolonged genital stimulation which she did not get from her husband. But, since she also participated in the regression from full genitality, her image of sex was a sado-masochistic one. Thus her great sexual experience, that of childbearing, was fraught with the dangers of killing and being killed. (While these dangers are actually present in childbirth, they do not under other circumstances assume such emotional importance.) If we suppose that these hypothetically reconstructed relations are exemplified in the case of Mrs. S, we can understand why she is impelled to repeat painful scenes with her son, scenes which have the conscious significance that he may kill her and thus also bring about his own death and which unconsciously reproduce the experience of childbirth.

In contrast to this, Mrs. L does not attribute to her children the power to destroy her. They can be a terrible nuisance and annoyance, but they are not that dangerous. Quarrels are less climactic, more trivial, and imminence of fatality does not haunt the daily routine. Mother and child are less isolated in intense struggle with each other; quarrels as recounted by Mrs. L appear to revolve around many external details and circumstances and to include other persons.[15] Thus Karen comes home from school and complains about her teacher; Mrs. L tries to justify the teacher, and Karen becomes enraged with the mother for taking the teacher's side. Karen and her sister get into a dispute about which one finished her milk first, and Karen shouts so loudly that her mother threatens her with the strap. On another occasion the little sister calls the mother an ass, and the mother spanks her. Karen yells that her mother is mean and cruel until the mother spanks her, too. There are daily quarrels about Karen's not getting dressed promptly enough in the morning, and so on. Mrs. L is exasperated with Karen, but she does not express the thought that Karen could aggravate her to death.

What are the emotional factors in this mother which make for this more moderate estimate of her child's power to damage her? Unlike Mrs. S, Mrs. L does not completely repress her own hostility toward either her mother or her children. She has many outspoken reproaches against her own mother. She does not maintain the same high level of filial piety which we noted in Mrs. S, who still lives on the closest terms with a good mother-figure, her older sister. Mrs. L frequently wards off with resentment what she takes to be unfair claims of her mother on her. She recalls how little her mother has helped her and holds many things against her mother from childhood days. Thus she justifies the negative feelings which she acknowledges toward her mother. Similarly in relation to her daughter, she admits that the child was, to begin with, a terrible burden which she resented. While she blames herself for having felt this way, she readily acknowledges how much of a burden Karen remains for her, and on one occasion confessed that she sometimes wishes that Karen were dead. Since these hostile feelings toward her own mother as well as toward her daughter are to some extent consciously acknowledged, they do not have to be projected onto the child. Thus the child is not invested with mother-killing or with self-destroying tendencies from the mother's own unconscious. As we noted before, Mrs. L is much less concerned than Mrs. S with her child's health and does not see Karen as wilfully exposing herself to colds or in other ways endangering her life.

Mother and child in the L family are not a symbiotic pair, with their fates inseparably intertwined, but two mutually independent persons. The mother is not fixated on the phase of the child's helpless infancy or the situation of childbirth but is urging her child toward increasing independence and looks forward eagerly to the greater independence she herself can enjoy, for instance, when she gets the children off to camp for the summer. Also, the mother's anger is less turned back against herself and less libidinized. When Mrs. L gets annoyed with Karen, she seethes inwardly until she cannot restrain herself from hitting the child; then she feels relieved. She experiences a catharsis. This seems to be in keeping with major American patterns about aggression. There is the feeling that aggression should be turned outward, that it is good to get things off your chest, and that an overt fight clears the air. The venting of anger seems to be experienced as a simple excretory act: something is got rid of, and one feels relieved. Anger here appears to be relatively uninvolved with sado-masochistic fantasies. Neither of the combatants is pictured as weak. The relation between parent and child is felt to be a symmetrical one. (When Karen's mother calls her a "nitwit," Karen calls her mother an "idiot." Karen also calls her mother a "brat.")

Karen, on her side, has the inevitable wishes, fantasies, and fears of her mother's death. But these are isolated from the day-to-day quarrels with the mother. They are expressed in reactions to movies and television shows which fascinate and sometimes frighten her, in which the wife dies and the husband marries his girl friend.

Karen writes a play in which a grown-up married daughter becomes enraged with her mother for trying to make her get a divorce (Karen has frequently urged her father to divorce her mother), and the daughter murders the mother. However, her actual quarrels with her mother do not appear to be a manifest dramatization of such fantasies. It is not as in the case of Stan who shouts "Drop dead!" to his mother and so induces in the mother an access of illness, when she retires to her bed and acts as if dead. Karen's mother remains upright and active; she does not comply with the child's unconscious fantasies.

In so far as the thought of killing enters into the quarrels between Karen and her mother, it takes the form of the child's fantasy that the mother is killing her. When the mother hits her, Karen sometimes screams: "You're killing me!" and in the next breath, "You can't hurt me!" Thus the child's death wishes toward the mother are projected onto the mother. It is again the reverse of the S family, where the mother's hostile impulses (toward both her mother and her child) were projected onto the child, who was seen as killing her. (We may also suppose that Mrs. S really believes that her son is bringing her to an early grave, while Karen has less of a serious anticipation of her own death when she accuses her mother in this way.) The projection of the child's bad wishes onto the parents has been observed to be a typical motive of American film plots. There, in oedipal dramas, a mother-figure tries to seduce the hero, and a father-figure tries to kill him. To take one example out of many, in *Gilda,* the beautiful wife of the hero's boss sought to win the hero's love, and the boss made an attempt on the hero's life. The hypothetical connection which we have suggested between this type of film plot and American family life is the following. American children are expected to surpass their parents. As the children see themselves as potentially on a higher level than their parents, they are more easily able to ascribe to the parents the bad impulses which they repudiate in themselves.[16] Karen seems to exemplify this American pattern in her projection of her bad impulses onto her mother. In the S family, on the other hand, where the European image of parental sanctity persists, bad impulses are seen as concentrated in the child.

While parents are inevitably moral authorities for their children, there are many variations in the manner of expressing and acknowledging this authority. Parents may be regarded with awe as righteous judges, or their fallibility may be unmasked. They may demand ceremonial respect, or they may feel uneasy in the role of authority and play it down. For Stan, his mother retains the power to pardon or condemn. After he has quarreled with her, he pleads for her forgiveness. If there have been angry words over breakfast, he cannot leave for school until she gives him a forgiving kiss. This reconciliation and pardon seem to have the effect of undoing the crime implicit in the quarrel. He is not only freed from the burden of his wickedness, but he is reassured that his mother does not remain in deathlike withdrawal. When his mother condemns him, he is liable to feel that this is a just sentence. In yelling dirty words at her he feels that he is implicitly confessing his masturbation and his bad sexual thoughts. The mother responds by calling down the punishment of God on him, and the boy feels that this is what he deserves. Thus his mother remains an external conscience for him, confirming the state of his soul. Mrs. S has no doubts about her own righteousness. She never alternates condemnations of her son with self-accusations. She recalls the respect she had for her own parents and cannot understand the lack of equal respect in her son.

Mrs. L is much less sure of being in the right. She acknowledges that her tolerance or intolerance of Karen's annoying behavior varies with her mood, whether she feels sick or well, or whether she has had a quarrel with her own mother. Karen is outspoken in her conviction that her mother's punishments are not an expression of superior justice but of impulsive feelings. When Mrs. L hits the children, Karen shouts that her mother is a maniac, "She hits because she likes to hit!" Karen never asks for her mother's forgiveness following a quarrel but after a short time "forgets" it (according to the mother) and is affectionate and cheerful again. The mother here is neither a just punisher nor a source of absolution. Just as the quarrel does not assume the significance of a crime, so also it is not a moral drama involving repentance and pardon.

It has been observed that in American families and in American life generally, no one likes to assume a role of authority.[17] A superordinate position makes one feel uneasy. There is a tendency to make all relationships approximate to symmetry. President Eisenhower's favorite news photograph of himself shows him laughingly shaking hands with his small grandson, who bows as the grandfather bows to him.[18] In American families the parents listen to the children rather than requiring the children to listen to them in quiet deference.[19] Parents who do not like to arrogate to themselves a superior authority tend to minimize moral justifications in their handling of their children. This is again reflected in the images of parent-figures in American films. Manifest parents of the hero or heroine are likely to be mild, ineffectual background figures. Characters who stand for the parents in a more disguised way, such as the hero's boss and the boss's wife, are often dangerous, violent, and immoral. Thus the punishing aspect of the parents is separated off as an attack without moral justification.[20] It is in this spirit that Karen takes the occasional angry blows of her mother: "She hits because she likes to hit."

The strong emotions engendered in family conflicts may be a source of intense (though unadmitted) gratification, or they may be felt as a disruption of a desirable façade of calm and efficiency, as senseless and exaggerated reactions, deprecated in retrospect as much ado about nothing. As might be inferred from what we already know, our two mothers differ greatly in their reactions to emotional scenes. Mrs. S preserves and repeatedly relives the intense emotions evoked by familial happenings. As she relates a quarrel with her son, the scene is alive for her, no word or gesture is forgotten, and her tears flow afresh as she exclaims: "I can't stand it, it hurts me, it's killing me." On the manifest level she suffers, but less consciously she enjoys these scenes and is thus impelled to re-evoke them so that she can feel again the gratifying pain which they arouse.

The emotional atmosphere of Mrs. L's discourse is quite different. There are no tears. Mrs. L's characteristic expression is an amused smile, and the tone she assumes as she recounts family upsets is a humorous one. The emotional quality of quarreling scenes is not re-evoked but is transformed in the retelling. In retrospect the feelings of anger and distress (especially of the child—the mother tends to minimize her own) appear unreasonable, disproportionate, absurd. Mrs. L strives to turn upsetting scenes into comic anecdotes. There is less enjoyment here of the painful feelings which a quarrel produces; to derive pleasure from it in retrospect, Mrs. L must transform the emotional tone of the scene and reduce its intensity by treating it humorously. Probably also Mrs. L experiences less pain in the quarrel itself than Mrs. S does, since Mrs. L assumes more the role of an aggressor than of a victim. In so far as quarrels are disturbing for Mrs. L, she tends to blank them out in memory. In her reports there is a displacement of emphasis from the central emotional drama to trivial peripheral details. Thus, if she and Karen have quarreled because she wanted Karen to try on a skirt she was making for her and Karen did not want to interrupt her play, Mrs. L goes into great detail about the pattern and the material she used for the skirt but forgets what she and Karen said to each other in their anger. The angry episode is like an alien thing which has obtruded itself into the reasonable and unemotional tenor of life; Mrs. L rectifies and smoothes over this break by eliminating it in memory.

Suffering is the major theme of Mrs. S's life. When she is not preoccupied with Stan's attacks on her, she recalls the misfortunes of her second son, who, after having started on a brilliant career, got into trouble and ruined his chances. Again and again she remembers with tears his early successes and re-evokes the tragedy of his downfall. "It hurts me, I have such pity on him, I could die." At other times she speaks of her eldest son, who has never caused her any trouble and who is doing quite well. But his wife makes unreasonable demands on him and does not understand him, and he is very hard pressed financially, and again it hurts Mrs. S. When family parties are organized on various occasions, there are always some painful repercussions as someone was not invited who should have been, or someone did not come who should have come, and Mrs. S participates in the hurt feelings which are thus engendered. Every encounter, fraught as it is with intense emotion, assumes a dramatic quality in Mrs. S's telling of it.

There is little of this dramatic quality in Mrs. L's account of her life. As she details the external aspects of events, playing down their emotional undertones, nothing seems very important. One wonders, What really matters here? If one looks for a pervasive theme, one finds it perhaps in the issue about order and disorder. Mrs. L feels that in her parents' house everything was in disorder. Her mother was a bad housekeeper. Innumerable relatives trouped in and out. The family was constantly moving. Nobody ever knew how much money they had. The father gambled. Escaping from this disorder, Mrs. L married an extremely meticulous, fussy, precise, methodical man. However, she is unable to meet successfully his requirements for perfect order; in her there persists an unresolved conflict on this issue. While she does not overtly rebel against her husband's standards, she derives great covert gratification from her daughter Karen's messiness. Over and over she relates Karen's feats of sloppiness. When Karen gets undressed, she leaves one shoe under the kitchen table, the other in the middle of the living-room floor, and so on. Karen eats mashed potatoes with her fingers. When she is supposed to take a bath, she sits in the tub reading a comic book and forgets to wash herself. These and other similar habits of Karen's exasperate her father. While Mrs. L repeatedly complained about them, she laughed so genuinely at the same time that when it was pointed out to her that she vicariously enjoyed Karen's sloppiness, she was able to acknowledge this to be true. Karen's inability to conform to time schedules (getting dressed in the morning, getting to bed at night) is a source of daily conflict, especially with the father.

The mother herself has residual difficulties about punctuality. But she finds relief from her inner conflicts about orderliness by externalizing them; Karen acts out disorderly impulses while the father embodies restraints against them. Mrs. L gives the impression of strong, persistent ambivalence toward early cleanliness training. On the one hand, she rebelled against it, this rebellion being justified by later disillusionment with her parents, who failed to live up to a high standard of orderliness. On the other hand, she felt impelled to strive toward such a standard and sought reinforcement for this striving in her husband. In Karen, understandably enough, there are similar conflicts. At the same time that she is so messy at home, she always has the job of the housekeeper at school. She manifests some very finicky reactions, becoming disgusted to the point of nausea at excretory smells, even her own, and expressing similar disgust at the sight of her little sister picking her nose.

I would suggest the following hypothetical basis for the emotional orientation of these two families. In both cases there seems to be a considerable concentration on motives of the anal phase.[21] But in the S family the sector of these motives which is emphasized is the sado-masochistic one. There are strongly libidinized fantasies of killing and being killed, with the mother's predominant image of herself as suffering and dying because of what her children do to her. In the L family, another sector of anal motives is in the ascendant, namely, those having to do with dirt and messiness and the defensive struggle toward cleanliness, neatness, and order.[22] This conflict between messiness and order lends itself less to melodramatic expressions. It is likely to take the form rather of endless, nonclimactic nagging about petty details. Instead of the tragic maternal reproach, "You are killing me," it is, "Take your bath, Karen. It's already quarter to nine. . . . Karen, take your bath. It's five minutes to nine."

In traditional Jewish culture, strong defenses were erected against aggression. Innumerable rituals guarded against the breakthrough of aggressive impulses.[23] One may suppose that the impulses thus warded off had a strong sadistic quality. These impulses were to a large extent turned inward. The Jews underwent endless sufferings, which they accepted in a spirit of exalted masochism as inflicted by a God who loved them above all others. This submission to paternal authority was haunted by rebellious impulses which appeared as doubts about religious rules, to which exceptions could always be found; and the doubts were in turn fought back by ever more refined formulations of the rules. The Jewish religion concentrated on regulating relations between men, between a sole father-god and his sons. There are covert indications of sadistic impulses of children toward mothers which also had to be held in check. Thus one motive behind the taboo against eating meat with milk may have been a defense against the impulse of the infant to bite and eat the milk-giving breast. Adam and Eve were expelled from Eden for having eaten the apple (a breast symbol). However, the major emphasis of religious ritual and observance was on male relationships. Women, excluded from study and argumentation about the law, may thus have expressed the same sado-masochistic motives, which men elaborated in highly ritualistic ways, in more free-flowing emotional relations with their children. Men accepted their sufferings from God, women from their children.

This sado-masochistic concentration appears to be absent in American culture. Opportunities for turning aggression outward have been manifold, nor does aggression seem fraught with terrible dangers. The possibility of injuring women has little plausibility where women appear as very strong.[24] On the other hand, cleanliness has been an outstanding American value. Current advertising for soaps and deodorants plays on the doubt about ever achieving perfect bodily cleanliness and the belief that one must be utterly clean in order to be loved. The emphasis on cleanliness training, which here seems so major, is one which involves, on the side of the mother, the image of the child as one who can learn and, on the side of the child, strong conflicts in relation to strict maternal demands.[25] These conflicts have in the past been notably resolved in reaction formations against the original messy impulses, giving rise to the clean, orderly, methodical, hard-working individual, who got things done when they had to be done. At present there is less maternal resoluteness in the demand for cleanliness, and the traditional reaction-formative type of character is no longer in the ascendant. However, I would suggest that there is a certain basic attitude toward excreta which remains the same. Excreta are impersonal things which one has to dispose of in appropriate ways. The relation between mother and child in which things play a major role provides a model for other relationships which are not sheerly between persons, but where persons are mutually involved in the management of things. I would speculate further that where a more sado-masochistic relation prevails, excreta are often equated with beloved persons who have been incorporated and who are being destructively got rid of.[26] This would fit the Eastern European Jewish pattern, in which there are few impersonalized quarrels about the orderly or disorderly management of things but where conflicts tend to have the significance of destroying the opponent.

I have tried to present here two contrasting pictures of some aspects of Eastern European Jewish and American Jewish mother-child relations. The question arises as to how the transition is achieved from the one to the other. Further investigation would be required to provide the answer to this. I have relatively little information about the mother of Mrs. L. From what I know, although she came to this country as a young girl, she seems to have perpetuated the Eastern European model of maternity less than Mrs. S. For instance, she was less anxious about her children and left them more to take care of themselves. As far as the S family is concerned, we can see a marked transition from the Eastern European Jewish pattern in the behavior of the son, in his overt expressions of aggression against the mother. Stan suffers severe conflicts about aggression. He strives to deny the mother's belief that his aggression can kill her. "Nobody ever died of aggravation," he argues. At the same time he tries to justify his aggressive feelings against his parents in terms of what he considers mistreatment in his childhood, and so on. He is striving for the American position that it is permissible to rebel against one's parents. But this remains difficult for him, since in the culture from which the parents come such rebellion is tantamount to murder.

In discussing the L family I have throughout referred to presumable general features of American culture. The question may be asked: What is Jewish in the L family? Here I must bring in the character of the father, whom I have dealt with very little. This father, of Eastern European Jewish origin, appears to exemplify a strong identification with his mother.[27] Thus, since he has been in bad health in recent years, he reproaches Karen for the aggravation she causes him by saying that it will shorten his life. However, he seems to have some conflicts about this, attempting at times to conceal from Karen that he feels exhausted after a prolonged dispute. Mrs. L is outspoken in her condemnation of her husband for attempting to impose such a burden of guilt on the child. Perhaps he realizes vicariously for her her residual masochistic tendencies, which she consciously repudiates. She denies any thoughts that annoyance with Karen can affect her health, and she does not recall any comparable reproaches from her own mother. We may note further that the strong mother–weak father combination which we find in the L family corresponds to a frequent American family constellation.[28] However, the specific qualities of this father, who is physically weak while he remains intellectually superior, have a marked Jewish aspect.

To sum up, we have seen here, in a fragmentary way and with much admittedly speculative interpretation, two contrasting maternal patterns. The Eastern European Jewish mother sees her child at any age as terribly vulnerable, a baby incapable of taking care of himself, who would perish without her constant vigilance.

At the same time the baby appears as terribly strong, capable of killing the mother. We saw in this a fixation of the mother on the earliest phase of the child's life, and particularly on the experience of giving birth, and also a tendency to project onto the child the mother's unacknowledged hostility toward him and toward her own mother. The mother is a righteous figure, capable of damning or giving absolution. She is a suffering person, being incessantly wounded and killed and deriving her major unacknowledged emotional gratification in this masochistic way. The American Jewish mother here described sees her child mainly as an independent being, who should stop as quickly as possible being babyish and proceed to acquire skills. A different aspect of the growing child is emphasized, that having to do with learning, and the child is not seen as fragile. The mother acknowledges hostility toward the child and toward her own mother and does not project them onto the child, who is accordingly not seen as self-damaging or as destroying the mother. In the conflicts between mother and child, the mother appears as less surely righteous, and the child can attribute gross unmoralized aggressive impulses to her. This is in keeping with American parents' avoidance of a dominant authoritative role, the tendency toward symmetry in parent-child relations, and the possibility for children to ascribe their own condemned motives to the parents. Instead of the sado-masochistic image of the quarrel as a murder, a central issue is the more impersonalized one about order and disorder. One of the foremost unsolved problems raised by this essay, as a subject for further research, is the question of how the transition from the Eastern European Jewish to the American Jewish family is achieved.

Notes

1. Zborowski and Herzog, 1952; also unpublished material in the files of Columbia University Research in Contemporary Cultures.
2. I refer to observations made during several years as a school psychologist in private schools in New York City, where the large majority of the families were American Jewish; also to other cases at the Jewish Board of Guardians.
3. Unpublished material in the files of Columbia University Research in Contemporary Cultures.
4. See "Fun Morality" in this volume (p. 168); also Wolfenstein, 1953.
5. Zborowski and Herzog, 1952.
6. An alternative has been observed to the tendency of this type of mother to see the child as always the same, namely, for the mother to hark back to the time of his early childhood as a golden age from which he has subsequently declined. It would seem that these two attitudes can also coexist: the child appearing invariant as far as health is concerned (always fragile and needing vigilant care) but changing in respect to goodness, becoming less loving toward the mother, less exclusively preoccupied with pleasing her.
7. Cf. Coleman, Kris, and Provence, 1953.
8. Infant mortality, however, is not decisive for the view that children are very

fragile. Many deep-lying fantasies contribute to the image of the child as weak or strong (cf. "Image of the Child in Contemporary Films" in this volume, p. 277).

9. *Infant Care,* 1945 and 1951.
10. Gorer, 1948.
11. Information about Eastern European Jewish mothers indicates much verbal expression of ambivalence toward their children. "In the mother's moods, opposites are almost simultaneous. If the child pesters her . . . her sharp 'devil take you!' or 'go into the ground!' will merge swiftly into a blessing, 'you shall grow strong and healthy for me!' " (Zborowski and Herzog, 1952, p. 334). Presumably in such swift undoing of the expression of a hostile wish, the mother did not allow herself to become aware of its significance. When the child turns such expressions of hostility back toward the mother (this being apparently an American development), her overwhelming sense of the seriousness of these words derives some of its force from her own unacknowledged hostility toward the child (as well as toward her own mother) which she projects. When the child says, "Drop dead!" the mother's reaction that this can kill her may not be a direct attribution of magical force to the words but rather the feeling that if the child is hostile toward her, this so wounds her to the heart that she can die. In the case of Mrs. S, it seems that she does on her side curse her son when provoked, but she does not acknowledge any feeling but that of wounded love toward him; her curses do not carry the force that his do.
12. This fantasy, that the mother will suffer and die if the son's self-damaging tendencies are carried through, may express an expiation: as if the mother unconsciously acknowledges her projected hostile tendencies and feels she must pay for them.
13. Zborowski and Herzog, 1952.
14. *Ibid.*
15. In contrast to this, typical quarrels in the S family are more narrowly focused in her mother-son relation. At a word from the mother—"Button your jacket" or "You should get some sleep now"—Stan flies into a rage—"Don't treat me like a baby!"—and the fight is on. Where, as in the L family, a larger sector of the external world is likely to be included in the terms of the quarrel, a greater sense of reality guards against the intrusion of melodramatic fantasies.
16. Wolfenstein and Leites, 1950.
17. Gorer, 1948.
18. *New York Times Magazine,* 1954.
19. Bateson, 1942.
20. Wolfenstein and Leites, 1950.
21. Freud, 1942*a*; Abraham, 1942; Jones, 1948.
22. In a similar way Rudolph Loewenstein (1951) contrasts German and Jewish characters, finding in the Germans a preponderance of defenses against dirtiness, in the Jews the concentration of defenses against aggression.
23. Freud, 1942*b*.
24. Similarly, one may contrast the attitudes toward women in British and American films. The British preoccupation with the danger of unleashing sadistic impulses toward women and the need to guard against such impulses find no counterpart in American films, where women are more than able to take care of themselves (cf. Wolfenstein and Leites, 1950).
25. Wolfenstein, 1953.
26. Cf. the little boy cited by Karl Abraham (1942, p. 427) who, when angry with his nurse, threatened to "ka-ka" her over the river. "According to the child's view the way to get rid of a person one no longer liked was by means of defecation."
27. As indicative of Mr. L's maternal identification, he says that he feels tied to Karen by an umbilical cord (when she is very demanding of his attention and he feels he cannot get away from her) and that he feels as if she had drained all the milk out of him (when he is exhausted by her demands).
28. Bibring, 1953.

List of References

ABRAHAM, KARL. 1942. *Selected Papers of Karl Abraham*. Translated by D. BRYANT and A. STRACHEY. London: Hogarth Press and Institute of Psychoanalysis.

BATESON, GREGORY. 1942. "Morale and National Character." In *Civilian Morale,* ed. GOODWIN WATSON, pp. 71–91. Boston: Houghton Mifflin Co.

BIBRING, GRETE. 1953. "On the 'Passing of the Oedipus Complex' in a Matriarchal Family Setting." In *Drives, Affects, Behavior,* ed. RUDOLPH LOEWENSTEIN, pp. 278-84. New York; International Universities Press.

COLEMAN, ROSE W., KRIS, ERNST, and PROVENCE, SALLY. 1953. "The Study of Variations of Early Parental Attitudes." In *The Psychoanalytic Study of the Child,* VIII, 20–47.

"Eisenhower's Favorite Picture of Himself," *New York Times Magazine*. January 10, 1954, cover photograph.

FREUD, SIGMUND. 1942*a*. "Character and Anal Eroticism." In *Collected Papers,* Vol. II. London: Hogarth Press and Institute of Psychoanalysis. ———. 1942*b*. "Obsessive Acts and Religious Practices," *ibid.*

GORER, GEOFFREY. 1948. *The American People: A Study in National Character*. New York: W. W. Norton & Co.

Infant Care. 1945 and 1951. Children's Bureau, Washington, D.C.

JONES, ERNEST. 1948. "Anal-erotic Character Traits," *Papers on Psychoanalysis,* pp. 413–37. London: Baillière, Tindall & Cox.

LOEWENSTEIN, RUDOLPH. 1951. *Christians and Jews: A Psychoanalytic Study*. New York: International Universities Press.

WOLFENSTEIN, MARTHA. 1953. "Trends in Infant Care," *American Journal of Orthopsychiatry,* XXIII, No. 1, 120–30.

WOLFENSTEIN, MARTHA, and LEITES, NATHAN. 1950. *Movies: A Psychological Study*. Glencoe, Ill.: Free Press.

ZBOROWSKI, MARK, and HERZOG, ELIZABETH. 1952. *Life Is with People: The Jewish Little Town in Eastern Europe*. New York: International Universities Press.

ALDOUS HUXLEY / The Claxtons

IN THEIR little house on the common, how beautifully the Claxtons lived, how spiritually! Even the cat was a vegetarian—at any rate officially—even the cat. Which made little Sylvia's behaviour really quite inexcusable. For after all little Sylvia was human and six years old, whereas Pussy was only four and an animal. If Pussy could be content with greens and potatoes and milk and an occasional lump of nut butter, as a treat—Pussy, who had a tiger in her blood—surely Sylvia might be expected to refrain from surreptitious bacon-eating. Particularly in somebody else's house. What made the incident so specially painful to the Claxtons was that it had occurred under Judith's roof. It was the first time they had stayed with Judith since their marriage. Martha Claxton was rather afraid of her sister, afraid of her sharp tongue and her laughter and her scarifying irreverence. And on her own husband's account she was a little jealous of Judith's husband. Jack Bamborough's books were not only esteemed; they also brought in money. Whereas poor Herbert . . . "Herbert's art is too *inward,*" his wife used to explain, "too spiritual for most people to understand." She resented Jack Bamborough's success; it was too complete. She wouldn't have minded so much if he had made pots of money in the teeth of critical contempt; or if the critics had approved and he had made nothing. But to earn praise *and* a thousand a year—that was too much. A man had no right to make the best of both worlds like that, when Herbert never sold anything and was utterly ignored. In spite of all which she had at last accepted Judith's often repeated invitation. After all, one ought to love one's sister and one's sister's husband. Also, all the chimneys in the house on the common needed sweeping, and the roof would have to be repaired where the rain was coming in. Judith's invitation arrived most conveniently. Martha accepted it. And then Sylvia went and did that really inexcusable thing. Coming down to breakfast before the others she stole a rasher from the dish of bacon with which her aunt and uncle unregenerately began the day. Her mother's arrival prevented her from eating it on the spot; she had to hide it. Weeks later, when Judith was looking for something in the inlaid Italian cabinet, a little pool of dried grease in one of the drawers bore eloquent witness to the crime. The day passed; but Sylvia found no opportunity to consummate the outrage she had begun. It was only in the evening, while her little brother Paul was being given his bath, that she was able to retrieve the now stiff and clammy-cold rasher. With guilty speed she hurried upstairs with it and hid it under her pillow. When the lights were turned out she ate it. In the morning, the grease stains and a piece of gnawed rind betrayed her. Judith went into fits of inextinguishable laughter.

"It's like the Garden of Eden," she gasped between the explosions of her mirth. "The meat of the Pig of the Knowledge of Good and Evil. But if you *will* surround bacon with categorical imperatives and mystery, what can you expect, my dear Martha?"

Martha went on smiling her habitual smile of sweet forgiving benevolence. But inside she felt extremely angry; the child had made a fool of them all in front of Judith and Jack. She would have liked to give her a good smacking. Instead of which—for one must never be rough with a child, one must never let it see that one is annoyed—she reasoned with Sylvia, she explained, she appealed, more in sorrow than in anger, to her better feelings.

"Your daddy and I don't think it's right to make animals suffer when we can eat vegetables which don't suffer anything."

"How do you know they don't?" asked Sylvia, shooting out the question malignantly. Her face was ugly with sullen ill-temper.

"We don't think it right, darling," Mrs. Claxton went on, ignoring the interruption. "And I'm sure you wouldn't either, if you realized. Think, my pet; to make that bacon, a poor little pig had to be killed. To be *killed,* Sylvia. Think of that. A poor innocent little pig that hadn't done anybody any harm."

"But I hate pigs," cried Sylvia. Her sullenness flared up into sudden ferocity; her eyes, that had been fixed and glassy with a dull resentment, darkly flashed. "I hate them, hate them, *hate* them."

"Quite right," said Aunt Judith, who had come in most inopportunely in the middle of the lecture. "Quite right. Pigs *are* disgusting. That's why people call them pigs."

Martha was glad to get back to the little house on the common and their beautiful life, happy to escape from Judith's irreverent laughter and the standing reproach of Jack's success. On the common she ruled, she was the mistress of the family destinies. To the friends who came to visit them there she was fond of saying, with that smile of hers, "I feel that, in our way and on a tiny scale, we've built Jerusalem in England's green and pleasant land."

It was Martha's great-grandfather who started the brewery business. Postgate's Entire was a household word in Cheshire and Derbyshire. Martha's share of the family fortune was about seven hundred a year. The Claxtons' spirituality and disinterestedness were the flowers of an economic plant whose roots were bathed in beer. But for the thirst of British workmen, Herbert would have had to spend his time and energies profitably doing instead of beautifully being. Beer and the fact that he had married Martha permitted him to cultivate the arts and the religions, to distinguish himself in a gross world as an apostle of idealism.

"It's what's called the division of labour," Judith would laughingly say. "Other people drink. Martha and I think. Or at any rate we think we think."

Herbert was one of those men who are never without a knapsack on their backs. Even in Bond Street, on the rare occasions when he went to London, Herbert looked as though he were just about to ascend Mont Blanc. The rucksack is a badge of spirituality. For the modern high-thinking, pure-hearted Teuton or Anglo-Saxon the scandal of the rucksack is what the scandal of the cross was to the Franciscans. When Herbert passed, long-legged and knickerbockered, his fair beard like a windy explosion round his face, his rucksack overflowing with the leeks and cabbages required in such profusion to support a purely graminivorous family, the street-boys yelled, the flappers whooped with laughter. Herbert ignored them, or else smiled through his beard forgivingly and with a rather studied humorousness. We all have our little rucksack to bear. Herbert bore his not merely with resignation, but boldly, provocatively, flauntingly in the faces of men; and along with the rucksack the other symbols of difference, of separation from ordinary, gross humanity—the concealing beard, the knickerbockers, the Byronic shirt. He was proud of his difference.

"Oh, I know you think us ridiculous," he would say to his friends of the crass materialistic world, "I know you laugh at us for a set of cranks."

"But we don't, we don't," the friends would answer, politely lying.

"And yet, if it hadn't been for the cranks," Herbert pursued, "where would you be now, what would you be doing? You'd be beating children and torturing animals and hanging people for stealing a shilling, and doing all the other horrible things they did in the good old days."

He was proud, proud; he knew himself superior. So did Martha. In spite of her beautiful Christian smile, she too was certain of her superiority. That smile of hers—it was the hall-mark of her spirituality. A more benevolent version of Mona Lisa's smile, it kept her rather thin, bloodless lips almost chronically curved into a crescent of sweet and forgiving charitableness, it surcharged the natural sullenness of her face with a kind of irrelevant sweetness. It was the product of long years of wilful self-denial, of stubborn aspirations towards the highest, of conscious and determined love for humanity and her enemies. (And for Martha the terms were really identical; humanity, though she didn't of course admit it, *was* her enemy. She felt it hostile and *therefore* loved it, consciously and conscientiously; loved it because she really hated it.)

In the end habit had fixed the smile undetachably to her face. It remained there permanently shining, like the head-lamps of a motor-car inadvertently turned on and left to burn, unnecessarily, in the daylight. Even when she was put out or downright angry, even when she was stubbornly, mulishly fighting to have her own will, the smile persisted. Framed between its pre-Raphaelitic loops of mouse-coloured hair the heavy, sullen-featured, rather unwholesomely pallid face continued to shine incongruously with forgiving love for the whole of hateful, hostile humanity; only in the grey eyes was there any trace of the emotions which Martha so carefully repressed.

It was her great-grandfather and her grandfather who had made the money. Her father was already by birth and upbringing the landed gentleman. Brewing was only the dim but profitable background to more distinguished activities as a sportsman, an agriculturist, a breeder of horses and rhododendrons, a member of parliament and the best London clubs.

The fourth generation was obviously ripe for Art and Higher Thought. And duly, punctually, the adolescent Martha discovered William Morris and Mrs. Besant, discovered Tolstoy and Rodin and Folk Dancing and Laotzse. Stubbornly, with all the force of her heavy will, she addressed herself to the conquest of spirituality, to the siege and capture of the Highest. And no less punctually than her sister, the adolescent Judith discovered French literature and was lightly enthusiastic (for it was in her nature to be light and gay) about Manet and Daumier, even, in due course, about Matisse and Cézanne. In the long run brewing almost infallibly leads to impressionism or theosophy or communism. But there are other roads to the spiritual heights; it was by one of these other roads that Herbert had travelled. There were no brewers among Herbert's ancestors. He came from a lower, at any rate a poorer, stratum of society. His father kept a drapery shop at Nantwich. Mr. Claxton was a thin, feeble man with a taste for argumentation and pickled onions. Indigestion had spoilt his temper and the chronic consciousness of inferiority had made him a revolutionary and a domestic bully. In the intervals of work he read the literature of socialism and unbelief and nagged at his wife, who took refuge in non-conformist piety. Herbert was a clever boy with a knack for passing examinations. He did well at school. They were very proud of him at home, for he was an only child.

"You mark my words," his father would say, prophetically glowing in that quarter of an hour of beatitude which intervened between the eating of his dinner and the beginning of his dyspepsia, "that boy'll do something remarkable."

A few minutes later, with the first rumblings and convulsions of indigestion, he would be shouting at him in fury, cuffing him, sending him out of the room.

Being no good at games Herbert revenged himself on his more athletic rivals by reading. Those afternoons in the public library instead of on the football field, or at home with one of his father's revolutionary volumes, were the beginning of his difference and superiority. It was, when Martha first knew him, a political difference, an anti-Christian superiority. Her superiority was mainly artistic and spiritual. Martha's was the stronger character; in a little while Herbert's interest in socialism was entirely secondary to his interest in art, his anti-clericalism was tinctured by Oriental religiosity. It was only to be expected.

What was not to be expected was that they should have married at all, that they should ever even have met. It is not easy for the children of land-owning brewers and shop-owning drapers to meet and marry.

Morris-dancing accomplished the miracle. They came together in a certain garden in the suburbs of Nantwich where Mr. Winslow, the Extension Lecturer, presided over the rather solemn stampings and prancings of all that was earnestly best among the youth of eastern Cheshire. To that suburban garden Martha drove in from the country, Herbert cycled out from the High Street. They met; love did the rest.

Martha was at that time twenty-four and, in her heavy, pallid style, not unhandsome. Herbert was a year older, a tall, disproportionately narrow young man, with a face strong-featured and equiline, yet singularly mild ("a sheep in eagle's clothing" was how Judith had once described him), and very fair hair. Beard at that time he had none. Economic necessity still prevented him from advertising the fact of his difference and superiority. In the auctioneer's office, where Herbert worked as a clerk, a beard would have been as utterly inadmissible as knickerbockers, an open shirt, and that outward and visible symbol of inward grace, the rucksack. For Herbert these things only became possible when marriage and Martha's seven hundred yearly pounds had lifted him clear of the ineluctable workings of economic law. In those Nantwich days the most he could permit himself was a red tie and some private opinions.

It was Martha who did most of the loving. Dumbly, with a passion that was almost grim in its stubborn intensity, she adored him—his frail body, his long-fingered, delicate hands, the aquiline face with its, for other eyes, rather spurious air of distinction and intelligence, all of him, all. "He has read William Morris and Tolstoy," she wrote in her diary, "he's one of the very few people I've met who feel *responsible* about things. Every one else is so terribly frivolous and self-centred and indifferent. Like Nero fiddling while Rome was burning. He isn't like that. He's conscious, he's aware, he accepts the burden. That's why I like him." That was why, at any rate, she thought she liked him. But her passion was really for the physical Herbert Claxton. Heavily, like a dark cloud charged with thunder, she hung over him with a kind of menace, ready to break out on him with the lightnings of passion and domineering will. Herbert was charged with some of the electricity of passion which he had called out of her. Because she loved, he loved her in return. His vanity, too, was flattered; it was only theoretically that he despised class-distinctions and wealth.

The land-owning brewers were horrified when they heard from Martha that she was proposing to marry the son of a shopkeeper. Their objections only intensified Martha's stubborn determination to have her own way. Even if she hadn't loved him, she would have married him on principle, just because his father *was* a draper and because all this class business was an irrelevant nonsense. Besides, Herbert had talents. What sort of talents it was rather hard to specify. But whatever the talents might be, they were being smothered in the auctioneer's office. Her seven hundred a year would give them scope. It was practically a duty to marry him.

"A man's a man for all that," she said to her father, quoting, in the hope of persuading him, from his favourite poet; she herself found Burns too gross and unspiritual.

"And a sheep's a sheep," retorted Mr. Postgate, "and a woodlouse is a woodlouse—for all that and all that."

Martha flushed darkly and turned away without saying anything more. Three weeks later she and the almost passive Herbert were married.

Well, now Sylvia was six years old and a handful, a little Paul, who was whiny and had adenoids, was just on five, and Herbert, under his wife's influence, had discovered unexpectedly enough that his talents were really artistic and was by this time a painter with an established reputation for lifeless ineptitude. With every reaffirmation of his lack of success he flaunted more defiantly than ever the scandal of the rucksack, the scandals of the knickerbockers and beard. Martha, meanwhile, talked about the inwardness of Herbert's art. They were able to persuade themselves that it was their superiority which prevented them from getting the recognition they deserved. Herbert's lack of success was even a proof (though not perhaps the most satisfactory kind of proof) of that superiority.

"But Herbert's time will come," Martha would affirm prophetically. "It's bound to come."

Meanwhile the little house on the Surrey common was overflowing with unsold pictures. Allegorical they were, painted very flatly in a style that was Early Indian tempered, wherever the Oriental originals ran too luxuriantly to breasts and wasp-waists and moonlike haunches, by the dreary respectability of Puvis de Chavannes.

"And let me beg you, Herbert"—those had been Judith's parting words of advice as they stood on the platform waiting for the train to take them back again to their house on the common—"let me implore you: try to be a little more *indecent* in your paintings. Not so shockingly pure. You don't know how happy you'd make me if you could really be obscene for once. Really obscene."

It was a comfort, thought Martha, to be getting away from that sort of thing. Judith was really too . . . Her lips smiled, her hand waved good-bye.

"Isn't it lovely to come back to our own dear little house!" she cried, as the station taxi drove them bumpily over the track that led across the common to the garden gate. "Isn't it lovely?"

"Lovely!" said Herbert, dutifully echoing her rather forced rapture.

"Lovely!" repeated little Paul, rather thickly through his adenoids. He was a sweet child, when he wasn't whining, and always did and said what was expected of him.

Through the window of the cab Sylvia looked critically at the long low house among the trees. "I think Aunt Judith's house is nicer," she concluded with decision.

Martha turned upon her the sweet illumination of her smile. "Aunt Judith's house is bigger," she said, "and much grander. But this is Home, my sweet. Our very own Home."

"All the same," persisted Sylvia, "I like Aunt Judith's house better."

Martha smiled at her forgivingly and shook her head. "You'll understand what I mean when you're older," she said. A strange child, she was thinking, a difficult child. Not like Paul, who was so easy. Too easy. Paul fell in with suggestions, did what he was told, took his colour from the spiritual environment. Not Sylvia. She had her own will. Paul was like his father. In the girl Martha saw something of her own stubbornness and passion and determination. If the will could be well directed . . . But the trouble was that it was so often hostile, resistant, contrary. Martha thought of that deplorable occasion, only a few months before, when Sylvia, in a fit of rage at not being allowed to do something she wanted to do, had spat in her father's face. Herbert and Martha had agreed that she ought to be punished. But how? Not smacked, of course; smacking was out of the question. The important thing was to make the child realize the heinousness of what she had done. In the end they decided that the best thing would be for Herbert to talk to her very seriously (but very gently, of course), and then leave her to choose her own punishment. Let her conscience decide. It seemed an excellent idea.

"I want to tell you a story, Sylvia," said Herbert that evening, taking the child on to his knees. "About a little girl, who had a daddy who loved her so much, so much." Sylvia looked at him suspiciously, but said nothing. "And one day that little girl, who was sometimes rather a thoughtless little girl, though I don't believe she was really naughty, was doing something that it wasn't right or good for her to do. And her daddy told her not to. And what do you think that little girl did? She spat in her daddy's face. And her daddy was very very sad. Because what his little girl did was wrong, wasn't it?" Sylvia nodded a brief defiant assent. "And when one has done something wrong, one must be punished, mustn't one?" The child nodded again. Herbert was pleased; his words had had their effect; her conscience was being touched. Over the child's head he exchanged a glance with Martha. "If you had been that daddy," he went on, "and the little girl you loved so much had spat in your face, what would you have done, Sylvia?"

"Spat back," Sylvia answered fiercely and without hesitation.

At the recollection of the scene Martha sighed. Sylvia was difficult, Sylvia was decidedly a problem. The cab drew up at the gate; the Claxtons unpacked themselves and their luggage. Inadequately tipped, the driver made his usual scene. Bearing his rucksack, Herbert turned away with a dignified patience. He was used to this sort of thing; it was a chronic martyrdom. The unpleasant duty of paying was always his. Martha only provided the cash. With what extreme and yearly growing reluctance! He was always between the devil of the undertipped and the deep sea of Martha's avarice.

"Four miles' drive and a tuppenny tip!" shouted the cab-driver at Herbert's receding and rucksacked back.

Martha grudged him even the twopence. But convention demanded that something should be given. Conventions are stupid things; but even the Children of the Spirit must make some compromise with the World. In this case Martha was ready to compromise with the World to the extent of twopence. But no more.

Herbert knew that she would have been very angry if he had given more. Not openly, of course; not explicitly. She never visibly lost her temper or her smile. But her forgiving disapproval would have weighed heavily on him for days. And for days she would have found excuses for economizing in order to make up for the wanton extravagance of a sixpenny instead of a twopenny tip. Her economies were mostly on the food, and their justification was always spiritual. Eating was gross; high living was incompatible with high thinking; it was dreadful to think of the poor going hungry while you yourself were living in luxurious gluttony. There would be a cutting down of butter and Brazil nuts, of the more palatable vegetables and the choicer fruits. Meals would come to consist more and more exclusively of porridge, potatoes, cabbages, bread. Only when the original extravagance had been made up several hundred times would Martha begin to relax her asceticism. Herbert never ventured to complain. After one of these bouts of plain living he would for a long time be very careful to avoid other extravagances, even when, as in this case, his economies brought him into painful and humiliating conflict with those on whom they were practised.

"Next time," the taxi-driver was shouting, "I'll charge extra for the whiskers."

Herbert passed over the threshold and closed the door behind him. Safe! He took off his rucksack and deposited it carefully on a chair. Gross, vulgar brute! But anyhow he had taken himself off with the twopence. Martha would have no cause to complain or cut down the supply of peas and beans. In a mild and spiritual way Herbert was very fond of his food. So was Martha—darkly and violently fond of it. That was why she had become a vegetarian, why her economies were always at the expense of the stomach—precisely because she liked food so much. She suffered when she deprived herself of some delicious morsel. But there was a sense in which she loved her suffering more than the morsel. Denying herself, she felt her whole being irradiated by a glow of power; suffering, she was strengthened, her will was wound up, her energy enhanced. The dammed-up instincts rose and rose behind the wall of voluntary mortification, deep and heavy with potentialities of force. In the struggle between the instincts Martha's love of power was generally strong enough to overcome her greed; among the hierarchy of pleasures, the joy of exerting the personal conscious will was more intense than the joy of eating even Turkish Delight or strawberries and cream. Not always, however; for there were occasions when, overcome by a sudden irresistible desire, Martha would buy and, in a single day, secretly consume a whole pound of chocolate creams, throwing herself upon the sweets with the same heavy violence as had characterized her first passion for Herbert. With the passage of time and the waning, after the birth of her two children, of her physical passion for her husband, Martha's orgies among the chocolates became more frequent. It was as though her vital energies were being forced, by the closing of the sexual channel, to find explosive outlet in gluttony. After one of these orgies Martha always tended to become more than ordinarily strict in her ascetic spirituality.

Three weeks after the Claxtons' return to their little house on the common, the War broke out.

"It's changed most people," Judith remarked in the third year, "it's altered some out of all recognition. Not Herbert and Martha, though. It's just made them more so—more like themselves than they were before. Curious." She shook her head. "Very curious."

But it wasn't really curious at all; it was inevitable. The War could not help intensifying all that was characteristically Herbertian and Martha-ish in Herbert and Martha. It heightened their sense of remote superiority by separating them still further from the ordinary herd. For while ordinary people believed in the War, fought and worked to win, Herbert and Martha utterly disapproved and, on grounds that were partly Buddhistic, partly Socialist-International, partly Tolstoyan, refused to have anything to do with the accursed thing. In the midst of universal madness they almost alone were sane. And their superiority was proved and divinely hallowed by persecution. Unofficial disapproval was succeeded, after the passing of the Conscription Act, by official repression. Herbert pleaded a conscientious objection. He was sent to work on the land in Dorset, a martyr, a different and spiritually higher being. The act of a brutal War Office had definitely promoted him out of the ranks of common humanity. In this promotion Martha vicariously participated. But what most powerfully stimulated her spirituality was not War-time persecution so much as War-time financial instability, War-time increase in prices. In the first weeks of confusion she had been panic-stricken; she imagined that all her money was lost, she saw herself with Herbert and the children, hungry and houseless, begging from door to door. She immediately dismissed her two servants, she reduced the family food supply to a prison ration. Time passed and her money came in very much as usual. But Martha was so much delighted with the economies she had made that she would not revert to the old mode of life.

"After all," she argued, "it's really not pleasant to have strangers in the house to serve you. And then, why should they serve us? They who are just as good as we are." It was a hypocritical tribute to Christian doctrine; they were really immeasurably inferior. "Just because we happen to be able to pay them—that's why they have to serve us. It's always made me feel uncomfortable and ashamed. Hasn't it you, Herbert?"

"Always," said Herbert, who always agreed with his wife.

"Besides," she went on, "I think one ought to do one's own work. One oughtn't to get out of touch with the humble small realities of life. I've felt really happier since I've been doing the housework, haven't you?"

Herbert nodded.

"And it's so good for the children. It teaches them humility and service. . . ."

Doing without servants saved a clear hundred and fifty a year. But the economies she made on food were soon counterbalanced by the results of scarcity and inflation. With every rise in prices Martha's enthusiasm for ascetic spirituality became more than ever fervid and profound. So too did her conviction that the children would be spoilt and turned into worldings if she sent them to an expensive boarding-school. "Herbert and I believe very strongly in home education, don't we, Herbert?" And Herbert would agree that they believed in it very strongly indeed. Home education without a governess, insisted Martha. Why should one let one's children be influenced by strangers? Perhaps badly influenced. Anyhow, not influenced in exactly the way one would influence them oneself. People hired governesses because they dreaded the hard work of educating their children. And of course it *was* hard work—the harder, the higher your ideals. But wasn't it worth while making sacrifices for one's children? With the uplifting question, Martha's smile curved itself into a crescent of more than ordinary soulfulness. Of course it was worth it. The work was an incessant delight—wasn't it, Herbert? For what could be more delightful, more profoundly soul-satisfying than to help your own children to grow up beautifully, to guide them, to mould their characters into ideal forms, to lead their thoughts and desires into the noblest channels? Not by any system of compulsion, of course; children must never be compelled; the art of education was persuading children to mould themselves in the most ideal forms, was showing them how to be the makers of their own higher selves, was firing them with enthusiasm for what Martha felicitously described as "self-sculpture."

On Sylvia, her mother had to admit to herself, this art of education was hard to practise. Sylvia didn't want to sculpture herself, at any rate into the forms which Martha and Herbert found most beautiful. She was quite discouragingly without that sense of moral beauty on which the Claxtons relied as a means of education. It was ugly, they told her, to be rough, to disobey, to say rude things and tell lies. It was beautiful to be gentle and polite, obedient and truthful. "But I don't mind being ugly," Sylvia would retort. There was no possible answer except a spanking; and spanking was against the Claxtons' principles.

Aesthetic and intellectual beauty seemed to mean as little to Sylvia as moral beauty. What difficulties they had to make her take an interest in the piano! This was the more extraordinary, her mother considered, as Sylvia was obviously musical; when she was two and a half she had already been able to sing "Three Blind Mice" in tune. But she didn't want to learn her scales. Her mother talked to her about a wonderful little boy called Mozart. Sylvia hated Mozart. "No, no!" she would shout, whenever her mother mentioned the abhorred name. "I don't want to hear." And to make sure of not hearing, she would put her fingers in her ears. Nevertheless, by the time she was nine she could play "The Merry Peasant" from beginning to end without a mistake. Martha still had hopes of turning her into the musician of the family. Paul, meanwhile, was the future Giotto; it had been decided that he inherited his father's talents. He accepted his career as docilely as he had consented to learn his letters. Sylvia, on the other hand, simply refused to read.

"But think," said Martha ecstatically, "how *wonderful* it will be when you can open any book and read all the *beautiful* things people have written!" Her coaxing was ineffective.

"I like playing better," said Sylvia obstinately, with that expression of sullen bad temper which was threatening to become as chronic as her mother's smile. True to their principles, Herbert and Martha let her play; but it was a grief to them.

"You make your daddy and mummy so sad," they said, trying to appeal to her better feelings. "So sad. Won't you try to read to make your daddy and mummy happy?" The child confronted them with an expression of sullen, stubborn wretchedness, and shook her head. "Just to please us," they wheedled. "You make us *so* sad." Sylvia looked from one mournfully forgiving face to the other and burst into tears.

"Naughty," she sobbed incoherently. "Naughty. Go away." She hated them for being sad, for making her sad. "No, go away, go away," she screamed when they tried to comfort her. She cried inconsolably; but still she wouldn't read.

Paul, on the other hand, was beautifully teachable and plastic. Slowly (for, with his adenoids, he was not a very intelligent boy) but with all the docility that could be desired, he learned to read about the lass on the ass in the grass and other such matters. "Hear how beautifully Paul reads," Martha would say, in the hope of rousing Sylvia to emulation. But Sylvia would only make a contemptuous face and walk out of the room. In the end she taught herself to read secretly, in a couple of weeks. Her parents' pride in the achievement was tempered when they discovered her motives for making the extraordinary effort.

"But what is this dreadful little book?" asked Martha, holding up the copy of "Nick Carter and the Michigan Boulevard Murderers" which she had discovered carefully hidden under Sylvia's winter underclothing. On the cover was a picture of a man being thrown off the roof of a skyscraper by a gorilla.

The child snatched it from her. "It's a lovely book," she retorted, flushing darkly with an anger that was intensified by her sense of guilt.

"Darling," said Martha, beautifully smiling on the surface of her annoyance, "you mustn't snatch like that. Snatching's *ugly.*" "Don't care." "Let me look at it, please." Martha held out her hand. She smiled, but her pale face was heavily determined, her eyes commanded.

Sylvia confronted her, stubbornly she shook her head. "No, I don't want you to."

"Please," begged her mother, more forgivingly and more commandingly than ever, "please." And in the end, with a sudden outburst of tearful rage, Sylvia handed over the book and ran off into the garden. "Sylvia, Sylvia!" her mother called. But the child would not come back. To have stood by while her mother violated the secrets of her private world would have been unbearable.

Owing to his adenoids Paul looked and almost was an imbecile. Without being a Christian Scientist, Martha disbelieved in doctors; more particularly she disliked surgeons, perhaps because they were so expensive. She left Paul's adenoids unextirpated; they grew and festered in his throat. From November to May he was never without a cold, a quinsy, an earache. The winter of 1921 was a particularly bad one for Paul. He began by getting influenza which turned into pneumonia, caught measles during his convalescence and developed at the New Year an infection of the middle ear which threatened to leave him permanently deaf. The doctor peremptorily advised an operation, treatment, a convalescence in Switzerland, at an altitude and in the sun. Martha hesitated to follow his advice. She had come to be so firmly convinced of her poverty that she did not see how she could possibly afford to do what the doctor ordered. In her perplexity she wrote to Judith. Two days later Judith arrived in person.

"But do you want to kill the boy?" she asked her sister fiercely. "Why didn't you get him out of this filthy dank hole weeks ago?"

In a few hours she had arranged everything. Herbert and Martha were to start at once with the boy. They were to travel direct to Lausanne by sleeper. "But surely a sleeper's hardly necessary," objected Martha. "You forget" (she beautifully smiled), "we're simple folk." "I only remember you've got a sick child with you," said Judith, and the sleeper was booked. At Lausanne he was to be operated on. (Expensive reply-paid telegram to the clinic; poor Martha suffered.) And when he was well enough he was to go to a sanatorium at Leysin. (Another telegram, for which Judith paid, however. Martha forgot to give the money back.) Martha and Herbert, meanwhile, were to find a good hotel, where Paul would join them as soon as his treatment was over. And they were to stay at least six months, and preferably a year. Sylvia, meanwhile, was to stay with her aunt in England; that would save Martha a lot of money. Judith would try to find a tenant for the house on the common.

"Talk of savages!" said Judith to her husband. "I've never seen such a little cannibal as Sylvia."

"It's what comes of having vegetarian parents, I suppose."

"Poor little creature!" Judith went on with an indignant pity. "There are times when I'd like to drown Martha, she's such a criminal fool. Bringing those children up without ever letting them go near another child of their own age! It's scandalous! And then talking to them about spirituality and Jesus and *ahimsa* and beauty and goodness knows what! And not wanting them to play stupid games, but be artistic! And always being sweet, even when she's furious! It's dreadful, really dreadful! And so silly. Can't she see that the best way of turning a child into a devil is to try to bring it up as an angel? Ah well . . ." She sighed and was silent, pensively; she herself had had no children and, if the doctors were right, never would have children.

The weeks passed and gradually the little savage was civilized. Her first lessons were lessons in the art of moderation. The food, which at the Bamboroughs' house was good and plentiful, was at the beginning a terrible temptation to a child accustomed to the austerities of the spiritual life.

"There'll be more to-morrow," Judith would say, when the child asked for yet another helping of pudding. "You're not a snake, you know; you can't store up to-day's over-eating for next week's dinners. The only thing you can do with too much food is to be sick with it."

At first Sylvia would insist, would wheedle and whine for more. But luckily, as Judith remarked to her husband, luckily she had a delicate liver. Her aunt's prophecies were only too punctually realized. After three or four bilious attacks Sylvia learned to control her greed. Her next lesson was in obedience. The obedience she was accustomed to give her parents was slow and grudging. Herbert and Martha never, on principle, commanded, but only suggested. It was a system that had almost forced upon the child a habit of saying no, automatically, to whatever proposition was made to her. "No, no, no!" she regularly began, and then gradually suffered herself to be persuaded, reasoned, or moved by the expression of her parents' sadness into a belated and generally grudging acquiescence. Obeying at long last, she felt an obscure resentment against those who had not compelled her to obey at once. Like most children, she would have liked to be relieved compulsorily of responsibility for her own actions; she was angry with her father and mother for forcing her to expend so much will in resisting them, such a quantity of painful emotion in finally letting her will be overcome. It would have been so much simpler if they had insisted from the first, had compelled her to obey at once, and so spared her all her spiritual effort and pain. Darkly and bitterly did she resent the incessant appeal they made to her better feelings. It wasn't fair, it wasn't fair. They had no right to smile and forgive and make her feel a beast, to fill her with sadness by being sad themselves. She felt that they were somehow taking a cruel advantage of her. And perversely, just because she hated their being sad, she deliberately went out of her way to say and do the things that would most sorely distress them. One of her favourite tricks was to threaten to "go and walk across the plank over the sluice." Between the smooth pond and the shallow rippling of the stream, the gentle water became for a moment terrible. Pent in a narrow channel of oozy brickwork six feet of cataract tumbled with unceasing clamour into a black and heaving pool. It was a horrible place. How often her parents had begged her not to play near the sluice! Her threat would make them repeat their recommendations; they would implore her to be reasonable. "No, I won't be reasonable," Sylvia would shout and run off towards the sluice. If, in fact, she never ventured within five yards of the roaring gulf, that was because she was much more terrified for herself than her parents were for her. But she would go as near as she dared for the pleasure (the pleasure which she hated) of hearing her mother mournfully express her sadness at having a little girl so disobedient, so selfishly reckless of danger. She tried the same trick with her Aunt Judith. "I shall go into the woods by myself," she menaced one day, scowling. To her great surprise, instead of begging her to be reasonable and not to distress the grown-ups by disobediently running into danger, Judith only shrugged her shoulders. "Trot along, then, if you want to be a little fool," she said without looking up from her letter. Indignantly, Sylvia trotted; but she was frightened of being alone in the huge wood. Only pride kept her from returning at once. Damp, dirty, tear-stained, and scratched, she was brought back two hours later by a gamekeeper.

"What luck," said Judith to her husband, "what enormous luck that the little idiot should have gone and got herself lost."

The scheme of things was marshalled against the child's delinquency. But Judith did not rely exclusively on the scheme of things to enforce her code; she provided her own sanctions. Obedience had to be prompt, or else there were prompt reprisals. Once Sylvia succeeded in provoking her aunt to real anger. The scene made a profound impression on her. An hour later she crept diffidently and humbly to where her aunt was sitting. "I'm sorry, Aunt Judith," she said, "I'm sorry," and burst into tears. It was the first time she had ever spontaneously asked for forgiveness.

The lessons which profited Sylvia most were those which she learned from other children. After a certain number of rather unsuccessful and occasionally painful experiments she learned to play, to behave as an equal among equals. Hitherto she had lived almost exclusively as a chronological inferior among grown-ups, in a state of unceasing rebellion and guerilla warfare. Her life had been one long *risorgimento* against forgiving Austrians and all too gentle, beautifully smiling Bourbons. With the little Carters from down the road, the little Holmeses from over the way, she was now suddenly required to adapt herself to democracy and parliamentary government. There were difficulties at first; but when in the end the little bandit had acquired the arts of civility, she was unprecedentedly happy. The grown-ups exploited the childish sociability for their own educational ends. Judith got up amateur theatricals; there was a juvenile performance of the *Midsummer Night's Dream*. Mrs. Holmes, who was musical, organized the children's enthusiasm for making a noise into part-singing. Mrs. Carter taught them country dances. In a few months Sylvia had acquired all that passion for the higher life which her mother had been trying to cultivate for years, always in vain. She loved poetry, she loved music, she loved dancing—rather platonically, it was true; for Sylvia was one of those congenitally clumsy and aesthetically insensitive natures whose earnest passion for the arts is always destined to remain unconsummated. She loved ardently, but hopelessly; yet not unhappily, for she was not yet, perhaps, conscious of the hopelessness of her passion. She even loved the arithmetic and geography, the English history and French grammar, which Judith had arranged that she should imbibe, along with the little Carters, from the little Carters' formidable governess.

"Do you remember what she was like when she arrived?" said Judith one day to her husband.

He nodded, comparing in his mind the sullen little savage of nine months before with the gravely, earnestly radiant child who had just left the room.

"I feel like a lion-tamer," Judith went on with a little laugh that covered a great love and a great pride. "But what does one do, Jack, when the lion takes to High Anglicanism? Dolly Carter's being prepared for confirmation and Sylvia's caught the infection." Judith sighed. "I suppose she's already thinking we're both damned."

"She'd be damned herself, if she didn't," Jack answered philosophically. "Much more seriously damned, what's more, because she'd be damned in *this* world. It would be a terrible flaw in her character if she didn't believe in some sort of rigmarole at this age."

"But suppose," said Judith, "she were to go on believing in it?"

Martha, meanwhile, had not been liking Switzerland, perhaps because it suited her, physically, too well. There was something, she felt, rather indecent about enjoying such perfect health as she enjoyed at Leysin. It was difficult, when one was feeling so full of animal spirits, to think very solicitously about suffering humanity and God, about Buddha and the higher life, and what not. She resented the genial care-free selfishness of her own healthy body. Waking periodically to conscience-stricken realizations that she had been thinking of nothing for hours and even days together but the pleasure of sitting in the sun, of breathing the aromatic air beneath the pines, of walking in the high meadows picking flowers and looking at the view, she would launch a campaign of intensive spirituality; but after a little while the sun and the bright eager air were too much for her, and she would relapse once more into a shamefully irresponsible state of mere well-being.

"I shall be glad," she kept saying, "when Paul is quite well again and we can go back to England."

And Herbert would agree with her, partly on principle, because, being resigned to his economic and moral inferiority, he always agreed with her, and partly because he too, though unprecedentedly healthy, found Switzerland spiritually unsatisfying. In a country where everybody wore knickerbockers, an open shirt, and a rucksack there was no superiority, no distinction in being so attired. The scandal of the top-hat would have been the equivalent at Leysin of the scandal of the cross; he felt himself undistinguishedly orthodox.

Fifteen months after their departure the Claxtons were back again in the house on the common. Martha had a cold and a touch of lumbago; deprived of mountain exercise, Herbert was already succumbing to the attacks of his old enemy, chronic constipation. They overflowed with spirituality.

Sylvia also returned to the house on the common, and, for the first weeks, it was Aunt Judith here and Aunt Judith there, at Aunt Judith's we did this, Aunt Judith never made me do that. Beautifully smiling, but with unacknowledged resentment at her heart, "Dearest," Martha would say, "I'm not Aunt Judith." She really hated her sister for having succeeded where she herself had failed. "You've done wonders with Sylvia," she wrote to Judith, "and Herbert and I can never be sufficiently grateful." And she would say the same in conversation to friends. "We can never be grateful enough to her, can we, Herbert?" And Herbert would punctually agree that they could never be grateful enough. But the more grateful to her sister she dutifully and even supererogatively was, the more Martha hated her, the more she resented Judith's success and her influence over the child. True, the influence had been unequivocally good; but it was precisely because it had been so good that Martha resented it. It was unbearable to her that frivolous, unspiritual Judith should have been able to influence the child more happily than she had ever done. She had left Sylvia sullenly ill-mannered and disobedient, full of rebellious hatred for all the things which her parents admired; she returned to find her well behaved, obliging, passionately interested in music and poetry, earnestly preoccupied with the newly discovered problems of religion. It was unbearable. Patiently Martha set to work to undermine her sister's influence on the child. Judith's own work had made the task more easy for her. For thanks to Judith, Sylvia was now malleable. Contact with children of her own age had warmed and softened and sensitized her, had mitigated her savage egotism and opened her up towards external influences. The appeal to her better feelings could now be made with the certainty of evoking a positive, instead of a rebelliously negative, response. Martha made the appeal constantly and with skill. She harped (with a beautiful resignation, of course) on the family's poverty. If Aunt Judith did and permitted many things which were not done and permitted in the house on the common, that was because Aunt Judith was so much better off. She could afford many luxuries which the Claxtons had to do without. "Not that your father and I mind doing without," Martha insisted. "On the contrary. It's really rather a blessing not to be rich. You remember what Jesus said about rich people." Sylvia remembered and was thoughtful. Martha would develop her theme; being able to afford luxuries and actually indulging in them had a certain coarsening, despiritualizing effect. It was so easy to become worldly. The implication, of course, was that Aunt Judith and Uncle Jack had been tainted by worldliness. Poverty had happily preserved the Claxtons from the danger—poverty, and also, Martha insisted, their own meritorious wish. For of course they could have afforded to keep at least one servant, even in these difficult times; but they had preferred to do without, "because, you see, serving is better than being served." Jesus had said that the way of Mary was better than the way of Martha. "But I'm a Martha," said Martha Claxton, "who tries her best to be a Mary too. Martha *and* Mary—that's the best way of all. Practical service *and* contemplation. Your father isn't one of those artists who selfishly detach themselves from all contact with the humble facts of life. He is a creator, but he is not too proud to do the humblest service." Poor Herbert! he couldn't have refused to do the humblest service, if Martha had commanded. Some artists, Martha continued, only thought of immediate success, only worked with an eye to profits and applause. But Sylvia's father, on the contrary, was one who worked without thought of the public, only for the sake of creating truth and beauty.

On Sylvia's mind these and similar discourses, constantly repeated with variations and in every emotional key, had a profound effect. With all the earnestness of puberty she desired to be good and spiritual and disinterested, she longed to sacrifice herself, it hardly mattered to what so long as the cause was noble. Her mother had now provided her with the cause. She gave herself up to it with all the stubborn energy of her nature. How fiercely she practised her piano! With what determination she read through even the dreariest books! She kept a notebook in which she copied out the most inspiring passages of her daily reading; and another in which she recorded her good resolutions, and with them, in an agonized and chronically remorseful diary, her failures to abide by the resolutions, her lapses from grace. "Greed. Promised I'd eat only one greengage. Took four at lunch. None to-morrow. O.G.H.M.T.B.G."

"What does O.G.H.M.T.B.G. mean?" asked Paul maliciously one day.

Sylvia flushed darkly. "You've been reading my diary!" she said. "Oh, you beast, you little beast." And suddenly she threw herself on her brother like a fury. His nose was bleeding when he got away from her. "If you ever look at it again, I'll kill you." And standing there with her clenched teeth and quivering nostrils, her hair flying loose round her pale face, she looked as though she meant it. "I'll kill you," she repeated. Her rage was justified; O.G.H.M.T.B.G. meant "O God, help me to be good."

That evening she came to Paul and asked his pardon.

Aunt Judith and Uncle Jack had been in America for the best part of a year.

"Yes, go; go by all means," Martha had said when Judith's letter came, inviting Sylvia to spend a few days with them in London. "You mustn't miss such a chance of going to the opera and all those lovely concerts."

"But is it quite fair, mother?" said Sylvia hesitatingly. "I mean, I don't want to go and enjoy myself all alone. It seems somehow . . ."

"But you ought to go," Martha interrupted her. She felt so certain of Sylvia now that she had no fears of Judith. "For a musician like you it's a necessity to hear *Parsifal* and the *Magic Flute*. I was meaning to take you myself next year; but now the opportunity has turned up this year, you must take it. Gratefully," she added, with a sweetening of her smile.

Sylvia went. *Parsifal* was like going to church, but much more so. Sylvia listened with a reverent excitement that was, however, interrupted from time to time by the consciousness, irrelevant, ignoble even, but oh, how painful! that her frock, her stockings, her shoes were dreadfully different from those worn by that young girl of her own age, whom she had noticed in the row behind as she came in. And the girl, it had seemed to her, had returned her gaze derisively. Round the Holy Grail there was an explosion of bells and harmonious roaring. She felt ashamed of herself for thinking of such unworthy things in the presence of the mystery. And when, in the entr'acte, Aunt Judith offered her an ice, she refused almost indignantly.

Aunt Judith was surprised. "But you used to love ices so much."

"But not now, Aunt Judith. Not now." An ice in church—what sacrilege! She tried to think about the Grail. A vision of green satin shoes and a lovely mauve artificial flower floated up before her inward eye.

Next day they went shopping. It was a bright cloudless morning of early summer. The windows of the drapers' shops in Oxford Street had blossomed with bright pale colours. The waxen dummies were all preparing to go to Ascot, to Henley, were already thinking of the Eton and Harrow match. The pavements were crowded; an immense blurred noise filled the air like a mist. The scarlet and golden buses looked regal and the sunlight glittered with a rich and oily radiance on the polished flanks of the passing limousines. A little procession of unemployed slouched past with a brass band at their head making joyful music, as though they were only too happy to be unemployed, as though it were a real pleasure to be hungry.

Sylvia had not been in London for nearly two years, and these crowds, this noise, this innumerable wealth of curious and lovely things in every shining window went to her head. She felt even more excited than she had felt at *Parsifal*.

For an hour they wandered through Selfridge's. "And now, Sylvia," said Aunt Judith, when at last she had ticked off every item on her long list, "now you can choose whichever of these frocks you like best." She waved her hand. A display of Summer Modes for Misses surrounded them on every side. Lilac and lavender, primrose and pink and green, blue and mauve, white, flowery, spotted—a sort of herbaceous border of young frocks. "Whichever you like," Aunt Judith repeated. "Or if you'd prefer a frock for the evening . . ."

Green satin shoes and a big mauve flower. The girl had looked derisively. It was unworthy, unworthy.

"No, really, Aunt Judith." She blushed, she stammered. "Really, I don't need a frock. Really."

"All the more reason for having it if you don't need it. Which one?"

"No, really. I don't, I can't . . ." And suddenly, to Aunt Judith's uncomprehending astonishment, she burst into tears.

The year was 1924. The house on the common basked in the soft late-April sunshine. Through the open windows of the drawing-room came the sound of Sylvia's practising. Stubbornly, with a kind of fixed determined fury, she was trying to master Chopin's Valse in D flat. Under her conscientious and insensitive fingers the lilt and languor of the dance rhythm was laboriously sentimental, like the rendering on the piano of a cornet solo outside a public house; and the quick flutter of semi-quavers in the contrasting passages was a flutter, when Sylvia played, of mechanical butterflies, a beating of nickel-plated wings. Again and again she played, again and again. In the little copse on the other side of the stream at the bottom of the garden the birds went about their business undisturbed. On the trees the new small leaves were like the spirits of leaves, almost immaterial, but vivid like little flames at the tip of every twig. Herbert was sitting on a tree stump in the middle of the wood doing those yoga breathing exercises, accompanied by auto-suggestion, which he found so good for his constipation. Closing his right nostril with a long forefinger, he breathed in deeply through his left—in, in, deeply, while he counted four heart-beats. Then through sixteen beats he held his breath and between each beat he said to himself very quickly, "I'm not constipated, I'm not constipated." When he had made the affirmation sixteen times, he closed his left nostril and breathed out, while he counted eight, through his right. After which he began again. The left nostril was the more favoured; for it breathed in with the air a faint cool sweetness of primroses and leaves and damp earth. Near him, on a camp stool, Paul was making a drawing of an oak tree. Art at all costs; beautiful, uplifting, disinterested Art. Paul was bored. Rotten old tree—what was the point of drawing it? All round him the sharp green spikes of the wild hyacinths came thrusting out of the dark mould. One had pierced through a dead leaf and lifted it, transfixed, into the air. A few more days of sunshine and every spike would break out into a blue flower. Next time his mother sent him into Godalming on his bicycle, Paul was thinking, he'd see if he couldn't overcharge her two shillings on the shopping instead of one, as he had done last time. Then he'd be able to buy some chocolate as well as go to the cinema; and perhaps even some cigarettes, though that might be dangerous. . . .

"Well, Paul," said his father, who had taken a sufficient dose of his mystical equivalent of Cascara, "how are you getting on?" He got up from the tree stump and walked across the glade to where the boy was sitting. The passage of time had altered Herbert very little; his explosive beard was still as blond as it had always been, he was as thin as ever, his head showed no signs of going bald. Only his teeth had visibly aged; his smile was discoloured and broken.

"But he really ought to go to a dentist," Judith had insistently urged on her sister, the last time they met.

"He doesn't want to," Martha had replied. "He doesn't really believe in them." But perhaps her own reluctance to part with the necessary number of guineas had something to do with Herbert's lack of faith in dentists. "Besides," she went on, "Herbert hardly notices such merely material, physical things. He lives so much in the noumenal world that he's hardly aware of the phenomenal. Really not aware."

"Well, he jolly well ought to be aware," Judith answered, "that's all I can say." She was indignant.

"How are you getting on?" Herbert repeated, and laid his hand on the boy's shoulder.

"The bark's most horribly difficult to get right," Paul answered in a complainingly angry voice.

"That makes it all the more worth while to get right," said Herbert. "Patience and work—they're the only things. Do you know how a great man once defined genius?" Paul knew very well how a great man had once defined genius; but the definition seemed to him so stupid and such a personal insult to himself, that he did not answer, only grunted. His father bored him, maddeningly. "Genius," Herbert went on, answering his own question, "genius is an infinite capacity for taking pains." At that moment Paul detested his father.

"One two-and three-and One-and two-and three-and . . ." Under Sylvia's fingers the mechanical butterflies continued to flap their metal wings. Her face was set, determined, angry; Herbert's great man would have found genius in her. Behind her stiff determined back her mother came and went with a feather brush in her hand, dusting. Time had thickened and coarsened her; she walked heavily. Her hair had begun to go grey. When she had finished dusting, or rather when she was tired of it, she sat down. Sylvia was laboriously cornet-soloing through the dance rhythm. Martha closed her eyes. "Beautiful, beautiful!" she said, and smiled her most beautiful smile. "You play it beautifully, my darling." She was proud of her daughter. Not merely as a musician; as a human being too. When she thought what trouble she had had with Sylvia in the old days . . . "Beautifully." She rose at last and went upstairs to her bedroom. Unlocking a cupboard, she took out a box of candied fruits and ate several cherries, a plum, and three apricots. Herbert had gone back to his studio and his unfinished picture of "Europe and America at the feet of Mother India." Paul pulled a catapult out of his pocket, fitted a buckshot into the leather pouch and let fly at a nuthatch that was running like a mouse up the oak tree on the other side of the glade. "Hell!" he said as the bird flew away unharmed. But the next shot was more fortunate. There was a spurt of flying feathers, there were two or three little squeaks. Running up Paul found a hen chaffinch lying in the grass. There was blood on the feathers. Thrilling with a kind of disgusted excitement Paul picked up the little body. How warm. It was the first time he had ever killed anything. What a good shot! But there was nobody he could talk to about it. Sylvia was no good: she was almost worse than mother about some things. With a fallen branch he scratched a hole and buried the little corpse, for fear somebody might find it and wonder how it had been killed. They'd be furious if they knew! He went into lunch feeling tremendously pleased with himself. But his face fell as he looked round the table. "Only this beastly cold stuff?"

"Paul, Paul," said his father reproachfully.

"Where's mother?"

"She's not eating to-day," Herbert answered.

"All the same," Paul grumbled under his breath, "she really might have taken the trouble to make something hot for us."

Sylvia meanwhile sat without raising her eyes from her plate of potato salad, eating in silence.

RUDYARD KIPLING / The Man Who Would Be King

"Brother to a Prince and fellow to a beggar if he be found worthy."

THE LAW, as quoted, lays down a fair conduct of life, and one not easy to follow. I have been fellow to a beggar again and again under circumstances which prevented either of us finding out whether the other was worthy. I have still to be brother to a Prince, though I once came near to kinship with what might have been a veritable King and was promised the reversion of a Kingdom—army, law-courts, revenue and policy all complete. But, to-day, I greatly fear that my King is dead, and if I want a crown I must go and hunt it for myself.

The beginning of everything was in a railway train upon the road to Mhow from Ajmir. There had been a Deficit in the Budget, which necessitated traveling, not Second-class, which is only half as dear as First-class, but by Intermediate, which is very awful indeed. There are no cushions in the Intermediate class, and the population are either Intermediate, which is Eurasian, or native, which for a long night journey is nasty, or Loafer, which is amusing though intoxicated. Intermediates do not patronize refreshment-rooms. They carry their food in bundles and pots, and buy sweets from the native sweet-meat-sellers, and drink the roadside water. That is why in the hot weather Intermediates are taken out of the carriages dead, and in all weathers are most properly looked down upon.

My particular Intermediate happened to be empty till I reached Nasirabad, when a huge gentleman in shirt-sleeves entered, and, following the custom of Intermediates, passed the time of day. He was a wanderer and a vagabond like myself, but with an educated taste for whiskey. He told tales of things he had seen and done, of out-of-the-way corners of the Empire into which he had penetrated, and of adventures in which he risked his life for a few days' food. "If India was filled with men like you and me, not knowing more than the crows where they'd get their next day's rations, it isn't seventy millions of revenue the land would be paying—it's seven hundred millions," said he; and as I looked at his mouth and chin I was disposed to agree with him. We talked politics—the politics of Loaferdom that sees things from the underside where the lath and plaster is not smoothed off—and we talked postal arrangements because my friend wanted to send a telegram back from the next station to Ajmir, which is the turning-off place from the Bombay to the Mhow line as you travel westward. My friend had no money beyond eight annas which he wanted for dinner, and I had no money at all, owing to the hitch in the Budget before mentioned. Further, I was going into a wilderness where, though I should resume touch with the Treasury, there were no telegraph offices. I was, therefore, unable to help him in any way.

"We might threaten a Station-master, and make him send a wire on tick," said my friend, "but that'd mean inquiries for you and for me, and I've got my hands full these days. Did you say you are traveling back along this line within any days?"

"Within ten," I said.

"Can't you make it eight?" said he. "Mine is rather urgent business."

"I can send your telegram within ten days if that will serve you," I said.

"I couldn't trust the wire to fetch him now I think of it. It's this way. He leaves Delhi on the 23d for Bombay. That means he'll be running through Ajmir about the night of the 23d."

"But I am going into the Indian Desert," I explained.

"Well and good," said he. "You'll be changing at Marwar Junction to get into Jodhpore territory—you must do that—and he'll be coming through Marwar Junction in the early morning of the 24th by the Bombay Mail. Can you be at Marwar Junction on that time? 'Twon't be inconveniencing you because I know that there's precious few pickings to be got out of these Central India States—even though you pretend to be correspondent of the *Backwoodsman*."

"Have you ever tried that trick?" I asked.

"Again and again, but the Residents find you out, and then you get escorted to the Border before you've time to get your knife into them. But about my friend here. I *must* give him a word o'mouth to tell him what's come to me or else he won't know where to go. I would take it more than kind of you if you was to come out of Central India in time to catch him at Marwar Junction, and say to him:—'He has gone South for the week.' He'll know what that means. He's a big man with a red beard, and a great swell he is. You'll find him sleeping like a gentleman with all his luggage round him in a Second-class compartment. But don't you be afraid. Slip down the window, and say:—'He has gone South for the week,' and he'll tumble. It's only cutting your time of stay in those parts by two days. I ask you as a stranger—going to the West," he said, with emphasis.

"Where have *you* come from?" said I.

"From the East," said he, "and I am hoping that you will give him the message on the Square—for the sake of my Mother as well as your own."

Englishmen are not usually softened by appeals to the memory of their mothers, but for certain reasons, which will be fully apparent, I saw fit to agree.

"It's more than a little matter," said he, "and that's why I ask you to do it—and now I know that I can depend on you doing it. A Second-class carriage at Marwar Junction, and a red-haired man asleep in it. You'll be sure to remember. I get out at the next station, and I must hold on there till he comes or sends me what I want."

"I'll give the message if I catch him," I said, "and for the sake of your Mother as well as mine I'll give you a word of advice. Don't try to run the Central India States just now as the correspondent of the *Backwoodsman*. There's a real one knocking about here, and it might lead to trouble."

"Thank you," said he, simply, "and when will the swine be gone? I can't starve because he's ruining my work. I wanted to get hold of the Degumber Rajah down here about his father's widow, and give him a jump."

"What did he do to his father's widow, then?"

"Filled her up with red pepper and slippered her to death as she hung from a beam. I found that out myself and I'm the only man that would dare going into the State to get hush-money for it. They'll try to poison me, same as they did in Chortumna when I went on the loot there. But you'll give the man at Marwar Junction my message?"

He got out at a little roadside station, and I reflected. I had heard, more than once, of men personating correspondents of newspapers and bleeding small Native States with threats of exposure, but I had never met any of the caste before. They lead a hard life, and generally die with great suddenness. The Native States have a wholesome horror of English newspapers, which may throw light on their peculiar methods of government, and do their best to choke correspondence with champagne, or drive them out of their mind with four-in-hand barouches. They do not understand that nobody cares a straw for the internal administration of

Native States so long as oppression and crime are kept within decent limits, and the ruler is not drugged, drunk, or diseased from one end of the year to the other. Native States were created by Providence in order to supply picturesque scenery, tigers, and tall-writing. They are the dark places of the earth, full of unimaginable cruelty, touching the Railway and the Telegraph on one side, and, on the other, the days of Harun-al-Raschid. When I left the train I did business with divers Kings, and in eight days passed through many changes of life. Sometimes I wore dress-clothes and consorted with Princes and Politicals, drinking from crystal and eating from silver. Sometimes I lay out upon the ground and devoured what I could get, from a plate made of a flapjack, and drank the running water, and slept under the same rug as my servant. It was all in the day's work.

Then I headed for the Great Indian Desert upon the proper date, as I had promised, and the Night Mail set me down at Marwar Junction, where a funny little, happy-go-lucky, native-managed railway runs to Jodhpore. The Bombay Mail from Delhi makes a short halt at Marwar. She arrived as I got in, and I had just time to hurry to her platform and go down the carriages. There was only one Second-class on the train. I slipped the window and looked down upon a flaming red beard, half covered by a railway rug. That was my man, fast asleep, and I dug him gently in the ribs. He woke with a grunt and I saw his face in the light of the lamps. It was a great and shining face.

"Tickets again?" said he.

"No," said I. "I am to tell you that he is gone South for the week. He is gone South for the week!"

The train had begun to move out. The red man rubbed his eyes. "He has gone South for the week," he repeated. "Now that's just like his impidence. Did he say that I was to give you anything?—'Cause I won't."

"He didn't," I said, and dropped away, and watched the red lights die out in the dark. It was horribly cold because the wind was blowing off the sands. I climbed into my own train—not an Intermediate Carriage this time—and went to sleep.

If the man with the beard had given me a rupee I should have kept it as a memento of a rather curious affair. But the consciousness of having done my duty was my only reward.

Later on I reflected that two gentlemen like my friends could not do any good if they foregathered and personated correspondents of newspapers, and might, if they "stuck up" one of the little rat-trap states of Central India or Southern Rajputana, get themselves into serious difficulties. I therefore took some trouble to describe them as accurately as I could remember to people who would be interested in deporting them: and succeeded, so I was later informed, in having them headed back from the Degumber border.

Then I became respectable, and returned to an Office where there were no Kings and no incidents except the daily manufacture of a newspaper. A newspaper office seems to attract every conceivable sort of person, to the prejudice of discipline. Zenana-mission ladies arrive, and beg that the Editor will instantly abandon all his duties to describe a Christian prize-giving in a back-slum of a perfectly inaccessible village; Colonels who have been over-passed for commands sit down and sketch the outline of a series of ten, twelve, or twenty-four leading articles on Seniority *versus* Selection; missionaries wish to know why they have not been permitted to escape from their regular vehicles of abuse and swear at a brother-missionary under special patronage of the editorial We; stranded theatrical companies troop up to explain that they cannot pay for their advertisements, but on their return from New Zealand or Tahiti will do so with interest; inventors of patent punkah-pulling machines, carriage couplings and unbreakable swords and axle-trees call with specifications in their pockets and hours at their disposal; tea-companies enter and elaborate their prospectuses with the office pens; secretaries of ball-committees clamor to have the glories of their last dance more fully expounded; strange ladies rustle in and say:—"I want a hundred lady's cards printed *at once,* please," which is manifestly part of an Editor's duty; and every dissolute ruffian that ever tramped the Grand Trunk Road makes it his business to ask for employment as a proofreader. And, all the time, the telephone-bell is ringing madly, and Kings are being killed on the Continent, and Empires are saying—"You're another," and Mister Gladstone is calling down brimstone upon the British Dominions, and the little black copy-boys are whining, *"kaa-pi-chay-ha-yeh"* (copy wanted) like tired bees, and most of the paper is as blank as Modred's shield.

But that is the amusing part of the year. There are other six months wherein none ever come to call, and the thermometer walks inch by inch up to the top of the glass, and the office is darkened to just above reading-light, and the press machines are red-hot to touch, and nobody writes anything but accounts of amusements in the Hill-stations or obituary notices. Then the telephone becomes a tinkling terror, because it tells you of the sudden deaths of men and women that you knew intimately, and the prickly-heat covers you as with a garment, and you sit down and write:—"A slight increase of sickness is reported from the Khuda Janta Khan District. The outbreak is purely sporadic in its nature, and, thanks to the energetic efforts of the District authorities, is now almost at an end. It is, however, with deep regret we record the death, etc."

Then the sickness really breaks out, and the less recording and reporting the better for the peace of the subscribers. But the Empires and the Kings continue to divert themselves as selfishly as before, and the Foreman thinks that a daily paper really ought to come out once in twenty-four hours, and all the people at the Hill-stations in the middle of their amusements say:—"Good gracious! Why can't the paper be sparkling? I'm sure there's plenty going on up here."

That is the dark half of the moon, and, as the advertisements say, "must be experienced to be appreciated."

It was in that season, and a remarkably evil season, that the paper began running the last issue of the week on Saturday night, which is to say Sunday morning, after the custom of a London paper. This was a great convenience, for immediately after the paper was put to bed, the dawn would lower the thermometer from 96° to almost 84° for half an hour, and in that chill—you have no idea how cold is 84° on the grass until you begin to pray for it—a very tired man could set off to sleep ere the heat roused him.

One Saturday night it was my pleasant duty to put the paper to bed alone. A King or courtier or a courtesan or a community was going to die or get a new Constitution, or do something that was important on the other side of the world, and the paper was to be held open till the latest possible minute in order to catch the telegram. It was a pitchy black night, as stifling as a June night can be, and the *loo,* the red-hot wind from the westward, was booming among the tinder-dry trees and pretending that the rain was on its heels. Now and again a spot of almost boiling water would fall on the dust with the flop of a frog, but all our weary world knew that was only pretence. It was a shade cooler in the press-room than the office, so I sat there, while the type ticked and clicked, and the night-jars hooted at the windows, and the all but naked compositors wiped the sweat from their foreheads and called for water. The thing that was keeping us back, whatever it was, would not come off, though the *loo* dropped and the last type was set, and the whole round earth stood still in the choking heat, with its finger on its lip, to wait the event. I drowsed, and wondered whether the telegraph was a blessing, and whether this dying man, or struggling people, was aware of the inconvenience the delay was causing. There was no special reason beyond the heat and worry to make tension, but, as the clock hands crept up to three o'clock and the machines spun their fly-wheels two and three times to see that all was in order, before I said the word that would set them off, I could have shrieked aloud.

Then the roar and rattle of the wheels shivered the quiet into little bits. I rose to go away, but two men in white clothes stood in front of me. The first one said:—"It's him!" The second said:—"So it is!" And they both laughed almost as loudly as the machinery roared, and mopped their foreheads. "We see there was a light burning across the road and we were sleeping in that ditch there for coolness, and I said to my friend here, The office is open. Let's come along and speak to him as turned us back from the Degumber State," said the smaller of the two. He was the man I had met in the Mhow train, and his fellow was the red-bearded man of Marwar Junction. There was no mistaking the eyebrows of the one or the beard of the other.

I was not pleased, because I wished to go to sleep, not to squabble with loafers. "What do you want?" I asked.

"Half an hour's talk with you cool and comfortable, in the office," said the red-bearded man. "We'd *like* some drink—the Contrack doesn't begin yet, Peachey, so you needn't look—but what we really want is advice. We don't want money. We ask you as a favor, because you did us a bad turn about Degumber."

I led from the press-room to the stifling office with the maps on the walls, and the red-haired man rubbed his hands. "That's something like," said he. "This was the proper shop to come to. Now, Sir, let me introduce to you Brother Peachey Carnehan, that's him, and Brother Daniel Dravot, that is *me,* and the less said about our professions the better, for we have been most things in our time. Soldier, sailor, compositor, photographer, proof-reader, street-preacher, and correspondents of the *Backwoodsman* when we thought the paper wanted one. Carnehan is sober, and so am I. Look at us first and see that's sure. It will save you cutting into my talk. We'll take one of your cigars apiece, and you shall see us light."

I watched the test. The men were absolutely sober, so I gave them each a tepid peg.

"Well *and* good," said Carnehan of the eyebrows, wiping the froth from his moustache. "Let me talk now, Dan. We have been all over India, mostly on foot. We have been boiler-fitters, engine-drivers, petty contractors, and all that, and we have decided that India isn't big enough for such as us."

They certainly were too big for the office. Dravot's beard seemed to fill half the room and Carnehan's shoulders the other half, as they sat on the big table. Carnehan continued:—"The country isn't half worked out because they that governs it won't let you touch it. They spend all their blessed time in governing it, and you can't lift a spade, nor chip a rock, nor look for oil, nor anything like that without all the Government saying—'Leave it alone and let us govern.' Therefore, such as it is, we will let it alone, and go away to some other place where a man isn't crowded and can come to his own. We are not little men, and there is nothing that we are afraid of except Drink, and we have signed a Contrack on that. *Therefore,* we are going away to be Kings."

"Kings in our own right," muttered Dravot.

"Yes, of course," I said. "You've been tramping in the sun, and it's a very warm night, and hadn't you better sleep over the notion? Come to-morrow."

"Neither drunk nor sunstruck," said Dravot. "We have slept over the notion half a year, and require to see Books and Atlases, and we have decided that there is only one place now in the world that two strong men can Sar-a-*whack*. They call it Kafiristan. By my reckoning it's the top right-hand corner of Afghanistan, not more than three hundred miles from Peshawur. They have two and thirty heathen idols there, and we'll be the thirty-third. It's a mountainous country, and the women of those parts are very beautiful."

"But that is provided against in the Contrack," said Carnehan. "Neither Women nor Liqu-or, Daniel."

"And that's all we know, except that no one has gone there, and they fight, and in any place where they fight a man who knows how to drill men can always be a King. We shall go to those parts and say to any King we find—'D' you want to vanquish your foes?' and we will show him how to drill men; for that we know better than anything else. Then we will subvert that King and seize his Throne and establish a Dynasty."

"You'll be cut to pieces before you're fifty miles across the Border," I said. "You have to travel through Afghanistan to get to that country. It's one mass of mountains and peaks and glaciers, and no Englishman has been through it. The people are utter brutes, and even if you reached them you couldn't do anything."

"That's more like it," said Carnehan. "If you could think us a little more mad we would be more pleased. We have come to you to know about this country, to read a book about it, and to be shown maps. We want you to tell us that we are fools and to show us your books." He turned to the bookcases.

"Are you at all in earnest?" I said.

"A little," said Dravot, sweetly. "As big a map as you have got, even if it's all blank where Kafiristan is, and any books you've got. We can read, though we aren't very educated."

I uncased the big thirty-two-miles-to-the-inch-map of India, and two smaller Frontier maps, hauled down volume INFKAN of the *Encyclopædia Britannica,* and the men consulted them.

"See here!" said Dravot, his thumb on the map. "Up to Jagdallak, Peachey and me know the road. We was there with Roberts's Army. We'll have to turn off to the right at Jagdallak through Laghmann territory. Then we get among the hills—fourteen thousand feet—fifteen thousand—it will be cold work there, but it don't look very far on the map."

I handed him Wood on the *Sources of the Oxus*. Carnehan was deep in the *Encyclopædia.*

"They're a mixed lot," said Dravot, reflectively; "and it won't help us to know the names of their tribes. The more tribes the more they'll fight, and the better for us. From Jagdallak to Ashang. H'mm!"

"But all the information about the country is as sketchy and inaccurate as can be," I protested. "No one knows anything about it really. Here's the file of the *United Services' Institute.* Read what Bellew says."

"Blow Bellew!" said Carnehan. "Dan, they're an all-fired lot of heathens, but this book here says they think they're related to us English."

I smoked while the men pored over *Raverty, Wood,* the maps and the *Encyclopædia.*

"There is no use your waiting," said Dravot, politely. "It's about four o'clock now. We'll go before six o'clock if you want to sleep, and we won't steal any of the papers. Don't you sit up. We're two harmless lunatics, and if you come, to-morrow evening, down to the Serai we'll say good-bye to you."

"You *are* two fools," I answered. "You'll be turned back at the Frontier or cut up the minute you set foot in Afghanistan. Do you want any money or a recommendation down-country? I can help you to the chance of work next week."

"Next week we shall be hard at work ourselves, thank you," said Dravot. "It isn't so easy being a King as it looks. When we've got our Kingdom in going order we'll let you know, and you can come up and help us to govern it."

"Would two lunatics make a Contrack like that?" said Carnehan, with subdued pride, showing me a greasy half-sheet of notepaper on which was written the following. I copied it, then and there, as a curiosity:

This Contrack between me and you persuing witnesseth in the name of God—Amen and so forth.

(*One*) *That me and you will settle this matter together:* i.e., *to be Kings of Kafiristan.*

(*Two*) *That you and me will not, while this matter is being settled, look at any Liquor, nor any Woman, black, white or brown, so as to get mixed up with one or the other harmful.*

(*Three*) *That we conduct ourselves with dignity and dis-*

cretion, and if one of us gets into trouble the other will stay by him.

Signed by you and me this day.

Peachey Taliaferro Carnehan.
Daniel Dravot.
Both Gentlemen at Large.

"There was no need for the last article," said Carnehan, blushing modestly; "but it looks regular. Now you know the sort of men that loafers are—we *are* loafers, Dan, until we get out of India—and *do* you think that we would sign a Contrack like that unless we was in earnest? We have kept away from the two things that make life worth having."

"You won't enjoy your lives much longer if you are going to try this idiotic adventure. Don't set the office on fire," I said, "and go away before nine o'clock."

I left them still poring over the maps and making notes on the back of the "Contrack." "Be sure to come down to the Serai to-morrow," were their parting words.

The Kumharsen Serai is the great four-square sink of humanity where the strings of camels and horses from the North load and unload. All the nationalities of Central Asia may be found there, and most of the folk of India proper. Balkh and Bokhara there meet Bengal and Bombay, and try to draw eye-teeth. You can buy ponies, turquoises, Persian pussy-cats, saddle-bags, fat-tailed sheep and musk in the Kumharsen Serai, and get many strange things for nothing. In the afternoon I went down there to see whether my friends intended to keep their word or were lying about drunk.

A priest attired in fragments of ribbons and rags stalked up to me, gravely twisting a child's paper whirligig. Behind him was his servant bending under the load of a crate of mud toys. The two were loading up two camels, and the inhabitants of the Serai watched them with shrieks of laughter.

"The priest is mad," said a horse-dealer to me. "He is going up to Kabul to sell toys to the Amir. He will either be raised to honor or have his head cut off. He came in here this morning and has been behaving madly ever since."

"The witless are under the protection of God," stammered a flat-cheeked Usbeg in broken Hindi. "They foretell future events."

"Would they could have foretold that my caravan would have been cut up by the Shinwaris almost within shadow of the Pass!" grunted the Eusufzai agent of a Rajputana trading-house whose goods had been feloniously diverted into the hands of other robbers just across the Border, and whose misfortunes were the laughing-stock of the bazaar. "Ohé, priest, whence come you and whither do you go?"

"From Roum have I come," shouted the priest, waving his whirligig; "from Roum, blown by the breath of a hundred devils across the sea! O thieves, robbers, liars, the blessing of Pir Khan on pigs, dogs, and perjurers! Who will take the Protected of God to the North to sell charms that are never still to the Amir? The camels shall not gall, the sons shall not fall sick, and the wives shall remain faithful while they are away, of the men who give me place in their caravan. Who will assist me to slipper the King of the Roos with a golden slipper with a silver heel? The protection of Pir Khan be upon his labors!" He spread out the skirts of his gaberdine and pirouetted between the lines of tethered horses.

"There starts a caravan from Peshawur to Kabul in twenty days, *Huzrut,*" said the Eusufzai trader. "My camels go therewith. Do thou also go and bring us good-luck."

"I will go even now!" shouted the priest. "I will depart upon my winged camels, and be at Peshawur in a day! Ho! Hazar Mir Khan," he yelled to his servant, "drive out the camels, but let me first mount my own."

He leaped on the back of his beast as it knelt, and, turning round to me, cried:—"Come thou also, Sahib, a little along the road and I will sell thee a charm—an amulet that shall make thee King of Kafiristan."

Then the light broke upon me and I followed the two camels out of the Serai till we reached open road and the priest halted.

"What d' you think o' that?" said he in English. "Carnehan can't talk their patter, so I've made him my servant. He makes a handsome servant. 'Tisn't for nothing that I've been knocking about the country for fourteen years. Didn't I do that talk neat? We'll hitch on to a caravan at Peshawur till we get to Jagdallak, and then we'll see if we can get donkeys for our camels, and strike into Kafiristan. Whirligigs for the Amir, O Lor! Put your hand under the camel-bags and tell me what you feel."

I felt the butt of a Martini, and another and another.

"Twenty of 'em," said Dravot, placidly. "Twenty of 'em, and ammunition to correspond, under the whirligigs and the mud dolls."

"Heaven help you if you are caught with those things!" I said. "A Martini is worth her weight in silver among the Pathans."

"Fifteen hundred rupees of capital—every rupee we could beg, borrow, or steal—are invested on these two camels," said Dravot. "We won't get caught. We're going through the Khaiber with a regular caravan. Who'd touch a poor mad priest?"

"Have you got everything you want?" I asked, overcome with astonishment.

"Not yet, but we shall soon. Give us a memento of your kindness, Brother. You did me a service yesterday, and that time in Marwar. Half my Kingdom shall you have, as the saying is." I slipped a small charm compass from my watch-chain and handed it up to the priest.

"Good-bye," said Dravot, giving me a hand cautiously. "It's the last time we'll shake hands with an Englishman these many days. Shake hands with him, Carnehan," he cried, as the second camel passed me.

Carnehan leaned down and shook hands. Then the camels passed away along the dusty road, and I was left alone to wonder. My eye could detect no failure in the disguises. The scene in Serai attested that they were complete to the native mind. There was just the chance, therefore, that Carnehan and Dravot would be able to wander through Afghanistan without detection. But, beyond, they would find death, certain and awful death.

Ten days later a native friend of mine, giving me the news of the day from Peshawur, wound up his letter with:—"There has been much laughter here on account of a certain mad priest who is going in his estimation to sell petty gauds and insignificant trinkets which he ascribes as great charms to H. H. the Amir of Bokhara. He passed through Peshawur and associated himself to the Second Summer caravan that goes to Kabul. The merchants are pleased because through superstition they imagine that such mad fellows bring good-fortune."

The two, then, were beyond the Border. I would have prayed for them, but, that night, a real King died in Europe and demanded an obituary notice.

The wheel of the world swings through the same phases again and again. Summer passed and winter thereafter, and came and passed again. The daily paper continued and I with it, and upon the third summer there fell a hot night, a night-issue, and a strained waiting for something to be telegraphed from the other side of the world, exactly as had happened before. A few great men had died in the past two years, the machines worked with more clatter, and some of the trees in the Office garden were a few feet taller. But that was all the difference.

I passed over to the press-room, and went through just such a scene as I have already described. The nervous tension was stronger than it had been two years before, and I felt the heat more acutely. At three o'clock I cried, "Print off," and turned to go, when there crept to my chair what was left of a man. He was bent into a circle, his head was sunk between his shoulders, and he moved his feet one over the other like a bear. I could hardly see whether he walked or crawled—this rag-wrapped, whining cripple who addressed me by name, crying that he was come back, "Can you give me a drink?" he whimpered. "For the Lord's sake, give me a drink!"

I went back to the office, the man following with groans of pain, and I turned up the lamp.

"Don't you know me?" he gasped, dropping into a chair, and he turned his drawn face, surmounted by a shock of grey hair, to the light.

I looked at him intently. Once before had I seen eyebrows that met over the nose in an inch-broad black band, but for the life of me I could not tell where.

"I don't know you," I said, handing him the whiskey. "What can I do for you?"

He took a gulp of the spirit raw, and shivered in spite of the suffocating heat.

"I've come back," he repeated; "and I was the King of Kafiristan—me and Dravot—crowned Kings we was! In this office we settled it—you setting there and giving us the books. I am Peachey—Peachey Taliaferro Carnehan, and you've been setting here ever since—O Lord!"

I was more than a little astonished, and expressed my feelings accordingly.

"It's true," said Carnehan, with a dry cackle, nursing his feet, which were wrapped in rags. "True as gospel. Kings we were, with crowns upon our heads—me and Dravot—poor Dan—oh, poor, poor Dan, that would never take advice, not though I begged of him!"

"Take the whiskey," I said, "and take your own time. Tell me all you can recollect of everything from beginning to end. You got across the border on your camels, Dravot dressed as a mad priest and you his servant. Do you remember that?"

"I ain't mad—yet, but I shall be that way soon. Of course I remember. Keep looking at me, or maybe my words will go all to pieces. Keep looking at me in my eyes and don't say anything."

I leaned forward and looked into his face as steadily as I could. He dropped one hand upon the table and I grasped it by the wrist. It was twisted like a bird's claw, and upon the back was a ragged, red, diamond-shaped scar.

"No, don't look there. Look at *me*," said Carnehan.

"That comes afterward, but for the Lord's sake don't distrack me. We left with that caravan, me and Dravot playing all sorts of antics to amuse the people we were with. Dravot used to make us laugh in the evenings when all the people were cooking their dinners—cooking their dinners, and . . . what did they do then? They lit little fires with sparks that went into Dravot's beard, and we all laughed—fit to die. Little red fires they was, going into Dravot's big red beard—so funny." His eyes left mine and he smiled foolishly.

"You went as far as Jagdallak with that caravan," I said, at a venture, "after you had lit those fires. To Jagdallak, where you turned off to try to get into Kafiristan."

"No, we didn't neither. What are you talking about? We turned off before Jagdallak, because we heard the roads was good. But they wasn't good enough for our two camels—mine and Dravot's. When we left the caravan, Dravot took off all his clothes and mine too, and said we would be heathen, because the Kafirs didn't allow Mohammedans to talk to them. So we dressed betwixt and between, and such a sight as Daniel Dravot I never saw yet nor expect to see again. He burned half his beard, and slung a sheep-skin over his shoulder, and shaved his head into patterns. He shaved mine, too, and made me wear outrageous things to look like a heathen. That was in a most mountainous country, and our camels couldn't go along any more because of the mountains. They were tall and black, and coming home I saw them fight like wild goats—there are lots of goats in Kafiristan. And these mountains, they never keep still, no more than the goats. Always fighting they are, and don't let you sleep at night."

"Take some more whiskey," I said, very slowly. "What did you and Daniel Dravot do when the camels could go no further because of the rough roads that led into Kafiristan?"

"What did which do? There was a party called Peachey Taliaferro Carnehan that was with Dravot. Shall I tell you about him? He died out there in the cold. Slap from the bridge fell old Peachey, turning and twisting in the air like a penny whirligig that you can sell to the Amir.—No; they was two for three ha'pence, those whirligigs, or I am much mistaken and woful sore. And then these camels were no use, and Peachey said to Dravot—'For the Lord's sake, let's get out of this before our heads are chopped off,' and with that they killed the camels all among the mountains, not having anything in particular to eat, but first they took off the boxes with the guns and the ammunition, till two men came along driving four mules. Dravot up and dances in front of them, singing,—'Sell me four mules.' Says the first man,—'If you are rich enough to buy, you are rich enough to rob'; but before ever he could put his hand to his knife, Dravot breaks his neck over his knee, and the other party runs away. So Carnehan loaded the mules with the rifles that was taken off the camels, and together we starts forward into those bitter cold mountainous parts, and never a road broader than the back of your hand."

He paused for a moment, while I asked him if he could remember the nature of the country through which he had journeyed.

"I am telling you as straight as I can, but my head isn't as good as it might be. They drove nails through it to make me hear better how Dravot died. The country was mountainous and the mules were most contrary, and the inhabitants was dispersed and solitary. They went up and up, and down and down, and that other party, Carnehan, was imploring of Dravot not to sing and whistle so loud, for fear of bringing down the tremenjus avalanches. But Dravot says that if a King couldn't sing it wasn't worth being King, and whacked the mules over the rump, and never took no heed for ten cold days. We came to a big level valley all among the mountains, and the mules were near dead, so we killed them, not having anything in special for them or us to eat. We sat upon the boxes, and played odds and even with the cartridges that was jolted out.

"Then ten men with bows and arrows ran down that valley, chasing twenty men with bows and arrows, and the row was tremenjus. They was fair men—fairer than you or me—with yellow hair and remarkable well built. Says Dravot, unpacking the guns —'This is the beginning of the business. We'll fight for the ten men,' and with that he fires two rifles at the twenty men, and drops one of them at two hundred yards from the rock where we was sitting. The other men began to run but Carnehan and Dravot sits on the boxes picking them off at all ranges, up and down the valley. Then we goes up to the ten men that had run across the snow too, and they fires a footy little arrow at us. Dravot he shoots above their heads and they all falls down flat. Then he walks over them and kicks them, and then he lifts them up and shakes hands all round to make them friendly like. He calls them and gives them the boxes to carry, and waves his hand for all the world as though he was King already. They takes the boxes and him across the valley and up the hill into a pine wood on the top, where there was half a dozen big stone idols. Dravot he goes to the biggest —a fellow they call Imbra—and lays a rifle and cartridge at his feet, rubbing his nose respectful with his own nose, patting him on the head, and saluting in front of it. He turns round to the men and nods his head, and says,—'That's all right. I'm in the know too, and all these old jim-jams are my friends.' Then he opens his mouth and points down it, and when the first man brings his food, he says—'No'; and when the second man brings him food, he says 'No'; but when one of the old priests and the boss of the village brings him food, he says—'Yes'; very haughty, and eats it slow. That was how we came to our first village, without any trouble, just as though we had tumbled from the skies. But we tumbled from one of those damned rope-bridges, you see, and you couldn't expect a man to laugh much after that."

"Take some more whiskey and go on," I said. "That was the first village you came into. How did you get to be King?"

"I wasn't King," said Carnehan. "Dravot he was the King, and a handsome man he looked with the gold crown on his head and all. Him and the other party stayed in that village, and every morning Dravot sat by the side of old Imbra, and the people came and worshipped. That was Dravot's order. Then a lot of men came into the valley, and Carnehan and Dravot picks them off with the rifles before they knew where they was, and runs down into the valley and up again the other side, and finds another village, same as the first one, and the people all falls down flat on their faces, and Dravot says,—'Now what is the trouble between you two villages?' and the people points to a woman, as fair as you or me, that was carried off, and Dravot takes her back to the first village and counts up the dead—eight there was. For each dead man Dravot pours a little milk on the ground and waves his arms like a whirligig and 'That's all right,' says he. Then he and Carnehan takes the big boss of each village by the arm and walks them down into the valley, and shows them how to scratch a line with a spear right down the valley, and gives each a sod of turf from both sides o' the line. Then all the people comes down and shouts like the devil and all, and Dravot says,—'Go and dig the land, and be fruitful and multiply,' which they did, though they didn't understand. Then we asks the names of things in their lingo—bread and water and fire and idols and such, and Dravot leads the priest of each village up to the idol, and says he must sit there and judge the people, and if anything goes wrong he is to be shot.

"Next week they was all turning up the land in the valley as quiet as bees and much prettier, and the priests heard all the complaints and told Dravot in dumb show what it was about. 'That's just the beginning,' said Dravot. 'They think we're Gods.' He and Carnehan picks out twenty good men and shows them how to click off a rifle, and form fours, and advance in line, and they was very pleased to do so, and clever to see the hang of it. Then he takes out his pipe and his baccy-pouch and leaves one at one village and one at the other, and off we two goes to see what was to be done in the next valley. That was all rock, and there was a little village there, and Carnehan says,—'Send 'em to the old valley to plant,' and takes 'em there and gives 'em some land that wasn't took before. They was a poor lot, and we blooded 'em with a kid before letting 'em into the new Kingdom. That was to impress the people, and then they settled down quiet, and Carnehan went back to Dravot who had got into another valley, all snow and ice and most mountainous. There was no people there and the Army got afraid, so Dravot shoots one of them, and goes on till he finds some people in a village, and the Army explains that unless the people wants to be killed they had better not shoot their little matchlocks; for they had matchlocks. We make friends with the priest and I stays there alone with two of the Army, teaching the men how to drill, and a thundering big Chief comes across the snow with kettle-drums and horns twanging, because he heard there was a new God kicking about. Carnehan sights for the brown of the men half a mile across the snow and wings one of them. Then he sends a message to the Chief that, unless he wished to be killed, he must come and shake hands with me and leave his arms behind. The chief comes alone first, and Carnehan shakes hands with him and whirls his arms about, same as Dravot used, and very much surprised that Chief was, and strokes my eyebrows. Then Carnehan goes alone to the Chief, and asks him in dumb show if he had an enemy he hated. 'I have,' says the Chief. So Carnehan weeds out the pick of his men, and sets the two of the Army to show them drill and at the end of two weeks the men can manœuvre about as well as Volunteers. So he marches with the Chief to a great big plain on the top of a mountain, and the Chief's men rushes into a village and takes it; we three Martinis firing into the brown of the enemy. So we took that village too, and I gives the Chief a rag from my coat and says, 'Occupy till I come': which was scriptural. By way of a reminder, when me and the Army was eighteen hundred yards away, I drops a bullet near him standing on the snow, and all the people falls flat on their faces. Then I sends a letter to Dravot, wherever he be by land or by sea."

At the risk of throwing the creature out of train I interrupted, "How could you write a letter up yonder?"

"The letter? Oh!—The letter! Keep looking at me between the eyes, please. It was a string-talk letter, that we'd learned the way of it from a blind beggar in the Punjab."

I remember that there had once come to the office a blind man with a knotted twig and a piece of string which he wound round the twig according to some cypher of his own. He could, after the lapse of days or hours, repeat the sentence which he had reeled up. He had reduced the alphabet to eleven primitive sounds; and tried to teach me his method, but failed.

"I sent that letter to Dravot," said Carnehan; "and told him to come back because this Kingdom was growing too big for me to handle, and then I struck for the first valley, to see how the priests were working. They called the village we took along with the Chief, Bashkai, and the first village we took, Er-Heb. The priests at Er-Heb were doing all right, but they had a lot of pending cases about land to show me, and some men from another village had been firing arrows at night. I went out and looked for that village and fired four rounds at it from a thousand yards. That used all the cartridges I cared to spend, and I waited for Dravot, who had been away two or three months, and I kept my people quiet.

"One morning I heard the devil's own noise of drums and horns, and Dan Dravot marches down the hill with his Army and a tail of hundreds of men, and, which was the most amazing—a great gold crown on his head. 'My Gord, Carnehan,' says Daniel, 'this is a tremendjus business, and we've got the whole country as far as it's worth having. I am the son of Alexander by Queen Semiramis, and you're my younger brother and a God too! It's the biggest thing we've ever seen. I've been marching and fighting for six weeks with the Army, and every footy little village for fifty miles has come in rejoiceful; and more than that, I've got the key of the whole show, as you'll see, and I've got a crown for you! I told 'em to make two of 'em at a place called Shu, where the gold lies in the rock like suet in mutton. Gold I've seen, and turquoise I've kicked out of the cliffs, and there's garnets in the sands of the river, and here's a chunk of amber that a man brought me. Call up all the priests and, here, take your crown.'

"One of the men opens a black hair bag and I slips the crown on. It was too small and too heavy, but I wore it for the glory. Hammered gold it was—five pound weight, like a hoop of a barrel.

" 'Peachey,' says Dravot, 'we don't want to fight no more. The Craft's the trick so help me!' and he brings forward that same Chief that I left at Bashkai—Billy Fish we called him afterward, because he was so like Billy Fish that drove the big tank-engine at Mach on the Bolan in the old days. 'Shake hands with him,' says Dravot, and I shook hands and nearly dropped, for Billy Fish gave me the Grip. I said nothing, but tried him with the Fellow Craft Grip. He answers, all right, and I tried the Master's Grip, but that was a slip. 'A Fellow Craft he is!' I says to Dan. 'Does he know the word?' 'He does,' says Dan, 'and all the priests know. It's a miracle! The Chiefs and the priests can work a Fellow Craft Lodge in a way that's very like ours, and they've cut the marks on the rocks, but they don't know the Third Degree, and they've come to find out. It's Gord's Truth. I've known these long years that the Afghans knew up to the Fellow Craft Degree, but this is a miracle. A God and a Grand-Master of the Craft am I, and a Lodge in the Third Degree I will open, and we'll raise the head priests and the Chiefs of the villages.'

" 'It's against all the law,' I says, 'holding a Lodge without warrant from any one; and we never held office in any Lodge.'

" 'It's a master-stroke of policy,' says Dravot. 'It means running the country as easy as a four-wheeled bogy on a down grade. We can't stop to inquire now, or they'll turn against us. I've forty chiefs at my heel, and passed and raised according to their merit they shall be. Billet these men on the villages and see that we run up a Lodge of some kind. The temple of Imbra will do for the Lodge-room. The women must make aprons as you show them. I'll hold a levee of Chiefs to-night and Lodge to-morrow."

"I was fair run off my legs, but I wasn't such a fool as not to see what a pull this Craft business gave us. I showed the priests' families how to make aprons of the degrees, but for Dravot's apron the blue border and marks was made of turquoise lumps on white hide, not cloth. We took a great square stone in the temple for the Master's chair, and little stones for the officer's chairs, and painted the black pavement with white squares, and did what we could to make things regular.

"At the levee which was held that night on the hillside with big bonfires, Dravot gives out that him and me were Gods and sons of Alexander, and Past Grand-Masters in the Craft, and was come to make Kafiristan a country where every man should eat in peace and drink in quiet, and specially obey us. Then the Chiefs come round to shake hands, and they was so hairy and white and fair it was just shaking hands with old friends. We gave them names according as they was like men we had known in India—Billy Fish, Holly Dilworth, Pikky Kergan that was Bazar-master when I was at Mhow, and so on and so on.

"The *most* amazing miracle was at Lodge next night. One of the old priests was watching us continuous, and I felt uneasy, for I knew we'd have to fudge the Ritual, and I didn't know what the men knew. The old priest was a stranger come in from beyond the village of Bashkai. The minute Dravot puts on the Master's apron that the girls had made for him, the priest fetches a whoop and a howl, and tries to overturn the stone that Dravot was sitting on. 'It's all up now,' I says. 'That comes of meddling with the Craft without warrant!' Dravot never winked an eye, not when ten priests took and tilted over the Grand-Master's chair—which was to say the stone of Imbra. The priest begins rubbing the bot-end of it to clear away the black dirt, and presently he shows all the other priests the Master's Mark, same as was on Dravot's apron, cut into the stone. Not even the priests of the temple of Imbra knew it was there. The old chap falls flat on his face at Dravot's feet and kisses 'em. 'Luck again,' says Dravot, across the Lodge to me, 'they say it's the missing Mark that no one could understand the why of. We're more than safe now.' Then he bangs the butt of his gun for a gavel and says:—'By virtue of the authority vested in me by my own right hand and the help of Peachey, I declare myself Grand-Master of all Freemasonry in Kafiristan in this the Mother Lodge o' the country, and King of Kafiristan equally with Peachey!' At that he puts on his crown and I puts on mine—I was doing Senior Warden—and we opens the Lodge in most ample form. It was an amazing miracle! The priests moved in Lodge through the first two degrees almost without telling, as if the memory was coming back to them. After that, Peachey and Dravot raised such as was worthy—high priests and Chiefs of far-off villages. Billy Fish was the first, and I can tell you we scared the soul out of him. It was not in any way according to Ritual, but it served our turn. We didn't raise more than ten of the biggest men because we didn't want to make the Degree common. And they was clamoring to be raised.

" 'In another six months,' says Dravot, 'we'll hold another Communication and see how you are working.' Then he asks them about their villages, and learns that they was fighting one against the other and were fair sick and tired of it. And when they wasn't doing that they was fighting with the Mohammedans. 'You can fight those when they come into our country,' says Dravot. 'Tell off every tenth man of your tribes for a Frontier guard, and send two hundred at a time to this valley to be drilled. Nobody is going to be shot or speared any more so long as he does well, and I know that you won't cheat me because you're white people—sons of Alexander—and not like common, black Mohammedans. You are my people and by God,' says he, running off into English at the end— 'I'll make a damned fine Nation of you, or I'll die in the making!'

"I can't tell all we did for the next six months because Dravot did a lot I couldn't see the hang of, and he learned their lingo in a way I never could. My work was to help the people plough, and now and again go out with some of the Army and see what the other villages were doing, and make 'em throw rope-bridges across the ravines which cut up the country horrid. Dravot was very kind to me, but when he walked up and down in the pine wood pulling that bloody red beard of his with both fists I knew he was thinking plans I could not advise him about, and I just waited for orders.

"But Dravot never showed me disrespect before the people. They were afraid of me and the Army, but they loved Dan. He was the best of friends with the priests and the Chiefs; but any one could come across the hills with a complaint and Dravot would hear him out fair, and call four priests together and say what was to be done. He used to call in Billy Fish from Bashkai, and Pikky Kergan from Shu, and an old Chief we called Kafuzelum—it was like enough to his real name—and hold councils with 'em when there was any fighting to be done in small villages. That was his Council of War, and the four priests of Bashkai, Shu, Khawak, and Madora was his Privy Council. Between the lot of 'em they send me, with forty men and twenty rifles, and sixty men carrying turquoises, into the Ghorband country to buy those hand-made Martini rifles, that come out of the Amir's workshops at Kabul, from one of the Amir's Herati regiments that would have sold the very teeth out of their mouths for turquoises.

"I stayed in Ghorband a month, and gave the Governor there the pick of my baskets for hush-money, and bribed the Colonel of the regiment some more, and, between the two and the tribes-people, we got more than a hundred hand-made Martinis, a hundred good Kohat Jezails, that'll throw to six hundred yards, and forty man-loads of very bad ammunition for the rifles. I came back with what I had, and distributed 'em among the men that the Chiefs sent to me to drill. Dravot was too busy to attend to those things, but the old Army that we first made helped me, and we turned out five hundred men that could drill, and two hundred that knew how to hold arms pretty straight. Even those cork-screwed, hand-made guns was a miracle to them. Dravot talked big about powder-shops and factories, walking up and down in the pine wood when the winter was coming on.

" 'I won't make a Nation,' says he, 'I'll make an Empire! These men aren't niggers; they're English! Look at their eyes—look at their mouths. Look at the way they stand up. They sit on chairs in their own houses. They're the Lost Tribes, or something like it, and they've grown to be English. I'll take a census in the spring if the priests don't get frightened. There must be a fair two million of 'em in these hills. The villages are full o' little children. Two million people—two hundred and fifty thousand fighting men—and all English! They only want the rifles and a little drilling. Two hundred and fifty thousand men, ready to cut in on Russia's right flank when she tries for India! Peachey, man,' he says, chewing his beard in great hunks, 'we shall be Emperors—Emperors of the Earth! Rajah Brooke will be a suckling to us. I'll treat with the Viceroy on equal terms. I'll ask him to send me twelve picked English—twelve that I know of—to help us govern a bit. There's Mackray, Sergeant-pensioner at Segowli—many's the good dinner he's given me, and his wife a pair of trousers. There's Donkin, the Warder of Tounghoo Jail; there's hundreds that I could lay my hand on if I was in India. The Viceroy shall do it for me. I'll send a man through in the spring for those men, and I'll write for a dispensation from the Grand Lodge for what I've done as Grand-Master. That—and all the Sniders that'll be thrown out when the native troops in India take up the Martini. They'll be worn smooth, but they'll do for fighting in these hills. Twelve English, a hundred thousand Sniders run through the Amir's country in driblets—I'd be content with twenty thousand in one year—and we'd be an Empire. When everything was shipshape, I'd hand over the crown—this crown I'm wearing now—to Queen Victoria on my knees, and she'd say: "Rise up, Sir Daniel Dravot." Oh, it's big! It's big, I tell you! But there's so much to be done in every place—Bashkai, Khawak, Shu, and everywhere else.'

" 'What is it?' I says. 'There are no more men coming in to be drilled this autumn. Look at those fat, black clouds. They're bringing the snow.'

" 'It isn't that,' says Daniel, putting his hand very hard on my shoulder; 'and I don't wish to say anything that's against you, for no other living man would have followed me and made me what I am as you have done. You're a first-class Commander-in-Chief, and the people know you; but—it's a big country, and somehow you can't help me, Peachey, in the way I want to be helped.'

" 'Go to your blasted priests then!' I said, and I was sorry when I made that remark, but it did hurt me sore to find Daniel talking so superior when I'd drilled all the men, and done all he told me.

" 'Don't let's quarrel, Peachey,' says Daniel, without cursing. 'You're a King too, and the half of this Kingdom is yours; but can't you see, Peachey, we want cleverer men than us now—three or four of 'em, that we can scatter about for our Deputies. It's a hugeous great State, and I can't always tell the right thing to do, and I haven't time for all I want to do, and here's the winter coming on and all.' He put half his beard into his mouth, and it was as red as the gold of his crown.

" 'I'm sorry, Daniel,' says I. 'I've done all I could. I've drilled the men and shown the people how to stack their oats better; and I've brought in those tinware rifles from Ghorband —but I know what you're driving at. I take it Kings always feel oppressed that way.'

" 'There's another thing too,' says Dravot, walking up and down. 'The winter's coming and these people won't be giving much trouble, and if they do we can't move about. I want a wife.'

" 'For God's sake leave the women alone!' I says. 'We've both got all the work we can, though I *am* a fool. Remember the Contrack, and keep clear o' women.'

" 'The Contrack only lasted till such time as we was Kings; and Kings we have been these months past,' says Dravot, weighing his crown in his hand. 'You go get a wife too, Peachey—a nice, strappin', plump girl that'll keep you warm in the winter. They're prettier than English girls, and we can take the pick of 'em. Boil 'em once or twice in hot water, and they'll come as fair as chicken and ham.'

" 'Don't tempt me!' I says. 'I will not have any dealings with a woman not till we are a dam' side more settled than we are now. I've been doing the work o' two men, and you've been doing the work o' three. Let's lie off a bit, and see if we can get some better tobacco from Afghan country and run in some good liquor; but no women.'

" 'Who's talking o' *women?*' says Dravot. 'I said *wife*—a Queen to breed a King's son for the King. A Queen out of the strongest tribe, that'll make them your blood-brothers, and that'll lie by your side and tell you all the people thinks about you and their own affairs. That's what I want.'

" 'Do you remember that Bengali woman I kept at Mogul Serai when I was a plate-layer?' says I. 'A fat lot o' good she was to me. She taught me the lingo and one or two other things; but what happened? She ran away with the Station Master's servant and half my month's pay. Then she turned up at Dadur Junction in tow of a half-caste, and had the impidence to say I was her husband—all among the drivers in the running-shed!'

" 'We've done with that,' says Dravot. 'These women are whiter than you or me, and a Queen I will have for the winter months.'

" 'For the last time o' asking, Dan, do *not,*' I says. 'It'll only bring us harm. The Bible says that Kings ain't to waste their strength on women, 'specially when they've got a new raw Kingdom to work over.'

" 'For the last time of answering I will,' said Dravot, and he went away through the pine-trees looking like a big red devil. The low sun hit his crown and beard on one side and the two blazed like hot coals.

"But getting a wife was not as easy as Dan thought. He put it before the Council, and there was no answer till Billy Fish said that he'd better ask the girls. Dravot damned them all round. 'What's wrong with me?' he shouts, standing by the idol Imbra. 'Am I a dog or am I not enough of a man for your wenches? Haven't I put the shadow of my hand over this country? Who stopped the last Afghan raid?' It was me really, but Dravot was too angry to remember. 'Who brought your guns? Who repaired the bridges? Who's the Grand-Master of the sign cut in the stone?' and he thumped his hand on the block that he used to sit on in Lodge, and at Council, which opened like Lodge always. Billy Fish said nothing and no more did the others. 'Keep your hair on, Dan,' said I; 'and ask the girls. That's how it's done at Home, and these people are quite English.'

" 'The marriage of the King is a matter of State,' says Dan, in a white-hot rage, for he could feel, I hope, that he was going against his better mind. He walked out of the Council-room, and the others sat still, looking at the ground.

" 'Billy Fish,' says I to the Chief of Bashkai, 'what's the difficulty here? A straight answer to a true friend.' 'You know,' says Billy Fish. 'How should a man tell you who knows everything? How can daughters of men marry Gods or Devils? It's not proper.'

"I remember something like that in the Bible; but, if, after seeing us as long as they had they still believed we were Gods, it wasn't for me to undeceive them.

" 'A God can do anything,' says I. 'If the King is fond of a girl he'll not let her die.' 'She'll have to,' said Billy Fish. 'There are all sorts of Gods and Devils in these mountains, and now and again a girl marries one of them and isn't seen any more. Besides, you two know the Mark cut in the stone. Only the Gods know that. We thought you were men till you showed the sign of the Master.'

"I wished then that we had explained about the loss of the genuine secrets of a Master-Mason at the first go-off; but I said nothing. All that night there was a blowing of horns in a little dark temple halfway down the hill, and I heard a girl crying fit to die. One of the priests told us that she was being prepared to marry the King.

" 'I'll have no nonsense of that kind,' says Dan. 'I don't want to interfere with your customs, but I'll take my own wife.' 'The girl's a little bit afraid,' says the priest. 'She thinks she's going to die, and they are a-heartening of her up down in the temple.'

" 'Hearten her very tender, then,' says Dravot, 'or I'll hearten you with the butt of a gun so that you'll never want to be heartened again.' He licked his lips, did Dan, and stayed up walking about more than half the night, thinking of the wife that he was going to get in the morning. I wasn't any means comfortable, for I knew that dealings with a woman in foreign parts, though you was a crowned King twenty times over, could not but be risky. I got up very early in the morning while Dravot was asleep, and I saw the priests talking together in whispers, and the Chiefs talking together too, and they looked at me out of the corners of their eyes.

" 'What is up, Fish?' I says to the Bashkai man, who was wrapped up in his furs and looking splendid to behold.

" 'I can't rightly say,' says he; 'but if you can induce the King to drop all this nonsense about marriage, you'll be doing him and me and yourself a great service.'

" 'That I do believe,' says I. 'But sure, you know, Billy, as well as me, having fought against and for us, that the King and me are nothing more than two of the finest men that God Almighty ever made. Nothing more, I do assure you.'

" 'That may be,' says Billy Fish, 'and yet I should be sorry if it was.' He sinks his head upon his great fur cloak for a minute and thinks. 'King,' says he, 'be you man or God or Devil, I'll stick by you to-day. I have twenty of my men with me, and they will follow me. We'll go to Bashkai until the storm blows over.'

"A little snow had fallen in the night, and everything was white except the greasy fat clouds that blew down and down from the north. Dravot came out with his crown on his head, swinging his arms and stamping his feet, and looking more pleased than Punch.

" 'For the last time, drop it, Dan,' says I, in a whisper. 'Billy Fish here says that there will be a row.'

" 'A row among my people!' says Dravot. 'Not much. Peachey, you're a fool not to get a wife too. Where's the girl?' says he, with a voice as loud as the braying of a jackass. 'Call up all the Chiefs and priests, and let the Emperor see if his wife suits him.'

"There was no need to call any one. They were all there leaning on their guns and spears round the clearing in the centre of the pine wood. A deputation of priests went down to the little temple to bring up the girl, and the horns blew up fit to wake the dead. Billy Fish saunters round and gets as close to Daniel as he could, and behind him stood his twenty men with matchlocks. Not a man of them under six feet. I was next to Dravot, and behind me was twenty men of the regular Army. Up comes the girl, and a strapping wench she was, covered with silver and turquoises but white as death, and looking back every minute at the priests.

" 'She'll do,' said Dan, looking her over. 'What's to be afraid of, lass? Come and kiss me.' He puts his arm round her. She shuts her eyes, gives a bit of a squeak, and down goes her face in the side of Dan's flaming red beard.

" 'The slut's bitten me!' says he, clapping his hand to his neck, and, sure enough, his hand was red with blood. Billy Fish and two of his matchlock-men catches hold of Dan by the shoulders and drags him into the Bashkai lot, while the priests howls in their lingo,—'Neither God nor Devil but a man!' I was all taken aback, for a priest cut at me in front, and the Army behind began firing into the Bashkai men.

" 'God A-mighty!' says Dan. 'What is the meaning o' this?'

" 'Come back! Come away!' says Billy Fish. 'Ruin and Mutiny is the matter. We'll break for Bashkai if we can.'

"I tried to give some sort of orders to my men—the men o' the regular Army—but it was no use, so I fired into the brown of 'em with an English Martini and drilled three beggars in a line. The valley was full of shouting, howling creatures, and every soul was shrieking, 'Not a God nor a Devil but only a man!' The Bashkai troops stuck to Billy Fish all they were worth, but their matchlocks wasn't half as good as the Kabul breach-loaders, and four of them dropped. Dan was bellowing like a bull, for he was very wrathy; and Billy Fish had a hard job to prevent him running out at the crowd.

" 'We can't stand,' says Billy Fish. 'Make a run for it down the valley! The whole place is against us.' The matchlock-men ran, and we went down the valley in spite of Dravot's protestations. He was swearing horribly and crying out that he was a King. The priests rolled great stones on us, and the regular Army fired hard, and there wasn't more than six men, not counting Dan, Billy Fish, and Me, that came down to the bottom of the valley alive.

"Then they stopped firing and the horns in the temple blew again. 'Come away—for Gord's sake come away!' says Billy Fish. 'They'll send runners out to all the villages before ever we get to Bashkai. I can protect you there, but I can't do anything now.'

"My own notion is that Dan began to go mad in his head from that hour. He stared up and down like a stuck pig. Then he was all for walking back alone and killing the priests with his bare hands; which he could have done. 'An Emperor am I,' says Daniel, 'and next year I shall be a Knight of the Queen.'

" 'All right, Dan,' says I; 'but come along now while there's time.'

" 'It's your fault,' says he, 'for not looking after your Army better. There was mutiny in the midst, and you didn't know—you damned engine-driving, plate-laying, missionary's-pass-hunting hound!' He sat upon a rock and called me every foul name he could lay tongue to. I was too heart-sick to care, though it was all his foolishness that brought the smash.

" 'I'm sorry, Dan,' says I, 'but there's no accounting for natives. This business is our Fifty-Seven. Maybe we'll make something out of it yet, when we've got to Bashkai.'

" 'Let's get to Bashkai, then,' says Dan, 'and, by God, when I come back here again I'll sweep the valley so there isn't a bug in a blanket left!'

"We walked all that day, and all that night Dan was stumping up and down on the snow, chewing his beard and muttering to himself.

" 'There's no hope o' getting clear,' said Billy Fish. 'The priests will have sent runners to the villages to say that you are only men. Why didn't you stick on as Gods till things was more settled? I'm a dead man,' says Billy Fish, and he throws himself down on the snow and begins to pray to his Gods.

"Next morning we was in a cruel bad country—all up and down, no level ground at all, and no food either. The six Bashkai men looked at Billy Fish hungry-wise as if they wanted to ask something, but they said never a word. At noon we came to the top of a flat mountain all covered with snow, and when we climbed up into it, behold, there was an Army in position waiting in the middle!

" 'The runners have been very quick,' says Billy Fish, with a little bit of a laugh. 'They are waiting for us.'

"Three or four men began to fire from the enemy's side, and a chance shot took Daniel in the calf of the leg. That brought him to his senses. He looks across the snow at the Army, and sees the rifles that we had brought into the country.

" 'We're done for,' says he. 'They are Englishmen, these people,—and it's my blasted nonsense that has brought you to this. Get back, Billy Fish, and take your men away; you've done what you could, and now cut for it. Carnehan,' says he, 'shake hands with me and go along with Billy. Maybe they won't kill you. I'll go and meet 'em alone. It's me that did it. Me, the King!'

" 'Go!' says I. 'Go to Hell, Dan. I'm with you here. Billy Fish, you clear out, and we two will meet those folk.'

" 'I'm a Chief,' says Billy Fish, quite quiet. 'I stay with you. My men can go.'

"The Bashkai fellows didn't wait for a second word but ran off, and Dan and Me and Billy Fish walked across to where the drums were drumming and the horns were horning. It was cold—awful cold. I've got that cold in the back of my head now. There's a lump of it there."

The punkah-coolies had gone to sleep. Two kerosene lamps were blazing in the office, and the perspiration poured down my face and splashed on the blotter as I leaned forward. Carnehan was shivering, and I feared that his mind might go. I wiped my face, took a fresh grip of the piteously mangled hands, and said:— "What happened after that?"

The momentary shift of my eyes had broken the clear current.

"What was you pleased to say?" whined Carnehan. "They took them without any sound. Not a little whisper all along the snow, not though the King knocked down the first man that set hand on him—not though old Peachey fired his last cartridge into the brown of 'em. Not a single solitary sound did those swines make. They just closed up tight, and I tell you their furs stunk. There was a man called Billy Fish, a good friend of us all, and they cut his throat, Sir, then and there, like a pig; and the King kicks up the bloody snow and says: 'We've had a dashed fine run for our money. What's coming next?' But Peachey, Peachey Taliaferro, I tell you, Sir, in confidence as betwixt two friends, he lost his head, Sir. No, he didn't neither. The King lost his head, so he did, all along o' one of those cunning rope-bridges. Kindly let me have the paper-cutter, Sir. It tilted this way. They marched him a mile across that snow to a rope-bridge over a ravine with a river at the bottom. You may have seen such. They prodded him behind like an ox. 'Damn your eyes!' says the King. 'D'you suppose I can't die like a gentleman?' He turns to Peachey—Peachey that was crying like a child. 'I've brought you to this, Peachey,' says he. 'Brought you out of your happy life to be killed in Kafiristan, where you was late Commander-in-Chief of the Emperor's forces. Say you forgive me, Peachey.' 'I do,' says Peachey. 'Fully and freely do I forgive you, Dan.' 'Shake hands, Peachey,' says he. 'I'm going now.' Out he goes, looking neither right nor left, and when he was plumb in the middle of those dizzy dancing ropes. 'Cut, you beggars,' he shouts; and they cut, and old Dan fell, turning round and round and round twenty thousand miles, for he took half an hour to fall till he struck the water, and I could see his body caught on a rock with the gold crown close beside.

"But do you know what they did to Peachey between two pine trees? They crucified him, Sir, as Peachey's hand will show. They used wooden pegs for his hands and his feet; and he didn't die. He hung there and screamed, and they took him down next day, and said it was a miracle that he wasn't dead. They took him down—poor old Peachey that hadn't done them any harm—that hadn't done them any. . . ."

He rocked to and fro and wept bitterly, wiping his eyes with the back of his scarred hands and moaning like a child for some ten minutes.

"They were cruel enough to feed him up in the temple, because they said he was more of a God than old Daniel that was a man. Then they turned him out on the snow, and told him to go home, and Peachey came home in about a year, begging along the roads quite safe; for Daniel Dravot he walked before and said:—'Come along, Peachey. It's a big thing we're doing.' The mountains they danced at night, and the mountains they tried to fall on Peachey's head, but Dan he held up his hand, and Peachey came along bent double. He never let go of Dan's hand, and he never let go of Dan's head. They gave it to him as a present in the temple, to remind him not to come again, and though the crown was pure gold, and Peachey was starving, never would Peachey sell the same. You knew Dravot, Sir! You knew Right Worshipful Brother Dravot! Look at him now!"

He fumbled in the mass of rags round his bent waist;

brought out a black horsehair bag embroidered with silver thread; and shook therefrom on to my table—the dried, withered head of Daniel Dravot! The morning sun that had long been paling the lamps struck the red beard and blind sunken eyes; struck, too, a heavy circlet of gold studded with raw turquoises, that Carnehan placed tenderly on the battered temples.

"You behold now," said Carnehan, "the Emperor in his habit as he lived—the King of Kafiristan with his crown upon his head. Poor old Daniel that was a monarch once!"

I shuddered, for, in spite of defacements manifold, I recognized the head of the man of Marwar Junction. Carnehan rose to go. I attempted to stop him. He was not fit to walk abroad. "Let me take away the whiskey and give me a little money," he gasped. "I was a King once. I'll go to the Deputy Commissioner and ask to set in the Poorhouse till I get my health. No, thank you, I can't wait till you get a carriage for me. I've urgent private affairs—in the south—at Marwar."

He shambled out of the office and departed in the direction of the Deputy Commissioner's house. That day at noon I had occasion to go down the blinding hot Mall, and I saw a crooked man crawling along the white dust of the roadside, his hat in his hand, quavering dolorously after the fashion of street-singers at Home. There was not a soul in sight and he was out of all possible earshot of the houses. And he sang through his nose, turning his head from right to left:

The Son of Man goes forth to war,
A golden crown to gain;
His blood-red banner streams afar—
Who follows in his train?

I waited to hear no more, but put the poor wretch into my carriage and drove him off to the nearest missionary for eventual transfer to the Asylum. He repeated the hymn twice while he was with me whom he did not in the least recognize, and I left him singing it to the missionary.

Two days later I inquired after his welfare of the Superintendent of the Asylum.

"He was admitted suffering from sun-stroke. He died early yesterday morning," said the Superintendent. "Is it true that he was half an hour bareheaded in the sun at midday?"

"Yes," said I, "but do you happen to know if he had anything upon him by any chance when he died!"

"Not to my knowledge," said the Superintendent.

And there the matter rests.

IV

THE GUILT-RIDDEN

With his ability to project, to look ahead, to move in the future, man posses equally the facility to look backward and to feel guilt. Guilt is such a human faculty that it is rarely attributed even anthropomorphically to either animals or gods. The preoccupation with guilt has colored our history, created some of our most beautiful literature. It is the central concern in most western religious systems.

Guilt, which has filled our asylums, our prisons, our psychiatric offices, seems to provide a formidable threat to the personality. Yet the feeling of guilt assures the personality of continued operation: without guilt, the individual may seek final renunciation. Indulgence in feelings of guilt is thus a necessary defense for the continuing life of the human being.

There are many different kinds of guilt: primal guilt and Oedipal guilt; guilt for real acts and neurotic guilt for fancied wrongdoings. There is guilt suffered for commission of an act and guilt suffered for the thought of it.

The problem of guilt and its expiation finds its highest expression in Christian myth. Its literary zenith is achieved in "Hamlet." Most recently, Philip Roth's "Eli, the Fanatic," offers us a brilliant and profound study of religious guilt: as another image of Christ, bearing the stigmata, carrying the guilt of the community, Eli is doomed by his own and his society's illicit desires.

ST. AUGUSTINE/The Confessions

HE SHOWS BY EXAMPLE THAT EVEN INFANCY IS PRONE TO SIN

HEARKEN, O God! Alas for the sins of men! Man saith this, and Thou dost compassionate him; for Thou didst create him, but didst not create the sin that is in him. Who bringeth to my remembrance the sin of my infancy? For before Thee none is free from sin, not even the infant which has lived but a day upon the earth. Who bringeth this to my remembrance? Doth not each little one, in whom I behold that which I do not remember of myself? In what, then, did I sin? Is it that I cried for the breast? If I should now so cry,—not indeed for the breast, but for the food suitable to my years,—I should be most justly laughed at and rebuked. What I then did deserved rebuke; but as I could not understand those who rebuked me, neither custom nor reason suffered me to be rebuked. For as we grow we root out and cast from us such habits. I have not seen any one who is wise, when "purging"[1] anything cast away the good. Or was it good, even for a time, to strive to get by crying that which, if given, would be hurtful—to be bitterly indignant that those who were free and its elders, and those to whom it owed its being, besides many others wiser than it, who would not give way to the nod of its good pleasure, were not subject unto it—to endeavour to harm, by struggling as much as it could, because those commands were not obeyed which only could have been obeyed to its hurt? Then, in the weakness of the infant's limbs, and not in its will, lies its innocency. I myself have seen and known an infant to be jealous though it could not speak. It became pale, and cast bitter looks on its foster-brother. Who is ignorant of this? Mothers and nurses tell us that they appease these things by I know not what remedies; and may this be taken for innocence, that when the fountain of milk is flowing fresh and abundant, one who has need should not be allowed to share it, though needing that nourishment to sustain life? Yet we look leniently on these things, not because they are not faults, nor because the faults are small, but because they will vanish as age increases. For although you may allow these things now, you could not bear them with equanimity if found in an older person.

Thou, therefore, O Lord my God, who gavest life to the infant, and a frame which, as we see, Thou hast endowed with senses, compacted with limbs, beautified with form, and, for its general good and safety, hast introduced all vital energies—Thou

[1] John xv. 2.

commandest me to praise Thee for these things, "to give thanks unto the Lord, and to sing praise unto Thy name, O Most High;"[2] for Thou art a God omnipotent and good, though Thou hadst done nought but these things, which none other can do but Thou, who alone madest all things, O Thou most fair, who madest all things fair, and orderest all according to Thy law. This period, then, of my life, O Lord, of which I have no remembrance, which I believe on the word of others, and which I guess from other infants, it chagrins me—true though the guess be—to reckon in this life of mine which I lead in this world; inasmuch as, in the darkness of my forgetfulness, it is like to that which I passed in my mother's womb. But if "I was shapen in iniquity, and in sin did my mother conceive me,"[3] where, I pray thee, O my God, where, Lord, or when was I, Thy servant, innocent? But behold, I pass by that time, for what have I to do with that, the memories of which I cannot recall?

He Advances to Puberty, and Indeed to the Early Part of the Sixteenth Year of His Age, in Which, Having Abandoned His Studies, He Indulged in Lustful Pleasures, and, With His Companions, Committed Theft.

HE DEPLORES THE WICKEDNESS OF HIS YOUTH.

I will now call to mind my past foulness, and the carnal corruptions of my soul not because I love them, but that I may love Thee, O my God. For love of Thy love do I it, recalling, in the very bitterness of my remembrance, my most vicious ways, that Thou mayest grow sweet to me,—Thou sweetness without deception! Thou sweetness happy and assured!—and re-collecting myself out of that my dissipation, in which I was torn to pieces, while, turned away from Thee the One, I lost myself among many vanities. For I even longed in my youth formerly to be satisfied with worldly things, and I dared to grow wild again with various and shadowy loves; my form consumed away,[4] and I became corrupt in Thine eyes, pleasing myself, and eager to please in the eyes of men.

STRICKEN WITH EXCEEDING GRIEF, HE REMEMBERS THE DISSOLUTE PASSIONS IN WHICH, IN HIS SIXTEENTH YEAR, HE USED TO INDULGE.

But what was it that I delighted in save to love and to be beloved? But I held it not in moderation, mind to mind, the bright path of friendship, but out of the dark concupiscence of the flesh and the effervescence of youth exhalations came forth which

[2] Ps. xcii. 4.
[3] Ps. li. 5.
[4] Ps. xxxix. 11.

obscured and overcast my heart, so that I was unable to discern pure affection from unholy desire. Both boiled confusedly within me, and dragged away my unstable youth into the rough places of unchaste desires, and plunged me into a gulf of infamy. Thy anger had overshadowed me, and I knew it not. I was become deaf by the rattling of the chains of my mortality, the punishment for my soul's pride; and I wandered farther from Thee, and Thou didst "suffer"[5] me; and I was tossed to and fro, and wasted, and poured out, and boiled over in my fornications, and Thou didst hold Thy peace, O Thou my tardy joy! Thou then didst hold Thy peace, and I wandered still farther from Thee, into more and more barren seed-plots of sorrows, with proud dejection and restless lassitude. . . .

HE COMMITS THEFT WITH HIS COMPANIONS, NOT URGED ON BY POVERTY, BUT FROM A CERTAIN DISTASTE OF WELL-DOING.

Theft is punished by Thy law, O Lord, and by the law written in men's hearts, which iniquity itself cannot blot out. For what thief will suffer a thief? Even a rich thief will not suffer him who is driven to it by want. Yet had I a desire to commit robbery, and did so, compelled neither by hunger, nor poverty, but through a distaste for well-doing, and a lustiness of iniquity. For I pilfered that of which I had already sufficient, and much better. Nor did I desire to enjoy what I pilfered, but the theft and sin itself. There was a pear-tree close to our vineyard, heavily laden with fruit, which was tempting neither for its colour nor its flavour. To shake and rob this some of us wanton young fellows went, late one night (having, according to our disgraceful habit, prolonged our games in the streets until then), and carried away great loads, not to eat ourselves, but to fling to the very swine, having only eaten some of them; and to do this pleased us all the more because it was not permitted. Behold my heart, O my God; behold my heart, which Thou hadst pity upon when in the bottomless pit. Behold, now, let my heart tell Thee what it was seeking there, that I should be gratuitously wanton, having no inducement to evil but the evil itself. It was foul, and I loved it. I loved to perish. I loved my own error—not that for which I erred, but the error itself. Base soul, falling from Thy firmament to utter destruction—not seeking aught through the shame but the shame itself!

CONCERNING THE MOTIVES TO SIN, WHICH ARE NOT IN THE LOVE OF EVIL, BUT IN THE DESIRE OF OBTAINING THE PROPERTY OF OTHERS.

There is a desirableness in all beautiful bodies, and in gold, and silver, and all things; and in bodily contact sympathy is powerful, and each other sense hath his proper adaptation of body.

[5] Matt. xvii. 17.

Worldly honour hath also its glory, and the power of command, and of overcoming; whence proceeds also the desire for revenge. And yet to acquire all these, we must not depart from Thee, O Lord, nor deviate from Thy law. The life which we live here hath also its peculiar attractiveness, through a certain measure of comeliness of its own, and harmony with all things here below. The friendships of men also are endeared by a sweet bond, in the oneness of many souls. On account of all these, and such as these, is sin committed; while through an inordinate preference for these goods of a lower kind, the better and higher are neglected,—even Thou, our Lord God, Thy truth, and Thy law. For these meaner things have their delights, but not like unto my God, who hath created all things; for in Him doth the righteous delight, and He is the sweetness of the upright in heart.[6]

When, therefore, we inquire why a crime was committed, we do not believe it, unless it appear that there might have been the wish to obtain some of those which we designated meaner things, or else a fear of losing them. For truly they are beautiful and comely, although in comparison with those higher and celestial goods they be abject and contemptible. A man hath murdered another; what was his motive? He desired his wife or his estate; or would steal to support himself; or he was afraid of losing something of the kind by him; or, being injured, he was burning to be revenged. Would he commit murder without a motive, taking delight simply in the act of murder? Who would credit it? For as for that savage and brutal man, of whom it is declared that he was gratuitously wicked and cruel, there is yet a motive assigned. "Lest through idleness," he says, "hand or heart should grow inactive."[7] And to what purpose? Why, even that, having once got possession of the city through that practice of wickedness, he might attain unto honours, empire, and wealth, and be exempt from the fear of the laws, and his difficult circumstances from the needs of his family, and the consciousness of his own wickedness. So it seems that even Catiline himself loved not his own villainies, but something else, which gave him the motive for committing them.

WHY HE DELIGHTED IN THAT THEFT, WHEN ALL THINGS WHICH UNDER THE APPEARANCE OF GOOD INVITE TO VICE ARE TRUE AND PERFECT IN GOD ALONE.

What was it, then, that I, miserable one, so doted on in thee, thou theft of mine, thou deed of darkness, in that sixteenth year of my age? Beautiful thou wert not, since thou wert theft. But art thou anything, that so I may argue the case with thee? Those pears that we stole were fair to the sight, because they were Thy

[6] Ps. lxiv. 10.

[7] Sallust, *De Bello Catil.* c. 9.

creation, Thou fairest[8] of all, Creator of all, Thou good God—God, the highest good, and my true good. Those pears truly were pleasant to the sight; but it was not for them that my miserable soul lusted, for I had abundance of better, but those I plucked simply that I might steal. For, having plucked them, I threw them away, my sole gratification in them being my own sin, which I was pleased to enjoy. For if any of these pears entered my mouth, the sweetener of it was my sin in eating it. And now, O Lord my God, I ask what it was in that theft of mine that caused me such delight; and behold it hath no beauty in it—not such, I mean, as exists in justice and wisdom; nor such as is in the mind, memory, senses, and animal life of man; nor yet such as is the glory and beauty of the stars in their courses; or the earth, or the sea, teeming with incipient life, to replace, as it is born, that which decayeth; nor, indeed, that false and shadowy beauty which pertaineth to deceptive vices. . . .

Thus doth the soul commit fornication when she turns away from Thee, and seeks without Thee what she cannot find pure and untainted until she returns to Thee. Thus all pervertedly imitate Thee who separate themselves far from Thee[9] and raise themselves up against Thee. But even by thus imitating Thee they acknowledge Thee to be the Creator of all nature, and so that there is no place whither they can altogether retire from Thee.[10] What, then, was it that I loved in that theft? And wherein did I, even corruptedly and pervertedly, imitate my Lord? Did I wish, if only by artifice, to act contrary to Thy law, because by power I could not, so that, being a captive, I might imitate an imperfect liberty by doing with impunity things which I was not allowed to do, in obscured likeness of Thy omnipotency?[11] Behold this servant of Thine, fleeing from his Lord, and following a shadow![12] O rottenness! O monstrosity of life and profundity of death! Could I like that which was unlawful only because it was unlawful?

HE GIVES THANKS TO GOD FOR THE REMISSION OF HIS SINS, AND REMINDS EVERY ONE THAT THE SUPREME GOD MAY HAVE PRESERVED US FROM GREATER SINS.

"What shall I render unto the Lord,"[13] that whilst my memory recalls these things my soul is not appalled at them? I

[8] Ps. xlv. 2.
[9] Ps. vii. 15.
[10] Ps. cxxxix. 7, 8.
[11] "For even souls, in their very sins, strive after nothing else but some kind of likeness of God, in a proud and preposterous, as if to say, slavish liberty. So neither could our first parents have been persuaded to sin unless it had been said, 'Ye shall be as gods.' "—AUG. *De Trin.* xi. 5.
[12] Jonah i. and iv.
[13] Ps. cxvi. 12.

will love Thee, O Lord, and thank Thee, and confess unto Thy name,[14] because Thou hast put away from me these so wicked and nefarious acts of mine. To Thy grace I attribute it, and to Thy mercy, that Thou hast melted away my sin as it were ice. To Thy grace also I attribute whatsoever of evil I have not committed; for what might I not have committed, loving as I did the sin for the sin's sake? Yea, all I confess to have been pardoned me, both those which I committed by my own perverseness, and those which, by Thy guidance, I committed not. Where is he who, reflecting upon his own infirmity, dares to ascribe his chastity and innocency to his own strength, so that he should love Thee the less, as if he had been in less need of Thy mercy, whereby Thou dost forgive the transgressions of those that turn to Thee? For whosoever, called by Thee, obeyed Thy voice, and shunned those things which he reads me recalling and confessing of myself, let him not despise me, who, being sick, was healed by that same Physician[15] by whose aid it was that he was not sick, or rather was less sick. And for this let him love Thee as much, yea, all the more, since by whom he sees me to have been restored from so great a feebleness of sin, by Him he sees himself from a like feebleness to have been preserved.

IN HIS THEFT HE LOVED THE COMPANY OF HIS FELLOW-SINNERS.

"What fruit had I then,"[16] wretched one, in those things which, when I remember them, cause me shame—above all in that theft, which I loved only for the theft's sake? And as the theft itself was nothing, all the more wretched was I who loved it. Yet by myself alone I would not have done it—I recall what my heart was—alone I could not have done it. I loved, then, in it the companionship of my accomplices with whom I did it. I did not, therefore, love the theft alone—yea, rather, it was that alone that I loved, for the companionship was nothing. What is the fact? Who is it that can teach me, but He who illuminateth mine heart and searcheth out the dark corners thereof? What is it that hath come into my mind to inquire about, to discuss, and to reflect upon? For had I at that time loved the pears I stole, and wished to enjoy them, I might have done so alone, if I could have been satisfied with the mere commission of the theft by which my pleasure was secured; nor needed I have provoked that itching of my own passions, by the encouragement of accomplices. But as my enjoyment was not in those pears, it was in the crime itself, which the company of my fellow-sinners produced.

[14] Rev. iii. 5.
[15] Luke iv. 23.
[16] Rom. vi. 21.

THEODOR REIK / Myth and Guilt

A HISTORIC short story, inserted into the novel *Sur La Pierre Blanche* by Anatole France, introduces Gallio, a highly educated Roman aristocrat who was nominated governor of ancient Greece and resided in Corinth. Gallio takes a walk in the garden of his beautiful cottage and discusses with his friends the present situation and the future of the Roman Empire. Some complain at the loss of the old virtues and hope that the young prince, who was just completing his sixteenth year and was known as modest and full of pity, would bring about an era of happiness when he became emperor. The hope of the world rests in that son of Agrippina, called Nero. The friends believe in the future of Rome although some of them doubt that Jupiter and Juno will always remain in power. A Greek philosopher, Apollodor, asserts that the regime of Jupiter approaches its end and Prometheus will be his successor. Gallio is rather inclined to believe that Hercules will succeed the son of Saturn.

The discussion is interrupted by an official who calls Gallio to the court before which two Jews appear as prosecutor and defendant. The head of the synagogue accuses another Jew of speaking each Saturday against the Mosaic law and asks the proconsul to protect the privileges of the children of Israel against the obnoxious preacher. The proconsul reluctantly goes to the tribunal while his friends express their regret that this stinking and ignorant race, the scum of the earth, had been permitted entrance into Roman and Greek cities.

The proconsul returning tells them that the issue was as unimportant and ridiculous as possible. The Jews accused a very ugly tent-weaver called Paul or Saul of atheism. This Jew had tried to persuade his coreligionists to worship their God in a way supposed to contradict their law. Since it was an argument about words or a difference of opinion about details of the Jewish law, Gallio had decided it did not concern him and left the shouting and fighting crowd. He speaks full of contempt of those Jewish quarrels about trifles.

By an odd accident Gallio had become witness to an argument that decided the future of the world. He had pondered the possibility that Hercules might become the successor of Jupiter. The shadow of the god who will be Lord on Earth and in Heaven had passed him by. Gallio had not the slightest notion that the divine figure took the shape of a Jew who was crucified in another, less important Roman province a few years ago, and that

that contemptible tent-maker had just now announced the coming of the Saviour.

With the discussion of the part and the personality of this Paul, who appears as an episodic figure in the gracious story of Anatole France, we abandon for the first time the area of general psychology and move to the field of exploration of the emotional life of an individual. Until now we were occupied with the research into productions of nations and masses, with the myths of people. In this part we are interested in the processes of a mythmaker. It cannot be denied that here is an inconsistency in the architectural style, a deviation from the plan. There is no sufficient justification for this faulty architecture. I can only plead mitigating circumstances. The first is that Paul of Tarsus is the only real, undoubtedly historic person to appear in the great drama of religious evolution we present. The person of Jesus Christ can be conceived as a mythological figure, while the figure of Saul the Pharisee has nothing mythical. It is a man of flesh and blood, even of a "thorn in the flesh" and of hot blood. The second factor to be brought forward is Paul's importance in the foundation of the new religion. Paul was not only the first and the greatest missionary of Christianity, but almost its founder.

It was justly said that the only Christian who ever lived had died on the cross. World history is little concerned with the biography of this rabbi, and not much more with his sayings and teachings—only in what the imagination of his disciples and apostles made of them. Let us compare the significance of this Galilean preacher with the character of the Jewish Messiah who preoccupied his people at the time before Christ and during His lifetime. The Messiah was in the thought of the contemporary Jews a kind of glorified, elevated Judas Maccabaeus. He was the hero of all hopes of his people who daydreamed of him, believed in him, and were convinced that he, chosen by Jahveh and endowed with superhuman powers, would defeat the Romans and free the nation. After that victory, which was conceived as the great deed of national liberation, peace, glory, and justice would rule in Israel, whereto all nations of the world would look for guidance. What became of this Jewish hope and daydream? It has vanished as the snow of yesteryear at the Scopus mountain. Nothing of it has survived. A few isolated attempts to revive it were fantastic and utopian and doomed to perish. Another Messiah, one not concerned with national and political aims of the Jews, had conquered the world.

Paul was not interested in the person of Jesus, whom he had never seen except in his "mind's eye" on that road to Damascus. Only three events of that sacred life preoccupy that pious

Jew of Tarsus: the Last Supper, the Crucifixion, and the Resurrection. It seems he considers all other events of Jesus' life—His miracles, His activities, and even His sayings—as of minor interest. Even His teachings are rarely and almost casually mentioned by the greatest apostle of Christianity. Only the figure of Christ, the Christology, or as we would prefer to say, the mythology of Christianism, is the point on which all thoughts and religious emotions of Paul are focused.

Only by reasoning, daydreaming, and fantasying about the final destiny of Christ as the "firstborn Son of God" did Paul arrive at his concept of a new religion. Did he think of a new religion when he first went out to speak of the crucified Jesus in the synagogues? Certainly not. Nothing was further from his pious mind, that could tolerate neither compromise nor concessions. He had most ardently studied the law with Rabbi Gamaliel in Jerusalem, and had developed an intensive hatred against those who had not obeyed it fully and to the letter. He hated especially those Essenes who confessed a faith he considered an aberration of the law, if not its perversion. Yet this man became not only the most ardent missionary of the new belief, he was much more: he was the builder, the architect, of what we now call Christianity, which is, in most of its essential features, his creation. That is true to such an extent that one can boldly assert that it had little in common with Christ.

A learned theologian asserts that Paul "organized Christ out of the Church," and seriously raises the question whether our churches of today are those of Jesus or Paul.[1] Paul, the mystic, brought the dying and risen Christ in conflict with the teaching and preaching Christ. Not what He said and did was decisive, but His death and resurrection, which brought salvation to mankind. What mattered was the "hanging upon Calvary of the emaciated figure of the ribbed Christ with the blood oozing from his pierced hands and sides and thorned brow."[2] Had this event and the resurrection not taken place, Christ, whom Paul transformed by interpolation and interpretation into the "only Son of God," would have been unable to redeem men, and would have had to leave them doomed to eternity.

The third factor in the decision to deal with Paul's personality within this investigation is the fact that the mystery of his conversion is still unsolved and tempts the curiosity of the psychologist to unravel it. In spite of innumerable attempts at explanation we still do not understand how the Christ-hater became the most ardent apostle of the crucified Son of Man. That great

[1] Desmond Shaw, *Jesus or Paulus* (London, 1945), p. 36.
[2] *Ibid.*, p. 80.

experience on the road to Damascus is still a psychological secret.

The bearing of that conversion upon the problem of the collective guilt feelings is obvious since it was Paul who first drew the conclusion that Christ's death was a ransom, and should atone for the crime of the first Adam. To return to a comparison that will illustrate the part of Paul within the investigation: it is as though, within a mystery story, the detective, eager to solve the crime, becomes intrigued by the strange behavior of the main witness: a witness used first by the attorney for the prosecution and then by the attorney for the defense—so to speak, a puzzle within the enigma. We would like to follow this thread.

The last but for us most important factor is the kind of psychological material presented by the development of the apostle. In his inner struggle a good portion of the religious evolution of mankind appears, in a sense recapitulated, reflected in an individual life in rapid abbreviation. There is the furious hatred against the Galilean and his followers, then the death of the accursed heretic—one would almost say his immolation. This is followed by increasing unconscious guilt feeling which, under the active support of emerging admiration and love, produces the conversion of Saul. The overwhelming guilt feeling results in full identification with the victim of the persecution.

The following analytic attempt does not aspire to analyze what made the great man tick, suffer, and act. This writer will be content if he succeeds in casting a new and surprising light on some facets of the psychological enigma of Paul's personality. He was a Jew of the tribe of Benjamin, living in Tarsus, and a Roman citizen. In the acts of Paul and Thecla, he is described as "of a low stature, bald on the head, crooked tights; handsome legs, hollow-eyed, had a crooked nose, full of grace." We have reason to assume that he must have suffered much under frustrated sexual drives. This man had seizures of a hysteric or hystero-epileptic type in which he spoke "in an unknown tongue unto God." He speaks of his emotional disturbance as "a messenger of Satan" and "a thorn in the flesh." In those attacks he suffered the tortures of the damned, all the terrors of annihilation, but enjoyed visions given only to those whom the Lord had called.

Argumentative, quarrelsome, a master of the art of making enemies and of making himself disliked, most sensitive and suspicious, intolerant and stubborn, sharply logical, often with a twist and turn of arguing later to be called talmudic, eloquent, stubborn as a mule, of a brilliant mind given to singleness of purpose and with an unique moral courage, he was ready to endure unlimited sufferings if he had to stand his ground and fight for his convictions. A conservative of most violent temperament and a hateful rebel preaching love of all men. Arthur Schnitzler once casually remarked that every nation in its pure characteristic traits is essentially unlikeable, the German as well as the French, the English as well as the American, and that only the individual can reconcile you with marked national peculiarities. This is perhaps too sharply expressed but it has a core of truth. Paul of Tarsus had in his personality a combination of the marked characteristics of the Jewish zealot in the diaspora, some of the worst and some of the best.

Only a few words on the outlook and the early training of Paul; he spoke Greek and Aramaic, he declared himself to be "an Hebrew of the Hebrews" (Philippians 3:5), but also emphasized his Roman citizenship, which he had from his birth (Acts 22:28). He was a child of a very strict Jewish home, well read in the history, the hopes, and the destiny of Israel. He went—perhaps when he was fourteen or fifteen—to Jerusalem to study with famous teachers. He boasts that he had "profited in the Jews' religion above many my equals in my own nation, being more exceedingly zealous of the tradition of my fathers" (Galatians 1:14). That Pharisean Jew, Saul, had absorbed all teachings of the synagogue, not only at the feet of Rabbi Gamaliel, but also in his native city of Tarsus. Tarsus was a Cilician city in which many gods were worshiped. The Romans, who were much more tolerant in religious things than other conquerors, had no objections to foreign cults.

Among them the worship of young gods who were beautiful youths, and had also died young as saviors, had a particularly great attraction for the imagination of the Mediterranean people of that period. The principal god of Tarsus, Sandan, was a figure of this type of dying and reviving deity. They had all been killed either by a wild beast, by being hanged on a tree or tied to a rock, or had been torn to pieces—Adonis, Attis, Osiris, Zagreus, Dionysus or Bacchus—only the names were different; their myths were almost the same. The Jewish boy who was told their stories had the impression that he heard variations on a single theme. Also, the ritual of those cults was very similar: there was mourning and lamentation, crying and other expressions of grief at the season when the young god was supposed to have died, and jubilation, joy, and triumph when he was supposed to have risen again and to have victoriously ascended to the gods.

The initiation rituals of young men into the mysteries of those religions were secret; but everybody knew that the novices were thought to die and be reborn in identification with the young god, and were resurrected with him. The young Jew Saul, born and bred in Tarsus, where some of those cults had their own places of worship, was of course as aware of their existence and meaning as a boy from an orthodox Jewish family who visits a public school in Manhattan is aware of Christian observances. He was repelled by the pagan superstitions, which appeared to him as stupid and despicable, but in his conversion and afterwards those old disavowed impressions from his childhood returned to his mind and memories of what he had heard and seen of those strange cults were fused with the rumors and messages of the death and resurrection of the young rabbi from Nazareth. Especially one of those cults is likely to have unconsciously occurred to the young Pharisean who had that shattering experience near the city of Damascus.

When, in the gracious story of Anatole France, the proconsul Gallio returns from the Basilica of Corinth, where he contemptuously dismissed the case of the Jews of the synagogue and of the other Jews who are followers of a certain Palestinian rabbi, he tells his friends about their trifling quarrels. From the confused talk in which that Syrian Jew answered his accusers, the proconsul got the vague impression that that tent-weaver worshiped Orpheus under some strange name he had forgotten. Perhaps he meant Adonis or Attis over whose sufferings and death the women cry.

The cults of several of those young gods spread from Asia over the whole Orient and were also brought to Rome and her provinces, as Vittorio Macchioro[3] and André Boulanger[4] convincingly showed. Judea and the neighboring countries in the last century before Christ were filled with believers in Orpheus' death and resurrection. Tarsus was one of the centers of that barbarian worship. A comparison between the Orphic theology and the Christology of Paul shows remarkable resemblance. According to Orphism, Zagreus, the young son of Zeus, is torn to pieces and killed by the Titans. Zeus calls him back to life and he takes him to Heaven.

The Christians of the first centuries were well aware of those striking resemblances of the Greek and Jewish myths. Justin Martyr assumes that the ancient poets had obtained knowledge of the future advent of the Saviour through prophets and invented the myth of Zagreus to make the Saviour Himself into a myth and to persuade Christians to doubt Him. Demons had invented the passion of Dionysus, but did not dare to create one thing: the Crucifixion. Justin adds that the demons introduced the story into the very country where the Saviour was born. He also notices that the story of Zagreus was widely accepted by the Hellenistic Jews and explains the popularity of the pagan myth by the fact that those shrewd demons substituted Zagreus for Christ.

The Orphic communion had the following elements: the

[3] *From Orpheus to Paul* (New York, 1930).
[4] *Orphée* (Paris, 1943).

human soul suffers from an inherited sin, but can be delivered from it by attaining divine life. New birth is achieved through communion with the dying Dionysus or Zagreus. For Orphism as for Paulinism, the aim is to deliver the souls from the burden of the flesh and to bring them into contact with God. Compare those essential features of Orphic belief with Paul's doctrine. Christ died in order to free mankind from the Adamic sin. Deliverance is attained by men through dying and being born again with Him. The body is the seat of sin. In being born again sin is destroyed in the body. The center of the mystery religions was to become similar to a god. The divine nature their worshipers had attained was sometimes expressed by the name attributed to them, which is nothing but the name of the deity. The neophytes of the Dionysus cult were called Bacchi as those of the Christ cult were called Christians.

According to the Orphic concept, mankind inherited an original sin from the murderous deed of the Titans, a sin from which each soul must be purged. During its earthly life, mankind has to serve sentence for the sins of the Titans who had torn to pieces and devoured Zagreus, son of Zeus and Persephone. Athena rescued the heart of the boy, which Zeus swallowed. Zagreus was reborn as Dionysus, child of Zeus and Semele. Mankind arose from the semen of the Titans, who were struck by the lightning of Zeus. That myth is similar to those of Negro-Australians, American Indians, Bushmen, and Eskimo and Zulu tales to be found in Andrew Lang's comparative work.[5] In Orphic theogony the myth of the swallowed god appears three times. First Kronos devours his children, then Zeus swallows Metis and Phanes, and then the Titans devour Zagreus. The savage character of that myth is obvious.

It cannot be our task to delineate how the combination of the Jewish traditions and of the doctrines of the mystery religions influenced the Christology of Paul. The character of the result of the different determined factors is not ambiguous. Seen from a merely historical view, Christianity is, to quote V. Macchioro's words, "an enormous Greek hero cult devoted to a Jewish Messiah." Another aspect of Paul's christology is more important for our inquiry. Although in a veiled and delusional form, Paul arrived at the sources of the original guilt.[6]

The Parisian criminals call conscience *"la muette."* Also mankind tried for many thousands of years to silence the signals of conscience emerging from unconscious depths. In the message

[5] *Myth, Ritual and Religion* (2d ed., London) I, p. 295.
[6] Compare Jacob Taubes' "Religion and the Future of Psychoanalysis" (*Psychoanalysis,* 1956/4).

of Paul the conscience of mankind obtained a voice. Formulated in the delusional shape of an evangel, Man confessed here his original guilt.

What happened? How did Saul the Christ-hater and Christ-baiter become the Christ-lover? The analytic interpretation that follows has, as far as I know, no predecessor in literature except Hanns Sachs' promising but unfinished attempt at Paul's characterization.[7] It cannot be denied that the interpretive attempt presented here has a provisional character, justifiable only by the very limited space granted to it within this book in which the figure of the apostle plays only an episodic part.

The following is an attempt to penetrate at least in some decisive points the psychological wall surrounding the mysterious change to which Saul was subjected. The experience to which he attributed his conversion is clearly described in the ninth chapter of the Acts. Saul was one of the most zealous and active persecutors of the Church in the making. A fanatic Jew, he "made havock of the church, entering into every house, and haling men and women committed them to prison." Saul, "yet breathing out threatenings and slaughter against the disciples of the Lord," went up from Jerusalem to Damascus, to bring the heretics back. When he came near Damascus, suddenly a light from Heaven shone around him and he heard a voice saying "Saul, Saul, why persecutest thou me?" Jesus told him who He was and added, "It is hard for thee to kick against the pricks." When Saul, trembling, arose from the earth, he saw no more. He was brought into Damascus where he remained three days "without sight and neither did eat nor drink." It is known that he then became the Apostle preaching Christ, the "Son of God," in the synagogues, and how confounded the Jews at Damascus had been who had known him as the destroyer of the Christians, and who now planned to kill him.

One is tempted to reconstruct or to guess at what the inner process was that took place in this tortured man when one considers his past history and certain features of the time after the conversion at Damascus. When one adds the insights psychology has gained into the unconscious dynamics of pathological phenomena, especially of hysteria and epilepsy, one will get a hypothesis which, if it does not hit the bull's eye, reaches its neighborhood. The scarcity of biographical and pathological data of course makes

[7] "At the Gates of Heaven" in *Masks of Love and Life* (Cambridge, 1948). Limited space does not allow me to give a critical survey of books on Paul's life, a *bibliographie raisonnée*. It should be mentioned that from the extended literature on Paul studied for this chapter, Albert Schweitzer's *The Mysticism of Paul the Apostle* (New York, 1955) was especially helpful.

the result of this attempt at analytic reconstruction doubtful; but my impression is that it comes closer to the historic reality than previous scientific endeavors of a similar kind.

I would like to preface the analytic interpretation of Paul by some remarks on fanaticism and enthusiasm. The two emotions are obviously akin and have an especially high intensity of feeling in common. They both have, it seems to me, to make an effort to suppress or drown opposite feelings. Enthusiasm has to ward off unconscious doubtful and aggressive tendencies directed against its object, and fanaticism has to reject trends of attraction to the object or cause that is fought and attacked. In the idea of enthusiasm we emphasize the positive, constructive side. Love for a cause or a person is a necessary ingredient of that emotion. We connect with fanaticism a critical note and see in a fanatic a person who is carried away by his beliefs beyond reason. While we in general consider enthusiasm as something desirable, we are inclined to frown upon fanaticism. The reason for this is that fanaticism does not denote only an extraordinary zeal or passionate partisanship for a cause, but also an equal or even more ardent rejection and repulsion of any different attitude or viewpoint.

Singleness of purpose is common to enthusiasm and fanaticism, but the first includes all appropriate things in its circle; the other excludes or rebuffs all that does not strictly belong to its sphere. The term "enthusiasm" has a positive, socially welcome tone—sometimes slightly ironic or condescending when we, for instance, smile at youthful enthusiasm—whereas the expression "fanaticism" has a by-character of rejecting, of ejecting hostility, of exclusiveness and narrow-mindedness. Although the two emotional manifestations are as dissimilar as only parts of the same kin can be, they have besides zeal or ardor other properties in common, for instance loyalty and long duration.

It is difficult to associate the term fanaticism with an emotion that is short-lived and almost as had to imagine enthusiasm for a cause lasting only for hours. It would be paradoxical to think of those emotions as fleeting and easily changeable. It is impossible to attribute to them an attitude similar to that of a certain woman about whom the Viennese writer Karl Kraus once remarked that she was faithful today to one man and faithful tomorrow to another. Yet there are sudden breakthroughs of disappointment and disillusion in enthusiasm, as there are unexpected disenchantments and dissociations in fanaticism. There are also sudden or gliding transitions from the one to the other; possible changes from enthusiasm to fanaticism, and, although more rarely, from fanaticism into enthusiasm.

It happens frequently that both manifestations are present in the same person, as though he had a Janus head whose one side is turned this way and the other the opposite. Finally, there is the frequently observed case of a turnabout in which a person is first enthusiastic, or even fanatic about a certain cause and then the opposite. In most of these cases, the turning point is brought about by a conversion, by a reversal of conviction, sometimes connected with a character transformation of the person. It is easy enough to say—and some theologians said it—that Paul's conversion means a transition from rigid fanaticism for Judaism to loving enthusiasm for the new religion of Christ. The ambiguity of these terms becomes obvious when you consider that it is possible to apply them the other way around.

In many cases of sudden conversion an intensive doubt, or even a rejection of a certain cause, is followed by an upsurge of passionate belief in it. The fanatical and persecutory zeal of Paul, his cruel and murderous wishes and hate for the Nazarene offenders and blasphemers neared their highest point when he, heading a group of men, went out to bring many of those criminal heretics, bound, back to Jerusalem. The message that Jesus, whose disciples he persecuted, had been crucified reached Paul two years after its occurrence. He had also heard many tales of the Saviour's resurrection. Still breathing slaughter, he thought many times of that crucified man and called his hateful image up. On the road to Damascus the inner situation suddenly changed. What had happened? We have only the description of Paul himself as the testimony of a highly introspective person, but his description is necessarily restricted and its value diminished by the fact that the most important part of the experience occurred in an epileptic or hystero-epileptic attack. In the seizure he, so to speak, died with Christ; or, as he would say, "in Christ." That is, he had identified with the man in whom so many Jews saw the Messiah.

At first Paul's hate for Christ had reached its peak and resulted in a vivid image of the Galilean. He seemed to see Him hanging on the cross with blood oozing from all His body, with the crown of thorns, in all His misery and last defamation and shame. But then it was no longer an image, produced by an act of thinking, but a vision, or better, a delusion in the sense of a pathological phenomenon, in which a person seems to be as real—I mean materially real—as the next man on the street. The vividly expressed murderous wish against the preacher who had declared himself the Son of God was replaced by the inner image of His death.

Then came the full identification with that dead man on the Cross in a vision. He saw, in his hysterical attack, Christ as a

Divine Being, radiant, all-powerful, with full knowledge of the secrets of the heart; not merely as a Jewish Messiah, but as exalted. Christ, conceived thus as a deity, spoke to him.

In that full identification Paul became this crucified heretic, in a sense, body and soul. It is obvious what determined this change from the cruel and sadistic into the masochistically suffering. In this reversal we have to recognize not only the operation of unconscious moral powers, of the forces that bring about an atonement for one's own cruel tendencies. There is also here the intensity of repressed feelings of love and admiration for that crucified young heretic—powerful emotions returning from the depth of the repressed. Yes, one can assert that this love turned the scales, decided the outcome of the unconscious conflict.

We cannot know if this reconstruction of the emotional processes during Paul's hystero-epileptic attack is psychologically correct. The similarity of Paul's description to the account Dostoevski gave of his own seizures is remarkable. If it is permitted to follow the analogy to the psychology of the attack, we would arrive at the conclusion that both neurotic men experienced in these seizures their own death in identification with another hated and loved person. Freud's interpretation[8] of Dostoevski's neurotic seizures is, to a great extent, also valid for the case of Paul of Tarsus.

Perhaps the indirect proof of this concept is to be seen in the behavior of the new apostle or, as we had better say, of the newborn Paul. I do not mean in the fact that he went out to the synagogue to preach Christ, but in what he said and how he said it. He speaks of himself as though he had lived and died in Christ, and as though he had been resurrected in Him. Only died with Him? "Know ye not, that so many of us as were baptized into Jesus Christ were baptized into his death? Therefore we are buried with him by baptism into death; that like as Christ was raised up from the dead by the glory of the Father, even so we also should walk in newness of life" (Romans 6:3, 4). It is as if—but this "if" approaches the character of full reality—he had experienced the tortures and the dying of Christ as his own. The metaphors he uses are more than that; they are reports of his own vividly felt experience—"whether in the body or out of the body, I cannot tell"—and have become only secondarily symbols. He had suffered death and had overcome the fear of dying, had triumphed over it: "Oh death, where is thy sting? Oh grave, where is thy victory?" (I Corinthians 15:55).

[8] *Dostojewski und die Vatertötung,* Gesammelte Schriften, XII (Vienna, 1934). The problem of guilt and atonement is also the central motif of the Russian writer. Dostoevski was as Paul "a man with a gift for religion, in the truest sense of the phrase. Dark traces of the past lay in his soul, ready to break through into the region of consciousness." (Freud, *Moses and Monotheism,* p. 137.)

The identification with Christ goes so far that he feels Him in himself, not as incorporated, but also as being Him: "I am crucified with Christ: nevertheless I live; yet not I, but Christ liveth in me: and the life which I now live in the flesh I live by the faith of the Son of God who loved me. . . . If we be dead with Christ, we believe that we shall also live with him." Those sentences have to be understood literally. The final resurrection appears, as Hanns Sachs[9] has aptly put it, "as a reproduction, enlarged to a grandiose size, of the experience that every man can find"—but, as we would add, of the experience of Paul on that road to Damascus. That "other self" in Paul had tried again and again to make itself known, but in vain. It could not penetrate the thick walls of loyalty to the past, the devotion to the law and tradition. When it succeeded in breaking through all resistances, it was with a forcefulness that did not allow contradiction any longer. The denied and repressed emotions knocked out everything Paul had learned to appreciate, and acknowledged only one power, the same that brought him to feel as one with Jesus: "And though I have the gift of prophecy, and understand all mysteries, and all knowledge; and though I have all faith so that I could remove mountains, and have not charity, I am nothing" (I Corinthians 13:2).

Many emotions, emerging from the dark underground into which they had been banned, worked together to produce that great about-face, but the strongest was love, that is greater than "faith and hope," love for a young prophet he had never seen and who had been crucified by the Romans. Paul does not speak of Eros, but uses the word "Agape," which means love in a desexualized form; but psychoanalysis knows from which hidden sources or deeper sensual desires this emotion is fed. That passion that had boiled up in hate against the new preacher, the Essenes, and the disciples of Johannes, that same zealous ardor of fanatic loathing has been reversed by the sudden emergence of a long-disavowed emotion of longing and belonging to that other rejected world and its priest. In identifying with the victim whom others had killed, but for whose agony and death he felt responsible, the persecutor became persecuted. In the intensity of an experience shared with the loved object, he knew he had to go out to convey to his people the death-conquering mysteries of the Last Supper, of the Crucifixion, and the Resurrection.

Paul's breakthrough to Jesus, the inner uproar produced by the assault of repressed emotions, also brought with it a revival and revision of thoughts long known and kept in the dark: the ideas of Orphic teachings, which now blended with the image of the Messiah as he lived in Hebrew literature and lore. Until then

[9] Hanns Sachs, *At the Gates of Heaven*, p. 100.

shadows vegetating in the underworld, those ideas gained a new life and significance in the light surrounding the drooping head of Jesus on the cross.

Much should be, but cannot be, said here about the changes in the personality of Paul subsequent to that vision; changes conditioned to a great extent by the reception he found when he told his people about the Messiah Jesus. The Jews could not stand the idea of another god besides Jahveh. Until Paul's death, Jesus was to Jewish Christians not another god, but the first-born of the sons of God who had sacrificed him for the salvation of mankind. Yet the way to deification of this contemporary son of God was opened by his sacrificial death and resurrection. Paul tried, for a long time, to reconcile his own overwhelming experience and the convictions resulting from it with the law. "A Hebrew of the Hebrews," proud of his nation as well as of his mission to the Jews, he desperately endeavored to show them the way to their salvation.

But there came a moment when a decision had to be made, when it became necessary to choose: the law or the faith. Paul could not remain with the Jews believing in God according to their law; he had to return to the Jews and Gentiles believing in Jehovah and in the Lord Jesus of Nazareth. More and more the death of Christ and His resurrection became the pivot of history for Paul. More and more the "new Adam" contrasted with the old Adam. The law has to yield to faith. Jahveh had, without knowing it, given His place to His firstborn son. It is unnecessary to be circumcised. What is needed is to be "baptized in Jesus," which means being reborn with Him and in Him. It presupposes dying with Him first in order to experience His resurrection as Paul did.

The totem meal was also renewed—no longer in the form of a communion in eating a sacred, otherwise forbidden animal, but in eating the God Himself and at His own explicit command. In these two acts the new Christians, and all Christians of future generations, became identified with Christ, renewing the oldest primitive ritual of many thousands of years ago. A ritual that had survived only in a symbolic and displaced form became again a material and "real" action in which the community was united with God whose body they eat and whose blood they drink in the most Holy Sacrament of the new religion. It is as though an essential part of the process that had once taken place in the brother horde had been repeated in its secondary phase, now displaced to the son figure. Jesus Christ, who appears as the firstborn son of God and His messenger in human form, was a rebel against Jahveh. Anatole France once aptly remarked that there are no victorious rebels. They are transformed into generally accepted and acknowledged authorities. After having atoned for His crime—in the myth the crime of all mankind—Jesus Christ becomes God Himself. The second round was won by the Son-God.

In Paul's conversion experience the world-historic essence of the Fall and of the Christ myth reappeared in individual reproduction. In his vision he again committed that first crime and suffered punishment for it. It is not accidental, but determined by his own experience, that he discovered that the two figures of Adam and Christ are intimately connected. Christ Himself did not mention Adam, but Paul taught that, as sin entered the world by one man, and also death by sin, so again by one man, Christ, was the Fall of Man converted into the Rise of Man, and sin eliminated by the shedding of His blood. If there had been no Fall, the salvation by Jesus, the coming of the Son of God would not have been necessary. In making Christ the antitype of Adam and in declaring that He atoned for the original sin, Paul has laid down the outline of the Christian Fall doctrine. The synoptic evidence shows that Jesus Christ never raised the question of the origin of sin, nor did He allude to the Fall of Adam. Again and again the contrast of the disobedience of Adam and the obedience of Christ is drawn by Paul (Romans 5:19). I Corinthians 15:22 proclaims: "For as in Adam all die, even so in Christ shall all be made alive."

The Fall finds then its predestined counterpart in the Redemption wrought by Christ in the writings of Augustine, perhaps the greatest man next to Paul in the history of Christianity, and by the other Fathers of the Church. Theology speaks of "the two complementary conceptions," of "the twin focal points which determine the ellipse of traditional theology," of the "two pillars of the Fall and of Redemption."[10] From the theologian's point of view human history begins with Adam and begins again with Christ, so much so that what happens in between occurs within an epoch of darkness. The two great events in the history of mankind, the Fall by Adam and the Redemption by Christ, became the double foundation of the Christian faith. St. Cyril of Alexandria only continues the line, introduced by the great apostles of the Gentiles, "We are all in Christ and the totality of mankind comes to life again in Him. For he is called the New Adam because by sharing in our nature He has enriched all unto happiness and glory, as the first Adam filled all with corruption and ignomy." (Comment in St. John Evang. I.1.24)

Paul's concept of the murder of God is, of course, not mentioned. It was replaced, as Freud said,[11] "by the tenet of the somewhat shadowy conception of the original sin." That conception

[10] N. P. Williams, *The Ideas of the Fall* (London, 1927), p. 8.
[11] *Moses and Monotheism*, p. 214.

did not remain shadowy. The Fathers of the Church made it definite and definable: Adam's sin was of the flesh, was a sexual transgression. Later generations of Christians willingly accepted that doctrine, following their priests as sheep the shepherd. Mankind accuses itself of concupiscence instead of murder. The sidetracking to sexuality which was the strongest motive of the primeval crime promised an easing of the collective guilt feeling. By confessing the minor offense one had avoided admitting the full gravity of the original deed. It seemed that mankind was released through salvation.

The emotional situation before Christianity resembled that in which a festering boil is felt. There is pressure and pain at the places where pus gathers. The unconscious guilt feeling of man thus was painfully experienced. Christianity can be compared to the lancing of the abscess and with it a relief from pressure was felt for a certain time. The deep abscess is still there.

Paul could not penetrate to the core of the Fall story. The true nature of the primal crime remained unconscious, but he pierced the amnesia of mankind at a certain point.

ERNEST JONES / The Death of Hamlet's Father

When a poet takes an old theme from which to create a work of art, it is always interesting, and often instructive, to note the respects in which he changes elements in the story. Much of what we glean of Shakespeare's personality is derived from such studies, the direct biographical details being so sparse. The difference in the accounts given in *Hamlet* of the way the King had died from that given in the original story is so striking that it would seem worth while to look closer at the matter.

The most obvious difference is that in the Saxo-Belleforest saga the murder is a public one, with Shakespeare a secret one. We do not know, however, who made this change, since an English play called *Hamlet,* thought to be written by Kyd, was extant some twelve years before Shakespeare wrote his; and he doubtless used it as well as the Belleforest version. That play no longer exists except in a much later and much distorted German version, but a Ghost probably appeared in it, and one can hardly imagine any other function for him than to disclose a secret murder. There is reason to suppose that Shakespeare may himself have had a hand in the Kyd play, but at all events he made the best possible use of the alteration.

In the old saga, Claudius (there called Feng) draws his sword on his brother the King (Horvendil)[1] at a banquet and slays him 'with many wounds'. He explains to the assembled nobles that he has done this to protect his sister-in-law (Geruth) from ill-treatment and imminent peril of her life at the hands of her husband—a pretext evidently, a reflection of the infant's sadistic conception of coitus. Incidentally, in the Saxon saga (though not with Belleforest), there had here been no previous adultery with the Queen, so that Feng is the sole villain, and Amleth, unlike Hamlet, unhesitatingly kills him and reigns in his stead as soon as he can overcome the external obstacles. In *Hamlet,* as is well known, the plot is intensified by the previous incestuous adultery of the Queen, which convulses Hamlet at least as much as his father's murder and results in an animus against women that complicates his previously simple task.

In the *Hamlet* play, on the other hand, Claudius disclaims all responsibility for his brother's death and spreads a somewhat improbable story of his having been stung to death by a serpent while sleeping in an orchard. How he knew this we are not told, nor why the adder possessed this quite unwonted deadliness. There is much to be said about that 'orchard', but we may assume that it symbolizes the woman in whose arms the king was murdered. The Ghost's version was quite different. According to him, Claudius had found him asleep and poured a juice of hebana into his ears, a still more improbable story from a medical point of view; he further tells us that the poison rapidly spread through his system resulting in 'all his smooth body being barked about most lazar-like with vile and loathsome crust'. Presumably its swift action prevented him from informing anyone of what had befallen him.

The source of this mysterious poison has been traced as follows.[2] Shakespeare seems to have taken the name, incidentally misspelling it, from the juice of 'hebon', mentioned in a play of Marlowe's, who himself had added an initial letter to the 'ebon' (ebony) of which the walls of the God of Sleep were composed (Ovid). Shakespeare apparently went on to confound this narcotic with henbane (hyoscyamus), which at that time was believed to cause mortification and turn the body black.[3] Two interesting beliefs about henbane are mentioned by Pliny: (1) that it is a remedy for earache, and (2) when poured into the ear it causes mental disorder.

[1] It was Shakespeare who changed this name to Hamlet, thus emphasizing the identification of son and father.
[2] See Hy. Bradley, *Modern Language Review* (1920), vol. xv, p. 85.
[3] W. Thistlton-Dyer, *Shakespeare's England,* vol. i, p. 509.

The coarse Northern butchery is thus replaced by a surreptitious Italianate form of murder, a fact that has led to many inquiries, which do not concern us here, concerning Italian influence on Shakespeare. The identical method is employed in the Play Scene, where a nephew murders his uncle, who was resting after coitus, by dropping poison into his ear and immediately afterwards espouses the widow *à la* Richard III. Hamlet says he got the Gonzago story from an Italian play, but no such play has yet been traced. There had, however, been two instances of murder in an unhappy Gonzaga family. In 1538 a famous Duke of Urbino, who was married to a Gonzaga, died under somewhat suspicious circumstances. Poison was suspected, and his barber was believed to have poured a lotion into his ears on a number of occasions. So the story goes: whether poison thus administered is lethal to anyone with intact tympani is a matter we must leave to the toxicologists. At all events the Duke's son got the unfortunate barber torn in pieces by pincers and then quartered. In the course of this proceeding the barber asserted he had been put on to commit the foul deed by a Luigi[4] Gonzaga, a relative of the Duke by marriage. For political and legal reasons, however, he was never brought to trial.[5] Furthermore, in 1592 the Marchese Rudolf von Castiglione got eight bravoes to murder his *uncle,* the Marchese Alfonso Gonzaga, a relative of the Duke of Mantua. Rudolf had wished to marry his uncle's daughter and had been refused; he himself was murdered eight months later.

The names used make it evident that Shakespeare was familiar with the story of the earlier Gonzaga murder, as he possibly was with the later one too. The 'poison in the ear' story must have appealed to him, since he not only used it in the Gonzago Play Scene—where it would be appropriate—but also in the account of Hamlet's father's death.

If we translate them into the language of symbolism the Ghost's story is not so dissimilar from that of Claudius. To the unconscious, 'poison' signifies any bodily fluid charged with evil intent, while the serpent has played a well-known rôle ever since the Garden of Eden. The murderous assault had therefore both aggressive and erotic components, and we note that it was Shakespeare who introduced the latter. Furthermore, that the ear is an unconscious equivalent for anus is a matter for which I have adduced ample evidence elsewhere.[6] So we must call Claudius' attack on his brother both a murderous aggression and a homosexual assault.

[4] From whom Shakespeare perhaps got the name Lucianus for the murderer in the Play Scene.

[5] See G. Bullough, 'The Murder of Gonzago', *Modern Language Review* (1935), vol. xxx, p. 433.

[6] *Essays in Applied Psycho-Analysis* (1923), pp. 341-6.

Why did Shakespeare give this curious turn to a plain story of envious ambition? The theme of homosexuality itself does not surprise us in Shakespeare. In a more or less veiled form a pronounced femininity and a readiness to interchange the sexes are prominent characteristics of his plays, and doubtless of his personality also. I have argued[7] that Shakespeare wrote *Hamlet* as a partly successful abreaction of the intolerable emotions aroused by the painful situation he depicts in his Sonnets, his betrayal by both his beloved young noble and his mistress. In life he apparently smothered his resentment and became reconciled to both betrayers. Artistically his response was privately to write the Sonnets (in the later publication of which he had no hand) and publicly to compose *Hamlet* not long afterwards—a play gory enough to satisfy all varieties of revenge.

The episode raises again the vexed question of the relation between active and passive homosexuality. Nonanalysts who write on this topic are apt to maintain that they represent two different inborn types, but this assertion gives one an unsatisfied feeling of improbability, and analytic investigation confirms these doubts by demonstrating numerous points of contact between the two attitudes. Certainly Claudius's assault was active enough; sexually it signified turning the victim into a female, *i.e.* castrating him. Hamlet himself, as Freud[8] pointed out long ago, was unconsciously identified with Claudius, which was the reason why he was unable to denounce and kill him. So the younger brother attacking the older is simply a replica of the son-father conflict, and the complicated poisoning story really represents the idea of the son castrating his father. But we must not forget that it is done in an erotic fashion. Now Hamlet's conscious attitude towards his father was a feminine one, as shown by his exaggerated adoration and his adjuring Gertrude to love such a perfect hero instead of his brother. In Freud's opinion homosexuality takes its origin in narcissism,[9] so that it is always a mirror-love; Hamlet's father would therefore be his own ideal of himself. That is why, in such cases, as with Hamlet, suicide is so close to murder.

My analytical experience, simplified for the present purpose, impels me to the following reconstruction of homosexual development. Together with the narcissism, a feminine attitude towards the father presents itself as an attempted solution of the intolerable murderous and castrating impulses aroused by jealousy. These may persist, but when the fear of the self-castration implied gains the upper hand, *i.e.* when the masculine impulse is strong,

[7] Ernest Jones, *Hamlet and Oedipus,* 1949.
[8] *Die Traumdeuting* (1900), p. 183.
[9] Freud, *Collected Papers,* vol. ii, p. 241.

the original aggression reasserts itself—but this time under the erotic guise of active homosexuality.

According to Freud, Hamlet was inhibited by his repressed hatred of his father. We have to add to this the homosexual aspect of his attitude, so that Love and Hate, as so often, both play their part.

PHILIP ROTH / Eli, The Fanatic

LEO TZUREF stepped out from back of a white column to welcome Eli Peck. Eli jumped back, surprised; then they shook hands and Tzuref gestured him into the sagging old mansion. At the door Eli turned, and down the slope of lawn, past the jungle of hedges, beyond the dark, untrampled horse path, he saw the street lights blink on in Woodenton. The stores along Coach House Road tossed up a burst of yellow—it came to Eli as a secret signal from his townsmen: "Tell this Tzuref where we stand, Eli. This is a modern community, Eli, we have our families, we pay taxes . . ." Eli, burdened by the message, gave Tzuref a dumb, weary stare.

"You must work a full day," Tzuref said, steering the attorney and his briefcase into the chilly hall.

Eli's heels made a racket on the cracked marble floor, and he spoke above it. "It's the commuting that's killing," he said, and entered the dim room Tzuref waved open for him. "Three hours a day . . . I came right from the train." He dwindled down into a harp-backed chair. He expected it would be deeper than it was and consequently jarred himself on the sharp bones of his seat. It woke him, this shiver of the behind, to his business. Tzuref, a bald shaggy-browed man who looked as if he'd once been very fat, sat back of an empty desk, halfway hidden, as though he were settled on the floor. Everything around him was empty. There were no books in the bookshelves, no rugs on the floor, no draperies in the big casement windows. As Eli began to speak Tzuref got up and swung a window back on one noisy hinge. "May and it's like August," he said, and with his back to Eli, he revealed the black circle on the back of his head. The crown of his head was missing! He returned through the dimness—the lamps had no bulbs—and Eli realized all he'd seen was a skullcap. Tzuref struck a match and lit a candle, just as the half-dying shouts of children at play rolled in through the open window. It was as though Tzuref had opened it so Eli could hear them.

"Aah, now," he said. "I received your letter."

Eli poised, waiting for Tzuref to swish open a drawer and remove the letter from his file. Instead the old man leaned forward onto his stomach, worked his hand into his pants pocket, and withdrew what appeared to be a week-old handkerchief. He uncrumpled it; he unfolded it; he ironed it on the desk with the side of his hand. "So," he said.

Eli pointed to the grimy sheet which he'd gone over word-by-word with his partners, Lewis and McDonnell. "I expected an answer," Eli said. "It's a week."

"It was so important, Mr. Peck, I knew you would come."

Some children ran under the open window and their mysterious babble—not mysterious to Tzuref, who smiled—entered the room like a third person. Their noise caught up against Eli's flesh and he was unable to restrain a shudder. He wished he had gone home, showered and eaten dinner, before calling on Tzuref. He was not feeling as professional as usual—the place was too dim, it was too late. But down in Woodenton they would be waiting, his clients and neighbors. He spoke for the Jews of Woodenton, not just himself and his wife.

"You understood?" Eli said.

"It's not hard."

"It's a matter of zoning . . ." and when Tzuref did not answer, but only drummed his fingers on his lips, Eli said, "We didn't make the laws . . ."

"You respect them."

"They protect us . . . the community."

"The law is the law," Tzuref said.

"Exactly!" Eli had the urge to rise and walk about the room.

"And then of course"—Tzuref made a pair of scales in the air with his hands—"The law is not the law. When is the law that is the law not the law?" He jiggled the scales. "And vice versa."

"Simply," Eli said sharply. "You can't have a boarding school in a residential area." He would not allow Tzuref to cloud the issue with issues. "We thought it better to tell you before any action is undertaken."

"But a house in a residential area?"

"Yes. That's what residential means." The DP's English was perhaps not as good as it seemed at first. Tzuref spoke slowly, but till then Eli had mistaken it for craft—or even wisdom. "Residence means home," he added.

"So this is my residence."

"But the children?"

"It is their residence."

"*Seventeen* children?"

"Eighteen," Tzuref said.

"But you *teach* them here."

"The Talmud. That's illegal?"

"That makes it school."

Tzuref hung the scales again, tipping slowly the balance.

"Look, Mr. Tzuref, in America we call such a place a boarding school."

"Where they teach the Talmud?"

"Where they teach period. You are the headmaster, they are the students."

Tzuref placed his scales on the desk. "Mr. Peck," he said, "I don't believe it . . ." but he did not seem to be referring to anything Eli had said.

"Mr. Tzuref, that is the law. I came to ask what you intend to do."

"What I *must* do?"

"I hope they are the same."

"They are." Tzuref brought his stomach into the desk. "We stay." He smiled. "We are tired. The headmaster is tired. The students are tired."

Eli rose and lifted his briefcase. It felt so heavy packed with the grievances, vengeances, and schemes of his clients. There were days when he carried it like a feather—in Tzuref's office it weighed a ton.

"Goodbye, Mr. Tzuref."

"Sholom," Tzuref said.

Eli opened the door to the office and walked carefully down the dark tomb of a corridor to the door. He stepped out on the porch and, leaning against a pillar, looked down across the lawn to the children at play. Their voices whooped and rose and dropped as they chased each other round the old house. The dusk made the children's game look like a tribal dance. Eli straightened up, started off the porch, and suddenly the dance was ended. A long piercing scream trailed after. It was the first time in his life anyone had run at the sight of him. Keeping his eyes on the lights of Woodenton, he headed down the path.

And then, seated on a bench beneath a tree, Eli saw him. At first it seemed only a deep hollow of blackness—then the figure emerged. Eli recognized him from the description. There he was, wearing the hat, that hat which was the very cause of Eli's mission, the source of Woodenton's upset. The town's lights flashed their message once again: "Get the one with the hat. What a nerve, what a nerve . . ."

Eli started towards the man. Perhaps he was less stubborn than Tzuref, more reasonable. After all, it was the law. But when he was close enough to call out, he didn't. He was stopped by the sight of the black coat that fell down below the man's knees, and the hands which held each other in his lap. By the round-topped, wide-brimmed Talmudic hat, pushed onto the back of his head. And by the beard, which hid his neck and was so soft and thin it fluttered away and back again with each heavy breath he took. He was asleep, his sidelocks curled loose on his cheeks. His face was no older than Eli's.

Eli hurried towards the lights.

The note on the kitchen table unsettled him. Scribblings on bits of paper had made history this past week. This one, however, was unsigned. "Sweetie," it said, "I went to sleep. I had a sort of Oedipal experience with the baby today. Call Ted Heller."

She had left him a cold soggy dinner in the refrigerator. He hated cold soggy dinners, but would take one gladly in place of Miriam's presence. He was ruffled, and she never helped that, not with her infernal analytic powers. He loved her when life was proceeding smoothly—and that was when she loved him. But sometimes Eli found being a lawyer surrounded him like quicksand—he couldn't get his breath. Too often he wished he were pleading for the other side; though if he were on the other side, then he'd wish he were on the side he was. The trouble was that sometimes the law didn't seem to be the answer, *law* didn't seem to have anything to do with what was aggravating everybody. And that, of course, made him feel foolish and unnecessary . . . Though that was not the situation here—the townsmen had a case. But not *exactly,* and if Miriam were awake to see Eli's upset, she would set about explaining his distress to him, understanding him, forgiving him, so as to get things back to Normal, for Normal was where they loved one another. The difficulty with Miriam's efforts was they only upset him more; not only did they explain little to him about himself or his predicament, but they convinced him of *her* weakness. Neither Eli nor Miriam, it turned out, was terribly strong. Twice before he'd faced this fact, and on both occasions had found solace in what his neighbors forgivingly referred to as "a nervous breakdown."

Eli ate his dinner with his briefcase beside him. Halfway through, he gave in to himself, removed Tzuref's notes, and put them on the table, beside Miriam's. From time to time he flipped through the notes, which had been carried into town by the one in the black hat. The first note, the incendiary:

To whom it may concern:

Please give this gentleman the following: Boys shoes with rubber heels and soles.

5 prs size 6c
3 prs size 5c
3 prs size 5b
2 prs size 4a
3 prs size 4c
1 pr size 7b
1 pr size 7c

Total 18 prs. boys shoes. This gentleman has a check already signed. Please fill in correct amount.

L. Tzuref
Director, Yeshivah of
Woodenton, N.Y.
(5/8/48)

"Eli, a regular greenhorn," Ted Heller had said. "He didn't say a word. Just handed me the note and stood there, like in the Bronx the old guys who used to come around selling Hebrew trinkets."

"A Yeshivah!" Artie Berg had said. "Eli, in Woodenton, a Yeshivah! If I want to live in Brownsville, Eli, I'll live in Brownsville."

"Eli," Harry Shaw speaking now, "the old Puddington place. Old man Puddington'll roll over in his grave. Eli, when I left the city, Eli, I didn't plan the city should come to me."

Note number two:

Dear Grocer:

Please give this gentleman ten pounds of sugar. Charge it to our account, Yeshivah of Woodenton, NY—which we will now open with you and expect a bill each month. The gentleman will be in to see you once or twice a week.

L. Tzuref, Director
(5/10/48)

P.S. Do you carry kosher meat?

"He walked right by my window, the greenie," Ted had said, "and he nodded, Eli. He's my *friend* now."

"Eli," Artie Berg had said, "he handed the damn thing to a *clerk* at Stop N' Shop—and in that hat yet!"

"Eli," Harry Shaw again, "it's not funny. Someday, Eli, it's going to be a hundred little kids with little *yamalkahs* chanting their Hebrew lessons on Coach House Road, and then it's not going to strike you funny."

"Eli, what goes on up there—my kids hear strange sounds."

"Eli, this is a modern community."

"Eli, we pay taxes."

"Eli."

"Eli!"

"Eli!"

At first it was only another townsman crying in his ear; but when he turned he saw Miriam, standing in the doorway, behind her belly.

"Eli, sweetheart, how was it?"

"He said no."

"Did you see the other one?" she asked.

"Sleeping, under a tree."

"Did you let him know how people feel?"

"He was sleeping."

"Why didn't you wake him up? Eli, this isn't an everyday thing."

"He was tired!"

"Don't shout, please," Miriam said.

" 'Don't shout. I'm pregnant. The baby is heavy.' " Eli found he was getting angry at nothing she'd said yet; it was what she was going to say.

"He's a very heavy baby the doctor says," Miriam told him.

"Then sit *down* and make my dinner." Now he found himself angry about her not being present at the dinner which he'd just been relieved that she wasn't present at. It was as though he had a raw nerve for a tail, that he kept stepping on. At last Miriam herself stepped on it.

"Eli, you're upset. I understand."

"You *don't* understand."

She left the room. From the stairs she called, "I do, sweetheart."

It was a trap! He would grow angry knowing she would be "understanding." She would in turn grow more understanding seeing his anger. He would in turn grow angrier . . . The phone rang.

"Hello," Eli said.

"Eli, Ted. So?"

"So nothing."

"Who is Tzuref? He's an American guy?"

"No. A DP. German."

"And the kids?"

"DP's too. He teaches them."

"What? What subjects?" Ted asked.

"I don't know."

"And the guy with the hat, you saw the guy with the hat?"

"Yes. He was sleeping."

"Eli, he sleeps with the *hat?*"

"He sleeps with the hat."

"Goddam fanatics," Ted said. "This is the twentieth century, Eli. Now it's the guy with the hat. Pretty soon all the little Yeshivah boys'll be spilling down into town."

"Next thing they'll be after our daughters."

"Michele and Debbie wouldn't look at them."

"Then," Eli mumbled, "you've got nothing to worry about, Teddie," and he hung up.

In a moment the phone rang. "Eli? We got cut off. We've got nothing to worry about? You worked it out?"

"I have to see him again tomorrow. We can work something out."

"That's fine, Eli. I'll call Artie and Harry."

Eli hung up.

"I thought you said *nothing* worked out." It was Miriam.

"I did."

"Then why did you tell Ted *something* worked out?"

"It did."

"Eli, maybe you should get a little more therapy."

"That's enough of that, Miriam."

"You can't function as a lawyer by being neurotic. That's no answer."

"You're ingenious, Miriam."

She turned, frowning, and took her heavy baby to bed.

The phone rang.

"Eli, Artie. Ted called. You worked it out? No trouble?"

"Yes."

"When are they going?"

"Leave it to me, will you, Artie? I'm tired. I'm going to sleep."

In bed Eli kissed his wife's belly and laid his head upon it to think. He laid it lightly, for she was that day entering the second week of her ninth month. Still, when she slept, it was a good place to rest, to rise and fall with her breathing and figure things out. "If that guy would take off that crazy hat. I know it, what eats them. If he'd take off that crazy hat everything would be all right."

"What?" Miriam said.

"I'm talking to the baby."

Miriam pushed herself up in bed. "Eli, please, baby, shouldn't you maybe stop in to see Dr. Eckman, just for a little conversation?"

"I'm fine."

"Oh, sweetie!" she said, and put her head back on the pillow.

"You know what your mother brought to this marriage—a sling chair and a goddam New School enthusiasm for Sigmund Freud."

Miriam feigned sleep, he could tell by the breathing.

"I'm telling the kid the truth, aren't I, Miriam? A sling chair, three months to go on a *New Yorker* subscription, and *An Introduction to Psychoanalysis*. Isn't that right?"

"Eli, must you be aggressive?"

"That's all you worry about, is your insides. You stand in front of the mirror all day and look at yourself being pregnant."

"Pregnant mothers have a relationship with the fetus that fathers can't understand."

"Relationship my ass. What is my liver doing now? What is my small intestine doing now? Is my island of Langerhans on the blink?"

"Don't be jealous of a little fetus, Eli."

"I'm jealous of your island of Langerhans!"

"Eli, I can't argue with you when I know it's not me you're really angry with. Don't you see, sweetie, you're angry with yourself."

"You and Eckman."

"Maybe he could help, Eli."

"Maybe he could help you. You're practically lovers as it is."

"You're being hostile again," Miriam said.

"What do you care—it's only *me* I'm being hostile towards."

"Eli, we're going to have a beautiful baby, and I'm going to have a perfectly simple delivery, and you're going to make a fine father, and there's absolutely no reason to be obsessed with whatever is on your mind. All we have to worry about—" she smiled at him "—is a name."

Eli got out of bed and slid into his slippers. "We'll name the kid Eckman if it's a boy and Eckman if it's a girl."

"Eckman Peck sounds terrible."

"He'll have to live with it," Eli said, and he went down to his study where the latch on his briefcase glinted in the moonlight that came through the window.

He removed the Tzuref notes and read through them all again. It unnerved him to think of all the flashy reasons his wife could come up with for his reading and rereading the notes. "Eli, why are you so *preoccupied* with Tzuref?" "Eli, stop getting *involved*. Why do you think you're getting *involved*, Eli?" Sooner or later, everybody's wife finds their weak spot. His goddam luck he had to be neurotic! Why couldn't he have been born with a short leg.

He removed the cover from his typewriter, hating Miriam for the edge she had. All the time he wrote the letter, he could hear what she would be saying about his not being *able* to let the matter drop. Well, her trouble was that she wasn't *able* to face the matter. But he could hear her answer already: clearly, he was guilty of "a reaction formation." Still, all the fancy phrases didn't fool Eli: all she wanted really was for Eli to send Tzuref and family on their way, so that the community's temper would quiet, and the calm circumstances of their domestic happiness return. All she wanted were order and love in her private world. Was she so wrong? Let the world bat its brains out—in Woodenton there should be peace. He wrote the letter anyway:

Dear Mr. Tzuref:

Our meeting this evening seems to me inconclusive. I don't think there's any reason for us not to be able to come up with some sort of compromise that will satisfy the Jewish community of Woodenton and the Yeshivah and yourself. It seems to me that what most disturbs my neighbors are the visits to town by the gentleman in the black hat, suit, etc. Woodenton is a progressive suburban community whose members, both Jewish and Gentile, are anxious that their families live in comfort and beauty and serenity. This is, after all, the twentieth century, and we do not think it too much to ask that the members of our community dress in a manner appropriate to the time and place.

Woodenton, as you may not know, has long been the home of well-to-do Protestants. It is only since the war that Jews have been able to buy property here, and for Jews and Gentiles to live beside each other in amity. For this adjustment to be made, both Jews and Gentiles alike have had to give up some of their more extreme practices in order not to threaten or offend the other. Certainly such amity is to be desired. Perhaps if such conditions had existed in prewar Europe, the persecution of the Jewish people, of which you and those 18 children have been victims, could not have been carried out with such success—in fact, might not have been carried out at all.

Therefore, Mr. Tzuref, will you accept the following conditions? If you can, we will see fit not to carry out legal action against the Yeshivah for failure to comply with township Zoning ordinances No. 18 and No. 23. The conditions are simply:

1. The religious, educational, and social activities of the Yeshivah of Woodenton will be confined to the Yeshivah grounds.

2. Yeshivah personnel are welcomed in the streets and

stores of Woodenton provided they are attired in clothing usually associated with American life in the 20th century.

If these conditions are met, we see no reason why the Yeshivah of Woodenton cannot live peacefully and satisfactorily with the Jews of Woodenton—as the Jews of Woodenton have come to live with the Gentiles of Woodenton. I would appreciate an immediate reply.

Sincerely,
ELI PECK, Attorney

Two days later Eli received his immediate reply:

Mr. Peck:

The suit the gentleman wears is all he's got.

Sincerely,
LEO TZUREF, Headmaster

Once again, as Eli swung around the dark trees and onto the lawn, the children fled. He reached out with his briefcase as if to stop them, but they were gone so fast all he saw moving was a flock of skullcaps.

"Come, come . . ." a voice called from the porch. Tzuref appeared from behind a pillar. Did he *live* behind those pillars? Was he just watching the children at play? Either way, when Eli appeared, Tzuref was ready, with no forewarning.

"Hello," Eli said.

"Sholom."

"I didn't mean to frighten them."

"They're scared, so they run."

"I didn't do anything."

Tzuref shrugged. The little movement seemed to Eli strong as an accusation. What he didn't get at home, he got here.

Inside the house they took their seats. Though it was lighter than a few evenings before, a bulb or two would have helped. Eli had to hold his briefcase towards the window for the last gleamings. He removed Tzuref's letter from a manila folder. Tzuref removed Eli's letter from his pants pocket. Eli removed the carbon of his own letter from another manila folder. Tzuref removed Eli's first letter from his back pocket. Eli removed the carbon from his briefcase. Tzuref raised his palms. ". . . It's all I've got . . ."

Those upraised palms, the mocking tone—another accusation. It was a crime to keep carbons! Everybody had an edge on him—Eli could do no right.

"I offered a compromise, Mr. Tzuref. You refused."

"Refused, Mr. Peck? What is, is."

"The man could get a new suit."

"That's all he's got."

"So you told me," Eli said.

"So I told you, so you know."

"It's not an insurmountable obstacle, Mr. Tzuref. We have stores."

"For that too?"

"On Route 12, a Robert Hall—"

"To take away the one thing a man's got?"

"Not take away, *replace*."

"But I tell you he has nothing. *Nothing*. You have that word in English? *Nicht? Gornisht?*"

"Yes, Mr. Tzuref, we have the word."

"A mother and a father?" Tzuref said. "No. A wife? No. A baby? A little ten-month-old baby? No! A village full of friends? A synagogue where you knew the feel of every seat under your pants? Where with your eyes closed you could smell the cloth of the Torah?" Tzuref pushed out of his chair, stirring a breeze that swept Eli's letter to the floor. At the window he leaned out, and looked, beyond Woodenton. When he turned he was shaking a finger at Eli. "And a medical experiment they performed on him yet! That leaves nothing, Mr. Peck. Absolutely nothing!"

"I misunderstood."

"No news reached Woodenton?"

"About the suit, Mr. Tzuref. I thought he couldn't afford another."

"He can't."

They were right where they'd begun. "Mr. Tzuref!" Eli demanded. *"Here?"* He smacked his hand to his billfold.

"Exactly!" Tzuref said, smacking his own breast.

"Then we'll buy him one!" Eli crossed to the window and taking Tzuref by the shoulders, pronounced each word slowly. "We-will-pay-for-it. All right?"

"Pay? What, diamonds!"

Eli raised a hand to his inside pocket, then let it drop. Oh stupid! Tzuref, father to eighteen, had smacked not what lay under his coat, but deeper, under the ribs.

"Oh . . ." Eli said. He moved away along the wall. "The suit is all he's got then."

"You got my letter," Tzuref said.

Eli stayed back in the shadow, and Tzuref turned to his chair. He swished Eli's letter from the floor, and held it up. "You say too much . . . all this reasoning . . . all these conditions . . ."

"What can I do?"

"You have the word 'suffer' in English?"

"We have the word suffer. We have the word law too."

"Stop with the law! You have the word suffer. Then try it. It's a little thing."

"They won't," Eli said.

"But you, Mr. Peck, how about you?"

"I am them, they are me, Mr. Tzuref."

"Aach! You are us, we are you!"

Eli shook and shook his head. In the dark he suddenly felt that Tzuref might put him under a spell. "Mr. Tzuref, a little light?"

Tzuref lit what tallow was left in the holders. Eli was afraid to ask if they couldn't afford electricity. Maybe candles were all they had left.

"Mr. Peck, who made the law, may I ask you that?"

"The people."

"No."

"Yes."

"Before the people."

"No one. Before the people there was no law." Eli didn't care for the conversation, but with only candlelight, he was being lulled into it.

"Wrong," Tzuref said.

"We make the law, Mr. Tzuref. It is our community. These are my neighbors. I am their attorney. They pay me. Without law there is chaos."

"What you call law, I call shame. The heart, Mr. Peck, the heart is law! God!" he announced.

"Look, Mr. Tzuref, I didn't come here to talk metaphysics. People use the law, it's a flexible thing. They protect what they value, their property, their well-being, their happiness—"

"Happiness? They hide their shame. And you, Mr. Peck, you are shameless?"

"We do it," Eli said, wearily, "for our children. This is the twentieth century . . ."

"For the goyim maybe. For me the Fifty-eighth." He pointed at Eli. "That is too old for shame."

Eli felt squashed. Everybody in the world had evil reasons for his actions. Everybody! With reasons so cheap, who buys bulbs. "Enough wisdom, Mr. Tzuref. Please. I'm exhausted."

"Who isn't?" Tzuref said.

He picked Eli's papers from his desk and reached up with them. "What do you intend for us to do?"

"What you must," Eli said. "I made the offer."

"So he must give up his suit?"

"Tzuref, Tzuref, leave me be with that suit! I'm not the

only lawyer in the world. I'll drop the case, and you'll get somebody who won't talk compromise. Then you'll have no home, no children, nothing. Only a lousy black suit! Sacrifice what you want. I know what I would do."

To that Tzuref made no answer, but only handed Eli his letters.

"It's not me, Mr. Tzuref, it's them."

"They are you."

"No," Eli intoned, "I am me. They are them. You are you."

"You talk about leaves and branches. I'm dealing with under the dirt."

"Mr. Tzuref, you're driving me crazy with Talmudic wisdom. This is that, that is the other thing. Give me a straight answer."

"Only for straight questions."

"Oh, God!"

Eli returned to his chair and plunged his belongings into his case. "Then, that's all," he said angrily.

Tzuref gave him the shrug.

"Remember, Tzuref, you called this down on yourself."

"*I* did?"

Eli refused to be his victim again. Double-talk proved nothing.

"Goodbye," he said.

But as he opened the door leading to the hall, he heard Tzuref.

"And your wife, how is she?"

"Fine, just fine." Eli kept going.

"And the baby is due when, any day?"

Eli turned. "That's right."

"Well," Tzuref said, rising. "Good luck."

"You know?"

Tzuref pointed out the window—then, with his hands, he drew upon himself a beard, a hat, a long, long coat. When his fingers formed the hem they touched the floor. "He shops two, three times a week, he gets to know them."

"He *talks* to them?"

"He sees them."

"And he can tell which is my wife?"

"They shop at the same stores. He says she is beautiful. She has a kind face. A woman capable of love . . . though who can be sure."

"*He* talks about *us,* to *you?*" demanded Eli.

"You talk about us, to her?"

"Goodbye, Mr. Tzuref."

Tzuref said, "Sholom. And good luck—I know what it is to have children. Sholom," Tzuref whispered, and with the whisper the candles went out. But the instant before, the flames leaped into Tzuref's eyes, and Eli saw it was not luck Tzuref wished him at all.

Outside the door, Eli waited. Down the lawn the children were holding hands and whirling around in a circle. At first he did not move. But he could not hide in the shadows all night. Slowly he began to slip along the front of the house. Under his hands he felt where bricks were out. He moved in the shadows until he reached the side. And then, clutching his briefcase to his chest, he broke across the darkest spots of the lawn. He aimed for a distant glade of woods, and when he reached it he did not stop, but ran through until he was so dizzied that the trees seemed to be running beside him, fleeing not towards Woodenton but away. His lungs were nearly ripping their seams as he burst into the yellow glow of the Gulf station at the edge of town.

"Eli, I had pains today. Where were you?"

"I went to Tzuref."

"Why didn't you call? I was worried."

He tossed his hat past the sofa and onto the floor. "Where are my winter suits?"

"In the hall closet. Eli, it's May."

"I need a strong suit." He left the room, Miriam behind him.

"Eli, talk to me. Sit down. Have dinner. Eli, what are you doing? You're going to get moth balls all over the carpet."

He peered out from the hall closet. Then he peered in again—there was a zipping noise, and suddenly he swept a greenish tweed suit before his wife's eyes.

"Eli, I love you in that suit. But not now. Have something to eat. I made dinner tonight—I'll warm it."

"You've got a box big enough for this suit?"

"I got a Bonwit's box, the other day. Eli, *why?*"

"Miriam, you see me doing something, let me do it."

"You haven't eaten."

"I'm *doing* something." He started up the stairs to the bedroom.

"Eli, would you please tell me what it is you want, and why?"

He turned and looked down at her. "Suppose this time you give me the reasons *before* I tell you what I'm doing. It'll probably work out the same anyway."

"Eli, I want to help."

"It doesn't concern you."

"But I want to help *you,*" Miriam said.

"Just be quiet, then."

"But you're upset," she said, and she followed him up the stairs, heavily, breathing for two.

"Eli, what now?"

"A shirt." He yanked open all the drawers of their new teak dresser. He extracted a shirt.

"Eli, batiste? With a tweed suit?" she inquired.

He was at the closet now, on his knees. "Where are my cordovans?"

"Eli, why are you doing this so compulsively? You look like you *have* to do something."

"Oh, Miriam, you're supersubtle."

"Eli, stop this and talk to me. Stop it or I'll call Dr. Eckman."

Eli was kicking off the shoes he was wearing. "Where's the Bonwit box?"

"Eli, do you want me to have the baby right *here!*"

Eli walked over and sat down on the bed. He was draped not only with his own clothing, but also with the greenish tweed suit, the batiste shirt, and under each arm a shoe. He raised his arms and let the shoes drop onto the bed. Then he undid his necktie with one hand and his teeth and added that to the booty.

"Underwear," he said. "He'll need underwear."

"Who!"

He was slipping out of his socks.

Miriam kneeled down and helped him ease his left foot out of the sock. She sat with it on the floor. "Eli, just lie back. Please."

"Plaza 9-3103."

"What?"

"Eckman's number," he said. "It'll save you the trouble."

"Eli—"

"You've got that goddam tender 'You need help' look in your eyes, Miriam, don't tell me you don't."

"I don't."

"I'm not flipping," Eli said.

"I know, Eli."

"Last time I sat in the bottom of the closet and chewed on my bedroom slippers. That's what I did."

"I know."

"And I'm not doing that. This is not a nervous breakdown, Miriam, let's get that straight."

"Okay," Miriam said. She kissed the foot she held. Then, softly, she asked, "What *are* you doing?"

"Getting clothes for the guy in the hat. Don't tell me why, Miriam. Just let me do it."

"That's all?" she asked.

"That's all."

"You're not leaving?"

"No."

"Sometimes I think it gets too much for you, and you'll just leave."

"What gets too much?"

"I don't *know,* Eli. Something gets too much. Whenever everything's peaceful for a long time, and things are nice and pleasant, and we're expecting to be even happier. Like now. It's as if you don't think we *deserve* to be happy."

"Damn it, Miriam! I'm giving this guy a new suit, is that all right? From now on he comes into Woodenton like everybody else, is that all right with you?"

"And Tzuref moves?"

"I don't even know if he'll take the suit, Miriam! What do you have to bring up moving!"

"Eli, I didn't bring up moving. Everybody did. That's what everybody wants. Why make everybody un*happy*. It's even a law, Eli."

"Don't tell me what's the law."

"All right, sweetie. I'll get the box."

"*I'll* get the box. Where is it?"

"In the basement."

When he came up from the basement, he found all the clothes neatly folded and squared away on the sofa: shirt, tie, shoes, socks, underwear, belt, and an old gray flannel suit. His wife sat on the end of the sofa, looking like an anchored balloon.

"Where's the green suit?" he said.

"Eli, it's your loveliest suit. It's my favorite suit. Whenever I think of you, Eli, it's in that suit."

"Get it out."

"Eli, it's a Brooks Brothers suit. You say yourself how much you love it."

"Get it out."

"But the gray flannel's more practical. For shopping."

"Get it out."

"You go overboard, Eli. That's your trouble. You won't do anything in moderation. That's how people destroy themselves."

"I do *everything* in moderation. That's my trouble. The suit's in the closet again?"

She nodded, and began to fill up with tears. "Why does it have to be *your* suit? Who are you even to decide to give a suit?

What about the others?" She was crying openly, and holding her belly. "Eli, I'm going to have a baby. Do we need all *this*?" and she swept the clothes off the sofa to the floor.

At the closet Eli removed the green suit. "It's a J. Press," he said, looking at the lining.

"I hope to hell he's happy with it!" Miriam said, sobbing.

A half hour later the box was packed. The cord he'd found in the kitchen cabinet couldn't keep the outfit from popping through. The trouble was there was too much: the gray suit *and* the green suit, an oxford shirt as well as the batiste. But let him have two suits! Let him have three, four, if only this damn silliness would stop! And a hat—of course! God, he'd almost forgotten the hat. He took the stairs two at a time and in Miriam's closet yanked a hatbox from the top shelf. Scattering hat and tissue paper to the floor, he returned downstairs, where he packed away the hat he'd worn that day. Then he looked at his wife, who lay outstretched on the floor before the fireplace. For the third time in as many minutes she was saying, "Eli, this is the real thing."

"Where?"

"Right under the baby's head, like somebody's squeezing oranges."

Now that he'd stopped to listen he was stupefied. He said, "But you have two more weeks . . ." Somehow he'd really been expecting it was to go on not just another two weeks, but another nine months. This led him to suspect, suddenly, that his wife was feigning pain so as to get his mind off delivering the suit. And just as suddenly he resented himself for having such a thought. God, what had he become! He'd been an unending bastard towards her since this Tzuref business had come up—just when her pregnancy must have been most burdensome. He'd allowed her no access to him, but still, he was sure, for good reasons: she might tempt him out of his confusion with her easy answers. He could be tempted all right, it was why he fought so hard. But now a sweep of love came over him at the thought of her contracting womb, and his child. And yet he would not indicate it to her. Under such splendid marital conditions, who knows but she might extract some promise from him about his concern with the school on the hill.

Having packed his second bag of the evening, Eli sped his wife to Woodenton Memorial. There she proceeded not to have her baby, but to lie hour after hour through the night having at first oranges, then bowling balls, then basketballs, squeezed back of her pelvis. Eli sat in the waiting room, under the shattering

African glare of a dozen rows of fluorescent bulbs, composing a letter to Tzuref.

Dear Mr. Tzuref:

The clothes in this box are for the gentleman in the hat. In a life of sacrifice what is one more? But in a life of no sacrifices even one is impossible. Do you see what I'm saying, Mr. Tzuref? I am not a Nazi who would drive eighteen children, who are probably frightened at the sight of a firefly, into homelessness. But if you want a home here, you must accept what we have to offer. The world is the world, Mr. Tzuref. As you would say, what is, is. All we say to this man is change your clothes. Enclosed are two suits and two shirts, and everything else he'll need, including a new hat. When he needs new clothes let me know.

We await his appearance in Woodenton, as we await friendly relations with the Yeshivah of Woodenton.

He signed his name and slid the note under a bursting flap and into the box. Then he went to the phone at the end of the room and dialed Ted Heller's number.

"Hello."

"Shirley, it's Eli."

"Eli, we've been calling all night. The lights are on in your place, but nobody answers. We thought it was burglars."

"Miriam's having the baby."

"At home?" Shirley said. "Oh, Eli, what a fun-idea!"

"Shirley, let me speak to Ted."

After the ear-shaking clatter of the phone whacking the floor, Eli heard footsteps, breathing, throat-clearing, then Ted. "A boy or a girl?"

"Nothing yet."

"You've given Shirley the bug, Eli. Now she's going to have *our* next one at home."

"Good."

"That's a terrific way to bring the family together, Eli."

"Look, Ted, I've settled with Tzuref."

"When are they going?"

"They're not exactly going, Teddie. I settled it—you won't even know they're there."

"A guy dressed like 1000 B.C. and I won't know it? What are you thinking about, pal?"

"He's changing his clothes."

"Yeah, to what? Another funeral suit?"

"Tzuref promised me, Ted. Next time he comes to town, he comes dressed like you and me."

"What! Somebody's kidding somebody, Eli."

Eli's voice shot up. "If he says he'll do it, he'll do it!"

"And, Eli," Ted asked, "he said it?"

"He said it." It cost him a sudden headache, this invention.

"And suppose he doesn't change, Eli. Just suppose. I mean that *might* happen, Eli. This might just be some kind of stall or something."

"No," Eli assured him.

The other end was quiet a moment. "Look, Eli," Ted said, finally, "he changes. Okay? All right? But they're still up there, aren't they? *That* doesn't change."

"The point is you won't know it."

Patiently Ted said, "Is this what we asked of you, Eli? When we put our faith and trust in you, is that what we were asking? We weren't concerned that this guy should become a Beau Brummel, Eli, believe me. We just don't think this is the community for them. And, Eli, we isn't me. The Jewish members of the community appointed me, Artie, and Harry to see what could be done. And we appointed you. And what's happened?"

Eli heard himself say, "What happened, happened."

"Eli, you're talking in crossword puzzles."

"My wife's having a baby," Eli explained, defensively.

"I realize that, Eli. But this is a matter of zoning, isn't it? Isn't that what we discovered? You don't abide by the ordinance, you go. I mean I can't raise mountain goats, say, in my backyard—"

"This isn't so simple, Ted. People are involved—"

"People? Eli, we've been through this and through this. We're not just dealing with people—these are religious fanatics is what they are. Dressing like that. What I'd really like to find out is what goes on up there. I'm getting more and more skeptical, Eli, and I'm not afraid to admit it. It smells like a lot of hocus-pocus abracadabra stuff to me. Guys like Harry, you know, they think and they think and they're afraid to admit what they're thinking. I'll tell you. Look, I don't even know about this Sunday school business. Sundays I drive my oldest kid all the way to Scarsdale to learn Bible stories . . . and you know what she comes up with? This Abraham in the Bible was going to kill his own *kid* for a sacrifice. She gets nightmares from it, for God's sake! You call that religion? Today a guy like that they'd lock him up. This is an age of science, Eli. I size people's feet with an X-ray machine, for God's sake. They've disproved all that stuff, Eli, and I refuse to sit by and watch it happening on my own front lawn."

"Nothing's happening on your front lawn, Teddie. You're exaggerating, nobody's sacrificing their kid."

"You're damn right, Eli—I'm not sacrificing mine. You'll see when you have your own what it's like. All the place is, is a hideaway for people who can't face life. It's a matter of *needs.* They have all these superstitions, and why do you think? Because they can't face the world, because they can't take their place in society. That's no environment to bring kids up in, Eli."

"Look, Ted, see it from another angle. We can convert them," Eli said, with half a heart.

"What, make a bunch of Catholics out of them? Look, Eli —pal, there's a good healthy relationship in this town because it's modern Jews and Protestants. That's the point, isn't it, Eli? Let's not kid each other, I'm not Harry. The way things are now are fine—like human beings. There's going to be no pogroms in Woodenton. Right? 'Cause there's no fanatics, no crazy people—" Eli winced, and closed his eyes a second—"just people who respect each other, and leave each other be. Common sense is the ruling thing, Eli. I'm for common sense. Moderation."

"Exactly, exactly, Ted. I agree, but common sense, maybe, says make this guy change his clothes. Then maybe—"

"Common sense says that? Common sense says to me they go and find a nice place somewhere else, Eli. New York is the biggest city in the world, it's only 30 miles away—why don't they go there?"

"Ted, give them a chance. Introduce them to common sense."

"Eli, you're dealing with *fanatics.* Do they display common sense? Talking a dead language, that makes sense? Making a big thing out of suffering, so you're going oy-oy-oy all your life, that's common sense? Look, Eli, we've been through all this. I don't know if you know—but there's talk that *Life* magazine is sending a guy out to the Yeshivah for a story. With pictures."

"Look, Teddie, you're letting your imagination get inflamed. I don't think *Life's* interested."

"But I'm interested, Eli. And we thought you were supposed to be."

"I am," Eli said, "I am. Let him just change the clothes, Ted. Let's see what happens."

"They live in the medieval ages, Eli—it's some superstition, some *rule.*"

"Let's just *see,*" Eli pleaded.

"Eli, every day—"

"One more day," Eli said. "If he doesn't change in one more day. . . ."

"What?"

"Then I get an injunction first thing Monday. That's that."

"Look, Eli—it's not up to me. Let me call Harry—"

"You're the spokesman, Teddie. I'm all wrapped up here with Miriam having a baby. Just give me the day—them the day."

"All right, Eli. I want to be fair. But tomorrow, that's all. Tomorrow's the judgment day, Eli, I'm telling you."

"I hear trumpets," Eli said, and hung up. He was shaking inside—Teddie's voice seemed to have separated his bones at the joints. He was still in the phone booth when the nurse came to tell him that Mrs. Peck would positively not be delivered of a child until the morning. He was to go home and get some rest, he looked like *he* was having the baby. The nurse winked and left.

But Eli did not go home. He carried the Bonwit box out into the street with him and put it in the car. The night was soft and starry, and he began to drive the streets of Woodenton. Square cool windows, apricot-colored, were all one could see beyond the long lawns that fronted the homes of the townsmen. The stars polished the permanent baggage carriers atop the station wagons in the driveways. He drove slowly, up, down, around. Only his tires could be heard taking the gentle curves in the road.

What peace. What incredible peace. Have children ever been so safe in their beds? Parents—Eli wondered—so full in their stomachs? Water so warm in its boilers? Never. Never in Rome, never in Greece. Never even did walled cities have it so good! No wonder then they would keep things just as they were. Here, after all, were peace and safety—what civilization had been working toward for centuries. For all his jerkiness, that was all Ted Heller was asking for, peace and safety. It was what his parents had asked for in the Bronx, and his grandparents in Poland, and theirs in Russia or Austria, or wherever else they'd fled to or from. It was what Miriam was asking for. And now they had it—the world was at last a place for families, even Jewish families. After all these centuries, maybe there just had to be this communal toughness—or numbness—to protect such a blessing. Maybe that was the trouble with the Jews all along—too soft. Sure, to live takes guts . . . Eli was thinking as he drove on beyond the train station, and parked his car at the darkened Gulf station. He stepped out, carrying the box.

At the top of the hill one window trembled with light. What *was* Tzuref doing up there in that office? Killing babies—probably not. But studying a language no one understood? Practicing customs with origins long forgotten? Suffering sufferings already suffered once too often? Teddie was right—why keep it up! However, if a man chose to be stubborn, then he couldn't expect to survive. The world is give-and-take. What sense to sit and brood over a suit. Eli would give him one last chance.

He stopped at the top. No one was around. He walked slowly up the lawn, setting each foot into the grass, listening to the shh shhh shhhh his shoes made as they bent the wetness into the sod. He looked around. Here there was nothing. Nothing! An old decaying house—and a suit.

On the porch he slid behind a pillar. He felt someone was watching him. But only the stars gleamed down. And at his feet, off and away, Woodenton glowed up. He set his package on the step of the great front door. Inside the cover of the box he felt to see if his letter was still there. When he touched it, he pushed it deeper into the green suit, which his fingers still remembered from winter. He should have included some light bulbs. Then he slid back by the pillar again, and this time there was something on the lawn. It was the second sight he had of him. He was facing Woodenton and barely moving across the open space towards the trees. His right fist was beating his chest. And then Eli heard a sound rising with each knock on the chest. And it did all three to Eli, plus more. Some feeling crept into him for whose deepness he could find no word. It was strange. He listened—it did not hurt to hear this moan. But he wondered if it hurt to make it. And so, with only stars to hear, he tried. And it did hurt. Not the bumblebee of noise that turned at the back of his throat and winged out his nostrils. What hurt buzzed down. It stung and stung inside him, and in turn the moan sharpened. It became a scream, louder, a song, a crazy song that whined through the pillars and blew out to the grass, until the strange hatted creature on the lawn turned and threw his arms wide, and looked in the night like a scarecrow.

Eli ran, and when he reached the car the pain was only a bloody scratch across his neck where a branch had whipped back as he fled the greenie's arms.

The following day his son was born. But not till one in the afternoon, and by then a great deal had happened.

First, at nine-thirty the phone rang. Eli leaped from the sofa—where he'd dropped the night before—and picked it screaming from the cradle. He could practically smell the hospital as he shouted into the phone, "Hello, yes!"

"Eli, it's Ted. Eli, he *did* it. He just walked by the store. I was opening the door, Eli, and I turned around and I swear I thought it was you. But it was him. He still walks like he did. but the clothes, Eli, the clothes."

"Who?"

"The greenie. He has on man's regular clothes. And the suit, it's a beauty."

The suit barreled back into Eli's consciousness, pushing all else aside. "What color suit?"

"Green. He's just strolling in the green suit like it's a holiday. Eli . . . is it a Jewish holiday?"

"Where is he now?"

"He's walking straight up Coach House Road, in this damn tweed job. Eli, it worked. You were right."

"We'll see."

"What next?"

"We'll see."

He took off the underwear in which he'd slept and went into the kitchen where he turned the light under the coffee. When it began to perk he held his head over the pot so it would steam loose the knot back of his eyes. It still hadn't when the phone rang.

"Eli, Ted again. Eli, the guy's walking up and down every street in town. Really, he's on a tour or something. Artie called me, Herb called me. Now Shirley calls that he just walked by our house. Eli, go out on the porch you'll see."

Eli went to the window and peered out. He couldn't see past the bend in the road, and there was no one in sight.

"Eli?" He heard Ted from where he dangled over the telephone table. He dropped the phone into the hook, as a few last words floated up to him—"Eliyousawhim . . . ?" He threw on the pants and shirt he'd worn the night before and walked barefoot on to his front lawn. And sure enough, his apparition appeared around the bend: in a brown hat a little too far down on his head, a green suit too far back on the shoulders, an unbuttoned-down button-down shirt, a tie knotted so as to leave a two-inch tail, trousers that cascaded onto his shoes—he was shorter than that black hat had made him seem. And moving the clothes was that walk that was not a walk, the tiny-stepped shlumpy gait. He came round the bend, and for all his strangeness—it clung to his whiskers, signaled itself in his locomotion—he looked as if he belonged. Eccentric, maybe, but he belonged. He made no moan, nor did he invite Eli with wide-flung arms. But he did stop when he saw him. He stopped and put a hand to his hat. When he felt for its top, his hand went up too high. Then it found the level and fiddled with the brim. The fingers fiddled, fumbled, and when they'd finally made their greeting, they traveled down the fellow's face and in an instant seemed to have touched each one of his features. They dabbed the eyes, ran the length of the nose, swept over the hairy lip, until they found their home in the hair that hid a little of his collar. To Eli the fingers said, *I have a face, I have a face at least.* Then his hand came through the beard and when it stopped at his chest it was like a pointer—and the eyes asked a question as tides of water shifted over them. *The face is all right, I can keep it?* Such a look was in those eyes that Eli was still seeing them when he turned his head away. They were the hearts of his jonquils, that only last week had appeared—they were the leaves on his birch, the bulbs in his coach lamp, the droppings on his lawn: those eyes were the eyes in his head. They were his, he had made them. He turned and went into his house and when he peeked out the side of the window, between shade and molding, the green suit was gone.

The phone.

"Eli, Shirley."

"I saw him, Shirley," and he hung up.

He sat frozen for a long time. The sun moved around the windows. The coffee steam smelled up the house. The phone began to ring, stopped, began again. The mailman came, the cleaner, the bakery man, the gardener, the ice cream man, the League of Women Voters lady. A Negro woman spreading some strange gospel calling for the revision of the Food and Drug Act knocked at the front, rapped the windows, and finally scraped a half-dozen pamphlets under the back door. But Eli only sat, without underwear, in last night's suit. He answered no one.

Given his condition, it was strange that the trip and crash at the back door reached his inner ear. But in an instant he seemed to melt down into the crevices of the chair, then to splash up and out to where the clatter had been. At the door he waited. It was silent, but for a fluttering of damp little leaves on the trees. When he finally opened the door, there was no one there. He'd expected to see green, green, green, big as the doorway, topped by his hat, waiting for him with those eyes. But there was no one out there, except for the Bonwit's box which lay bulging at his feet. No string tied it and the top rode high on the bottom.

The coward! He couldn't do it! He couldn't!

The very glee of that idea pumped fuel to his legs. He tore out across his back lawn, past his new spray of forsythia, to catch a glimpse of the bearded one fleeing naked through yards, over hedges and fences, to the safety of his hermitage. In the distance a pile of pink and white stones—which Harriet Knudson had painted the previous day—tricked him. "Run," he shouted to the rocks, "Run, you . . ." but he caught his error before anyone else did, and though he peered and craned there was no hint anywhere of a man about his own size, with white, white, terribly white skin (how white must be the skin of his body!) in cowardly retreat.

He came slowly, curiously, back to the door. And while the trees shimmered in the light wind, he removed the top from the box. The shock at first was the shock of having daylight turned off all at once. Inside the box was an eclipse. But black soon sorted from black, and shortly there was the glassy black of lining, the coarse black of trousers, the dead black of fraying threads, and in the center the mountain of black: the hat. He picked the box from the doorstep and carried it inside. For the first time in his life he *smelled* the color of blackness: a little stale, a little sour, a little old, but nothing that could overwhelm you. Still, he held the package at arm's length and deposited it on the dining room table.

Twenty rooms on a hill and they store their old clothes with me! What am I supposed to do with them? Give them to charity? That's where they came from. He picked up the hat by the edges and looked inside. The crown was smooth as an egg, the brim practically threadbare. There is nothing else to do with a hat in one's hands but put it on, so Eli dropped the thing on his head. He opened the door to the hall closet and looked at himself in the full-length mirror. The hat gave him bags under the eyes. Or perhaps he had not slept well. He pushed the brim lower till a shadow touched his lips. Now the bags under his eyes had inflated to become his face. Before the mirror he unbuttoned his shirt, unzipped his trousers, and then, shedding his clothes, he studied what he was. What a silly disappointment to see yourself naked in a hat. Especially in that hat. He sighed, but could not rid himself of the great weakness that suddenly set on his muscles and joints, beneath the terrible weight of the stranger's strange hat.

He returned to the dining room table and emptied the box of its contents: jacket, trousers, and vest (*it* smelled deeper than blackness). And under it all, sticking between the shoes that looked chopped and bitten, came the first gleam of white. A little fringed serape, a gray piece of semi-underwear, was crumpled at the bottom, its thready border twisted into itself. Eli removed it and let it hang free. What is it? For warmth? To wear beneath underwear in the event of a chest cold? He held it to his nose but it did not smell from Vick's or mustard plaster. It was something special, some Jewish thing. Special food, special language, special prayers, why not special BVD's? So fearful was he that he would be tempted back into wearing his traditional clothes—reasoned Eli—that he had carried and buried in Woodenton everything, including the special underwear. For that was how Eli now understood the box of clothes. The greenie was saying, Here, I give up. I refuse even to be tempted. We surrender. And that was how Eli continued to understand it until he found he'd slipped the white fringy surrender flag over his hat and felt it clinging to his chest. And now, looking at himself in the mirror, he was momentarily uncertain as to who was tempting who into what. Why *did* the greenie leave his clothes? Was it even the greenie? Then who was it? And why? But, Eli, for Christ's sake, in an age of science things don't happen like that. Even the goddam pigs take drugs . . .

Regardless of who was the source of the temptation, what was its end, not to mention its beginning, Eli, some moments later, stood draped in black, with a little white underneath, before the full-length mirror. He had to pull down on the trousers so they would not show the hollow of his ankle. The greenie, didn't he wear socks? Or had he forgotten them? The mystery was solved when Eli mustered enough courage to investigate the trouser pockets. He had expected some damp awful thing to happen to his fingers should he slip them down and out of sight—but when at last he jammed bravely down he came up with a khaki army sock in each hand. As he slipped them over his toes, he invented a genesis: a G.I.'s present in 1945. Plus everything else lost between 1938 and 1945, he had also lost his socks. Not that he had lost the socks, but that he'd had to stoop to accepting these, made Eli almost cry. To calm himself he walked out the back door and stood looking at his lawn.

On the Knudson back lawn, Harriet Knudson was giving her stones a second coat of pink. She looked up just as Eli stepped out. Eli shot back in again and pressed himself against the back door. When he peeked between the curtain all he saw were paint bucket, brush, and rocks scattered on the Knudsons' pink-spattered grass. The phone rang. Who was it—Harriet Knudson? Eli, there's a Jew at your door. *That's me*. Nonsense, Eli, I saw him with my own eyes. *That's me, I saw you too, painting your rocks pink*. Eli, you're having a nervous breakdown again. Jimmy, Eli's having a nervous breakdown again. Eli, this is Jimmy, hear you're having a little breakdown, anything I can do, boy? Eli, this is Ted, Shirley says you need help. Eli, this is Artie, you need help. Eli, Harry, you need help you need help . . . The phone rattled its last and died.

"God helps them who help themselves," intoned Eli, and once again he stepped out the door. This time he walked to the center of his lawn and in full sight of the trees, the grass, the birds, and the sun, revealed that it was he, Eli, in the costume. But nature had nothing to say to him, and so stealthily he made his way to the hedge separating his property from the field beyond and he cut his way through, losing his hat twice in the underbrush. Then, clamping the hat to his head, he began to run, the threaded tassels jumping across his heart. He ran through the weeds and wild flowers, until on the old road that skirted the town he slowed up. He was walking when he approached the Gulf station from the back. He supported himself on a huge tireless truck rim, and among tubes, rusted engines, dozens of topless oil cans, he rested. With a kind of brainless cunning, he readied himself for the last mile of his journey.

"How are you, Pop?" It was the garage attendant, rubbing his greasy hands on his overalls, and hunting among the cans.

Eli's stomach lurched and he pulled the big black coat round his neck.

"Nice day," the attendant said and started around to the front.

"Sholom," Eli whispered and zoomed off towards the hill.

The sun was directly overhead when Eli reached the top. He had come by way of the woods, where it was cooler, but still he was perspiring beneath his new suit. The hat had no sweatband and the cloth clutched his head. The children were playing. The children were always playing, as if it was that alone that Tzuref had to teach them. In their shorts, they revealed such thin legs that beneath one could see the joints swiveling as they ran. Eli waited for them to disappear around a corner before he came into the open. But something would not let him wait—his green suit. It was on the porch, wrapped around the bearded fellow, who was painting the base of a pillar. His arm went up and down, up and down, and the pillar glowed like white fire. The very sight of him popped Eli out of the woods onto the lawn. He did not turn back, though his insides did. He walked up the lawn, but the children played on; tipping the black hat, he mumbled, "Shhh . . . shhhh," and they hardly seemed to notice.

At last he smelled paint.

He waited for the man to turn to him. He only painted. Eli felt suddenly that if he could pull the black hat down over his eyes, over his chest and belly and legs, if he could shut out all light, then a moment later he would be home in bed. But the hat wouldn't go past his forehead. He couldn't kid himself—he was there. No one he could think of had forced him to do this.

The greenie's arm flailed up and down on the pillar. Eli breathed loudly, cleared his throat, but the greenie wouldn't make life easier for him. At last, Eli had to say "Hello."

The arm swished up and down; it stopped—two fingers went out after a brush hair stuck to the pillar.

"Good day," Eli said.

The hair came away; the swishing resumed.

"Sholom," Eli whispered and the fellow turned.

The recognition took some time. He looked at what Eli wore. Up close, Eli looked at what he wore. And then Eli had the strange notion that he was two people. Or that he was one person wearing two suits. The greenie looked to be suffering from a similar confusion. They stared long at one another. Eli's heart shivered, and his brain was momentarily in such a mixed-up condition that his hands went out to button down the collar of his shirt that somebody else was wearing. What a mess! The greenie flung his arms over his face.

"What's the matter . . ." Eli said. The fellow had picked up his bucket and brush and was running away. Eli ran after him.

"I wasn't going to hit . . ." Eli called. "Stop . . ." Eli caught up and grabbed his sleeve. Once again, the greenie's hands flew up to his face. This time, in the violence, white paint spattered both of them.

"I only want to . . ." But in that outfit Eli didn't really know what he wanted. "To talk . . ." he said finally. "For you to look at me. Please, just *look* at me . . ."

The hands stayed put, as paint rolled off the brush onto the cuff of Eli's green suit.

"Please. . . please," Eli said, but he did not know what to do. "Say something, speak *English,*" he pleaded.

The fellow pulled back against the wall, back, back, as though some arm would finally reach out and yank him to safety. He refused to uncover his face.

"Look," Eli said, pointing to himself. "It's your suit. I'll take care of it."

No answer—only a little shaking under the hands, which led Eli to speak as gently as he knew how.

"We'll . . . we'll moth-proof it. There's a button missing" —Eli pointed—"I'll have it fixed. I'll have a zipper put in . . . Please, please—just look at me . . ." He was talking to himself, and yet how could he stop? Nothing he said made any sense—that alone made his heart swell. Yet somehow babbling on, he might babble something that would make things easier between them. "Look . . ." He reached inside his shirt to pull the frills of underwear into the light. "I'm wearing the special underwear, even . . . Please," he said, *"please, please, please"* he sang, as if it were some sacred word. "Oh, *please* . . ."

Nothing twitched under the tweed suit—and if the eyes watered, or twinkled, or hated, he couldn't tell. It was driving him crazy. He had dressed like a fool, and for what? For this? He reached up and yanked the hands away.

"There!" he said—and in that first instant all he saw of

the greenie's face were two white droplets stuck to each cheek.

"Tell me—" Eli clutched his hands down to his sides—"Tell me, what can I do for you, I'll do it . . ."

Stiffly, the greenie stood there, sporting his two white tears.

"Whatever I can do . . . Look, look, what I've done *already*." He grabbed his black hat and shook it in the man's face.

And in exchange, the greenie gave him an answer. He raised one hand to his chest, and then jammed it, finger first, towards the horizon. And with what a pained look! As though the air were full of razors! Eli followed the finger and saw beyond the knuckle, out past the nail, Woodenton.

"What do you want?" Eli said. "I'll bring it!"

Suddenly the greenie made a run for it. But then he stopped, wheeled, and jabbed that finger at the air again. It pointed the same way. Then he was gone.

And then, all alone, Eli had the revelation. He did not question his understanding, the substance or the source. But with a strange, dreamy elation, he started away.

On Coach House Road, they were double-parked. The Mayor's wife pushed a grocery cart full of dog food from Stop N' Shop to her station wagon. The President of the Lions Club, a napkin around his neck, was jamming pennies into the meter in front of the Bit-in-Teeth Restaurant. Ted Heller caught the sun as it glazed off the new Byzantine mosaic entrance to his shoe shop. In pinkened jeans, Mrs. Jimmy Knudson was leaving Halloway's Hardware, a paint bucket in each hand. Roger's Beauty Shoppe had its doors open—women's heads in silver bullets far as the eye could see. Over by the barbershop the pole spun, and Artie Berg's youngest sat on a red horse, having his hair cut; his mother flipped through *Look,* smiling: the greenie had changed his clothes.

And into this street, which seemed paved with chromium, came Eli Peck. It was not enough, he knew, to walk up one side of the street. That was not enough. Instead he walked ten paces up one side, then on an angle, crossed to the other side, where he walked ten more paces, and crossed back. Horns blew, traffic jerked, as Eli made his way up Coach House Road. He spun a moan high up in his nose as he walked. Outside no one could hear him, but he felt it vibrate the cartilage at the bridge of his nose.

Things slowed around him. The sun stopped rippling on spokes and hubcaps. It glowed steadily as everyone put on brakes to look at the man in black. They always paused and gaped, whenever he entered the town. Then in a minute, or two, or three, a light would change, a baby squawk, and the flow continue. Now, though lights changed, no one moved.

"He shaved his beard," Eric the barber said.

"Who?" asked Linda Berg.

"The . . . the guy in the suit. From the place there."

Linda looked out the window.

"It's Uncle Eli," little Kevin Berg said, spitting hair.

"Oh, God," Linda said, "Eli's having a nervous breakdown."

"A nervous breakdown!" Ted Heller said, but not immediately. Immediately he had said "Hoooly . . ."

Shortly, everybody in Coach House Road was aware that Eli Peck, the nervous young attorney with the pretty wife, was having a breakdown. Everybody except Eli Peck. He knew what he did was not insane, though he felt every inch of its strangeness. He felt those black clothes as if they were the skin of his skin—the give and pull as they got used to where he bulged and buckled. And he felt eyes, every eye on Coach House Road. He saw headlights screech to within an inch of him, and stop. He saw mouths: first the bottom jaw slides forward, then the tongue hits the teeth, the lips explode, a little thunder in the throat, and they've said it: Eli Peck Eli Peck Eli Peck Eli Peck. He began to walk slowly, shifting his weight down and forward with each syllable: E–li–Peck–E–li–Peck–E–li–Peck. Heavily he trod, and as his neighbors uttered each syllable of his name, he felt each syllable shaking all his bones. He knew who he was down to his marrow—they were telling him. Eli Peck. He wanted them to say it a thousand times, a million times, he would walk forever in that black suit, as adults whispered of his strangeness and children made "Shame . . . shame" with their fingers.

"It's going to be all right, pal . . ." Ted Heller was motioning to Eli from his doorway. "C'mon, pal, it's going to be all right . . ."

Eli saw him, past the brim of his hat. Ted did not move from his doorway, but leaned forward and spoke with his hand over his mouth. Behind him, three customers peered through the doorway. "Eli, it's Ted, remember Ted . . ."

Eli crossed the street and found he was heading directly towards Harriet Knudson. He lifted his neck so she could see his whole face.

He saw her forehead melt down to her lashes. "Good morning, Mr. Peck."

"Sholom," Eli said, and crossed the street where he saw the President of the Lions.

"Twice before . . ." he heard someone say, and then he

crossed again, mounted the curb, and was before the bakery, where a delivery man charged past with a tray of powdered cakes twirling above him. "Pardon me, Father," he said, and scooted into his truck. But he could not move it. Eli Peck had stopped traffic.

He passed the Rivoli Theater, Beekman Cleaners, Harris' Westinghouse, the Unitarian Church, and soon he was passing only trees. At Ireland Road he turned right and started through Woodenton's winding streets. Baby carriages stopped whizzing and creaked—"Isn't that . . ." Gardeners held their clipping. Children stepped from the sidewalk and tried the curb. And Eli greeted no one, but raised his face to all. He wished passionately that he had white tears to show them . . . And not till he reached his own front lawn, saw his house, his shutters, his new jonquils, did he remember his wife. And the child that must have been born to him. And it was then and there he had the awful moment. He could go inside and put on his clothes and go to his wife in the hospital. It was not irrevocable, even the walk wasn't. In Woodenton memories are long but fury short. Apathy works like forgiveness. Besides, when you've flipped, you've flipped—it's Mother Nature.

What gave Eli the awful moment was that he turned away. He knew exactly what he could do but he chose not to. To go inside would be to go halfway. There was more . . . So he turned and walked towards the hospital and all the time he quaked an eighth of an inch beneath his skin to think that perhaps he'd chosen the crazy way. To think that he'd *chosen* to be crazy! But if you chose to be crazy, then you weren't crazy. It's when you didn't choose. No, he wasn't flipping. He had a child to see.

"Name?"

"Peck."

"Fourth floor." He was given a little blue card.

In the elevator everybody stared. Eli watched his black shoes rise four floors.

"Four."

He tipped his hat, but knew he couldn't take it off.

"Peck," he said. He showed the card.

"Congratulations," the nurse said. ". . . the grandfather?"

"The father. Which room?"

She led him to 412. "A joke on the Mrs?" she said, but he slipped in the door without her.

"Miriam?"

"Yes?"

"Eli."

She rolled her white face towards her husband. "Oh, Eli . . . Oh, Eli."

He raised his arms. "What could I do?"

"You have a son. They called all morning."

"I came to see him."

"Like *that!*" she whispered harshly. "Eli, you can't go around like that."

"I have a son. I want to see him."

"Eli, why are you doing this to me!" Red seeped back into her lips. *"He's* not your fault," she explained. "Oh, Eli, sweetheart, why do you feel guilty about everything. Eli, change your clothes. I forgive you."

"Stop forgiving me. Stop understanding me."

"But I love you."

"That's something else."

"But, sweetie, you *don't* have to dress like that. You didn't do anything. You don't have to feel guilty because . . . because everything's all right. Eli, can't you see that?"

"Miriam, enough reasons. Where's my son?"

"Oh, please, Eli, don't flip now. I need you now. Is that why you're flipping—because I need you?"

"In your selfish way, Miriam, you're very generous. I want my son."

"Don't flip now. I'm afraid, now that he's out." She was beginning to whimper. "I don't know if I love him, now that he's out. When I look in the mirror, Eli, he won't be there . . . Eli, Eli, you look like you're going to your own funeral. Please, can't you leave well enough *alone?* Can't we just have a family?"

"No."

In the corridor he asked the nurse to lead him to his son. The nurse walked on one side of him, Ted Heller on the other.

"Eli, do you want some help? I thought you might want some help."

"No."

Ted whispered something to the nurse; then to Eli he whispered, "Should you be walking around like this?"

"Yes."

In his ear Ted said, "You'll . . . you'll frighten the kid . . ."

"There," the nurse said. She pointed to a bassinet in the second row and looked, puzzled, to Ted. "Do I go in?" Eli said.

"No," the nurse said. "She'll roll him over." She rapped on the enclosure full of babies. "Peck," she mouthed to the nurse on the inside.

Ted tapped Eli's arm. "You're not thinking of doing something you'll be sorry for . . . are you, Eli? Eli—I mean you know you're still Eli, don't you?"

In the enclosure, Eli saw a bassinet had been wheeled before the square window.

"Oh, Christ. . . ." Ted said. "You don't have this Bible stuff on the brain—" And suddenly he said, "You wait, pal." He started down the corridor, his heels tapping rapidly.

Eli felt relieved—he leaned forward. In the basket was what he'd come to see. Well, now that he was here, what did he think he was going to say to it? I'm your father, Eli, the Flipper? I am wearing a black hat, suit, and fancy underwear, all borrowed from a friend? How could he admit to this reddened ball—*his* reddened ball—the worst of all: that Eckman would shortly convince him he wanted to take off the whole business. He couldn't admit it! He wouldn't do it!

Past his hat brim, from the corner of his eye, he saw Ted had stopped in a doorway at the end of the corridor. Two interns stood there smoking, listening to Ted. Eli ignored it.

No, even Eckman wouldn't make him take it off! No! He'd wear it, if he chose to. He'd make the kid wear it! Sure! Cut it down when the time came. A smelly hand-me-down, whether the kid liked it or not!

Only Teddie's heels clacked; the interns wore rubber soles—for they were there, beside him, unexpectedly. Their white suits smelled, but not like Eli's.

"Eli," Ted said, softly, "visiting time's up, pal."

"How are you feeling, Mr. Peck? First child upsets everyone. . . ."

He'd just pay no attention; nevertheless, he began to perspire, thickly, and his hat crown clutched his hair.

"Excuse me—Mr. Peck. . . ." It was a new rich bass voice. "Excuse me, rabbi, but you're wanted . . . in the temple." A hand took his elbow, firmly; then another hand, the other elbow. Where they grabbed, his tendons went taut.

"Okay, rabbi. Okay okay okay okay okay okay. . . ." He listened; it was a very soothing word, that okay. "Okay okay everything's going to be okay." His feet seemed to have left the ground some, as he glided away from the window, the bassinet, the babies. "Okay easy does it everything's all right all right—"

But he rose, suddenly, as though up out of a dream, and flailing his arms, screamed: *"I'm the father!"*

But the window disappeared. In a moment they tore off his jacket—it gave so easily, in one yank. Then a needle slid under his skin. The drug calmed his soul, but did not touch it down where the blackness had reached.

V

THE ALIENATED

The argument between the social psychologists and the individual psychologists is not based on the dissimilarity of their respective goals, but rather on differences of approach. Individual psychologists have viewed adjustment in terms of the internal factors: the social psychologists tend to look at the individual as an expression of, or a subordinate part of, the group.

John Locke's idea of the "tabula rasa" was once the war cry of the social psychologist: man was merely the receptor of the culture or group mores, and he could be reproduced in the group image without much difficulty if only the group utilized the proper techniques. The unique heredity of each human being, and the possibility of interplay between this heredity and the environment, was for the most part ignored. Freud's emphasis on the internalization of the mores of society within the personality through the development of the superego recognized the role played by external factors in conditioning human behavior. But Freud tended to regard social forces as the essentially negative producers of repressions, disease, and neurosis. Man was described as the "neurotic animal."

Today's social psychologists are groping toward a new model of the human personality: one in which all factors receive their due weight, and the interplay between individual and society becomes neither a picture of instinct determining social adjustment nor of society warping instinct, but rather a picture of the balanced conditioning of the libido by ego and superego, and ego and superego by libido. This new model revolves around reciprocating and supporting relationships: the effect of the mother in civilizing the child is seen as but one half of the picture; the effect of the child in altering the role, identity, and position of the mother is the other.

The utilization of this new model may help us to discover the sources of alienation in our own culture. The inability of large groups of our population to find satisfying roles within the society is cause for much concern. In art, we have moved from the sexual alienation of the romantic, through the Lost Generation of Hemingway, to the Beat Bohemia of the 60's. In politics we have been faced with revolution on the left and reactionary upheaval on the right. In our daily lives, we are constantly made aware of the enormous increase in crime rates and dope addiction.

There can be little doubt that the loss of a traditional mode of thinking has been responsible for some of this antisocial activity. But even more crucial than these rebellions is the lack of communication among men—and it is just this lack that is exemplified in the artistic productions of our time. The artist, who was once an integral part of society, who communicated its objectives to other men, is today beyond society. He lives in a despairing and anguished world; his concept of art is individualistic and not comprehensible to his public.

The mechanisms involved in the alienation of the human being from his group do not vary much from reactionary to revolutionary, criminal to artist. A disturbed family constellation, a sick society, an era without an orientation will produce alienation in all the forms in which we know it today.

There can be no doubt that in the end individual factors play an enormous role in human development. But the impact of a cultural heritage that lacks cohesion and structure, that promotes destructive goals, or, like our own society, that seems unable to reconcile the needs of a great many of its individuals with the group, can only result in the tragedy of alienation.

MARGARET MEAD / Art and Reality

THE STUDY of primitive cultures, themselves highly integrated wholes which satisfy aesthetic as well as analytical scientific impulses, throws most light upon the problems of the relation of art to present-day society when we study primitive religions, rather than when we follow our present limited categories and try to talk of primitive music or primitive design. In the close inter-relationships between a phrase of Balinese music, the design on a Balinese frieze, or the pattern on the border of a cloth, we find a clue to the relationship between Art and Reality for which our own culture is striving to find new formulations. Within the short space of this discussion, I wish to focus on only a few of the many points which suggest themselves when one analyzes any primitive culture.

First, the art of a primitive culture, seen now as the whole ritual, the symbolic expression of the meaning of life, appeals to all of the senses, just as also a mediaeval high mass involved all the senses, through the eye and ear to the smell of incense, the kinaesthetisia of genuflection and kneeling or swaying to the passing procession, to the cool touch of holy water on the forehead. For Art to be Reality, the whole sensuous being must be caught up in the experience. Our present practices, by which people sit on stiff chairs and listen in constrained silence to a piece of music, or wander in desultory unpatterned groups in an art gallery looking at framed pictures hung in desperate disregard of any relevance which might exist among them, is the very opposite process. One sense may be heightened, one emotion sharpened, but, except in rare cases, there is no increase in the whole individual's relationship to the whole of life.

Second, in primitive societies, the artist is not a separate person, having no immediate close relationship to the economic processes and everyday experiences of his society. The concept of the artist whose gift sets him apart, or who only becomes an artist because his life history has set him apart, is almost wholly lacking. The artist, instead, is the person who does best something that other people, many other people, do less well. His products, whether he be choreographer or dancer, flutist or pot-maker, or carver of the temple gate, are seen as differing in degree but not in kind from the achievements of the less gifted among his fellow citizens. The concept of the artist as different in kind is fatal to the development of any adequate artistic form which will satisfy all of the sensibilities which are developed in individuals reared under the impact of these forms.

Both of these differences, the difference between a ritual which involves all of the senses and our present artistic practices which fractionate the sensuous man, and the difference between an artist who is merely the best of a host of fellow practitioners and the artist who is different in kind from men who are hardly his fellows at all, are not inherent in the nature of civilization as compared with the nature of primitive society. Our own Middle Ages, as well as many great cultures of the past, developed complete, harmonious rituals which involved every type of sense experience, and the concept of the artist and the related concept of the fine arts are both special bad accidents of our own local European tradition.

There is, however, another difference which is due, not merely to the accidents of a particular local historical development, but to the nature of any modern cosmopolitan civilization of the type towards which the world appears to be tending. This is the discrepancy between the experience of one man and the experience of another, so that artists paint and poets sing almost for themselves alone, or for some slender band of fellow deviants, children of the same exact historical accident which produced them, becoming unintelligible even to those who are temperamentally akin, five to ten years after they have created what seemed to them an abiding formal statement of some great truth. One of the problems of our emerging culture is to learn ways, which have never even been approximated yet, of blending the essence of permanent human preoccupations with the accidents of idiosyncratic, local, time-limited experience. This need raises a multitude of problems, such as how to establish a balance between ephemeral, highly perishable, immediate expressions, and forms which will have sufficient duration to become strong and valid, or how to educate a generation with potentialities for multiple and diversified aesthetic responses without at the same time having these diversifications cancel each other out or merely produce confusion. It is possible that one answer lies in developing art forms in which there is a new relationship between those parts which are contributed by the highly gifted and keyed to the longer-time preoccupations of man, and the improvisations which embody the special tone and meaning of a half generation's experience in the cane-fields of the South or the stock-yards of Chicago, so that each local group of actors or dancers or scene designers could find full expression within a form which dignified their own efforts but did not dwarf them or make them ridiculous.

Finally, we need to break down the present dichotomy between the artist, the work of art, and the spectator, and realize that any patterned activity of a people—a football match, the group of bowlers in a bowling alley—is closer to an art form than a group of dubiously reverent attendants at an art gallery or in a concert hall, even when the masterpiece of paint or musical composition is included. By making Art a specially precious part of life, we have demoted it from being all of life, seen from one point of view. When this is done, everyone suffers—the "artists" and all the people to whose lives significance might have been given.

MASON GRIFF / The Commercial Artist

WHAT HAPPENS to art and creativity, freedom and self-expression, in a mass society? Do they become routinized and rationalized like so many other phenomena? And what of the artist? How does he maintain his identity? How does he preserve his independence and continue to be creative? How is he drawn into the field of art in the first place? What are some of the tensions and anxieties accompanying his recruitment? These are questions which will be discussed in this paper.

The material on which this discussion is based comes from two studies. The first studied a group of students attending a large art school in Chicago.[1] One of the objectives of that study was to discover the reasons for students entering the field of art when the possibilities for success in it are so limited. For example, the estimates of the number of those who are able to support themselves exclusively from the sale of their paintings in this country range from five to fifteen persons.[2] The results of this study revealed that these students understood the difficulties an artist faced and that it would be necessary for them to supplement their income from some other source.

These findings led directly to a second study of what the artist does when he finishes his formal training.[3] One alternative, and the one studied, is to work as a commercial artist. However, the role of the commercial artist is contrary in many fundamental respects to the role of the fine artist. Ideally, the fine artist is free from any restrictions on his work. The commercial artist is restricted by his clients. How then, do artists resolve this conflict in roles? This was the major question asked in the second study.

The charge that commercial art has a corrupting influence

on the artist is an old one. Michelangelo rebelled against the Pope's attempt to restrict his paintings, and Rembrandt turned his back on the burghers who had given him wealth and recognition to paint as he wished in solitary poverty. Furthermore, the general problem implied here is not confined only to painters; the same problem can be found among most artists in other fields, such as writers, musicians, and dancers.[4] Finally, it may be seen as a general problem extending beyond the artistic occupations. One can see parallels in the comparison of the pure mathematician or the theoretical physicist with those working in the applied fields. On a more abstract level, the problem can be seen as a general dilemma: the wish to carry out an action in its pure form, as opposed to attempts to qualify the action in some way.[5]

Identity, Recruitment, and Self

Identity, and its connection with an occupation, has many dimensions. If a person identifies with an occupation that is socially sanctioned, the members of that society are supportive of him. If the occupation is not socially sanctioned, the members of the society attempt to prevent, persuade, or erect obstacles to keep him from pursuing that occupation. The legitimacy of the pursuit, from the point of view of society, is the key to understanding the present role and status of the artist in contemporary society. In turn, this explains the reasons for tensions arising in the career of the artist, and the reasons these tensions arise when they do.

Tension points may be described as points of decision. Not all decisions, however, have equal tension-producing force. Some, such as the decision of whom and when to marry, or when and where to move, or what career to follow, are usually more crucial than other decisions. These tension points, which are produced and decided in a social context, i.e., in interrelationships to and with significant others and groups, can be called social tension points, as distinguished from individual tension points. With reference to occupations, such tension points are particularly crucial, since the social meaning of work is pervasive in a society based upon achieved, rather than ascribed status. In such a society, it is through a person's work that he belongs to a specific social class and enjoys, or does not enjoy, certain rewards which society has established as goals: material rewards, in the form of money and the symbols of success which money can buy; and immaterial rewards, in the forms of prestige, status, and pride in accomplishment, which are derived from identification with a socially sanctioned occupation.

The attitude of our society toward art and the artist, specifically toward painting and the painter, is ambivalent. The painter and his work are sanctioned, but only when painting is pursued as an avocation rather than as a vocation. Artistic talents in children are encouraged by teachers, parents, and the community. Presidents, prime ministers, doctors, housewives, and friends who paint are respected for their talent. In short, the pursuit of art is sanctioned when it is undertaken by people who have already achieved identification with some other socially sanctioned role. The vocation itself is even sanctioned when it remains at a safe distance. The lives of Van Gogh and Gauguin have been the subjects of popular novels and movies.

However, difficulties reflecting this ambivalence arise when some member of a family wishes to pursue a career in art. Then two very strong objections present themselves. The first is the fact that the painter cannot hope to support himself solely from the sale of his paintings and that this inability will make it impossible for him to attain many of the symbols of success which the family cherishes. The second is the Bohemian stereotype of the artist, with which the family does not want to be identified because it violates the professed mores, morals, and values of our culture.

The Bohemian stereotype of the artist is, of course, closely related to the financial problems that art as a vocation presents. How did this stereotype arise, and how has it affected the public image of the artist, his recruitment, and his identity?

A century and a half ago, the artist became alienated from his society. The French Revolution, with the destruction of the nobility and the subsequent loss of aristocratic patronage, was the precipitating factor. There were people who could have created a market for paintings, but these people, the bourgeois, were products of a way of life and an ideology antithetical to the support of, or sympathy with, art. Their philosophy was essentially utilitarian. The work of the artist and his ideology are nonutilitarian. Outside of their investment potential, paintings have no utility. Some paintings were purchased, but these were, as they frequently are today, paintings produced in the past with a market value certified by time. Hence they represented a rational purchase involving no gamble on an uncertain commodity such as a purchase from a contemporary, and as yet unknown, artist would entail.

Out of this period and these conditions emerged the stereotype image of the artist which has continued down to the present time: the artist as starving and dying; the artist as a deviant and a suicide; the artist as insane and alcoholic; the artist as an undiscovered genius whose greatness is not recognized until after his death. One is reminded of Van Gogh, Modigliani, and Utrillo—the insane, the alcoholic, and the drug addict, respectively.

Emerging with this stereotype was the Bohemian ideology that was to become so closely attached to the artist. It is an ideology which not only expresses antinomianism—moral, aesthetic, and social—which is central to its ethos, but also implies an active conflict, a war with civil society.[6] The function of the ideology was to give the artist an identity and a sanction justifying his alienation. This was done by affirming certain values—freedom of self-expression, and the realization of self through artistic fulfillment—as transcending and antithetical to the values supported by bourgeois society. As a consequence, although the artist was in this way able to achieve identity and a sense of community with other artists, he was also committed to alienation and opposition to bourgeois values. Thus, an artist who has accepted this identity and commitment, which is really the only one open to the fine artist in bourgeois society, is presented with new conflicts and tensions should he wish to return to the bourgeois community. This is essentially the problem of the fine artist who, unable to support himself by his work, decides to turn to commercial art. His reasons for doing so are usually associated with the wish to support a family and to have some of the symbols of success which money can provide, such as a comfortable home, a car, and the opportunity to travel. The affirmation of these values, however, conflicts with the Bohemian ideology and consequently challenges his identity as a fine artist. How this problem of identification is resolved is the central subject of this paper.

The reader may protest that the stereotype given above is, after all, only a stereotype which may or may not be valid. He may further question whether or not the Bohemian ideology actually functions in the artist's identity. There is no scientific evidence to document the public stereotype of the artist, but we do have indirect evidence. Hardly an issue of any of a number of popular weekly magazines appears without some caricature of the artist. Everyone is familiar with the painter and his nude model and all the associated implications of immorality. There is the starving painter who absurdly refuses to eat the food serving as a model for his canvas, and the starving and irresponsible artist who is deaf to the common sense pleas of his wife and family and is merely laughable from a practical point of view. Furthermore, evidence gathered from interviews with art students and artists confirms the potency of this stereotype; this is what they believe is the public's image of them. More important, this is what their families believe the artist to be.

How has this stereotype affected the recruitment of people into the art profession? The artist occupies an ambivalent position. Supposedly, both the artist and his work are valued; yet the artist is not rewarded. Consequently his recruitment and identity involve conflicts within himself, and between himself and significant others. Both the Bohemian stereotype, posing the problem of identity, and the recruitment phenomena, posing the problem of a socially sanctioned occupation and the particular significance this has in our society, are relevant to the tensions which occupy his career.

Since the image of the artist as a Bohemian is one which respectable bourgeois society rejects, and since the vocation of artist offers negligible hope for financial security or success, one would imagine that there would be consistency in the *discouragement* of children from becoming artists. On the contrary, however, one finds evidence that both parents and other social agents nourish and *encourage* the complete fulfillment of the child's talents. This fact is reflected in the early career of the artist, where there are no tensions in his incipient career, at least none attributable to a discrepancy between encouragement and reward. This is reflected in such statements as, "When I was in kindergarten, I was separated from the rest of my class and left to paint by myself"; or, "I was always being asked to paint pictures for my relatives and friends"; or, "I was considered the artist among the people I hung around with." This encouragement of the young artist was further suggested by many statements referring to the fact that parents had prominently displayed the child's paintings and had shown them with pride to friends and relatives.

It may be seen that when a teacher separates a child in class or encourages him in some similar manner, the teacher is defining art and artists as valuable. By endowing the young artist with social recognition and esteem, the teacher is implicitly saying that the artist is to be rewarded; this serves to convince the child that he and his creations are acceptable to social authority. When the child is separated from his classmates, the fact that he is in some way distinguished is reinforced in front of his peers. The child begins to understand that his ability to paint is an unusual one which not everyone possesses, and which entitles him to prestige, special consideration, and recognition. Thus, in every way, the child is encouraged to exercise freely that which he most basically feels is himself. He learns that he has the freedom to create, and that the volition to do this is an inherent attribute of the artist. He also learns that his contribution is socially meaningful and constructive. The accumulating social experiences of the child, and the picture which emerges of these early years, is one of congruence between aspiration and fulfillment, encouragement and reward. Tensions or anxieties, which one would expect if there were discrepancies between these variables, are absent. Outside of the normal tensions of childhood and adolescence, all the factors favoring the retention and nourishment of an artist's career are present.

Discontinuities in this process begin abruptly at either of two points: at the end of high school or at the end of art school, usually the former. At these points, parents increase pressure on the child to commit himself to an occupation. Whenever the pressures begin, they become oppressive when the parents discover that the child has the intention of pursuing a career in the fine arts, since they are aware of the financial difficulties he will face. The discovery may be made when the child makes a public declaration that he is going to be an artist, when he enrolls in an art school, or, if he is already in art school, when he breaks an informal agreement to pursue commercial art or art education.

When the student's intention to become an artist is discovered, there is a reversal in the attitude of his parents toward him. A crisis is engendered which becomes greatly aggravated during the period beginning with the announcement of his intentions and ending with the termination of his formal education. The entire family turns against him in a determined effort to dissuade him. Parents and brothers and sisters may realize for the first time that he wishes to enter a profession associated with deviancy. Now he, and with him his family, is identified with the objects of innumerable jokes in the newspapers and magazines. In a word, "the world is laughing at them," and the family feels personally attacked and humiliated. The family begins to remove the student's paintings from the walls where they were once prominently displayed. The student's artistic achievements and the large salaries received by artists become topics to be avoided.

The common reaction to, and resolution of, the crisis may be classified into two major forms. The parents may blame the child, and, if so, disown him; or they may assume personal culpability and declare that they have failed him in some way. Those parents who feel personally culpable for the child's "deviancy" or realize that the child cannot be persuaded to alter his career, accept the situation with the mental reservation that somehow they or some unknown intervening force will induce the individual to renounce his pursuit. At this time, the parents and other members of the family reply to inquiries concerning the future of the young artist by telling the truth, by rationalizing, or by lying.

When members of the family tell the truth, they do so by

fortifying themselves against the ridicule and censure of their friends and admitting that they have failed. The constant questions concerning the future of the child generate, and add to, the bitterness of the family. These questions are frequent because, until the time of his decision to make art his life's work, this child had been the member of the family with the greatest prestige, precisely because of his unusual gift.

If the parents rationalize the intentions of the student they do so by telling the truth, but at the same time pointing to past masters and to present-day ones who are internationally famous and receive thousands of dollars for a single painting. In time, they may actually believe that this will come true for their child, and thus reduce their antagonism towards him. At the same time, they avoid mentioning the overwhelming number of painters who have been or are unable to support themselves by their work, or who have attained recognition only after death.

The family that lies about the true situation will convey the impression that their child is pursuing commercial art, usually adding "the respectable aspects," meaning, nothing pertaining to sex or pornography. They imply that he is doing work comparable to that of Norman Rockwell for national magazines, with the added implication of a large salary. In time, the parents may come to believe that this is the true intent of the child, despite contrary evidence which they witness every day.

But isn't there an inconsistency here? Hasn't it been stated that the young artist is a success and that he is encouraged and rewarded for his ability? Hasn't it been stated that his success has been a source of gratification for his parents as well as for him? There is an inconsistency, but one which becomes understandable if the great difference between school success and occupational success is considered. School success is confined to the yardstick of the report card: "My son can paint. He has his posters displayed." "My daughter gets all A's in art." There is recognition in the form of prizes, articles in the local newspaper, or acknowledgment on graduation programs. Yet, the totality of prestige and the measures of success attained from these sources are confined to school. When a child graduates from high school, new standards and criteria of judgment are applied, which are associated with symbols of financial success and social prestige. Art, particularly fine art, is not an avenue conducive to the attainment of these success symbols, and parents and families know this. Moreover, these reactions reflect some significant attitudes toward the fine artist and toward art in contemporary culture.

Contemporary culture stresses conformity, respectability,

rationality, practicality, and security. These are a few of the essential values which are incorporated in the cultural complex called by Max Weber, rational bourgeois capitalism.[7] Art and the life of the artist are antinomies of this. Fine art is nonutilitarian. The artist is a nonconformist and violates many of the behavioral patterns set down by society. His choice of career also opposes the success theme so strongly stressed and so pervasive. To parents who value success for their children, as an affirmation and confirmation of their worthiness as parents, there is little comfort in the notion that the young artist may achieve recognition after his death; yet, this is very often all the young artist has to offer as justification for the sacrifices he proposes to make. Is it any wonder that, given the tremendous ideological emphasis on success, parents oppose a child's commitment to a career in art?

Not all students enter art school under conditions of parental opposition or personal rebellion.[8] This is especially true of those who enroll with the express intention of becoming commercial artists. Their career is straightforward. They take commercial art courses, graduate from school with this identity, and immediately enter the commercial art world. A second group are those who enter with the intention of teaching art. They enroll in the required courses, graduate, and pursue an academic career.

The group with which we are concerned, however, is composed of those who pursue fine art throughout their formal training, graduate, and are then confronted with the problem of how to earn a living. Some solve the problem by returning to graduate school, many to qualify for teaching certificates. Others move over to schools like the Institute of Design in Chicago, which teaches commercial and industrial art with a fine-arts ideology. There is still another group who take jobs outside of the art field and continue to paint after work, on week-ends, and during vacations. Most of these, however, eventually return to art in some capacity, many as commercial artists. This change in roles confronts the artist with many of the questions asked at the beginning of this paper. What will working as a commercial artist do to his identity as a fine artist, his freedom for self-expression, and his independence? How will his creativity be affected by using his talents to produce commercial art? The misgivings concerning this step are resolved in various ways described below. The artist's identity undergoes changes which range in type from those who still symbolically accept the role of fine artist to those who reject it completely. Between these two extremes lies a third group which identifies with both roles.

Alternate Role Styles

The *traditional-role* artist works as a commercial artist, but subjectively identifies himself as a fine artist. In enacting this role, he withdraws symbolically from the role of commercial artist and states that he is only temporarily engaged in commercial art, as an expedient until he can accumulate enough money to be financially independent. He feels that only if he is financially independent will he have the freedom and time necessary for his work.

His justification for working in the field of commercial art is that the standards of contemporary society preclude any suitable alternative, since there is not a large enough market to support any but a very small number of artists. Underlying this assumption is the belief that society will give lip-service to, but in reality will not support, his primary identity as a fine artist who lives only from, and solely for, his art. The Bohemian ideology supports him in this belief.

To defend his premise, he cites numerous examples, both past and present, of artists who have attempted but failed to live exclusively from the sale of their paintings, *e.g.*, Van Gogh and Albert Ryder, Pissarro and Cezanne. Coupled with this belief is the fact that many of this group actually attempted to live from the sale of their paintings, and finding this impossible, have turned to the commercial art field. Before doing this, some worked in factories, the post office, or within another field unrelated to art. They have specifically avoided working in fields related to art, because they have felt that to do so would channel some of their creative energy into these other artistic activities. Many of them still do feel that art-related jobs can affect their paintings, because of the habits one falls victim to.

This is the group which suffers the most and has the deepest guilt feelings about working in the commercial art field. These are the artists who left school with the intention of remaining dedicated to art but, through a number of discouraging experiences, felt it was useless to pursue this course. The alternative they have chosen is a difficult one, since the switch to commercial art means that they are accepting a role which they formerly actively rejected.

In this respect they are faced with three important identity problems which they must resolve: (1) they must legitimize relinquishing their former identity as fine artists; (2) they must legitimize the meaning of their new self-conceptions, *i.e.*, they must make their new identity bearable, and they must find rewards in their new role; (3) they must legitimize their new identity as commercial artists to their significant others. Let us examine each of these problems in order.

One basic consideration regarding the abandonment of former roles is evident: the career of the artist is precarious and success uncertain. Of greatest importance here is the fact that, in the recapitulation of their achievements, these artists can find no confirmation of their abilities from others, such as normally functions to indicate progress. Indicative of the importance of this are the statements they make in explaining how they arrived at the decision to leave their former roles; *e.g.*, "I always sold a few but never enough to keep me going"; or "I sell a little but I don't know whether or not my level of painting is improving"; or "You say to yourself, what will I be like when I'm fifty?" or "Painting drives you to a certain madness."

These statements not only indicate uncertainty and the absence of confirmation by significant others, but also that the painter does not have the usual marks indicative of progress such as promotions, raises in pay, and awards to rely upon which are institutionally structured in most occupations. These devices function to communicate, confirm, and be supportive of the fact that the individual is making some progress toward the goals of the institution. The fine artist lacks any such stable frame of reference.

Involved in this is a certain incongruity. The artist, as a member of society, incorporates a future goal-orientation and makes this part of his frame of reference, since he has been inculcated with it as part of his socialization process. Yet, his occupation does not have clear-cut goals toward which he may strive. The ones that do exist are precarious and virtually unattainable. After all, how many artists out of the thousands who have pursued art create an immortal painting? Certainly there are a few markers, such as one-man exhibits, acceptance by a gallery, sales, and commissions, but even these are tenuous. In the totality of an artist's career, they have so little remunerative value and are achieved only after such a long, arduous, and often painful struggle that they cannot compensate for the great insecurity which his career involves. Too many great artists have failed to attain them in their lifetimes to go unnoticed by others in the profession. The possibility of being discovered and recognized after death turns out to be of small comfort, especially when the artist and the people with whom he interacts and from whom he seeks confirmation are under the influence of a society oriented toward remunerative occupations and the rewards and recognition which such occupations provide. The precarious future of the fine artist clashes with the institutional challenges of his culture, *e.g.*, family and dependents and the questions stemming from responsibilities to them. How fair is it to ask them to sacrifice the comforts of life so that the artist may pursue a goal so uncertain of attainment? Very often the artist has deep misgivings about his own abilities, and few are self-confident enough to suggest to themselves or to others that they possess the gifts of a Cezanne, a Picasso, or a Rembrandt.

The second problem which the traditional-role artist faces, legitimizing his new identity as a commercial artist, is essentially one of justifying the pursuit of the new role, without damaging his ego too greatly. The justifications are in the form of recriminations against his former role and those who are still pursuing it. In many cases these justifications are the same, but with a contrary twist, as those once used to justify his identity as a fine artist. He talks of pain when he sees the things that others must do in order to continue to live while pursuing the role of fine artist, *e.g.*, "I was tired of being a bastard from society." He contrasts his work as a commercial artist with the occupations of those with whom he formerly identified, and declares that he is much better off as a commercial artist, even with the liabilities the new role involves.

As time passes, as these artists continue in commercial art, and as they move from one status to another, passing milestones and being occupationally mobile, their change in identity becomes more consistent, integrated, and reinforced. This is especially so as they interact with others and form primary relationships with others who, like themselves, have faced the same dilemma and have resolved it in the same manner. With these added experiences, the justifications become more positive and more sophisticated. For example, they state: "Now I know where commercial art fits in"; "Commercial art is used to beautify the industrial world"; "Commercial art is getting better all he time"; "We raise the standard of living of people." As these quotations indicate, the guilt feelings which were first associated with abjuring to the "enemy's camp" have been dissipated.

In connection with the third problem, that of legitimizing the new role to significant others, the traditional-role artist must satisfy two groups: his former colleagues who are still enacting the fine artist role, and his family and relatives.

In justifying himself to his former colleagues, there is the feeling that he is deserting and betraying them. He has two alternatives in overcoming the bitterness and recriminations against him from former colleagues. Either he can remove himself physically from the geographical location, thereby avoiding interacting with them as would be inevitable if he remained in the area, or he can escape symbolically. The latter appears to be the more difficult alternative, since the artist must always be defensive about working in commercial art.

In justifying himself to his family and relatives, the artist must be prepared to answer questions concerning his reasons for having changed his mind about commercial art. Furthermore, if his feelings were intense and opinionated against commercial art before he entered the field, he very probably alienated his family. If this was the case he must be prepared, like the prodigal son returning home, to face such taunts as "I thought you were so sure of yourself!" or "I see you weren't so clever as you thought!" and the vicious innuendos of those whose sensibilities he offended. The usual solution is to accept this in silence.

Since the traditional-role artists identify themselves as fine artists temporarily engaged in commercial art, they admit that a role conflict exists, that they are aware of it, and that they have personally experienced it. They verbalize this experience in terms of guilt and frustration and they symbolize it in terms of (1) a time problem and (2) an ethical problem. The first concerns the fact that their jobs as commercial artists do not allow them sufficient time to paint. The second concerns the concept of their talent as a "gift" and stems from the belief that the ability to paint is of supernatural or divine origin and is a blessing. If one's parents cannot paint, and if there is no evidence that the ability to paint is inherited, how then can the ability to paint be explained? The answer is that it is a gift from the *deity*. The argument then is that, if the artist is a person who has been endowed with a God-given talent, this gift places an obligation on the artist not to use the gift for anything but the greater glory of God and Man. Since, theoretically, religion and the secular world have, as Durkheim has pointed out, antithetical goals and rewards, then the talent is not supposed to be dissipated, especially in the realm of the material or profane world.

The implication is that when the artist becomes introspective he will be confronted with the above considerations and say to himself, "Is this what the *deity* meant for me to do with my gift which was so carefully rationed out to a chosen few both in the past and in the present?" The fact that the artist is not devoting as much time and energy to the development of the gift as he should is sinful enough, but, in addition, he is using it to sell things and is, therefore, perverting it.

To illustrate further the problem of guilt and conflict, one can examine the interaction of the traditional-role artist with his colleague groups. Since he belongs to two social systems, that of the fine artist and that of the commercial artist, one would expect that within each colleague group he would find support for his self-conceptions and identity. However, since the role of commercial artist has no significance for him and he does not identify with his colleagues in that field, he has little interaction with them except for the exchange of normal amenities. Indeed, any attempt on their part to assuage his feelings has no mitigating effect, since their opinions are not significant to him. As a matter of fact, encouragement from them may only aggravate his conflict, since they represent a group from which he has withdrawn and symbolically rejected.

Neither does he find comfort when he turns to the fine-arts group. Normally one would expect that his former colleagues would be the ones to give him the greatest support, but in fact they are the ones who condemn him the most and are his most severe critics. Since these are the artists whom he considers his peers and the people whose criticism he honors most, their condemnation is devastating to his self-conceptions. These artists regard his working in the field of commercial art as reprehensible and define this in terms of *betrayal to the cause of fine art and the prostitution of a God-given talent.*

The reaction of the traditional-role artist to these attacks is to withdraw and to seek membership in other groups which will not condemn him or may actually reinforce and define his actions as logical and justifiable.

A second mechanism, in addition to withdrawal, which he uses to save his original identity is that of compartmentalization. By means of this, he is able to cope with the serious charge levelled against him by fine artists, art educators, dealers, and gallery owners who maintain that commercial art carries over to fine art. This position holds that the two arts are fundamentally different and that therefore any carry-over from commercial art destroys the artist's ability in fine art. Those who hold this view contend that if an artist continually creates commercial art, his perception and mental processes will unavoidably and irreversibly become habituated to seeing and thinking within the framework of commercial art.

Thus, it is essential for the traditional-role artist to institute both compartmentalization and withdrawal; if he did not, his identity as a fine artist would become untenable. If, for example, he did not compartmentalize, but admitted that commercial art carries over and does affect his perception and thinking, then he would be saying that he is painting from the point of view of his clients or prospective buyers, and that he is inevitably using such common commercial art techniques as making art immediately recognizable and creating a desire in the viewer.

The traditional-role artist reinforces his position that there is no carry-over from commercial art to fine art, by pointing out that the work he does in commercial art is closely related to fine art and that he is relatively free from restrictions. For example, if he is a lay-out man, he points to the fact that the lay-out man is considered the thinker of the studio and that it is he who dictates to others rather than others who dictate to him. Thus, he excludes himself from restrictions. He points out that it is he who tells the illustrators how the ad should appear, what it should contain, and what colors should be used. The illustrator, on the other hand, points out that he is doing finished art work and is therefore as close to painting as it is possible to be in commercial art. The letter man points out that lettering cannot possibly affect his work in fine art because lettering has nothing to do with art. This same point is made by the production men, the paste-up men, and the art directors. They point out that they are never responsible for the creation of the ad, except in a superficial way.

At the other extreme of role identification are those whom I have called the *commercial-role* artists. They organize their role on the basis that both fine art and commercial art are utilitarian. As commercial artists they think of themselves as instruments for the transformation of verbal symbols into visual ones, as dictated by a client, such as an advertising studio, a manufacturer, or a merchant. As a result, their ideological orientation is committed to expectations deriving from the commercial field, especially pleasing and satisfying clients. In conceiving of their role in this manner, the commercial-role artists refrain from interjecting or altering in any way the expressed wishes of their clients, unless specifically asked by the clients to do so. As passive agents, they accept the occupational imperative that "the customer is always right." After all, they state, it is the customer who is paying for the ad.

The consequence of this belief is that the commercial-role artist defines his role as having been successfully fulfilled when the requirements of the client have been met as parsimoniously as possible. This means the creation and execution of illustrations or lay-outs as quickly and cheaply as possible. The major reason for this is that time and deadlines dominate the commercial-art world and have the same meaning as they do in such fields as transportation and newspaper work. Meeting deadlines implies meeting advertising campaigns which are aimed and co-ordinated from a number of standpoints. For example, clothing ads must be ready for the right season. Bathing suit ads must appear in late spring and early summer, and fur coat ads in late autumn and early winter. The importance of time and the synchronization of all phases of advertising can be understood, when it is realized that some advertising campaigns have very large budgets. In some campaigns, not only huge sums of money are at stake, but the very survival of the client, the ad agency, the studio, and the artist. Commercial artists state that one can move, from an income of 50,000 dollars a year, to an income of nothing overnight. It is no accident that part of the culture of this group includes talk about stomach troubles, ulcers, and mental breakdowns. What does one tell his wife and children, his neighbors, the private school his child is attending, when such a disaster strikes?

In contrast to the traditional-role artists, the commercial-role artists reject the idea that they are working in commercial art because of extenuating circumstances. On the contrary, they believe that the traditional-role artists are pursuing a nineteenth-century anachronism which should be discarded as the role of the contemporary artist.

Although it is difficult to say that these artists are faced with a role conflict, since they do not perceive it as such, it is nevertheless valuable to consider their reactions to the role conflict as perceived by the traditional-role artists.

For example, when they are confronted with the fact that their clients dictate to them and that this is contrary to the classical concept of the fine artist, they thoroughly agree that this is so. However they transform what, to the traditional-role artist, is distasteful into a *positive attribute actually having functional significance* for them as artists. They state that restrictions are beneficial to an artist because they provide him with discipline. So, for example, when they do paint they can begin immediately because they know where they are going. They also believe that these restrictions are responsible for the fact that the commercial artist is more creative than the fine artist, because restrictions impose greater problems which require greater ingenuity and creativity to solve. They not only have to work with restrictions on color, subject matter, and budgets, but they must also please a client. Furthermore, they point out that the dangers and the consequences of failing are greater for the commercial artist than for the fine artist. If a commercial artist fails he may lose his job, his income, and his reputation, whereas if a fine artist fails his only penalty is a damaged ego.

When asked about the problem of carry-over, the commercial-role artist admits that carry-over does occur and further states that this is beneficial, since there is basically no difference between the two art forms. As with restrictions, the carry-over is considered desirable because it contributes to the artist's progress and to his ability to produce a painting that will sell. Art is regarded as a utilitarian product no matter what objective the artist may have in painting. Since commercial art is a field producing a product to be sold, and since art is a utilitarian product, knowledge and skills acquired in commercial art constitute a desirable carry-over in any direction, because they will help the artist produce paintings that will sell.

Between the traditional role at one end of role identification and the commercial role at the other, is a third one called the *compromise-role,* a mixture of both the traditional and the commercial roles. Like the commercial artists, the compromise artists believe that they are instruments of the client, but, unlike them, they do not conceive of themselves as passive agents completely at the mercy of the client. They regard themselves as active agents and carry out their role conceptions of themselves by obeying the wishes of the clients, but at the same time trying to persuade them at every opportunity to accept innovations of all types, especially the introduction into their ads of fine arts symbols. In this latter respect they also differ from the commercial artists, since, by conceiving of themselves as active agents, they also imply that they view the client as maneuverable and therefore a personal object, rather than an immovable, impersonal object which is the view of the client held by the commercial-role artists.

In order to implement one of their objectives—"putting art into advertising"—it is essential for them to escape the arbitrariness of the client and, if possible, to attain a degree of social control over him. In order to do this, the status of the artist in relationship to the client must change from that of a subordinate to that of a superior.

There are several ways in which this objective may be accomplished. The most practical is for the artist to win the confidence of his clientele, and this is best accomplished by successfully fulfilling their demands. The limitations of this method are that confidence bears fruit only after a long and enduring relationship and that the relationship between artist and client is still one-sided since the power still ultimately remains with the client.

A more satisfactory solution occurs when the artist achieves a reputation in commercial art, fine art, or both. This may be accomplished by: (1) receiving certain honors in the commercial art field, such as winning an exhibition sponsored by a commercial artists' guild; (2) having a fine arts painting exhibited in a museum; or (3) landing a national account, such as the Container

Corporation of America or one of the large weekly magazines, such as the cover of *Time* or *Fortune* or certain parts of the *Reader's Digest*.

Once the artist has achieved a reputation, his relationship to the client is either balanced or reversed. If it is reversed, the client becomes the passive agent and the artist the active one. The artist is then in a position to be selective, rejecting those clients whose work is not amenable to the dictates of progressive commercial art. The greatest achievement in this respect would be to work for clients such as the Container Corporation of America (specifically their *Great Ideas of Western Man* series), the John Hancock Life Insurance Company, or the West Virginia Pulp and Paper Company.

A corollary to the above aspect of the role is that many compromise-role artists feel that they are involved in a crusade for better art. They believe that by raising the standards of their client's art they are at the same time raising the level of the public's taste for art. These feelings become transfigured into their future goal-orientation, and they symbolize this in terms of contributions to and improvements of society in the future. One way of realizing this ambition is by staking out a claim for themselves in an area of advertising art which they believe has been backward and could stand considerable improvement. For example, they will point to an area like heavy industry and say that this is an area in which they would like to make their major contribution to society, by innovating new methods of illustrating the industry. They mention that their ambition is to convince a client that he will eventually increase his sales in this way.

These artists are aware that a conflict exists between commercial art and fine art and feel that their development is hampered by their lack of time to paint and by the fact that they have given a higher priority to their commercial art work than to their fine art work. They do not express these feelings in terms of guilt, as the traditional-role artists do, but rather in terms of regret, and express their lack of time for painting in terms of frustration. They also point out that a person who devotes himself exclusively to painting may make a greater contribution to society than one who remains in the commercial art field. However, they make this statement on a comparative and relative basis aimed at answering the question of who contributes the most to society. They feel that by improving the level of commercial art, and by bringing it closer to fine art, they are making a major contribution to such universals as truth and beauty. They qualify this, however, by saying that perhaps the contribution is not as great as that of the fine artist, *if* he can paint *one* masterpiece.

Another interesting reaction of the compromise-role artists, which reveals their awareness of conflict, is the transformation of symbols. In interviews, they strongly rejected the terms "commercial art" and "commercial artist" and substituted for them "advertising art" and "advertising artist." The intensity and consistency with which they did this suggested that the connotations of the term "commercial artist" were incompatible with their role-identification and self-conceptions. My analysis of this is that there is a stereotype of the commercial artist which operates rather powerfully within the profession and that the image conveyed is that of the self-conception of the commercial-role artist. The connotations of the term are those of typing, of the artist as merely an instrument of the client, and of the work produced as completely utilitarian. The commercial artist functions as an instrument of buying and selling in an impersonal market.

By calling themselves "advertising artists," the compromise-role artists are able to asert their identity *as artists* and their function as creative rather than merely utilitarian. Thus, they can conceive of themselves as responsible for improving the public's taste in art and raising the standard of living, by creating new and better desires. It appears that the term "advertising" is easier for them to rationalize than the term "commercial," and that this rationalization is a crucial mechanism in resolving their role conflicts.

The term compromise-role has been used to indicate that this group employs the mechanism of compromise to resolve the conflict situation. In doing this, the members identify themselves as fine artists and as advertising artists, and state that one can work in both fields and contribute to both fields at the same time. They state further that growth and development in one field helps growth and development in the other. Since compromise implies bringing together at least two viewpoints, this mechanism precludes the use of both withdrawal, which would involve withdrawing from one viewpoint, and compartmentalization, which would involve separating the two roles.

The attitude of the compromise-role artist, *i.e.,* that this linkage is desirable, is in contrast to that of the traditional-role artist and very similar to that of the commercial-role artist. The view is that the artist, by meeting many problems in his commercial work, acquires speed and certainty in solving them. This enables him to reduce delays and, consequently to devote more time to painting. Furthermore, by constantly being faced with problems which not only have to be solved, but must be solved within a short space of time, the artist acquires an ability that is useful in his fine art work. Thus the time spent in commercial art, which appears to be wasted from the point of view of the traditional-role artist, is in reality productive and beneficial. Unlike the commercial-role artist, however, the compromise-role artist is not particularly interested in selling his paintings. He does, of course, sell them if he can. However, in most instances he prefers using them as a method of advertising himself to prospective clients. He is more concerned than the members of the other two groups to exhibit his paintings where there is the possibility that they will attract a new client or an art director of an ad agency.

Another way in which these artists compromise the situation is related directly to their central role-conception and to their attempts to restrict their clientele. If they were able to have only clients who were good clients and who would be willing to accept innovations and grant the artist the mandate he wants—the right to determine how the ads should appear—then there would be very little difference between what they produce in advertising art and what they produce as fine art.

In this connection, they point out that the two fields are progressively coming together and that more art is continually being added to advertising, so that eventually the two fields will be one field, or, in any event, the differences between the two will be slight.

Their strongest argument for refuting the charge that the two fields are divergent and irreconcilable is to cite examples of artists who have done both, or are doing both, and have still managed to be great painters. If working for clients who impose restrictions is harmful, they argue, then how can one account for the fact that great artists of the past, such as Leonardo and Michelangelo, worked under restrictions and had clients and still managed to produce masterpieces. If it is objected that these examples go back too far in the past, they point to more recent examples, such as Remington and Winslow Homer, who worked as magazine illustrators and yet painted at the same time and produced great works of art. They also like to point to contemporary artists like Picasso and Miró.

The resemblance between the compromise-role and the traditional-role lies in the fact that the members of both groups are concerned with fine art. The difference is that those who adopt the compromise-role do not consider their commercial art work onerous or harmful to their fine art work, nor do they feel their status as artists should be autonomous and independent of the secular world. They believe, as do the commercial-role artists, that their legitimate position in society lies in the commercial field.

Motives for Painting and Painting Styles

Why do artists who are working in commercial art continue to paint in the fine arts tradition? Is there any connection between role-identity and painting styles?

The painting of the *traditional-role* artist is oriented away from the commercial market and his position is antithetical to that of the other two groups with respect to utilitarian art. He views his work not as a means to further his position in the commercial art world, but as a method of perfecting himself as a fine artist. His explanations are couched in terms of improving and perfecting his ability to depict fine-arts symbols. The predominating themes encompassing and organizing his behavior are self-improvement, correcting mistakes, overcoming unresolved problems, creating an original style, and deriving new forms of aesthetic expression. He refers frequently to the fact that he feels an intrinsic need to paint (which resembles catharsis), and that this is a need which he feels must be fulfilled even at the expense of reducing his income. This reinforces his aim to accumulate enough money so that he will be independent and can then devote his time exclusively to painting. One point should be noted here: although all three groups mention that their background in fine arts has been helpful to their careers in commercial art, the traditional-role artist is the only one who never refers to his paintings in relation to commercial art and never speaks of the benefits that commercial art may have for his fine-arts painting.

These artists emphasize that their paintings serve as lessons. They learn by painting, and, by studying their paintings, they discover errors and how to correct them. They never paint with the idea of selling their paintings or try to paint what would be attractive to the public. Many, as a matter of fact, become emotionally attached to their work and will not part with it, even though opportunities may arise to do so. If the paintings are exhibited, they will often place sold signs on them even though they are not sold in order to retain them, or in other cases place prices on them high enough to insure their retention.

The *commercial-role* artist's characteristic motive for painting is to supplement his income. This motive is congruent with his role-definition, the only difference being that the client has now become an unknown purchaser.

The second motive, which is closely related to the first, centers on the manifest function of perfecting new styles in order to keep abreast of the changes in art fashions which occur so frequently in this field. The latent function stems from the nature of much commercial art, which is extremely exacting and repetitious and often imposes an overwhelming number of restrictions on the artist. As some artists complain, "You can almost feel the client guiding your hand as you draw." Clients also have idiosyncrasies. There is the humorous anecdote of the client who told his artist that he approved of his illustration, but "couldn't he just widen, a little more, the ass of the girl sitting on the fence."

If the artist is to divorce himself from this confining work and in that way find new and better-paying clients, and if, in addition, he is not to be behind the times in art fashion, he must during some part of his career develop an original style. To realize this goal he has only one alternative: find time! However, free time can be found only on week-ends and vacations, and infringing on his free time are his obligations to his primary and secondary groups. He cannot arbitrarily ignore his wife, his children, his parents, his friends and neighbors, no matter how much he may want to or how urgent it may be for his career to do so. Certainly he cannot ignore his business associates, upon whom he depends for routine work, and he cannot neglect his regular commercial-art work because it provides him with a steady income. If he is required to meet a deadline he must do so, even if it means infringing on his nonvocational time such as evenings, week-ends, and vacations. Furthermore, there is an occupational imperative which commands the artist to get as much work as he can, because styles and fashions change so frequently that plenty is often followed by prolonged want. An artist who has a distinctive and popular style may be in great demand at one time, only to be completely forgotten and by-passed at a later date.

Another problem which the commercial-role artist faces is that of typing, which stems from the minute specialization which is prevalent in some areas of commercial art. Thus, the individual artist is labeled as a specialist possessing a circumscribed skill and capable of only that skill. Once this has occurred the artist finds it extremely difficult to escape his specialty. The following interview illustrates this problem.

"... I had a friend who could do beer bottles well. Perspiration on beer bottles was his specialty. You know, of course, how broken down it is? One person does the head, another the arms, another the furniture, etc. Well, his specialty was beer bottles. He tried to get out of it. He would go to a new client and ask for work and they would ask him what kind of work he had done. He would tell them 'perspiration on beer bottles.' They would say, 'We have work for you on that.' He couldn't get out of it."

As a result of all these factors, the artist is faced with a number of paradoxes and dilemmas. The method of resolving them lies in originating a new style. If he succeeds, he can show present and prospective clients the new style and thereby induce them to give him new types of work. Furthermore, the clients begin to change their conception of the artist and the type of work they associate with him. Should these efforts prove fruitful, the artist is on his way toward improving the quality of his work, toward reaching new markets, and toward increasing his income.

One of the most interesting observations is that, in many cases, the paintings of the commercial-role artists are more real than real life. There is a greater exactness of detail than would be true if one took a photograph. This is in keeping with the commercial-art folkways, because one of the common tendencies in commercial art is to over-exaggerate the details of subject matter so that the viewer can recognize immediately the objects of the illustration and the message they are intended to convey.

The *compromise-role* artist paints for a number of reasons, the most important being that he can, in this way, advertise his work and attract desirable clients. A second reason is the desire to improve his advertising-art style. The third reason is that he has a "need disposition" to paint. All of the artists interviewed, regardless of their role-identifications, stated that they felt an intrinsic need to paint and that they experienced a satisfaction from painting, because this was their only opportunity to paint without restrictions imposed by a client or by the technical processes.

As stated above, the major reason for the *compromise-role* artist's fine arts painting is that it enables him to promote his name and produce a specific style. By having his paintings displayed at exhibitions, he is able to attract the attention of significant persons in advertising and to demonstrate his continued interest in painting. They, in turn, by their criticism and conversations, confirm and reinforce his self-conception as an artist. Furthermore, there is always the possibility that one or more of his paintings may receive honors or citations, not only from peer groups but from the media devoted to both fine and commercial art, such as art magazines and trade journals. Finally, there is always the possibility that one of his paintings may be hung as either a temporary or a permanent part of the collection of a fine-arts museum. This is the highest achievement for the compromise-role artist because it not only confirms his conception of himself as an artist, but also his conception of himself as a crusader for higher artistic standards in the commercial art world.

To understand fully the importance to the compromise-role artist of attracting the attention of significant others in the commercial-art world, it is necessary to understand the highly competitive nature of his occupation. Commercial art places a premium on new ideas and new methods of presenting visual phenomena, especially those having the ability to direct the attention of new customers to a company's product, in such a way that they will buy the product. By exhibiting, the artist is experimenting with new styles, testing these new approaches in competition with other artists, and attracting the attention of art directors of major firms. To do this is essential to the reinforcement of his role-conceptions for several reasons. The first is related to the constant injunction to derive new styles. The only method available is that of constant experimentation. Such experimentation, however, takes time, and since the commercial artist has little spare time, he must use what he has judiciously. He can do this only by making his free-time painting serve several needs simultaneously. It must serve as a device to attract better clients; it must serve as a means to derive new styles; it must satisfy the artist's need to paint; finally, it must serve as a device to support the artist's self-conception as an artist in the advertising field. By painting and exhibiting, the compromise-role artist not only satisfies these needs but demonstrates objectively, to his peers and to himself, that he is still interested in the sacred aspects of art.

Conclusions

On the basis of this study, together with others in the field of occupations and professions, several conclusions may be drawn about the phenomenon of identity. Identity, despite many of its changes, nuances, and adumbrations of contrary roles, has a fairly stable core of persistent characteristics. How and why this small core-area persists is still unclear, although the importance of cultural imperatives and social agents in reinforcing these imperatives is incontrovertible. As illustrated in this paper, many obstacles may present themselves to change an individual once committed to a role; yet the persistency prevails. The most amazing aspect of the group studied is their continued persistency in identification, even though their objective behavior would preclude their continuance in a given role. Such persistency is commonly referred to as deluding oneself or harboring an illusion. Whatever the label, the phenomenon functions to enable the individual to persist in his identity, and, as such, constitutes an important aspect of human behavior which must be accounted for in any study of identity and human behavior.

Fulfillment of the role of artist may be only one small aspect of a person's total behavior, but the retention of that role may still be the most important aspect of his behavior. Its most positive function would appear to be that it answers the question of who he is.

This statement, however, is not adequate for an understanding of identity, since there are a number of peripheral and inferential questions proceeding from this basic concept. One important series pertains to the retention of an original identity, in those situations where the individual is conscious that his identity will be questioned by significant others, for example in choosing between remaining a fine artist or changing his role to that of a commercial artist or an art educator. The field for future research would seem to include classifying these questions, and the situations in which they are asked and answered, to see what similarities and differences emerge.

Several conclusions were reached concerning role-conflict, perhaps the most important being that entrance into commercial art alone was *not* significant in creating conflict. The significant factor was the identity the individual held when he made the decision to enter the field. Concurrent with identity is the experience of conflict and the use of various mechanisms, such as withdrawal, compartmentalization, and compromise, to resolve the conflict. Those individuals who identified as fine artists (the traditional-role) were the ones most apt to experience guilt and conflict, whereas those who identified with the commercial-role experienced the least guilt and conflict. Furthermore, styles of painting were directly related to role-identification. Although this correlation was based on a very limited number of examples, there was definite evidence of observable differences. The paintings of the traditional-role artists were least affected by the commercial-art ideology and its accompanying styles and techniques; whereas, the paintings of the commercial-role artists, except for the fact that there was no specific client to satisfy or product to advertise, were almost exactly a commercial-art product.

A final consideration concerns the broad implications of the inconsistencies, and attendant tensions, produced by the discrepancies between our cultural values and the economic facts and demands of our social structure. Artists and members of other professions are inculcated with belief in the value of creative activity and complete role fulfillment. At the same time, the realities of the situations in which they must work and earn a living preclude, in many ways, the realization of these values. The artist must restrict his freedom; the writer must keep the market in mind or subsidize himself in some way; the scholar must teach first and do the basic research for which he has been trained in his "spare" time; and the student must be tempted to pass courses, even if this means cheating. These antinomies constantly threaten the individual's attempt to achieve not only a stable identity, but one in accord with the ideology that motivates him. How constructive or how destructive the tension resulting from the conflict may be, is a subject that merits further study. It is apparent that some persons are more able than others to resolve role-conflict and make substantial contributions to the arts and sciences, by using the mechanisms of withdrawal, compartmentalization, and compromise. Why this should be so, with its resulting cost to both society and the individual, is a subject with broad implications for the future of our civilization.

References

1. MASON GRIFF, "The Recruitment of the Artist" (unpublished manuscript, 1955). Also see Anselm Strauss, "The Art School and Its Students: A Study and Interpretation" (unpublished manuscript.)
2. The number is not large in any country.
3. MASON GRIFF, "The Commercial Artist: A Study in Role Conflict and Career Development (Unpublished Ph.D. dissertation, University of Chicago, 1958).
4. See, for example, Howard S. Becker, "The Jazz Musician and His Audience" (Unpublished Master's thesis, University of Chicago, 1949).
5. In this connection, see Talcott Parsons and Edward Shils (eds.), *Toward a General Theory of Action* (Cambridge: Harvard University Press, 1951). See especially the discussion of the pattern variable called universalistic-particularistic.
6. EDWARD SHILS, "Ideology and Civility," *The Sewanee Review,* LXVI (Summer, 1958), 467-68.
7. TALCOTT PARSONS, *The Structure of Social Action.* (Glencoe, Ill.: The Free Press, 1949), pp. 503-16.
8. For an extended discussion of the Art School, its importance in defining roles, and its implication for the art world, see Anselm Strauss, *op. cit.*

DOLLARD, DOOB, MILLER, MOWRER, & SEARS / Criminality*

The literature on the topic of criminality reveals a great diversity of factors which have been shown to correlate statistically with this phenomenon; there is, however, no generally accepted conceptual system of crime causation. Atomistic explanations stressing the etiological importance of now one isolated factor, now another, have repeatedly been put forward, but only to be sooner or later discredited. Many excellent empirical studies have been reported and a great many solid facts discovered, but the meaning of these facts remains largely to be determined. Criminology, as a science, seems still to be in that stage, which all sciences pass through, of collecting data and shuffling them about in more or less random fashion, without any well-defined natural categories into which they may be sorted and systematically dealt with. Until such categories have been established, scientific principles and laws can scarcely be expected to evolve; and the current view that "causes are multiple [and] grow out of the total situation" (1, p. vii) will continue to represent the ultimate in crime-causation theory. What would seem most urgently needed, therefore, in this field is the discovery of a few *common denominators* which will comprise as many of the isolated yet relevant factors as possible. As an exploratory step in this direction, two such common denominators are here proposed, the first of which is *frustration,* as previously defined in this book, and the second is what has been termed *anticipation of punishment.*[1]

The present chapter will be devoted to an attempt to determine how adequately these two concepts actually serve their intended purpose. More specifically, the plan will be to examine those measurable characteristics in which criminals have been

* Reprinted from John Dollard, Leonard W. Doob, Neal E. Miller, O. H. Mowrer, and Robert R. Sears, *Frustration and Aggression*.

[1] The term "punishment" is here used to include not only the external infliction of injury but also the loss of accustomed gratifications, valued personal relationships, special privileges, etc. It is also important to keep in mind that punishment is no less a form of aggression than is crime. The fact that the latter is "anti-social" and the former is what may be called "pro-social," i.e., is aligned with and directed toward the enforcement and perpetuation of the mores of a group, does not alter the essentially aggressive character of both; crime and punishment both injure other persons and therefore qualify, according to the definition employed in this study, as forms of aggression. This tendency for aggression to be patterned along opposing, i.e., socially approved and socially disapproved, lines has numerous implications for social theory which will be considered in detail at another time.

found to deviate significantly from the population at large and to ascertain to what degree these deviations imply either higher-than-average frustration or lower-than-average anticipation of punishment, the underlying assumption being that criminality, as a species of aggression,[2] will vary positively with the former and negatively with the latter.

This approach, necessarily cross-sectional and statistical, is fraught with many dangers, not the least of which in this case is the inadequacy of the available data.[3] Many of the sources which must be relied upon are old and especially unsatisfactory since they lack indices of reliability. Data reported by different investigators have often been selected according to widely divergent criteria; hence inter-comparison and refined correlational treatment are frequently impossible. Many otherwise valuable findings that have been reported regarding criminals are rendered useless for present purposes because of a lack of comparable observations for the non-criminal population. Certain selective factors are also often operative, such as the fact that criminal statistics are derived in most instances from convicts (in prison or on parole) and do not, therefore, characterize offenders in general, including those who elude apprehension or else come to trial but are not convicted. In view of these and other limitations which might be enumerated, the following analysis is not to be regarded as in any sense definitive but rather as a means of stating and tentatively exploring the possibilities of an hypothesis and of posing some of its research implications.

(a) Economic Status. The most comprehensive survey of the relation between poverty and crime is that reported by Bonger (2), who concluded from an analysis of data collected from various countries that "the poor supply a very great proportion of the convicts, in every case a greater proportion than they bear to the population in general, and the well-to-do form only a small part." Bonger found, for example, that in Italy during the years 1887-1889, 60 per cent of the population, classified as indigent or poor, contributed 88 per cent of the convicts. Other investigators[4] have

[2] In the following pages an attempt will be made to show that criminal behavior qualifies as aggression in the one respect that it is a reaction to frustration; and the simple fact that a given type of behavior is forbidden and is therefore termed criminal is almost axiomatic proof that it is directly or indirectly hurtful to some one or more members of the group in which it is forbidden. The problem of distinguishing between behavior which is "accidentally" injurious and behavior which is "intentionally" (criminally) injurious has already been dealt with and will not be reconsidered here.

[3] References to criminological literature will necessarily be incomplete; works selected for citation will be, in the main, either comprehensive surveys and summaries or of such a character as to typify other representative investigation on the same topic.

[4] Reviewed by Gillin (4).

studied this problem, but their findings have been in essential agreement with those of Bonger. To cite but one of the more recent studies, Shaw and McKay (3) found that in Chicago the coefficient of correlation by square-mile areas between delinquency rates and rates of financial aid to families by the United Charities and the Jewish Charities was +.74, between delinquency cases and dependency cases in the juvenile court was +.82, and between delinquency cases and mothers' pension cases was +.63.

It has sometimes been argued that poverty is correlated with crime, not because of any direct causal relationship, but because both phenomena are the common consequences of stupidity, laziness, or some similar trait. But the force of this contention is weakened by the observation, reported by various writers (5; 6; 7), that criminality tends to decrease during periods of prosperity and to increase during depressions; it can scarcely be maintained that either stupidity or laziness likewise follows the economic cycle.

That poverty is a source of more or less constant frustration is indicated by the fact that when individuals have money their goal-responses are different from those which they manifest when they do not have it.[5] On the basis of assumptions stated elsewhere in this study, poverty would therefore be expected to lead, other factors being held constant, to an increase in criminality, as in fact appears to be the case.

But not only does low economic status lead to a heightened expectation of criminality because of higher-than-average frustration; it also tends to lower the inhibiting influence of anticipated punishment. Fines cannot be collected from penniless persons; and the threat of imprisonment has little deterring effect upon the individual who habitually experiences scarcely less deprivation outside of prison than he would inside. Human beings do not dread the loss of privileges and material advantages which they do not possess.

(*b*) *Vocational Status.* Bonger (2) has reported that unskilled male workers are implicated in all crimes (except "insult") more often in proportion to their incidence in the general population than are independent merchants, professional men, and "students and persons with income."[6] Fernald, Holmes, Hayes, and

[5] In modern civilized societies the total amount of frustration experienced on this score is probably greatly increased by advertising, by the movies, and perhaps to a less extent by the schools. Any agency which portrays other persons behaving differently from the way in which the mass of people are accustomed or financially able to behave and which gives the impression that anyone who does not behave in this different way is "missing something" can scarcely fail to have such an effect. Experienced poverty is obviously a function of one's relative as well as absolute level of achievement and possession.

[6] See also Shield (8), Sullenger (9), and Gillin (4; 6).

Dawley (10) found that 40.4 per cent of 517 female offenders studied in five New York State penal institutions had been engaged as domestic servants; about 24 per cent of the general female population was engaged in this type of work at the time this study was conducted. On the other hand, these writers found that only .8 per cent of their subjects had engaged in professional work, as against 8.0 per cent of the female population at large. Sutherland (11, p. 160) has reviewed the more recent evidence in this connection and concludes that "such comparisons show a disproportionately large representation in prisons from the unskilled and semi-skilled occupations, but the statistics are relatively unreliable and the comparisons are difficult. Furthermore, it is probable that arrest and convictions and commitments to prisons are distinctly biased against the unskilled and semi-skilled classes because of their helplessness to resist arrest and conviction."

That certain types of occupation are more arduous, disagreeable, or dangerous than others is obvious; by implication, persons who are forced into these intrinsically less desirable kinds of work will experience, other things being equal, a higher-than-average amount of frustration and will therefore show a heightened tendency toward criminality. However, since the various occupations also differ greatly in their remunerativeness and since no attempt has apparently ever been made to ascertain the criminality of groups in which vocational and economic status are independently controlled, substantiation of the foregoing deduction will have to wait upon further inquiry.

(*c*) *Educational Status.* The existence of an inverse relationship between criminality and educational achievement has long been suspected and has been substantiated by a variety of studies. Bonger (2) reported that of 1,209 juvenile delinquents in the English prisons during the years 1898-1899, only 9.1 per cent could be said to have had a "good education," but he gave no figures for the population at large with which this finding could be compared. Statistics published by the United States Government for the American prison population as of 1923 disclosed the following facts:

> The figures . . . show, in general, a decidedly lower educational status for the prisoners than for the population as a whole. For example, the ratio of commitments per 100,000 of the adult population was 42.7 for the illiterate as against 27.3 for those able to read and write. Among the literate group the commitment ratio is highest (31.4) for those of only elementary school education and lowest (14.3) for prisoners who had had some college training. The commitment ratio is about three times as high for the illiterate as for the college group. (12, p. 19)

Brearley has reported that "for the 43 states for which homicide rates are available, the coefficient of correlation between the main rate of homicide, . . . and the percentage of illiteracy on January 1, 1920, was +.658 with a probable error of +.06" (13, p. 147). Sutherland has reviewed the more recent findings and states that "the conclusion is that crime decreases with the amount of formal education" (11, p. 177).[7]

Measures of educational achievement usually include or imply not only training in the technological sense, which tends to decrease frustration (through increased earning capacity), but moral training as well, which makes for increased anticipation of punishment. It is thus evident that the inverse correlation between criminality and educational achievement, as ordinarily judged, probably exists for two distinguishable reasons; but further research will be required to demonstrate the extent to which each is responsible for the observed relationship.

It seems evident that low educational achievement is not in itself frustrating. This is shown by the tenacity with which children normally resist the educational process. Deficient education is a source of frustration only at the adult level and then only to the extent that it leads to low income, inferior social status, or other conditions interfering with the performance of goal-responses. The fact that an education, once acquired, tends to reduce frustration is thus in no way inconsistent with the statement, stressed elsewhere in this study, that the acquisition of an education is always more or less frustrating.

(*d*) *Intelligence*. As Murchison (16, p. 28) has pointed out, there is a natural inclination to assume that wickedness and stupidity go hand in hand: "The author is not acquainted with any historical religion that has an intelligent and wise devil. Only the good are wise and intelligent. The devil and his followers are always foolish and idiotic."[8] Following an earlier period when feeblemindedness was regarded by many writers as virtually the exclusive explanation of criminality, the present consensus of opinion is that the low intelligence is much less of a cause of crime than was formerly supposed. On the basis of an analysis of 350 reports on the subject of criminal intelligence, involving data accrued from the examination of approximately 175,000 individuals, Sutherland (11, p. 96) has shown that "the relationship between crime and feeblemindedness is, in general, comparatively slight.

[7] *Cf.* also Glueck and Glueck (14), Pilcher (15), and Shield (8).

[8] "Comparing normal and criminal persons of the same age, Carrara found the *wisdom* tooth much more frequently present among normal persons. The percentage number of criminals showing no last molars is nearly quadruple that of normal individuals, according to Carrara's figures" (17, p. 65; italics added).

Certainly it is a much less important factor than age or sex. This does not, however, mean that it may not be a very important factor in individual cases."[9]

On the basis of the assumptions underlying the present analysis, it may seem surprising that stupidity is not correlated with criminality to a greater degree than the findings indicate. Not only would low intelligence seem likely to increase the amount of frustration experienced by an individual; it would also be expected to diminish the effectiveness of the socializing forces in that it would imply a lowered capacity to appreciate the consequences of specific acts and a less keen anticipation of impending punishment. But since the normally intelligent man is instigated both by needs which are actually present and also, perhaps to an even greater extent, by anticipated wants, the person with blunted capacity for looking into the future is likely to have a relatively low level of aspiration and to find acceptable a life status which would be intolerable to a more intelligent person. The same limitation of intelligence which restricts an individual's learning and earning capacities may also make the ensuing low level of accomplishment far less frustrating than it would otherwise be.

(*e*) *Age*. Attention has repeatedly been called to the fact that crime is characteristically a youthful occupation (20; 15). Statistics show that deliquency as well as the more serious crimes increases among male offenders fairly steadily during adolescence, reaching a peak at the age of about twenty-five years, after which there is a negatively accelerated decline. The rate for all crimes for persons between twenty and twenty-four years of age is approximately five times as great as for persons over fifty; serious crimes are about fifteen times as frequent at the earlier ages (11). Fernald, Holmes, Hayes, and Dawley (10), in the study of delinquent women already cited, found that upon classifying their subjects according to four-year groups between seventeen and seventy-four years of age, the greatest number of offenders were between eighteen and twenty-two years.[10]

The fact that criminality reaches a peak during the twenties and thereafter declines has been explained in a variety of ways, none of which seems entirely satisfactory. It has been suggested, for example, that as human beings grow older they cease to commit crimes for the same reason that they cease to play strenuous

[9] Doll (18) and Erickson (19) have argued for the existence of a somewhat closer relationship between intelligence and crime than Sutherland assumes.

[10] Shield (8) calls attention to the fact that, although the incidence of criminal behavior in general declines after a youthful peak occurring between the ages of fifteen and twenty-four, some types of crime, notably sex crimes and murder (as contrasted to property offenses), increase with age at least up to the forty-fifth year. Why this state of affairs should exist has apparently not been determined.

games and drive automobiles recklessly, namely, because of a decline in physical vigor and emotional buoyance. The hypothesis here offered is that the pattern of variation in criminality in relation to age reflects a corresponding pattern in the general level of frustration experienced by the average individual during his life cycle. With the approach of adulthood, the youth is forced to rely more and more upon his own resources; having enjoyed during earlier years a relatively sheltered existence, the young man or woman must sooner or later pass through a period of more or less profound readjustment on the road to self-sufficiency and independence. By the time the average man is twenty-five or thirty years old he has usually married, gained some degree of economic security, and established himself as a person of some importance in his community. From this time on, the discrepancy between his wants and his means of gratifying them normally lessens, having achieved by middle life a relatively stable equilibrium in this respect. Furthermore, as his possessions and means of securing gratification increase, man becomes increasingly conservative, having now much to lose through social retribution for wrongdoing. Thus, with advancing age, not only does man's general level of frustration tend to decrease but his responsiveness to the threat of punishment also increases, thereby providing discouragement against criminality from two sources.

On theoretical grounds, the relation of crime to the life history of women would be expected to follow a somewhat different course from the one it does in men. The fact that women usually marry men a few years their senior means that they achieve a comparable degree of economic security and impulse gratification correspondingly sooner than do men. One would consequently expect to find that the incidence of delinquency and crime among them would begin to diminish at an earlier age than it does in men, which, as the statistics already cited show, is actually the case. In societies in which woman's status depends largely on her physical attractiveness, it might also be expected that her tendencies toward criminality would be highest relatively late in life. The validity of this inference apparently cannot be established on the basis of data now available; but the fact that prison commitments for females is greatest in Finland between the age of thirty-five and forty-five instead of during the twenties as in America shows that variations of this kind do occur (11).

(*f*) *Physical Size*. Smaller-than-average stature is quite generally regarded by men as a disadvantage and must be in some degree frustrating for a great many individuals. Although inferior size alone would not be expected to "produce" criminality in any given individual, it should show its influence statistically. Goring summarizes the findings of his monumental study of the physique of the English convict as follows:

> To sum up: all English criminals, with the exception of those technically convicted of fraud, are markedly differentiated from the general population in stature and body-weight; in addition, offenders convicted of violence to the person are characterized by an average degree of strength and of constitutional soundness considerably above the average of other criminals, and of the law-abiding community; finally, thieves and burglars (who constitute, it must be borne in mind, 90 per cent of all criminals), and also incendiaries, as well as being inferior in stature and weight, are also, relatively to other criminals and the population at large, puny in their general bodily habit. (21, pp. 200–201)

Weidenshall (22) has likewise reported that the inmates of an American female reformatory are shorter than the average working girl of fifteen.[11]

It may well be that in some cases the inferior stature of criminals is due to race, malnutrition reflecting low economic status, or some other factor which is independently correlated with criminality; to the extent that this is true, criminals are not criminal because they are undersized but they are both criminal and undersized for the same reason or reasons. However, it seems safe to predict that further research, in which this ambiguity is adequately controlled, will nevertheless reveal at least a slight connection between physical size and criminality, as originally postulated above.

The tendency for inferior stature to lead to increased criminality through a heightening of frustration may actually be lessened somewhat by the opposing tendency for smaller individuals to be less bold and more readily deterred by the prospect of retaliation. This supposition is supported by Goring's observation, already cited, that English criminals "convicted of violence . . . are characterized by an average degree of strength and of constitutional soundness considerably above the average of other criminals." However, the factor of size as a source of frustration is probably more important as a determiner of criminality than the influence of size upon the individual's reaction to the threat of punishment; for the latter is largely a product of childhood training, and during childhood the individual is always smaller than the surrounding adults, even though he be unusually large for his age.

[11] With the decline of the Italian school of "criminal anthropology," which held that crime was directly and more or less exclusively due to "congenital degeneracy," relatively little interest has been shown in the physique of criminals.

A number of writers, notably Healy (23) and Slawson (24), have remarked upon the tendency for delinquent children to be either conspicuously larger or conspicuously smaller than their classmates and playfellows of the same age. Marked aberration in either direction would be expected to be somewhat frustrating for children, although variation above the average would be expected to be less so than deviation below the average.

(g) *Personal Appearance and Physical Defects.* "I have wondered a great deal about the connection between crime and physical ugliness and deformity. That there is such a connection I have no faintest doubt" (25, p. 135).

There are probably two distinct reasons for the popular assumption that criminals differ from non-criminals in personal appearance, the one reason existing only in fancy, the other existing in fact. As Alexander and Staub (26) have shown, the villainy of the criminals in a given society regularly tends to be overestimated; for reasons which cannot be dealt with here, criminals are seen as personifications of all that is evil and odious and when so viewed are felt to deserve even worse treatment than is actually accorded them. They become scapegoats and whipping boys for the group as a whole and are commonly conceived as being in some vague sense not quite human. The atavistic theory of criminal types advanced by Lombroso and his school can now be seen in retrospect as primarily an attempt to give scientific status to this widespread social compulsion. Ellis (17) has reproduced thirty "authentic" pen sketches of "typical" criminals drawn by the governor of an English prison more than half a century ago; modern motion-picture portrayals of criminals seem to show that their appearance has not altered much in popular imagination during the interim.

Not only is there a tendency for criminals to be thought of as more repulsive-looking and misformed than they are, but there is also some evidence that they actually do deviate somewhat from the general run of individuals in the matter of personal appearance. It seems likely, on the basis of evidence reviewed by Ellis (17) at a time when the theory of atavistic criminal types was at its zenith of popularity, that an unusually large proportion of criminals have lower jaws which either recede or protrude to an excessive degree; and other peculiarities of physiognomy, such as overlarge or misshapen ears, were also reported as unusually common. That these findings were not entirely a product of the preconceptions of the time is indicated by the work of a number of recent investigators, such as Kilmer (27), for example, who reports that 44 per cent of a criminal group examined by him had "flap ears" as compared with 23 per cent of a non-criminal control group.[12] But it is not necessary to fall back upon Lombroso's theory of criminal degeneracy to explain the apparent connection between personal appearance and criminality. As various writers (25; 11) have pointed out, personal appearance is an important factor, particularly in women, in determining whether an individual will be able to gratify his desires and needs by legitimate, socially accepted methods or will have to resort to illegal procedures. It is easy to imagine the rebuffs and failures which offensive-looking individuals are likely to encounter in attempting to pursue many of the socially desirable walks of life and to understand why such individuals are prone to gravitate to the "underworld."

That the amount of frustration experienced by an individual is increased not only by unfortunate facial conformations and expressions, but also by bodily incapacities and defects, is obvious; that individuals who are so afflicted show an exaggerated tendency toward criminality is therefore not remarkable. Citing the Massachusetts Census of 1905, Sutherland (11, p. 84) says: "The number of lame, deformed, and maimed was 39 per 10,000 population of the state, while among the offenders it was 150; the number of deaf or dumb was 19 in the general population and 31 among offenders." The same census shows no greater incidence of blindness among delinquents and criminals than among the population at large; but blindness is so generally incapacitating and it so greatly reduces the individual's chances of successfully eluding apprehension that the fact that the blind are not more regularly deterred from criminal behavior than they actually are seems quite remarkable.

(*h*) *Health.* Since ill-health usually prevents the afflicted person from carrying out many goal-responses which seem important to him, it is unquestionably a source of serious frustration in the lives of a great many individuals; and the expectation would be, therefore, that such individuals would be represented in greater proportion among criminals than among the non-criminal population. Although Goring (21), Healy (23), Sullenger (1), and various other writers have interested themselves in ill-health as a factor in crime, the data necessary for arriving at any definite conclusion in this connection have apparently never been collected; in securing them care would have to be taken to distinguish between the effects of ill-health *per se* and of factors such as low economic status (resulting in undernourishment, exposure,

[12] Bridges (28) has likewise commented upon the relation of strabismus and certain other physical deformities to delinquency.

and inadequate medical attention) which might be associated with it.

(*i*) *Hyperactivity.* It has been noted by numerous writers that delinquents and criminals are likely to be unusually restless and overactive. Post-encephalitic individuals have been found especially often to present such a picture and seem to find their way into court in disproportionately large numbers. Instead of supposing, however, that hyperactivity as such is a factor in the causation of misconduct, Sutherland (11, p. 99) has suggested that "the inferiority resulting from [post-encephalitic] lesions in the central nervous system lowers the status of the child, and the criticisms of parents and teachers when the child does not do as well as previously drive the child desperate."[13] Healy and Bronner have taken the position that the hyperactivity so often noted in delinquents who have never had encephalitis may be a consequence of fundamental maladjustment rather than a cause of it. They say:

> A highly debatable question is whether or not such uninhibited behavior as we have just enumerated is caused by structural or functional peculiarities of the central nervous system, by obscure malfunctioning of other organs, or is the expression of emotional tensions occurring at even an early period of life as the result of situational experiences. . . . Evidently the question cannot be answered, but from some special observations we are forced to conclude that there is evidence that emotional thwartings and dissatisfactions, themselves dating back to very early years, may be the inciting cause of hyperactivity. (30, p. 45)

The primary purpose of calling attention to the frequently noted connection between criminality and hyperactivity is to show that even such an obscure relationship as this one need not be thought of as necessarily falling outside the scope of the present conception of criminality as a function of the two basic variables of frustration and anticipation of punishment.

(*j*) *Race and Nationality.* There is no serious contention among modern criminologists that individuals of any given race or nationality are *congenitally* either more or less prone to criminality than are those of any other group. But a mass of evidence has been accumulated to show that race, as a factor conditioning an individual's economic and social status in a given society, may play a very important rôle in this respect. American Indian men "were committed to prisons in 1923 3.1 times as frequently as American-born white men in proportion to the population, and Indian women 5.4 times as frequently as white women" (11, p. 112). Negro men in America are likewise arrested and committed

[13] *Cf.* Kahn and Cohen (29).

to prison about three times as frequently as native-born white men in proportion to the population; and Negro women show an even higher incidence of criminality in proportion to white women. That both the Indian and Negro groups in America experience a relatively great amount of frustration is commonly acknowledged; and Dollard (31) has advanced reasons for supposing that among the Negroes there is also a calculated weakening (by the whites) of the socializing forces as far as at least certain forms of criminality are concerned.

Certain immigrant groups, notably the Italian and the Irish, show a somewhat higher crime rate than do native-born Americans; but the factor of nationality shows its greatest influence upon criminality in the offspring of the foreign-born. "Special studies have indicated that the delinquency rates of the second generation are comparatively low when an immigrant group first settles in a community and increase as contacts with the surrounding culture multiply. The rate remains low in these foreign colonies which are comparatively isolated from the surrounding culture. The rate is low in the heart of the colony but increases on the borderlines where the group comes into contact with other groups" (11, p. 114).[14]

It can scarcely be supposed that the economic status of the offspring of the foreign-born is actually worse than that of their parents or that they live at a really inferior level of material comfort; but what seems to happen characteristically is that, as Americanization proceeds, an ever widening discrepancy is created between existing living conditions and the ideal standards of living which are created by American schools, American advertising, and other powerful institutions, with a resulting increase of discontent. This heightening of frustration would be expected to make, therefore, for increased criminality; but this is not the only way in which the process works. Various writers have called attention to the fact that the socializing influence of the family upon oncoming generations breaks down in periods of transition from one culture to another (28).[15] Parents stand for the old and the inadequate; and the normal process of identification with them, now recognized as of the greatest importance in character formation (34), occurs to a very incomplete and socially insufficient degree. The "clash of cultures," as Glueck and Glueck (14) have called it, is thus to be seen as not only increasing the amount of experi-

[14] See also Beynon (32).

[15] Ross (33) has taken the position, not easy to maintain, that economic factors are alone operative in this connection.

enced frustration but as also seriously lessening one of the major socializing forces, *viz.*, anticipation of punishment.

(*k*) *Illegitimacy*. The earlier data on the relationship between criminality and illegitimacy of birth have been reviewed by Bonger, who found that in France, as an example, during the years 1890-1895, "a natural son runs twice as much danger of becoming a criminal as he would if legitimate, and that this danger is even four times as great in the case of a natural daughter" (2, p. 494). Of the various countries for which statistics were available, Italy alone showed no heightening of criminality as a function of illegitimacy. Sullenger has surveyed the more recent data and concludes that "children born out of wedlock have a much higher expectancy of delinquency than other children" (1, p. 29).

As in the case of race and nationality, illegitimacy as such can scarcely be supposed to have any bearing upon an individual's becoming or not becoming a criminal; but the consequences and implications of illegitimacy are such as to make for both increased frustration and lowered anticipation of punishment. Unwanted, neglected, and ostracized, the illegitimate child has a distinctly inferior chance of identifying with suitable persons and of gaining those internalized restraints which are essential to satisfactory character formation; and much the same forces also increase his difficulties in school and in earning a livelihood.[16] If every illegitimate child could be adopted into a satisfactory home, thereby insuring adequate socialization and no more than an average amount of frustration, the connection between illegitimacy and criminality should, according to the present hypothesis, be greatly lessened, if not completely eliminated.

(*l*) *Marital Status*. Perhaps the most dramatic demonstration of all of the rôle of frustration in the causation of criminality is afforded by the data concerning the marital status of criminals as compared with non-criminals. The following quotation from a United States Government bulletin dealing with the antecedents of American prison inmates as of 1920 shows this relationship with remarkable clarity:

> A striking fact shown by the figures . . . is that, for both sexes and for all age groups for which significant comparisons can be made, the divorced population furnished a disproportionate number of prisoners. For divorced males the commitment ratio was 201.9 per 100,000, or nearly three times the ratio of 72 for single males, and about six times the ratio for married and for widowed

[16] Bridges (28) has given especial attention to the psychological effects of ostracism, humiliation, and other depressing experiences which illegitimate individuals are likely to encounter.

males. For divorced females the ratio of 24.1 per 100,000 was six times as large as the ratio of 4 for single, eight times the ratio for married, and ten times the ratio for the widowed. (12, pp. 23–24) [17]

That married persons enjoy, on the average, greater satisfaction of the important sexual and reproductive impulses than do unmarried persons is an assumption that can scarcely be questioned; and the data presented in the preceding quotation show the extent to which frustration in this sphere seems to increase the tendency toward criminality. Loss of accustomed satisfactions through divorce is exceptionally frustrating, and it is therefore not surprising that divorcees—who are often more or less chronically maladjusted in other ways—should show an unusually high crime rate. The only respect in which the facts are not immediately seen to fit the theory that increased frustration tends to increase criminality is that both men and women who have lost their mates *due to death* show an exceptionally low crime rate. That the loss of a husband or wife through death is ordinarily a source of serious frustration, i.e., disrupts many long-established and important habits, cannot be doubted.[18] Why, then, do persons who are thus affected not show an increase in outward aggression?

A perusal of anthropological literature reveals that if a people believe, as many primitive peoples do, that a person's death may be due to some agency outside himself (such as sorcery), individuals who are deprived of a loved (or useful) relative or friend show the clearest kind of aggressive behavior, relatively unmixed with anything resembling mourning, and set out to avenge the loss (frustration) which they have sustained.[19] On the other hand, in a culture such as our own, where death is seen as usually due to impersonal forces or is attributed to "destiny," to the "will of God," or to some other cause which man feels helpless or even fearful to combat, the resulting aggressive impulses apparently "turn inward" and give rise to the special

[17] Erickson (19), in his study of the intelligence of criminals, has likewise made the incidental observation that there is a higher-than-average incidence of single, separated, and divorced individuals among criminal populations ("for each level of intelligence") than in the population at large.

[18] The marriage relationship, like all other intimate human associations, is necessarily somewhat ambivalent. Every man and every woman presumably finds some features of married life frustrating. To the extent that this is true, every married person may be expected to find release from marriage—however satisfactory it may have been in general—something of a relief. But since the losses sustained through the death of a spouse ordinarily exceed the gains, the experience of frustration predominates over the gratification which is also present; and since the individual usually cannot bear to acknowledge this latter aspect of his reaction, the total psychological picture is still further complicated by marked guilt feelings.

[19] Several good examples of this are given by Sumner and Keller (35).

experience of mourning or grief. In such a mood human beings are very little disposed to show criminal aggressiveness.

Frustration may also arise in the sex sphere, not only as a result of a person's being unmarried, divorced, or widowed, but also because of incompatibility between sex partners within marriage. Having found, in keeping with the United States Government statistics already cited, that a greater percentage of male prisoners are unmarried or divorced than their non-criminal brothers,[20] Gillin also reports "greater disharmony between the [married] prisoners and their wives than between the brothers and their wives" (36, p. 208). Marital compatibility or harmony was judged not only on the basis of the responses obtained to direct questioning but was also inferred from the degree of similarity or dissimilarity of the background and cultural peculiarities of the husband and wife. Gillin concludes as follows:

> Thus, on four points—economic status, education, nationality, and religion—the prisoners and their wives show greater differences [statistically significant] than the brothers and their wives. These findings suggest the possibility that these differences in background between the prisoners and their wives may account for the greater disharmony between prisoners and their wives than that found between brothers and their wives. (36, p. 211)

There is, of course, the logical possibility that some special type of childhood experience or an hereditary "taint" which makes for heightened criminality also creates an aversion to the married state and that the factor of frustration in the realm of sexual adjustment has no direct causal connection with criminality. The facts, however, do not seem to favor such an interpretation.

(*m*) *Sex Ratio*. Although the ratio of male and female criminals varies considerably in different countries—from 3:1 in Belgium to 22.5:1 in Finland—men are found consistently to be the more frequent offenders (2; 11). It is true that in certain respects men carry heavier social and economic responsibilities, yet it can hardly be supposed that the amount of frustration experienced by them is greater in the same proportion that their criminality exceeds that of women. Other considerations also have to be taken into account. It has been suggested that women are naturally less prone to react aggressively than are men, but writers who have given the most careful attention to this question agree that such variations as exist between the sexes in this respect are largely socially determined. Physically smaller and weaker and periodically incapacitated during an important period of their

[20] *Cf.* Bonger (2), Fernald, Holmes, Hayes, and Dawley (10).

lives by pregnancy and, to a less extent, by menstruation, women are taught to accept a protected albeit subservient position within the group. Lack of boldness and aggressiveness which would bring the greatest contempt upon a man is accepted as entirely natural and becoming in a woman. Bender, Kaiser, and Schilder have given especial attention to the reasons for greater criminality in men and conclude that the difference in the social expectations for men and women is of great importance in this connection; they say: "A fundamental causative factor seems to be our socially conditioned concepts regarding masculinity and femininity. Thus, passivity is felt to be feminine, aggressivity, masculine. A male needs to fight off any sense of femininity by physical activity—a masculine trait" (37, p. 408).[21]

Another important factor conditioning the incidence of criminality in men and women is the fact that when faced by adversity women can often find in the various forms of prostitution a solution to their problems that is not open to men. Although sometimes legally defined as a crime, prostitution is more likely to be treated as a form of immorality and tolerated as a necessary evil. Women who try to solve difficult life situations in this way are likely to lose social status, but with reasonable discretion they can usually avoid imprisonment. That prostitution probably saves a great many women from becoming criminals in the stricter sense of the term is indicated by a variety of facts. As women become less economically dependent upon men in a society, chastity seems to be less highly valued and the need for prostitution accordingly diminishes; as this occurs and women are forced to turn to other resources, their crime rate shows a decided tendency to increase. Although reliable statistics are not as yet apparently available, this process has undoubtedly taken place in the United States within recent decades (38; 9). Comparative statistics from other countries show that as men and women approach a single standard of sexual morality, the crime rate for the two sexes also becomes more nearly comparable; for example, in Denmark during the years 1876-1885 the number of women convicted of crimes with respect to the number of men was more than eight times as great as in Algeria for the same period, in which country the standards of sexual conduct for men and women were far more divergent than in Denmark (2). Statistics also show that, whereas Negro women in America are committed to all types of prisons seventeen times as frequently as white women, Negro men are

[21] It is interesting to note the exaggerated masculinity affected by many criminals; the writers cited suggest that criminality in men is commonly due to reaction-formation against latent homosexuality and passivity.

committed only five times as frequently as white men (11); and it is well known that Negro women are relatively little dependent economically upon Negro men and that their standards of sexual conduct do not differ materially.[22]

Although the foregoing analysis is necessarily incomplete, it will suffice to indicate the way in which the greater incidence of crime among men than among women can be brought into line with the hypothesis that the two basic variables controlling criminality are frustration and the prospect of punishment in its varied guises.

(*n*) *Home Conditions.* So much attention has already been given (28; 39) to the rôle of the home in determining the criminality or non-criminality of the children reared therein that this topic can be treated here somewhat summarily. The results of Glueck and Glueck (14), which are typical of those obtained by other investigators, show that of a thousand delinquent boys studied by them in Boston only 7.9 per cent had homes which were intact and afforded good supervision. In the remaining 92.1 per cent of the cases, one or both parents were gone from the home due to death, divorce, desertion, or imprisonment, or else the discipline and harmony of the home were impaired by incompatibility between parents or by the necessity for the mother to seek outside employment. These and similar unwholesome home conditions are likely to be associated with low economic status and privation of various kinds and thus to lead to an increase in the general level of frustration of the children affected by them; but probably more important is their effect upon the socialization of the developing individual. Superego or conscience is now believed to be established primarily through the existence of affectional bonds (i.e., expectations of reward and security) between a child and his parents; when these are weak or lacking or when parents are not fit models to pattern after, character formation does not proceed normally and the individual grows up deficient in those internalized restraints which, when combined with external social forces, ordinarily keep most individuals within the bounds of conventional conduct.

(*o*) *Neighborhood Conditions.* Despite the great importance of conditions within the home in determining the character development of children, the standards and practices of neighborhood contemporaries also have a significant influence. An isolated family usually encounters serious difficulty, at least in urban areas, in attempting to maintain for its children stronger anticipation of

[22] This statement applies only to lower-class Negroes. Upper-class Negroes approximate white standards in this connection (31).

punishment than prevail in the rest of the neighborhood. Shaw and his fellow workers (3) have made a detailed study of the so-called "delinquency areas" in Chicago and have found that when families of relatively high standards are forced to move into demoralized neighborhoods, there is a definitely disintegrative effect upon the conduct of the younger members of the family. Playmates and school associates exercise a strong leveling influence which is sometimes so great as to be a source of considerable conflict for families with high standards of conduct but lacking sufficient income to avoid low-standard neighborhoods. Ridicule and disapproval from other children can either strengthen or weaken the socializing efforts of the home in respect to anticipation of punishment, and it is natural that an attempt should be made to keep both the home and the neighborhood ideals fairly comparable. Although socially inferior neighborhoods are also likely to be areas of deprivation and frustration, their main contribution to the ranks of criminality probably results from the fact that the extra-legal penalties for misconduct are less than in other communities.

(*p*) *Regional Conditions.* Numerous writers have remarked upon the higher crime rate in cities than in rural areas;[23] and one explanation which has frequently been offered is that the anonymity of the city offers greater opportunity for persons to commit crimes and avoid both legal and extra-legal punishment than exists in the country. Another factor which is less frequently taken into account is that in rural areas human relations are greatly simplified (20), man's major struggles being against nature instead of against other men; accordingly when man encounters frustration in a rural environment his aggressions are more likely to be directed against hostile environmental forces than toward other men, as occurs in city life; aggressions directed toward nature—such as imprecations and grumbling concerning the weather—are rarely regarded as criminal.[24] There seems to be no reliable way of determining whether the amount of frustration experienced by city dwellers is also greater than that experienced by rural dwellers or whether the difference in the incidence of crime is largely dependent upon the factors just cited.

Brearley has shown that not only is the homicide rate a function of the absolute density of population in a given area, but that it is also dependent upon the rate at which the population is increasing. He says:

[23] See the review by Ross (33).

[24] It should also be recalled that, as previously noted (in Chapter III), farmers sometimes displace their aggressions inspired by frustrations due to crop failure to other men, such as politicians and Negroes.

> An indication that rapidly growing cities may expect an increase in homicide is shown by the data for Florida cities for the years 1920 to 1925. By the latter date the "Florida boom" in land values and population was well under way. In the six cities of the state there were 57 homicides in 1920 and 208 in 1925. An analysis of the individual cities shows even more clearly the effect of increasing numbers etc. (p. 149)
>
> The data for counties, exclusive of cities of 10,000 or more, indicate the same tendency for growth of population to increase homicide [disproportionately to the absolute increase in population]. (13, p. 151)

This writer believes that "inadequate housing facilities, an increase of immigrants, and the social disorganization accompanying an influx of strangers" are the main reasons for the higher homicide rates in rapidly growing cities. These factors all clearly represent either frustrations or conditions conducive to frustration. The socializing forces are also undoubtedly weakened under these conditions: government regulatory facilities are often taxed to the limit and the greater mobility of a rapidly growing population also tends to weaken the force of custom and of community sanctions. Outsiders are ordinarily attracted to a given community in great numbers only when unusual economic gains are in prospect. The number of persons who look forward to profiting by such a situation is always greater than the number who actually realize their expectations, with consequent frustration of a fairly large number of individuals and an increase in criminal tendencies.

(*q*) *Alcoholism and Drug Addiction.* Alcohol has been called the superego solvent, and to the extent that it weakens internal restraints and also deadens anticipation of external punishment its use might be expected to correlate with criminality. On these grounds it has often been condemned as one of the major causes of crime, but actually it may be more of a substitute for than a cause of crime. Freud (40) has concluded that intoxication is one of man's trusted methods of rendering frustration tolerable ("drowning one's sorrows"); if anticipation of punishment for misconduct is thereby weakened, so also is the frustration lessened. Sutherland has analyzed the statistics on crime and drunkenness in relation to the business cycle and has concluded that "In general these correlations are large enough and consistent enough to indicate that serious crimes increase in periods of depression, and that drunkenness increases in prosperity" (11, p. 161), thus lending support to the supposition, advanced by recent writers on the psychology of alcoholism (41; 42), that it is a reaction to frustration which is safer than crime and actually preferred by many individuals when the necessary money for indulging in it is available.

The bearing of drug addiction upon criminality seems to be not greatly different from that of alcoholism (43) and will not be given special consideration here.

(*r*) *Militarism and Moral Holidays.* Although the existing statistics are by no means complete, there is evidence that military life is likely to result in increased criminality. Bonger (2, p. 517) cites Hausner for the statement that during peacetime the criminality of soldiers "is 25 times as great as the criminality of civilians." Subjected to strict discipline, which may reactivate early childhood attitudes of resentment (44), and deprived of many normal opportunities for self-expression and impulse gratification, the soldier seems almost certain to find life in barracks unusually frustrating; the fact that formal penalties for misconduct are often exceptionally severe indicates that this frustration produces strong instigation to criminal aggression which requires strong restraints. Even so, these restraints do not seem capable of completely stemming the aggressive reactions to this state of affairs.

The incidence of criminality among soldiers during wartime is virtually impossible to determine. Standards of conduct are so disorganized and inverted that it is only by the most arbitrary definitions that anyone can say what is criminal and what is not. Behavior for which a civilian in peacetime would be severely punished may be encouraged during war, and normally innocuous actions may become highly reprehensible. That this confusion as to what punishments may be anticipated tends to have persisting effects upon soldiers is indicated by the fact that nations have always found it difficult to assimilate and re-socialize the men who return from wars. Corroborative of this common historical observation is the finding that in America in 1923 there was an unduly large proportion of ex-service men in prison (12).[25] This fact is probably to be explained not only as due to the disruption of traditional taboos and inhibitions but also, at least in part, as reflecting increased frustration through loss of jobs, disrupted personal relationships, or the like.[26]

All human societies set aside certain days or seasons during which behavior that is ordinarily forbidden is permitted; this arrangement, allowing periodic release of pent-up instigation, seems essential to the stability of any social group. It might be conjectured that this relaxation of moral vigilance and temporary lowering of standards would mean a reduction in behavior which

[25] See also Erickson (19).

[26] The fact that criminality among the civilian population of a warring country tends to decline (2) may be due either to displacement of aggression or to less systematic prosecution of crimes than normally occurs in peacetime.

would be called criminal, but this is not actually the case. Statistics show that a disproportionate number of crimes are committed on holidays (13); it is as if the forces of repression, once weakened, are likely to give way more or less completely. The increased number of arrests which are made on holidays has sometimes been attributed to the effect of heightened consumption of alcohol on these occasions, or to the fact that more persons are at leisure; but other considerations suggest that the mechanism already mentioned is probably also operative here.

(*s*) *Form of Government.* The total amount of frustration experienced by a given group is obviously influenced by the prevailing form of government. Other things being equal, an oppressive, inadequate government would be expected to result in increased criminality, and a just, efficient government would be expected to result in reduced criminality (45). A government, however, not only has the power to influence the amount of frustration experienced by the governed, but it also controls the severity of the punishment administered for aggressive reactions to the existing frustration. It is thus possible that a tyrannical government might greatly increase frustration and yet at the same time actually lower the incidence of criminality. This process can presumably go only so far without laying the basis for ultimate revolution or war. Obviously the problems involved here are complex and empirical data are difficult to obtain and interpret, as will be pointed out in Chapter VII.

(*t*) *Psychopathology.* By legal definition a criminal is a person who has committed a socially prohibited act and is judged to have been mentally and morally responsible at the time he committed it; such an offender is thus distinguished from a demonstrably insane offender and given somewhat different treatment from that which the latter would receive for objectively similar behavior. This fact accounts, at least in part, for the not very surprising finding that not more than 1 to 5 per cent of most prison and reformatory populations are psychotic in the traditionally accepted sense of the term. There is, nevertheless, a school of writers —notably, Alexander and Staub (26), Aichhorn (34), Lippman (46), and others—who believe that much, if not all, delinquent and criminal behavior is instigated by psychological mechanisms (mainly unconscious) which are basically similar to those believed to be operative in the neuroses and functional psychoses. In reading the works of the authors cited, the conviction cannot be escaped that they have often obtained exceptional insight in individual cases; but their findings do not justify the conclusion that all criminals are mentally disordered. Sutherland says:

> The preconception is shown in extreme form in the editorial in the *Journal of the American Medical Association*, Aug. 2, 1930, which was approved by the sub-committee on the medical aspects of crime, to the effect that a diagnosis of mental disease is "permissible even when the criminal has shown no evidence of mental disease other than his criminal behavior." A diagnosis of mental pathology assumes a criterion of the normal, and the normal in regards to thoughts, feelings, and sentiments is not stated in objective terms but is determined by the psychiatrist's preconceptions. (11, pp. 105–106)

More defensible than the position that mental abnormality causes criminality is the hypothesis that both of these phenomena are *alternative* reactions to frustration, the occurrence of the one or the other being determined by the entire structure of the individual's entire personality. According to this view, of two individuals who have experienced equal amounts of frustration, the one with a particular personality organization will be prone to react criminally, whereas the other with a different organization will be likely to show some form of psychopathology.

In the preceding pages an attempt has been made to marshal support for the hypothesis that all of the factors which have been found to be causally related to criminality derive this connection because of implying, directly or indirectly, on the part of the offending individual either higher-than-average frustration, lower-than-average anticipation of punishment, or both. This conclusion, once it has been arrived at, seems to sink almost to the level of a truism; but its validity has not always been so obvious. It must be remembered that a few decades ago the most widely accepted view of crime held that it was a mark of congenital degeneracy.

That criminality tends to vary inversely with anticipation of punishment is widely recognized by common sense. When crime increases there is a demand for more severe laws and for stricter law enforcement; and the home, school, church, and other character-forming institutions are looked at askance. This relation of the breakdown of the forces of social control to the incidence of crime in a given community has been formulated by Shaw as follows:

> In short, with the process of growth of the city the invasion of residential communities by business and industry causes a disintegration of the community as a unit of social control. This disorganization is intensified by the influx of foreign national and racial groups whose old cultural and social controls break down in the new cultural and racial situation of the city. In this state of social disorganization, community resistance is low. Delinquent

and criminal patterns arise and are transmitted socially just as any other cultural and social pattern is transmitted. In time these delinquent patterns may become dominant and shape the attitudes and behavior of persons living in the area. Thus the section becomes an area of delinquency. (47, pp. 205–206) [27]

Focusing attention upon the preëminent importance of the home as a socializing institution, Healy and Bronner say:

> As we looked into the lives of these young people, it was clear, for one thing, that social restraints and inhibitions were in many instances absent because of poor formation of what is so aptly termed an ego-ideal. There had been no strong emotional tie-up to any one who presented a pattern of satisfactory social behavior. To put it in another way, the child had never had an affectional identification with one who seemed to him a good parent. The father or mother either had not played a rôle that was admired by the child or else on account of the lack of a deep love relationship was not accepted as an ideal. (30, p. 10)

If there is thus no novelty in the proposition that criminality varies inversely with the anticipation of punishment that is built up and reinforced through socialization, neither is there anything new in the suggestion that it varies positively with frustration. Bonger (2, p. 462) long ago cited the old Dutch proverb that "Happy people are not wicked" and pivoted almost the whole argument of his monumental book on the contention that criminality is a reflection of deprivations and dissatisfactions. This assertion, however, has certain discomforting implications and has not been as widely accepted as the logic of the situation would seem to warrant. As an illustration of this general tendency to neglect the importance and relevance of the frustration concept in the field of criminality, one finds Glueck and Glueck (14, p. 80) reporting that "on the whole we are dealing with parents and homes that in many respects must be characterized as unwholesome or underprivileged," but at the same time insisting that of the one thousand delinquent boys forming the basis of their study only 5 per cent evidenced marked "dissatisfactions" (p. 109).

Healy and Bronner have faced the problem of frustration in relation to delinquency more squarely and find that it is of major importance. They say:

> It is through the lack of satisfying human relationships that feelings of inadequacy, deprivation, or thwarting are created. When these discomforts are powerfully experienced, the driving forces of wishes and desires naturally develop into urges for substitute satis-

[27] For a discussion of the relation of crime to radicalism (reform) and social change, see Katz and Schanck (48).

> factions. When the young individual does not then find satisfactions enough in socially acceptable behavior (or does not develop inhibiting neurosis), he may find an alternative mode of self-expression through seizing upon the idea of delinquency. Thus delinquency really represents a portion of the stream of human activities which has a strong current behind it. Beginning with various types of discontents at frustration and continued as a drive for substitute satisfactions, the current has turbulently flowed along into the forms of self-expression that ideas of delinquency have suggested. (30, p. 201)

Although no claim to originality can be made in stressing the rôle of either anticipation of punishment or frustration as a major determinant of criminality, this phenomenon has not previously been seen and defined as a function of the dynamic interaction and balance existing between these two factors. Criminality is here viewed, not as a function of the absolute level of frustration nor of the absolute degree of anticipated punishment, but as a function of the discrepancy between the two. With a low degree of anticipated punishment, criminality does not result if frustration is also sufficiently low; likewise, given a high degree of frustration, criminality does not result if anticipation of punishment is sufficiently high. But when anticipation of punishment deviates in the downward direction and frustration deviates upward, the magnitude of the resulting discrepancy carries with it a correspondingly increasing expectancy of criminality.

References

1. Sullenger, T. E. *Social Determinants in Juvenile Delinquency.* New York: Wiley, 1936.
2. Bonger, W. A. *Criminality and Economic Conditions.* Boston: Little, Brown, 1916.
3. Shaw, C. R. and McKay, H. D. Social Factors in Juvenile Delinquency. Vol. II in, National Commission on Law Observance and Enforcement. *Report on the Causes of Crime.* Washington: U. S. Government Printing Office, 1931.
4. Gillin, J. L. Some Economic Factors in the Making of the Criminal, *J. soc. Forces,* 1923-24, 2, 689-691.
5. Bonger, W. A. *An Introduction to Criminology.* London: Methuen, 1936.
6. Gillin, J. L. Economic Factors in the Making of Criminals. *J. soc. Forces,* 1924-25, *3,* 248-255.
7. Sellin, T. *Research Memorandum on Crime in the Depression.* New York: Social Science Research Council, 1937.

8. Shield, J. A. Twelve Thousand Criminals. *J. crim. Law Criminol.*, 1937-38, *28*, 806-814.
9. Sullenger, T. E. Female Criminality in Omaha. *J. crim. Law Criminol.*, 1936-37, *27*, 706-711.
10. Fernald, M. R., Holmes, M., Hayes, S., and Dawley, A. *A Study of Women Delinquents in New York State.* New York: Century, 1920.
11. Sutherland, E. H. *Principles of Criminology.* Philadelphia: Lippincott, 1934.
12. U. S. Bureau of the Census. *The Prisoner's Antecedents.* Washington: U. S. Government Printing Office, 1929.
13. Brearley, H. C. *Homicide in the United States.* Chapel Hill: University of North Carolina Press, 1932.
14. Glueck, S. and Glueck, E. T. *One Thousand Juvenile Delinquents.* Cambridge, Mass.: Harvard University Press, 1934.
15. Pilcher, E. Relation of Mental Disease to Crime. *J. crim. Law Criminol.*, 1930-31, *21*, 212-246.
16. Murchison, C. *Criminal Intelligence.* Worcester, Mass.: Clark University Press, 1926.
17. Ellis, H. *The Criminal.* (Fourth Edition). London: Walter Scott, 1910.
18. Doll, E. A. The Relation of Intelligence to Criminality. *J. soc. Psychol.*, 1930, *1*, 527-531.
19. Erickson, M. H. A Study of the Relationship Between Intelligence and Crime. *J. crim. Law Criminol.*, 1928-29, *19*, 592-635.
20. Hacker, E. Criminality and Immigration. *J. crim. Law Criminol.*, 1929-30, *20*, 429-438.
21. Goring, C. *The English Convict.* London: H. M. Stationery Office, 1913.
22. Weidensall, J. The Mentality of the Criminal Woman. Baltimore: Warwick and York, 1916.
23. Healy, W. *The Individual Delinquent.* Boston: Little, Brown, 1929.
24. Slawson, J. *The Delinquent Boy,* Boston: Badger, 1926.
25. Nelson, V. F. *Prison Days and Nights.* Boston: Little, Brown, 1933.
26. Alexander, F. and Staub, H. *The Criminal, the Judge, and the Public.* New York: Macmillan, 1931.
27. Kilmer, T. W. A Study of the Human Ear from the Standpoint of Identification and Criminality. *Correction,* 1932, *2,* 12.
28. Bridges, K. M. B. Factors Contributing to Juvenile Delinquency. *J. crim. Law Criminol.*, 1926-27, 17, 531-580.

29. Kahn, E. and Cohen, L. H. Organic Drivenness: A Brain-stem Syndrome and an Experience. *N. E. J. Med.*, 1934, *210*, 748-756.
30. Healy, W. and Bronner, A. F. *New Light on Delinquency and Its Treatment*. New Haven: Yale University Press, 1936.
31. Dollard, J. *Caste and Class in a Southern Town*. New Haven: Yale University Press, 1937.
32. Beynon, E. D. Crime and Custom of the Hungarians of Detroit. *J. crim. Law Criminol.*, 1934-35, *25*, 755-774.
33. Ross, H. Crime and the Native Born Sons of European Immigrants. *J. crim. Law Criminol.*, 1937-38, *28*, 202-209.
34. Aichhorn, A. *Wayward Youth*. New York: Viking, 1935.
35. Sumner, W. G. and Keller, A. G. *The Science of Society*. (Four Vols.) New Haven: Yale University Press, 1927.
36. Gillin, J. L. Backgrounds of Prisoners in the Wisconsin State Prison and of Their Brothers. *Amer. sociol. Rev.*, 1937, *2*, 204-212.
37. Bender, L., Keiser, S. and Schilder, P. Studies in Aggressiveness. *Genet. Psychol. Monog.*, 1936, *18*, 357-564.
38. Potter, E. C. The Problem of Women in Penal and Correctional Institutions. *J. crim. Law Criminol.*, 1934-35, *25*, 65-75.
39. Sullenger, T. E. Juvenile Delinquency. A Product of the Home. *J. crim. Law Criminol.*, 1933-34, *24*, 1088-1092.
40. Freud, S. *Civilization and Its Discontents*. (Trans. by Joan Riviere) . London: Hogarth Press, 1930.
41. Knight, R. P. The Psychoanalytic Treatment in a Sanatorium of Chronic Addiction to Alcohol. *J. Amer. med. Asso.*, 1938, *111*, 1443-1448.
42. Miles, W. R. Psychological Factors in Alcoholism. *Ment. Hyg., N. Y.*, 1937, *21*, 529-548.
43. Kolb, L. Drug Addiction in Its Relation to Crime. *Ment. Hyg., N. Y.*, 1925, *9*, 74-89.
44. Mowrer, O. H. and Mowrer, W. M. Enuresis—A Method for Its Study and Treatment. *Amer. J. Orthopsychiat.*, 1938, *8*, 436-459.
45. Bruce, A. A. One Hundred Years of Criminological Development in Illinois. *J. crim. Law Crimonol.*, 1933-34, *24*, 11-49.
46. Lippman, H. S. The Neurotic Delinquent. *Amer. J. Orthopsychiat.*, 1937, *7*, 114-121.
47. Shaw, C. R. *Delinquency Areas*. Chicago: University of Chicago Press, 1929.
48. Katz, D. and Schanck, R. L. *Social Psychology*. New York: Wiley, 1938.

JEAN-PAUL SARTRE / Childhood of a Leader

LUCIEN WAS very satisfied with himself he had conducted himself like a *chic type* and that repaid many errors. "She was ripe for it," he told himself with a little regret, but on reconsidering it, he thought, "It's the same as though I had her: she offered herself and I didn't want her." And henceforth he no longer considered himself a virgin. These slight satisfactions occupied his mind for several days. Then they, too, melted into the fog. Returning to school in October, he felt as dismal as at the beginning of the previous year.

Berliac had not come back and no one had heard anything about him. Lucien noticed several unknown faces. His right hand neighbor whose name was Lemordant had taken a year of special mathematics in Poitiers. He was even bigger than Lucien, and with his black moustache, already looked like a man. Lucien met his friends again without pleasure: they seemed childish to him and innocently boisterous: schoolboys. He still associated himself with their collective manifestation but with nonchalance, as was permitted him by his position of *carré*. Lemordant would have attracted him more, because he was mature; but, unlike Lucien, he did not seem to have acquired that maturity through multiple and painful experiences: he was an adult by birth. Lucien often contemplated with a full satisfaction that voluminous, pensive head, neckless, planted awry on the shoulders: it seemed impossible to get anything into it, neither through the ears, nor the tiny slanting eyes, pink and glassy: "man with convictions," Lucien thought with respect; and he wondered, not without jealousy, what that certitude could be that gave Lemordant such a full consciousness of self. "That's how I should be; a rock." He was even a little surprised that Lemordant should be accessible to mathematical reasoning; but M. Husson convinced him when he gave back the first papers: Lucien was seventh and Lemordant had been given a "5" and 78th place; all was in order. Lemordant gave no sign, he seemed to expect the worst. His tiny mouth, his heavy cheeks, yellow and smooth, were not made to express feelings: he was a Buddha. They saw him angry only once, the day Loewy bumped into him in the cloakroom. First, he gave a dozen sharp little growls, and blinked his eyes; "Back to Poland," he said at last, "to Poland you dirty kike and don't come crapping around here with us." He dominated Loewy with his whole form and his massive chest swayed on his long legs. He finished up by slapping him and little Loewy apologized: the affair ended there.

On Thursdays, Lucien went out with Guigard who took him dancing with his sister's girl friends. But Guigard finally confessed that these hops bored him. "I've got a girl," he confided, "a *première* in Plisnier's, Rue Royale. She has a friend who doesn't have anybody: you ought to come with us Saturday night." Lucien made a scene with his parents and got permission to go out every Saturday; they left the key under the mat for him. He met Guigard around nine o'clock in a bar on the Rue Saint-Honorée. "You wait and see," Guigard said, "Fanny is charming and what's nice about her is she really knows how to dress." "What about mine?" "I don't know her; I know she's an apprentice dressmaker and she's just come to Paris from Angoulême. By the way." he added, "don't pull any boners. My name's Pierre Daurat. You, because you're blond, I said you were part English, it's better. Your name's Lucien Bonnières." "But why?" asked Lucien, intrigued. "My boy," Guigard answered, "it's a rule. You can do what you like with these girls but never tell your name." "All right," Lucien said, "What do I do for a living?" "You can say you're a student, that's better, you understand, it flatters them and then you don't have to spend much money. Of course, we share the expenses; but let me pay this evening; I'm in the habit: I'll tell you what you owe me on Monday." Immediately Lucien thought Guigard was trying to get a rake-off. "God, how distrustful I've gotten!" he thought with amusement. Just then Fanny came in: a tall, thin brunette with long thighs and a heavily rouged face. Lucien found her intimidating. "Here's Bonnières I was telling you about," Guigard said. "Pleased to meet you," Fanny said with a myopic look. "This is my girl friend Maud." Lucien saw an ageless little woman wearing a hat that looked like an overturned flower pot. She was not rouged and appeared greyish after the dazzling Fanny. Lucien was bitterly disappointed but he saw she had a pretty mouth—and then there was no need to be embarrassed with her. Guigard had taken care to pay for the beers in advance so that he could profit from the commotion of their arrival to push the two girls gaily toward the door without allowing them the time for a drink. Lucien was grateful to him: M. Fleurier only gave him 125 francs a week and out of this money he had to pay carfare. The evening was amusing; they went dancing in the Latin Quarter in a hot, pink little place with dark corners and where a cocktail cost five francs. There were many students with girls of the same type as Fanny but not as good looking. Fanny was superb: she looked straight in the eyes of a big man with a beard who smoked a pipe and said very loudly, "I hate people who smoke pipes at dances." The man turned crimson and put the lighted pipe back in his pocket. She treated Guigard and Lucien with a certain condescension and sometimes told them, "You're a couple of kids" with a gentle, maternal air. Lucien felt full of ease and sweetness; he told Fanny several amusing little things and smiled while telling them. Finally, the smile never left his face and he was able to hit on a refined tone of voice with touches of devil-may-care and tender courtesy tinged with irony. But Fanny spoke little to him; she took Guigard's chin and pulled his cheeks to make his mouth stand out; when the lips were full and drooling a little, like fruit swollen with juice or like snails, she licked them, saying "Baby." Lucien was horribly annoyed and thought Guigard was ridiculous: Guigard had rouge near his lips and fingermarks on his cheeks. But the behavior of the other couples was even more negligent: everyone kissed; from time to time the girl from the checkroom passed among them with a little basket, throwing streamers and multicolored balls shouting, *"Olè, les enfants, amusez-vous, olè, olè!"* and everybody laughed. At last Lucien remembered the existence of Maud and he said to her, smiling, "Look at those turtle doves . . ." He pointed to Fanny and Guigard and added, *"nous autres, nobles viellards . . ."* He did not finish the phrase but smiled so drolly that Maud smiled too. She removed her hat and Lucien saw with pleasure that she was somewhat better than the other women in the dance hall; then he asked her to dance and told her the jokes he played on his professors the year of his baccalaureat. She danced well, her eyes were black and serious and she had an intelligent look. Lucien told her about Berthe and said he was full of remorse. "But," he added, "it was better for her." Maud thought the story about Berthe was poetic and sad, she asked how much Berthe earned from Lucien's parents. "It's not always funny," she added, "for a young girl to be in the family way." Guigard and Fanny paid no more attention to them, they caressed each other and Guigard's face was covered with moisture. From time to time Lucien repeated, "Look at those turtle doves, just look at them!" and he had his sentence ready, "They make me feel like doing it too." But he dared not say it and contented himself with smiling, then he pretended that he and Maud were old friends, disdainful of love and he called her "brother" and made as if to slap her on the back. Suddenly, Fanny turned her head and looked at them with surprise, "Well," she said, "first-graders, how're you doing? Why don't you kiss, you're dying to." Lucien took Maud in his arms; he was a little annoyed because Fanny was watching them: he wanted the kiss to be long and successful but he wondered how people breathed. Finally, it was not as difficult as he thought, it was enough to kiss on an angle, leaving the nostrils clear. He heard Guigard counting "one—two —three—four—" and he let go of Maud at 52. "Not bad for a beginning," Guigard said. "I can do better." Lucien looked at his wrist watch and counted: Guigard left Fanny's mouth at the 159th second. Lucien was furious and thought the contest was stupid. "I let go of Maud just to be safe," he thought, "but that's nothing, once you know how to breathe you can keep on forever." He proposed a second match and won. When it was all over, Maud looked at Lucien and said seriously, "You kiss well." Lucien blushed with pleasure. "At your service," he answered, bowing. Still he would rather have kissed Fanny. They parted around half past twelve because of the last metro. Lucien was joyful; he leaped and danced in the Rue Raynouard and thought, "It's in the bag." The corner of his mouth hurt because he had smiled so much.

He saw Maud every Thursday at six and on Saturday evening. She let herself be kissed but nothing more. Lucien complained to Guigard who reassured him, "Don't worry," Guigard said, "Fanny's sure she'll lay; but she's young and only had two boys; Fanny says for you to be very tender with her." "Tender?" Lucien said, "Get a load of that!" They both laughed and Guigard concluded, "That's what you've got to do." Lucien was very tender. He kissed Maud a lot and told her he loved her, but after a while it became a little monotonous and then he was not too proud of going out with her: he would have liked to give her advice on how she should dress, but she was full of prejudices and angered quickly. Between kisses, they were silent, gazing at each other and holding hands. "God knows what she's thinking with those strict eyes she has," Lucien still thought of the same thing: This small existence, sad and vague, which was his own, and told himself, "I wish I were Lemordant, there's a man who's found his place!" During those times he saw himself as though he were another person: sitting near a woman who loved him, his hand in hers, his lips still wet from kisses, refusing the humble happiness she offered him: alone. Then he clasped Maud's fingers tightly and tears came to his eyes: he would have liked to make her happy.

One morning in December, Lemordant came up to Lucien; he held a paper. "You want to sign?" he asked. "What is it?" "Because of the kikes at the Normale Sup; they sent the *Oeuvre* a petition against compulsory military training with 200 signatures. So we're protesting; we need a thousand names at least: we're going to get the *cyrards,* the *flottards,* the *agros,* the *X's,* and the whole works." Lucien was flattered. "Is it going to be printed?" "Surely in *Action.* Maybe in *Echo de Paris* besides." Lucien wanted to sign on the spot but he thought it would not be wise. He took the paper and read it carefully. Lemordant added, "I hear you don't have anything to do with politics; that's your business. But you're French and you've got a right to have your say." Lucien felt an inexplicable and rapid joy. He signed. The next day he bought *Action Française* but the proclamation was not there. It didn't appear until Thursday, Lucien found it on the second page under the headline: YOUTH OF FRANCE SCORES IN TEETH OF INTERNATIONAL JEWRY. His name was there, compressed, definitive, not far from Lemordant's, almost as strange as the names *Fleche* and *Flipot* which surrounded it; it looked unreal. "Lucien Fleurier" he thought, "A peasant name, a real French name." He read the whole series of names starting with F aloud and when it came to his turn he pronounced it as if he did not recognize it. Then he stuffed the newspaper in his pocket and went home happily.

A few days later he sought out Lemordant. "Are you active in politics?" he asked. "I'm in the League," Lemordant said, "Ever read *Action Française*?" Not much," Lucien confessed, "Up to now it didn't interest me but I think I'm changing my mind." Lemordant looked at him without curiosity, with his impenetrable air. Lucien told him in a few words, what Bergère had called his "Disorder." "Where do you come from?" Lemordant asked. "Férolles. My father has a factory there." "How long did you stay there?" "Till second form." "I see," Lemordant said, "it's very simple, you're uprooted. Have you read Barrès?" "I read *Colette Baudoche*." "Not that," Lemordant said impatiently, "I'll bring you the *Deracinés* this afternoon. That's your story. You'll find the cause and cure." The book was bound in green leather. On the first page was an "*ex libris* André Lemordant" in gothic letters. Lucien was surprised; he had never dreamed Lemordant could have a first name.

He began reading it with much distrust: it had been explained to him so many times: so many times had he been lent books with a "Read this, it fits you perfectly," Lucien thought with a sad smile that he was not someone who could be set down in so many pages. The Oedipus complex, the Disorder: what childishness, and so far away! But, from the very first, he was captivated: in the first place, it was not psychology—Lucien had a bellyful of psychology—the young people Barrès described were not abstract individuals or declassed like Rimbaud or Verlaine, nor sick like the unemployed Viennese who had themselves psychoanalyzed by Freud. Barrès began by placing them in their milieu, in their family: they had been well brought up, in the provinces, in solid traditions. Lucien thought Sturel resembled himself. "It's true," he said, "I'm uprooted." He thought of the moral health of the Fleuriers, a health acquired only in the land, their physical strength (his grandfather used to twist a bronze sou between his fingers) ; he remembered with emotion the dawns in Férolles: he rose, tiptoed down the stairs so as not to wake his family, straddled his bicycle and the soft countryside of the Ile de France enveloped him in its discreet caresses. "I've always hated Paris," he thought with force. He also read the *Jardin de Bérénice* and, from time to time, stopped reading and began to ponder, his eyes vague; thus they were again offering him a character and a destiny, a means of escaping the inexhaustible gossip of his conscience, a method of defining and appreciating himself. And how much he preferred the unconscious, reeking of the soil, which Barrès gave him, to the filthy, lascivious images of Freud. To grasp it, Lucien had only to turn himself away from a sterile and dangerous contemplation of self: he must study the soil and subsoil of Férolles, he must decipher the sense of the rolling hills which descended as far as the Sernette, he must apply himself to human geography and history. Or, simply return to Férolles and live there: he would find it harmless and fertile at his feet, stretched across the countryside, mixed in the woods, the springs, and the grass like nourishing humus from which Lucien could at last draw the strength to become a leader. Lucien left these long dreams exalted, and sometimes felt as if he had found his road. Now he was silent close to Maud, his arm about her waist, the words, the scraps of sentences resounding in him: "renew tradition," "the earth and the dead"; deep, opaque words, inexhaustible. "How tempting it is," he thought. Yet he dared not believe it: he had already been disappointed too often. He opened up his fears to Lemordant: "It would be too good." "My boy," Lemordant answered, "You don't believe everything you want to right away: you need practice." He thought a little and said, "You ought to come with us." Lucien accepted with an open heart, but he insisted on keeping his liberty, "I'll come," he said, "but I won't be involved. I want to see and think about it."

Lucien was captivated by the camaraderies of the young *camelots;* they gave him a cordial, simple welcome and he immediately felt at ease in their midst. He soon knew Lemordant's "gang," about 20 students almost all of whom wore velvet berets. They held their meetings on the second floor of the Polder beer-hall where they played bridge and billiards. Lucien often went there to meet them and soon he realized they had adopted him for he was always greeted with shouts of *"Voilà le plus beau!"* or

"Our National Fleurier!" But it was their good humor which especially captured Lucien: nothing pedantic or austere; little talk of politics. They laughed and sang, that was all, they shouted or beat the tables in honor of the student youth. Lemordant himself smiled without dropping an authority which no one would have dared question. Lucien was more often silent, his look wandering over these boisterous, muscular young people. "This is strength," he thought. Little by little he discovered the true sense of youth in the midst of them: it was not in the affected grace Bergère appreciated; youth was the future of France. However, Lemordant's friends did not have the troubled charm of adolescence: they were adults and several wore beards. Looking closely he found an air of parenthood in all of them: they had finished with the wanderings and uncertainties of their age, they had nothing more to learn, they were made. In the beginning their lighthearted, ferocious jokes somewhat shocked Lucien: one might have thought them without conscience. When Rémy announced that Mme. Dubus, the wife of the radical leader had her legs cut off by a truck, Lucien expected them to render a brief homage to their unfortunate adversary. But they all burst out laughing and slapped their legs saying: "The old carrion!" and "What a fine truck driver!" Lucien was a little taken back but suddenly he understood that this great, purifying laughter was a refusal: they had scented danger, they wanted no cowardly pity and they were firm. Lucien began to laugh too. Little by little their pranks appeared to him in their true light: there was only the shell of frivolity; at heart it was the affirmation of a right: their conviction was so deep, so religious, that it gave them the right to appear frivolous to dismiss all that was not essential with a whim, a pirouette. Between the icy humor of Charles Maurras and the jokes of Desperreau, for instance (he carried in his pocket an old condom end which he called Blum's foreskin) there was only a difference of degree. In January the University announced a solemn meeting in the course of which the degree of *doctor honoris causa* was to be bestowed on two Swedish mineralogists. "You're going to see something good," Lemordant told Lucien, giving him an invitation card. The big amphitheatre was packed. When Lucien saw the President of the Republic and the Rector enter at the sound of the *Marseillaise,* his heart began to pound, he was afraid for his friends. Just then a few young people rose from their seats and began to shout. With sympathy Lucien recognized Rémy, red as a beet, struggling between two men who were pulling his coat, shouting "France for the French!" But he was especially pleased to see an old gentleman, with the air of a precocious child, blowing a little horn.

"How healthy it is," he thought. He keenly tasted this odd mixture of headstrong gravity and turbulence which gave the youngest an air of maturity and the oldest an impish air. Soon Lucien himself tried to joke. He had some success and when he said of Herriot, "There's no more God if he dies in his bed," he felt the birth of a sacred fury in him. Then he gritted his teeth and, for a moment, felt as convinced, as strict, as powerful as Rémy or Desperreau. "Lemordant is right," he thought, "you need practice, it's all there." He also learned to avoid discussions: Guigard, who was only a republican, overwhelmed him with objections. Lucien listened to him politely but, after a while, shut up. Guigard was still talking, but Lucien did not even look at him any more: he smoothed the fold in his trousers and amused himself by blowing smoke rings with his cigarette and looking at women. Nevertheless, he heard a few of Guigard's objections, but they quickly lost their weight and slipped off him, light and futile. Guigard finally was quiet, quite impressed. Lucien told his parents about his new friends and M. Fleurier asked him if he was going to be a *camelot*. Lucien hesitated and gravely said, "I'm tempted, I'm really tempted." "Lucien, I beg you, don't do it," his mother said, "they're very excitable and something bad can happen so quickly. Don't you see you can get in trouble or be put in prison? Besides, you're much too young to be mixed up in politics." Lucien answered her only with a firm smile and M. Fleurier intervened. "Let him alone, dear," he said gently, "let him follow his own ideas; he has to pass through it." From that day on it seemed to Lucien that his parents treated him with a certain consideration. Yet he did not decide; these few weeks had taught him much: by turn he considered the benevolent curiosity of his father, Mme. Fleurier's worries, the growing respect of Guigard, the insistence of Lemordant and the impatience of Rémy and, nodding his head, he told himself, "This is no small matter." He had a long conversation with Lemordant and Lemordant well understood his reasons and told him not to hurry. Lucien still was nostalgic: he had the impression of being only a small gelatinous transparency trembling on the seat in a café and the boisterous agitation of the *camelots* seemed absurd to him. But at other times he felt hard and heavy as a rock and he was almost happy.

He got along better and better with the whole gang. He sang them the *Noce à Rebecca* which Hébrard had taught him the previous vacation and everyone thought it was tremendously amusing. Lucien threw out several biting reflections about the Jews and spoke of Berliac who was so miserly: "I always asked myself: why is he so cheap, it isn't possible to be that cheap. Then one day I understood: he was one of the tribe." Everybody began to laugh and a sort of exaltation came over Lucien: he felt truly furious about the Jews and the memory of Berliac was deeply unpleasant to him. Lemordant looked him in the eyes and said, "You're a real one, you are." After that they often asked Lucien: "Fleurier, tell us a good one about the kikes." And Lucien told the Jewish jokes he learned from his father; all he had to do was begin, "Vun day Levy met Bloom . . ." to fill his friends with mirth. One day Rémy and Patenotre told how they had come across an Algerian Jew by the Seine and how they had almost frightened him to death by acting as if they were going to throw him in the water: "I said to myself," Rémy concluded, "what a shame it was Fleurier wasn't with us." "Maybe it was better he wasn't there," Desperreau interrupted, "he'd have chucked him in the water for good!" There was no one like Lucien for recognizing a Jew from the nose. When he went out with Guigard he nudged his elbow: "Don't turn around now: the little short one, behind us, he's one of them!" "For that," Guigard said, "you can really smell 'em out." Fanny could not stand the Jews either; all four of them went to Maud's room one Thursday and Lucien sang the *Noce à Rebecca*. Fanny could stand no more, she said, "Stop, stop, or I'll wet my pants." And when he had finished, she gave him an almost tender look. They played jokes on him in the Polder beerhall. There was always someone to say, negligently, "Fleurier who likes the Jews so much . . ." or "Leon Blum, the great friend of Fleurier . . ." and the others waited, in stitches, holding their breath, open mouthed. Lucien grew red and struck the table, shouting. "God damn . . . !" and they burst out laughing and said, "He bit! He bit! He didn't bite —he swallowed it!"

He often went to political meetings with them and heard Professor Claude and Maxime Real Del Sarte. His work suffered a little from these new obligations, but, since Lucien could not count on winning the Centrale scholarship anyhow, that year, M. Fleurier was indulgent. "After all," he told his wife, "Lucien must learn the job of being a man." After these meetings Lucien and his friends felt hotheaded and were given to playing tricks. Once about ten of them came across a little, olive skinned man who was crossing the Rue Saint-André-des-Arts, reading *Humanité*. They shoved him into a wall and Rémy ordered "Throw down that paper." The little man wanted to act up but Desperreau slipped behind him and grabbed him by the waist while Lemordant ripped the paper from his grasp with a powerful fist. It was very amusing. The little man, furious, kicked the air and shouted "Let go of me! Let go!" with an odd accent and Lemordant, quite calm tore up the paper. But things were spoiled when Desperreau wanted to let the man go: he threw himself on Lemordant and would have struck him if Rémy hadn't landed a good punch behind his ear just in time. The man fell against the wall and looked at them all evilly, saying, *"Sales Français!"* "Say that again," Marchesseau demanded coldly. Lucien realized there was going to be some dirty work: Marchesseau could not take a joke when it was a question of France. *"Sales Français!"* the dago said. He was slapped again and threw himself forward, his head lowered, *"Sales Français, sales bourgeois,* I hate you, I hope you croak, all of you, all of you!" and a flood of other filthy curses with a violence that Lucien never imagined possible. Then they lost patience and all had to step in and give him a good lesson. After a while they let him go and the man dropped against the wall: his breath was a whistle, one punch had closed his left eye and they were all around him, tired of striking him, waiting for him to fall. The man twisted his mouth and spat: *"Sales Français, sales Français."* There was a moment of hesitation and Lucien realized his friends were going to give it up. Then it was stronger than he was, he leaped forward and struck with all his might. He heard something crack and the little man looked at him with surprise and weakness. *"Sales . . ."* he muttered, but his puffed eye began to open on a red, sightless globe; he fell to his knees and said nothing more. "Get the hell out," Rémy hissed. They ran, stopping only at Place Saint-Michel: no one was following them. They straightened their ties and brushed each other off.

The evening passed without mention of the incident and the young men were especially nice to each other: they had abandoned the modest brutality which usually veiled their feelings. They spoke politely to each other and Lucien thought that for the first time they were acting as they acted with their families; but he was ennervated: he was not used to fighting thugs in the middle of the street. He thought tenderly of Maud and Fanny.

He could not sleep. "I can't go on," he thought, "following them like an amateur. Everything has been weighed, I *must* join!" He felt grave and almost religious when he announced the good news to Lemordant. "It's decided," he said, "I'm with you." Lemordant slapped him on the shoulder and the gang celebrated the event by polishing off several bottles. They had recovered their gay and brutal tone and talked only about the incident of the night before. As they were about to leave, Marchesseau told Lucien simply, "You've got a terrific punch!" and Lucien answered, "He was a Jew."

The day after that he went to see Maud with a heavy

malacca cane he had bought in a store on the Boulevard St. Michel. Maud understood immediately: she looked at the cane and said, "So you did it?" "I did it," Lucien smiled. Maud seemed flattered; personally, she favored the ideas of the Left, but she was broad minded. "I think," she said, "there's good in all parties." In the course of the evening, she scratched his neck several times and called him "My little *camelot*." A little while after that, one Saturday night, Maud felt tired. "I think I'll go back," she said, "but you can come up with me if you're good: you can hold my hand and be real nice to your little Maud who's so tired, and you can tell her stories." Lucien was hardly enthusiastic: Maud's room depressed him with its careful poverty: it was like a maid's room. But it would have been criminal to let such an opportunity pass by. Hardly in the room, Maud threw herself on the bed, saying, "Whew! it feels so good!" Then she was silent, gazing into Lucien's eyes, and puckered her lips. He stretched himself out near her and she put her hand over his eyes, spreading her fingers and saying. "Peekaboo, I see you, you know I see you, Lucien!" He felt soft and heavy, she put her fingers in his mouth and he sucked them, then spoke to her tenderly, "Poor little Maud's sick, does little Maud have a pain?" and he caressed her whole body; she had closed her eyes and was smiling mysteriously. After a moment he raised her skirt and they made love; Lucien thought, "What a break!" When it was over Maud said, "Well, if I'd thought that!" She looked at Lucien with a tender reproach." "Naughty boy, I thought you were going to be good!" Lucien said he was as surprised as she was. "That's the way it happens," he said. She thought a little and then told him seriously, "I don't regret anything. Before maybe it was purer but it wasn't so complete."

In the métro, Lucien thought "I have a mistress." He was empty and tired, saturated with a smell of absinthe and fresh fish; he sat down, holding himself stiffly to avoid contact with his sweat-soaked shirt; he felt his body to be curdled milk. He repeated forcefully, "I have a mistress." But he felt frustrated: what he desired in Maud the night before was her narrow, closed face which seemed so unattainable, her slender silhouette, her look of dignity, her reputation for being a serious girl, her scorn of the masculine sex, all those things that made her a strange being, truly *someone else,* hard and definitive, always out of reach, with her clean little thoughts, her modesties, her silk stockings and crepe dresses, her permanent wave. And all this veneer had melted under his embrace, the flesh remained, he had stretched his lips toward an eyeless face, naked as a belly, he had possessed a great flower of moist flesh. Again he saw the blind beast throbbing in the sheets with rippling, hairy yawns and he thought: that was *us two*. They had made a single one, he could no longer distinguish his flesh from that of Maud; no one had ever given him that feeling of sickening intimacy, except possibly Riri, when Riri showed him his wee-wee behind a bush or when he had forgotten himself and stayed resting on his belly, bouncing up and down, his behind naked, while they dried out his pants. Lucien felt some comfort thinking about Guigard: tomorrow he would tell him: "I slept with Maud, she's a sweet little kid, old man it's in her blood." But he was uncomfortable, and felt naked in the dusty heat of the métro, naked beneath a thin film of clothing, stiff and naked beside a priest, across from two mature women, like a great, soiled beanpole.

Guigard congratulated him vehemently. He was getting a little tired of Fanny. "She really has a rotten temper. Yesterday she gave me dirty looks all evening." They both agreed: there have to be women like that, because, after all, you couldn't stay chaste until you got married and then they weren't in love and they weren't sick but it would be a mistake to get attached to them. Guigard spoke of real girls with delicacy and Lucien asked him news of his sister. "She's fine," said Guigard, "She says you're a quitter. You know," he added, with a little abandon, "I'm not sorry I have a sister: you find out things you never could imagine." Lucien understood him perfectly. As a result they spoke often of girls and felt full of poetry and Guigard loved to recite the words of one of his uncles who had had much success with women. "Possibly I haven't always done the right thing in my dog's life, but there's one thing God will witness: I'd rather cut my hands off than touch a virgin." Sometimes they went to see Pierrette, Guigard's girl friend. Lucien liked Pierrette a lot, he talked to her like a big brother, teased her a little and was grateful to her because she had not cut her hair. He was completely absorbed in his political activities; every Sunday morning he went to sell *Action Française* in front of the church in Neuilly. For more than two hours, Lucien walked up and down, his face hard. The girls coming out of mass sometimes raised beautiful frank eyes toward him; then Lucien relaxed a little and felt pure and strong; he smiled at them. He explained to the gang that he respected women and he was glad to find in them the understanding he had hoped for. Besides, they almost all had sisters.

On the 17th of April, the Guigards gave a dance for Pierrette's 18th birthday and naturally Lucien was invited. He was already quite good friends with Pierrette, she called him her dancing partner and he suspected her of being a little bit in love with him. Mme. Guigard had brought in a caterer and the afternoon promised to be quite gay. Lucien danced with Pierrette several times, then went to see Guigard who was receiving his friends in the smoking room. "Hello," Guigard said, "I think you all know each other: Fleurier, Simon, Vanusse, Ledoux." While Guigard was naming his friends, Lucien saw a tall young man with red, curly hair, milky skin and hard black eyelashes, approaching them hesitantly and he was overcome with rage. "What's this fellow doing here," he wondered, "Guigard knows I can't stand Jews!" He spun on his heels and withdrew rapidly to avoid introduction. "Who is that Jew?" he asked Pierrette a moment later. "It's Weill, he's at the Hautes Etudes Commercial; my brother met him in fencing class." "I hate Jews" Lucien said. Pierrette gave a little laugh. "This one's a pretty good chap," she said, "Take me in to the buffet." Lucien drank a glass of champagne and only had time to set it down when he found himself nose to nose with Guigard and Weill. He glared at Guigard and turned his back, but Pierrette took his arm and Guigard aproached him openly: "My friend Fleurier, my friend Weill," he said easily, "there, you're introduced." Weill put out his hand and Lucien felt miserable. Luckily, he suddenly remembered Desperreau: "Fleurier would have chucked the Jew in the water for good." He thrust his hands in his pockets, turned his back on Guigard and walked away. "I can never set foot in this house again," he thought, getting his coat. He felt a bitter pride. "That's what you call keeping your ideals; you can't live in society any more." Once in the street his pride melted and Lucien grew worried. "Guigard must be furious!" He shook his head and tried to tell himself with conviction, "He didn't have the right to invite a Jew if he invited me!" But his rage had left him; he saw the surprised face of Weill again with discomfort, his outstretched hand, and he felt he wanted a reconciliation: "Pierrette surely thinks I'm a heel. I should have shaken hands with him. After all, it didn't involve me in anything. Say hello to him and afterwards go right away: that's what I should have done." He wondered if he had time to go back to Guigard's. He would go up to Weill and say, "Excuse me, I wasn't feeling well." He would shake hands and say a few nice words. No. It was too late, his action was irreparable. He thought with irritation, "Why did I need to show my opinions to people who can't understand them." He shrugged his shoulders nervously: it was a disaster. At that very instant Guigard and Pierrette were commenting on his behavior, Guigard was saying, "He's completely crazy!" Lucien clenched his fists. "Oh God," he thought, "how I hate them! God how I hate Jews!" and he tried to draw strength from the contemplation of this immense hatred. But it melted away under his look, in vain he thought of Leon Blum who got money from Germany and hated the French, he felt nothing more than a dismal indifference. Lucien was lucky to find Maud home. He told her he loved her and possessed her several times with a sort of rage. "It's all screwed up," he told himself, "I'll never be *anybody*." "No, no," Maud said, "stop that, my big darling, it's forbidden!" But at last she let herself go: Lucien wanted to kiss her everywhere. He felt childish and perverse; he wanted to cry.

At school, next morning, Lucien's heart tightened when he saw Guigard. Guigard looked sly and pretended not to see him. Lucien was so enraged that he could not take notes: "The bastard," he thought, "the bastard!" At the end of the class, Guigard came up to him, he was pale. "If he says a word," thought Lucien, "I'll knock his teeth in." They stayed side by side for an instant, each looking at the toes of their shoes. Finally, Guigard said in an injured voice, "Excuse me, old man, I shouldn't have done that to you." Lucien started and looked at him with distrust. But Guigard went on painfully, "I met him in the class, you see, so I thought . . . we fenced together and he invited me over to his place, but I understand, you know, I shouldn't have . . . I don't know how it happened, but when I wrote the invitations I didn't think for a second . . ." Lucien still said nothing because the words would not come out, but he felt indulgent. Guigard, his head bowed, added, "Well, what a boner . . ." "You big hunk of baloney!" Lucien said, slapping his shoulder, "of course I know you didn't do it on purpose." He said generously, "I was wrong, too. I acted like a heel. But what do you expect—it's stronger than I am. I can't stand them—it's physical. I feel as though they had scales on their hands. What did Pierette say?" "She laughed like mad," Guigard said pitifully. "And the guy?" "He caught on. I said what I could, but he took off fifteen minutes later." Still humble, he added, "My parents say you were right and you couldn't have done otherwise because of your convictions." Lucien savored the word "convictions"; he wanted to hug Guigard: "It's nothing, old man," he told him; "It's nothing because we're still friends." He walked down the Boulevard Saint-Michel in a state of extraordinary exaltation: he seemed to be himself no longer.

He told himself, "It's funny, it isn't *me* any more. I don't recognize myself!" It was hot and pleasant; people strolled by, wearing the first astonished smile of springtime on their faces; Lucien thrust himself into this soft crowd like a steel wedge; he thought, "It's not me any more. Only yesterday I was a big, bloated bug like the crickets in *Férolles*." Now Lucien felt clean and sharp as a chronometer. He went into La Source and ordered a pernod. The gang didn't hang around the Source because the place swarmed with dagos; but dagos and Jews did not disturb Lucien that day. He felt unusual and threatening in the midst of these olive-tinted bodies which rustled like a field of oats in the wind; a monstrous clock leaning on the bar, shining red. He recognized with amusement a little Jew the J. P. had roughed up last semester in the Faculté de Droit corridors. The fat and pensive little monster had not kept the mark of the blows, he must have stayed laid up for a while and then regained his round shape; but there was a sort of obscene resignation in him.

He was happy for the time being: he yawned voluptuously; a ray of sunlight tickled his nostrils; he scratched his nose and smiled. Was it a smile? Or rather a little oscillation which had been born on the outside, somewhere in a corner of the place and which had come to die on his mouth? All the dagos were floating in dark, heavy water whose eddies jolted their flabby flesh, raised their arms, agitated their fingers and played a little with their lips. Poor bastards! Lucien almost pitied them. What did they come to France for? What sea currents had brought them and deposited them here? They could dress in clothes from tailors on the Boulevard Saint-Michel in vain; they were hardly more than jellyfish, Lucien thought, he was not a jellyfish, he did not belong to that humiliated race, he told himself, "I'm a diver." Then he suddenly forgot the Source and the dagos, he only saw a back, a wide back hunched with muscles going further and further away, losing itself, implacable, in the fog. He saw Guigard: Guigard was pale, he followed the back with his eyes and said to an invisible Pierrette, "Well, what a boner . . . !" Lucien was flooded with an almost intolerable joy: this powerful, solitary back was *his own!* And the scene happened yesterday! For an instant, at the cost of a violent effort, he was Guigard, he saw the humility of Guigard and felt himself deliciously terrified. "Let that be a lesson to them!" he thought. The scene changed: it was Pierrette's boudoir, it was happening in the future, Pierrette and Guigard were pointing out a name on the list of invitations. Lucien was not there but his power was over them. Guigard was saying, "Oh no! Not that one! That would be fine for Lucien. Lucien can't stand Jews." Lucien studied himself once more; he thought "I am Lucien! Somebody who can't stand Jews." He had often pronounced this sentence but today was unlike all other times. Not at all like them. Of course, it was apparently a simple statement, as if someone had said "Lucien doesn't like oysters" or "Lucien likes to dance." But there was no mistaking it: love of dancing might be found in some little Jew who counted no more than a fly: all you had to do was look at that damned kike to know that his likes and dislikes clung to him like his odor, like the reflections of his skin, that they disappeared with him like the blinking of his heavy eyelids, like his sticky, voluptuous smiles. But Lucien's anti-semitism was of a different sort: unrelenting and pure, it stuck out of him like a steel blade menacing other breasts. "It's . . . sacred," he thought. He remembered his mother when he was little, sometimes speaking to him in a certain special tone of voice: "Papa is working in his office." This sentence seemed a sacramental formula to him which suddenly conferred a halo of religious obligations on him, such as not playing with his air gun and not shouting. "Tarara-boom!"; he walked down the hall on tiptoes as if he were in a cathedral. "Now it's my turn," he thought with satisfaction. Lowering their voices, they said, "Lucien doesn't like Jews," and people would feel paralysed, their limbs transfixed by a swarm of aching little arrows. "Guigard and Pierette," he said tenderly, "are children." They had been guilty but it sufficed for Lucien to show his teeth and they were filled with remorse, they had spoken in a low voice and walked on tiptoe.

Lucien felt full of self respect for the second time. But this time he no longer needed the eyes of Guigard: he appeared respectable in his own eyes—in his own eyes which had finally pierced his envelope of flesh, of likes and dislikes, habits and humors. "Where I sought myself," he thought "I could not find myself." In good faith he took a detailed counting of all he *was*. "But if I could only be what I am I wouldn't be worth any more than that little kike." What could one discover searching in this mucous intimacy if not the sorrow of flesh, the ignoble lie of equality and disorder? "First maxim," Lucien said, "Not to try and see inside yourself; there is no mistake more dangerous." The real Lucien—he knew now—had to be sought in the eyes of others, in the frightened obedience of Pierrette and Guigard, the hopeful waiting of all those beings who grew and ripened for him, these young apprentice girls who would become *his* workers, people of Férolles, great and small, of whom he would one day be the master. Lucien was almost afraid, he felt almost too great for himself. So many people were waiting for him, at attention: and he was and always would be this immense waiting of others. "That's a leader," he thought. And he saw a hunched, muscular back re-appear, then, immediately afterwards, a cathedral. He was inside, walking on tiptoe beneath the sifted light that fell from the windows. "Only this time I am the cathedral!" He stared intently at his neighbor, a tall Cuban, brown and mild as a cigar. He must absolutely find words to express this extraordinary discovery. Quietly, cautiously, he raised his hand to his forehead, like a lighted candle, then drew into himself for an instant, thoughtful and holy, and the words came of themselves. "I HAVE RIGHTS!" Rights! Something like triangles and circles: it was so perfect that it didn't exist, you could trace thousands of circles with a compass in vain, you could never make a single circle. Generations of workers could even scrupulously obey the commands of Lucien, they would never exhaust his right to command, rights were beyond existence, like mathematical objects and religious dogma. And now Lucien was just that: an enormous bouquet of responsibilities and rights. He had believed that he existed by chance for a long time, but it was due to a lack of sufficient thought. His place in the sun was marked in Férolles long before his birth. They were *waiting* for him long before his father's marriage: if he had come into the world it was to occupy that place: "I exist," he thought, "because I have the right to exist." And, perhaps for the first time, he had a flashing, glorious vision of his destiny. Sooner or later he would go to the Centrale (it made no difference). Then he would drop Maud (she always wanted to sleep with him, it was tiresome, their confused flesh giving off an odor of scorched rabbit stew in the torrid heat of springtime. "And then, Maud belongs to everybody. Today me, tomorrow somebody else, none of it makes any sense"); he would go and live in Férolles. Somewhere in France there was a bright young girl like Pierrette, a country girl with eyes like flowers who would stay chaste for him: sometimes she tried to imagine her future master, this gentle and terrible man; but she could not. She was a virgin; in the most secret part of her body she recognized the right of Lucien alone to possess her. He would marry her, she would be *his* wife, the tenderest of his rights. When, in the evening, she would undress with slender, sacred gestures, it would be like a holocaust. He would take her in his arms with the approval of everyone, and tell her "You belong to me!" What she would show him she would have the right to show him alone and for him the act of love would be a voluptuous counting of his goods. His most tender right, his most intimate right: the right to be respected to the very flesh, obeyed to the very bed. "I'll marry young," he thought. He thought too that he would like to have many children; then he thought of his father's work; he was impatient to continue it and wondered if M. Fleurier was not going to die soon.

A clock struck noon; Lucien rose. The metamorphosis was complete: a graceful, uncertain adolescent had entered this café one hour earlier; now a man left, a leader among Frenchmen. Lucien took a few steps in the glorious light of a French morning.

At the corner of Rue des Ecoles and the Boulevard Saint-Michel he went towards a stationery shop and looked at himself in the mirror: he would have liked to find on his own face the impenetrable look he admired on Lemordant's. But the mirror only reflected a pretty, headstrong little face that was not yet terrible. "I'll grow a moustache," he decided.

ALLEN GINSBERG / Howl (For Carl Solomon)

I

I saw the best minds of my generation destroyed by madness, starving hysterical naked,
dragging themselves through the negro streets at dawn looking for an angry fix,
angelheaded hipsters burning for the ancient heavenly connection to the starry dynamo in the machinery of night,
who poverty and tatters and hollow-eyed and high sat up smoking in the supernatural darkness of cold-water flats floating across the tops of cities contemplating jazz,
who bared their brains to Heaven under the El and saw Mohammedan angels staggering on tenement roofs illuminated,
who passed through universities with radiant cool eyes hallucinating Arkansas and Blake-light tragedy among the scholars of war,
who were expelled from the academies for crazy & publishing obscene odes on the windows of the skull,
who cowered in unshaven rooms in underwear, burning their money in wastebaskets and listening to the Terror through the wall,
who got busted in their pubic beards returning through Laredo with a belt of marijuana for New York,
who ate fire in paint hotels or drank turpentine in Paradise Alley, death, or purgatoried their torsos night after night
with dreams, with drugs, with waking nightmares, alcohol and cock and endless balls,
incomparable blind streets of shuddering cloud and lightning in the mind leaping toward poles of Canada & Paterson, illuminating all the motionless world of Time between,
Peyote solidities of halls, backyard green tree cemetery dawns, wine

drunkenness over the rooftops, storefront boroughs of teahead joyride neon blinking traffic light, sun and moon and tree vibrations in the roaring winter dusks of Brooklyn, ashcan rantings and kind king light of mind,

who chained themselves to subways for the endless ride from Battery to holy Bronx on benzedrine until the noise of wheels and children brought them down shuddering mouth-wracked and battered bleak of brain all drained of brilliance in the drear light of Zoo,

who sank all night in submarine light of Bickford's floated out and sat through the stale beer afternoon in desolate Fugazzi's, listening to the crack of doom on the hydrogen jukebox,

who talked continuously seventy hours from park to pad to bar to Bellevue to museum to the Brooklyn Bridge,

a lost battalion of platonic conversationalists jumping down the stoops off fire escapes off windowsills off Empire State out of the moon,

yacketayakking screaming vomiting whispering facts and memories and anecdotes and eyeball kicks and shocks of hospitals and jails and wars,

whole intellects disgorged in total recall for seven days and nights with brilliant eyes, meat for the Synagogue cast on the pavement,

who vanished into nowhere Zen New Jersey leaving a trail of ambiguous picture postcards of Atlantic City Hall,

suffering Eastern sweats and Tangerian bone-grindings and migraines of China under junk-withdrawal in Newark's bleak furnished room,

who wandered around and around at midnight in the railroad yard wondering where to go, and went, leaving no broken hearts,

who lit cigarettes in boxcars boxcars boxcars racketing through snow toward lonesome farms in grandfather night,

who studied Plotinus Poe St. John of the Cross telepathy and bop kaballa because the cosmos instinctively vibrated at their feet in Kansas,

who loned it through the streets of Idaho seeking visionary indian angels who were visionary indian angels,

who thought they were only mad when Baltimore gleamed in supernatural ecstasy,

who jumped in limousines with the Chinaman of Oklahoma on the impulse of winter midnight streetlight smalltown rain,

who lounged hungry and lonesome through Houston seeking jazz or sex or soup, and followed the brilliant Spaniard to converse about America and Eternity, a hopeless task, and so took ship to Africa, who disappeared into the volcanoes of Mexico leaving behind nothing but the shadow of dungarees and the lava and ash of poetry scattered in fireplace Chicago,

who reappeared on the West Coast investigating the F.B.I. in beards and shorts with big pacifist eyes sexy in their dark skin passing out incomprehensible leaflets,

who burned cigarette holes in their arms protesting the narcotic tobacco haze of Capitalism,

who distributed Supercommunist pamphlets in Union Square weeping and undressing while the sirens of Los Alamos wailed them down, and wailed down Wall, and the Staten Island ferry also wailed,

who broke down crying in white gymnasiums naked and trembling before the machinery of other skeletons,

who bit detectives in the neck and shrieked with delight in policecars for committing no crime but their own wild cooking pederasty and intoxication,

who howled on their knees in the subway and were dragged off the roof waving genitals and manuscripts,

who let themselves be fucked in the ass by saintly motorcyclists, and screamed with joy,

who blew and were blown by those human seraphim, the sailors, caresses of Atlantic and Caribbean love,

who balled in the morning in the evenings in rosegardens and the grass of public parks and cemeteries scattering their semen freely to whomever come who may,

who hiccupped endlessly trying to giggle but wound up with a sob behind a partition in a Turkish Bath when the blonde & naked angel came to pierce them with a sword,

who lost their loveboys to the three old shrews of fate the one eyed shrew of the heterosexual dollar the one eyed shrew that winks out of the womb and the one eyed shrew that does nothing but sit on her ass and snip the intellectual golden threads of the craftsman's loom,

who copulated ecstatic and insatiate with a bottle of beer a sweetheart a package of cigarettes a candle and fell off the bed, and continued along the floor and down the hall and ended fainting on the wall with a vision of ultimate cunt and come eluding the last gyzym of consciousness,

who sweetened the snatches of a million girls trembling in the sunset, and were red eyed in the morning but prepared to sweeten the snatch of the sunrise, flashing buttocks under barns and naked in the lake,

who went out whoring through Colorado in myriad stolen nightcars, N.C., secret hero of these poems, cocksmen and Adonis of Denver—joy to the memory of his innumerable lays of girls in empty lots & diner backyards, moviehouses' rickety rows, on mountaintops in caves or with gaunt waitresses in familiar roadside lonely petticoat upliftings & especially secret gas-station solipisisms of johns, & hometown alleys too,

who faded out in vast sordid movies, were shifted in dreams, woke on a sudden Manhattan, and picked themselves up out of basements hungover with heartless Tokay and horrors of Third Avenue iron dreams & stumbled to unemployment offices,

who walked all night with their shoes full of blood on the snow-bank docks waiting for a door in the East River to open to a room full of steamheat and opium,

who created great suicidal dramas on the apartment cliff-banks of the Hudson under the wartime blue floodlight of the moon & their heads shall be crowned with laurel in oblivion,

who ate the lamb stew of the imagination or digested the crab at the muddy bottom of the rivers of Bowery,

who wept at the romance of the streets with their pushcarts full of onions and bad music,

who sat in boxes breathing in the darkness under the bridge, and rose up to build harpsichords in their lofts,

who coughed on the sixth floor of Harlem crowned with flame under the tubercular sky surrounded by orange crates of theology,

who scribbled all night rocking and rolling over lofty incantations which in the yellow morning where stanzas of gibberish,

who cooked rotten animals lung heart feet tail borsht & tortillas dreaming of the pure vegetable kingdom,

who plunged themselves under meat trucks looking for an egg,

who threw their watches off the roof to cast their ballot for Eternity outside of Time, & alarm clocks fell on their heads every day for the next decade,

who cut their wrists three times successively unsuccessfully, gave up and were forced to open antique stores where they thought they were growing old and cried,

who were burned alive in their innocent flannel suits on Madison Avenue amid blasts of leaden verse & the tanked-up clatter of the iron regiments of fashion & the nitroglycerine shrieks of the fairies of advertising & the mustard gas of sinister intelligent editors, or were run down by the drunken taxicabs of Absolute Reality,

who jumped off the Brooklyn Bridge this actually happened and walked away unknown and forgotten into the ghostly daze of Chinatown soup alleyways & firetrucks, not even one free beer,

who sang out of their windows in despair, fell out of the subway window, jumped in the filthy Passaic, leaped on negroes, cried all over the street, danced on broken wineglasses barefoot smashed phonograph records of nostalgic European 1930's German jazz finished the whiskey and threw up groaning into the bloody toilet, moans in their ears and the blast of colossal steamwhistles,

who barreled down the highways of the past journeying to each other's hotrod-Golgotha jail-solitude watch or Birmingham jazz incarnation,

who drove crosscountry seventytwo hours to find out if I had a vision or you had a vision or he had a vision to find out Eternity,

who journeyed to Denver, who died in Denver, who came back to Denver & waited in vain, who watched over Denver & brooded & loned in Denver and finally went away to find out the Time, & now Denver is lonesome for her heroes,

who fell on their knees in hopeless cathedrals praying for each other's salvation and light and breasts, until the soul illuminated its hair for a second,

who crashed through their minds in jail waiting for impossible criminals with golden heads and the charm of reality in their hearts who sang sweet blues to Alcatraz,

who retired to Mexico to cultivate a habit, or Rocky Mount to tender Buddha or Tangiers to boys or Southern Pacific to the black locomotive or Harvard to Narcissus to Woodlawn to the daisychain or grave,

who demanded sanity trials accusing the radio of hypnotism & were left with their insanity & their hands & a hung jury,

who threw potato salad at CCNY lecturers on Dadaism and subsequently presented themselves on the granite steps of the madhouse with shaven heads and harlequin speech of suicide, demanding instantaneous lobotomy,

and who were given instead the concrete void of insulin metrasol electricity hydrotherapy psychotherapy occupational therapy pingpong & amnesia,

who in humorless protest overturned only one symbolic pingpong table, resting briefly in catatonia,

returning years later truly bald except for a wig of blood, and tears and fingers, to the visible madman doom of the wards of the madtowns of the East,

Pilgrim State's Rockland's and Greystone's foetid halls, bickering with the echoes of the soul, rocking and rolling in the midnight solitude-bench dolmen-realms of love, dreams of life a nightmare, bodies turned to stone as heavy as the moon,

with mother finally ******, and the last fantastic book flung out of the tenement window, and the last door closed at 4 AM and the last telephone slammed at the wall in reply and the last furnished room emptied down to the last piece of mental furniture, a yellow paper rose twisted on a wire hanger in the closet, and even that imaginary, nothing but a hopeful little bit of hallucination—

ah, Carl, while you are not safe I am not safe, and now you're really in the total animal soup of time—

and who therefore ran through the icy streets obsessed with a sudden flash of the alchemy of the use of the ellipse the catalog the meter & the vibrating plane,

who dreamt and made incarnate gaps in Time & Space through images juxtaposed, and trapped the archangel of the soul between 2 visual images and joined the elemental verbs and set the noun and dash of consciousness together jumping with sensation of Pater Omnipotens Aeterna Deus

to recreate the syntax and measure of poor human prose and stand before you speechless and intelligent and shaking with shame, rejected yet confessing out the soul to conform to the rhythm of thought in his naked and endless head,

the madman bum and angel beat in Time, unknown, yet putting down here what might be left to say in time come after death,

and rose reincarnate in the ghostly clothes of jazz in the goldhorn shadow of the band and blew the suffering of America's naked mind for love into an eli eli lamma lamma sabacthani saxophone cry that shivered the cities down to the last radio

with the absolute heart of the poem of life butchered out of their own bodies good to eat a thousand years.

II

What sphinx of cement and aluminum bashed open their skulls and ate up their brains and imagination?

Moloch! Solitude! Filth! Ugliness! Ashcans and unobtainable dollars! Children screaming under the stairways! Boys sobbing in armies! Old men weeping in the parks!

Moloch! Moloch! Nightmare of Moloch! Moloch the loveless! Mental Moloch! Moloch the heavy judger of men!

Moloch the incomprehensible prison! Moloch the crossbone soulless jailhouse and Congress of sorrows! Moloch whose buildings are judgment! Moloch the vast stone of war! Moloch the stunned governments!

Moloch whose mind is pure machinery! Moloch whose blood is running money! Moloch whose fingers are ten armies! Moloch whose breast is a cannibal dynamo! Moloch whose ear is a smoking tomb!

Moloch whose eyes are a thousand blind windows! Moloch whose skyscrapers stand in the long streets like endless Jehovahs! Moloch whose factories dream and croak in the fog! Moloch whose smokestacks and antennae crown the cities!

Moloch whose love is endless oil and stone! Moloch whose soul is electricity and banks! Moloch whose poverty is the specter of genius! Moloch whose fate is a cloud of sexless hydrogen! Moloch whose name is the Mind!

Moloch in whom I sit lonely! Moloch in whom I dream Angels! Crazy in Moloch! Cocksucker in Moloch! Lacklove and manless in Moloch!

Moloch who entered my soul early! Moloch in whom I am a consciousness without a body! Moloch who frightened me out of my natural ecstasy! Moloch whom I abandon! Wake up in Moloch! Light streaming out of the sky!

Moloch! Moloch! Robot apartments! invisible suburbs! skeleton treasuries! blind capitals! demonic industries! spectral nations! invincible madhouses! granite cocks! monstrous bombs!

They broke their backs lifting Moloch to Heaven! Pavements, trees, radios, tons! lifting the city to Heaven which exists and is everywhere about us!

Visions! omens! hallucinations! miracles! ecstasies! gone down the American river!

Dreams! adorations! illuminations! religions! the whole boatload of sensitive bullshit!

Breakthroughs! over the river! flips and crucifixions! gone down the flood! Highs, Epiphanies! Despairs! Ten years' animal screams and suicides! Minds! New loves! Mad generation! down on the rocks of Time!

Real holy laughter in the river! They saw it all! the wild eyes! the holy yells! They bade farewell! They jumped off the roof! to solitude! waving! carrying flowers! Down to the river! into the street!

ROBERT LOUIS STEVENSON / A Lodging for the Night

It was late in November, 1456. The snow fell over Paris with rigourous, relentless persistence; sometimes the wind made a sally and scattered it in flying vortices; sometimes there was a lull, and flake after flake descended out of the black night air, silent, circuitous, interminable. To poor people, looking up under moist eyebrows, it seemed a wonder where it all came from. Master Francis Villon had propounded an alternative that afternoon at a tavern window: was it only Pagan Jupiter plucking geese upon Olympus? or were the holy angels moulting? He was only a poor Master of Arts, he went on; and as the question somewhat touched upon divinity, he durst not venture to conclude. A silly old priest from Montargis, who was among the company, treated the young rascal to a bottle of wine in honor of the jest and grimaces with which it was accompanied, and swore on his own white beard that he had been just such another irreverent dog when he was Villon's age.

The air was raw and pointed, but not far below freezing; and the flakes were large, damp, and adhesive. The whole city was sheeted up. An army might have marched from end to end and not a footfall given the alarm. If there were any belated birds in heaven, they saw the island like a large white patch, and the bridges like slim white spars, on the black ground of the river. High up overhead the snow settled among the tracery of the cathedral towers. Many a niche was drifted full; many a statue wore a long white bonnet on its grotesque or sainted head. The gargoyles had been transformed into great false noses, drooping towards the point. The crockets were like upright pillows swollen on one side. In the intervals of the wind, there was a dull sound of dripping about the precincts of the church.

The cemetery of St. John had taken its own share of the snow. All the graves were decently covered; tall white housetops stood around in grave array; worthy burghers were long ago in bed, be-nightcapped like their domiciles; there was no light in all the neighborhood but a little peep from a lamp that hung swinging in the church choir, and tossed the shadows to and fro in time to its oscillations. The clock was hard on ten when the patrol went by with halberds and a lantern, beating their hands; and they saw nothing suspicious about the cemetery of St. John.

Yet there was a small house, backed up against the cemetery wall, which was still awake, and awake to evil purpose, in that snoring district. There was not much to betray it from without; only a stream of warm vapor from the chimney-top, a patch where the snow melted on the roof, and a few half-obliterated footprints at the door. But within, behind the shuttered windows, Master Francis Villon the poet, and some of the thievish crew with whom he consorted, were keeping the night alive and passing round the bottle.

A great pile of living embers diffused a strong and ruddy glow from the arched chimney. Before this straddled Dom Nicolas, the Picardy monk, with his skirts picked up and his fat legs bared to the comfortable warmth. His dilated shadow cut the room in half; and the firelight only escaped on either side of his broad person, and in a little pool between his outspread feet. His face had the beery, bruised appearance of the continual drinker's; it was covered with a network of congested veins, purple in ordinary circumstances, but now pale violet, for even with his back to the fire the cold pinched him on the other side. His cowl had half fallen back, and made a strange excrescence on either side of his bull neck. So he straddled, grumbling, and cut the room in half with the shadow of his portly frame.

On the right, Villon and Guy Tabary were huddled together over a scrap of parchment; Villon making a ballade which he was to call the "Ballade of Roast Fish," and Tabary spluttering admiration at his shoulder. The poet was a rag of a man, dark, little, and lean, with hollow cheeks and thin black locks. He carried his four-and-twenty years with feverish animation. Greed had made folds about his eyes, evil smiles had puckered his mouth. The wolf and pig struggled together in his face. It was an eloquent, sharp, ugly, earthly countenance. His hands were small and prehensile, with fingers knotted like a cord; and they were continually flickering in front of him in violent and expressive pantomime. As for Tabary, a broad, complacent, admiring imbecility breathed from his squash nose and slobbering lips: he had become a thief, just as he might have become the most decent of burgesses, by the imperious chance that rules the lives of human geese and human donkeys.

At the monk's other hand, Montigny and Thevenin Pensete played a game of chance. About the first there clung some flavour of good birth and training, as about a fallen angel; something long, lithe, and courtly in the person; something aquiline and darkling in the face. Thevenin, poor soul, was in great feather: he had done a good stroke of knavery that afternoon in the Faubourg St. Jacques, and all night he had been gaining from Montigny. A flat smile illuminated his face; his bald head shone rosily in a garland of red curls; his little protuberant stomach shook with silent chucklings as he swept in his gains.

"Doubles or quits?" said Thevenin.

Montigny nodded grimly.

"Some may prefer to dine in state," wrote Villon, *"on bread and cheese on silver plate.* Or, or—help me out, Guido!"

Tabary giggled.

"Or parsley on a golden dish," scribbled the poet.

The wind was freshening without; it drove the snow before it, and sometimes raised its voice in a victorious whoop, and made sepulchral grumblings in the chimney. The cold was growing sharper as the night went on. Villon, protruding his lips, imitated the gust with something between a whistle and a groan. It was an eerie, uncomfortable talent of the poet's, much detested by the Picardy monk.

"Can't you hear it rattle in the gibbet?" said Villon. "They are all dancing the devil's jig on nothing, up there. You may dance, my gallants, you'll be none the warmer! Whew! what a gust! Down went somebody just now! A medlar the fewer on the three-legged medlar-tree!—I say, Dom Nicolas, it'll be cold to-night on the St. Denis Road?" he asked.

Dom Nicolas winked both his big eyes, and seemed to choke upon his Adam's apple. Montfaucon, the great grisly Paris gibbet, stood hard by the St. Denis Road, and the pleasantry touched him on the raw. As for Tabary, he laughed immoderately over the medlars; he had never heard anything more light-hearted; and he held his sides and crowed. Villon fetched him a fillip on the nose, which turned his mirth into an attack of coughing.

"Oh, stop that row," said Villon, "and think of rhymes to 'fish.' "

"Doubles or quits," said Montigny doggedly.

"With all my heart," quoth Thevenin.

"Is there any more in that bottle?" asked the monk.

"Open another," said Villon. "How do you ever hope to fill that big hogshead, your body, with little things like bottles? And how do you expect to get to heaven? How many angels, do you fancy, can be spared to carry up a single monk from Picardy? Or do you think yourself another Elias—and they'll send the coach for you?"

"Hominibus impossibile," replied the monk as he filled his glass.

Tabary was in ecstasies.

Villon filliped his nose again.

"Laugh at my jokes, if you like," he said.

"It was very good," objected Tabary.

Villon made a face at him. "Think of rhymes to 'fish,'" he said. "What have you to do with Latin? You'll wish you knew none of it at the great assizes, when the devil calls for Guido Tabary, clericus—the devil with the hump-back and red-hot finger-nails. Talking of the devil," he added in a whisper, "look at Montigny!"

All three peered covertly at the gamester. He did not seem to be enjoying his luck. His mouth was a little to a side; one nostril nearly shut, and the other much inflated. The black dog was on his back, as people say, in terrifying nursery metaphor; and he breathed hard under the gruesome burden.

"He looks as if he could knife him," whispered Tabary, with round eyes.

The monk shuddered, and turned his face and spread his open hands to the red embers. It was the cold that thus affected Dom Nicolas, and not any excess of moral sensibility.

"Come now," said Villon—"about this ballade. How does it run so far?" And beating time with his hand, he read it aloud to Tabary.

They were interrupted at the fourth rhyme by a brief and fatal movement among the gamesters. The round was completed, and Thevenin was just opening his mouth to claim another victory, when Montigny leaped up, swift as an adder, and stabbed him to the heart. The blow took effect before he had time to utter a cry, before he had time to move. A tremor or two convulsed his frame; his hands opened and shut, his heels rattled on the floor; then his head rolled backward over one shoulder with the eyes wide open, and Thevenin Pensete's spirit had returned to Him who made it.

Everyone sprang to his feet; but the business was over in two two's. The four living fellows looked at each other in rather a ghastly fashion; the dead man contemplating a corner of the roof with a singular and ugly leer.

"My God!" said Tabary; and he began to pray in Latin.

Villon broke out into hysterical laughter. He came a step forward and ducked a ridiculous bow at Thevenin, and laughed still louder. Then he sat down suddenly, all of a heap, upon a stool, and continued laughing bitterly as though he would shake himself to pieces.

Montigny recovered his composure first.

"Let's see what he has about him," he remarked, and he picked the dead man's pockets with a practised hand, and divided the money into four equal portions on the table. "There's for you," he said.

The monk received his share with a deep sigh, and a single

stealthy glance at the dead Thevenin, who was beginning to sink into himself and topple sideways off the chair.

"We're all in for it," cried Villon, swallowing his mirth. "It's a hanging job for every man jack of us that's here—not to speak of those who aren't." He made a shocking gesture in the air with his raised right hand, and put out his tongue and threw his head on one side, so as to counterfeit the appearance of one who has been hanged. Then he pocketed his share of the spoil, and executed a shuffle with his feet as if to restore the circulation.

Tabary was the last to help himself; he made a dash at the money, and retired to the other end of the apartment.

Montigny stuck Thevenin upright in the chair, and drew out the dagger, which was followed by a jet of blood.

"You fellows had better be moving," he said, as he wiped the blade on his victim's doublet.

"I think we had," returned Villon, with a gulp. "Damn his fat head!" he broke out. "It sticks in my throat like phlegm. What right has a man to have red hair when he is dead?" And he fell all of a heap again upon the stool, and fairly covered his face with his hands.

Montigny and Dom Nicolas laughed aloud, even Tabary feebly chiming in.

"Cry-baby," said the monk.

"I always said he was a woman," added Montigny, with a sneer. "Sit up, can't you?" he went on, giving another shake to the murdered body. "Tread out that fire, Nick!"

But Nick was better employed; he was quietly taking Villon's purse, as the poet sat limp and trembling on the stool where he had been making a ballade not three minutes before. Montigny and Tabary dumbly demanded a share of the booty, which the monk silently promised as he passed the little bag into the bosom of his gown. In many ways an artistic nature unfits a man for practical existence.

No sooner had the theft been accomplished than Villon shook himself, jumped to his feet, and began helping to scatter and extinguish the embers. Meanwhile Montigny opened the door and cautiously peered into the street. The coast was clear; there was no meddlesome patrol in sight. Still it was judged wiser to slip out severally; and as Villon was himself in a hurry to escape from the neighbourhood of the dead Thevenin, and the rest were in a still greater hurry to get rid of him before he should discover the loss of his money, he was the first by general consent to issue forth into the street.

The wind had triumphed and swept all the clouds from heaven. Only a few vapours, as thin as moonlight, fleeted rapidly across the stars. It was bitter cold; and by a common optical effect, things seemed almost more definite than in the broadest daylight. The sleeping city was absolutely still; a company of white hoods, a field full of little alps, below the twinkling stars. Villon cursed his fortune. Would it were still snowing! Now, wherever he went, he left an indelible trail behind him on the glittering streets; wherever he went he was still tethered to the house by the cemetery of St. John; wherever he went he must weave, with his own plodding feet, the rope that bound him to the crime and would bind him to the gallows. The leer of the dead man came back to him with a new significance. He snapped his fingers as if to pluck up his own spirits, and choosing a street at random, stepped boldly forward in the snow.

Two things preoccupied him as he went; the aspect of the gallows at Montfaucon in this bright, windy phase of the night's existence, for one; and for another, the look of the dead man with his bald head and garland of red curls. Both struck cold upon his heart, and he kept quickening his pace as if he could escape from unpleasant thoughts by mere fleetness of foot. Sometimes he looked back over his shoulder with a sudden nervous jerk; but he was the only moving thing in the white streets, except when the wind swooped round a corner and threw up the snow, which was beginning to freeze, in spouts of glittering dust.

Suddenly he saw, a long way before him, a black clump and a couple of lanterns. The clump was in motion, and the lanterns swung as though carried by men walking. It was a patrol. And though it was merely crossing his line of march he judged it wiser to get out of eyeshot as speedily as he could. He was not in the humour to be challenged, and he was conscious of making a very conspicuous mark upon the snow. Just on his left hand there stood a great hotel, with some turrets and a large porch before the door; it was half-ruinous, he remembered, and had long stood empty; and so he made three steps of it, and jumped into the shelter of the porch. It was pretty dark inside, after the glimmer of the snowy streets, and he was groping forward with outspread hands, when he stumbled over some substance which offered an indescribable mixture of resistances, hard and soft, firm and loose. His heart gave a leap, and he sprang two steps back and stared dreadfully at the obstacle. Then he gave a little laugh of relief. It was only a woman, and she dead. He knelt beside her to make sure upon this latter point. She was freezing cold, and rigid like a stick. A little ragged finery fluttered in the wind about her hair and her cheeks had been heavily rouged that same afternoon. Her pockets were quite empty; but in her stocking, underneath the garter, Villon found two of the small coins that went by the name of whites. It was little enough; but it was always something; and the poet was moved with a deep sense of pathos that she should have died before she had spent her money. That seemed to him a dark and pitiable mystery; and he looked from the coins in his hand to the dead woman, and back again to the coins, shaking his head over the riddle of man's life. Henry V. of England, dying at Vincennes just after he had conquered France, and this poor jade cut off by a cold draught in a great man's doorway, before she had time to spend her couple of whites—it seemed a cruel way to carry on the world. Two whites would have taken such a little while to squander; and yet it would have been one more good taste in the mouth, one more smack of the lips, before the devil got the soul, and the body was left to birds and vermin. He would like to use all his tallow before the light was blown out and the lantern broken.

While these thoughts were passing through his mind, he was feeling, half mechanically, for his purse. Suddenly his heart stopped beating; a feeling of cold scales passed up the back of his legs, and a cold blow seemed to fall upon his scalp. He stood petrified for a moment; then he felt again with one feverish movement; and then his loss burst upon him, and he was covered at once with perspiration. To spendthrifts money is so living and actual—it is such a thin veil between them and their pleasures! There is only one limit to their fortune—that of time; and a spendthrift with only a few crowns is the Emperor of Rome until they are spent. For such a person to lose his money is to suffer the most shocking reverse, and fall from heaven to hell, from all to nothing, in a breath. And all the more if he has put his head in the halter for it; if he may be hanged to-morrow for that same purse, so dearly earned, so foolishly departed! Villon stood and cursed; he threw the two whites into the street; he shook his fist at heaven; he stamped, and was not horrified to find himself trampling the poor corpse. Then he began rapidly to retrace his steps towards the house beside the cemetery. He had forgotten all fear of the patrol, which was long gone by at any rate, and had no idea but that of his lost purse. It was in vain that he looked right and left upon the snow; nothing was to be seen. He had not dropped it in the streets. Had it fallen in the house? He would have liked dearly to go in and see; but the idea of the grisly occupant unmanned him. And he saw besides, as he drew near, that their efforts to put out the fire had been unsuccessful; on the contrary, it had broken into a blaze, and a changeful light played in the chinks of door and window, and revived his terror for the authorities and Paris gibbet.

He returned to the hotel with the porch, and groped about upon the snow for the money he had thrown away in his childish passion. But he could only find one white; the other had probably struck sideways and sunk deeply in. With a single white in his pocket, all his projects for a rousing night in some wild tavern vanished utterly away. And it was not only pleasure that fled laughing from his grasp; positive discomfort, positive pain, attacked him as he stood ruefully before the porch. His perspiration had dried upon him; and although the wind had now fallen, a binding frost was setting in stronger with every hour, and he felt benumbed and sick at heart. What was to be done? Late as was the hour, improbable as was success, he would try the house of his adopted father, the chaplain of St. Benoît.

He ran there all the way, and knocked timidly. There was no answer. He knocked again and again, taking heart with every stroke; and at last steps were heard approaching from within. A barred wicket fell open in the iron-studded door, and emitted a gush of yellow light.

"Hold up your face to the wicket," said the chaplain from within.

"It's only me," whimpered Villon.

"Oh, it's only you, is it?" returned the chaplain; and he cursed him with foul unpriestly oaths for disturbing him at such an hour, and bade him be off to hell, where he came from.

"My hands are blue to the wrist," pleaded Villon; "my feet are dead and full of twinges; my nose aches with the sharp air; the cold lies at my heart. I may be dead before morning. Only this once, father, and before God, I will never ask again!"

"You should have come earlier," said the ecclesiastic coolly. "Young men require a lesson now and then." He shut the wicket and retired deliberately into the interior of the house.

Villon was beside himself; he beat upon the door with his hands and feet, and shouted hoarsely after the chaplain.

"Wormy old fox!" he cried. "If I had my hand under your twist, I would send you flying headlong into the bottomless pit."

A door shut in the interior, faintly audible to the poet down long passages. He passed his hand over his mouth with an oath. And then the humour of the situation struck him, and he laughed and looked lightly up to heaven, where the stars seemed to be winking over his discomfiture.

What was to be done? It looked very like a night in the frosty streets. The idea of the dead woman popped into his imagination, and gave him a hearty fright; what had happened to her in the early night might very well happen to him before morning. And he so young! and with such immense possibilities of disorderly amusement before him! He felt quite pathetic over the notion of his own fate, as if it had been some one else's, and made a little imaginative vignette of the scene in the morning when they should find his body.

He passed all his chances under review, turning the white between his thumb and forefinger. Unfortunately he was on bad terms with some old friends who would once have taken pity on him in such a plight. He had lampooned them in verses; he had beaten and cheated them; and yet now, when he was in so close a pinch, he thought there was at least one who might perhaps relent. It was a chance. It was worth trying at least, and he would go and see.

On the way, two little accidents happened to him which coloured his musings in a very different manner. For, first, he fell in with the track of a patrol, and walked in it for some hundred yards, although it lay out of his direction. And this spirited him up; at least he had confused his trail; for he was still possessed with the idea of people tracking him all about Paris over the snow, and collaring him next morning before he was awake. The other matter affected him quite differently. He passed a street corner, where, not so long before, a woman and her child had been devoured by wolves. This was just the kind of weather, he reflected, when wolves might take it into their heads to enter Paris again; and a lone man in these deserted streets would run the chance of something worse than a mere scare. He stopped and looked upon the place with an unpleasant interest—it was the centre where several lanes intersected each other; and he looked down them all, one after another, and held his breath to listen, lest he should detect some galloping black things on the snow or hear the sound of howling between him and the river. He remembered his mother telling him the story and pointing out the spot, while he was yet a child. His mother! If he only knew where she lived, he might make sure at least of shelter. He determined he would inquire upon the morrow; nay, he would go and see her, too, poor old girl! So thinking, he arrived at his destination—his last hope for the night.

The house was quite dark, like its neighbors; and yet after a few taps, he heard a movement overhead, a door opening, and a cautious voice asking who was there. The poet named himself in a loud whisper, and waited, not without some trepidation, the result. Nor had he to wait long. A window was suddenly opened, and a pailful of slops splashed down upon the doorstep. Villon had not been unprepared for something of the sort, and had put himself as much in shelter as the nature of the porch admitted; but for all that, he was deplorably drenched below the waist. His hose began to freeze almost at once. Death from cold and exposure stared him in the face; he remembered he was of phthisical tendency, and began coughing tentatively. But the gravity of the danger steadied his nerves. He stopped a few hundred yards from the door where he had been so rudely used, and reflected with his finger to his nose. He could only see one way of getting a lodging and that was to take it. He had noticed a house not far away, which looked as if it might be easily broken into, and thither he betook himself promptly, entertaining himself on the way with the idea of a room still hot, with a table still loaded with the remains of supper, where he might pass the rest of the black hours and whence he should issue, on the morrow, with an armful of valuable plate. He even considered on what viands and what wines he should prefer; and as he was calling the roll of his favourite dainties, roast fish presented itself to his mind with an odd mixture of amusement and horror.

"I shall never finish that ballade," he thought to himself; and then, with another shudder at the recollection, "Oh, damn his fat head!" he repeated fervently, and spat upon the snow.

The house in question looked dark at first sight; but as Villon made a preliminary inspection in search of the handiest point of attack, a little twinkle of light caught his eye from behind a curtained window.

"The devil!" he thought. "People awake! Some student or some saint, confound the crew. Can't they get drunk and lie in bed snoring like their neighbors! What's the good of curfew, and poor devils of bellringers jumping at a rope's end in bell-towers? What's the use of day, if people sit up all night? The gripes to them!" He grinned as he saw where his logic was leading him. "Every man to his business, after all," added he, "and if they're awake, by the Lord, I may come by a supper honestly for once, and cheat the devil."

He went boldly to the door and knocked with an assured hand. On both previous occasions, he had knocked timidly and with some dread of attracting notice; but now when he had just discarded the thought of a burglarious entry, knocking at a door seemed a mighty simple and innocent proceeding. The sound of his blows echoed through the house with thin, phantasmal reverberations, as though it were quite empty; but these had scarcely died away before a measured tread drew near, a couple of bolts were withdrawn, and one wing was opened broadly, as though no guile or fear of guile were known to those within. A tall figure of a man, muscular and spare, but a little bent, confronted Villon. The head was massive in bulk, but finely sculptured; the nose blunt at the bottom, but refining upward to where it joined a pair of strong and honest eyebrows; the mouth and eyes surrounded with delicate markings, and the whole face based upon a thick white beard, boldly and squarely trimmed. Seen as it was by the light of a flickering handlamp, it looked perhaps nobler than it had a right to do; but it was a fine face, honourable, rather than intelligent, strong, simple, and righteous.

"You knock late, sir," said the old man in resonant, courteous tones.

Villon cringed, and brought up many servile words of apology; at a crisis of this sort, the beggar was uppermost in him, and the man of genius hid his head with confusion.

"You are cold," repeated the old man, "and hungry? Well, step in." And he ordered him into the house with a noble enough gesture.

"Some great seigneur," thought Villon, as his host, setting down the lamp on the flagged pavement of the entry, shot the bolts once more into their places.

"You will pardon me if I go in front," he said, when this was done; and he preceded the poet up-stairs into a large apartment, warmed with a pan of charcoal and lit by a great lamp hanging from the roof. It was very bare of furniture: only some gold plate on a sideboard; some folios; and a stand of armour between the windows. Some smart tapestry hung upon the walls, representing the crucifixion of our Lord in one piece, and in another a scene of shepherds and shepherdesses by a running stream. Over the chimney was a shield of arms.

"Will you seat yourself," said the old man, "and forgive me if I leave you? I am alone in my house to-night, and if you are to eat I must forage for you myself."

No sooner was his host gone than Villon leaped from the chair on which he had just seated himself, and began examining the room, with the stealth and passion of a cat. He weighed the gold flagons in his hand, opened all the folios, and investigated the arms upon the shield, and the stuff with which the seats were lined. He raised the window curtains, and saw that the windows were set with rich stained glass in figures, so far as he could see, of martial import. Then he stood in the middle of the room, drew a long breath and retaining it with puffed cheeks, looked round and round him, turning on his heels, as if to impress every feature of the apartment on his memory.

"Seven pieces of plate," he said. "If there had been ten, I would have risked it. A fine house, and a fine old master, so help me all the saints!"

And just then, hearing the old man's tread returning along the corridor, he stole back to his chair, and began humbly toasting his wet legs before the charcoal pan.

His entertainer had a plate of meat in one hand and a jug

of wine in the other. He sat down the plate upon the table, motioning Villon to draw in his chair, and going to the sideboard, brought back two goblets, which he filled.

"I drink to your better fortune," he said gravely touching Villon's cup with his own.

"To our better acquaintance," said the poet, growing bold. A mere man of the people would have been awed by the courtesy of the old seigneur, but Villon was hardened in that matter; he had made mirth for great lords before now, and found them as black rascals as himself. And so he devoted himself to the viands with a ravenous gusto, while the old man, leaning backward, watched him with steady, curious eyes.

"You have blood on your shoulder, my man," he said.

Montigny must have laid his wet hand upon him as he left the house. He cursed Montigny in his heart.

"It was none of my shedding," he stammered.

"I had not supposed so," returned his host quietly. "A brawl?"

"Well, something of that sort," Villon admitted with a quaver.

"Perhaps a fellow murdered?"

"Oh, no, not murdered," said the poet, more and more confused. "It was all fair play—murdered by accident. I had no hand in it, God strike me dead!" he added fervently.

"One rogue the fewer, I dare say," observed the master of the house.

"You may dare to say that," agreed Villon, infinitely relieved. "As big a rogue as there is between here and Jerusalem. He turned up his toes like a lamb. But it was a nasty thing to look at. I dare say you've seen dead men in your time, my lord?" he added, glancing at the armour.

"Many," said the old man. "I have followed the wars, as you imagine."

Villon laid down his knife and fork, which he had just taken up again.

"Were any of them bald?" he asked.

"Oh, yes; and with hair as white as mine."

"I don't think I should mind the white so much," said Villon. "His was red." And he had a return of his shuddering and tendency to laughter, which he drowned with a great draught of wine. "I'm a little put out when I think of it," he went on. "I knew him—damn him! And then the cold gives a man fancies—or the fancies give a man cold, I don't know which."

"Have you any money?" asked the old man.

"I have one white," returned the poet, laughing. "I got it

out of a dead jade's stocking in a porch. She was as dead as Caesar, poor wench, and as cold as a church, with bits of ribbon sticking in her hair. This is a hard world in winter for wolves and wenches and poor rogues like me."

"I," said the old man, "am Enguerrand de la Feuillèe, seigneur de Brisetout, bailly du Patatrac. Who and what may you be?"

Villon rose and made a suitable reverence. "I am called Francis Villon," he said, "a poor Master of Arts of this university. I know some Latin, and a deal of vice. I can make chansons, ballades, lais, virelais, and roundels, and I am very fond of wine. I was born in a garret, and I shall not improbably die upon the gallows. I may add, my lord, that from this night forward I am your lordship's very obsequious servant to command."

"No servant of mine," said the knight; "my guest for this evening, and no more."

"A very grateful guest," said Villon politely, and he drank in dumb show to his entertainer.

"You are shrewd," began the old man, tapping his forehead, "very shrewd; you have learning; you are a clerk; and yet you take a small piece of money off a dead woman in the street. Is it not a kind of theft?"

"It is a kind of theft much practised in the wars, my lord."

"The wars are the field of honour," returned the old man proudly. "There a man plays his life upon the cast; he fights in the name of his lord the king, his Lord God, and all their lordships the holy saints and angels."

"Put it," said Villon, "that I were really a thief, should I not play my life also, and against heavier odds?"

"For gain but not for honour."

"Gain?" repeated Villon with a shrug. "Gain! The poor fellow wants supper, and takes it. So does the soldier in a campaign. Why, what are all these requisitions we hear so much about? If they are not gain to those who take them, they are loss enough to the others. The men-at-arms drink by a good fire, while the burgher bites his nails to buy them wine and wood. I have seen a good many ploughmen swinging on trees about the country; ay, I have seen thirty to one elm, and a very poor figure they made; and when I asked someone how all these came to be hanged, I was told it was because they could not scrape together enough crowns to satisfy the men-at-arms."

"These things are a necessity of war, which the low-born must endure with constancy. It is true that some captains drive overhard; there are spirits in every rank not easily moved by pity; and, indeed, many follow arms who are no better than brigands."

"You see," said the poet, "you cannot separate the soldier from the brigand; and what is a thief but an isolated brigand with circumspect manners? I steal a couple of mutton chops, without so much as disturbing people's sleep; the farmer grumbles a bit, but sups none the less wholesomely on what remains. You come up blowing gloriously on a trumpet, take away the whole sheep, and beat the farmer pitifully into the bargain. I have no trumpet; I am only Tom, Dick, or Harry; I am a rogue and a dog, and hanging's too good for me—with all my heart; but just ask the farmer which of us he prefers, just find out which of us he lies awake to curse on cold nights."

"Look at us two," said his lordship. "I am old, strong, and honoured. If I were turned from my house tomorrow, hundreds would be proud to shelter me. Poor people would go out and pass the night in the streets with their children, if I merely hinted that I wished to be alone. And I find you up, wandering homeless, and picking farthings off dead women by the wayside! I fear no man and nothing; I have seen you tremble and lose countenance at a word. I wait God's summons contentedly in my own house, or, if it please the king to call me out again, upon the field of battle. You look for the gallows; a rough, swift death, without hope or honour. Is there no difference between these two?"

"As far as to the moon," Villon acquiesced. "But if I had been born lord of Brisetout, and you had been the poor scholar Francis, would the difference have been any the less? Should not I have been warming my knees at this charcoal pan, and would not you have been groping for farthings in the snow? Should not I have been the soldier, and you the thief?"

"A thief?" cried the old man. "I a thief! If you understood your words, you would repent them."

Villon turned out his hands with a gesture of inimitable impudence. "If your lordship had done me the honour to follow my argument!" he said.

"I do you too much honour in submitting to your presence," said the knight. "Learn to curb your tongue when you speak with old and honourable men, or some one hastier than I may reprove you in a sharper fashion." And he rose and paced the lower end of the apartment, struggling with anger and antipathy. Villon surreptitiously refilled his cup, and settled himself more comfortably in the chair, crossing his knees and leaning his head upon one hand and the elbow against the back of the chair. He was now replete and warm, and he was in no-wise frightened for his host, having gauged him as justly as was possible between two such different characters. The night was far spent, and in a very comfortable fashion after all; and he felt morally certain of a safe departure on the morrow.

"Tell me one thing," said the old man, pausing in his walk. "Are you really a thief?"

"I claim the sacred right of hospitality," returned the poet. "My lord, I am."

"You are very young," the knight continued.

"I should never have been so old," replied Villon, showing his fingers, "if I had not helped myself with these ten talents. They have been my nursing mothers and my nursing fathers."

"You may still repent and change."

"I repent daily," said the poet. "There are few people more given to repentance than poor Francis. As for change, let somebody change my circumstances. A man must continue to eat, if it were only that he may continue to repent."

"The change must begin in the heart," returned the old man solemnly.

"My dear lord," answered Villon, "do you really fancy that I steal for pleasure? I hate stealing, like any other piece of work or of danger. My teeth chatter when I see a gallows. But I must eat, I must drink, I must mix in society of some sort. What the devil! Man is not a solitary animal—*Cui Deus fœminam tradit.* Make me king's pantler—make me abbot of St. Denis; make me bailly of the Patatrac; and then I shall be changed indeed. But as long as you leave me the poor scholar Francis Villon, without a farthing, why, of course, I remain the same."

"The Grace of God is all-powerful."

"I should be a heretic to question it," said Francis. "It has made you lord of Brisetout and bailly of the Patatrac; it has given me nothing but the quick wits under my hat and these ten toes upon my hands. May I help myself to wine? I thank you respectfully. By God's grace, you have a very superior vintage."

The lord of Brisetout walked to and fro with his hands behind his back. Perhaps he was not yet quite settled in his mind about the parallel between thieves and soldiers; perhaps Villon had interested him by some cross-thread of sympathy; perhaps his wits were simply muddled by so much unfamiliar reasoning; but whatever the cause, he somehow yearned to convert the young man to a better way of thinking, and could not make up his mind to drive him forth again into the street.

"There is something more than I can understand in this," he said at length. "Your mouth is full of subtleties, and the devil has led you very far astray; but the devil is only a very weak spirit before God's truth, and all his subtleties vanish at a word of true honour, like darkness at morning. Listen to me once more. I learned long ago that a gentleman should live chivalrously and lovingly to God, and the king, and his lady; and though I have seen many strange things done, I have still striven to command my ways upon that rule. It is not only written in all noble histories, but in every man's heart if he will take care to read. You speak of food and wine, and I know very well that hunger is a difficult trial to endure; but you do not speak of other wants; you say nothing of honour, of faith to God and other men, of courtesy, of love without reproach. It may be that I am not very wise—and yet I think I am—but you seem to me like one who has lost his way and made a great error in life. You are attending to the little wants, and you have totally forgotten the great and only real ones, like a man who should be doctoring toothache on the Judgment Day. For such things as honour and love and faith are not only nobler than food and drink, but indeed I think we desire them more, and suffer more sharply for their absence. I speak to you as I think you will most easily understand me. Are you not, while careful to fill your belly, disregarding another appetite in your heart, which spoils the pleasure of your life and keeps you continually wretched?"

Villon was sensibly nettled under all this sermonizing.

"You think I have no sense of honour!" he cried. "I'm poor enough, God knows! It's hard to see rich people with their gloves, and you blowing in your hands. An empty belly is a bitter thing, although you speak so lightly of it. If you had had as many as I, perhaps you would change your tune. Any way I'm a thief—make the most of that—but I'm not a devil from hell, God strike me dead. I would have you to know I've an honour of my own, as good as yours, though I don't prate about it all day long, as if it was a God's miracle to have any. It seems quite natural to me; I keep it in its box till it's wanted. Why now, look you here, how long have I been in this room with you? Did you not tell me you were alone in the house? Look at your gold plate! You're strong, if you like, but you're old and unarmed, and I have my knife. What did I want but a jerk of the elbow and here would have been you with the cold steel in your bowels, and there would have been me, linking in the streets, with an armful of golden cups! Did you suppose I hadn't wit enough to see that? And I scorned the action. There are your damned goblets, as safe as in a church; there are you, with your heart ticking as good as new; and here am I, ready to go out again as poor as I came in, with my one white that you threw in my teeth! And you think I have no sense of honour—God strike me dead!"

The old man stretched out his right arm. "I will tell you what you are," he said. "You are a rogue, my man, an impudent and black-hearted rogue and vagabond. I have passed an hour with you. Oh! believe me, I feel myself disgraced! And you have eaten and drunk at my table. But now I am sick of your presence; the day has come, and the night-bird should be off to his roost. Will you go before, or after?"

"Which you please," returned the poet, rising. "I believe you to be strictly honourable." He thoughtfully emptied his cup. "I wish I could add you were intelligent," he went on, knocking on his head with his knuckles. "Age! age! the brains stiff and rheumatic."

The old man preceded him from a point of self-respect; Villon followed, whistling, with his thumbs in his girdle.

"God pity you," said the lord of Brisetout at the door.

"Good-bye, papa," returned Villon with a yawn. "Many thanks for the cold mutton."

The door closed behind him. The dawn was breaking over the white roofs. A chill, uncomfortable morning ushered in the day. Villon stood and heartily stretched himself in the middle of the road.

"A very dull old gentleman," he thought. "I wonder what his goblets may be worth."

HENRY JAMES / The Figure in the Carpet

I HAD done a few things and earned a few pence —I had perhaps even had time to begin to think I was finer than was perceived by the patronising; but when I take the little measure of my course (a fidgety habit, for it's none of the longest yet) I count my real start from the evening George Corvick, breathless and worried, came in to ask me a service. He had done more things than I, and earned more pence, though there were chances for cleverness I thought he sometimes missed. I could only, however, that evening declare to him that he never missed one for kindness. There was almost rapture in hearing it proposed to me to prepare for *The Middle,* the organ of our lucubrations, so called from the position in the week of its day of appearance, an article for which he had made himself responsible and of which, tied up with a stout string, he laid on my table the subject. I pounced upon my opportunity—that is on the first volume of it—and paid scant attention to my friend's explanation of his appeal. What explanation could be more to the point than my obvious fitness for the task? I had written on Hugh Vereker, but never a word in *The Middle,* where my dealings were mainly with the ladies and the minor poets. This was his new novel, an advance copy, and whatever much or little it should do for his reputation I was clear on the spot as to what it should do for mine. Moreover if I always read him as soon as I could get hold of him I had a particular reason for wishing to read him now: I had accepted an invitation to Bridges for the following Sunday, and it had been mentioned in Lady Jane's note that Mr. Vereker was to be there. I was young enough to have an emotion about meeting a man of his renown, and innocent enough to believe the occasion would demand the display of an acquaintance with his "last."

Corvick, who had promised a review of it, had not even had time to read it; he had gone to pieces in consequence of news requiring—as on precipitate reflection he judged—that he should catch the night-mail to Paris. He had had a telegram from Gwendolen Erme in answer to his letter offering to fly to her aid. I knew already about Gwendolen Erme; I had never seen her, but I had my ideas, which were mainly to the effect that Corvick would marry her if her mother would only die. That lady seemed now in a fair way to oblige him; after some dreadful mistake about some climate or some waters she had suddenly collapsed on the return from abroad. Her daughter, unsupported and alarmed, desiring to make a rush for home but hesitating at the risk, had accepted our friend's assistance, and it was my secret belief that at sight of him Mrs. Erme would pull round. His own belief was scarcely to be called secret; it discernibly at any rate differed from mine. He had showed me Gwendolen's photograph with the remark that she wasn't pretty but was awfully interesting; she had published at the age of nineteen a novel in three volumes, "Deep Down," about which, in *The Middle,* he had been really splendid. He appreciated my present eagerness and undertook that the periodical in question should do no less; then at the last, with his hand on the door, he said to me: "Of course you'll be all right, you know." Seeing I was a trifle vague he added: "I mean you won't be silly."

"Silly—about Vereker! Why what do I ever find him but awfully clever?"

"Well, what's that but silly? What on earth does 'awfully clever' mean? For God's sake try to get *at* him. Don't let him suffer by our arrangement. Speak of him, you know, if you can, as *I* should have spoken of him."

I wondered an instant. "You mean as far and away the biggest of the lot—that sort of thing?"

Corvick almost groaned. "Oh you know, I don't put them

back to back that way; it's the infancy of art! But he gives me a pleasure so rare; the sense of"—he mused a little—"something or other."

I wondered again. "The sense, pray, of what?"

"My dear man, that's just what I want *you* to say!"

Even before Corvick had banged the door I had begun, book in hand, to prepare myself to say it. I sat up with Vereker half the night; Corvick couldn't have done more than that. He was awfully clever—I stuck to that, but he wasn't a bit the biggest of the lot. I didn't allude to the lot, however; I flattered myself that I emerged on this occasion from the infancy of art. "It's all right," they declared vividly at the office; and when the number appeared I felt there was a basis on which I could meet the great man. It gave me confidence for a day or two—then that confidence dropped. I had fancied him reading it with relish, but if Corvick wasn't satisfied how could Vereker himself be? I reflected indeed that the heat of the admirer was sometimes grosser even than the appetite of the scribe. Corvick at all events wrote me from Paris a little ill-humouredly. Mrs. Erme was pulling around, and I hadn't at all said what Vereker gave him the sense of.

The effect of my visit to Bridges was to turn me out for more profundity. Hugh Vereker, as I saw him there, was of a contact so void of angles that I blushed for the poverty of imagination involved in my small precautions. If he was in spirits it wasn't because he had read my review; in fact on the Sunday morning I felt sure he hadn't read it, though *The Middle* had been out three days and bloomed, I assured myself, in the stiff garden of periodicals which gave one of the ormolu tables the air of a stand at a station. The impression he made on me personally was such that I wished him to read it, and I corrected to this end with a surreptitious hand what might be wanting in the careless conspicuity of the sheet. I'm afraid I even watched the result of my manœuvre, but up to luncheon I watched in vain.

When afterwards, in the course of our gregarious walk, I found myself for half an hour, not perhaps without another manœuvre, at the great man's side, the result of his affability was a still livelier desire that he shouldn't remain in ignorance of the peculiar justice I had done him. It wasn't that he seemed to thirst for justice; on the contrary I had not yet caught in his talk the faintest grunt of a grudge—a note for which my young experience had already given me an ear. Of late he had had more recognition, and it was pleasant, as we used to say in *The Middle,* to see that it drew him out. He wasn't of course popular, but I judged one of the sources of his good humour to be precisely that his success was independent of that. He had none the less become in a manner the fashion; the critics at least had put on a spurt and caught up with him. We had found out at last how clever he was, and he had had to make the best of the loss of his mystery. I was strongly tempted, as I walked beside him, to let him know how much of that unveiling was my act; and there was a moment when I probably should have done so had not one of the ladies of our party, snatching a place at his other elbow, just then appealed to him in a spirit comparatively selfish. It was very discouraging: I almost felt the liberty had been taken with myself.

I had had on my tongue's end, for my own part, a phrase or two about the right word at the right time; but later on I was glad not to have spoken, for when on our return we clustered at tea I perceived Lady Jane, who had not been out with us, brandishing *The Middle* with her longest arm. She had taken it up at her leisure; she was delighted with what she had found, and I saw that, as a mistake in a man may often be a felicity in a woman, she would practically do for me what I hadn't been able to do for myself. "Some sweet little truths that needed to be spoken," I heard her declare, thrusting the paper at rather a bewildered couple by the fireplace. She grabbed it away from them again on the reappearance of Hugh Vereker, who after our walk had been upstairs to change something. "I know you don't in general look at this kind of thing, but it's an occasion really for doing so. You *haven't* seen it? Then you must. The man has actually got *at* you, at what *I* always feel, you know." Lady Jane threw into her eyes a look evidently intended to give an idea of what she always felt; but she added that she couldn't have expressed it. The man in the paper expressed it in a striking manner. "Just see there, and there, where I've dashed it, how he brings it out." She had literally marked for him the brightest patches of my prose, and if I was a little amused Vereker himself may well have been. He showed how much he was when before us all Lady Jane wanted to read something aloud. I liked at any rate the way he defeated her purpose by jerking the paper affectionately out of her clutch. He'd take it upstairs with him and look at it on going to dress. He did this half an hour later—I saw it in his hand when he repaired to his room. That was the moment at which, thinking to give her pleasure, I mentioned to Lady Jane that I was the author of the review. I did give her pleasure, I judged, but perhaps not quite so much as I had expected. If the author was "only me" the thing didn't seem quite so remarkable. Hadn't I had the effect rather of diminishing the lustre of the article than of adding to my own? Her ladyship was subject to the most extraordinary drops. It didn't matter; the only effect I cared about was the one it would have on Vereker up there by his bedroom fire.

At dinner I watched for the signs of this impression, tried to fancy some happier light in his eyes; but to my disappointment Lady Jane gave me no chance to make sure. I had hoped she'd call triumphantly down the table, publicly demand if she hadn't been right. The party was large—there were people from outside as well, but I had never seen a table long enough to deprive Lady Jane of a triumph. I was just reflecting in truth that this interminable board would deprive *me* of one when the guest next me, dear woman—she was Miss Poyle, the vicar's sister, a robust unmodulated person—had the happy inspiration and the unusual courage to address herself across it to Vereker, who was opposite, but not directly, so that when he replied they were both leaning forward. She inquired, artless body, what he thought of Lady Jane's "panegyric," which she had read—not connecting it however with her right-hand neighbour; and while I strained my ear for his reply I heard him, to my stupefaction, call back gaily, his mouth full of bread: "Oh it's all right—it's the usual twaddle!"

I had caught Vereker's glance as he spoke, but Miss Poyle's surprise was a fortunate cover for my own. "You mean he doesn't do you justice?" said the excellent woman.

Vereker laughed out, and I was happy to be able to do the same. "It's a charming article," he tossed us.

Miss Poyle thrust her chin half across the cloth. "Oh you're so deep!" she drove home.

"As deep as the ocean! All I pretend is that the author doesn't see—"

A dish was at this point passed over his shoulder, and we had to wait while he helped himself.

"Doesn't see what?" my neighbor continued.

"Doesn't see anything."

"Dear me—how very stupid!"

"Not a bit," Vereker laughed again. "Nobody does."

The lady on his further side appealed to him and Miss Poyle sank back to myself. "Nobody sees anything!" she cheerfully announced; to which I replied that I had often thought so too, but had somehow taken the thought for a proof on my own part of a tremendous eye. I didn't tell her the article was mine; and I observed that Lady Jane, occupied at the end of the table, had not caught Vereker's words.

I rather avoided him after dinner, for I confess he struck me as cruelly conceited, and the revelation was a pain. "The usual twaddle"—my acute little study! That one's admiration should have had a reserve or two could gall him to that point? I had thought him placid, and he was placid enough; such a surface was the hard polished glass that encased the bauble of his vanity. I was really ruffled, and the only comfort was that if nobody saw anything George Corvick was quite as much out of it as I. This comfort however was not sufficient, after the ladies had dispersed, to carry me in the proper manner—I mean in a spotted jacket and humming an air—into the smoking-room. I took my way in some dejection to bed; but in the passage I encountered Mr. Vereker, who had been up once more to change, coming out of his room. *He* was humming an air and had on a spotted jacket, and as soon as he saw me his gaiety gave a start.

"My dear young man," he exclaimed, "I'm so glad to lay hands on you! I'm afraid I most unwittingly wounded you by those words of mine at dinner to Miss Poyle. I learned but half an hour ago from Lady Jane that you wrote of the little notice in *The Middle*."

I protested that no bones were broken; but he moved with me to my own door, his hand, on my shoulder, kindly feeling for a fracture; and on hearing that I had come up to bed he asked leave to cross my threshold and just tell me in three words what his qualification of my remarks had represented. It was plain he really feared I was hurt, and the sense of his solicitude suddenly made all the difference to me. My cheap review fluttered off into space, and the best things I had said in it became flat enough beside the brilliancy of his being there. I can see him there still, on my rug, in the firelight and his spotted jacket, his fine clear face all bright with the desire to be tender to my youth. I don't know what he had at first meant to say, but I think the sight of my relief touched him, excited him, brought up words to his lips from far within. It was so these words presently conveyed to me something that, as I afterwards knew, he had never uttered to any one. I've always done justice to the generous impulse that made him speak: it was simply compunction for a snub unconsciously administered to a man of letters in a position inferior to his own, a man of letters moreover in the very act of praising him. To make the thing right he talked to me exactly as an equal and on the ground of what we both loved best. The hour, the place, the unexpectedness deepened the impression: he couldn't have done anything more exquisitely successful.

"I don't quite know how to explain it to you," he said, "but it was the very fact that your notice of my book had a spice of intelligence, it was just your exceptional sharpness, that produced the feeling—a very old story with me, I beg you to believe—under the momentary influence of which I used in speaking to that good lady the words you so naturally resent. I don't read the things in the newspapers unless they're thrust upon me as that one was—it's always one's best friend who does it! But I used to read them sometimes—ten years ago. I dare say they were in general rather stupider then; at any rate it always struck me they missed my little point with a perfection exactly as admirable when they patted me on the back as when they kicked me in the shins. Whenever since I've happened to have a glimpse of them they were still blazing away—still missing it, I mean, deliciously. *You* miss it, my dear fellow, with inimitable assurance; the fact of your being awfully clever and your article's being awfully nice doesn't make a hair's breadth of difference. It's quite with you rising young men," Vereker laughed, "that I feel most what a failure I am!"

I listened with intense interest; it grew intenser as he talked. "*You* a failure—heavens! What then may your 'little point' happen to be?"

"Have I got to *tell* you, after all these years and labours?" There was something in the friendly reproach of this—jocosely exaggerated—that made me, as an ardent young seeker for truth, blush to the roots of my hair. I'm as much in the dark as ever, though I've grown used in a sense to my obtuseness; at that moment, however, Vereker's happy accent made me appear to myself, and probably to him, a rare donkey. I was on the point of exclaiming "Ah yes, don't tell me: for my honour, for that of the craft, don't!" when he went on in a manner that showed he had read my thought and had his own idea of the probability of our some day redeeming ourselves. "By my little point I mean—what shall I call it?—the particular thing I've written my books most *for*. Isn't there for every writer a particular thing of that sort, the thing that most makes him apply himself, the thing without the effort to achieve which he wouldn't write at all, the very passion of his passion, the part of the business in which, for him, the flame of art burns most intensely? Well, it's *that!*"

I considered a moment. I was fascinated—easily, you'll say; but I wasn't going after all to be put off my guard. "Your description's certainly beautiful, but it doesn't make what you describe very distinct."

"I promise you it would be distinct if it should dawn on you at all." I saw that the charm of our topic overflowed for my companion into an emotion as lively as my own. "At any rate," he went on, "I can speak for myself: there's an idea in my work without which I wouldn't have given a straw for the whole job. It's the finest fullest intention of the lot, and the application of it has been, I think, a triumph of patience, of ingenuity. I ought to leave that to somebody else to say; but that nobody does say it is precisely what we're talking about. It stretches, this little trick of mine, from book to book, and everything else, comparatively, plays over the surface of it. The order, the form, the texture of my books will perhaps someday constitute for the initiated a complete representation of it. So, it's naturally the thing for the critic to look for. It strikes me," my visitor added, smiling, "even as the thing for the critic to find."

This seemed a responsibility indeed. "You call it a little trick?"

"That's only my little modesty. It's really an exquisite scheme."

"And you hold that you've carried the scheme out?"

"The way I've carried it out is the thing in life I think a bit well of myself for."

I had a pause. "Don't you think you ought—just a trifle —to assist the critic?"

"Assist him? What else have I done with every stroke of my pen? I've shouted my intention in his great blank face!" At this, laughing out again, Vereker laid his hand on my shoulder to show the allusion was not to my personal appearance.

"But you talk about the initiated. There must therefore, you see, be initiation."

"What else in heaven's name is criticism supposed to be?" I'm afraid I coloured at this too; but I took refuge in repeating that his account of his silver lining was poor in something or other that a plain man knows things by. "That's only because you've never had a glimpse of it," he returned. "If you had had one the element in question would soon have become practically all you'd see. To me it's exactly as palpable as the marble of this chimney. Besides, the critic just *isn't* a plain man: if he were, pray, what would he be doing in his neighbour's garden? You're anything but a plain man yourself, and the very *raison d'être* of you all is that you're little demons of subtlety. If my great affair's a secret, that's only because it's a secret in spite of itself—the amazing event has made it one. I not only never took the smallest precaution to keep it so, but never dreamed of any such accident. If I had I shouldn't in advance have had the heart to go on. As it was, I only became aware little by little, and meanwhile I had done my work."

"And now you quite like it?" I risked.

"My work?"

"Your secret. It's the same thing."

"Your guessing that," Vereker replied, "is a proof that you're as clever as I say!" I was encouraged by this to remark that he would clearly be pained to part with it, and he confessed that it was indeed with him now the great amusement of life. "I live almost to see if it will ever be detected." He looked at me for a jesting challenge; something far within his eyes seemed to peep out. "But I needn't worry—it won't!"

"You fire me as I've never been fired," I declared; "you make me determined to do or die." Then I asked: "Is it a kind of esoteric message?"

His countenance fell at this—he put out his hand as if to bid me good-night. "Ah my dear fellow, it can't be described in cheap journalese!"

I knew of course he'd be awfully fastidious, but our talk had made me feel how much his nerves were exposed. I was unsatisfied—I kept hold of his hand. "I won't make use of the expression then," I said, "in the article in which I shall eventually announce my discovery, though I dare say I shall have hard work to do without it. But meanwhile, just to hasten that difficult birth, can't you give a fellow a clue?" I felt much more at my ease.

"My whole lucid effort gives him the clue—every page and line and letter. The thing's as concrete there as a bird in a cage, a bait on a hook, a piece of cheese in a mousetrap. It's stuck into every volume as your foot is stuck into your shoe. It governs every line, it chooses every word, it dots every i, it places every comma."

I scratched my head. "Is it something in the style or something in the thought? An element of form or an element of feeling?"

He indulgently shook my hand again, and I felt my questions to be crude and my distinctions pitiful. "Good-night, my dear boy—don't bother about it. After all, you do like a fellow."

"And a little intelligence might spoil it?" I still detained him.

He hesitated. "Well, you've got a heart in your body. Is that an element of form or an element of feeling? What I contend that nobody has ever mentioned in my work is the organ of life."

"I see—it's some idea about life, some sort of philosophy. Unless it be," I added with the eagerness of a thought perhaps still happier, "some kind of game you're up to with your style, something you're after in the language. Perhaps it's a preference for the letter P!" I ventured profanely to break out. "Papa, potatoes, prunes—that sort of thing?" He was suitably indulgent: he only said I hadn't got the right letter. But his amusement was over; I could see he was bored. There was nevertheless something else I had absolutely to learn. "Should you be able, pen in hand, to state it clearly yourself—to name it, phrase it, formulate it?"

"Oh," he almost passionately sighed, "if I were only, pen in hand, one of *you* chaps!"

"That would be a great chance for you of course. But why should you despise us chaps for not doing what you can't do yourself?"

"Can't do?" He opened his eyes. "Haven't I done it in twenty volumes? I do it in my way," he continued. "You don't do it in yours."

"Ours is so devilish difficult," I weakly observed.

"So is mine! We each choose our own. There's no compulsion. You won't come down and smoke?"

"No. I want to think this thing out."

"You'll tell me then in the morning that you've laid me bare?"

"I'll see what I can do; I'll sleep on it. But just one word more," I added. We had left the room—I walked again with him a few steps along the passage. "This extraordinary 'general intention,' as you call it—for that's the most vivid description I can induce you to make of it—is then, generally, a sort of buried treasure?"

His face lighted. "Yes, call it that, though it's perhaps not for me to do so."

"Nonsense!" I laughed. "You know you're hugely proud of it."

"Well, I didn't propose to tell you so; but it *is* the joy of my soul!"

"You mean it's a beauty so rare, so great?"

He waited a little again. "The loveliest thing in the world!" We had stopped, and on these words he left me; but at the end of the corridor, while I looked after him rather yearningly, he turned and caught sight of my puzzled face. It made him earnestly, indeed I thought quite anxiously, shake his head and wave his finger. "Give it up—give it up!"

This wasn't a challenge—it was fatherly advice. If I had had one of his books at hand I'd have repeated my recent act of faith—I would have spent half the night with him. At three o'clock in the morning, not sleeping, remembering moreover how indispensable he was to Lady Jane, I stole down to the library with a candle. There wasn't, so far as I could discover, a line of his writing in the house.

Returning to town I feverishly collected them all; I picked out each in its order and held it up to the light. This gave me a maddening month, in the course of which several things took place. One of these, the last, I may as well immediately mention, was that I acted on Vereker's advice: I renounced my ridiculous attempt. I could really make nothing of the business; it proved a dead loss. After all, before, as he had himself observed, I liked him; and what now occurred was simply that my new intelligence and vain preoccupation damaged my liking. I not only failed to find his general intention, I found myself missing the subordinate intentions I had formerly found. His books didn't even remain the charming things they had been for me; the exasperation of my search put me out of conceit of them. Instead of being a pleasure the more they became a resource the less; for from the moment I was unable to follow up the author's hint I of course felt it a point of honour not to make use professionally of my knowledge of them. I *had* no knowledge—nobody had any. It was humiliating, but I could bear it—they only annoyed me now. At last they even bored me, and I accounted for my confusion—perversely, I allow—by the idea that Vereker had made a fool of me. The buried treasure was a bad joke, the general intention a monstrous *pose*.

The great point of it all is, however, that I told George Corvick what had befallen me and that my information had an immense effect upon him. He had at last come back, but so, unfortunately, had Mrs. Erme, and there was as yet, I could see, no question of his nuptials. He was immensely stirred up by the anecdote I had brought from Bridges; it fell in so completely with the sense he had had from the first that there was more in Vereker than met the eye. When I remarked that the eye seemed what the printed page had been expressly invented to meet he immediately accused me of being spiteful because I had been foiled. Our commerce had always that pleasant latitude. The thing Vereker had mentioned to me was exactly the thing he, Corvick, had wanted me to speak of in my review. On my suggesting at last that with the assistance I had now given him he would doubtless be prepared to speak of it himself he admitted freely that before doing this there was more he must understand. What he would have said, had he reviewed the new book, was that there was evidently in the writer's inmost art something to *be* understood. I hadn't so much as hinted at that: no wonder the writer hadn't been flattered! I asked Corvick what he really considered he meant by his own supersubtlety, and, unmistakably kindled, he replied: "It isn't for the vulgar—it isn't for the vulgar!" He had hold of the tail of something: he would pull hard, pull it right out. He pumped me dry on Vereker's strange confidence and, pronouncing me the luckiest of mortals, mentioned half-a-dozen questions he wished to goodness I had had the gumption to put. Yet on the other hand he didn't want to be told too much—it would spoil the fun of seeing what would come. The failure of *my* fun was at the moment of our meeting not complete, but I saw it ahead, and Corvick saw that I saw it. I, on my side, saw likewise that one of the first things he would do would be to rush off with my story to Gwendolen.

On the very day after my talk with him I was surprised by the receipt of a note from Hugh Vereker, to whom our encounter at Bridges had been recalled, as he mentioned, by his falling, in a magazine, on some article to which my signature was appended. "I read it with great pleasure," he wrote, "and remembered under its influence our lively conversation by your bedroom fire. The consequence of this has been that I begin to measure the temerity of my having saddled you with a knowledge that you may find something of a burden. Now that the fit's over I can't imagine how I came to be moved so much beyond my wont. I had never before mentioned, no matter in what expansion, the history of my little secret, and I shall never speak of the business again. I was accidentally so much more explicit with you than it had ever entered into my game to be, that I find this game—I mean the pleasure of playing it—suffers considerably. In short, if you can understand it, I've spoiled a part of my fun. I really don't want to give anybody what I believe you clever young men call the tip. That's of course a selfish solicitude, and I name it to you for what it may be worth to you. If you're disposed to humour me don't repeat my revelation. Think me demented—it's your right; but don't tell anybody why."

The sequel to this communication was that as early on the morrow as I dared I drove straight to Mr. Vereker's door. He occupied in those years one of the honest old houses in Kensington-Square. He received me immediately, and as soon as I came in I saw I had not lost my power to minister to his mirth. He laughed out at sight of my face, which doubtless expressed my perturbation. I had been indiscreet—my compunction was great. "I *have* told somebody," I panted, "and I'm sure that person will by this time have told somebody else! It's a woman, into the bargain."

"The person you've told?"

"No, the other person. I'm quite sure he must have told her."

"For all the good it will do her—or do *me!* A woman will never find out."

"No, but she'll talk all over the place: she'll do just what you don't want."

Vereker thought a moment, but was not so disconcerted as I had feared: he felt that if the harm was done it only served him right. "It doesn't matter—don't worry."

"I'll do my best, I promise you, that your talk with me shall go no further."

"Very good; do what you can."

"In the meantime," I pursued, "George Corvick's possession of the tip may, on his part, really lead to something."

"That will be a brave day."

I told him about Corvick's cleverness, his admiration, the intensity of his interest in my anecdote; and without making too much of the divergence of our respective estimates mentioned that my friend was already of opinion that he saw much further into a certain affair than most people. He was quite as fired as I had been at Bridges. He was moreover in love with the young lady: perhaps the two together would puzzle something out.

Vereker seemed struck with this. "Do you mean they're to be married?"

"I dare say that's what it will come to."

"That may help them," he conceded, "but we must give them time!"

I spoke of my own renewed assault and confessed my difficulties; whereupon he repeated his former advice: "Give it up, give it up!" He evidently didn't think me intellectually equipped for the adventure. I stayed half an hour, and he was most good-natured, but I couldn't help pronouncing him a man of shifting moods. He had been free with me in a mood, he had repented in a mood, and now in a mood he had turned indifferent. This general levity helped me to believe that, so far as the subject of the tip went, there wasn't much in it. I contrived however to make him answer a few more questions about it, though he did so with visible impatience. For himself, beyond doubt, the thing we were all so blank about was vividly there. It was something, I guessed, in the primal plan; something like a complex figure in a Persian carpet. He highly approved of this image when I used it, and he used another himself. "It's the very string," he said, "that my pearls are strung on!" The reason of his note to me had been that he really didn't want to give us a grain of succour—our density was a thing too perfect in its way to touch. He had formed the habit of depending on it, and if the spell was to break it must break by some force of its own. He comes back to me from that last occasion—for I was never to speak to him again—as a man with some safe secret for enjoyment. I wondered as I walked away where he had got *his* tip.

When I spoke to George Corvick of the caution I had received he made me feel that any doubt of his delicacy would be almost an insult. He had instantly told Gwendolen, but Gwendolen's ardent response was in itself a pledge of discretion. The question would now absorb them and they would enjoy their fun too much to wish to share it with the crowd. They appeared to have caught instinctively Vereker's peculiar notion of fun. Their intellectual pride, however, was not such as to make them indifferent to any further light I might throw on the affair they had in hand. They were indeed of the "artistic temperament," and I was freshly struck with my colleague's power to excite himself over a question of art. He called it letters, he called it life, it was all one thing. In what he said I now seemed to understand that he spoke equally for Gwendolen, to whom, as soon as Mrs. Erme was sufficiently better to allow her a little leisure, he made a point of introducing me. I remember our calling together one Sunday in August at a huddled house in Chelsea, and my renewed envy of Corvick's possession of a friend who had some light to mingle with his own. He could say things to her that I could never say to him. She had indeed no sense of humour and, with her pretty way of holding her head on one side, was one of those persons whom you want, as the phrase is, to shake, but who have learnt Hungarian by themselves. She conversed perhaps in Hungarian with Corvick; she had remarkably little English for his friend. Corvick afterwards told me that I had chilled her by my apparent indisposition to oblige them with the detail of what Vereker had said to me. I allowed that I felt I had given thought enough to that indication: hadn't I even made up my mind that it was hollow and wouldn't stand the test? The importance they attached to it was irritating—it rather envenomed my doubts.

That statement looks unamiable, and what probably happened was that I felt humiliated at seeing other persons derive a daily joy from an experiment which had brought me only chagrin. I was out in the cold while, by the evening fire, under the lamp, they followed the chase for which I myself had sounded the horn. They did as I had done, only more deliberately and sociably—they went over their author from the beginning. There was no hurry, Corvick said—the future was before them and the fascination could only grow; they would take him page by page, as they would take one of the classics, inhale him in slow draughts and let him sink deep in. I doubt whether they would have got so wound up if they had not been in love: poor Vereker's secret gave them endless occasion to put their young heads together. None the less it represented the kind of problem for which Corvick had a special aptitude, drew out the particular pointed patience of which, had he lived, he would have given more striking and, it is to be hoped, more fruitful examples. He at least was, in Vereker's words, a little demon of subtlety. We had begun by disputing, but I soon saw that without my stirring a finger his infatuation would have its bad hours. He would bound off on false scents as I had done—he would clap his hands over new lights and see them blown out by the wind of the turned page. He was like nothing, I told him, but the maniacs who embrace some bedlamitical theory of the cryptic character of Shakespeare. To this he replied that if we had had Shakespeare's own word for his being cryptic he would at once have accepted it. The case there was altogether different—we had nothing but the word of Mr. Snooks. I returned that I was stupefied to see him attach such importance even to the word of Mr. Vereker. He wanted thereupon to know if I treated Mr. Vereker's word as a lie. I wasn't perhaps prepared, in my unhappy rebound, to go so far as that, but I insisted that till the contrary was proved I should view it as too fond an imagination. I didn't, I confess, say—I didn't at that time quite know—all I felt. Deep down, as Miss Erme would have said, I was uneasy, I was expectant. At the core of my disconcerted state—for my wonted curiosity lived in its ashes—was the sharpness of a sense that Corvick would at last probably come out somewhere. He made, in defence of his credulity, a great point of the fact that from of old, in his study of this genius, he had caught whiffs and hints of he didn't know what, faint wandering notes of a hidden music. That was just the rarity, that was the charm: it fitted so perfectly into what I reported.

If I returned on several occasions to the little house in Chelsea I dare say it was as much for news of Vereker as for news of Miss Erme's mamma. The hours spent there by Corvick were present to my fancy as those of a chess-player bent with a silent scowl, all the lamplit winter, over his board and his moves. As my imagination filled it out the picture held me fast. On the other side of the table was a ghostlier form, the faint figure of an antagonist good-humouredly but a little wearily secure—an antagonist who leaned back in his chair with his hands in his pockets and a smile on his fine clear face. Close to Corvick, behind him, was a girl who had begun to strike me as pale and wasted and even, on more familiar view, as rather handsome, and who rested on his shoulder and hung on his moves. He would take up a chessman and hold it poised a while over one of the little squares, and then he would put it back in its place with a long sigh of disappointment. The young lady, at this, would slightly but uneasily shift her position and look across, very hard, very long, very strangely, at their dim participant. I had asked them at an early stage of the business if it mightn't contribute to their success to have some closer communication with him. The special circumstances would surely be held to have given me a right to introduce them. Corvick immediately replied that he had no wish to approach the altar before he had prepared the sacrifice. He quite agreed with our friend both as to the sport and as to the honour—he would bring down the animal with his own rifle. When I asked him if Miss Erme were as keen a shot he said after thinking: "No, I'm ashamed to say she wants to set a trap. She'd give anything to see him; she says she requires another tip. She's really quite morbid about it. But she must play fair—she *shan't* see him!" he emphatically added. I wondered if they hadn't even quarrelled a little on the subject—a suspicion not corrected by the way he more than once exclaimed to me: "She's quite incredibly literary, you know—quite fantastically!" I remember his saying of her that she felt in italics and thought in capitals. "Oh when I've run him to earth," he also said, "then, you know, I shall knock at his door. Rather—I beg you to believe. I'll have it from his own lips: 'Right you are, my boy; you've done it this time!' He shall crown me victor—with the critical laurel."

Meanwhile he really avoided the chances London life might have given him of meeting the distinguished novelist; a danger, however, that disappeared with Vereker's leaving England for an indefinite absence, as the newspapers announced—going to the south for motives connected with the health of his wife, which had long kept her in retirement. A year—more than a year—had elapsed since the incident at Bridges, but I had not encountered him again. I think at bottom I was rather ashamed—I hated to remind him that, though I had irremediably missed his point, a reputation for acuteness was rapidly overtaking me. This scruple led me a dance; kept me out of Lady Jane's house, made me even decline, when in spite of my bad manners she was a second time so good as to make me a sign, an invitation to her beautiful seat. I once saw her with Vereker at a concert, and was sure I was seen by them, but I slipped out without being caught. I felt, as on that occasion I splashed along in the rain, that I couldn't have done anything else; and yet I remember saying to myself that it was hard, was even cruel. Not only had I lost the books, but I had lost the man himself: they and their author had been alike spoiled for me. I knew too which was the loss I most regretted. I had liked the man still better than I had liked the books.

Six months after Vereker had left England George Corvick, who made his living by his pen, contracted for a piece of work which imposed on him an absence of some length and a journey of some difficulty, and his undertaking of which was much of a surprise to me. His brother-in-law had become editor of a great provincial paper, and the great provincial paper, in a fine flight of fancy, had conceived the idea of sending a "special commissioner" to India. Special commissioners had begun, in the "metropolitan press," to be the fashion, and the journal in question must have felt it had passed too long for a mere country cousin. Corvick had no hand, I knew, for the big brush of the correspondent, but that was his brother-in-law's affair, and the fact that a particular task was not in his line was apt to be with himself exactly a reason for accepting it. He was prepared to out-Herod the metropolitan press; he took solemn precautions against priggishness, he exquisitely outraged taste. Nobody ever knew it—the taste was all his own. In addition to his expenses he was to be conveniently paid, and I found myself able to help him, for the usual fat book, to a plausible arrangement with the usual fat publisher. I naturally inferred that his obvious desire to make a little money was not unconnected with the prospect of a union with Gwendolen Erme. I was aware that her mother's opposition was largely addressed to his want of means and of lucrative abilities, but it so happened that, on my saying the last time I saw him something that bore on the question of his separation from our young lady, he exclaimed with an emphasis that startled me: "Ah I'm not a bit engaged to her, you know!"

"Not overtly," I answered, "because her mother doesn't like you. But I've always taken for granted a private understanding."

"Well, there *was* one. But there isn't now." That was all he said save something about Mrs. Erme's having got on her feet again in the most extraordinary way—a remark from which I gathered he wished me to think he meant that private understandings were of little use when the doctor didn't share them. What I took the liberty of really thinking was that the girl might in some way have estranged him. Well, if he had taken the turn of jealousy, for instance, it could scarcely be jealousy of me. In that case (beside the absurdity of it) he wouldn't have gone away to leave us together. For some time before his going we had indulged in no allusion to the buried treasure, and from his silence, of which mine was the consequence, I had drawn a sharp conclusion. His courage had dropped, his ardour had gone the way of mine—this inference at least he left me to enjoy. More than that he couldn't do; he couldn't face the triumph with which I might have greeted an explicit admission. He needn't have been afraid, poor dear, for I had by this time lost all need to triumph. In fact I considered I showed magnanimity in not reproaching him with his collapse, for the sense of his having thrown up the game made me feel more than ever how much I at last depended on him. If Corvick had broken down I should never know; no one would be of any use if *he* wasn't. It wasn't a bit true I had ceased to care for knowledge; little by little my curiosity not only had begun to ache again, but had become the familiar torment of my consciousness. There are doubtless people to whom torments of such an order appear hardly more natural than the contortions of disease; but I don't after all know why I shold in this connexion so much as mention them. For the few persons, at any rate, abnormal or not, with whom my anecdote is concerned, literature was a game of skill, and skill meant courage, and courage meant honour, and honour meant passion, meant life. The stake on the table was a special substance and our roulette the revolving mind, but we sat round the green board as intently as the grim gamblers at Monte Carlo. Gwendolen Erme, for that matter, with her white face and her fixed eyes, was of the very type of the lean ladies one had met in the temples of chance. I recognised in Corvick's absence that she made this analogy vivid. It was extravagant, I admit, the way she lived for the art of the pen. Her passion visibly preyed on her, and in her presence I felt almost tepid. I got hold of "Deep Down" again: it was a desert in which she had lost herself, but in which too she had dug a wonderful hole in the sand—a cavity out of which Corvick had still more remarkably pulled her.

Early in March I had a telegram from her, in consequence of which I repaired immediately to Chelsea, where the first thing she said to me was: "He has got it, he has got it!"

She was moved, as I could see, to such depths that she must mean the great thing. "Vereker's idea?"

"His general intention. George has cabled from Bombay."

She had the missive open there; it was emphatic though concise. "Eureka. Immense." That was all—he had saved the cost of the signature. I shared her emotion, but I was disappointed. "He doesn't say what it is."

"How could he—in a telegram? He'll write it."

"But how does he know?"

"Know it's the real thing? Oh I'm sure that when you see it you do know. *Vera incessu patuit dea!*"

"It's you, Miss Erme, who are a 'dear' for bringing me such news!"—I went all lengths in my high spirits. "But fancy finding our goddess in the temple of Vishnu! How strange of George to have been able to go into the thing again in the midst of such different and such powerful solicitations!"

"He hasn't gone into it, I know; it's the thing itself, let severely alone for six months, that has simply sprung out at him like a tigress out of the jungle. He didn't take a book with him—on purpose; indeed he wouldn't have needed to—he knows every page, as I do, by heart. They all worked in him together, and some day somewhere, when he wasn't thinking, they fell, in all their superb intricacy, into the one right combination. The figure in the carpet came out. That's the way he knew it would come and the real reason—you didn't in the least understand, but I suppose I may tell you now—why he went and why I consented to his going. We knew the change would do it—that the difference of thought, of scene, would give the needed touch, the magic shake. We had perfectly, we had admirably calculated. The elements were all in his mind, and in the *secousse* of a new and intense experience they just struck light." She positively struck light herself—she was literally, facially luminous. I stammered something about unconscious cerebration, and she continued: "He'll come right home—this will bring him."

"To see Vereker, you mean?"

"To see Vereker—and to see *me*. Think what he'll have to tell me!"

I hesitated. "About India?"

"About fiddlesticks! About Vereker—about the figure in the carpet."

"But, as you say, we shall surely have that in a letter."

She thought like one inspired, and I remember how Corvick had told me long before that her face was interesting. "Perhaps it can't be got into a letter if it's 'immense.' "

"Perhaps not if it's immense bosh. If he has hold of something that can't be got into a letter he hasn't hold of *the* thing. Vereker's own statement to me was exactly that the 'figure' *would* go a letter."

"Well, I cabled to George an hour ago—two words," said Gwendolen.

"Is it indiscreet of me to ask what they were?"

She hung fire, but at last brought them out. " 'Angel, write.' "

"Good!" I cried. "I'll make it sure—I'll send him the same."

My words however were not absolutely the same—I put something instead of "angel"; and in the sequel my epithet seemed the more apt, for when eventually we heard from Corvick it was merely, it was thoroughly to be tantalised. He was magnificent in his triumph, he described his discovery as stupendous; but his ecstasy only obscured it—there were to be no particulars till he should have submitted his conception to the supreme authority. He had thrown up his commission, he had thrown up his book, he had thrown up everything but the instant need to hurry to Rapallo, on the Genoese shore, where Vereker was making a stay. I wrote him a letter which was to await him at Aden—I besought him to relieve my suspense. That he had found my letter was indicated by a telegram which, reaching me after weary days and in the absence of any answer to my laconic dispatch at Bombay, was evidently intended as a reply to both communications. Those few words were in familiar French, the French of the day, which Corvick often made use of to show he wasn't a prig. It had for some persons the opposite effect, but his message may fairly be paraphrased. "Have patience; I want to see, as it breaks on you, the face you'll make!" "Tellement envie de voir ta tête!"—that was what I had to sit down with. I can certainly not be said to have sat down, for I seem to remember myself at this time as rattling constantly between the little house in Chelsea and my own. Our impatience, Gwendolen's and mine, was equal, but I kept hoping her light would be greater. We all spent during this episode, for people of our means, a great deal of money in telegrams and cabs, and I counted on the receipt of news from Rapallo immediately after the junction of the discoverer with the discovered. The interval seemed an age, but late one day I heard a hansom precipitated to my door with the crash engendered by a hint of liberality. I lived with my heart in my mouth and accordingly bounded to the window—a movement which gave me a view of a young lady erect on the footboard of the vehicle and eagerly looking up at my house. At sight of me she flourished a paper with a movement that brought me straight down, the movement with which, in melodramas, handkerchiefs and reprieves are flourished at the foot of the scaffold.

"Just seen Vereker—not a note wrong. Pressed me to bosom—keeps me a month." So much I read on her paper while the cabby dropped a grin from his perch. In my excitement I paid him profusely and in hers she suffered it; then as he drove away we started to walk about and talk. We had talked, heaven knows, enough before, but this was a wondrous lift. We pictured the whole scene at Rapallo, where he would have written, mentioning my name, for permission to call; that is *I* pictured it, having more material than my companion, whom I felt hang on my lips as we stopped on purpose before shop-windows we didn't look into. About one thing we were clear: if he was staying on for fuller communication we should at least have a letter from him that would help us through the dregs of delay. We understood his staying on, and yet each of us saw, I think, that the other hated it. The letter we were clear about arrived; it was for Gwendolen, and I called on her in time to save her the trouble of bringing it to me. She didn't read it out, as was natural enough; but she repeated to me what it chiefly embodied. This consisted of the remarkable statement that he'd tell her after they were married exactly what she wanted to know.

"Only when we're married—not before," she explained. "It's tantamount to saying—isn't it?—that I must marry him straight off!" She smiled at me while I flushed with disappointment, a vision of fresh delay that made me at first unconscious of my surprise. It seemed more than a hint that on me as well he would impose some tiresome condition. Suddenly, while she reported several more things from his letter, I remembered what he had told me before going away. He had found Mr. Vereker deliriously interesting and his own possession of the secret a real intoxication. The buried treasure was all gold and gems. Now that it was there it seemed to grow and grow before him; it was in all time, in all tongues, one of the most wonderful flowers of art. Nothing, above all, when once one was face to face with it, had been more consummately *done*. When once it came out it came out, was there with a splendour that made you ashamed; and there hadn't been, save in the bottomless vulgarity of the age, with every one tasteless and tainted, every sense stopped, the smallest reason why it should have been overlooked. It was immense, but it was simple —it was simple, but it was immense, and the final knowledge of it was an experience quite apart. He intimated that the charm of such an experience, the desire to drain it, in its freshness, to the last drop, was what kept him there close to the source. Gwendolen, frankly radiant as she tossed me these fragments, showed the elation of a prospect more assured than my own. That brought me back to the question of her marriage, prompted me to ask if what she meant by what she had just surprised me with was that she was under an engagement.

"Of course I am!" she answered. "Didn't you know it?" She appeared astonished, but I was still more so, for Corvick had told me the exact contrary. I didn't mention this, however; I only reminded her how little I had been on that score in her confidence, or even in Corvick's, and that moreover I wasn't in ignorance of her mother's interdict. At bottom I was troubled by the disparity of the two accounts; but after a moment I felt that Corvick's was the one I least doubted. This simply reduced me to asking myself if the girl had on the spot improvised an engagement—vamped up an old one or dashed off a new—in order to arrive at the satisfaction she desired. She must have had resources of which I was destitute, but she made her case slightly more intelligible by returning presently: "What the state of things has been is that we felt of course bound to do nothing in mamma's lifetime."

"But now you think you'll just dispense with mamma's consent?"

"Ah it mayn't come to that!" I wondered what it might come to, and she went on: "Poor dear, she may swallow the dose. In fact, you know," she added with a laugh, "she really *must!*"—a proposition of which, on behalf of every one concerned, I fully acknowledged the force.

Nothing more annoying had ever happened to me than to become aware before Corvick's arrival in England that I should not be there to put him through. I found myself abruptly called to Germany by the alarming illness of my younger brother, who, against my advice, had gone to Munich to study, at the feet indeed of a great master, the art of portraiture in oils. The near relative who made him an allowance had threatened to withdraw it if he should, under specious pretexts, turn for superior truth to Paris—Paris being somehow, for a Cheltenham aunt, the school of evil, the abyss. I deplored this prejudice at the time, and the deep injury of it was now visible—first in the fact that it hadn't saved the poor boy, who was clever, frail and foolish, from congestion of the lungs, and second in the greater break with London to which the event condemned me. I'm afraid that what was uppermost in my mind during several anxious weeks was the sense that if we had only been in Paris I might have run over to see Corvick. This was actually out of the question from every point of view: my brother, whose recovery gave us both plenty to do, was ill for three months, during which I never left him and at the end of which we had to face the absolute prohibition of a return to England. The consideration of climate imposed itself, and he was in no state to meet it alone. I took him to Meran and there spent the summer with him, trying to show him by example how to get back to work and nursing a rage of another sort that I tried *not* to show him.

The whole business proved the first of a series of phenomena so strangely interlaced that, taken all together (which was how I had to take them) they form as good an illustration as I can recall of the manner in which, for the good of his soul doubtless, fate sometimes deals with a man's avidity. These incidents certainly had larger bearings than the comparatively meagre consequence we are here concerned with—though I feel that consequence also a thing to speak of with some respect. It's mainly in such a light, I confess, at any rate, that the ugly fruit of my exile is at this hour present to me. Even at first indeed the spirit in which my avidity, as I have called it, made me regard that term owed no element of ease to the fact that before coming back from Rapallo George Corvick addressed me in a way I didn't like. His letter had none of the sedative action I must to-day profess myself sure he had wished to give it, and the march of occurrences was not so ordered as to make up for what it lacked. He had begun on the spot, for one of the quarterlies, a great last word on Vereker's writings, and this exhaustive study, the only one that would have counted, have existed, was to turn on the new light, to utter—oh so quietly!—the unimagined truth. It was in other words to trace the figure in the carpet through every convolution, to reproduce it in every tint. The result, according to my friend, would be the greatest literary portrait ever painted, and what he asked of me was just to be so good as not to trouble him with questions till he should hang up his masterpiece before me. He did me the honour to declare that, putting aside the great sitter himself, all aloft in his indifference, I was individually the connoisseur he was most working for. I was therefore to be a good boy and not try to peep under the curtain before the show was ready: I should enjoy it all the more if I sat very still.

I did my best to sit very still, but I couldn't help giving a jump on seeing in *The Times,* after I had been a week or two in Munich and before, as I knew, Corvick had reached London, the announcement of the sudden death of poor Mrs. Erme. I instantly, by letter, appealed to Gwendolen for particulars, and she wrote me that her mother had yielded to long-threatened failure of the heart. She didn't say, but I took the liberty of reading into her words, that from the point of view of her marriage and also of her eagerness, which was quite a match for mine, this was a solution more prompt than could have been expected and more radical than waiting for the old lady to swallow the dose. I candidly admit indeed that at the time—for I heard from her repeatedly—I read some singular things into Gwendolen's words and some still more extraordinary ones into her silences. Pen in hand, this way, I live the time over, and it brings back the oddest sense of my having been, both for months and in spite of myself a kind of coerced spectator. All my life had taken refuge in my eyes, which the procession of events appeared to have committed itself to keep astare. There were days when I thought of writing to Hugh Vereker and simply throwing myself on his charity. But I felt more deeply that I hadn't fallen quite so low—besides which, quite properly, he would send me about my business. Mrs. Erme's death brought Corvick straight home, and within the month he was united "very quietly"—as quietly, I seemed to make out, as he meant in his article to bring out his *trouvaille*—to the young lady he had loved and quitted. I use this last term, I may parenthetically say, because I subsequently grew sure that at the time he went to India, at the time of his great news from Bombay, there was no engagement whatever. There was none at the moment she affirmed me the opposite. On the other hand he certainly became engaged the day he returned. The happy pair went down to Torquay for their honeymoon, and there, in a reckless hour, it occurred to poor Corvick to take his young bride for a drive. He had no command of that business: this had been brought home to me of old in a little tour we had once made together in a dogcart. In a dogcart he perched his companion for a rattle over Devonshire hills, on one of the likeliest of which he brought his horse, who, it was true, had bolted, down with such violence that the occupants of the cart were hurled forward and that he fell horribly on his head. He was killed on the spot; Gwendolen escaped unhurt.

I pass rapidly over the question of this unmitigated tragedy, of what the loss of my best friend meant for me, and I complete my little history of my patience and my pain by the frank statement of my having, in a postscript to my very first letter to her after the receipt of the hideous news, asked Mrs. Corvick whether her husband had not at least finished the great article on Vereker. Her answer was as prompt as my question: the article, which had been barely begun, was a mere heartbreaking scrap. She explained that Corvick had just settled down to it when interrupted by her mother's death, and that then, on his return, he had been kept from work by the engrossments into which that calamity plunged them. The opening pages were all that existed; they were striking, they were promising, but they didn't unveil the idol. That great intellectual feat was obviously to have formed his climax. She said nothing more, nothing to enlighten me as to the state of her own knowledge—the knowledge for the acquisition of which I had conceived her doing prodigious things. This was above all what I wanted to know: had *she* seen the idol unveiled? Had there been a private ceremony for a palpitating audience of one? For what else but that ceremony had the previous ceremony been enacted? I didn't like as yet to press her, though when I thought of what had passed between us on the subject in Corvick's absence her reticence surprised me. It was therefore not till much later, from Meran, that I risked another appeal, risked it in some trepidation, for she continued to tell me nothing. "Did you hear in those few days of your blighted bliss," I wrote, "what we desired so to hear?" I said "we" as a little hint; and she showed me she could take a little hint. "I heard everything," she replied, "and I mean to keep it to myself!"

It was impossible not to be moved with the strongest sympathy for her, and on my return to England I showed her every kindness in my power. Her mother's death had made her means sufficient, and she had gone to live in a more convenient quarter. But her loss had been great and her visitation cruel; it never would have occurred to me, moreover, to suppose she could come to feel the possession of a technical tip, of a piece of literary experience, a counterpoise to her grief. Strange to say, none the less, I couldn't help believing after I had seen her a few times that I caught a glimpse of some such oddity. I hasten to add that there had been other things I couldn't help believing, or at least imagining; and as I never felt I was really clear about these, so, as to the point I here touch on, I give her memory the benefit of the doubt. Stricken and solitary, highly accomplished and now, in her deep mourning, her maturer grace and her uncomplaining sorrow, incontestably handsome, she presented herself as leading a life of singular dignity and beauty. I had at first found a way to believe that I should soon get the better of the reserve formulated, the week after the catastrophe, in her reply to an appeal as to which I was not unconscious that it might strike her as mistimed. Certainly that reserve was something of a shock to me—certainly it puzzled me the more I thought of it and even though I tried to explain it, with moments of success, by an imputation of exalted sentiments, of superstitious scruples, of a refinement of loyalty. Certainly it added at the same time hugely to the price of Vereker's secret, precious as this mystery already appeared. I may as well confess abjectly that Mrs. Corvick's unexpected attitude was the final tap on the nail that was to fix fast my luckless idea, convert it into the obsession of which I'm for ever conscious.

But this only helped me the more to be artful, to be adroit, to allow time to elapse before renewing my suit. There were plenty of speculations for the interval, and one of them was deeply absorbing. Corvick had kept his information from his young friend till after the removal of the last barrier to their intimacy—then only had he let the cat out of the bag. Was it Gwendolen's idea, taking a hint from him, to liberate this animal only on the basis of the renewal of such a relation? Was the figure in the carpet traceable or describable only for husbands and wives—for lovers supremely united? It came back to me in a mystifying manner that in Kensington Square, when I mentioned that Corvick would have told the girl he loved, some word had dropped from Vereker that gave colour to this possibility. There might be little in it, but there was enough to make me wonder if I should have to marry Mrs. Corvick to get what I wanted. Was I prepared to offer her this price for the blessing of her knowledge? Ah that way madness lay! —so I said to myself at least in bewildered hours. I could see meanwhile the torch she refused to pass on flame away in her chamber of memory—pour through her eyes a light that made a glow in her lonely house. At the end of six months I was fully sure of what this warm presence made up to her for. We had talked again and again of the man who had brought us together—of his talent, his character, his personal charm, his certain career, his dreadful doom, and even of his clear purpose in that great study which was to have been a supreme literary portrait, a kind of critical Vandyke or Velasquez. She had conveyed to me in abundance that she was tongue-tied by her perversity, by her piety, that she would never break the silence it had not been given to the "right person," as she said, to break. The hour, however, finally arrived. One evening when I had been sitting with her longer than usual I laid my hand firmly on her arm.

"Now at last what *is* it?"

She had been expecting me; she was ready. She gave a long slow soundless headshake, merciful only in being inarticulate. This mercy didn't prevent its hurling at me the largest finest coldest "Never!" I had yet, in the course of a life that had known denials, had to take full in the face. I took it and was aware that with the hard blow the tears had come into my eyes. So for a while we sat and looked at each other; after which I slowly rose. I was wondering if some day she would accept me; but this was not what I brought out. I said as I smoothed down my hat: "I know what to think then. It's nothing!"

A remote disdainful pity for me gathered in her dim smile; then she spoke in a voice that I hear at this hour. "It's my *life!*" As I stood at the door she added: "You've insulted him!"

"Do you mean Vereker?"

"I mean the Dead!"

I recognised when I reached the street the justice of her charge. Yes, it was her life—I recognised that too; but her life none the less made room with the lapse of time for another interest. A year and a half after Corvick's death she published in a single volume her second novel, "Overmastered," which I pounced on in the hope of finding in it some tell-tale echo or some peeping face. All I found was a much better book than her younger performance, showing I thought the better company she had kept. As a tissue tolerably intricate it was a carpet with a figure of its own; but the figure was not the figure I was looking for. On sending a review of it to *The Middle* I was surprised to learn from the office that a notice was already in type. When the paper came out I had no hesitation in attributing this article, which I thought rather vulgarly overdone, to Drayton Deane, who in the old days had been something of a friend of Corvick's, yet had only within a few weeks made the acquaintance of his widow. I had had an early copy of the book, but Deane had evidently had an earlier. He lacked all the same the light hand with which Corvick had gilded the gingerbread—he laid on the tinsel in splotches.

Six months later appeared "The Right of Way," the last chance, though we didn't know it, that we were to have to redeem ourselves. Written wholly during Vereker's sojourn abroad, the book had been heralded, in a hundred paragraphs, by the usual ineptitudes. I carried it, as early a copy as any, I this time flattered myself, straightway to Mrs. Corvick. This was the only use I had for it; I left the inevitable tribute of *The Middle* to some more ingenious mind and some less irritated temper. "But I already have it," Gwendolen said. "Drayton Deane was so good as to bring it to me yesterday, and I've just finished it."

"Yesterday? How did he get it so soon?"

"He gets everything so soon! He's to review it in *The Middle.*"

"He—Drayton Deane—review Vereker?" I couldn't believe my ears.

"Why not? One fine ignorance is as good as another."

I winced but I presently said: "You ought to review him yourself!"

"I don't 'review,' " she laughed. "I'm reviewed!"

Just then the door was thrown open. "Ah yes, here's your reviewer!" Drayton Deane was there with his long legs and his tall forehead: he had come to see what she thought of "The Right of Way," and to bring news that was singularly relevant. The evening papers were just out with a telegram on the author of that work, who, in Rome, had been ill for some days with an attack of malarial fever. It had at first not been thought grave, but had taken, in consequence of complications, a turn that might give rise to anxiety. Anxiety had indeed at the latest hour begun to be felt.

I was struck in the presence of these tidings with the fundamental detachment that Mrs. Corvick's overt concern quite failed to hide: it gave me the measure of her consummate independence. That independence rested on her knowledge, the knowledge which nothing now could destroy and which nothing could make different. The figure in the carpet might take on another twist or two, but the sentence had virtually been written. The writer might go down to his grave: she was the person in the world to whom—as if she had been his favoured heir—his continued existence was least of a need. This reminded me how I had observed at a particular moment—after Corvick's death—the drop of her desire to see him face to face. She had got what she wanted without that. I had been sure that if she hadn't got it she wouldn't have been restrained from the endeavour to sound him personally by those superior reflexions, more conceivable on a man's part than on a woman's, which in my case had served as a deterrent. It wasn't however, I hasten to add, that my case, in spite of this invidious comparison, wasn't ambiguous enough. At the thought that Verecker was perhaps at that moment dying there rolled over me a wave of anguish—a poignant sense of how inconsistently I still depended on him. A delicacy that it was my one compensation to suffer to rule me had left the Alps and the Apennines between us, but the vision of the waning opportunity made me feel as if I might in my despair at last have gone to him. Of course I would really have done nothing of the sort. I remained five minutes, while my companions talked of the new book, and when Drayton Deane appealed to me for my opinion of it I made answer, getting up, that I detested Hugh Vereker—simply couldn't read him. I departed with the moral certainty that as the door closed behind me Deane would remark that I was awfully superficial. His hostess wouldn't contradict *that* at least.

I continue to trace with a briefer touch our intensely odd concatenations. Three weeks after this came Vereker's death, and before the year was out the death of his wife. That poor lady I had never seen, but I had had a futile theory that, should she survive him long enough to be decorously accessible, I might approach her with the feeble flicker of my petition. Did she know and if she knew would she speak? It was much to be presumed that for more reasons than one she would have nothing to say; but when she passed out of all reach I felt that renouncement was indeed my appointed lot. I was shut up in my obsession for ever—my gaolers had gone off with the key. I find myself quite as vague as a captive in a dungeon about the time that further elapsed before Mrs. Corvick became the wife of Drayton Deane. I had foreseen, through my bars, this end of the business, though there was no indecent haste and our friendship had rather fallen off. They were both so "awfully intellectual" that it struck people as a suitable match, but I had measured better than any one the wealth of understanding the bride would contribute to the partnership. Never, for a marriage in literary circles—so the newspapers described the alliance—had a lady been so bravely dowered. I began with due promptness to look for the fruit of the affair—that fruit, I mean, of which the premonitory symptoms would be peculiarly visible in the husband. Taking for granted the splendour of the other party's nuptial gift, I expected to see him make a show commensurate with his increase of means. I knew what his means had been—his article on "The Right of Way" had distinctly given one the figure. As he was now exactly in the position in which still more exactly I was not I watched from month to month, in the likely periodicals, for the heavy message poor Corvick had been unable to deliver and the responsibility of which would have fallen on his successor. The widow and wife would have broken by the rekindled hearth the silence that only a widow and wife might break, and Deane would be as aflame with the knowledge as Corvick in his own hour, as Gwendolen in hers, had been. Well, he was aflame doubtless, but the fire was apparently not to become a public blaze. I scanned the periodicals in vain: Drayton Deane filled them with exuberant pages, but he withheld the page I most feverishly sought. He wrote on a thousand subjects, but never on the subject of Vereker. His special line was to tell truths that other people either "funked," as he said, or overlooked, but he never told the only truth that seemed to me in these days to signify. I met the couple in those literary circles referred to in the papers: I have sufficiently intimated that it was only in such circles we were all constructed to revolve. Gwendolen was more than ever committed to them by the publication of her third novel, and I myself definitely classed by holding the opinion that this work was inferior to its immediate precedessor. Was it worse because she had been keeping worse company? If her secret was, as she had told me, her life—a fact discernible in her increasing bloom, an air of conscious privilege that, cleverly corrected by pretty charities, gave distinction to her appearance—it had yet not a direct influence on her work. That only made one—everything only made one—yearn the more for it; only rounded it off with a mystery finer and subtler.

It was therefore from her husband I could never remove my eyes: I hovered about him in a manner that might have made him uneasy. I went even so far as to engage him in conversation. *Didn't* he know, hadn't he come into it as a matter of course?—that question hummed in my brain. Of course he knew; otherwise he wouldn't return my stare so queerly. His wife had told him what I wanted and he was amiably amused at my impotence. He didn't laugh—he wasn't a laugher: his system was to present to my irritation, so that I should crudely expose myself, a conversational blank as vast as his big bare brow. It always happened that I turned away with a settled conviction from these unpeopled expanses, which seemed to complete each other geographically and to symbolise together Drayton Deane's want of voice, want of form. He simply hadn't the art to use what he knew; he literally was incompetent to take up the duty where Corvick had left it. I went still further—it was the only glimpse of happiness I had. I made up my mind that the duty didn't appeal to him. He wasn't interested, he didn't care. Yes, it quite comforted me to believe him too stupid to have joy of the thing I lacked. He was as stupid after as before, and that deepened for me the golden glory in which the mystery was wrapped. I had of course none the less to recollect that his wife might have imposed her conditions and exactions. I had above all to remind myself that with Vereker's death the major incentive dropped. He was still there to be honoured by what might be done—he was no longer there to give it his sanction. Who alas but he had the authority?

Two children were born to the pair, but the second cost the mother her life. After this stroke I seemed to see another ghost of a chance. I jumped at it in thought, but I waited a certain time for manners, and at last my opportunity arrived in a remunerative way. His wife had been dead a year when I met Drayton Deane in the smoking-room of a small club of which we both were members, but where for months—perhaps because I rarely entered it—I hadn't seen him. The room was empty and the occasion propitious. I deliberately offered him, to have done with the matter for ever, that advantage for which I felt he had long been looking.

"As an older acquaintance of your late wife's than even you were," I began, "you must let me say to you something I have on my mind. I shall be glad to make any terms with you that you see fit to name for the information she must have had from George Corvick—the information, you know, that he, poor fellow, in one of the happiest hours of his life, had straight from Hugh Vereker."

He looked at me like a dim phrenological bust. "The information—?"

"Vereker's secret, my dear man—the general intention of his books: the string the pearls were strung on, the buried treasure, the figure in the carpet."

He began to flush—the numbers on his bumps to come out. "Vereker's books had a general intention?"

I stared in my turn. "You don't mean to say you don't know it?" I thought for a moment he was playing with me. "Mrs. Deane knew it; she had it, as I say, straight from Corvick, who had, after infinite search and to Vereker's own delight, found the very mouth of the cave. Where *is* the mouth? He told after their marriage—and told alone—the person who, when the circumstances were reproduced, must have told *you.* Have I been wrong in taking for granted that she admitted you, as one of the highest privileges of the relation in which you stood to her, to the knowledge of which she was after Corvick's death the sole depository? All *I* know is that that knowledge is infinitely precious, and what I want you to understand is that if you'll in your turn admit me to it you'll do me a kindness for which I shall be lastingly grateful."

He had turned at last very red; I dare say he had begun by thinking I had lost my wits. Little by little he followed me; on my own side I stared with a livelier surprise. "I don't know what you're talking about," he said.

He wasn't acting—it was the absurd truth. "She *didn't* tell you—?"

"Nothing about Hugh Vereker."

I was stupefied; the room went round. It had been too good even for that!" "Upon your honour?"

"Upon my honour. What the devil's the matter with you?" he growled.

"I'm astounded—I'm disappointed. I wanted to get it out of you."

"It isn't *in* me!" he awkwardly laughed. "And even if it were—"

"If it were you'd let me have it—oh yes, in common humanity. But I believe you. I see—I see!" I went on, conscious, with the full turn of the wheel, of my great delusion, my false view of the poor man's attitude. What I saw, though I couldn't say it, was that his wife hadn't thought him worth enlightening. This struck me as strange for a woman who had thought him worth marrying. At last I explained it by the reflexion that she couldn't possibly have married him for his understanding. She had married him for something else. He was to some extent enlightened now, but he was even more astonished, more disconcerted: he took a moment to compare my story with his quickened memories. The result of his meditation was his presently saying with a good deal of rather feeble form:

"This is the first I hear of what you allude to. I think you must be mistaken as to Mrs. Drayton Deane's having had any unmentioned, and still less any unmentionable, knowledge of Hugh Vereker. She'd certainly have wished it—if it bore on his literary character—to be used."

"It *was* used. She used it herself. She told me with her own lips that she 'lived' on it."

I had no sooner spoken than I repented of my words; he grew so pale that I felt as if I had struck him. "Ah 'lived'—!" he murmured, turning short away from me.

My compunction was real; I laid my hand on his shoulder. "I beg you to forgive me—I've made a mistake. You *don't* know what I thought you knew. You could, if I had been right, have rendered me a service; and I had my reasons for assuming that you'd be in a position to meet me."

"Your reasons?" he echoed. "What were your reasons?"

I looked at him well; I hesitated; I considered. "Come and sit down with me here and I'll tell you." I drew him to a sofa, I lighted another cigar and, beginning with the anecdote of Vereker's one descent from the clouds, I recited to him the extraordinary chain of accidents that had, in spite of it, kept me till that hour in the dark. I told him in a word just what I've written out here. He listened with deepening attention, and I became aware, to my surprise, by his ejaculations, by his questions, that he would have been after all not unworthy to be trusted by his wife. So abrupt an experience of her want of trust had an agitating effect on him; but I saw that immediate shock throb away little by little and then gather again into waves of wonder and curiosity—waves that promised, I could perfectly judge, to break in the end with the fury of my own highest tides. I may say that to-day as victims of unappeased desire there isn't a pin to choose between us. The poor man's state is almost my consolation; there are indeed moments when I feel it to be almost my revenge.

VI

THE RELIGIOUS MAN

Jung's theory of the racial unconscious illuminates yet another aspect of unconscious psychology. Jung's objections to the strictures of orthodox Freudianism led him to his idea of the collective unconscious. This collective unconscious has produced the idea of God who thus becomes the image of a numinosum or dynamic agency or effect which is not caused by an act of will but controls its subject. All ritual practice—whether it involves dancing, drug-taking, or the consumption of alcohol—is carried out to reproduce the effect of the numinosum or mystic experience. This unseen, inner force, says Jung, may not be manipulated by man: it is the product of racial memory, is born with him and follows its own immutable laws. It produces in the conscious mind a desire for mystic or religious experience which cannot be invoked except under abnormal conditions in which there is a loss of consciousness, through sleep, hypnosis, trance, emotional stress, or physical frenzy. This desire, says Jung in contradistinction to Freud, is in no way neurotic but is a natural part of human behavior.

Unamuno's priest, like Jung himself, is aware of the necessity for this mystic experience. Because he is a man whose excessive rationalism has split him from his numinous or religious self, however, Father Manuel Bueno has lost the ability to make contact with this spiritual self. His excessive rationalism seems to preclude any direct knowledge of the mystic experience of God—yet in his life and even in his disbelief we can see the distorted image of this irrational power which Jung calls the collective unconscious, and which is reflected in society by the institution of religion.

ST. AUGUSTINE/The Vision at Ostia*

A Conversation He Had With His Mother Concerning The Kingdom of Heaven

As THE day now approached on which she was to depart this life (which day Thou knewest, we did not), it fell out—Thou, as I believe, by Thy secret ways arranging it—that she and I stood alone, leaning in a certain window, from which the garden of the house we occupied at Ostia could be seen; at this place, removed from the crowd, we were resting ourselves for the voyage, after the fatigues of a long journey. We then were conversing alone very pleasantly; and, forgetting those things which are behind, and reaching forth unto those things which are before,[1] we were seeking between ourselves in the presence of the Truth, which Thou art, of what nature the eternal life of the saints would be, which eye hath not seen, nor ear heard, neither hath entered into the heart of man.[2] But yet we opened wide the mouth of our heart, after those supernal streams of Thy fountain, the fountain of life, which is with Thee;[3] that being sprinkled with it according to our capacity, we might in some measure weigh so high a mystery.

And when our conversation had arrived at that point, that the very highest pleasure of the carnal senses, and that in the very brightest material light, seemed by reason of the sweetness of that life not only not worthy of comparison, but not even of mention, we, lifting ourselves with a more ardent affection towards the Selfsame, did gradually pass through all corporeal things, and even the heaven itself, whence sun, and moon, and stars shine upon the earth; yea, we soared higher yet by inward musing, and discoursing, and admiring Thy works; and we came to our own minds, and went beyond them, that we might advance as high as that region of unfailing plenty, where Thou feedest Israel[4] for ever with the food of truth, and where life is that Wisdom by whom all these things are made, both which have been, and which are to come; and she is not made, but is as she hath been, and so shall ever be; yea, rather, to have been, and to be hereafter, are not in her, but only to be, seeing she is eternal, for to have been and to be hereafter are not eternal. And while we were thus speaking, and strain-

* St. Augustine, *The Confessions,* Book IX, chap. X (ed. Schaff).
[1] Phil. iii. 13.
[2] I Cor. ii. 9; Isa. lxiv. 4.
[3] Ps. xxxvi. 9.
[4] Ps. lxxx. 5.

ing after her, we slightly touched her with the whole effort of our heart; and we sighed, and there left bound the first-fruits of the Spirit;[5] and returned to the noise of our own mouth, where the word uttered has both beginning and end. And what is like unto Thy Word, our Lord, who remaineth in Himself without becoming old, and maketh all things new?[6]

We were saying, then, If to any man the tumult of the flesh were silenced—silenced the phantasies of earth, waters, and air—silenced, too, the poles; yea, the very soul be silenced to herself, and go beyond herself by not thinking of herself—silenced fancies and imaginary revelations, every tongue, and every sign, and whatsoever exists by passing away, since, if any could hearken, all these say, "We created not ourselves, but were created by Him who abideth for ever:" If, having uttered this, they now should be silenced, having only quickened our ears to Him who created them, and He alone speak not by them, but by Himself, that we may hear His word, not by fleshly tongue, nor angelic voice, nor sound of thunder, nor the obscurity of a similitude, but might hear Him—him whom in these we love—without these, as we two now strained ourselves, and with rapid thought touched on that Eternal Wisdom which remaineth over all. If this could be sustained, and other visions of a far different kind be withdrawn, and this one ravish, and absorb, and envelope its beholder amid these inward joys, so that his life might be eternally like that one moment of knowledge which we now sighed after, were not this "Enter thou into the joy of Thy Lord"?[7] And when shall that be? When we shall all rise again; but all shall not be changed.[8]

Such things was I saying; and if not after this manner, and in these words, yet, Lord, Thou knowest, that in that day when we were talking thus, this world with all its delights grew contemptible to us, even while we spake. Then my mother said, "Son, for myself, I have no longer any pleasure in aught in this life. What I want here further, and why I am here, I know not, now that my hopes in this world are satisfied. There was indeed one thing for which I wished to tarry a little in this life, and that was that I might see thee a Catholic Christian before I died. My God has exceeded this abundantly, so that I see thee despising all earthly felicity, made His servant—what do I do here?"

[5] Rom. viii. 23.
[6] Wisd. vii. 27.
[7] Matt. xxv. 21.
[8] I Cor. xv. 51.

ST. JOHN OF THE CROSS/Advice to the Religious

Cautions

which any who would be a true religious and would quickly attain to perfection must needs bear ever in mind. Addressed to the Carmelite Nuns of Beas.

The religious who desires to attain quickly to holy recollection, silence, spiritual detachment and poverty of spirit, wherein is enjoyed the peaceful refreshment of the Holy Spirit and whereby the soul reaches union with God, and is freed from the hindrances of all creatures of this world, and is defended from the wiles and deceits of the devil and is disencumbered of itself, must needs practise the following instructions.

With habitual care and with no further labour or other kind of exercise, failing not of his own part to do that which his state enjoins on him, he will progress very quickly to great perfection, gaining all the virtues together and attaining to holy peace.

To this end it must first be noted that the evils which the soul receives come from the enemies aforementioned—namely, the world, the devil and the flesh. The world is the least difficult enemy. The devil is the hardest to understand. The flesh is the most tenacious of all and its assaults continue for so long as the old man exists.

In order to conquer any of these three enemies, it is necessary to conquer them all three; and, if one is weakened, the other two are weakened: and, when all three are conquered, no more war remains in the soul.

Against the World

In order to free thyself perfectly from the evil which the world can do to thee, thou shalt use three cautions.

CAUTION THE FIRST

The first caution is that for all persons thou shalt have equal love and equal forgetfulness, whether they be thy relatives

Reprinted from Saint John of the Cross, *Complete Works.* Translated from the critical edition of P. Silverio de Santa Teresa, C.D., and edited by E. Allison Peers, Vol. III (London: Burns Oates & Washbourne Ltd., 1935), pp. 220-226.

or no; withdrawing thy heart from these as much as from those; more so, indeed, in some ways, from thy kinsmen, lest flesh and blood quicken with natural love, which is ever alive among kinsfolk, the which thou must ever mortify for spiritual perfection. Hold them all as strangers to thee; in this way thou dost serve them better than by setting upon them the affection which thou owest to God. Love not one person better than another or thou shall go astray, for he whom God loves best is worthy to be loved best, and thou knowest not who it is that God best loveth. But if thou are equally forgetful of them all, as befits thee for holy recollection, thou shalt free thyself from going astray with respect to them, whether little or much. Think not of them at all, neither good things nor evil things; flee from them in so far as thou fairly canst. And, if thou observe not this, thou hast not learned to be a religious, neither shalt be able to attain to holy recollection, nor to free thyself from the imperfections that come to thee hereby. And if in this matter thou desire to allow thyself a certain licence, the devil will deceive thee in one way or in another, or thou wilt deceive thyself, under some colour of good or of evil. In doing that which has been described lies security, for in no other way canst thou free thyself from the imperfections and evils which the soul obtains from creatures.

CAUTION THE SECOND

The second caution against the world is with respect to temporal blessings. Herein it is needful, if thou wouldst truly free thyself from this kind of evil and moderate the excesses of thine appetite, to abhor all kinds of possession and to have no care for them—neither as to food, nor clothing, nor any other created thing, nor as to the morrow. Thou must direct this care to something higher, namely, to seeking the kingdom of God—that is, to not failing God—and the rest, as His Majesty says, shall be added unto us. For He that cares for the beasts will not be forgetful of thee. In this way shalt thou attain silence and peace in the senses.

CAUTION THE THIRD

The third caution is very necessary if thou art to learn to guard thyself in the convent from all evil with respect to the religious. Many, through not observing it, have not only lost the peace and blessing of their souls, but have fallen, and habitually fall, into many evils and sins. This caution is that thou shouldst keep thyself with all diligence from setting thy thoughts upon what happens in the community, and still more from speaking of it. This may concern, or may have concerned, some religious in particular: thou shalt say naught of his character, or of his manner of life, or of any of his business, however grave it be, either under pretext of zeal or of desire to remedy matters, save to that person to whom it is right that thou shouldst speak of it, and this at its proper time. Nor shouldst thou ever be shocked or marvel at aught that thou seest or hearest, but shouldst strive to keep thy soul in forgetfulness of it all.

For if thou desirest to consider any of these things, even though thou live among angels, many of them will seem to thee to be amiss, since thou wilt not understand the substance of them. Take thou here for an example Lot's wife, who, because she was troubled at the perdition of the Sodomites and looked backward to see what was happening, was punished by God, who turned her into a pillar of salt. By this understand that, even though thou live among devils, God wills thee to live among them in such a way that thou look not back in thy thought at their business, but abandon them wholly, striving to keep thy soul pure and sincere with God, undisturbed by thoughts either of one thing or of another. Thou mayest take it for certain that convents and communities will never be without some occasion of stumbling, since there are never wanting devils who strive to overthrow the saints, and God permits this in order to exercise them and prove them. And if thou keep not thyself, as has been said, as though thou wert not in the house, thus canst never be a religious, however much thou doest, nor attain to holy detachment and recollection, nor free thyself from the evils that lie herein. For, if thou do not this, however good may be thy intention and however great thy zeal, the devil will entrap thee either in one place or in another, and thou art already securely entrapped when thou dost permit thy soul to be distracted in any of these ways. Remember that which is said by the apostle S. James: If any man thinketh himself to be religious and bridleth not his tongue, that man's religion is vain. This is to be understood no less of inward speech than of outward.

Against the Devil

These three cautions should be used by him that aspires to perfection, in order to free himself from the devil, his second enemy. To this end it must be noted that, among the many wiles used by the devil to deceive spiritual persons, the most ordinary is that of deceiving them under an appearance of what is good and not under an appearance of what is evil; for he knows that if they recognize evil they will scarcely touch it. And thus thou must ever have misgivings concerning that which seems good, when it is not commanded thee by obedience. Security and success in this matter come from taking proper counsel in it.

CAUTION THE FIRST

Let the first caution, then, be that, save when thou art so commanded by obligation, thou be moved to nothing, however good and full of charity it may seem, whether it be for thyself or for anyone within or without the house, without being ordered by obedience. In observing this thou gainest merit and security. Avoid attachment and thou shalt flee from the devil and from evils of which thou knowest not, but whereof God shall call for an account of thee in His time. And if thou observe not this caution, both in little things and in great, however successful thou seem to be, thou canst not fail, either to a small or to a great degree, to be deceived by the devil. And, although thou do no worse than fail to be ruled in all things by obedience, thou strayest and art therefore to be blamed; for God prefers obedience to sacrifice, and the actions of a religious are not his own but belong to obedience, and if thou withdraw them from obedience, thou wilt have to account them as lost.

CAUTION THE SECOND

Let the second caution be that thou never consider thy superior as less than if he were God, be the superior who he may, for to thee he stands in the place of God. And observe that the devil, the enemy of humility, meddles herein greatly. If thou consider thy superior as has been said, thou gainest and profitest greatly, but otherwise thy loss and harm are great. Keep thyself, therefore, with great vigilance from considering his character, his ways or his habits or any of his other characteristics, for, if thou do this, thou wilt do thyself the harm of exchanging Divine obedience for human, by being moved, or not being moved, only by the visible characteristics of thy superior, instead of by the invisible God Whom thou servest in his person. And thy obedience will be vain, or will be the more unfruitful, if thou take offence at any unpleasing characteristic in thy superior, or rejoice when thou findest him good and pleasant. For I tell thee that the devil has ruined the perfection of a great multitude of religious by causing them to consider these characteristics, and their obedience is of very little worth in the eyes of God, because they have considered these things and not paid sole respect to obedience. If thou strive not until thou come to regard no one superior as of more importance than another, in so far as thine own feelings are concerned, thou canst in no wise become a spiritual person nor keep thy vows well.

CAUTION THE THIRD

The third caution aimed directly against the devil is that thou strive ever to humble thy heart in word and in deed, rejoicing at the good of others as at thine own, and desiring that others be preferred to thyself in all things, and this with all thy heart. And in this way shalt thou overcome evil with good and shalt cast the devil far from thee and shalt have joy of heart; and strive thou to practise this most with respect to those who least attract thee. And know that, if thou practise it not thus, thou shalt not attain to true charity neither shalt make progress therein. And love ever to be taught by all men rather than to desire to teach him that is least of all.

Against the Flesh

Three further cautions should be observed by him that desires to conquer himself and his sensual nature, which is his third enemy.

CAUTION THE FIRST

The first caution is that thou shouldst understand that thou hast come to the convent only that all may fashion thee and try thee. And thus, in order to free thyself from the imperfections and disturbances that may arise from the temperaments and habits of the religious, and to pluck advantage from every happening, thou must think that all who are in the convent are workmen who are to try thee, as in truth they are. For some have to fashion thee in thy words, others in thy deeds and others in thy thoughts; and thou must be subject to them in all things even as an image is subject to him that fashions it and to him that paints it and to him that gilds it. And, if thou observe not this, thou shalt not be able to overcome thy sensual nature and thy feelings, neither shalt thou be able to conduct thyself well in the convent with the religious, nor shall attain holy peace nor free thyself from many evils and occasions of stumbling.

CAUTION THE SECOND

The second caution is that thou never fail to perform any good works because of the lack of pleasure or sweetness that thou findest therein, if it be fit that they should be done in the service of Our Lord; neither perform thou them only for the sweetness and pleasure that they give thee. On the contrary, it behooves thee equally to perform these and others that are distasteful to thee, for otherwise it is impossible for thee to gain constancy and overcome thy weakness.

CAUTION THE THIRD

Let the third caution be that the spiritual man must never in his exercises set his eyes upon that which is delectable in them and thence derive attachment to them, and perform them for this reason only; neither must he flee from that which is displeasing to him in them, but rather he must seek that which is toilsome and distasteful. In this way he bridles his sensual nature; and if thou do otherwise thou wilt neither lose the love of thyself, nor wilt win and attain the love of God.

C. G. JUNG / Psychology and Religion

IT WILL be my task to show what psychology, or rather that special branch of medical psychology which I represent, has to do with or to say about religion. Since religion is incontestably one of the earliest and most universal activities of the human mind, it is self-evident that any kind of psychology which touches upon the psychological structure of human personality cannot avoid at least observing the fact that religion is not only a sociological or historical phenomenon, but also something of considerable personal concern to a great number of individuals.

Notwithstanding the fact that I have often been called a philosopher, I am an empiricist and adhere to the phenomenological standpoint. I trust that it does not collide with the principles of scientific empiricism if one occasionally makes certain reflections which go beyond a mere accumulation and classification of experience. As a matter of fact I believe that an experience is not even possible without reflection, because "experience" is a process of assimilation, without which there could be no understanding. As this statement indicates, I approach psychological matters from a scientific and not from a philosophical standpoint. In as much as religion has a very important psychological aspect, I am dealing with it from a purely empirical point of view, that is, I restrict myself to the observation of phenomena and I refrain from any application of metaphysical or philosophical considerations. I do not deny the validity of other considerations, but I cannot claim to be competent to apply them correctly. I am aware that most people believe they know all there is to be known about psychology, because they think that psychology is nothing but what they know of themselves. But I am afraid psychology is a good deal more than that. While having little to do with philosophy, it has much to do with empirical facts, many of which are not easily accessible to the average experience. . . .

Since I am going to present a rather unusual argument, I cannot assume that my audience is completely aware of the methodological standpoint of that kind of psychology which I represent. This standpoint is exclusively phenomenological, that is, it is concerned with occurrences, events, experiences, in a word, with facts. Its truth is a fact and not a judgment. Speaking for instance of the motive of the virgin birth, psychology is only concerned with the fact that there is such an idea, but it is not concerned with the question whether such an idea is true or false in any other sense. It is psychologically true in as much as it exists. Psychological existence is subjective in so far as an idea occurs in only one individual. But it is objective in so far as it is established by a society—by a consensus gentium.

This point of view is the same as that of natural science. Psychology deals with ideas and other mental contents as zoology for instance deals with different species of animals. An elephant is true because it exists. The elephant, moreover, is neither a conclusion nor a statement nor a subjective judgment of a creator. It is a phenomenon. But we are so used to the idea that psychical events are wilful and arbitrary products, even inventions of the human creator, that we can hardly liberate ourselves from the prejudiced view that the psyche and its contents are nothing but our own arbitrary invention or the more or less illusory product of assumption and judgment. The fact is that certain ideas exist almost everywhere and at all times and they can even spontaneously create themselves quite apart from migration and tradition. They are not made by the individual, but they rather happen—they even force themselves upon the individual's consciousness. This is not platonic philosophy but empirical psychology.

In speaking of religion I must make clear from the start what I mean by that term. Religion, as the Latin word denotes, is a careful and scrupulous observation of what Rudolf Otto[1] aptly termed the "numinosum," that is, a dynamic existence or effect, not caused by an arbitrary act of will. On the contrary, it seizes and controls the human subject, which is always rather its victim than its creator. The numinosum is an involuntary condition of the subject, whatever its cause may be. At all events, religious teaching as well as the consensus gentium always and everywhere explains this condition as being due to a cause external to the individual. The numinosum is either a quality of a visible object or the influence of an invisible presence causing a peculiar alteration of consciousness. This is, at least, the general rule.

There are, however, certain exceptions when it comes to the question of practice or ritual. A great many ritualistic performances are carried out for the sole purpose of producing at will the effect of the numinosum by certain devices of a magic nature, such as invocation, incantation, sacrifice, meditation and other yoga practices, self-inflicted tortures of various descriptions and so forth. But a religious belief in an external and objective divine cause always precedes any such performance. The Catholic church, for instance, administers the sacraments with the purpose of bestowing their spiritual blessings upon the believer; but since this act would amount to enforcing the presence of divine grace by an indubitably magic procedure, it is logically argued that nobody is able to compel divine grace to be present in the sacramental act, but that it is nevertheless inevitably present, the sacrament being a divine institution which God would not have caused to be if he had not had it in mind to support it.[2]

Religion appears to me to be a peculiar attitude of the human mind, which could be formulated in accordance with the original use of the term "religio," that is, a careful consideration and observation of certain dynamic factors, understood to be "powers," spirits, demons, gods, laws, ideas, ideals or whatever name man has given to such factors as he has found in his world powerful, dangerous or helpful enough to be taken into careful consideration, or grand, beautiful and meaningful enough to be devoutly adored and loved. In colloquial language one often says of somebody who is enthusiastically interested in a certain pursuit, that he is almost "religiously devoted" to his cause; William James, for instance, remarks that a scientist often has no creed, but "his temper is devout."[3]

I want to make clear that by the term "religion"[4] I do not mean a creed. It is, however, true that on the one hand every confession is originally based upon the experience of the numinosum and on the other hand upon Πίστις, the loyalty, trust, and confidence toward a definitely experienced numinous effect and the subsequent alteration of consciousness: the conversion of Paul is a striking example of this. "Religion," it might be said, is the term that designates the attitude peculiar to a consciousness which has been altered by the experience of the numinosum.

Creeds are codified and dogmatized forms of original religious experience.[5] The contents of the experience have become sanctified and usually congealed in a rigid, often elaborate, structure. The practice and the reproduction of the original experience have become a ritual and an unchangeable institution. This does not necessarily mean a lifeless petrification. On the contrary it can become the form of religious experience for ages of time and for millions of people without there being any vital necessity for alterations. Although the Catholic church has often been blamed for a particular rigidity, it admits nevertheless that the dogma has its life and hence is capable of undergoing change and development. Even the number of dogmas is unlimited and can be augmented in the course of time. The same holds true of the ritual. Yet all changes and developments are confined within the frame of the originally experienced facts, thereby involving a particular kind of dogmatic content and emotional value. Even Protestantism —which has surrendered apparently to an almost unlimited liberation from dogmatic tradition and from codified ritual and has thus split into more than four hundred denominations—even Protestantism is bound at least to be Christian and to express itself within the frame of the conviction that God has revealed himself in Christ, who suffered for mankind. This is a definite frame, with definite contents, which cannot be coupled with or amplified by Buddhistic or Islamic ideas and emotions. Yet it is unquestionable that not only Buddha or Mohammed or Confucius or Zarathustra represents religious phenomena, but that Mithras, Attis, Kybele, Mani, Hermes and many exotic cults do so as well. The psychologist, in as much as he assumes a scientific attitude, has to disregard the claim of every creed to be the unique and eternal truth. He must keep his eye on the human side of the religious problem, in that he is concerned with the original religious experience quite apart from what the creeds have made of it.

Being a doctor and a specialist in nervous and mental diseases my point of departure is not any creed, but the psychology of the homo religiosus, the man who takes into account and carefully observes certain factors which influence him and, through him, his general condition. It is easy to denominate and define those factors according to historical tradition or anthropological knowledge, but to do the same thing from the standpoint of psychology is an uncommonly difficult task. What I can contribute to the question of religion is derived entirely from my practical experience, both with my patients and with so-called normal beings. As our experience with people depends considerably upon what we do with them, I can see no other way of proceeding than to give you at least a general idea of the line I take in my professional work.

Since every neurosis is connected with man's most intimate life, there will always be some hesitation when a patient has to give a complete account of all the circumstances and complications which have originally led him into a morbid condition. But why shouldn't he be able to talk freely? Why should he be afraid or shy or prudish? The reason is that he is "carefully observing" certain external factors which form important constituents of what one calls public opinion or respectability or reputation. And even if he trusts his doctor, and if he is no longer shy of him, he will be reluctant or even afraid to admit certain things to *himself,* as if it were dangerous to become conscious of himself. One is usually afraid of things which seem to be overpowering. But is there anything in man that is stronger than himself? We should not forget that any neurosis means a corresponding amount of demoralization. In so far as man is neurotic, he has lost confidence in himself. A neurosis is a humiliating defeat and is felt as such by people who are not entirely unconscious of their own psychology. And one is defeated by something "unreal." Doctors may have assured the patient, long ago, that there is nothing the matter with him, that he does not suffer from a real heart disease or from a real cancer. His symptoms are quite imaginary. The more he believes that he is a "malade imaginaire," the more a feeling of inferiority permeates his whole personality. "If my symptoms are imaginary," he will say, "where have I caught such a confounded imagination and why should I cherish such a perfect nuisance?" It is indeed pathetic to have an intelligent man almost imploringly assure you that he is suffering from an intestinal cancer and declare at the same time in a despondent voice that of course he knows his cancer to be a merely imaginary affair.

Our usual materialistic conception of the psyche is, I am afraid, not particularly helpful in neurotic cases. If only the soul were endowed with a subtle body, then one could say, at least, that this breath or smoke body was suffering from a real though somewhat airy cancer, in much the same way as the gross material body could be subject to a similar ailment. There would, at least, be something real. Medicine therefore feels a strong dislike toward anything of a psychical nature—either the body is ill or there is nothing the matter. And if you cannot prove that the body is really diseased, that is because our present means do not enable the physician to find the true nature of the undoubtedly organic trouble.

But what is the psyche after all? A materialistic prejudice explains it as a merely epiphenomenal by-product of organic processes in the brain. Any psychic disturbance must be an organic or physical disorder which is undiscoverable only because of the insufficiency of our actual diagnostic means. The undeniable connection between psyche and brain gives this point of view a certain strength, but not enough to make it an unshakable truth. We do not know whether there is a real disturbance of the organic processes of the brain in a case of neurosis, and if there are disorders of an endocrine nature it is impossible to say whether they are not effects rather than causes.

On the other hand it is indubitable that the real causes of neuroses are psychological. It is indeed very difficult to imagine that an organic or physical disorder can be cured in a moment by a mere confession. But I have seen a case of hysterical fever, with a temperature as high as 102°, which was cured in a few minutes by a confession of the psychological cause. And how should we explain cases of manifest physical diseases that are influenced and even cured by a mere discussion of certain painful psychological conflicts? I have seen a case of psoriasis, extending practically over the whole body, which was reduced by nine-tenths after a few weeks of psychological treatment. In another case, a patient had recently undergone an operation for distention of the colon, forty centimeters of which had been removed, but this was followed by another extraordinary distention of the colon. The patient was desperate and refused to permit a second operation, though the surgeon thought it indispensable. As soon as certain intimate psychological facts were discovered, the colon began to function normally.

Such experiences, which are by no means rare, make it exceedingly difficult to believe that the psyche is nothing, or that an imaginary fact is unreal. It is only not there where a nearsighted mind seeks it. It is existent but not in a physical form. It is an almost ridiculous prejudice to assume that existence can only be physical. As a matter of fact the only form of existence we know of immediately is psychic. We might well say, on the contrary, that physical existence is merely an inference, since we know of matter only in so far as we perceive psychic images transmitted by the senses.

We are surely making a great mistake when we forget this simple yet fundamental truth. If a neurosis should have no other cause at all than imagination, it would, none the less, be a very real thing. If a man imagined that I was his arch-enemy and killed me, I should be dead on account of mere imagination. Imaginations do exist and they may be just as real and just as obnoxious or dangerous as physical conditions. I even believe that psychical dangers are much more dangerous than epidemics or earthquakes. Not even the medieval epidemics of bubonic plague or smallpox killed as many people as certain differences of opinion in 1914 or certain political ideals in Russia.

Although our mind cannot grasp its own form of existence, owing to the lack of the Archimedean point outside, it nevertheless exists. Psyche is existent, it is even existence itself.

What shall we now reply to our patient with the imaginary cancer? I would tell him: "Yes, my friend, you are really suffering from a cancer-like thing, you really harbor a deadly evil which, however, will not kill your body, because it is imaginary. But it will eventually kill your soul. It has already spoilt and has even poisoned your human relations and your personal happiness and it will go on thus ever increasing until it has swallowed your whole psychic existence. So that in the end you will not be human any more, but will be an evil destructive tumor."

It is obvious to our man that he is not the originator of his morbid imagination, although his theoretical mind will certainly suggest that he is the owner and maker of his own imagination. If one is suffering from a real cancer, one never believes oneself to be the responsible originator of such an evil, despite the fact that the cancer is in one's own body. But when it comes to the psyche we instantly feel a kind of responsibility, as if we were the makers of our psychical conditions. This prejudice is of relatively recent date. Not very long ago even highly civilized people believed that psychic agencies could influence our mind and feeling. There were ghosts, wizards and witches, demons and angels, and even gods, that could produce certain psychological alterations in man. In former times the man with the idea that he had cancer might have felt quite differently about his idea. He would probably have assumed that somebody had worked witchcraft against him or that he was possessed. He never would have thought himself to be the originator of such a phantasy.

As a matter of fact I assume that his cancer idea is a spontaneous growth, originating in that part of the psyche which is not identical with consciousness. It appears to be an autonomous development intruding upon consciousness. Of consciousness one might say that it is our own psychical existence, but the cancer is *its* own psychical existence, independent of ourselves. This statement seems to formulate the observable facts completely. If we submit such a case to an association experiment,[6] we soon discover that the man is not master in his own house. His reactions will be delayed, altered, suppressed or replaced by autonomous intruders. There will be a number of stimulus words which cannot be answered by his conscious intention. They will be answered by certain autonomous contents, which are very often unconscious even to the test person. In our case we will certainly discover answers which come from the psychic complex at the root of the cancer idea. Whenever a stimulus word touches something connected with the hidden complex, the reaction of the ego consciousness will be disturbed, or even replaced, by an answer coming from the complex. It is just as if the complex were an autonomous being capable of interfering with the intentions of the ego. Complexes indeed behave like secondary or partial personalities in possession of a mental life of their own.

Many complexes are merely split from consciousness because the latter preferred to get rid of them by repression. But there are others that have never been in consciousness before and that therefore could never have been arbitrarily repressed. They grow out of the unconscious mind and invade consciousness with their weird and unassailable convictions and impulses. Our patient's case belonged in the latter category. Despite his culture and intelligence, he was a helpless victim of something which obsessed or possessed him. He was utterly unable to help himself in any way against the demoniacal power of his morbid idea. It overgrew him indeed like a carcinoma. One day the idea had appeared and from then on it remained unshakably; there were only short free intervals.

The existence of such cases explains, to a certain extent, why people are afraid of becoming conscious of themselves. There might really be something behind the screen—one never knows—and thus people prefer "to take into account and to observe carefully" factors external to their consciousness. In most people there is a sort of primitive δεισιδαιμονία concerning the possible contents of the unconscious. Beyond all natural shyness, shame and tact, there is a secret fear of the unknown "perils of the soul." Of course one is reluctant to admit such a ridiculous fear. But one should realize that this fear is by no means unjustifiable; on the contrary, it is only too well founded. We are never sure that a new idea will not seize either upon ourselves or upon our neighbors. We know from modern as well as from ancient history that such ideas can be rather strange, so peculiar, indeed, that not everybody can agree with them. The result may be that all dissenters, no matter how well meaning or reasonable they are, get burnt alive or have their heads cut off or are disposed of in masses by the more modern machine gun. We cannot even calm ourselves with the idea that such things belong to a remote past. Unfortunately they seem to belong not only to the present moment, but, quite particularly, to the future. "Homo homini lupus" is a sad, yet eternal truism. There is indeed reason enough why man should be afraid of those nonpersonal forces dwelling in the unconscious mind. We are blissfully unconscious of those forces because they never, or almost never, appear in our personal dealings and under ordinary circumstances. But if, on the other hand, people crowd together and form a mob, then the dynamics of the collective man are set free—beasts or demons which lie dormant in every person till he is part of a mob. Man in the crowd is unconsciously lowered to an inferior moral and intellectual level, to that level which is always there, below the threshold of consciousness, ready to break forth as soon as it is stimulated through the formation of a crowd.

It is, to my mind, a fatal mistake to consider the human psyche as a merely personal affair and to explain it exclusively from a personal point of view. Such a mode of explanation is only applicable to the individual in his ordinary everyday occupations and relationships. If, however, some slight trouble occurs, perhaps in the form of an unforeseen and somewhat extraordinary event, instantly instinctive forces are called up, forces which appear to be wholly unexpected, new, and even strange. They can no longer be explained by personal motives, being comparable rather to certain primitive occurrences like panics at solar eclipses and such things. To explain the murderous outburst of Bolshevistic ideas by a personal father complex appears to me as singularly inadequate.

The change of character that is brought about by the uprush of collective forces is amazing. A gentle and reasonable being can be transformed into a maniac or a savage beast. One is always inclined to lay the blame on external circumstances, but nothing could explode in us if it had not been there. As a matter of fact, we are always living upon a volcano and there is, as far as we know, no human means of protection against a possible outburst which will destroy everybody within its reach. It is certainly a good thing to preach reason and common sense, but what if your audience is a lunatic asylum or a crowd in a collective seizure? There is not much difference either, because the madman as well as the mob is moved by nonpersonal, overwhelming forces.

As a matter of fact, it needs as little as a neurosis to conjure up a force that cannot be dealt with by reasonable means. Our cancer case shows clearly how impotent human reason and intellect are against the most palpable nonsense. I always advise my patients to take such obvious but invincible nonsense as the manifestations of a power and a meaning not yet understood. Experience has taught me that it is a much more effective method of procedure to take such a fact seriously and to seek for a suitable explanation. But an explanation is suitable only when it produces a hypothesis equal to the morbid effect. Our case is confronted with a will power and a suggestion more than equal to anything his consciousness can put against it. In this precarious situation it would be bad strategy to convince the patient that he is somehow, though in a highly incomprehensible way, at the back of his own symptom, secretly inventing and supporting it. Such a suggestion would instantly paralyze his fighting spirit, and he would get demoralized. It is much better if he understands that his complex is an autonomous power directed against his conscious personality. Moreover, such an explanation fits the actual facts much better than a reduction to personal motives. An apparent personal motivation does exist, but it is not made by intention, it just happens to the patient.

When in the Babylonian Epos Gilgamesh's arrogance and ὕβρις defy the gods, they invent and create a man equal in strength to Gilgamesh in order to check the hero's unlawful ambition. The very same thing has happened to our patient: he is a thinker who has settled, or is always going to settle, the world by the power of his intellect and reason. His ambition has at least succeeded in carving his own personal fate. He has forced everything under the inexorable law of his reason, but somewhere nature escaped and came back with a vengeance in the form of perfectly unassailable nonsense, the cancer idea. This clever device was formed by the unconscious mind to keep him on a merciless and cruel leash. It was the worst blow which could be given to all his reasonable ideals and above all to his belief in the all-powerful human will. Such an obsession can only occur in a person who makes a habitual misuse of reason and intellect for an egotistical power purpose.

Gilgamesh, however, escaped the revenge of the gods. He had warning dreams to which he paid attention. They showed him how he could overcome his foe. Our patient, living in an age where the gods have become extinct and are even in bad repute, also had such dreams, but he did not listen to them. How could an intelligent man be so superstitious as to take dreams seriously! The very common prejudice against dreams is but one of the symptoms of a far more serious undervaluation of the human soul in general. The marvelous development of science and technics has been counterbalanced on the other side by an appalling lack of wisdom and introspection. It is true that our religious teaching speaks of an immortal soul; but it has very few kind words for the actual human psyche, which would go straight to eternal damnation if it were not for a special act of Divine Grace. Those two important factors are largely responsible for the general undervaluation of the psyche, but not entirely. Much older than those relatively recent developments are the primitive fear of and aversion to everything that borders on the unconscious.

Consciousness must have been a very precarious thing in its beginnings. In relatively primitive societies we can still observe how easily consciousness is lost. One of the "perils of the soul"[7] is, for instance, the loss of a soul. This is a case of a part of the psyche becoming unconscious again. Another example is the amok condition,[8] the equivalent of the berserk condition in the Germanic saga.[9] This is a more or less complete trance, often accompanied by devastating social effects. Even an ordinary emotion can cause a considerable loss of consciousness. Primitives therefore cherish elaborate forms of politeness, speaking with a hushed voice, laying down their weapons, crouching, bowing the head, showing the palms. Even our own forms of politeness still show a "religious" observation of possible psychical dangers. We propitiate the fates by wishing magically a good day. It is not good form to keep the left hand in your pocket or behind your back when shaking hands. If you want to be particularly propitiating you use both hands. Before people of great authority we bow with uncovered head, i.e., we offer our head unprotected, in order to propitiate the powerful one, who might quite easily fall suddenly a prey to a fit of uncontrollable violence. In war dances primitives can become so excited that they may shed blood.

The life of the primitive is filled with constant regard for the ever-lurking possibility of psychical dangers, and the attempts and procedures employed to diminish the risks are very numerous. The creation of tabooed areas is an external evidence of this fact. The innumerable taboos are delimited psychical areas, meticulously and fearfully observed. I made a terrific mistake once when I was with a tribe on the southern slopes of Mt. Elgon. I wanted to inquire about the ghost houses I frequently found in the woods and during a palaver I mentioned the word "selelteni" meaning "ghost." Instantly everybody was silent and painfully embarrassed. They all looked away from me because I had spoken aloud a carefully hushed-up word, and had thus invited most dangerous consequences. I had to change the subject in order to be able to continue the meeting. The same men assured me that they never had dreams; they were the prerogative of the chief and of the medicine man. The medicine man then confessed to me that he no longer had any dreams, for they had the District Commissioner now instead. "Since the English are in the country we have no dreams any more," he said. "The District Commissioner knows everything about war and diseases, and about where we have got to live." This strange statement is based upon the fact that dreams were formerly the supreme political guide, the voice of "mungu." Therefore it would have been unwise for an ordinary man to suggest that he had dreams.

Dreams are the voice of the Unknown, that ever threatens with new schemes, new dangers, sacrifices, warfare and other troublesome things. An African negro once dreamt that his enemies had taken him prisoner and burnt him alive. The next day he called his relatives together and implored them to burn him. They consented to do so to the extent that they bound his feet together and put them in the fire. He was of course badly crippled but had escaped his foes.[10]

There are any amount of creeds and ceremonies that exist for the sole purpose of forming a defense against the unexpected, dangerous tendencies of the unconscious. The peculiar fact that the dream is the divine voice and messenger and yet an unending source of trouble, does not disturb the primitive mind. We still find obvious remnants of this primitive fact in the psychology of the Jewish prophets.[11] Often enough they hesitate to listen to the voice. And it was, we must admit, rather hard on a pious man like Hosea to marry the prostitute in order to obey the Lord's command. Since the dawn of mankind there has been a marked tendency to delimit the unruly and arbitrary "supernatural" influence by definite forms and laws. And this process has gone on in history by the multiplication of rites, institutions and creeds. In the last two thousand years we find the institution of the Christian church assuming a mediating and protective function between these influences and man. It is not denied in medieval ecclesiastical writings that a divine influx could take place in dreams, for instance, but this view is not exactly encouraged and the church reserves the right to decide whether a revelation is to be considered authentic or not.[12] In spite of the fact that the church recognizes the undeniable emanation of certain dreams from God, it is disinclined, even positively averse, to any serious occupation with dreams, while admitting that some might contain an immediate revelation. Thus the change in mental attitudes which has taken place in recent centuries is, from this point of view at least, not wholly unwelcome to the church, because it has effectively discouraged the former introspective attitude which was favorable to a serious consideration of dreams and inner experiences.

Protestantism, having pulled down many a wall which had been carefully erected by the church, began immediately to experience the disintegrating and schismatic effect of individual revelation. As soon as the dogmatic fence was broken down and as soon as the ritual had lost the authority of its efficiency, man was confronted with an inner experience, without the protection and the guidance of a dogma and a ritual which are the unparalleled quintessence of Christian as well as of pagan religious experience. Protestantism has, in the main, lost all the finer shades of the dogma: the mass, the confession, the greater part of the liturgy and the sacrificial importance of priesthood.

I must emphasize the point that this statement is not a judgment of values and has no intention of being one. I merely state the facts. Protestantism has, however, intensified the authority of the Bible as a substitute for the lost authority of the church. But as history has shown, one can interpret certain biblical texts in many ways. Nor has the scientific criticism of the New Testament been very helpful in enhancing the divine character of the holy writings. It is also a fact that under the influence of a so-called scientific enlightenment great masses of educated people have either left the church or have become profoundly indifferent to it. If they were all dull rationalists or neurotic intellectuals the loss would not be regrettable. But many of them are religious people, only incapable of agreeing with the actually existing forms of creed. If this were not so, one could hardly explain the remarkable effect of the Buchman movement on the more or less educated Protestant classes. The Catholic who has turned his back on the church usually develops a secret or manifest inclination toward atheism, whereas the Protestant follows, if possible, a sectarian movement. The absolutism of the Catholic church seems to demand an equally absolute negation, while Protestant relativism permits variations.

It may perhaps be thought that I have gone a bit far into the history of Christianity for no other purpose than to explain the prejudice against dreams and individual inner experience. But what I have just said might have been a part of my conversation with our cancer patient. I told him that it would be better to take his obsession seriously instead of reviling it as pathological nonsense. But to take it seriously would mean acknowledging it as a sort of diagnostic information of the fact that, in a psyche which really existed, trouble had arisen in the form of a cancer-like growth. "But," he will certainly ask, "what could that growth be?" And I shall answer: "I do not know," as indeed I do not. Although, as I mentioned before, it is surely a compensatory or complementary unconscious development, nothing is yet known about its specific nature or about its content. It is a spontaneous manifestation of the unconscious mind, based upon contents which are not to be found in consciousness.

My patient is now very curious how I shall set about getting at those contents which form the root of the obsession. I then inform him, at the risk of shocking him severely, that his dreams will provide us with all the necessary information. We will take them as if they issued from an intelligent, purposive and, as it were, personal source. This is of course a bold hypothesis and at the same time an adventure, because we are going to give extraordinary credit to a discreditable entity, whose very existence is still denied by not a few contemporary psychologists as well as by philosophers. A famous anthropologist, to whom I had demonstrated my way of proceeding, made the typical remark: "That's all very interesting indeed, but dangerous." Yes, I admit, it is dangerous, just as dangerous as a neurosis. When you want to cure a neurosis, you have to risk something. To do something without risk is merely ineffectual, as we know only too well. A surgical operation for cancer is a risk too and yet it is what has to be done. For the sake of a better understanding I have often felt tempted to advise my patients to conceive of the psyche as of a subtle body, in which subtle tumors can grow. The prejudiced belief that the psyche is unimaginable and consequently less than air or that it is a more or less philosophic system of logical concepts, is so great that, when people are not conscious of certain contents, they assume that they do not exist. There is no confidence and no belief in a reliable psychical functioning outside consciousness, and dreams are thought to be only ridiculous. Under such conditions my proposal arouses the worst suspicions. And indeed I have heard every conceivable argument under the sun that man has ever invented used against the vague specters of dreams.

Yet in dreams we find, without any profound analysis, the same conflicts and complexes whose existence can also be ascertained by the association test. Moreover, those complexes form an integral part of the existing neurosis. We have, therefore, reason to believe that dreams can give us at least as much information about the content of a neurosis as the association test. As a matter of fact they give very much more. The symptom is like the shoot above ground, yet the main plant is an extended rhizoma underground. The rhizoma represents the content of a neurosis; it is the matrix of complexes, of symptoms and of dreams. We have every reason, even, to believe that dreams mirror exactly the underground processes of the psyche. And if we get there, we literally get at the "roots" of the disease.

As it is not my intention to go further into the psychopathology of neuroses, I propose to choose another case as an example of how dreams reveal the unknown inner facts of the psyche and of what these facts consist. The dreamer is also an intellectual, of remarkable intelligence and learning. He was neurotic and was seeking my help because he felt that his neurosis had become overpowering and was slowly but surely undermining his morale. Fortunately his intellectual integrity had not yet suffered and he had the free use of his fine intelligence. On account of that I set him the task of observing and recording his dreams himself. The dreams were not analyzed or explained to him and it was only very much later that we began with their analysis. Thus the dreams I am going to demonstrate have not been tampered with at all. They represent an entirely uninfluenced natural sequence of events. The patient had never read psychology, not to speak of analytical psychology.

Since the series consists of over four hundred dreams, I could not possibly give an impression of the whole material; but I have published a selection of seventy-four of these dreams containing motives of a peculiar religious interest.[13] The dreamer, it should be said, is a Catholic by education, but he is no longer a practicing one, nor is he interested in religious problems. He belongs to those intellectuals or scientists who would be simply amazed if anybody should saddle them with religious views of any kind. If one holds that the unconscious mind is a psychical existence independent of consciousness, a case such as that of our dreamer might be of particular interest, provided we are not mistaken in our opinion about the religious character of certain dreams. And if one lays stress on the conscious mind alone and does not credit the unconscious with an independent existence, it will be interesting to find out whether or not the dream has really derived its material from conscious contents. Should the facts be in favor of the hypothesis which includes the unconscious, one can use dreams as sources of information about the possible religious tendencies of the unconscious mind.

One cannot expect that dreams will manifestly speak of religion as we know it. There are, however, just two dreams among the four hundred that obviously deal with religion. I will now give the text which the dreamer himself had taken down.

"There are many houses which have a theatrical character, a sort of stage scenery. Somebody mentions the name of Bernard Shaw. It is also mentioned that the play which is to follow refers to a remote future. One of the houses is distinguished by a signboard with the following inscription:

This is the universal Catholic church.
It is the church of the Lord.
All those who feel themselves to be instruments of the Lord may enter.

And below in smaller letters:

The church is founded by Jesus and Paul.

—it is as if a firm boasted of its old standing. I say to my friend: 'Let us go in and have a look.' He replies: 'I do not see why many people should be together in order to have religious feelings.' But I say: 'You are a Protestant so you will never understand it.' There is a woman nodding approval. I now become aware of a bill posted on the wall of the church. It reads as follows:

'Soldiers!

'When you feel that you are under the power of the Lord avoid talking directly to him. The Lord is not accessible to words. We also recommend urgently that you should not indulge in discussions about the attributes of the Lord among yourselves. It would be fruitless, as anything of value and importance is ineffable.

'Signed: Pope . . .' (The name, however, is not decipherable.)

"We now enter the church. The interior resembles a mosque rather than a church, as a matter of fact it is particularly like the Hagia Sophia. There are no chairs, which produces a wonderful effect of space. There are also no images. There are only framed sentences on the walls (like those in the Hagia Sophia). One of these sentences reads: 'Do not flatter your benefactor.' The same woman who nodded approval to me before begins to weep and says: 'Then there is nothing left at all.' I reply: 'I think that it is perfectly all right,' but she vanishes.

"At first I am right in front of a pillar which obliterates the view, then I change my position and I see a crowd of people in front of me. I do not belong to them and I am standing alone. But I see them clearly and I also see their faces. They pronounce the following words: 'We confess that we are under the power of the Lord. The Kingdom of Heaven is within ourselves.' They repeat this thrice in a most solemn way. Then the organ plays a fugue by Bach and a choir sings. Sometimes it is music alone, sometimes the following words are repeated: 'Everything else is paper,' which means that it does not produce a living impression.

"When the music is finished the second part of the ceremony begins, as is the custom at students' meetings where the dealing with serious affairs is followed by the gay part of the gathering. There are serene and mature human beings. One walks to and fro, others talk together, they welcome each other, and wine from the episcopal seminary and other drinks are served. In the form of a toast one wishes the church a favorable development and a radio amplifier plays a ragtime melody with the refrain: 'Charles is now also in the game.' It is as if the pleasure concerning some new member of the society were to be expressed by that performance. A priest explains to me: 'These somewhat futile amusements are officially acknowledged and admitted. We must adapt a little to American methods. If you have to deal with big crowds, as we have, it is inevitable. We differ however on principle from the American churches in that we cherish an emphatically antiascetic tendency.' Whereupon I woke up with a feeling of great relief."

There are numerous works, as you know, concerning the phenomenology of dreams, but very few that deal with their psychology. This for the obvious reason that it is a most ticklish and risky business. Freud has made a courageous effort to elucidate the intricacies of dream psychology by the aid of views which he has gathered in the field of psychopathology.[14] Much as I admire the boldness of his attempt, I cannot agree with his method and its results. He explains the dream as a mere façade, behind which something has been carefully hidden. There is no doubt that neurotics hide disagreeable things, probably just as much as normal people do. But it is a serious question whether this category can be applied to such a normal and world-wide phenomenon as the dream. I am doubtful whether we can assume that a dream is something else than it appears to be. I am rather inclined to quote another Jewish authority, the Talmud, which says: "The dream is its own interpretation." In other words I take the dream for granted. The dream is such a difficult and intricate subject, that I do not dare to make any assumptions about its possible cunning. The dream is a natural event and there is no reason under the sun why we should assume that it is a crafty device to lead us astray. The dream occurs when consciousness and will are to a great extent extinguished. It seems to be a natural product which is also to be found in people who are not neurotic. Moreover, we know so little about the psychology of the dream process that we must be more than careful when we introduce elements foreign to the dream itself into its explanation.

For all these reasons I hold that our dream really speaks of religion and that it means to do so. Since the dream is elaborate and consistent it suggests a certain logic and a certain intention, that is, it is preceded by a motivation in the unconscious which finds direct expression in the dream content.

The first part of the dream is a serious statement in favor of the Catholic church. A certain Protestant point of view—that religion is an individual experience—is discouraged by the dreamer. The second, more grotesque part, is an adaptation by the church to a decidedly worldly point of view and the end is a statement in favor of an anti-ascetic tendency which would not and could not be backed up by the real church. But the dreamer's anti-ascetic priest makes it a matter of principle. Spiritualization and sublimation are emphatically Christian principles and any insistence upon the contrary would amount to a blasphemous paganism. Christianity has never been worldly nor has it ever cherished a friendly neighborliness with good wine and food, and it is more than doubtful whether the introduction of jazz music into the cult would be a particular asset. The "serene and mature" personalities, that peripatetically converse with each other in a more or less Epicurean style, remind one much more of an antique philosophic ideal, which is rather distasteful to the contemporary Christian. In the first as well as in the second part the importance of masses or crowds is stressed.

Thus the Catholic church, though it is strongly recommended, appears to be coupled with a strange pagan point of view which is irreconcilable to a fundamentally Christian attitude. The real irreconcilability does not appear in the dream. It is hushed up as it were by a "gemütliche" atmosphere, in which dangerous contrasts are blurred and blended. The Protestant point of view of an individual relationship to God is overpowered by mass organization and correspondingly collective religious feeling. The insistence upon crowds and the insinuation of a pagan ideal are peculiar parallels to things that actually happen in Europe. Everybody wondered about paganism in modern Germany, because nobody knew how to interpret Nietzsche's Dionysian experience. Nietzsche was but one case among thousands and millions of then future Germans in whose unconscious the Germanic cousin of Dionysos, that is, Wotan, developed during the Great War.[15] In the dreams of the Germans whom I treated then I could see clearly the Wotanistic revolution coming on, and in 1918 I published an article in which I pointed out the peculiar kind of new development which was to be expected in Germany.[16] Those Germans were by no means people who had studied *Thus Spake Zarathustra,* and surely those young people who started the pagan sacrifices of sheep did not know of Nietzsche's experience.[17] Therefore they called their god Wotan and not Dionysos. In Nietzsche's biography you will find irrefutable proofs that the god he originally meant was really Wotan, but, being a philologist and living in the seventies and eighties of the nineteenth century, he called him Dionysos. Looked at from a comparative standpoint, the two gods have indeed much in common.

There is apparently no opposition to collective feeling, mass religion and paganism in the whole dream of my patient, except the soon-silenced Protestant friend. There is only one curious incident deserving our attention: that is the unknown woman who first supports the eulogy of Catholicism and then suddenly weeps, saying: "Then there is nothing left at all," and vanishes without returning.

Who is this woman? She is to the dreamer a vague and unknown person, but when he had that dream he was already well acquainted with her as the "unknown woman" who had frequently appeared in previous dreams.

As this figure plays a great role in men's dreams, it carries the technical designation "anima,"[18] owing to the fact that since time immemorial man in his myths always manifested the idea of a coexistence of male and female in the same body. Such psychological intuitions were usually projected in the form of the divine Syzygia, the divine pair, or of the idea of the hermaphroditic nature of the creator.[19] Edward Maitland, the biographer of Anna Kingsford, relates in our own day an inner experience of the bisexual nature of the Deity,[20] then there is Hermetic philosophy with its hermaphrodite and its androgynous inner man,[21] the "homo Adamicus," who "though he appears in male form, always carries Eve, that is, his woman, with him, concealed in his body," as a medieval commentator of the *Hermetic Tractatus Aureus* says.[22]

The anima is presumably a psychical representation of the minority of female genes in a male body. This is all the more probable as the same figure is not to be found in the imagery of a feminine unconscious. There is a corresponding figure, however, that plays an equivalent role, yet it is not a woman's image but a man's. This male figure in a woman's psychology has been designated "animus."[23] One of the most typical manifestations of both figures is what has long been called "animosity." The anima causes illogical moods, and the animus produces irritating topics and unreasonable opinions. Both are frequent dream figures. As a rule they personify the unconscious and give it its peculiarly disagreeable or irritating character. The unconscious in itself has no such negative qualities. They appear only when it is personified by those figures and they begin to influence consciousness. Being only partial personalities they have the character either of an inferior woman or of an inferior man, hence their irritating influence. A man experiencing this will be subject to unaccountable moods and a woman will be argumentative and will produce opinions which are beside the mark.

The wholly negative reaction of the anima to the church dream points out that the dreamer's feminine, that is, his unconscious, side disagrees with his attitude. The disagreement originates with the sentence on the wall: "Do not flatter your benefactor," with which the dreamer agrees. The meaning of the sentence seems to be sound enough, so that one does not understand why the woman should feel so desperate about it. Without delving further into this mystery, we must content ourselves for the time being with the fact that there is a contradiction in the dream and that a very important minority has left the stage under vivid protest and gives no more attention to the further proceedings.

We gather, then, from the dream, that the unconscious functioning of the dreamer's mind produces a pretty flat compromise between Catholicism and a pagan joie de vivre. The product of the unconscious is manifestly not expressing a point of view or a definite opinion, it is rather a dramatic exposition of an act of deliberation. It could be formulated perhaps in the following way: "Now what about this religious business? You are a Catholic, are you not? Is that not good enough? But asceticism—well, well, even the church has to adapt a little—movies, radio, spiritual five o'clock tea and all that—why not some ecclesiastical wine and gay acquaintances?" But for some secret reason this awkward mystery woman, well known from many former dreams, seems to be deeply disappointed and quits.

I must confess I find myself in sympathy with the anima. Obviously the compromise is too cheap and too superficial, but characteristic of the dreamer as well as of many other people to whom religion does not matter very much. Religion was of no concern to my patient and he certainly never expected that it would concern him in any way. But he had come to me because of a very serious experience. Being highly rationalistic and intellectual he had found that his attitude of mind and his philosophy forsook him completely in the face of his neurosis and its demoralizing forces. He found nothing in his whole Weltanschauung that would help him to gain a sufficient control over himself. He therefore was very much in the situation of a man deserted by his heretofore cherished convictions and ideals. It is by no means an extraordinary case that under such conditions a man should return to the religion of his childhood in the hope of finding something helpful there. It was, however, not a conscious attempt or a decision to revivify former religious beliefs. He merely dreamed it; that is, his unconscious produced a peculiar statement about his religion. It is just as if the spirit and the flesh, the eternal enemies in Christian consciousness, had made peace with each other in the form of a curious mitigation of their contradictory nature. Spirituality and worldliness come together in unexpected peacefulness. The effect is somewhat grotesque and comical. The inexorable severity of the spirit seems to be undermined by an almost antique gaiety, perfumed by wine and roses. The dream certainly describes a spiritual and worldly atmosphere that dulls the sharpness of a moral conflict and swallows up in oblivion all mental pain and distress.

If this was a wish fulfilment, it was surely a conscious one, for it was precisely what the patient had already overdone. And he was not unconscious about this either, since wine was one of his most dangerous enemies. The dream is, on the contrary, an impartial statement of the patient's spiritual condition. It is the picture of a degenerate religion corrupted by worldliness and mob instincts. There is religious sentimentality instead of the numinosum of divine experience. This is the well-known characteristic of a religion that has lost the living mystery. It is easily understandable that such a religion is incapable of giving help or of having any other moral effect.

The general aspect of the dream is surely unfavorable although certain other aspects of a more positive nature are dimly visible. It rarely occurs that dreams are either exclusively positive or exclusively negative. As a rule one finds both aspects, but usually one is stronger than the other. It is obvious that such a dream provides the psychologist with enough material to raise the problem of a religious attitude. If our dream were the only one we possess, we could hardly hope to unlock its innermost meaning, but we have quite a number of dreams in our series which suggest a strange religious problem. I never, if I can help it, interpret one dream by itself. As a rule a dream belongs in a series. As there is a continuity in consciousness, despite the fact that it is regularly interrupted by sleep, there is probably also a continuity of unconscious processes and perhaps even more so than with the events of consciousness. In any case my experience is in favor of the probability that dreams are the visible links in a chain of unconscious events. If we want any light on the question of the deeper reasons for the dream, we must go back to the series and find out where it has its position in the long chain of the four hundred dreams.

We find our dream wedged in between two important dreams of an uncanny quality. The dream before reports that there is a gathering of many people and that a peculiar ceremony is taking place, apparently of magic character, with the purpose of "reconstructing the gibbon." The dream after is occupied with a similar theme—the magic transformation of animals into human beings.

Both dreams are intensely disagreeable and very alarming to the patient. Whereas the church dream manifestly moves on the surface and exhibits opinions which in other circumstances could as well be thought consciously, these two dreams are strange and remote in character and their emotional effect is such that the dreamer would avoid them if possible. As a matter of fact, the text of the second dream literally says: "If one runs away, everything is lost." This remark coincides curiously with that of the unknown woman: "Then there is nothing left at all." The inference we draw from these remarks is that the church dream was an attempt at escape from other dream thoughts of a much deeper significance. Those thoughts appear spuriously in the dreams occurring before and after it.

Notes

1. Rudolph Otto, *Das Heilige* (1917).
2. The gratia adiuvans and the gratia sanctificans are the effects of the sacramentum ex opere operato. The sacrament owes its efficiency to the fact that it is immediately instituted by Christ himself. The church is unable to connect the

rite with grace, so that the actus sacramentalis would produce the presence and the effect of grace, i.e., res et sacramentum. Thus the ritual carried out by the priest is not causa instrumentalis, but merely causa ministerialis.

3. "But our esteem for facts has not neutralized in us all religiousness. It is itself almost religious. Our scientific temper is devout" (William James, *Pragmatism* [1911], p. 14 *et seq.*).
4. "Religio est, quae superioris cujusdam naturae (quam divinam vocant) curam caerimoniamque affert" (Cicero, *De invent. Rhetor.*, Lib. II); "Religiose testimonium dicere ex jurisjurandi fide" (Cicero, *Pro Coel.*, 55).
5. Heinrich Scholz (*Religionsphilosophie*, 1921) insists upon a similar point of view; see also H. R. Pearcy, *A Vindication of Paul* (1936).
6. Jung, *Studies in Word-Association* (London, 1918).
7. J. G. Frazer, *Taboo and the Perils of the Soul* (1911), p. 30 *et seq.*; A. E. Crawley, *The Idea of the Soul* (London, 1909), p. 82 *et seq.*; *L. Lévy-Bruhl, La Mentalité Primitive* (Paris, 1922), passim.
8. Feun, *Running Amok* (1901).
9. M. Ninck, *Wodan und germanischer Schicksalsglaube* (Jena, 1935).
10. L. Lévy-Bruhl, *Les Fonctions Mentales dans les Sociétés Inférieures Idem, Mental. Prim.* chap. III, "Les Rêves."
11. Fr. Haeussermann, *Wortempfang und Symbol in der alttestamentlichen Prophetie* (Giessen, 1932).
12. In an excellent tract about dreams and their functions Benedictus Pererius, S. J. (*De Magia. De Observatione Somniorum et de Divinatione Astrologica libri tres* [Coloniae Agripp., 1598], p. 114 *et seq.*), says: "Deus nempe, istius modi temporum legibus non est alligatus nec opportunitate temporum eget ad operandum, ubicunque enim vult, quandocumque, et quibuscumque vult, sua inspirat somnia . . ." (p. 147). The following passage casts an interesting light on the relation between the church and the problem of dreams: "Legimus enim apud Cassianum in collatione 22. veteres illos monachorum magistros et rectores, in perquirendis, et excutiendis quorundam somniorum causis, diligenter esse versatos" (p. 142). Pererius classifies dreams in the following manner: "Multa sunt naturalia, quaedam humana, nonnulla etiam divina" (p. 145). There are four causes of dreams: I. An affection of the body. II. An affect or vehement commotion of the mind through love, hope, fear or hatred (p. 126 *et seq.*). III. The power and cunning of the demon, meaning a pagan god or the Christian devil. (Potest enim daemon naturales effectus ex certis causis aliquando necessario proventuros, potest quaecunque ipsemet postea facturus est, potest tam prasentia quam praeterita, quae hominibus occulta sunt, cognoscere, et hominibus per somnium indicare [p. 129].) Concerning the interesting diagnosis of demonic dreams, the author says: ". . . conjectari potest, quae somnia missa sint a daemone: primo quidem, si frequenter accidant somnia significantia res futuras, aut occultas, quarum cognitio non ad utilitatem vel ipsius, vel aliorum, sed ad inanem curiosae scientiae ostentationem, vel etiam ad aliquid mali faciendum conferat . . ." (p. 130). IV. Dreams sent by God. Concerning the signs indicating the divine nature of a dream the author says: ". . . ex praestantia rerum, quae per somnium significantur: nimirum, si ea per somnium innotescant homini, quorum certa cognitio, solius Dei concessu ac munere potest homini contingere, hujus modi sunt, quae vocantur in scolis Theologorum, futura contingentia, arcana item cordium, quaeque intimis animorum recessibus, ab omni penitus mortalium intelligentia oblitescunt, denique praecipua fidei nostrae mysteria, nulli, nisi Deo docente manifesta (!!)" ". . . deinde, hoc ipsum (divinum esse) maxime declaratur interiori quadam animorum illuminatione atque commotione, qua Deus sic mentem illustrat, sic voluntatem afficit, sic hominem de fide et auctoritate eius somnii certiorem facit, ut Deum esse ipsius auctorem, ita perspicue agnoscat et liquido iudicet, ut id sine dubitatione ulla credere et velit et debeat" (p. 131 *et seq.*). Since the demon, as mentioned above, is also liable to produce dreams accurately predicting future events, the author adds a quotation from Gregory (*Dialog.*, Lib. IV, cap 48): "Sancti viri illusiones atque revelationes, ipsas visionum voces et imagines, quondam intimo sapore discernunt, ut sciant quid

a bono spiritu percipiant et quid ab illusore patiantur. Nam si erga haec mens hominis cauta non esset, per deceptorem spiritum, multis se vanitatibus immergeret, qui nonnumquam solet multa vera praedicere, ut ad extremum valeat animam ex una aliqua falsitate laqueare" (p. 132). It seemed to be a welcome safeguard against this uncertainty if dreams occupied themselves with the "main mysteries of our faith." Athanasius, in his biography of St. Anthony, gives us some idea of how clever the devils are in predicting future events (cf. E. A. Wallis Budge, *The Book of Paradise* [London, 1904], I, p. 37 *et seq.*). According to the same author they appear sometimes even in the shape of monks, singing psalms, reading the Bible aloud and making confusing comments about the moral conduct of the brethren (pp. 33 *et seq.*, 47). Pererius, however, seems to trust his criterium and he continues: "Quemadmodum igitur naturale mentis nostrae lumen facit nos evidenter cernere veritatem primorum principiorum, namque statim citra ullam argumentationem, assensu nostro complecti: sic enim somniis a Deo datis, lumen divinum animis nostris affulgens, perficit, ut ea somnia et vera et divina esse intelligamus certoque credamus." Pererius does not touch the dangerous question of whether any unshakable conviction, derived from a dream, necessarily proves the divine origin of the dream. He merely takes it for granted that a dream of this sort would naturally exhibit a character conforming to the "main mysteries of our faith," and not by any chance with those of another one. The humanist Caspar Peucer (in his *Commentarius de Praecipuis Generibus Divinationum,* etc. Witebergae 1560 de divinat. ex somn., p. 270) is far more definite and restrictive in that respect. He says: "Divina somnia sunt, quae divinitus immissa sacrae literae affirmant, nonquibusvis promiscue, nec captantibus aut expectantibus peculiares ἀποχαλύψεις sua opinione, sed sanctis Patribus et Prophetis Dei arbitrio et voluntate, nec de levibus negociis, aut rebus nugacibus et momentaneis, sed de Christo, de gubernatione Ecclesiae, de imperiis et eorundem ordine, de aliis mirandis eventibus: et certa his semper addidit Deus testimonia, ut donum interpretationis et alia, quo constaret non temere ea objici ex natura nasci, sed inseri divinitus." His crypto-Calvinism tangibly manifests itself in his words, particularly if they are compared with the theologia naturalis of his Catholic contemporary. It is probable that Peucer's hint at "revelations" alludes to heretical innovations. In the next paragraph at least, where he deals with somnia diabolici generis, he says: "Quaeque nunc Anabaptistis et omni tempore Enthusiastis et similibus fanaticis . . . diabolus exhibet." Pererius with more perspicacity and human understanding devotes a chapter to the question: "An licitum sit christiano homini, observare somnia?" and another one to the question: "Cuius hominis sit rite interpretari somnia?" In the first one he reaches the conclusion that important dreams should be considered. I quote his words: "Denique somnia, quae nos saepe commovent, et incitant ad flagitia, considerare num a daemone nobis subjiciantur, sicut contra, quibus ad bona provocamur et instigamur, veluti ad caelibatum, largitionem eleemosynarum et ingressum in religionem, ea ponderari num a Deo nobis missa sint, non est superstiosi animi, sed religiosi, prudentis ac salutis suae satagentis atque solliciti." But only stupid people would observe all the other futile dreams. In the second chapter he answers that nobody should or could interpret dreams "nisi divinitus afflatus et eruditus." "Nemo enim," he adds, "novit quae Dei sunt, nisi spiritus Dei" (*R. Cor.*, I, 2.11). This statement, eminently true in itself, reserves the art of interpretation to such persons as are ex officio endowed with the donum spiritus sancti. It is obvious, however, that a Jesuit author could not envisage a descensus spiritus sancti extra ecclesiam.

13. Jung, "Traumsymbole des Individuationsprozesses," *Eranos-Jahrbuch 1935* (Zürich, 1936). Although the dreams I quote are mentioned in this publication, they have been examined there from another angle. As dreams have many aspects, they can be studied from different sides.

14. Freud, *Traumdeutung* (Vienna, 1900). Eng. trans., *Interpretation of Dreams.* Herbert Silberer, *Der Traum* (1919), represents a more cautious and a more balanced point of view. Concerning the difference between Freud's and my own views, I refer the reader to my little essay on this subject in *Modern Man in*

Search of a Soul (London, 1933), p. 132. Further material in *Two Essays on Analytical Psychology* (1928), p. 83 *et seq.;* W. M. Kranefeldt, *Secret Ways of the Mind* (New York, 1932); Gerhard Adler, *Entdeckung der Seele* (Zürich, 1934); T. Wolff, "Einführung in die Grundlagen der Komplexen Psychologie," *Die Kulturelle Bedeutung der Komplexen Psychologie* (Berlin, 1935), pp. 1-168.

15. Cf. the relation of Odin as a god of poets, seers and raving enthusiasts, and Mimir, the wise one, to Dionysos and Silenos. The word Odin has a root connection with Gall. οὐατεις, Jr. fāith, Lat. Vates, similar to μάντις and μαlνομαι. Martin Ninck, *Wodan und germanischer Schicksalsglaube* (1935), p. 30 *et sqq.*
16. In *Ueber das Unbewusste* (Schweizerland, 1918).
17. In "Wotan," *Neue Schweizer Rundschau,* Heft 11 (1936).
    An abbreviated edition in *Saturday Review of Literature* (Oct. 16, 1937). The Wotan parallels in Nietzsche's work are to be found (1) in the poem of 1863-64 "To the Unknown God"; (2) in "Klage der Ariadne," *Also sprach Zarathustra,* p. 366; (3) *Also sprach Zarathustra,* p. 143 and p. 200; (4) The Wotan dream of 1859 in E. Foerster-Nietzsche, *Der werdende Nietzsche* (1924), p. 84 *et sqq.*
18. *Two Essays,* p. 202 *et sqq.; Psychological Types* (1923), pp. 588, 593 *et sqq.;* "Ueber die Archetypen des collectiven Unbewussten," *Eranos-Jahrbuch 1934,* p. 204 *et sqq.;* "Ueber den Archetypus mit besonderer Berücksichtigung des Animabegriffes," *Zentralblatt für Psychotherapie,* IX (1936), 259 *et sqq.*
19. *Zentralbl. f. Psychotherapie,* IX, 259 *et sqq.*
20. Edward Maitland, *Anna Kingsford, Her Life, Letters, Diary and Work* (London, 1896), p. 129 *et seq.*
21. The statement, concerning the hermaphroditic nature of the Deity in *Corpus Hermeticum,* Lib. I (ed. W. Scott, *Hermetica,* I, p. 118: ὁ δὲ νοῦς ὁ πρῶτος ἀρρενόθηλυς ὤν), is probably derived from Plato, *Symposium XIV.* It is questionable whether the later medieval representatives of the hermaphrodite are derived from the "Poimandres" (*Corp. Herm.,* Lib. I) since it was practically unknown in the West before it was printed by Marsilius Ficinus in 1471. There is a possibility, however, that a Greek scholar, though rare in those days, has gleaned the idea from one of the then existing codices graeci, as, for instance, the *Cod. Laurentianus* 71, 33 of the fourteenth century, the *Parisinus Graec.* 1220, fourteenth century, the *Vaticanus Graec.* 237 and 951, fourteenth century. There are no older codices. The first Latin translation by Marsilius Ficinus had a sensational effect. But before that date we have the hermaphroditic symbols of the *Cod. Germ. Monac.,* 598 of 1417. It seems more probable to me that the hermaphroditic symbol is derived from Arabic or Syriac Mss. translated in the eleventh or twelfth century. In the old Latin *Tractatulus Avicennae,* strongly influenced by Arabic tradition, we find: "(Elixir) Ipsum est serpens luxurians, seipsum impraegnans (*Artis Auriferae,* etc. [1593], T. I., p. 406). Although it is matter of a Pseudo-Avicenna and not of the authentic Ibn Sina (970-1037), he belongs to the Arabo-Latin sources of the medieval Hermetic philosophy. We find the same passage in the tractatus "Rosinus ad Sarratantam" (*Art Aurif.* [1593], I, 309): "Et ipsum est serpens seipsum luxurians, seipsum impraegnans, etc." "Rosinus" is an Arabo-Latin corruption of "Zosimos," the Greek neo-Platonic philosopher of the third century. His tract *Ad Sarratantam* belongs to the same class of literature and since the history of these texts is still completely in the dark, nobody can say who copied from whom. The *Turba Philosophorum,* Sermo LXV, a Latin text of Arabic origin, also makes the allusion: "compositum germinat se ipsum" (J. Ruska, *Turba Philosophorum. Quellen und Studien zur Geschichte der Naturwissenschaften und der Medizin* [1931], p. 165). As far as I can make out, the first text definitely mentioning the hermaphrodite is the "Liber de Arte Chimica incerti autoris," sixteenth century (in *Art. Aurif.* [1593], I, 575 *et sqq.*), p. 610: "Is vero mercurius est omnia metalla, masculus et foemina, et monstrum Hermaphroditum in ipso animae et corporis matrimonio." Of later literature I mention only: *Pandora* (a German text, 1588); "Splendor Solis" in *Aureum Vellus,* etc. (1598); Michael Majer, *Symbola aureae mensae duodecim nationum*

(1617); *idem, Atalanta Fugiens* (1618). J. D. Mylius, *Philosophia Reformata* (1622).

22. The *Tractatus Aureus Hermetis* is of Arabic origin and does not belong to the *Corpus Hermeticum*. Its history is unknown (first printed in the *Ars Chemica*, 1566). Dominicus Gnosius has written a commentary to the text in *Hermetis Trismegisti Tractatus vere Aureus de Lapidis Philosophici Secreto cum Scholiis Dominici Gnosii*, 1610. He says (p. 101): "Quem ad modum in sole ambulantis corpus continuo sequitur umbra . . . sic hermaphroditus noster Adamicus, quamvis in forma masculi appareat semper tamen in corpore occultatam Evam sive foeminam suam secum circumfert." This commentary, together with the text, is reproduced in J. J. Mangeti, *Bibl. Chem.* (1702), I, 401 *et sqq*.

23. A description of both types in *Two Essays*, II, 202 *et sqq*. See also *Psychological Types*, Definition No. 48, p. 588 *et sqq*.; also Emma Jung, "Ein Beitrag zum Problem des Animus," in *Wirklichkeit der Seele* (1934) p. 296 *et sqq*.

MIGUEL DE UNAMUNO / Saint Manuel Bueno, Martyr

If in this life only we have hope in Christ, we are of all men most miserable.

—I Corinthians XV, 19

NOW THAT the Bishop of the diocese of Renada, to which this my loved village of Valverde de Lucerna belongs, has, so they say, instituted proceedings to have our Don Manuel, or, to be more accurate, Saint Manuel Bueno, who was priest of this parish, beatified, I want to set down here by way of confession, and to what end only God, not I, knows, all I know and remember of that man who filled all the deepest life of my soul, who was my true spiritual father, the father of my spirit, mine, that of Angela Carballino.

The other, my temporal father, my father in the flesh, I hardly knew, for he died when I was still very young. I know that he was a stranger who came to our Valverde de Lucerna, that he settled here when he married my mother. He brought with him a few books, the *Quixote*, some of the classic dramas, a few novels, books of history, all jumbled together, and these books, almost the only ones the village possessed, fed my dreams as a child. My good mother told me hardly any of my father's words or deeds. Those of Don Manuel, whom she, like everyone in the village, adored, loved—in all chasteness, of course—had effaced the memory of those of her husband, whose soul she fervently commended to God every night as she said the rosary.

I remember Don Manuel as though it were yesterday when I was a child, ten years old, before I went to the convent school in the cathedral city of Renada. He, our saint, would have been about thirty-seven years old at the time. He was tall, slender, erect; he carried his head the way our Peña del Buitre bears its peak, and in his eyes there was all the bottomless blue of our lake. He drew the eyes of all, and with them the hearts, and when he looked at us it seemed that the flesh became as transparent as glass to reveal our hearts to him. We all loved him, but the children most of all. The things he said to us—not words, things! The village began to note an odor of sanctity about him; it felt drenched and drunk with his aroma.

It was at this time that my brother Lázaro, who was in America and sent us from there the money that permitted us to live comfortably, urged my mother to send me to the convent school to complete my education outside the village, and this despite the fact that he had his reservations about the nuns. "But as there are no good lay schools there, so far as I know, and certainly not for girls," he wrote to us, "we have to make do with what we have. The important thing is to polish off Angelita's rough edges and get her away from the uncouth village girls." And so I entered the school, thinking at first that I would become a teacher, but pedagogy stuck in my throat.

At school I came to know the girls of the city and made friends with some of them. But I never lost touch with the affairs and people of our village, from whom I received frequent letters and an occasional visit. And the fame of our priest, who was attracting attention in the cathedral city, reached even our school. The nuns were always asking about him.

From the time I was very small, my mind was filled with questions, concerns, doubts, owing in part, I suppose, to that conglomeration of books my father had left, and all this took increment at school, particularly in my association with a classmate who took a great fancy to me. At times she proposed that we should enter the same convent together, swearing perpetual sisterhood, and sealing the oath with our blood, and at others she talked to me, with her eyes half-closed, dreamily, of sweethearts and marital adventures. I have never learned since what became of her or what she did. And this in spite of that fact that when Don Manuel's name came up, or when my mother referred to him in her letters —and this happened in nearly all of them—which I read to my friend, she would say almost ecstatically: "What luck to be able to live near a saint like that, a living, flesh-and-blood saint, and kiss his hand! When you go back to your village, be sure to write me long, long letters and tell me all about him."

I spent about five years at the school, and now they are like a morning dream lost in the far-off horizon of memory, and when I was fifteen I came back to my Valverde de Lucerna. Now it had become Don Manuel—Don Manuel and the lake and the mountain. I came longing to know him, to put myself under his guidance, to have him show me the path my life should take.

People said that he had entered the seminary to study for the priesthood in order to provide for the children of a widowed sister, to be a father to them; that he had made a name for himself at the seminary by reason of his keen mind and his ability, and that he had turned down offers of a brilliant future in the Church because he wanted nothing but to be in Valverde de Lucerna, in his remote village lying like a link between the lake and the mountain reflected in it.

And how he loved his flock! He spent his life patching up unhappy marriages, making refractory children submissive to their parents, reducing stiff-necked parents, and, above all, comforting the suffering and heavy-burdened and ministering to all in the hour of death.

I recall, among other incidents, that when the unfortunate daughter of old Rabona, who had run away, returned from the city unmarried and cast off, with her baby, Don Manuel never rested until he persuaded her former sweetheart, Perote, to marry her and adopt the child, saying to him:

"Come now, give this poor waif a father, for the only one he has is the one in heaven."

"But, Don Manuel, I am not to blame for it."

"Who knows, my son, who knows? . . . Above all, it's not a question of blame."

And today the staff and comfort of poor Perote, sick and paralyzed, is the son who was not his, whom he recognized, inspired by the example of Don Manuel's saintliness.

On Midsummer's Night, the shortest of the year, it was and still is the custom for all the poor crones, and not a few men, who believe themselves bewitched or possessed of a devil, and who are for the most part hysteric and at times epileptic, to gather about our lake. Don Manuel undertook the task of making of himself a lake, a fountain of cleansing water, to alleviate their sufferings and, if possible, heal them. And such was the effect of his presence, his regard, and, above all, the unspeakably gentle authority of his words and his voice—the miracle of that voice!—that he achieved amazing cures. With this his fame grew, drawing to our lake and to him all the sick of the vicinity. On one occasion a mother came, begging him to work a miracle with her son, and he replied with a sad smile: "I have no permission from the Bishop to work miracles."

He was particularly concerned that all should go clean. If he saw someone with a tear in his clothes, he would say to him: "Go and see the sexton and ask him to mend it for you." The sexton was a tailor. And when on New Year's Day people called to congratulate him on his saint's day—his patron saint was Our Lord Jesus—Don Manuel wanted everyone to come wearing a new shirt, and those who had none received one from his own hands.

He treated all with the same affection, and if he showed any partiality, it was toward the more unfortunate and those who seemed more rebellious. There was a poor idiot in the village, Blasillo the Fool, and it was he whom he treated with the greatest tenderness, and he even managed to teach him things that it seemed a miracle he could have learned. It was that the few feeble embers of intelligence the imbecile possessed took fire as he imitated his Don Manuel like a pitiful monkey.

The marvel of the man was his voice, a divine voice that brought tears to the eyes. When in the High Mass he intoned the prelude, a ripple ran through the congregation, and all who heard him were moved to the depths of their being. His chant overflowed the temple and lost itself in the air over the lake and the foot of the mountain. And when in the sermon on Good Friday he cried out the "My God, my God, why hast Thou forsaken me?" a shudder went through the whole congregation, like the waters of the lake when the frozen north wind whips it. It was as though they were hearing Our Lord Himself speak, as though the voice came from the old crucifix at whose feet so many generations of mothers had laid their sorrows. Once when his mother, Don Manuel's mother, heard him, she could not contain herself, and from the floor of the church where she sat she cried out: "My son!" And there was not a dry eye in the church. It was as if the maternal cry had come from the parted lips of the Mater Dolorosa—her heart transfixed by seven swords—in one of the chapels of the church. Then Blasillo the Fool went wandering up and down the streets repeating pathetically and like an echo: "My God, my God, why hast Thou forsaken me?" and when the tears came to people's eyes as they heard him, the imbecile was suffused with delight over his triumph of imitation.

So great was Don Manuel's power that nobody ever ventured to lie in his presence, and all confessed without having to go to the confessional. Once when a revolting crime had been committed in a neighboring village, a fool who did not know what Don Manuel was really like sent for him, and said:

"Don Manuel, let's see if you can make this scoundrel tell the truth."

"So then you can punish him for it?" answered the saintly man. "No, Your Honor, no; I do not get from a man the truth that may send him to his death. That is a matter between him and God. Human justice is not my affair. 'Judge not that ye be not judged,' said Our Lord."

"But what about me, Father . . ."

"I understand; you, Your Honor, will render unto Caesar that which is Caesar's, and I will render unto God what is God's."

And as he left, he looked long at the suspected malefactor, and said to him:

"Make sure that God has forgiven you, for that is the only thing that matters."

The entire village attended Mass, if only to hear and see him at the altar, where he seemed to become transfigured, his face all alight. He had introduced a practice in the rite, which was to have us all gather in the church, men and women, old folk and children, several thousand of us, to recite together, in a single voice, the Apostles' Creed: "I believe in God the Father, Maker of heaven and earth," and the rest of it. It was not a chorus, but a single voice, a simple, united voice, all blended in one, and forming a mountain whose peak, lost at times in the clouds, was Don Manuel. And when we came to "I believe in the resurrection of the flesh and the life everlasting," Don Manuel's voice became lost, as in a lake, in that of the entire village, and what happened was that he fell silent. And I could hear the pealing of the bells of the town that was said to be buried at the bottom of the lake—bells that it was said could be heard on Midsummer's Night, too—and they were the bells of the town buried in the spiritual lake of our village; I could hear the voice of our dead who were resurrected in us in the communion of the saints. Later, when I came to understand the secret of our saint, I understood that it was as if the leader of a caravan crossing the desert should have died within sight of his goal, and his people should lift him on their shoulders to bring his lifeless body into the promised land.

Most of the people in the village, when their time came, wanted to die holding fast to his hand as to an anchor.

Never in his sermons did he fulminate against unbelievers, Masons, liberals, or heretics. Why, when there were none in the village? And even less against the evils of the press. But one of the most frequent themes in his sermons was that of the evils of the tongue. He found an excuse for everything and for all. He refused to believe in the evil intention of any.

"Envy," he never tired of repeating, "is kept alive by those who are bent on believing themselves envied, and most persecutions are due more to the persecutory mania than to persecution."

"But, Don Manuel, just see what she meant to say to me. . . ."

"We should care less about what people mean to say than about what they say without meaning to."

He led an active, not a contemplative life, fleeing in every possible way from having nothing to do. When he heard someone say that idleness is the mother of all vices, he would answer: "And of the worst of them all, which is idle thinking." And when I once asked him what he meant by that, he replied: "Idle thinking is thinking to keep from doing anything, or thinking too much about what one has done instead of what one has to do. What's done is done, and on to the next thing, for there is nothing worse than remorse without amends." To do, to do! From that time I grasped clearly that Don Manuel fled from idle and solitary thinking, that some thought tormented him.

And so it was that he was always occupied, and not infrequently with inventing occupations. He wrote very little of his own, so that he has left us hardly any writings or notes; but he was the scribe of others, and especially of mothers for whom he wrote letters to their children who were away.

He also did manual work, helping out with certain of the village tasks. At threshing time he went to the threshing floor to help with the flailing and winnowing, and while he did this he instructed or entertained the workers. At times he took the place of a sick laborer.

One bitter winter day he came upon a child shivering with cold, whose father had sent him into the woods a long way off to bring back a stray cow. "You go home," he said to the child, "and get warm, and tell your father that I will find the cow." And when he came back with the animal, he met the father, who, all abashed, had come to meet him.

In winter he chopped wood for the poor. When the great chestnut tree died—"a matriarchal chestnut," he called it—under whose shade he had played as a child, and whose nuts had delighted him for so many years, he asked for the trunk, took it home, and after sawing six boards from it, which he kept at the foot of his bed, he cut up the rest for the poor. He also made handballs for the boys and many toys for the children.

He used to accompany the doctor on his rounds and add his advice to the doctor's prescriptions. He took special interest in pregnancies and the raising of babies, and he considered the saying "Dead children are angels for heaven" nothing short of blasphemy. The death of a child moved him deeply.

"A stillborn child or a child who dies at birth, and a suicide," he said to me once, "are the most terrible mysteries to me. A child crucified!"

And once, when a man had taken his own life, and the father of the suicide, who was not of our village, asked him if he could be buried in consecrated ground, he replied: "Certainly, for at the last moment, in the instant of his death, he repented, beyond the shadow of a doubt."

He often went to the school, too, to help out the teacher, to teach with him, and not only the catechism. The fact is that he fled both idleness and solitude. And for the sake of being with the village, and especially with the young people and the children, he would go to the dances. And more than once he played the drum himself so the young men and girls could dance. This, which in another would have seemed a grotesque profanation of his calling, in him acquired a sacred character, like a religious rite. When the Angelus sounded, he would put down the drum and sticks, bare his head, and all the others with him, and pray: "The angel of the Lord declared unto Mary . . . Hail Mary. . . ." And then: "Now to rest for tomorrow."

"The first thing," he would say, "is for people to be happy, for them all to be happy to be alive. The joy of living comes first of all. Nobody should wish to die until it is God's will."

"I do," a recently widowed woman said to him once, "I want to follow my husband."

"What for?" he answered. "You stay here to commend his soul to God."

At a wedding he once said: "If I could only change all the water of our lake to wine, to a wine that, no matter how much one drank, would always cheer and never intoxicate . . . or at least bring a happy intoxication."

Once a team of poor circus-performers came through the village. The leader, who took the part of the clown, had with him his wife, who was pregnant and gravely ill, and three children who helped him in his act. While he was in the village square, amusing the children, and even the grown-ups, she became very ill and had to leave, followed by the anguished eyes of the clown and the laughter of the children. Don Manuel accompanied her and later, in a corner of the inn stable, comforted her in her dying moments. And when the show was over, the village and the clown learned of the tragedy, and they all went to the inn, where the poor man, his voice choked with tears, said: "They are right, Father, when they call you a saint," and he took Don Manuel's hand to lift it to his lips; but before he could do so, Don Manuel had taken the hand of the clown in his and, turning to the onlookers, said:

"You are the saint, good clown; I saw you working and I understood that you do this not only to give your children bread, but also to give joy to the children of others, and I tell you that your wife, the mother of your children, whom I have sent on her way to God while you were working and giving happiness, is at rest in the Lord, and you will go to join her, and the angels whom you will make laugh in heaven will pay you with their laughter."

Everybody, children and grown-ups, wept and wept, as much with sorrow as with a strange contentment in which the sorrow was swallowed up. Later, recalling that solemn moment, I understood that the unvarying cheerfulness of Don Manuel was the temporal and earthly form of an infinite, eternal sadness that he veiled from the eyes and the ears of others with heroic saintliness.

With that constant activity of his, with that sharing in the tasks and diversions of all, it was as though he was trying to flee himself, to flee his solitude. "I am afraid of solitude," he would repeat. But even so, from time to time he went alone, skirting the lake, to the ruins of that old abbey where the souls of the devout Cistercian monks rest whom history has buried in forgetfulness. There was the cell of the one called Father Captain, and on the walls it was said there were still stains of the blood with which he spattered them in his flagellations. What were Don Manuel's thoughts there? What I remember is that once when he was talking about the abbey, I asked him how it was that he had never thought of entering a monastery, and he answered me:

"It is not primarily because I have to take care of my widowed sister and my nephews, for God looks after the poor, but because I was not born to be a hermit, an anchorite. Solitude would kill my soul, and as for a monastery, Valverde de Lucerna is my monastery. I was not meant to live alone, to die alone. I was meant to live for my village, die for my village. How am I going to save my soul if I do not save that of my people?"

"But there have been saintly hermits," I said.

"True. The Lord blessed them with the grace of solitude, which He has denied me, and I must resign myself. I must not lose my flock to save my soul. God made me like that. I could not resist the temptations of the desert. I could not carry unaided the cross of being."

I have endeavored in these recollections, these which my faith lives on, to portray our Don Manuel as he was when I, a girl almost sixteen, returned from the convent school of Renada to our monastery of Valverde de Lucerna. And I knelt once more at the feet of its abbot.

"Well, here is Simona's daughter," he said as soon as he laid eyes on me, "and become a young lady who plays the piano, knows French and heaven knows what else. Now it's time to start thinking about giving us a new family. And your brother Lázaro, when is he coming back? He's still in the New World, isn't he?"

"Yes, Father. He's still in America."

"The New World. And we in the Old. When you write him, tell him for me that I should like to know when he is coming back from the New World to this Old one, bringing us what is new from there. And tell him that he will find the lake and the mountain as he left them."

When I went to confession to him, I was so upset that I could hardly bring out a word. I stammered out the act of contrition, almost sobbing. He said, watching me:

"But what's the matter, lamb? Of what or of whom are you afraid? Because it is not the weight of your sins or the fear of God that is distressing you; you are trembling because of me, isn't that it?"

I burst into tears.

"But what have they been telling you about me? What kind of fairy stories have you been hearing? Was it your mother? Come now, calm yourself, and imagine that you are talking to your brother. . . ."

With this I plucked up courage and began to confide to him my preoccupations, my doubts, my discouragements.

"Bah, bah! Where did you read all that nonsense? All that is literature. Don't swallow too much of that, not even Saint Theresa. If you need to amuse yourself, read *Bertoldo,* as your father did."

I came away from my first confession with that saintly man profoundly comforted. And that initial fear I felt—that more than respect, fear—turned into a deep pity. I was just a young girl then, a child, you might say, but I was on the threshold of womanhood, I felt within me the stirrings of motherhood, and there in the confessional beside that holy man I sensed a kind of unspoken confession on his part in the humble murmur of his voice. And I recalled how he uttered the words of Jesus Christ: "My God, my God, why hast Thou forsaken me?" how his mother answered him from the floor of the church where she sat: "My son," and I could hear the cry that rent the hush of the temple. And I confessed with him again to console him.

Once when I was explaining one of those doubts of mine to him in the confessional, he answered me:

"You have your answer in the catechism: do not ask me that, for I am ignorant; the Holy Mother Church has doctors who will know what to answer you."

"But the doctor here is you, Don Manuel."

"Me a doctor, me? What an idea! I, my little Miss Doctor, am nothing but a poor village priest. And do you know who whispers those doubts into your ear, who lays them as snares for you? The Devil!"

Taking my courage in my hands, I asked him point-blank: "What if he whispered them to you, Don Manuel?"

"To whom? To me? The Devil? We're not acquainted, my child, we're not acquainted."

"But what if he did?"

"I wouldn't pay any attention to him. And that's enough of that. Let's get through, for some really sick people are waiting for me."

I left, thinking to myself, I don't know why, that our Don Manuel, for all his reputation as a caster-out of devils, did not believe in the Devil. And as I started home I met Blasillo the Fool, who was never far away from the church, and who when he saw me, to show off his accomplishments, began to repeat—and how poignantly!—"My God, my God, why hast Thou forsaken me?" I was so overcome that when I got home I shut myself up in my room to cry until my mother came.

"I am afraid, Angelita, that with all these confessions, you are going to want to profess."

"Don't worry, Mother," I answered, "I have plenty to do here in the village, which is my convent."

"Until you marry."

"I'm not thinking of that."

On another occasion when I met Don Manuel, I asked him, looking him straight in the eyes: "Is there a hell, Don Manuel?"

With complete calm, he answered: "For you, my child? No."

"And for the others?"

"What do you care, if you are not going there?"

"I care about the others. Is there?"

"Believe in heaven, in the heaven that we can see. Look at it," and he pointed to it above the mountain and reflected below in the lake.

"But one must believe in hell, the same as in heaven," I replied.

"Yes, one must believe all the Holy Apostolic Roman Catholic Church believes and teaches. And that is enough!"

I read a profound sadness in his eyes, as blue as the waters of the lake.

Those years went by like a dream. The image of Don Manuel was growing in me without my realizing it, for he was such an everyday man, like the daily bread we ask for in the Lord's Prayer. I helped him all I could in his duties, I visited his sick, our sick, the school, took care of the church ornaments and linen. I was, as he called me, his deaconess. I went for a few days to visit a school-friend in the city, and I had to come back, for I felt smothered in the city, I lacked something, I thirsted for the sight of the waters of the lake, hungered for the sight of the mountain. Above all, I felt the lack of my Don Manuel, and it was as though he was calling me, as though he was in danger away from me, as though he needed me. I was beginning to feel a kind of maternal affection for my spiritual father. I wanted to help him bear the cross of being.

My twenty-fourth birthday was approaching when my brother Lázaro, with a tidy fortune he had saved, came back from America. He came here to Valverde de Lucerna with the idea of taking our mother and me to live in the city, perhaps to Madrid.

"In the village," he said, "a person becomes dull and stupid." And he went on: "Civilization is the opposite of rustication. Enough of the country. I did not send you off to school for you to rot away here, among these clodhoppers."

I said nothing, though I was prepared to put up a resistance to the idea of moving; but our mother, who was over sixty, took a firm stand from the start. "Change pastures at my age?" was her immediate answer; and then she made it clear that she could not live without the sight of her lake, her mountain, and, above all, of her Don Manuel.

"You're like cats who hate to move," my brother repeated over and over.

As he became aware of the sway Don Manuel exerted over the whole village, and especially over us, my mother and me, he came to feel a resentment toward him. Don Manuel seemed to him the personification of that obscurant theocracy in which he believed Spain to be submerged. And he began to lash out with all the anticlerical clichés and the antireligious and progressive shibboleths he had brought back, strengthened, from the New World.

"In this Spain of milksops," he would say, "the priests lead the women around by the nose, and the women, the men. And then the country, this feudal backwater!"

On his lips "feudal" was a term to strike fear to the heart; "feudal" and "medieval" were the epithets he used when he wanted to condemn a thing.

It disconcerted him to see how unimpressed we were by his diatribes, and the respectful indifference of the village. "Nobody could change these boors." But as he was good, because he was intelligent, it did not take him long to realize the kind of ascendancy Don Manuel held over the village, and he soon took in what the priest did for his parish.

"No, no, he is not like the others," he said. "He is a saint."

"But do you know what the other priests are like?" I asked him.

"I can imagine."

But, for all this, he did not set foot in the church and never missed an occasion to boast of his lack of belief, even though he always had a good word to say for Don Manuel. And in the village, I don't quite know how, a state of expectancy was building up of some kind of duel between my brother Lázaro and Don Manuel, or rather of my brother's conversion by the priest. Nobody doubted that he would finally bring him into the fold. Lázaro—as he told me later—was longing to see and hear Don Manuel, to see and hear him in the church, to know him and talk with him, to learn the secret of his spiritual power. Finally, after much urging, he went to hear him, out of curiosity—so he said.

"Yes, this is a horse of a different color," he said to me after he had heard him. "He's not like the others, but he doesn't take me in. He is too intelligent to believe all he has to teach."

"Then do you think he is a hypocrite?" I asked.

"Not a hypocrite, no, but it's the job at which he makes his living."

As for me, my brother was determined that I should read the books he had brought with him, and others that he urged me to buy.

"So your brother Lázaro," said Don Manuel to me, "wants you to read. Well, read, my child, read and make him happy. I know you are not going to read anything that is not good; read novels if you want to. They are no worse than histories that are called true. It is better for you to read than to fill your head with the village gossip and tittle-tattle. But, above all, read pious works that will bring you contentment of living, a gentle, silent contentment."

Did he have it?

It was at this time that our mother became gravely ill and died, and in her last days her one desire was that Don Manuel should convert Lázaro, whom she hoped to meet one day in heaven, in some corner of the stars from which she could see the lake and the mountain of Valverde de Lucerna. She was going now to see God.

"You're not going," Don Manuel said to her, "you're staying here. Your body here, in this earth, and your soul here, too, in this house, seeing and hearing your children even though they neither see nor hear you."

"But, Father, I am going to see God."

"God, my daughter, is here and everywhere, and you will see Him from here, from here. And all of us in Him, and Him in us."

"May God repay you," I said to him.

"The happiness with which your mother dies," he answered, "will be her life eternal."

And turning to my brother Lázaro: "Her heaven is to go on seeing you, and it is now that she must be saved. Tell her that you will pray for her."

"But—"

"But what? Tell her you will pray for her, who gave you life, and I know that once you have promised, you will pray, and after you have prayed . . ."

My brother, his eyes filled with tears, knelt beside our dying mother and gave her his solemn promise to pray for her.

"And I in heaven for you, for all of you," she answered, and kissing the crucifix, and with her eyes on Don Manuel's, she gave her soul to God.

"Into Thy hands I commend thy spirit," murmured the saintly man.

My brother and I stayed on alone in the house. The death of our mother had established a bond between Lázaro and Don Manuel, who seemed to neglect his other patients somewhat, his other needy, to look after my brother. Afternoons they went for walks beside the lake or toward the ivy-covered ruins of the old Cistercian abbey.

"He is an extraordinary man," Lázaro told me. "You know they say there is a submerged town at the bottom of this lake, and that on Midsummer's Night at twelve o'clock one can hear the pealing of its church bells."

"Yes," I answered, "a feudal, medieval city . . ."

"And I think," he went on, "that at the bottom of our Don Manuel's soul there is also a submerged, drowned city, and that sometimes the pealing of its bells can be heard."

"Yes," I replied. "This submerged city in Don Manuel's soul—and why not in yours, too?—is the cemetery of the souls of our forebears, those of this our Valverde de Lucerna . . . feudal and medieval!"

My brother finally came to go to Mass regularly to hear Don Manuel, and when word got around that he would fulfill his spiritual obligations, that he would take communion along with the others, the whole village felt a secret delight, as though he had been restored to it. But it was so honest, so unaffected a delight that Lázaro felt neither conquered nor humiliated.

And the day of his communion came, in the sight of all, in the company of all. When it was my brother's turn, I could see that Don Manuel was white as the January snow on the mountain and trembling like the waters of the lake when the north wind buffets them. As he approached him with the sacred form in his hand, it shook so as he raised it to Lázaro's lips that he dropped it as a fit of giddiness came over him. And it was my brother who picked it up and carried it to his mouth. And the village, seeing Don Manuel's tears, wept too, saying to itself: "How much he loves him!" And as it was the first hour of morning, a cock crowed.

When we came back home and I was alone with my brother, I put my arms around his neck and said, as I kissed him:

"Oh, Lázaro, Lázaro, the pleasure you have given us today, all of us, the village, everybody, the living and the dead, and especially Mamma, our mother! Did you see? Poor Don Manuel was weeping for joy. The pleasure you have given us all!"

"That's why I did it," he answered.

"For that reason? To give us pleasure? You did it first of all for yourself, because of your conversion."

Then Lázaro, my brother, as pale and trembling as Don Manuel when he was giving him communion, made me sit down in the chair in which our mother used to sit, took a deep breath, and, as though in intimate confession, said to me:

"Angelita, the time has come to tell you the truth, the whole truth, and I am going to tell it to you because I should, because I cannot, should not, keep it from you, and because, sooner or later, you would divine it anyway, and partially, which is worse."

And then, serenely and calmly, in a low voice he told me something that plunged me into a lake of sadness. How Don Manuel had been appealing to him, especially on those walks to the ruins of the old Cistercian abbey, not to shock people, to give a good example, to participate in the religious life of the village, to pretend to believe even if he didn't, to keep his ideas on the matter to himself, but all without attempting to win him over or convert him in any other fashion.

"But is that possible?" I cried out in consternation.

"All too possible, sister, all too possible! And when I said to him: 'But are you, the priest, advising me to pretend?' he stammered out: 'Pretend? No, not pretend, that is not pretending. Dip your fingers in holy water, someone said, and you will end by believing.' And when I, looking him right in the eye, said: "So you by saying Mass have ended by believing?' he looked away over the lake, and his eyes filled with tears. That is how I wrested his secret from him."

"Lázaro," I groaned.

At that very moment Blasillo the Fool came through the street, crying out his "My God, my God, why hast Thou forsaken me?" and Lázaro shivered, thinking he was hearing the voice of Don Manuel, perhaps that of Our Lord Jesus Christ.

"It was then," my brother went on, "that I understood his motives, and with them his saintliness. For he is a saint, sister, a true saint. In trying to win me to his saintly cause—for it is a saintly cause, the most saintly—he was not trying to chalk up a triumph for himself; he was doing it for the peace, the happiness, the illusion, if you like, of those entrusted to his care. I realized that if he deceives them in this manner—if it is deceit—it is not for his own benefit. I surrendered to his arguments, and there you have my conversion. And I shall never forget the day when I said to him: 'But, Don Manuel, the truth, the truth above all,' and he, trembling, whispered to me, in spite of the fact that we were alone, in the middle of the fields: 'The truth? The truth, Lázaro, is something so terrible, so unbearable, so deadly, that perhaps simple people could not live with it.' 'And why do you let me get a glimpse of it here, as though in the confessional?' I asked him. And he answered: 'Because if I didn't, it would torment me so much, so much that I would finally shout it in the middle of the square, and that never, never, never. I am here to make the souls of my faithful live, to make them happy, to make them dream they are immortal, and not to destroy them. What is needed here is for them to live in health, to live in unity of feeling, and with the truth; with my truth they would not live. Let them live. And that is what the Church does, make them live. True religion? All religions are true in so far as they make the people who profess them live spiritually, in so far as they console them for having had to be born to die, and the truest religion for every people is its own, the one that has made it. And mine? Mine is consoling myself by consoling others, even if the consolation I give them is not mine.' I shall never forget these words of his."

"But then this communion of yours has been a sacrilege," I broke in, regretting my words the minute I had said them.

"Sacrilege? And the one who administred it? And his Masses?"

"What martyrdom!"

"And now," my brother went on, "there is another to console the people."

"To deceive them?"

"Not to deceive them," he answered, "but to corroborate their faith."

"And what about the village people," I asked, "do they really believe?"

"How do I know! They believe without thinking, out of habit, tradition. The important thing is not to awaken them. Let them live in the poverty of their emotions so they will not acquire the torments of abundance. Blessed are the poor in heart!"

"You have picked that up, brother, from Don Manuel. And now, tell me, have you fulfilled your promise to our mother on her deathbed, when you said you would pray for her?"

"But of course I have. Whom do you take me for? Do you think I would break my word, the solemn promise given in her last moments to a mother?"

"I don't know. You might have wanted to deceive her so she would die comforted."

"If I did not fulfill the promise, I would live without comfort."

"So?"

"I have carried out my promise and I have not failed to pray for her a single day."

"Only for her?"

"Well, for whom else?"

"For yourself, and from now on for Don Manuel."

We separated, and each went to his own room, I to weep all

night and pray for the conversion of my brother and Don Manuel, and he, Lázaro, I don't know for what.

After that day I was fearful of finding myself alone with Don Manuel, whom I continued to help in his tasks. And he seemed to sense what was going on inside me and to divine its cause. When finally I came to him at the penitential bar—who was the judge and who the offender?—we both, he and I, silently bowed our heads and began to weep. And it was he, Don Manuel, who broke the terrible silence to say to me with a voice that seemed to come from a tomb:

"But you, Angelina, you have the same faith as when you were ten years old. Isn't that so? You do believe?"

"I do believe, Father."

"Then go on believing. And if doubts come to you, silence them even to yourself. We have to live. . . ."

Mustering my courage, and trembling, I said to him: "But, Father, do you believe?"

He hesitated for a moment, and mastering himself, he said: "I believe!"

"But in what, Father, in what? Do you believe in the other life? Do you believe that when we die we do not die completely? Do you believe that we will meet again, that we will love again in the other world to come? Do you believe in the other life?"

A sob shook the poor saint. "My child, let's not talk about that."

Now, as I set down these memories, I ask myself: Why did he not deceive me? Why did he not deceive me as he did the others? Why could he not deceive himself or why could he not deceive me? And I want to think that his suffering came from not being able to deceive himself in order to deceive me.

"And now," he added, "pray for me, for your brother, for yourself, for all. We must live. And we must give life."

Then, after a pause: "Why don't you marry, Angelina?"

"You know why, Father."

"No, no. You must marry. Between Lázaro and me we will find you a husband. Because you should get married to rid yourself of these preoccupations."

"Preoccupations, Don Manuel?"

"I know what I am saying. And don't suffer too much for others, for each of us has more than enough with having to answer for himself."

"That you should tell me this, Don Manuel! That you

should advise me to get married to answer for myself, and not worry myself about others! That it should be you!"

"You are right, Angelina. I don't know what I am saying, I don't know what I am saying any more since I am making my confession to you. But yes, yes, one must live, one must live."

And when I was getting to my feet to leave the church, he said to me:

"Now, Angelina, in the name of the village, do you absolve me?"

I felt as though filled with a mysterious sacerdocy, and I said to him:

"In the name of the Father, the Son, and the Holy Ghost, I absolve you, Father."

We left the church, and as we went out, I felt a maternal quickening within me.

My brother, now completely given over to furthering Don Manuel's work, was his most assiduous collaborator and companion. Moreover, their common secret was a link between them. He went with him to visit the sick, the schools, and put his money at the saintly man's disposal. A little more and he would have learned to help him with the Mass. And he penetrated deeper and deeper into Don Manuel's unfathomable soul.

"What a man!" he said to me. "Yesterday as we were walking along the shore of the lake, he said to me: 'This is my sorest temptation.' And as I looked at him inquiringly, he went on: 'My poor father, who was close to ninety when he died, was tormented all his life, so he told me himself, by the temptation of suicide, which had haunted him since he could not remember when, from birth, he said, and fighting it off. And this fight was responsible for his life. In order not to yield to the temptation, he exaggerated all precautions to preserve his life. He told me of terrible scenes. It seemed to me a form of madness, and I have inherited it. If you knew how this water, which reflects the sky in its apparent calm—the current is hidden—calls to me. My life, Lázaro, is a form of continual suicide, a struggle against suicide, which is the same thing; but just so they live, just so our people live!' And then he added: 'Here the river opens out into a lake, and then, flowing down the plateau, hurls itself in cascades, falls, and torrents through gorges and chasms, until it reaches the city. In the same way our life here in the village is a still pool. But the temptation of suicide is greater here, beside the still waters that reflect the stars at night, than beside the cascades, which cause fear. Listen, Lázaro, I have been at the deathbed of poor ignorant peasants who had hardly ever been away from their village, and I have heard from their own lips, or could guess it, the real cause of their sickness unto death, and I have seen there, at the head of their deathbed, the unmitigated blackness of the chasm of weariness of living. It is a thousand times worse than hunger. So let us go on, Lázaro, suiciding ourselves in our work and in our village, and let it dream this its life as the lake dreams the sky.'

"On another occasion," my brother told me, "we saw a young lass, a goat-girl, who, standing on a pinnacle of the mountain slope looking over the lake, was singing in a voice fresher than its waters. Don Manuel stopped me and, pointing her out, said: 'Look, it is as though time had stopped, as though that lass had always been there as she is, and singing, and as though she would always be there, as she was when my senses began, as she will be when they leave me. This girl forms a part of nature, along with the rocks, the clouds, the trees, the waters, and not of history.' How Don Manuel loves, how he personifies nature! I shall never forget the day of the snowstorm when he said to me: 'Lázaro, have you ever seen a greater mystery than that of the snow falling on the lake, and dying in it, while it spreads a coif over the mountain?' "

Don Manuel had to restrain my brother in his zeal and inexperience of a neophyte. When he learned that he was going about inveighing against certain generally held superstitions, he said to him:

"Let them be. It is so hard to make them understand where orthodox belief ends and superstition begins. Most of all, for us. Let them be, as long as they find comfort. It is better for them to believe everything, even things that contradict one another, than to believe nothing. This idea that the one who believes too much ends by believing nothing, is a Protestant concept. Let us not protest. The protest kills happiness."

My brother told me, too, that one night when the moon was full they were returning to the village along the lake, whose surface was rippled by the mountain breeze, and each ripple was capped with moonglow, Don Manuel said to him:

"Look, the water is reciting the litany, and saying now: *ianua cœli, ora pro nobis,* gate of heaven, pray for us!"

Two furtive tears clung to his lashes and fell to the grass, like dew, catching the trembling radiance of the full moon.

Time went flowing by, and my brother and I noticed that Don Manuel's strength was beginning to decline, that he could no longer completely restrain the unfathomable sadness that devoured him. Perhaps some treacherous illness was gnawing at his body and soul. Lázaro, perhaps with the idea of giving him something to think about, suggested that it might be a good idea for the church to organize a kind of Catholic Agrarian union.

"A union?" Don Manuel answered sadly. "What is a union? I know of no other union than the Church, and you know what it says: 'My kingdom is not of this world.' Our kingdom, Lázaro, is not of this world. . . ."

"Is it of the other?"

Don Manuel's head drooped. "The other, Lázaro, is here, too, because there are two kingdoms in this world. Or rather, the other world—Oh, I don't know what I am talking about. And as for the union, that is a holdover from your days of belief in progress. No, Lázaro; it is not religion's place to settle the economic or political conflicts of this world, which God left to the disputations of men. Let men think and act as they will, let them console themselves for having been born, let them live as happily as they can in the illusion that all this has a purpose. I have not come to preach the submission of the poor to the rich or the rich to the poor. Resignation and charity in all and toward all. Because the rich man must resign himself to his riches, and to life, and the poor must also have charity toward the rich. The social problem? Forget about that; that is not our business. Suppose they bring about a new society in which there are no longer rich or poor, in which wealth is equitably distributed, in which all is for all, then what? Don't you think that this general well-being will engender an even greater tedium of life? Yes, I know, one of the leaders of what they call the social revolution has said that religion is the opiate of the people. Opiate—opiate—yes, opiate. Let us give them an opiate, and let them sleep and dream. What is this frenzied activity of mine but an opiate? And despite it I neither sleep nor dream well. This terrible nightmare. I, too, can say with the Divine Master: 'My soul is sick unto death.' No, Lázaro, no, we will organize no unions. If they want to establish them, I'm in favor of it, for it gives them something to put their minds to. Let them play at unions if it makes them happy."

It became evident to the village that Don Manuel's strength was waning, that he tired easily. His voice, that miracle of a voice, took on a kind of inner tremor. And above all, when he talked to the people about the other world, the other life, he would pause at intervals, closing his eyes. "He is seeing it," they would say. And at such times it was Blasillo the Fool who wept as though his heart would break. For Blasillo had come to weep more than he laughed, and even his laughter had an echo of tears.

The last week of the Passion at which Don Manuel officiated among us, in our world, in our village, the whole congregation sensed that the tragedy was approaching its end. What a sound those words took on: "My God, my God, why hast Thou forsaken me?" as Don Manuel uttered them for the last time in public. And when he came to the promise of the Divine Master to the good thief—"All thieves are good," Don Manuel used to say—"Today shalt thou be with me in paradise!" And the last general communion our saint gave. When it came my brother's turn, with a steady hand this time he gave it to him, and after the liturgical ". . . *in vitam æternam,*" he bent down and whispered to him: "There is no eternal life but this . . . let them dream it eternal—eternal for a few years." And when he came to me, he said: "Pray, my child, pray for us." And then something so extraordinary that I bear it in my heart like the greatest of all mysteries, and it was the words he said to me in a voice that seemed of the other world: "And pray, too, for Our Lord Jesus Christ."

I rose, my strength gone, like a sleepwalker. Everything about me seemed a dream. And I thought: "I will have to pray for the lake and the mountain, too." And then I said to myself: "Can I be possessed of a devil?" And, home at last, I picked up the crucifix my mother had held in her hands as she yielded up her soul to God, and looked at it through my tears, recalling the "My God, my God, why hast Thou forsaken me?" of our two Christs, the one of this earth and the one of this village, and prayed: "Thy will be done on earth as it is in heaven," and then: ". . . lead us not into temptation. Amen." Then turning to the image of the Mater Dolorosa with her heart transfixed by seven swords which had been the most sorrowful consolation of my poor mother, I prayed: "Holy Mary, Mother of God, pray for us sinners, now and in the hour of our death. Amen." I had no more than said the words when I asked myself: "Sinners? Us sinners? What is our sin? What?" The question gave me no rest all day.

The next day I went to see Don Manuel, who was taking on the solemnity of a religious sunset, and I said to him:

"Do you remember, my Father, when I asked you a question years ago and you answered me: 'Do not ask me that for I am ignorant; the Holy Mother Church has doctors who will know how to answer you'?"

"Do I remember! And I remember that I told you those were questions put into your mind by the Devil."

"Well, Father, I, possessed of a devil, come to ask you another question put into my mind by my guardian devil."

"Ask it."

"Yesterday, when you gave me communion, you told me to pray for all of us and even for—"

"Don't say it, and go on."

"I got home and started to pray, and when I came to 'Pray for us sinners, now and in the hour of our death,' a voice inside me said: 'Sinners? Us sinners? And what is our sin?' What is our sin, Father?"

"Our sin?" he replied. "A great doctor of the Spanish Apostolic Church said what it was; the great doctor of *Life Is a Dream* said that 'Man's greatest sin is having been born.' That is our sin, my child; having been born."

"Can it be atoned for, Father?"

"Go and pray again! Pray once more for us sinners now and in the hour of our death. Yet, finally the dream can be atoned for, finally life can be atoned for . . . finally the calvary of birth comes to an end. And as Calderón said, to do good—to feign good—is not lost even in dreams."

And the hour of his death came at last. The whole village saw it come. And this was his finest lesson. He did not wish to die idle or alone. He died preaching to his people, in the church. First, before asking to be carried there because his paralysis made it impossible for him to move, he sent for Lázaro and me to come to his house. And there, the three of us alone, he said to us:

"Listen, tend these poor sheep, let them console themselves for living, let them believe what I have been unable to believe. And when your hour comes, Lázaro, die like me, as our Angela will die, in the bosom of the Holy Roman Catholic Church; that is to say, the Holy Mother Church of Valverde de Lucerna. And farewell until we never meet again, for this dream of life is coming to an end. . . ."

"Father, Father," I groaned.

"Don't be troubled, Angela, and go on praying for all sinners, for all who have been born. And let them dream, let them dream. What longings I have to sleep, sleep, sleep without end, sleep for all eternity, and without dreaming, forgetting the dream. When I am buried let it be in a box made of those six planks I sawed out of the old chestnut in whose shade I played as a child, when I was beginning to dream. Then I did believe in the life everlasting. That is to say, it seems to me now that I believed then. For a child, to believe is the same as to dream. And for a people. You will find the six planks I sawed with my own hands at the foot of my bed."

He was overcome by dizziness, and when it had passed, he went on:

"You remember that when we all, as one, the whole village, recited the creed together, when we came to the end of it I was silent? When the Israelites were reaching the end of their wandering in the wilderness, the Lord said to Aaron and to Moses that because they had rebelled against his word they should not lead their people into the Promised Land, and he commanded them to go up into Mount Hor, where Moses stripped Aaron of his garments, and Aaron died there, and then Moses went up from the plains of Moab to Mount Nebo, to the top of Pisgah, which is over against Jericho, and the Lord showed him all the land He had promised to His people, but saying to him: 'Thou shalt not go over thither!' And Moses died there, and no man knew of his sepulcher. And he left Joshua as leader. You, Lázaro, be my Joshua, and if you can make the sun stand still, stop it, and never mind progress. Like Moses, I have looked upon the face of God, our supreme dream, and you know how it says in the Bible that who shall look upon the face of God, that he who sees the eyes of the face of the dream with which he looks upon us, shall surely die and forever. So let not this our people see the face of God as long as they live, for after they are dead it does not matter, for they will see nothing. . . ."

"Father, Father, Father," I groaned again.

"You, Angela, pray, go on praying that sinners may all dream until they die the resurrection of the flesh and the life everlasting. . . ."

I was waiting for "and who knows?" when Don Manuel had another sinking spell.

"And now," he went on, "now, in the hour of my death, the time has come for you to have me carried in this chair to the church, to take leave of my people who are waiting for me."

He was carried to the church and placed, in his armchair, in the presbytery, at the foot of the altar. In his hands he held a crucifix. My brother and I stood near him, but it was Blasillo the Fool who was closest to him. He tried to take Don Manuel's hand and kiss it. And when some of those near tried to prevent him, Don Manuel rebuked them, saying:

"Let him come near me. Come, Blasillo, give me your hand."

The idiot wept with joy.

And then Don Manuel said: "Only a few words, my children, for I have barely enough strength left to die. I have nothing new to say to you. Live in peace and contentment, and with the hope that we will all see one another one day, in the Valverde de

Lucerna up there among the stars that at night shine high above the reflection of the mountain in the lake. And pray, pray to Blessed Mary, to Our Lord. Be good, and that is enough. Forgive me the evil I may have done you without meaning to and without knowing it. And now, after I give you my blessing, let us all say together the Lord's Prayer, the Hail Mary, the Salve, and finally the Apostles' Creed."

With the crucifix he held in his hand he gave the people his blessing, the women, the children, and not a few men weeping, and then the prayers began, to which Don Manuel listened in silence, holding Blasillo's hand, and to the sound of the prayers he was falling asleep. First the Lord's Prayer, with its "Thy will be done, on earth as it is in heaven," then the "Holy Mary, pray for us sinners now and in the hour of our death," then the Salve with its "weeping and groaning in this vale of tears," and, last of all, the Creed. And when they came to the "resurrection of the flesh and life everlasting," all the people felt that their saint had yielded his soul to God. It was not necessary to close his eyes, for he died with them closed. And when we tried to wake Blasillo, we found that he had fallen asleep in the Lord forever. So we had two bodies to bury.

The whole village went at once to the house of the saint to carry away relics, to divide up the pieces of his garments, to keep everything they could find as a memento of the blessed martyr. My brother took his breviary, and between the pages he found a dried carnation, fastened to a paper, and on the paper a cross with a date.

Nobody in the village seemed able to believe that Don Manuel was dead; all of them expected to see him, and perhaps they did, on his daily walk along the lake reflecting the image of the mountain or lying against it. Everyone continued to hear his voice, and everyone visited his grave, around which a veritable cult sprang up. The afflicted came to touch the chestnut cross, the work of his hands, too, and carved from the same tree that had furnished the six planks in which he was buried. And the ones who least of all could believe that he had died were my brother and I.

Lázaro carried on the tradition of the saint, and began to set down all he had heard, the notes that I have made use of in this my record.

"He made a new man of me, a real Lazarus, raised from the dead," he said to me. "He gave me faith."

"Faith?" I interrupted.

"Yes, faith, faith in the consolation of life, faith in the happiness of life. He cured me of my belief in progress. Because, Angela, there are two kinds of dangerous, harmful men: those who, convinced of the other life, of the resurrection of the flesh, torment, like the inquisitors they are, their fellow men so that by spurning this life as a passing thing they may gain the other; and those who believing only in this world—"

"Like you perhaps."

"Yes, like me, and like Don Manuel. But who believing only in this world await some kind of future society, and make every effort to deny people the comfort of believing in the other world—"

"So—"

"So one must give them illusion to live by."

The poor priest who came to replace Don Manuel in his cure of souls was overpowered by the memory of the saint, and he put himself into the hands of my brother and myself for guidance. He wanted only to walk in the footsteps of the saint. And my brother said to him: "Very little theology, Father; religion, religion." And listening to him, I smiled to myself, wondering if this was not a kind of theology, too.

I began to fear for my poor brother from that time. Ever since Don Manuel's death his life could hardly be called living. He visited his grave every day, and spent hour after hour gazing out over the lake. He had a nostalgic longing for abiding peace.

"Don't look at the lake so much," I said to him.

"Don't be afraid, sister. It is another lake that is calling to me, another mountain. I cannot live without him."

"What about the contentment of living, Lázaro, the contentment of living?"

"That is for other sinners, not for us who have looked upon the face of God, who has seen with His eyes the dream of life."

"Then are you getting ready to go to see Don Manuel?"

"No, sister, no; now, here in the house, just between the two of us, the whole truth, bitter though it be, bitter as the sea into which the sweet waters of this lake flow, the whole truth for you, who are armored against it . . ."

"No, no, Lázaro, that is not the truth!"

"It is my truth."

"Yours, but what about—"

"And his, too."

"Not any more, Lázaro, not any more! Now believe something else, now believe . . ."

"Look, Angela, one of the times when Don Manuel said to

me that there are thing which, even though a person admits them to himself, he should keep from others, and I answered that he said this to me really saying it—these very things—to himself, he finally confessed to me that he believed that more than one of the greatest saints, perhaps the greatest of all, had died without believing in the life to come."

"Is that possible?"

"All too possible. And now, sister, take care that no one here in the village suspects our secret."

"Suspects it?" I answered him. "Even if, in a fit of madness, I should try to explain it to them, they would not understand. The people do not understand by words; the people have understood only by your acts. To try to explain this to them would be like reading an eight-year-old child a page of Saint Thomas Aquinas —in Latin."

"All right, then when I am gone, pray for me and for him and for all."

And finally his hour came, too. An illness that had been undermining his strong constitution seemed to grow more acute with Don Manuel's death.

"I do not so much mind dying," he said to me during his last days, "as that with me another piece of Don Manuel's soul dies. But he will still go on living in you. Until the day finally comes when all we dead will die completely."

When he lay in the throes of death, the people, as is the custom in our villages, came in to see him, and commended his soul to Don Manuel, to Saint Manuel Bueno, Martyr. My brother said nothing to them, he had nothing more to say; he had already said all there was to be said. He was another link between the two Valverdes de Lucerna, that at the bottom of the lake and that which is reflected in its surface; he was another of us who had died of life—another, in his way, of our saints.

I was left more than bereft, but in my village and with my village. And now that I have lost my Saint Manuel, the father of my soul, and my Lázaro, my brother not only in the flesh but also in the spirit, it is now that I realize that I have aged and how I have aged. But have I lost them? Have I grown old? Am I approaching death?

One must live! And he taught me to live, he taught us to live, to feel life, to feel the meaning of life, to merge ourselves in the soul of the mountain, in the soul of the lake, in the soul of the people of the village, to lose ourselves in them to remain in them. He taught me by his life to lose myself in the life of the people of my village, and I felt the passing of the hours, the days, the years, no more than the passing of the waters of the lake. It seemed as if my life would always be the same. I did not feel myself grow old. I no longer lived in myself, but in my people, and my people lived in me. I tried to say what they, most of them, said without trying. I went out to the street, which was the road, and as I knew everybody, I lived in them, and forgot myself, while in Madrid, where I had gone at times with my brother, as I knew nobody, I felt a horrible loneliness, tortured by the sight of so many people I did not know.

And now, as I set down this memory, this intimate confession of my experience with saintliness, I believe that Don Manuel Bueno, that my Saint Manuel, and my brother Lázaro died believing they did not believe in the thing that most concerns us; but without believing, they believed it, believing it with active, resigned desolation.

But why, I have asked myself time and again, didn't Don Manuel try to convert my brother by a subterfuge, a lie, pretending to be a believer without being one? And I have understood that it was because he knew that he would not deceive him, that deception would not work with him, that he could convert him only with the truth, with his truth; that he would have accomplished nothing if he had tried to play the comedy—better, the tragedy—he put on to save the village. And in this way he won him over to his pious fraud; in this way he won him to the reason of life with the truth of death. And thus he won me, who never let anyone else see his divine, his saintly game. And I firmly believed and believe that Our Lord God, for one of His holy and inscrutable purposes, made them believe they did not believe. And that perhaps at the moment of their passing the blind dropped from their eyes. And I, do I believe?

As I write this now, here, in my mother's old home, now that more than fifty years lie behind me, and my memories are turning white together with my hair, it is snowing, snowing over the lake, snowing over the mountain, snowing over the memory of my father, the outsider, of my mother, of my brother Lázaro, of my village, of my Saint Manuel, and also over the memory of poor Blasillo, my Saint Blasillo, may he watch over me from heaven! And this snow wipes out the roughnesses and wipes out the shadows, for even at night the snow gives light. And I do not know what is truth and what is lie, nor what I saw or what I only dreamed—or rather what I dreamed and what I only saw—nor what I knew or what I believed. Nor do I know if I am transferring to this paper, as white as the snow, my conscience, which will go into it, leaving me without it. What do I want with it now?

Do I know anything? Do I believe anything? Did what I am putting down here really happen, and did it happen as I am telling it? Can such things happen? Is all this more than a dream dreamed within another dream? Can I, Angela Carballino, a woman over fifty, be the only person in this village assailed by these thoughts alien to the others? And the others, those who surround me, do they believe? What is believing? At least they live. And now they believe in Saint Manuel Bueno, Martyr, who, without hoping for immortality, kept them in hope of it.

It seems that His Reverence the Bishop, who has set on foot the beatification of our saint of Valverde de Lucerna, is planning to write his life, a kind of handbook of the perfect priest, and is gathering information of every sort for it. He has come to see me several times, he has asked me for everything I knew, I have given him all sorts of data, but I have always kept to myself the tragic secret of Don Manuel and of my brother. And it is strange that he has not suspected it. And I hope that what I have set down in this memoir will never come to his knowledge. I am afraid of the authorities of the earth, the temporal authorities, even those of the Church.

But here I leave this, and let its fate be what it will.

How did this document come into my hands, this memoir of Angela Carballino's? That, reader, is something I must keep a secret. I give it to you just as it came to me, with a few—only a few—changes in the wording. You find that it closely resembles other things that I have written? That is no proof against its objectivity, its originality. Do I know, anyway, whether I have not created outside myself real, authentic beings with an immortal soul? As for the reality of this Saint Manuel Bueno, Martyr, as revealed to me by his disciple and spiritual daughter, Angela Carballino, this is a reality it does not cross my mind to doubt. I believe in it more than the saint himself did; I beleve in it more than in my own reality.

And now, before bringing this epilogue to a close, patient reader, I want to recall to you the ninth verse of the Epistle of the forgotten apostle, Saint Judas—what is in a name!—in which we are told that my celestial patron, Saint Michael Archangel—Michael means "Who like God?" and archangel, archmessenger—disputed with the Devil—devil means accuser, public prosecutor—for the body of Moses, and would not allow him to carry it off to damnation, saying to him: "The Lord rebukes you." And let him who wishes to understand, understand.

I also wish, because Angela Carballino put her own emotions into her account—I don't know what else she could have put—to comment here on what she said as to whether, if Don Manuel and his disciple Lázaro had confessed to the people the state of their belief, they would have understood them. I would add, they would not even have believed them. They would have believed in their works and not in their words, because words are not needed to support works, for the works are sufficient to themselves. And for a village like Valverde de Lucerna, the only confession is one's conduct. People do not know what faith is, and perhaps they don't care much.

I am well aware of the fact that in what has been told in this account, novelized, if you like—and the novel is the most intimate, the truest history, and for that reason I cannot understand why there are those who take it amiss that the Bible should be called a novel, which is, in reality, to set it above a mere chronicle—nothing passes; but I hope this is because everything remains, like the lakes and the mountains and the blessed simple souls firmly set, beyond faith and despair, who come together in them, in the lakes and the mountains, outside history, in a divine novel and there have their refuge.

VII

THE WHOLE MAN

Dr. Maslow's introduction of the concept of the "Whole Man" into psychology derives from the same rationalist tradition discussed in earlier pages. Its major value lies in its emphasis on health as a possible condition of the human mind.

It is almost impossible, however, to discuss the whole man without conjuring up a vision of Pollyanna. We are so accustomed to thinking in terms of hatred and repression, of neurotic sublimation or compensation, of disease as the jumping-off place for our psychology, that the idea of a healthy human being seems almost simple-minded.

Yet the whole man—functioning, productive, striving—does exist. He is not to be confused with the completely happy man, or the well-adjusted citizen. He may often be only a peripheral member of his social group: he may observe none of its social amenities and may live in a manner that is far from his cultural norm. He may be rebel or artist, a genius or a man with grace. His rebellion, however, will never result in hatred or destruction; his art may provide the basis for a new way of thinking; his genius or his grace may make life better for those around him. He represents a balance between the forces of libido and aggression.

Ralph Waldo Emerson's nineteenth-century transcendentalism, his emphasis on self-reliance, his recognition of the possibility of happiness, embodies a good many of Dr. Maslow's ideals. Robert Browning's proud and functioning "Rabbi Ben Ezra" is yet another "whole" man. And in C. E. Montague's "Action," we get a glimmer of the possibilities inherent in all human beings—beings who may be functioning at half their potentialities, and who may, by a careful husbanding of their psychological abilities, achieve a level of personality integration that we can, at this time, hardly conceive.

JOHN STUART MILL / Individuality*

SUCH BEING the reasons which make it imperative that human beings should be free to form opinions, and to express their opinions without reserve; and such the baneful consequences to the intellectual, and through that to the moral nature of man, unless this liberty is either conceded, or asserted in spite of prohibition; let us next examine whether the same reasons do not require that men should be free to act upon their opinions—to carry these out in their lives, without hindrance, either physical or moral, from their fellow-men, so long as it is at their own risk and peril. This last proviso is of course indispensable. No one pretends that actions should be as free as opinions. On the contrary, even opinions lose their immunity, when the circumstances in which they are expressed are such as to constitute their expression a positive instigation to some mischievous act. An opinion that corn-dealers are starvers of the poor, or that private property is robbery, ought to be unmolested when simply circulated through the press, but may justly incur punishment when delivered orally to an excited mob assembled before the house of a corn-dealer, or when handed about among the same mob in the form of a placard. Acts, of whatever kind, which, without justifiable cause, do harm to others, may be, and in the more important cases absolutely require to be, controlled by the unfavourable sentiments, and, when needful, by the active interference of mankind. The liberty of the individual must be thus far limited; he must not make himself a nuisance to other people. But if he refrains from molesting others in what concerns them, and merely acts according to his own inclination and judgment in things which concern himself, the same reasons which show that opinion should be free, prove also that he should be allowed, without molestation, to carry his opinions into practice at his own cost. That mankind are not infallible; that their truths, for the most part, are only half-truths; that unity of opinion, unless resulting from the fullest and freest comparison of opposite opinions, is not desirable, and diversity not an evil, but a good, until mankind are much more capable than at present of recognising all sides of the truth, are principles applicable to men's modes of action, not less than to their opinions. As it is useful that while mankind are imperfect there should be different opinions, so it is that there should be different experiments of living; that free scope should be given to varieties of character, short of injury to others; and that the worth of different modes of life should be

* Reprinted from John Stuart Mill, *On Liberty*.

proved practically, when any one thinks fit to try them. It is desirable, in short, that in things which do not primarily concern others, individuality should assert itself. Where, not the person's own character, but the traditions or customs of other people are the rule of conduct, there is wanting one of the principal ingredients of human happiness, and quite the chief ingredient of individual and social progress.

In maintaining this principle, the greatest difficulty to be encountered does not lie in the appreciation of means towards an acknowledged end, but in the indifference of persons in general to the end itself. If it were felt that the free development of individuality is one of the leading essentials of well-being; that it is not only a co-ordinate element with all that is designated by the terms civilization, instruction, education, culture, but is itself a necessary part and condition of all those things; there would be no danger that liberty should be undervalued, and the adjustment of the boundaries between it and social control would present no extraordinary difficulty. But the evils is, that individual spontaneity is hardly recognized by the common modes of thinking, as having any intrinsic worth, or deserving any regard on its own account. The majority, being satisfied with the ways of mankind as they now are (for it is they who make them what they are), cannot comprehend why those ways should not be good enough for everybody; and what is more, spontaneity forms no part of the ideal of the majority of moral and social reformers, but is rather looked on with jealousy, as a troublesome and perhaps rebellious obstruction to the general acceptance of what these reformers, in their own judgment, think would be best for mankind. Few persons, out of Germany, even comprehend the meaning of the doctrine which Wilhelm Von Humboldt, so eminent both as a *savant* and as a politician, made the text of a treatise—that 'the end of man, or that which is prescribed by the eternal or immutable dictates of reason, and not suggested by vague and transient desires, is the highest and most harmonious development of his powers to a complete and consistent whole;' that, therefore, the object 'towards which every human being must ceaselessly direct his efforts, and on which especially those who design to influence their fellow-men must ever keep their eyes, is the individuality of power and development;' that for this there are two requisites, 'freedom, and a variety of situations;' and that from the union of these arise 'individual vigour and manifold diversity,' which combine themselves in 'originality.'[1]

[1] *The Sphere and Duties of Government,* from the German of Baron Wilhelm von Humboldt, pp. 11-13.

Little, however, as people are accustomed to a doctrine like that of Von Humboldt, and surprising as it may be to them to find so high a value attached to individuality, the question, one must nevertheless think, can only be one of degree. No one's idea of excellence in conduct is that people should do absolutely nothing but copy one another. No one would assert that people ought not to put into their mode of life, and into the conduct of their concerns, any impress whatever of their own judgment, or of their own individual character. On the other hand, it would be absurd to pretend that people ought to live as if nothing whatever had been known in the world before they came into it; as if experience had as yet done nothing towards showing that one mode of existence, or of conduct, is preferable to another. Nobody denies that people should be so taught and trained in youth, as to know and benefit by the ascertained results of human experience. But it is the privilege and proper condition of a human being, arrived at the maturity of his faculties, to use and interpret experience in his own way. It is for him to find out what part of recorded experience is properly applicable to his own circumstances and character. The traditions and customs of other people are, to a certain extent, evidence of what their experience has taught *them;* presumptive evidence, and as such, have a claim to his deference; but, in the first place, their experience may be too narrow; or they may not have interpreted it rightly. Secondly, their interpretation of experience may be correct, but unsuitable to him. Customs are made for customary circumstances, and customary characters: and his circumstances or his character may be uncustomary. Thirdly, though the customs be both good as customs, and suitable to him, yet to conform to custom, merely *as* custom, does not educate or develop in him any of the qualities which are the distinctive endowment of a human being. The human faculties of perception, judgment, discriminative feeling, mental activity, and even moral preference, are exercised only in making a choice. He who does anything because it is the custom, makes no choice. He gains no practice either in discerning or in desiring what is best. The mental and moral, like the muscular powers, are improved only by being used. The faculties are called into no exercise by doing a thing merely because others do it, no more than by believing a thing only because others believe it. If the grounds of an opinion are not conclusive to the person's own reason, his reason cannot be strengthened, but is likely to be weakened by his adopting it: and if the inducements to an act are not such as are consentaneous to his own feelings and character (where affection, or the rights of others, are not concerned) it is so much done towards rendering his feelings and character inert and torpid, instead of active and energetic. . . .

It is not by wearing down into uniformity all that is individual in themselves, but by cultivating it and calling it forth, within the limits imposed by the rights and interests of others, that human beings become a noble and beautiful object of contemplation; and as the works partake the character of those who do them, by the same process human life also becomes rich, diversified, and animating, furnishing more abundant aliment to high thoughts and elevating feelings, and strengthening the tie which binds every individual to the race, by making the race infinitely better worth belonging to. In proportion to the development of his individuality, each person becomes more valuable to himself, and is therefore capable of being more valuable to others. There is a greater fulness of life about his own existence, and when there is more life in the units there is more in the mass which is composed of them. As much compression as is necessary to prevent the stronger specimens of human nature from encroaching on the rights of others, cannot be dispensed with; but for this there is ample compensation even in the point of view of human development. The means of development which the individual loses by being prevented from gratifying his inclinations to the injury of others, are chiefly obtained at the expense of the development of other people. And even to himself there is a full equivalent in the better development of the social part of his nature, rendered possible by the restraint put upon the selfish part. To be held to rigid rules of justice for the sake of others, develops the feelings and capacities which have the good of others for their object. But to be restrained in things not affecting their good, by their mere displeasure, develops nothing valuable, except such force of character as may unfold itself in resisting the restraint. If acquiesced in, it dulls and blunts the whole nature. To give any fair play to the nature of each, it is essential that different persons should be allowed to lead different lives. In proportion as this latitude has been exercised in any age, has that age been noteworthy to posterity. Even despotism does not produce its worst effects, so long as Individuality exists under it; and whatever crushes individuality is despotism, by whatever name it may be called, and whether it professes to be enforcing the will of God or the injunctions of men. . . .

A. H. MASLOW / Self-Actualizing People*

Personal Foreword

THE STUDY to be reported . . . is unusual in various ways. It was not planned as an ordinary research; it was not a social venture but a private one, motivated by my own curiosity and pointed toward the solution of various personal moral, ethical, and scientific problems. I sought only to convince and to teach myself (as is quite proper in a personal quest) rather than to prove or to demonstrate to others.

Quite unexpectedly, however, these studies have proved to be so enlightening to me, and so laden with exciting implications, that it seems fair that some sort of report should be made to others in spite of its methodological shortcomings.

In addition, I consider the problem of psychological health to be so pressing, that *any* suggestions, *any* bits of data, however moot, are endowed with great heuristic value. This kind of research is in principle so difficult—involving as it does a kind of lifting oneself by one's axiological bootstraps—that if we were to wait for conventionally reliable data, we should have to wait forever. It seems that the only manly thing to do is not to fear mistakes, to plunge in, to do the best that one can, hoping to learn enough from blunders to correct them eventually. At present the only alternative is simply to refuse to work with the problem. Accordingly, for whatever use can be made of it, the following report is presented with due apologies to those who insist on conventional reliability, validity, sampling, etc.

Subjects and Methods

The subjects were selected from among personal acquaintances and friends, and from among public and historical figures. In addition, in a first research with young people, three thousand college students were screened, but yielded only one immediately usable subject and a dozen or two possible future subjects.

I had to conclude that self-actualization of the sort I had found in my older subjects was not possible in our society for young, developing people.

Accordingly, in collaboration with Dr. Evelyn Raskin and

* Reprinted from "Self-Actualization: a study in psychological health" in W. Wolff, ed., *Symposia on Topical Issues,* Vol. I, "Values in Personality Research," pp. 11-34. Published by Grune and Stratton, 1950. By permission of A. H. Maslow and the publisher.

Dan Freedman, a search was begun for a panel of *relatively* healthy college students. We arbitrarily decided to choose the healthiest 1 percent of the college population. This research, pursued over a two-year period as time permitted, had to be interrupted before completion, but it was, of course, very instructive at the clinical level. It is hoped that the subjects selected may yet be followed up for our further instruction.

It was also hoped that figures created by novelists or dramatists could be used for demonstration purposes, but none were found that were usable in our culture and our time (in itself a thought-provoking finding).

The first clinical definition, on the basis of which subjects were finally chosen or rejected, had a positive as well as a merely negative side. The negative criterion was an absence of neurosis, psychopathic personality, psychosis, or strong tendencies in these directions. Possible psychosomatic illness called forth closer scrutiny and screening. Wherever possible, Rorschach tests were given, but turned out to be far more useful in revealing concealed psychopathology than in selecting healthy people. The positive criterion for selection was positive evidence of self-actualization (SA), as yet a difficult syndrome to describe accurately. For the purposes of this discussion, it may be loosely described as the full use and exploitation of talents, capacities, potentialities, etc. Such people seem to be fulfilling themselves and to be doing the best that they are capable of doing, reminding us of Nietzsche's exhortation, "Become what thou art!" They are people who have developed or are developing to the full stature of which they are capable (1, 2, 3, 4, 5). These potentialities may be either idiosyncratic or species-wide, so that the self in self-actualization must not have too individualistic a flavor.

This criterion implies also either gratification, past or present, of the basic emotional needs for safety, belongingness, love, respect, and self-respect, and of the cognitive needs for knowledge and for understanding, or in a few cases, conquest of these needs. This is to say that all subjects felt safe and unanxious, accepted, loved and loving, respect-worthy and respected, and that they had worked out their philosophical, religious, or axiological bearings. It is still an open question as to whether this basic gratification is a sufficient or only a prerequisite condition of self-actualization. It may be that self-actualization means basic gratification plus at least minimum talent, capacity, or richness.

In general, the technique of selection used was that of *iteration,* previously used in studies of the personality syndromes of self-esteem and of security. . . . This consists briefly in starting with the personal or cultural nontechnical state of belief, collating the various extant usages and definitions of the syndrome, and then defining it more carefully, still in terms of actual usage (what might be called the lexicographical stage), with, however, the elimination of the logical and factual inconsistencies customarily found in folk definitions.

On the basis of the corrected folk definition, the first groups of subjects are selected, a group who are high in the quality and a group who are low in it. These people are studied as carefully as possible in the clinical style, and on the basis of this empirical study the original corrected folk definition is further changed and corrected as required by the data now in hand. This gives the first clinical definition. On the basis of this new definition, the original group of subjects is reselected, some being retained, some being dropped, and some new ones being added. This second level group of subjects is then in its turn clinically, and if possible, experimentally and statistically studied, which in turn causes modification, correction, and enrichment of the first clinical definition, with which in turn a new group of subjects is selected and so on. In this way an originally vague and unscientific folk concept can become more and more exact, more and more operational in character, and therefore more scientific.

Of course, external, theoretical, and practical considerations may intrude into this spiral-like process of self-correction. For instance, early in this study, it was found that folk usage was so unrealistically demanding that no living human being could possibly fit the definition. We had to stop excluding a possible subject on the basis of single foibles, mistakes, or foolishness; or to put it in another way, we could not use perfection as a basis for selection, since no subject was perfect.

Another such problem was presented by the fact that in all cases it was impossible to get full and satisfactory information of the kind usually demanded in clinical work. Possible subjects, when informed of the purpose of the research, became self-conscious, froze up, laughed off the whole effort, or broke off the relationship. As a result, since this early experience, all older subjects have been studied indirectly, indeed almost surreptitiously. Only younger people can be studied directly.

Since living people were studied whose names could not be divulged, two desiderata or even requirements of ordinary scientific work became impossible to achieve: namely, repeatability of the investigation and public availability of the data upon which conclusions were made. These difficulties are partly overcome by the inclusion of public and historical figures, and by the supplementary study of young people and children who could conceivably be used publicly.

The subjects have been divided into the following categories:

Cases:	3	fairly sure and 2 highly probable contemporaries
	2	fairly sure historical figures (Lincoln in his last years and Thomas Jefferson)
	6	highly probable public and historical figures (Einstein, Eleanor Roosevelt, Jane Addams, William James, and Spinoza)
Partial Cases:	5	contemporaries who fairly certainly fall short somewhat but who can yet be used for study
	7	historical figures who probably or certainly fall short, but who can yet be used for study (Walt Whitman, Henry Thoreau, Beethoven, F. D. Roosevelt, Freud)
Potential or Possible Cases:	20	younger people who seem to be developing in the direction of self-actualization, and G. W. Carver, Eugene V. Debs, Albert Schweitzer, Thomas Eakins, Fritz Kreisler, Goethe

Gathering and Presentation of the Data

Data here consist not so much in the usual gathering of specific and discrete facts as in the slow development of a global or holistic impression of the sort that we form of our friends and acquaintances. It was rarely possible to set up a situation, to ask pointed questions, or to do any testing with my older subjects (although this *was* possible and was done with younger subjects). Contacts were fortuitous and of the ordinary social sort. Friends and relatives were questioned where this was possible.

Because of this and also because of the small number of subjects as well as the incompleteness of the data for many subjects, any quantitative presentation is impossible: only composite impressions can be offered for whatever they may be worth (and of course they are worth much less than controlled objective observation, since the investigator is never *quite* certain about what is description and what is projection).

The holistic analysis of these total impressions yields, as the most important and useful whole characteristics of self-actualizing people for further clinical and experimental study, the following:

More Efficient Perception of Reality and More Comfortable Relations with It

The first form in which this capacity was noticed was as an unusual ability to detect the spurious, the fake, and the dishonest in personality, and in general to judge people correctly and efficiently. In an informal experiment with a group of college students, a clear tendency was discerned for the more secure (the more healthy) to judge their professors more accurately than did the less secure students, i.e., high scorers in the S-I test (6).

As the study progressed, it slowly became apparent that this efficiency extended to many other areas of life—indeed *all* areas that were tested. In art and music, in things of the intellect, in scientific matters, in politics and public affairs, they seemed as a group to be able to see concealed or confused realities more swiftly and more correctly than others. Thus an informal experiment indicated that their predictions of the future from whatever facts were in hand at the time seemed to be more often correct, because less based upon wish, desire, anxiety, fear, or upon generalized, character-determined optimism or pessimism.

At first this was phrased as good taste or good judgment, the implication being relative and not absolute. But for many reasons (some to be detailed below), it has become progressively more clear that this had better be called perception (not taste) of something that was absolutely there (reality, not a set of opinions). It is hoped that this conclusion—or hypothesis—can soon be put to the experimental test.

If this is so, it would be impossible to overstress its importance. Recently Money-Kyrle (7), an English psychoanalyst, has indicated that he believes it possible to call a neurotic person not only *relatively* but *absolutely* inefficient, simply because he does not perceive the real world so accurately or so efficiently as does the healthy person. The neurotic is not only emotionally sick—he is cognitively *wrong*! If health and neurosis are, respectively, correct and incorrect perceptions of reality, propositions of fact and propositions of value merge in this area, and in principle, value propositions should then be empirically demonstrable rather than merely matters of taste or exhortation. For those who have wrestled with this problem it will be clear that we may have here a partial basis for a true science of values, and consequently of ethics, social relations, politics, religion, etc.

It is definitely possible that maladjustment or even extreme neurosis would disturb perception enough to affect acuity of perception of light or touch or odor. But it is *probable* that this effect can be demonstrated in spheres of perception removed from the merely physiological, e.g., *Einstellung* experiment (8), etc. It should also follow that the effects of wish, desire, prejudice, upon perception as in many recent experiments should be very much less in healthy people than in sick. A priori considerations encourage the hypothesis that this superiority in the perception of reality eventuates in a superior ability to reason, to perceive the truth, to come to conclusions, to be logical and to be cognitively efficient, in general. . . .

It was found that self-actualizing people distinguished far more easily than most the fresh, concrete, and idiographic from the generic, abstract, and rubricized. The consequence is that they live more in the real world of nature than in the man-made mass of concepts, abstractions, expectations, beliefs, and stereotypes that most people confuse with the world. They are therefore far more apt to perceive what is there rather than their own wishes, hopes, fears, anxieties, their own theories and beliefs, or those of their cultural group. "The innocent eye," Herbert Read has very effectively called it.

The relationship with the unknown seems to be of exceptional promise as another bridge between academic and clinical psychology. Our healthy subjects are uniformly unthreatened and unfrightened by the unknown, being therein quite different from average men. They accept it, are comfortable with it, and, often are even *more* attracted by it than by the known. They not only tolerate the ambiguous and unstructured (9); they like it. Quite characteristic is Einstein's statement, "The most beautiful thing we can experience is the mysterious. It is the source of all art and science."

These people, it is true, are the intellectuals, the researchers, and the scientists, so that perhaps the major determinant here is intellectual power. And yet we all know how many scientists with high IQ, through timidity, conventionality, anxiety, or other character defects, occupy themselves exclusively with what is known, with polishing it, arranging and rearranging it, classifying it, and otherwise puttering with it instead of discovering, as they are supposed to do.

Since, for healthy people, the unknown is not frightening, they do not have to spend any time laying the ghost, whistling past the cemetery, or otherwise protecting themselves against imagined dangers. They do not neglect the unknown, or deny it, or run away from it, or try to make believe it is really known, nor do they organize, dichotomize, or rubricize it prematurely. They do not cling to the familiar, nor is their quest for the truth a catastrophic need for certainty, safety, definiteness, and order, such as we see in an exaggerated form in Goldstein's brain-injured or in the compulsive-obsessive neurotic. They can be, when the total objective situation calls for it, comfortably disorderly, sloppy, anarchic, chaotic, vague, doubtful, uncertain, indefinite, approximate, inexact, or inaccurate (all, at certain moments in science, art, or life in general, quite desirable).

Thus it comes about that doubt, tentativeness, uncertainty, with the consequent necessity for abeyance of decision, which is for most a torture, can be for some a pleasantly stimulating challenge, a high spot in life rather than a low.

Acceptance (Self, Others, Nature)

A good many personal qualities that can be perceived on the surface and that seem at first to be various and unconnected may be understood as manifestations or derivatives of a more fundamental single attitude, namely, of a relative lack of overriding guilt, of crippling shame, and of extreme or severe anxiety. This is in direct contrast with the neurotic person who in every instance may be described as crippled by guilt and/or shame and/or anxiety. Even the normal member of our culture feels unnecessarily guilty or ashamed about too many things and has anxiety in too many unnecessary situations. Our healthy individuals find it possible to accept themselves and their own nature without chagrin or complaint or, for that matter, even without thinking about the matter very much.

They can accept their own human nature in the stoic style, with all its shortcomings, with all its discrepancies from the ideal image without feeling real concern. It would convey the wrong impression to say that they are self-satisfied. What we must say rather is that they can take the frailties and sins, weaknesses, and evils of human nature in the same unquestioning spirit with which one accepts the characteristics of nature. One does not complain about water because it is wet, or about rocks because they are hard, or about trees because they are green. As the child looks out upon the world with wide, uncritical, innocent eyes, simply noting and observing what is the case, without either arguing the matter or demanding that it be otherwise, so does the self-actualizing person look upon human nature in himself and in others. This is of course not the same as resignation in the eastern sense, but resignation too can be observed in our subjects, especially in the face of illness and death.

Be it observed that this amounts to saying in another form what we have already described; namely, that the self-actualized person sees reality more clearly: our subjects see human nature as it *is* and not as they would prefer it to be. Their eyes see what is before them without being strained through spectacles of various sorts to distort or shape or color the reality (10).

The first and most obvious level of acceptance is at the so-called animal level. Those self-actualizing people tend to be good and lusty animals, hearty in their appetites and enjoying themselves mightily without regret or shame or apology. They seem to have a uniformly good appetite for food; they seem to sleep well; they seem to enjoy their sexual lives without unnecessary inhibition and so on for all the relatively physiological impulses. They are able to accept themselves not only on these low levels, but at all levels as well; e.g., love, safety, belongingness, honor, self-respect. All of these are accepted without question as worth while, simply because these people are inclined to accept the work of nature rather than to argue with her for not having constructed things to a different pattern. This shows itself in a relative lack of the disgusts and aversions seen in average people and especially in neurotics, e.g., food annoyances, disgust with body products, body odors, and body functions.

Closely related to self-acceptance and to acceptance of others is (1) their lack of defensiveness, protective coloration, or pose, and (2) their distaste for such artificialities in others. Cant, guile, hypocrisy, front, face, playing a game, trying to impress in conventional ways: these are all absent in themselves to an unusual degree. Since they can live comfortably even with their own shortcomings, these finally come to be perceived, especially in later life, as not shortcomings at all, but simply as neutral personal characteristics.

This is not an absolute lack of guilt, shame, sadness, anxiety, defensiveness; it is a lack of unnecessary (because unrealistic) guilt, etc. The animal processes, e.g., sex, urination, pregnancy, menstruation, growing old, etc., are part of reality and so must be accepted. Thus no healthy woman feels guilty or defensive about being female or about any of the female processes.

What healthy people *do* feel guilty about (or ashamed, anxious, sad, or defensive) are (1) improvable shortcomings, e.g., laziness, thoughtlessness, loss of temper, hurting others; (2) stubborn remnants of psychological ill health, e.g., prejudice, jealousy, envy; (3) habits, which, though relatively independent of character structure, may yet be very strong, or (4) shortcomings of the species or of the culture or of the group with which they have identified. The general formula seems to be that healthy people will feel bad about discrepancies between what is and what might very well be or ought to be (11, 1, 12).

Spontaneity

Self-actualizing people can all be described as relatively spontaneous in behavior and far more spontaneous than that in their inner life, thoughts, impulses, etc. Their behavior is marked by simplicity and naturalness, and by lack of artificiality or straining for effect. This does not necessarily mean consistently unconventional behavior. If we were to take an actual count of the number of times that the self-actualizing person behaved in an unconventional manner the tally would not be high. His unconventionality is not superficial but essential or internal. It is his impulses, thought, consciousness that are so unusually unconventional, spontaneous, and natural. Apparently recognizing that the world of people in which he lives could not understand or accept this, and since he has no wish to hurt them or to fight with them over every triviality, he will go through the ceremonies and rituals of convention with a good-humored shrug and with the best possible grace. Thus I have seen a man accept an honor he laughed at and even despised in private, rather than make an issue of it and hurt the people who thought they were pleasing him.

That this conventionality is a cloak that rests very lightly upon his shoulders and is easily cast aside can be seen from the fact that the self-actualizing person practically never allows convention to hamper him or inhibit him from doing anything that he considers very important or basic. It is at such moments that his essential lack of conventionality appears, and not as with the average Bohemian or authority-rebel, who makes great issues of trivial things and who will fight against some unimportant regulation as if it were a world issue.

This same inner attitude can also be seen in those moments when the person becomes keenly absorbed in something that is close to one of his main interests. He can then be seen quite casually to drop off all sorts of rules of behavior to which at other times he conforms; it is as if he has to make a conscious effort to be conventional; as if he were conventional voluntarily and by design.

Finally, this external habit of behavior can be voluntarily dropped when in the company of people who do not demand or expect routine behavior. That this relative control of behavior is felt as something of a burden is seen by our subjects' preference for such company as allows them to be more free, natural, and spontaneous, and that relieves them of what they find sometimes to be effortful conduct.

One consequence or correlate of this characteristic is that these people have codes of ethics that are relatively autonomous and individual rather than conventional. The unthinking observer might sometimes believe them to be unethical, since they can break not only conventions but laws when the situation seems to demand it. But the very opposite is the case. They are the most ethical of people even though their ethics are not necessarily the same as those of the people around them. It is this kind of observation that leads us to understand very assuredly that the ordinary ethical behavior of the average person is largely conventional behavior rather than truly ethical behavior, e.g., behavior based on fundamentally accepted principles.

Because of this alienation from ordinary conventions and from the ordinarily accepted hypocrisies, lies, and inconsistencies of social life, they sometimes feel like spies or aliens in a foreign land and sometimes behave so.

I should not give the impression that they try to hide what they are like. Sometimes they let themselves go deliberately, out of momentary irritation with customary rigidity or with conventional blindness. They may, for instance, be trying to teach someone or they may be trying to protect someone from hurt or injustice or they may sometimes find emotions bubbling up from within them that are so pleasant or even ecstatic that it seems almost sacrilegious to suppress them. In such instances I have observed that they are not anxious or guilty or ashamed of the impression that they make on the onlooker! It is their claim that they usually behave in a conventional fashion simply because no great issues are involved or because they know people will be hurt or embarrassed by any other kind of behavior.

Their ease of penetration to reality, their closer approach to an animal-like or childlike acceptance and spontaneity imply a superior awareness of their own impulses, desires, opinions, and subjective reactions in general (1, 13, 14). Clinical study of this capacity confirms beyond a doubt the opinion, e.g., of Fromm (15) that the average normal, well-adjusted person often has not the slightest idea of what he is, of what he wants, of what his own opinions are.

It was such findings as these that led ultimately to the discovery of a most profound difference between self-actualizing people and others; namely, that the motivational life of self-actualizing people is not only quantitatively different but also qualitatively different from that of ordinary people. It seems probable that we must construct a profoundly different psychology of motivation for self-actualizing people, e.g., expression motivation or growth motivation, rather than deficiency motivation. Perhaps it will be useful to make a distinction between living and *preparing* to live. Perhaps the concept of motivation should apply *only* to non-self-actualizers. Our subjects no longer strive in the ordinary sense, but rather develop. They attempt to grow to perfection and to develop more and more fully in their own style. The motivation of ordinary men is a striving for the basic need gratifications that they lack. But self-actualizing people in fact lack none of these gratifications; and yet they have impulses. They work, they try, and they are ambitious, even though in an unusual sense. For them motivation is just character growth, character expression, maturation, and development; in a word self-actualization. Could these self-actualizing people be more human, more revealing of the original nature of the species, closer to the species type in the taxonomical sense? Ought a biological species to be judged by its crippled, warped, only partially developed specimens, or by examples that have been overdomesticated, caged, and trained?

Problem Centering

Our subjects are in general strongly focused on problems outside themselves. In current terminology they are problem centered rather than ego centered. They generally are not problems for themselves and are not generally much concerned about themselves; e.g., as contrasted with the ordinary introspectiveness that one finds in insecure people. These individuals customarily have some mission in life, some task to fulfill, some problem outside themselves which enlists much of their energies (16).

This is not necessarily a task that they would prefer or choose for themselves; it may be a task that they feel is their responsibility, duty, or obligation. This is why we use the phrase "a task that they must do" rather than the phrase "a task that they want to do." In general these tasks are nonpersonal or unselfish, concerned rather with the good of mankind in general, or of a nation in general, or of a few individuals in the subject's family.

With a few exceptions we can say that our subjects are ordinarily concerned with basic issues and eternal questions of the type that we have learned to call philosophical or ethical. Such people live customarily in the widest possible frame of reference. They seem never to get so close to the trees that they fail to see the forest. They work within a framework of values that are broad and not petty, universal and not local, and in terms of a century rather than the moment. In a word, these people are all in one sense or another philosophers, however homely.

Of course, such an attitude carries with it dozens of implications for every area of daily living. For instance, one of the main presenting symptoms originally worked with (bigness, lack of smallness, triviality, pettiness) can be subsumed under this more general heading. This impression of being above small things, of having a larger horizon, a wider breadth of vision, of living in the widest frame of reference, *sub specie aeternitatis,* is of the utmost social and interpersonal importance; it seems to impart a certain serenity and lack of worry over immediate concerns that make life easier not only for themselves but for all who are associated with them.

The Quality of Detachment; The Need for Privacy

For all my subjects it is true that they can be solitary without harm to themselves and without discomfort. Furthermore, it is true for almost all that they positively *like* solitude and privacy to a definitely greater degree than the average person. The dichotomy introvert-extrovert applies hardly at all to these people, and will not be used here. The term that seems to be most useful is detachment.

It is often possible for them to remain above the battle, to remain unruffled, undisturbed by that which produces turmoil in others. They find it easy to be aloof, reserved, and also calm and serene; thus it becomes possible for them to take personal misfortunes without reacting violently as the ordinary person does. They seem to be able to retain their dignity even in undignified surroundings and situations. Perhaps this comes in part from their tendency to stick by their own interpretation of a situation rather than to rely upon what other people feel or think about the matter. This reserve may shade over into austerity and remoteness.

This quality of detachment may have some connection with certain other qualities as well. For one thing it is possible to call my subjects more objective (in *all* senses of that word) than average people. We have seen that they are more problem centered than ego centered. This is true even when the problem concerns themselves, their own wishes, motives, hopes, or aspirations. Consequently, they have the ability to concentrate to a degree not usual for ordinary men. Intense concentration produces as a by-product such phenomena as absent-mindedness, the ability to forget and to be oblivious of outer surroundings. Examples are the ability to sleep soundly, to have undisturbed appetite, to be able to smile and laugh through a period of problems, worry, and responsibility.

In social relations with most people, detachment creates certain troubles and problems. It is easily interpreted by "normal" people as coldness, snobbishness, lack of affection, unfriendliness, or even hostility. By contrast, the ordinary friendship relationship is more clinging, more demanding, more desirous of reassurance, compliment, support, warmth, and exclusiveness. It is true that self-actualizing people do not need others in the ordinary sense. But since this being needed or being missed is the usual earnest of friendship, it is evident that detachment will not easily be accepted by average people.

Autonomy; Independence of Culture and Environment

One of the characteristics of self-actualizing people, which to a certain extent crosscuts much of what we have already described, is their relative independence of the physical and social environment. Since they are propelled by growth motivation rather than by deficiency motivation, self-actualizing people are not dependent for their main satisfactions on the real world, or other people or culture or means to ends or, in general, on extrinsic satisfactions. Rather they are dependent for their own development and continued growth on their own potentialities and latent resources. Just as the tree needs sunshine and water and food, so do most people need love, safety, and the other basic need gratifications that can come only from without. But once these external satisfiers are obtained, once these inner deficiencies are satiated by outside satisfiers, the true problem of individual human development begins, e.g., self-actualization.

This independence of environment means a relative stability in the face of hard knocks, blows, deprivations, frustrations, and the like. These people can maintain a relative serenity and happiness in the midst of circumstances that would drive other people to suicide; they have also been described as "self-contained."

Deficiency-motivated people *must* have other people available, since most of their main need gratifications (love, safety, respect, prestige, belongingness) can come only from other human beings. But growth-motivated people may actually be *hampered* by others. The determinants of satisfaction and of the good life are for them now inner-individual and *not* social. They have become strong enough to be independent of the good opinion of other people, or even of their affection. The honors, the status, the rewards, the prestige, and the love they can bestow must have become less important than self-development and inner growth (17, 18, 13, 19, 20, 21). We must remember that the best technique we know, even though not the only one, for getting to this point of independence from love and respect, is to have been given plenty of this very same love and respect in the past.

Continued Freshness of Appreciation

Self-actualizing people have the wonderful capacity to appreciate again and again, freshly and naïvely, the basic goods of life, with awe, pleasure, wonder, and even ecstasy, however stale these experiences may have become to others. Thus for such a person, any sunset may be as beautiful as the first one, any flower may be of breath-taking loveliness, even after he has seen a million flowers. The thousandth baby he sees is just as miraculous a product as the first one he saw. He remains as convinced of his luck in marriage thirty years after his marriage and is as surprised by his wife's beauty when she is sixty as he was forty years before. For such people, even the casual workaday, moment-to-moment business of living can be thrilling, exciting, and ecstatic. These intense feelings do not come all the time; they come occasionally rather than usually, but at the most unexpected moments. The person may cross the river on the ferry ten times and at the eleventh crossing have a strong recurrence of the same feelings, reaction of beauty, and excitement as when he rode the ferry for the first time (22).

There are some differences in choice of beautiful objects. Some subjects go primarily to nature. For others it is primarily children, and for a few subjects it has been primarily great music; but it may certainly be said that they derive ecstasy, inspiration, and strength from the basic experiences of life. No one of them, for instance, will get this same sort of reaction from going to a night club or getting a lot of money or having a good time at a party.

Perhaps one special experience may be added. For several of my subjects the sexual pleasures and particularly the orgasm provided, not passing pleasure alone, but some kind of basic strengthening and revivifying that some people derive from music or nature. I shall say more about this in the section on the mystic experience.

It is probable that this acute richness of subjective experience is an aspect of closeness of relationship to the concrete and fresh, *per se* reality discussed above. Perhaps what we call staleness in experience is a consequence of ticketing off a rich perception into one or another category or rubric as it proves to be no longer advantageous, or useful, or threatening or otherwise ego involved (10).

The Mystic Experience; The Oceanic Feeling

Those subjective expressions that have been called the mystic experience and described so well by William James (23) are a fairly common experience for our subjects. The strong emotions described in the previous section sometimes get strong enough, chaotic, and widespread enough to be called mystic experiences. My interest and attention in this subject was first enlisted by several of my subjects who described their sexual orgasms in vaguely familiar terms which later I remembered had been used by various writers to describe what *they* called the mystic experience. There were the same feelings of limitless horizons opening up to the vision, the feeling of being simultaneously more powerful and also more helpless than one ever was before, the feeling of great ecstasy and wonder and awe, the loss of placing in time and space with, finally, the conviction that something extremely important and valuable had happened, so that the subject is to some extent transformed and strengthened even in his daily life by such experiences.

It is quite important to dissociate this experience from any theological or supernatural reference, even though for thousands of years they have been linked. None of our subjects spontaneously made any such tie-up, although in later conversation some semi-religious conclusions were drawn by a few, e.g., "life must have a meaning," etc. Because this experience is a natural experience, well within the jurisdiction of science, it is probably better to use Freud's term for it, e.g., the oceanic feeling.

We may also learn from our subjects that such experiences can occur in a lesser degree of intensity. The theological literature has generally assumed an absolute, qualitative difference between the mystic experience and all others. As soon as it is divorced from supernatural reference and studied as a natural phenomenon, it becomes possible to place the mystic experience on a quantitative continuum from intense to mild. We discover then that the *mild* mystic experience occurs in many, perhaps even most individuals, and that in the favored individual it occurs dozens of times a day.

Apparently the acute mystic experience is a tremendous intensification of *any* of the experiences in which there is loss of self or transcendance of it, e.g., problem centering, intense concentration, muga behavior, as described by Benedict (24), intense sensuous experience, self-forgetful and intense enjoyment of music or art.

Gemeinschaftsgefühl

This word, invented by Alfred Adler (11), is the only one available that describes well the flavor of the feelings for mankind expressed by self-actualizing subjects. They have for human beings in general a deep feeling of identification, sympathy, and affection in spite of the occasional anger, impatience, or disgust described below. Because of this they have a genuine desire to help the human race. It is as if they were all members of a single family. One's feelings toward his brothers would be on the whole affectionate, even if these brothers were foolish, weak, or even if they were sometimes nasty. They would still be more easily forgiven than strangers.

If one's view is not general enough and if it is not spread over a long period of time, then one may not see this feeling of identification with mankind. The self-actualizing person is after all very different from other people in thought, impulse, behavior, emotion. When it comes down to it, in certain basic ways he is like an alien in a strange land. Very few really understand him, however much they may like him. He is often saddened, exasperated, and even enraged by the shortcomings of the average person, and while they are to him ordinarily no more than a nuisance, they sometimes become bitter tragedy. However far apart he is from them at times, he nevertheless feels a basic underlying kinship with these creatures whom he must regard with, if not condescension, at least the knowledge that he can do many things better than they can, that he can see things that they cannot see, that the truth that is so clear to him is for most people veiled and hidden. This is what Adler called the older-brotherly attitude.

Interpersonal Relations

Self-actualizing people have deeper and more profound interpersonal relations than any other adults (although not necessarily deeper than those of children). They are capable of more fusion, greater love, more perfect identification, more obliteration of the ego boundaries than other people would consider possible. There are, however, certain special characteristics of these relationships. In the first place, it is my observation that the other members of these relationships are likely to be healthier and closer to self-actualization than the average, often *much* closer. There is high selectiveness here, considering the small proportion of such people in the general population.

One consequence of this phenomenon and of certain others as well is that self-actualizing people have these especially deep ties with rather few individuals. Their circle of friends is rather small. The ones that they love profoundly are few in number. Partly this is for the reason that being very close to someone in this self-actualizing style seems to require a good deal of time. Devotion is not a matter of a moment. One subject expressed it so: "I haven't got time for many friends. Nobody has, that is, if they are to be *real* friends." The only possible exception in my group was one woman who seemed to be especially equipped socially. It was almost as if her appointed task in life was to have close and warm and beautiful relations with all the members of her family and their families as well as all her friends and theirs. Perhaps this was because she was an uneducated woman who had no formal task or career. This exclusiveness of devotion can and does exist side by side with a widespreading *Gemeinschaftsgefühl,* benevolence, affection, and friendliness (as qualified above). These people *tend* to be kind or at least patient to almost everyone. They have an especially tender love for children and are easily touched by them. In a very real even though special sense, they love or rather have compassion for all mankind.

This love does not imply lack of discrimination. The fact is that they can and do speak realistically and harshly of those who deserve it, and especially of the hypocritical, the pretentious, the pompous, or the self-inflated. But the face-to-face relationships even with these people do not always show signs of realistically low evaluations. One explanatory statement was about as follows: "Most people, after all, do not amount to much but they *could* have. They make all sorts of foolish mistakes and wind up being miserable and not knowing how they got that way when their intentions were good. Those who are not nice are usually paying for it in deep unhappiness. They should be pitied rather than attacked."

Perhaps the briefest possible description is to say that their hostile reactions to others are (1) deserved, (2) for the good of the person attacked or for someone else's good. This is to say, with Fromm, that their hostility is not character based, but is reactive or situational.

All the subjects for whom I have data show in common another characteristic that is appropriate to mention here, namely, that they attract at least some admirers, friends or even disciples or worshippers. The relation between the individual and his train of admirers is apt to be rather one-sided. The admirers are apt to demand more than our individual is willing to give. And furthermore, these devotions are apt to be rather embarrassing, distressing, and even distasteful to the self-actualizing person, since they often go beyond ordinary bounds. The usual picture is of our subject being kind and pleasant when forced into these relationships, but ordinarily trying to avoid them as gracefully as possible.

The Democratic Character Structure

All my subjects without exception may be said to be democratic people in the deepest possible sense. I say this on the basis of a previous analysis of authoritarian (25) and democratic character structures that is too elaborate to present here; it is possible only to describe some aspects of this behavior in short space. These people have all the obvious or superficial democratic characteristics. They can be and are friendly with anyone of suitable character regardless of class, education, political belief, race, or color. As a matter of fact it often seems as if they are not even aware of these differences, which are for the average person so obvious and so important.

They have not only this most obvious quality but their democratic feeling goes deeper as well. For instance they find it possible to learn from anybody who has something to teach them—no matter what other characteristics he may have. In such a learning relationship they do not try to maintain any outward dignity or to maintain status or age prestige or the like. It should even be said that my subjects share a quality that could be called humility of a certain type. They are all quite well aware of how little they know in comparison with what *could* be known and what *is* known by others. Because of this it is possible for them without pose to be honestly respectful and even humble before people who can teach them something that they do not know or who have a skill they do not possess. They give this honest respect to a carpenter who is a good carpenter; or for that matter to anybody who is a master of his own tools or his own craft.

The careful distinction must be made between this democratic feeling and a lack of discrimination in taste, of an undiscriminating equalizing of any one human being with any other. These individuals, themselves elite, select for their friends elite, but this is an elite of character, capacity, and talent, rather than of birth, race, blood, name, family, age, youth, fame, or power.

Most profound, but also most vague is the hard-to-get-at tendency to give a certain quantum of respect to *any* human being just because he is a human individual; our subjects seem not to wish to go beyond a certain minimum point, even with scoundrels, of demeaning, of derogating, of robbing of dignity.

Discrimination Between Means and Ends

I have found none of my subjects to be chronically unsure about the difference between right and wrong in his actual living. Whether or not they could verbalize the matter, they rarely showed in their day-to-day living the chaos, the confusion, the inconsistency, or the conflict that are so common in the average person's ethical dealings. This may be phrased also in such terms as: these individuals are strongly ethical, they have definite moral standards, they do right and do not do wrong. Needless to say, their notions of right and wrong are often not the conventional ones.

One way of expressing the quality I am trying to describe was suggested by Dr. David Levy, who pointed out that a few centuries ago these would all have been described as men who walk in the path of God or as godly men. So far as religion is concerned, none of my subjects is orthodoxly religious, but on the other hand I know of only one who describes himself as an atheist (four of the total group studied). The few others for whom I have information hesitate to call themselves atheists. They say that they believe in a God, but describe this God more as a metaphysical concept than as a personal figure. Whether or not they could be called religious people as a group must then depend entirely on the concept or definition of religion that we choose to use. If religion is defined only in social-behavioral terms, then these are all religious people, the atheists included. But if more conservatively we use the term religion so as to include and stress the supernatural element and institutional orthodoxy (certainly the more common usage) then our answer must be quite different, for then almost none of them is religious.

Self-actualizing people most of the time behave as though, for them, means and ends are clearly distinguishable. In general, they are fixed on ends rather than on means, and means are quite definitely subordinated to these ends. This, however, is an oversimple statement. Our subjects make the situation more complex by often regarding as ends in themselves many experiences and activities that are, for other people, only means to ends. Our subjects are somewhat more likely to appreciate for its own sake, and in an absolute way, the doing itself; they can often enjoy for its own sake the getting to some place as well as the arriving. It is occasionally possible for them to make out of the most trivial and routine activity an intrinsically enjoyable game or dance or play. Wertheimer pointed out that most children are so creative that they can transform hackneyed routine, mechanical, and rote experiences, e.g., as in one of his experiments, transporting books from one set of shelves to another, into a structured and amusing game of a sort by doing this according to a certain system or with a certain rhythm.

Philosophical, Unhostile Sense of Humor

One very early finding that was quite easy to make, because it was common to all my subjects, was that their sense of humor is not of the ordinary type. They do not consider funny what the average man considers to be funny. Thus they do not laugh at hostile humor (making people laugh by hurting someone) or superiority humor (laughing at someone else's inferiority) or authority-rebellion humor (the unfunny, smutty joke). Characteristically what they consider humor is more closely allied to philosophy than to anything else. It may also be called the humor of the real because it consists in large part in poking fun at human beings in general when they are foolish, or forget their place in the universe, or try to be big when they are actually small. This can take the form of poking fun at themselves, but this is not done in any masochistic or clownlike way. Lincoln's humor can serve as a suitable example. Probably Lincoln never made a joke that hurt anybody else; it is also likely that many or even most of his jokes had something to say, had a function beyond just producing a laugh. They often seemed to be education in a more palatable form, akin to parables or fables.

On a simple quantitative basis, our subjects may be said to be humorous less often than the average of the population. Punning, joking, witty remarks, gay repartee, persiflage of the ordinary sort is much less often seen than the rather thoughtful, philosophical humor that elicits a smile more usually than a laugh, that is intrinsic to the situation rather than added to it, that is spontaneous rather than planned, and that very often can never be repeated. It should not be surprising that the average man, accustomed as he is to joke books and belly laughs, considers our subjects to be rather on the sober and serious side.

Creativeness

This is a universal characteristic of all the people studied or observed. There is no exception. Each one shows in one way or another a special kind of creativeness or originality or inventiveness that has certain peculiar characteristics. These special characteristics can be understood more fully in the light of discussion later in this chapter. For one thing, it is different from the special-talent creativeness of the Mozart type. We may as well face the fact that the so-called geniuses display ability that we do not understand. All we can say of them is that they seem to be specially endowed with a drive and a capacity that may have rather little relationship to the rest of the personality and with which, from all evidence, the individuals seem to be born. Such talent we have no concern with here since it does not rest upon psychic health or basic satisfaction. The creativeness of the self-actualized man seems rather to be kin to the naïve and universal creativeness of unspoiled children. It seems to be more a fundamental characteristic of common human nature—a potentiality given to all human beings at birth. Most human beings lose this as they become enculturated, but some few individuals seem either to retain this fresh and naïve, direct way of looking at life, or if they have lost it, as most people do, they later in life recover it.

This creativeness appears in some of our subjects not in the usual forms of writing books, composing music, or producing artistic objects, but rather may be much more humble. It is as if this special type of creativeness, being an expression of healthy personality, is projected out upon the world or touches whatever activity the person is engaged in. In this sense there can be creative shoemakers or carpenters or clerks. Whatever one does can be done with a certain attitude, a certain spirit that arises out of the nature of the character of the person performing the act. One can even *see* creatively as the child does.

This quality is differentiated out here for the sake of discussion, as if it were something separate from the characteristics that precede it and follow it, but this is not actually the case. Perhaps when we speak of creativeness here we are simply describing from another point of view, namely, from the point of view of consequences, what we have described above as a greater freshness, penetration, and efficiency of perception. These people seem to see the true and the real more easily. It is because of this that they seem to other more limited men creative.

Furthermore, as we have seen, these individuals are less inhibited, less constricted, less bound, in a word, less enculturated. In more positive terms, they are more spontaneous, more natural, more human. This too would have as one of its consequences what would seem to other people to be creativeness. If we assume, as we may from our study of children, that all people were once spontaneous, and perhaps in their deepest roots still are, but that these people have in addition to their deep spontaneity a superficial but powerful set of inhibitions, then this spontaneity must be checked so as not to appear very often. If there were no choking-off forces, we might expect that every human being would show this special type of creativeness.

Resistance to Enculturation

Self-actualizing people are not well adjusted (in the naïve sense of approval of and identification with the culture). They get along with the culture in various ways, but of all of them it may be said that in a certain profound and meaningful sense they resist enculturation and maintain a certain inner detachment from the culture in which they are immersed. Since in the culture-and-personality literature very little has been said about resistance to molding by the culture, and since, as Riesman (251) has clearly pointed out, the saving remnant is especially important for American society, even our meager data are of some importance.

On the whole the relationship of these healthy people with their much less healthy culture is a complex one; from it can be teased out at least the following components.

1. All these people fall well within the limits of apparent conventionality in choice of clothes, of language, of food, of ways of doing things in our culture. And yet they are not *really* conventional, certainly not fashionable or smart or chic.

The expressed inner attitude is usually that it is ordinarily of no great consequence which folkways are used, that one set of traffic rules is as good as any other set, that while they make life smoother they do not really matter enough to make a fuss about. Here again we see the general tendency of these people to accept most states of affairs that they consider unimportant or unchangeable or not of primary concern to them as individuals. Since choice of shoes, or style of haircut or politeness, or manner of behaving at a party are not of primary concern to any of the individuals studied, they are apt to elicit as a reaction only a shrug of the shoulders.

But since this tolerant acceptance is not warm approval with identification, their yielding to convention is apt to be rather casual and perfunctory, with cutting of corners in favor of directness, honesty, saving of energy, etc. In the pinches, when yielding to conventions is too annoying or too expensive, the apparent conventionality reveals itself for the superficial thing that it is, and is tossed off as easily as a cloak.

2. Hardly any of these people can be called authority rebels in the adolescent or hot sense. They show no active impatience or moment-to-moment, chronic, long-time discontent with the culture or preoccupation with changing it quickly, although they often enough show bursts of indignation with injustice. One of these subjects, who was a hot rebel in his younger days, a union organizer in the days when this was a highly dangerous occupation, has given up in disgust and hopelessness. As he became resigned to the slowness of social change (in this culture and in this era) he turned finally to education of the young. All the others show what might be called a calm, long-time concern with culture improvement that seems to me to imply an acceptance of slowness of change along with the unquestioned desirability and necessity of such change.

This is by no means a lack of fight. When quick change is possible or when resolution and courage are needed, it is available in these people. Although they are not a radical group of people in the ordinary sense, I think they easily *could* be. First of all, this is primarily an intellectual group (it must be remembered who selected them), most of whom already have a mission, and feel that they are doing something really important to improve the world. Second, they are a realistic group and seem to be unwilling to make great but useless sacrifices. In a more drastic situation it seems very likely that they would be willing to drop their work in favor of radical social action, e.g., the anti-Nazi underground in Germany or in France. My impression is that they are not against fighting but only against ineffective fighting.

Another point that came up very commonly in discussion was the desirability of enjoying life and having a good time. This seems to all but one to be incompatible with hot and full-time rebelliousness. Furthermore, it seems to them that this is too great a sacrifice to make for the small returns expected. Most of them have had their episodes of fighting, impatience, and eagerness in youth, and in most cases have learned that their optimism about quick change was unwarranted. What they settled down to as a group was an accepting, calm, good-humored everyday effort to improve the culture, usually from within, rather than to reject it and fight it from without.

3. An inner feeling of detachment from the culture is not necessarily conscious but is displayed by almost all, particularly in discussions of the American culture as a whole, in various comparisons with other cultures, and in the fact that they very frequently seem to be able to stand off from it as if they did not quite belong to it. The mixture of varying proportions of affection or approval and hostility or criticism indicated that they select from American culture what is good in it by their lights and reject what they think bad in it. In a word they weigh it, assay it, taste it, and then make their own decisions.

This is certainly very different from the ordinary sort of passive yielding to cultural shaping displayed for instance by the ethnocentric subjects of the many studies of authoritarian personalities.

Detachment from the culture is probably also reflected in our self-actualizing subjects' detachment from people and their liking for privacy, which has been described above, as also in their lesser than average need for and liking for the familiar and customary.

4. For these and other reasons they may be called autonomous, i.e., ruled by the laws of their own character rather than by the rules of society. It is in this sense that they are not only or merely Americans, but also to a greater degree than others, members at large of the human species. To say that they are above or beyond the American culture would be misleading if interpreted strictly, for after all they speak American, act American, have American characters, etc.

And yet if we compare them with the oversocialized, the robotized, or the ethnocentric, we are irresistibly tempted to hypothesize that this group is not simply another subcultural group, but rather less enculturated, less flattened out, less molded. This implies degree, and placing on a continuum that ranges from relative acceptance of the culture to relative detachment from it.

If this turns out to be a tenable hypothesis, at least one other hypothesis can be deduced from it, that those individuals in different cultures who are more detached from their own culture should not only have less national character but also should be more like each other in certain respects than they are like the less developed members of their own societies. Of course this raises questions about what constitutes the good American.

In summary the perennial question, Is it possible to be a good or healthy man in an imperfect culture? has been answered by the observation that it *is* possible for relatively healthy people to develop in the American culture. They manage to get along by a complex combination of inner autonomy and outer acceptance that of course will be possible only so long as the culture remains tolerant of this kind of detached withholding from complete cultural identification.

Of course this is not ideal health. Our imperfect society clearly forces inhibitions and restraints upon our subjects. To the extent that they have to maintain their little secrecies, to that extent is their spontaneity lessened and to that extent are some of their potentialities not actualized. And since only few people can attain health in our culture, those who do attain it are lonely for their own kind and therefore again less spontaneous and less actualized.[1]

The Imperfections of Self-Actualizing People

The ordinary mistake that is made by novelists, poets, and essayists about the good human being is to make him so good that he is a caricature, so that nobody would like to be like him. The individual's own wishes for perfection, and his guilt and shame about shortcomings are projected upon various kinds of people from whom the average man demands much more than he himself gives. Thus teachers and ministers are ordinarily conceived to be rather joyless people who have no mundane desires and who have no weaknesses. It is my belief that most of the novelists who have attempted to portray good (healthy) people did this sort of thing, making them into stuffed shirts or marionettes or unreal projections of unreal ideals, rather than into the robust, hearty, lusty individuals they really are. Our subjects show many of the lesser human failings. They too are equipped with silly, wasteful, or thoughtless habits. They can be boring, stubborn, irritating. They are by no means free from a rather superficial vanity, pride, par-

[1] I am indebted to Dr. Tamara Dembo for her help with this problem.

tiality to their own productions, family, friends, and children. Temper outbursts are not rare.

Our subjects are occasionally capable of an extraordinary and unexpected ruthlessness. It must be remembered that they are very strong people. This makes it possible for them to display a surgical coldness when this is called for, beyond the power of the average man. The man who found that a long-trusted acquaintance was dishonest cut himself off from this friendship sharply and abruptly and without any pangs whatsoever. Another woman who was married to someone she did not love, when she decided on divorce, did it with a decisiveness that looked almost like ruthlessness. Some of them recover so quickly from the death of people close to them as to seem heartless.

Not only are these people strong but also they are independent of the opinions of other people. One woman, extremely irritated by the stuffy conventionalism of some individuals she was introduced to at a gathering, went out of her way to shock these people by her language and behavior. One might say it was all right for her to react to irritation in this way, but another result was that these people were completely hostile not only to the woman but to the friends in whose home this meeting took place. While our subject *wanted* to alienate these people, the host and hostess did not.

We may mention one more example that arises primarily from the absorption of our subjects in an impersonal world. In their concentration, in their fascinated interest, in their intense concentration on some phenomenon or question, they may become absent-minded or humorless and forget their ordinary social politeness. In such circumstances, they are apt to show themselves more clearly as essentially not interested in chatting, gay conversation, party-going, or the like, they may use language or behavior that may be very distressing, shocking, insulting, or hurtful to others. Other undesirable (at least from the point of view of others) consequences of detachment have been listed above.

Even their kindness can lead them into mistakes, e.g., marrying out of pity, getting too closely involved with neurotics, bores, unhappy people, and then being sorry for it, allowing scoundrels to impose on them for a while, giving more than they should so that occasionally they encourage parasites and psychopaths, etc.

Finally, it has already been pointed out that these people are *not* free of guilt, anxiety, sadness, self-castigation, internal strife, and conflict. The fact that these arise out of nonneurotic sources is of little consequence to most people today (even to most psychologists) who are therefore apt to think them *un*healthy for this reason.

Values and Self-Actualization

A firm foundation for a value system is automatically furnished to the self-actualizer by his philosophic acceptance of the nature of his self, of human nature, of much of social life, and of nature and physical reality. These acceptance values account for a high percentage of the total of his individual value judgments from day to day. What he approves of, disapproves of, is loyal to, opposes or proposes, what pleases him or displeases him can often be understood as surface derivations of this source trait of acceptance.

Not only is this foundation automatically (and universally) supplied to *all* self-actualizers by their intrinsic dynamics (so that in at least this respect fully developed human nature may be universal and cross-cultural); other determiners are supplied as well by these same dynamics. Among these are (1) his peculiarly comfortable relationships with reality, (2) his *Gemeinschaftsgefühl,* (3) his basically satisfied condition from which flow, as epiphenomena, various consequences of surplus, of wealth, overflowing abundance, (4) his characteristically discriminating relations to means and ends, etc. (see above).

One most important consequence of this attitude toward the world—as well as a validation of it—is the fact that conflict and struggle, ambivalence and uncertainty over choice lessen or disappear in many areas of life. Apparently "morality" is largely an epiphenomenon of nonacceptance or dissatisfaction. Many problems are seen to be gratuitous and fade out of existence in the atmosphere of pagan acceptance. It is not so much that the problem is solved as that it becomes clearly seen that it never was an intrinsic problem in the first place, but only a sick-man-created one, e.g., card-playing, dancing, wearing short dresses, exposing the head (in some churches) or *not* exposing the head (in others), drinking wine, or eating some meats and not others, or eating them on some days but not on others. Not only are such trivialities deflated; the process also goes on at a more important level, e.g., the relations between the sexes, attitudes toward the structure of the body and toward its functioning, and toward death itself.

The pursuit of this finding to more profound levels has suggested to the writer that much else of what passes for morals, ethics, and values may be the gratuitous epiphenomena of the pervasive psychopathology of the average. Many conflicts, frustrations, and threats (which force the kind of choice in which value is expressed), evaporate or resolve for the self-actualizing person in the same way as do, let us say, conflicts over dancing. For him the seemingly irreconcilable battle of the sexes becomes no conflict at all but rather a delightful collaboration. The antagonistic interests of adults and children turn out to be not so antagonistic after all. Just as with sex and age differences, so also is it with natural differences, class and caste differences, political differences, role differences, religious differences, etc. As we know, these are each fertile breeding grounds for anxiety, fear, hostility, aggression, defensiveness, and jealousy. But it begins to appear that they *need not be,* for our subjects' reaction to differences is much less often of this undesirable type.

To take the teacher-student relationship as a specific paradigm, our teacher subjects behaved in a very unneurotic way simply by interpreting the whole situation differently, e.g., as a pleasant collaboration rather than as a clash of wills, of authority, of dignity, etc.; the replacement of artificial dignity—that is easily and inevitably threatened—with the natural simplicity that is *not* easily threatened; the giving up of the attempt to be omniscient and omnipotent; the absence of student-threatening authoritarianism; the refusal to regard the students as competing with each other or with the teacher; the refusal to assume the professor stereotype and the insistence on remaining as realistically human as, say, a plumber or a carpenter; all of these created a classroom atmosphere in which suspicion, wariness, defensiveness, hostility, and anxiety disappeared. So also do similar threat responses tend to disappear in marriages, in families and in other interpersonal situations when threat itself is reduced.

The principles and the values of the desperate man and of the psychologically healthy man must be different in at least some ways. They have profoundly different perceptions (interpretations) of the physical world, the social world and the private psychological world, whose organization and economy is in part the responsibility of the person's value system. For the basically deprived man the world is a dangerous place, a jungle, an enemy territory populated by (1) those whom he can dominate and (2) those who can dominate him. His value system is of necessity, like that of any jungle denizen, dominated and organized by the lower needs, especially the creature needs and the safety needs. The basically satisfied person is in a different case. He can afford out of his abundance to take these needs and their satisfaction for granted and can devote himself to higher gratifications. This is to say that their value systems are different, in fact *must* be different.

The topmost portion of the value system of the self-actualized person is entirely unique and idiosyncratic-character-structure-expressive. This must be true by definition, for self-actualization is actualization of a self, and no two selves are altogether alike. There is only one Renoir, one Brahms, one Spinoza. Our subjects had very much in common, as we have seen, and yet at the same time were more completely individualized, more unmistakably themselves, less easily confounded with others than any average control group could possibly be. That is to say, they are simultaneously very much alike and very much unlike each other. They are more completely individual than any group that has ever been described, and yet are also more completely socialized, more identified with humanity than any other group yet described.

The Resolution of Dichotomies in Self-Actualization

As this point we may finally allow ourselves to generalize and underscore a very important theoretical conclusion derivable from the study of self-actualizing people. At several points in this chapter—and in other chapters as well—it was concluded that what had been considered in the past to be polarities or opposites or dichotomies were so *only in unhealthy people*. In healthy people, these dichotomies were resolved, the polarities disappeared, and many oppositions thought to be intrinsic merged and coalesced with each other to form unities.

For example the age-old opposition between heart and head, reason and instinct, or cognition and conation was seen to disappear in healthy people where they become synergic rather than antagonists, and where conflict between them disappears because they say the same thing and point to the same conclusion. In a word in these people, desires are in excellent accord with reason. St. Augustine's "Love God and do as you will" can easily be translated, "Be healthy and then you may trust your impulses."

The dichotomy between selfishness and unselfishness disappears altogether in healthy people because in principle every act is *both* selfish and unselfish. Our subjects are simultaneously very spiritual and very pagan and sensual. Duty cannot be contrasted with pleasure nor work with play when duty *is* pleasure, when work *is* play, and the person doing his duty and being virtuous is simultaneously seeking his pleasure and being happy. If the most socially identified people are themselves also the most individualistic people, of what use is to retain the polarity? If the most mature are also childlike? And if the most ethical and moral people are also the lustiest and most animal?

Similar findings have been reached for kindness-ruthlessness, concreteness-abstractness, acceptance-rebellion, self-society, adjustment-maladjustment, detachment from others-identification with others, serious-humorous, Dionysian-Apollonian, introverted-extroverted, intense-casual, serious-frivolous, conventional-unconventional, mystic-realistic, active-passive, masculine-feminine, lust-love, and Eros-Agape. In these people, the id, the ego, and the superego are collaborative and synergic; they do not war with each other nor are their interests in basic disagreement as they are in neurotic people. So also do the cognitive, the conative, and the emotional coalesce into an organismic unity and into a non-Aristotelian interpenetration. The higher and the lower are not in opposition but in agreement, and a thousand serious philosophical dilemmas are discovered to have more than two horns, or, paradoxically, no horns at all. If the war between the sexes turns out to be no war at all in matured people, but only a sign of crippling and stunting of growth, who then would wish to choose sides? Who would deliberately and knowingly choose psychopathology? Is it necessary to choose between the good woman and the bad, as if they were mutually exclusive, when we have found that the really healthy woman is both at the same time?

In this, as in other ways, healthy people are so different from average ones, not only in degree but in kind as well, that they generate two very different kinds of psychology. It becomes more and more clear that the study of crippled, stunted, immature, and unhealthy specimens can yield only a cripple psychology and a cripple philosophy. The study of self-actualizing people must be the basis for a more universal science of psychology.

Bibliography

1. Fromm, E., *Man for Himself,* Rinehart, 1947.
2. Goldstein, K., *The Organism,* American Book, 1939.
3. May, R., *Man's Search for Himself,* Norton, 1953.
4. Mumford, L., *The Conduct of Life,* Harcourt, Brace, 1951.
5. Riesman, D., *The Lonely Crowd,* Yale University Press, 1950.
6. Maslow, A. H., *The S-I Test: A Measure of Psychological Security-Insecurity,* Stanford University Press, 1952.
7. Money-Kyrle, R. E., Towards a common aim—a psycho-analytical contribution to ethics, *Brit. J. med. Psychol.,* 1944, *20,* 105-117.
8. Luchins, A., Mechanization in problem solving: the effect of *Einstellung, Psychol. Monogr.,* 1942, *54,* No. 6.
9. Frenkel-Brunswik, E., Intolerance of ambiguity as an emotional and perceptual personality variable, *J. Personality,* 1949, *18,* 108-143.
10. Bergson, H., *Creative Evolution,* Modern Library, 1944.
11. Adler, A., *Social Interest,* Putnam, 1939.
12. Horney, K., *Our Inner Conflicts,* Norton, 1945.
13. Rand, A., *The Fountainhead,* Bobbs-Merrill, 1943.
14. Reik, T., *Listening With the Third Ear,* Farrar and Straus, 1948.
15. Fromm, E., *Escape From Freedom,* Farrar and Rinehart, 1941.

16. Angyal, A., *Foundations for a Science of Personality,* Commonwealth Fund, 1941.
17. Huxley, A., *The Perennial Philosophy,* Harper, 1944.
18. Northrop, F.S.C., *The Logic of the Sciences and the Humanities,* Macmillan, 1947.
19. Rogers, C., The concept of the fully functioning person (mimeographed).
20. Taylor, E., *Richer By Asia,* Houghton Mifflin, 1947.
21. Wolfe, T., *You Can't Go Home Again,* Harper, 1949.
22. Eastman, M., *The Enjoyment of Poetry,* Scribner, 1928.
23. James, W., *The Varieties of Religious Experience,* Modern Library, 1943.
24. Benedict, R., *The Chrysanthemum and the Sword,* Houghton Mifflin, 1946.
25. Maslow, A. H., The authoritarian character structure, *J. social Psychol.,* 1943, *18,* 401-411.

RALPH WALDO EMERSON / Ode Inscribed to W. H. Channing

THOUGH LOATH to grieve
The evil time's sole patriot,
I cannot leave
My honied thought
For the priest's cant,
Or statesman's rant.

If I refuse
My study for their politique,
Which at the best is trick,
The angry Muse
Puts confusion in my brain.

But who is he that prates
Of the culture of mankind,
Of better arts and life?
Go, blindworm, go,
Behold the famous States
Harrying Mexico
With rifle and with knife!

Or who, with accent bolder,
Dare praise the freedom-loving mountaineer?
I found by thee, O rushing Contoocook!
And in thy valleys, Agiochook!
The jackals of the Negro-holder.

The God who made New Hampshire
Taunted the lofty land
With little men;
Small bat and wren
House in the oak:
If earth-fire cleave
The upheaved land, and bury the folk,
The southern crocodile would grieve.
Virtue palters; Right is hence;
Freedom praised, but hid;
Funeral eloquence
Rattles the coffin-lid.

What boots thy zeal,
O glowing friend,
That would indignant rend
The northland from the south?
Wherefore? to what good end?
Boston Bay and Bunker Hill
Would serve things still;
Things are of the snake.

The horseman serves the horse,
The neatherd serves the neat,
The merchant serves the purse,
The eater serves his meat;
'Tis the day of the chattel,
Web to weave, and corn to grind,
Things are in the saddle,
And ride mankind.

There are two laws discrete,
Not reconciled,
Law for man, and law for thing;
The last builds town and fleet,
But it runs wild,
And doth the man unking.

'Tis fit the forest fall,
The steep be graded,
The mountain tunnelled,
The sand shaded,
The orchard planted,
The glebe tilled,
The prairie granted,
The steamer built.

Let man serve law for man;
Live for friendship, live for love,
For truth's and harmony's behoof;
The state may follow how it can,
As Olympus follows Jove.

Yet do not I implore
The wrinkled shopman to my sounding woods,
Nor bid the unwilling senator
Ask votes of thrushes in the solitudes.
Every one to his chosen work;
Foolish hands may mix and mar;
Wise and sure the issues are.
Round they roll till dark is light,
Sex to sex, and even to odd;
The over-god
Who marries Right to Might,
Who peoples, unpeoples,
He who exterminates
Races by stronger races,
Black by white faces,
Knows to bring honey
Out of the lion;
Grafts gentlest scion
On pirate and Turk.

The Cossack eats Poland,
Like stolen fruit;
Her last noble is ruined,
Her last poet mute:
Straight, into double band
The victors divide;
Half for freedom strike and stand;
The astonished Muse finds thousands at her side.

ROBERT BROWNING / Rabbi Ben Ezra

I

GROW OLD along with me!
The best is yet to be,
The last of life, for which the first was made:
Our times are in His hand
Who saith "A whole I planned,
Youth shows but half; trust God: see all nor be afraid!"

II

Not that, amassing flowers,
Youth sighed "Which rose make ours,
Which lily leave and then as best recall?"
Not that, admiring stars,
It yearned "Nor Jove, nor Mars;
Mine be some figured flame which blends, transcends them all!"

III

Not for such hopes and fears
Annulling youth's brief years,
Do I remonstrate: folly wide the mark!
Rather I prize the doubt
Low kinds exist without,
Finished and finite clods, untroubled by a spark.

IV

Poor vaunt of life indeed,
Were man but formed to feed
On joy, to solely seek and find and feast:
Such feasting ended, then
As sure an end to men;
Irks care the crop-full bird? Frets doubt the maw-crammed beast?

V

Rejoice we are allied
To That which doth provide
And not partake, effect and not receive!
A spark disturbs our clod;
Nearer we hold of God
Who gives, than of His tribes that take, I must believe.

VI

Then, welcome each rebuff
That turns earth's smoothness rough,
Each sting that bids nor sit nor stand but go!
Be our joys three-parts pain!
Strive, and hold cheap the strain;
Learn, nor account the pang; dare, never grudge the throe!

VII

For thence,—a paradox
Which comforts while it mocks,—
Shall life succeed in that it seems to fail:
What I aspired to be,
And was not, comforts me:
A brute I might have been, but would not sink i' the scale.

VIII

What is he but a brute
Whose flesh has soul to suit,
Whose spirit works lest arms and legs want play?
To man, propose this test—
Thy body at its best,
How far can that project thy soul on its lone way?

IX

Yet gifts should prove their use:
I own the Past profuse
Of power each side, perfection every turn:
Eyes, ears took in their dole,
Brain treasured up the whole;
Should not the heart beat once "How good to live and learn"?

X

Not once beat "Praise be Thine!
I see the whole design,
I, who saw power, see now love perfect too:
Perfect I call Thy plan:
Thanks that I was a man!
Maker, remake, complete,—I trust what Thou shalt do!"

XI

For pleasant is this flesh;
Our soul, in its rose-mesh
Pulled ever to the earth, still yearns for rest;
Would we some prize might hold
To match those manifold
Possessions of the brute,—gain most, as we did best!

XII

Let us not always say
"Spite of this flesh to-day
I strove, made head, gained ground upon the whole!"
As the bird wings and sings,
Let us cry "All good things
Are ours, nor soul helps flesh more, now, than flesh helps soul!"

XIII

Therefore I summon age
To grant youth's heritage,

Life's struggle having so far reached its term:
Thence shall I pass, approved
A man, for aye removed
From the developed brute; a god though in the germ.

XIV

And I shall thereupon
Take rest, ere I be gone
Once more on my adventure brave and new:
Fearless and unperplexed,
When I wage battle next,
What weapons to select, what armor to indue.

XV

Youth ended, I shall try
My gain or loss thereby;
Leave the fire ashes, what survives is gold:
And I shall weigh the same,
Give life its praise or blame:
Young, all lay in dispute; I shall know, being old.

XVI

For note, when evening shuts,
A certain moment cuts
The deed off, calls the glory from the gray:
A whisper from the west
Shoots—"Add this to the rest,
Take it and try its worth: here dies another day."

XVII

So, still within this life,
Though lifted o'er its strife,
Let me discern, compare, pronounce at last,
"This rage was right i' the main,
That acquiescence vain:
The Future I may face now I have proved the Past."

XVIII

For more is not reserved
To man, with soul just nerved
To act to-morrow what he learns to-day:
Here, work enough to watch
The Master work, and catch
Hints of the proper craft, tricks of the tool's true play.

XIX

As it was better, youth
Should strive, through acts uncouth,
Toward making, than repose on aught found made:
So, better, age, exempt
From strife, should know, than tempt
Further. Thou waitedest age: wait death nor be afraid!

XX

Enough now, if the Right
And Good and Infinite
Be named here, as thou callest thy hand thine own,
With knowledge absolute,
Subject to no dispute
From fools that crowded youth, nor let thee feel alone.

XXI

Be there, for once and all,
Severed great minds from small,
Announced to each his station in the Past!
Was I, the world arraigned,
Were they, my soul disdained,
Right? Let age speak the truth and give us peace at last!

XXII

Now, who shall arbitrate?
Ten men love what I hate,
Shun what I follow, slight what I receive;
Ten, who in ears and eyes
Match me: we all surmise,
They this thing, and I that: whom shall my soul believe?

XXIII

Not on the vulgar mass
Called "work," must sentence pass,
Things done, that took the eye and had the price;
O'er which, from level stand,
The low world laid its hand,
Found straightway to its mind, could value in a trice:

XXIV

But all, the world's coarse thumb
And finger failed to plumb,
So passed in making up the main account;
All instincts immature,
All purposes unsure,
That weighed not as his work, yet swelled the man's amount:

XXV

Thoughts hardly to be packed
Into a narrow act,
Fancies that broke through language and escaped;
All I could never be,
All, men ignored in me,
This, I was worth to God, whose wheel the pitcher shaped.

XXVI

Ay, note that Potter's wheel,
That metaphor! and feel
Why time spins fast, why passive lies our clay,—

Thou, to whom fools propound,
When the wine makes its round,
"Since life fleets, all is change; the Past gone, seize to-day!"

XXVII

Fool! All that is, at all,
Lasts ever, past recall;
Earth changes, but thy soul and God stand sure:
What entered into thee,
That was, is, and shall be:
Time's wheel runs back or stops: Potter and clay endure.

XXVIII

He fixed thee 'mid this dance
Of plastic circumstance,
This Present, thou, forsooth, wouldst fain arrest:
Machinery just meant
To give thy soul its bent,
Try thee and turn thee forth, sufficiently impressed.

XXIX

What though the earlier grooves
Which ran the laughing loves
Around thy base, no longer pause and press?
What though, about thy rim,
Skull-things in order grim
Grow out, in graver mood, obey the sterner stress?

XXX

Look not thou down but up!
To uses of a cup,
The festal board, lamp's flash and trumpet's peal,
The new wine's foaming flow,
The Master's lips a-glow!
Thou, heaven's consummate cup, what need'st thou with earth's wheel?

XXXI

But I need, now as then,
Thee, God, who mouldest men;
And since, not even while the whirl was worst,
Did I,—to the wheel of life
With shapes and colors rife,
Bound dizzily,—mistake my end, to slake Thy thirst:

XXXII

So, take and use Thy work:
Amend what flaws may lurk,
What strain o' the stuff, what warpings past the aim!
My times be in Thy hand!
Perfect the cup as planned!
Let age approve of youth, and death complete the same!

C. E. MONTAGUE / Action

WHEN Christopher Bell was just fifty-two he woke up one September morning to feel a slight numbness all down his right side. Some of the numbness was in his right arm; a good deal of it in his right thigh, along its outside, rather less in his right foot; and just a little in his head—all over the hinterland of his right ear.

It seemed a big percentage of a man to "go to sleep" at one time. He lay still for a minute, to let it pass off. But it didn't. So he began to speculate. When he got up, would he be able to stand? And to walk straight? Would his head go on working all right, with that bit of it stiff? Just how hard a punch would it turn out to be, that some god or devil had given him in the night?

He tried. Yes, he could stand, walk, dress and shave. No portion of him was absolutely on strike. But the numbness went on. And somehow he couldn't feel sure that some part of the right flank of his body or brain would not give way, without notice, and give him a cropper. You never know how deliciously sure you have been of yourself, of every scrap of yourself, all the days of your health, till some small gadget inside you is put out of action: Bell made this deep reflection while going downstairs to his solitary breakfast. He kept one hand on the banisters.

Christopher Bell was the reigning sovereign of a respectable dynasty of "merchant princes" in Manchester. For several generations his clan had embraced the higher civilisation so far as English Public schools and universities lead to such embraces. He had read with understanding and relish, and he had travelled with open eyes. He could value the great things in the arts and in science—indeed, in the whole ampler life of the race. And always, till now, his blood had pretty well bubbled with health. He had rowed, run, swum and ridden well. To his body, at forty years old, the War had brought a second boyhood of happy absorption in efforts merely physical.

Half-way through the war, the wife he had loved in every tissue of body and soul had died of something brought on by too passionate overwork for the cause. The news came to Bell in a hospital where he had just begun to grow a new skin on a face and hands well flayed and charred by chemical warfare. He could not see at the time, so a nurse read the telegram out. His face was buried deep in a canary-coloured mask of wadding stained with picric acid, so the nurse could not see how he took it—only knew that he thanked her very civilly through the little blow-hole left for his mouth. I fancy Bell was hanging on hard to the thought that he still had two children, a boy and a girl, both in their teens. Soldiers, even educated ones, are apt to grow sentimental, especially when wounded. Bell, the war widower, lay, week by week, behind his fancy-dress mask, staying his mind on an ingenious vision of an improved world, to come after the war. He saw it as a young man and a young woman standing in summer twilight, under the stars, with their eyes all a-shine at the loveliness of the life which it had taken so much pain and shame to make possible for them.

Many soldiers hugged these quaint fancies, in their bad times. They helped, for the moment. It was afterwards that they had to be paid for. In the foul enervatory air that filled England and Europe just after the war Bell's boy and girl drifted feebly into failure. Both were married lovelessly now, each to another small waste product of that waste-producing time. Somewhere out of Bell's sight these forfeited objects of his pride and joy were shuffling punily through life. He gathered that they were rather ashamed of him as an old slow-coach provincial.

Bell was not given to wallowing in self-pity. Still, as you see, he had had his losses, like another.

Your merchant prince, in these days, is prone to lose heart, get himself up as an owner of land and beeves, and melt weakly into the common herd of squires who know not, poor fellows, what it is to go on 'Change. Bell was different. He had pride. He stuck, as his father had done, to his post among the garrison of the smutty city that had done well by them. He lived where he could hear the Town Hall clock strike twelve when the traffic was quiet at night, and a North wind blowing. He liked the sound, he was so oddly civic a person.

To this old-fashioned hobby Bell added some cheap habits less rare in rich men. He stood on guard against his wealth, lest it should cut him off from the sight and sound of ordinary and unprincely men, for whom his regard had been re-doubled by four years of living with them in the war. Because of this fad he nearly always went in to the city by tram. This morning he walked the three hundred yards from his house to the tram's stopping-place with deliberate caution. He could not be sure of that sleepy right leg. He was still distrusting it temperately when he had taken his seat and was tendering his fare to town.

The conductor rejected the tender, at sight. "We doan't taäke bootons," he said with civil composure.

Bell examined the bright disc that he had offered as a sixpence.

Behold! a silvery trouser-button. Last night it had come off and he had slipped it into a pocket. He put his finger-tips ruefully up to his eyes. "I'm sorry," he said to the man, as he gave the right coin.

"It's aal reet, Sir," the conductor said quietly. Once he saw that no pulling of legs had been intended, his tact and sympathy were perfect.

He passed on to collect other fares. But a new care remained in Bell's mind. Sight, too? Was that going? Sight, touch, the whole sensory business, losing precision, entering on the long slope to decay—the silver cord going loose and the golden bowl cracking? When a man who has known how to read feels the first clap of the hand of Time on his shoulder, he has plenty of ready prompters to ruefulness; so many excellent poets have found handsome words for the mists and mellow poignancy of man's autumn, the lapse from old vigour and vision into mere drug-takers' dreams while we are led down the avenue lined with overblown roses, to lie in the dust at its end.

Bell kept his head. But his memory was beginning to bulge with lovely quotations not conducive to high spirits—"Bare ruined choirs where late the sweet birds sang," and all that lot.

The morning's office work did him good, while it lasted. He had more than most men of the gift of forgetting himself in the excitement of getting a job to come right—any old job, the dictating of letters, anything. And just now the affairs of his firm were of quite stirring interest. Like many others it had been making large losses for several years. Bell's game was to keep these losses as low as he could without stopping the work and wages of a moorland village-ful of people who spun and wove cotton for Bell to sell for less than it cost to make it. This unacquisitive practice brought Bell into great infamy. Most of his fellow-employers wanted to close all the factories down, or half close them down, and leave the work-people to live on their fat. So Bell was an arrant traitor to them. Still, he was an employer: and so, to ardent Socialist eyes, he was a sucker of blood, *ex officio*. This lively cross-fire of censures braced Bell. If it had to be woe unto you when all men spoke well of you, it might be safer when everyone slated you hard. Anyhow it livened you up, like a good stinging wind that has blown across snow. While he schemed to find some not quite ruinous sale for the stuff that piled itself up at the mills, Bell could forget the thing that had clawed him in its clutch during the night.

But the clouds return after the rain: luncheon-time set his mind free to worry, the way your sore tongue returns and returns to the amusement of hurting itself on the sharp point of a tooth lately broken. He lunched at the club; and twice in the one hour it took him, his mind accused younger members of paying him the pestilential kind of unarguing deference which is really the civil refusal of youth to keep its communications open with age. Could they have noticed the way he walked down the stairs—a canny way, like a horse's when it is afraid on a slippery slope? One younger man opened the door of the billiard-room for him. Damn these good manners that ain't good at all.

Going home at twilight, in the tram, Bell thought over all this so absorbedly that he kept his legs crossed the whole way. So, when he stood up, to get off, his right leg had gone clean asleep. It was only asleep in the common and blameless way. Still he couldn't know that, at first. For all he could tell, a second stroke might have fallen, and this time a real knock-out. Of course he kept his fears dark; still, he stepped off the car with such unconcealable care that the conductor slipped a friendly hand under his arm and led him slowly to the safety of the footpath, like a blind man or a drunk.

When Bell had walked a few yards by himself the extra numbness was gone. But the other numbness remained. And so did the feel of that patiently guarding hand under his arm. Of course he had not needed it. Still, perhaps he would, presently. *Mene, mene, etc.*—every wall seemed to be covered with sinister shreds of writing. An object for everybody's protection, a call on everyone's forbearance—that was the kind of pest that he might become. Soon, too, perhaps. This kind of plague crept on and on. It never turned back. Five years might bring an invalid-chair and a male nurse to put him to bed and to see that he was carted securely about from place to place, to sprawl in the sun—Mentone, the Canaries, Egypt, all the places to which the *passés* butterflies of our commonwealth were brought to lie out and doze in the warmth when too much eating and idling had brought them back all the way to the status of larvae. Disgusting!

Bell gazed steadily into this smiling future, while eating his dinner alone. From the table he went straight, like a man who knew what he needed, to that shelf in his study on which there were all his pet Alpine books. No other sport had ever so wholly ravished his soul as mountaineering. On the high snows it seemed as if magical fires were lit in your blood; the flame of life burned amazingly; something was added unto a man as divine as whatever it is that makes its way into the vapid juice of a fruit and turns it to wine. Nowhere else in the world was the taste of success so wholly and indefeasibly sweet as it was on the tip of some spire of granite and ice that had all but turned you back in despair by the Daphnean rigour of its resistance. There, uplifted on the swell of the round earth, you could see how men had come to dream Gardens of Eden and Ages of Gold.

He took from the shelf a great climber's narratives of his greatest adventures. Two of these, in especial, could always entrance Bell as soon as he had read a few lines: their vividness gave him an almost physical sense of what they described. Each was a case of cutting steps up a long and extremely steep slope of ice. And in each case the slope had, at one point, ceased even to slope. For just a few feet of its height it had become as vertical as the wall of a house: each man of the party had had to hold himself in to the perpendicular wall by sheer strength and good hand-hold, against gravitation.

In each case the party had come safely through. But with how big a margin of safety, as engineers say? Bell wondered. A pretty big one, he fancied. Few good climbers slipped in really difficult places; all their faculties were bent up too intently for that, with danger about; they were above their own everyday form. But what if such a party were to try paring and paring away at that pretty wide margin? Something like an experiment, that! To what untold heights of achievement might not the party attain before all the margin was gone! And of course the party might be a party of one.

Bell had once had a holiday dream of climbing a crag that grew steeper and steeper till it was vertical first, and then overhung, more and more, but still he climbed on and on because the crag beetled out over a warm summer sea, so that, when he lost hold in the end, he would only fall from one pleasure into another, out of a mountaineer's paradise into a swimmer's. Cut out the old fear of death in that way, or some other, and—why, you could do anything.

As he sat back with the open book on his knees, a light wind stirred the trees in the garden. It may have been this that called up another old notion of his. This one had visited him in a wood close to Arras, in 1916. During some dark windless weeks of that autumn the unfallen leaves had been fading inertly from green to a dull rusty red, and so down to a dead russet brown; the whole burning heart of the year was collapsing into shabby ashes. Then a night of frost came and then a gale on a day of broken sunshine thrown wildly about between clouds. As the gale stripped the trees it had seemed almost to blow them aflame; sparks of brave yellow flew in the air; the dun beech-leaves took light and fell lustrously. Somehow the sight had filled Bell, at the time, with a wish that, when he had to go, he might do it like that—all a-stir and a-glow, by one of the "violent" deaths, as most of the easy ones seemed to be called. Anything but to lie on a bed in a hushed room, with the lights low and life's jolly noises shut out, and people whispering among the shadows. One wrench for the undecayed body, and then unbreakable sleep—what end could equal it?

Now, almost suddenly, these several notions ran into one, as raindrops do on a newly wet window. Here was the moment to put into practice that old and sound choice of his between the long decrepitude of the flesh and the one clean cut and summary pang that save you it all. Suicide? Oh! no. But just to carry on, right to the end, the piquant experiment of paring and paring away that limiting and restraining margin of safety which mountaineers, even the boldest, keep in reserve. Had not all things conspired to free him from too much love of remaining alive—bereavement and baulked hope and now this first lick of fire from heaven, soon to blast the whole of him by degrees? Why, fate had brought him the fulfilment of his old dream. No precipice in the world would now have an abhorred death waiting at its foot—merely a warm quiet sea of painless forgetfulness.

Only—he must be quick, before the accursed thing that was setting to work on him could pith so much of the vigour out of his body that he could not make his own way to a place—already he had a good place in his mind—where he might try the thing out.

At the end of September a savoursome blend of jollity and melancholy pervades the little Val d'Anniviers. The summer hotels of Zinal at the head of the valley, are closing. Down the bridle-path, through forests of fir, the hotel staffs stream along joyously, laden with the year's vintage of tips, to their snug winter homes in the Rhone Valley below. Reconverted, after four months of restraint and disguise, into young, natural Swiss men and women, they caper like Alpine cows let out in the spring. Shouting, chaffing and singing, they seem to flout with their merriment Nature's yearly menace to marmots and men. And Nature answers them back. Almost hour by hour the new snow creeps down the forested slopes of the valley and grizzles more of its firs; the morning dew lies late, and even at noon the weakening sun hangs lazily low above the main chain of the Alps. You feel, all about you, a big closing-in, the rustle of a heavy curtain falling upon a good time that is played out at last.

As Bell walked the six miles up from Vissoye to Zinal, he breasted that jovial current of waiters and chamber-maids thawed and re-humanised. Jove! they were good to see and to hear, with their jokes and catches and bold, friendly, unobsequious looks at any man and brother they met. But everything was good in this place. Even the smell of Vissoye and its pigs, as he passed, had been the smell of the best holiday of his boyhood. How he had liked life—every bit of it, coloured or plain, the high lights and the low! Even the jars had been part of the makings of the incomparable adventure. He wondered whether the mere feel of things—common things, all sorts of things—could ever have given anyone else such raptures of secret contentment as they had given to him.

He had made sure of a room at Zinal. He dined by the light of one lamp in a corner of the hotel's dining-room, now empty and shadowy. An elderly woman waited upon him; everyone else in the house had gone down the valley; she had been left for a week or two more, to cook, wait, make a bed and draw out a bill for anyone mad enough to turn up so belatedly. Bell had known her for thirty years—ever since her marriage to an old guide of his, recently killed on the Meije. She told him how their son Pierre was now a guide too, rather to her alarm. She seemed amazingly glad to see Bell, as if he were a bit of some good old world that had been slipping away. And he——? she asked. Was he making a *grande course,* as always? Surely not, at this time of year?

He fenced with her apt, friendly questions. He felt like a liar. Indeed, he was one, pretty well; for he fully meant to deceive. He would go for a walk by himself, he said, after breakfast tomorrow—perhaps to the Arpitetta Alp only, perhaps rather further.

She looked at him sadly, with pleasant directness. "All alone now!" she said simply. "And once it was you and Madame—and Gaspard and me. Ah! the good times." She had all humanity's fate in her face, like an old woman drawn by Rembrandt—hopes and happy love and then the dust of the day, dimming the roses, and then great loneliness and unconsolable tears. Would Monsieur have coffee she asked.

Bell could face her no longer. It was too treacherous. No, he said, he would want nothing more. Let her go to bed early, like all the good marmots. So would he too, when he had smoked a little end of tobacco.

When she was gone, he sat by a fire of logs she had lit for him in the small smoking-room. To his surprise he found he had nothing to do. There could be no saying good-bye, no specious last letter to write, no will to be made, no manifesto of any sort to be left. People do not do such things just before unforeseen accidents—for the wood must look raw at the break. A real good tip for the widow of Gaspard would have to be left in an obvious place: that was all.

It went beyond having nothing to do. There was nothing to think. He had no fear of *post mortem* torture to busy his brain, for the God of his faith was no fiend. He was equally void of covetous hopes of a sensational "good time" when the breath should be out of his body. So far he might have expected his mind to be free. The strange thing was to find how much of one's usual matter for thought is taken away if, in twenty hours or so, one will have nothing whatever to fix up or to see to, no house or business to run, no social beat to patrol, no arts or letters to care for, nor "public duties" to mind. It was a release. But it was a queer one—a kind of vacuous and disquieting freedom, such as a man might attain who was suddenly let off the pressure of gravitation, so that he needn't keep his feet down to the earth any more—in fact couldn't press on it hard if he tried, and so couldn't get any purchase for putting forth his strength upon anything at all. Bell's released mind did its best to think firmly of what he was going to do the next day. But no firmness came: the levers of thought could not find any fulcrum; they worked at a loss feebly and fumblingly.

He brought over the lamp to review the Inn's tiny library—two shelves freakishly peopled with the printed leavings of guests lettered, half-lettered, unlettered, conventional, independent and odd. There was the common aphrodisiac novel of commerce; there was *The Vicar of Wakefield,* all golden sunshine and wit; there were Nat Gould and the wise, humane book of the great William James on the incessant endeavour of men to find or to imagine some larger life on which to rest the frail and soon-tired figure of their own. Yes, that was it: something to lean against: something sure not to give when you put your whole weight on it, in any state of yourself: that was where peace and strength were to be had; nowhere else. So he fancied, at least: he could not be sure: he was still in that vacuum where his thought had no pivot to work on: the wheels did not bite on the road; the cogs would not engage; he thought and he felt, but gropingly, not with the sure and eager drive of a mind and heart that have found themselves by forgetting themselves.

The place that Bell had picked for his purpose was on the West side of the Schallijoch. The Schallijoch, as you may know, is a dip in the ridge that joins the Weisshorn to the Schallihorn. Even the lowest point of the dip is more than 12,000 feet high. The last part of the rise to the ridge from the West is up one of the steepest slopes of ice that are climbed. That is if you mount it where it is least steep. At some other points it is steeper than any slope that is climbed, or thought to be climbable. The surface of this wall of ice undulates like a sheet of hammered copper—here a concave patch and there a convex one. Though the wall, at its steepest, leans back from the straight, as a whole, it has parts—the upper halves of these hollows and lower of these bulges—at which it is vertical for some feet at a time; and at two or three parts it even overhangs slightly. These last, avoided by climbers happily wedded to life, were what Bell had in mind. He would start up the wall at the steepest part he could find; as he went on, he would make, at each stage, for the point where there seemed to be most an overhang. He would do the thing honestly—try all that was in him to bring the climb off, reach the ridge and prove that, in this small matter, man could do more than he knew. With careful timing he would be up, if up at all, about dusk. In that unlikely event he would carry the test a step further and try to come down his ice ladder by feel, in the dark, instead of descending the gentle snow slopes on the Eastern side of the pass.

He worked out a time-table. Three hours' walk up to the Arpitetta Alp from Zinal. Three more up from the Alp to the foot of the final icewall. Half an hour for eating; another half hour for sundries and lateage. Four for the ultimate work on the wall. Eleven hours in all. Tomorrow's evening dusk would be over by seven. He would push off at eight in the morning.

Probably you would have thought him rather a pleasant sight as he quitted Zinal—the outward figure of a hale, fit mountaineer; just a little stricken with years, but vigorous; brindled but not at all bald; leanly and brownly good-looking, turning out by himself, with his axe under his arm and a little luncheon in his pocket, for a walk among the feet of sporting old friends like the Weisshorn and Roth-horn. How can you tell by the looks of a man that he would not feel the point of a pin if you ran it into his thigh, or that this exemption from pain is causing any disturbance of his spirits?

Nobody was to be seen at the emerald Alp of Arpitetta. Like the almost deserted Zinal, like yesterday's valley path streaming with walkers carrying bundles, the empty hovels on the Alp recalled the sight of a whole countryside in flight before the army of an invader. The ashes left from the cheesemaker's fire were wet with drippings from the roof; the rough wooden crane used for swinging the cauldron over the flames flapped in a draught from the door. Outside, the intoxicant beauty of gentian and orchis was over for the year; the rich grass had spread back over the trodden mud of the milking-place; but snow was lying a few hundred feet higher up. The invader was near.

Bell's legs were liking the work. The numb one was numb, but it did not give out: it would not let him down. By one o'clock he had reached the tail end—some would call it the snout—of the big Weisshorn Glacier, eaten his rations and set a first foot on the rough convex swell of honey-combed ice with water flushing out its millions of cells; for the sun was on it. He pawed the stuff tenderly with his axe. Perdition catch his soul but he did love it—strong as iron, carvable as cheese; what genius could have conceived so delicious a union of opposites if, by some disaster, no glaciers had been made?

By three o'clock he was through the freak shapes of the ice-fall, across the snowfield above it and close to the wall that he sought. Yes, its great width and height had the wavy surface that he remembered. It showed like a vast relief map of some low rolling downland, modelled in ice and then set up to stand on its edge. Off to his right, as he looked up, the general angle was easiest. That was the regular way—very steep but quite practicable. That was of no use for his purpose. Far away to his left the slope looked ferocious enough. But down it an almost continuous fall of stones of all sizes, broken away from the sun-warmed rocks of the Weisshorn, came sliding and hissing, or bounding and smashing explosively. That was no use either. That way would be suicide, not experiment.

He soon saw what he wanted—almost directly above him. There, nearly all the way up to the ridge, the ice was steep and bare and blue, and the face of it waved more at this place than anywhere else. Several broad bosses of rocks must have underlain the smooth surface. Over these the close-fitting ice swelled like a stocking upon a bent knee. Up to the centre of each of these bosses it bulged out overhangingly; just above each centre it would recede at a more merciful angle; but nowhere in the whole thousand feet of ascent would a man have a foothold to stand on, unless he made it.

Bell conscientiously tightened each boot-lace and puttee-string. Then he set off for the point where he had descried the best overhangs. It was half-way, as he judged, to the top of the wall. If he should conquer that one, then he would look for another, more bulgy.

He cut his steps with almost fanatical care. He had a disagreeable sense of doing something furtive: he couldn't help asking himself, against his own will, "What if somebody saw?" Damn somebody, another part of him said. Still, he cut every step as if he defied the whole solar system to say that it was not the work of a good craftsman bent upon keeping alive. So he rose slowly. It took a good two hours' work to mount a third of the way to the ridge. But then he was close to what mattered more—the great bulge that he was making for.

The bulge stood out like a gigantic blister upon the face of the ice. It must have been forty feet in diameter and it jutted so much that a stone dropped from its outermost point would only have touched the slope again some fifty feet lower. So the climax had come. To reach that outermost point he would have to climb for about twenty feet as you climb up the under side of a ladder that leans against a wall. And he would have to make the ladder, rung by rung, as he climbed it—fashion each rung out of the ice with his axe, held in one hand, while with the other hand and both feet he clung to three of the rungs made already, and held up the body against the drag of its weight. Every rung would have to be made like a letter-box in a door, big enough for the toe of a boot to go in, but so shaped that, when a hand entered, the fingers could bend down inside and grip as you grip the top of a fence. The grand, the crucial question was how long one hand and one arm could hold the body in to the projecting ice-wall. For what part of the two hours or so that the other labouring hand might require to cut that fantastical staircase? Of course, if his axe should slip out of his hand, or if one step should break, that would end the affair. But away with the thought of any such bungling.

The moment the overhang started Bell discovered the theory of gravitation to be exceedingly true. The work was amazingly hard. When he had carved five letter-boxes, and used them, an hour had gone. He carved five more and observed that daylight was failing. Behind his back an unsensational sunset was going on at its ease. His left hand was chilled almost dead with all the ice it had gripped; his right wrist was swollen and sore with the intensity of the axe-work; his right knee had begun to shake as uncontrollably as chattering teeth; he heard his breath as if it were somebody else's: it made a dry rustling noise, like a bird struggling silently in the hand.

The centre of the boss was now, he reckoned, some eight feet above his head. Beyond it he could see nothing as yet, but a tranquil sky with a rose-coloured flush dying out of it. Five letter-boxes more, he thought, might take him up to the nipple of this frozen breast and bring the receding slope of its upper half into his sight. It was just at this point that it struck him as a clear, sober matter of fact that he could not get up those eight feet. His strength was running out fast: one more good letter-box was all that he could conceive himself able to make. He made it, hacking away with slow, painful strokes, his axe-handle slippery with his sweat. He reached up his left hand to grab the new hold and dragged a foot up to its new place below. Then, just to go down fighting, he went through the movements of starting to chip out yet another step. Second by second the effort held out; his strokes were the taps of a child; his wrist felt like breaking; yet somehow he finished the hole and forced his left hand to rise up to it: then he even hauled up in its turn a right foot of infinite weight: the poor quivering knee had to straighten out next, and did it, after a long, doubtful struggle. But that was the end, he felt, of all possible effort.

By this time all his senses had the morbid exultation that will sometimes come of fierce physical effort. His mind was at leisure, after a fashion. He was fully aware of the sunset; he did not miss the charm of its sabbatical calm: the majesty and mystery of mountains were still there, all right. A verse he had liked as a boy came into his head, as beautiful things that have built themselves into your mind are apt to do at a crisis—as people who once went to church will cry out "Oh! God!" when a smash comes.

And here indeed might death be fair
If death be dying into air
And souls evanished mix with the
Illumined sky, eternal sea.

But no pretty dying for him, if death could be still headed off. He started desperately to try again, sweating and straining. No good: the feeble strokes of his axe scarcely scratched the bare ice; his left hand was frost-bitten now, past feeling anything. Only five feet to relative safety, but five more than any spur worn by his will could drive the spent body. "I'm done," he said, and ceased to struggle upwards.

Some innate impulse to take the thing well and not let human dignity down at a pinch kept him resolved to hold on, foot and hand, to the last moment possible.

While he clung so, the sun left him. A high Alpine sunset is sudden, like tropical ones. A cold, sharp-edged shadow raced up from the valley, chasing the sunlight before it. Pursuer and fugitive scudded up over the tops of the firs and across the bright green of the Alp Bell had passed, and then up the ice-fall and on up the wall till the shadow came down like a great frigid hand on the sweaty back of his neck. Next moment the last warmth and light fleeted up out of sight, over the bulge. As his gaze followed, his cheeks felt the sting of a few falling granules of ice; little chips of it, rather; even a few rather big ones. A trickle of ice scraps seemed to be sliding down the upper half of the bulge, to dive into space on reaching its centre—most of them clear of his back.

Queer! Was an ice avalanche coming? No need to suppose it, though. Glaciers, crushed and huddled things, always heaving and cracking, played curious tricks and ground out all sorts of freak rubbish. Oh! let the ice do what it liked, all his business with it was done; all that he could now attend to was a kind of dream noise, big, muted and almost asleep, that the torrent was making, enormously far off, down in the blackening trench of the valley—that and a kind of emotional dream of himself, the dying man doing his best to take leave as was meet—a figure at which he could look, as it were, from outside, and dreamily feel it to be rather touching.

Into this semi-dream there managed to enter, also, a sound more abrupt—a little noise like the low startled cry that some women give when they see a horse fall or a big window is smashed. The cry worked itself into his dream, but also it roused him. "Getting light-headed," he thought. But he wasn't. Almost as quick as that thought, a new sound, a light hissing rub, rushed down to his ears and an ice-axe slid over the bulge overhead and out into the air: it whizzed past the back of his head.

To anyone versed in high mountains an ice-axe loose and falling in any such place is a portent of horror, like a child's pony galloping riderless home or a boat adrift, bottom uppermost in a Thames lasher. It means that somebody may have just lost the power to move, without help, at a place where a man unable to move will soon be unable to live. Suddenly Bell's mind took eyes to itself; it saw a party of some sort above him, trying to cut its way down the ice wall, straight towards the deadly bulge that now beetled over himself. At this hour! And by such a route! They must be mad; so he thought—forgetting himself. And now one of them was disabled—perhaps had disabled the whole of his party—tethered it to the ice-wall. The idea was frightful to Bell.

Another sound came. From somewhere not far overhead there broke, like an explosion, the singular cry that Swiss peasants and some mountaineers employ as a long-distance hail. No other noise of purely human production will carry so far. Harsh, wild and long, it starts, as the noise of a rocket does, at its maximum loudness, and then wails itself out in a dying fall that has an effect of collapse into despair. Though commonly uttered on quite cheerful occasions, it might be the passionate scream of some wretched animal terrified by the solitude of a desolate place and trying to empty into one impetuous lamentation all its burden of loneliness and desire.

Bell held his breath as the sinking shriek thinned away into silence. Then he counted off the seconds half-aloud, by guess work, as bomb-throwers learnt how to do in the war. The count ran to seven—eight—nine—and, just as Bell was muttering "Ten," the great yell smashed into the silence again. Yes: he had expected that. Someone above was in the last extremity of danger—was trying the last shift of all, the most all-but-hopeless of all—was sending out the Alpine signal of distress into this stone and snow desert where autumn and night had joined to make it utterly certain that no answer could come. It was like praying to God, for dear life, that a well of fresh water might open itself in the dry middle of the Sahara.

Up to that point of time, as you have seen, Bell had been the kind of dual creature that most of us are for nearly the whole of our days. Part of him had toiled, sweated and ached, and another part of him had been sorry for that one. But, from the moment the second yell came, this twofold arrangement was somehow abolished. All craving or need for any part of himself to be troubled about any other was over; now there was nothing at all to work out any more, no next move to be consciously planned, nor hesitant will to be coaxed or hustled, nor any plaguey choice to be made. All of the man was one unit at last, and it lived intently and intensely, moved by some force which it had no more desire to question than flames have to ask "Why burn upward?"

The next mystery was that out of the mind so suddenly lightened there seemed, as it were, to overflow lightness into Bell's body of lead. Strangely empowered, his left foot was rising already to thrust itself into the next letter-box; almost gaily his right arm, freed from its pre-occupation with pain, was beginning to hack a new hand-hold above. How long it took him to make he could not have told, then or after. For time, too, was abolished; long trains of executive, practical thought could run on to their end instantaneously; courses, whole courses, of study of relevant things—of the state of the ice, minute changes of gradient, the swift regelation following sundown—were carried out without any sense of duration. One of the revelatory trances had come, in which even a plain man sees for once that an eternity need not be long and that in a single moment he may have everlasting life.

A minor, but still a piquant, discovery was that he had never really known till now what it was to cut a good sizable strip off that old margin of safety which he had imagined himself to have all but used up. His new letter-boxes were marvels of sketchy adequacy; they were high art in the skimpiness of the means that they took to their end; triumphs of confident "cheek" to Nature, they bluffed that august power quite wittily. Almost before the vocalist overhead had completed the long S.O.S. of the mountains—it takes three minutes in all—Bell had his chest up to the dead centre of the bulge and saw what he had come for.

Some thirty feet higher up, a woman in mountain kit, with no axe and no hold for hand or foot, was dangling at a long rope's end. Her body revolved a little as it hung against the steep ice, but she was making no voluntary movement. The rope constricting her chest was held with one straining hand by a man perched eighty feet higher up. He was clearly unable to move, hand or foot, without being dragged off his stance by the weight of the woman. He stood on one foot—his right: it seemed to be firmly placed, on a tiny step; and a little above his hand, he had the pick of his axe driven well into the ice. To the steel bracket thus formed by the axe-head the man was holding on stoutly with his right hand.

The sorry sight explained itself. The woman must have been cutting steps down the slope; she must have slipped from a step, and dropped her axe with the shock. The man had checked her fall well, but both were hung up as immovably as a couple of stoats nailed to a gamekeeper's door. And now the rope must be slowly killing the woman. Just as Bell's head topped the bulge she called out in a strangled voice to the man, "Can you cut the rope, Teddy? I'm done, anyhow. Think of the kiddies. You *must.*" The man held on.

Bell gave tongue as loud as the dry brown fur lining his mouth would allow. "Well held, Sir," he roared. "It's all right, I'm coming."

Not once in a long and respectable Alpine career had Bell thought he would ever entrust his person to ledges quite so narrow as those on which he made the rest of his way up to that pendant woman. And yet he had never, in any hard place, felt such absolute freedom from any uneasiness. As he romped up, he sang out, at intervals "There in three minutes," "Just two minutes more," "Only one minute more," "Half a shake—I'm just there." Then he arrived. He cut a big step close to where the woman's feet hung, planted his own firmly on it, and then stooping and straightening up again, took the weight of her, sitting, on his right shoulder. Lest she be fainting he put up his right hand behind her, to hold her in place.

She was no fainter, though she was white, yellow, greenish all the bad colours that beauty itself may have to put on in bad times. "She's a good 'un," Bell thought, as she sat quiet, panting.

"*You're* a great sportsman," she gasped, when she had breath enough.

Feeling all the weight off the rope of a sudden, the man above shouted down thickly, "Sure you have got her, Sir?"

"Right as rain," she called up from her perch.

Bell added, "Leave the rope slack, and dig in. We'll come up when you're comfy."

The man gave a tuneless yodel of joy and was plying his axe the same instant; chips and wedges of ice came pelting down from the great step that he must be cutting, from which to make the whole caravan fast. In five minutes he ceased hacking, braced himself, drew in the slack of the rope and announced that now he could hold up a cow for a day.

Bell let the woman cannily down till her feet found a trim

ledge that he had managed to scratch out while holding her up. But some four or five feet of smooth ledgeless ice intervened between this and the lowest step the woman had cut, coming down, before she slipped off. Some new ones had to be made. "Care to cut 'em?" Bell asked. "Or shall I?"

She ruefully opened the hands in which no axe was now held. "I dropped it," she said, "like a mug. I feel sick with shame."

"Have mine," he said holding it out.

Her open boy face shone with joyous relief, as if at a gift of free absolution from sin. Even now their lives hung on this axe that he was entrusting to her, the convicted axe-dropper. She took it. "You are a very generous person," she said. "Now I'll unrope, and go up by myself, and you shall tie on."

He shook his head firmly. "You mustn't unrope."

Her eyes broke out in a quick sparkle of anger. "You've *got* to rope up," she said, flushing. "I know that I've done a dud thing and can't preach. But what about you? Climbing alone! coming up out of nowhere, almost at night. Up a worse slope than this beast! Think it bears looking into? Eh? Well, do you mean to rope up, or shall both of us climb in this way that you seem to think right?"

Bell fairly funked the scrutiny of the young woman's spirited simplicity. When once simplicity sets out to inquire, what else is so penetrating? "Well, you tie on in the middle," he said, "and I at the end."

"That's fair," she agreed. A few feet of spare rope were let down by her husband. In two or three minutes, at most, the man who would have shuffled off the mortal coil was securely girt with the most delectable of its loops, the cheerfullest symbol of human determination not to withdraw from the banquet of life—only to salt a dish now and then with a few little hazards.

The last daylight was gone when the three stood safe on the level roof of the ridge, scrunching its gritty granular snow somewhat shyly, though partly kept in countenance by the dark, which is itself a shy, friendly thing. Bell, now a mere dual creature again, had been wondering, all the way up the last flight of ice stairs, how he should give these married lovers a chance to re-assert their lately threatened right to possession of each other's lips. Best, he thought, just to turn his back on them when he got up, and try to look busy, coiling the rope.

But they also seemed to have some sort of plan. The man was waiting above the last step, to shake Bell by the hand—really to shake him—and mumbling something which Bell did not desire to make out more clearly. The cup of his consternation was filled when the lady raised his disengaged hand to her lips, a gesture for which he had not been prepared by her vivacity lower down.

Then, with one silent consent, they all stampeded away from the key of emotion. "You travel light, Sir," said Bell, just to say something trivial. The other two seemed to carry not so much as a prune or a biscuit between them.

"Well——" said the man, and then Bell imagined the man must be having a quiet laugh in the dark.

"Oh! I know I can't talk," Bell admitted. "The fact is I didn't expect to be coming right over the Pass."

"Same here," said the man. "We just walked up from Randa—meant to go only as far as the hut for the Weisshorn, eat our sandwiches there and go back to dinner. Then—it *was* rather mad, but the snow was so toppingly good—we thought we might just rush the Schallijoch before dark, sleep at Zinal and come back to-morrow."

"Gosh! it was rash!" exclaimed Bell, off his guard. He felt sure the next instant, the man was quite seeing the humour of such a rebuke from such a sinner. Hastily trying to cover the slip, Bell made another. He asked, "How on earth did you miss the way down?"

The man didn't exactly say, "How did *you* miss the way up?" but he did say, "Yes, it was stupid, but—well you know how it isn't so easy to see a way down from above as it is from below?"

"Hadn't we better push off?" said Bell rather hurriedly. "We'll be getting friz, up here." But it was not the cold that he minded. It was the heat. It felt as if he couldn't move his tongue without burning his fingers.

The three truants had luck. Just such a full moon as they needed, not having a lantern, was on the point of rising from behind the snowy mass of the Mischabel, beyond the forest glen of the Visp. The mounting light could no longer contain itself. Its bright animation was pulsing up the dark violet of the sky in tremulous waves. It would be easy, by such a light as was coming, to follow the downward track left by the couple, on their way up, almost to the door of the old Weisshorn hut, a refuge squat, squalid, flea-haunted and cramped, but divinely rich in raw materials for manufacturing heat, against a long night of hard frost.

At any time it is rather exciting to walk in the dark, and in silence, with anyone whom you like but don't yet know very well. What is he thinking about? You? And, if so, in what way? Barring you? Liking you? Wanting to throw down the conventional fence and talk frankly? An hour or two of this blindfold contact between mind and mind may so work on them both that when their eyes meet under a lamp at the end of the walk it may feel as if they had

had a long and intimate conversation, leaving each of them just slightly anxious to know that the other has taken nothing amiss. Even thus, with friendly and deprecatory looks, did Bell and the strangers regard each other by candle-light two hours later, among the strong shadows and smells of the hut.

In ten minutes more the man's wife, who had walked like a true Joan of Arc, was exercising the blessed privilege of healthy and tired young people of thirty or so. While she slept like a prosperous babe, her man and Bell smoked as they lay in the hay at the big sleeping-shelf's other end. Smoking helps to keep talk good. A man can puff at his pipe between each thing he really wants to say and the next. No gap-filling rubble is required.

Bell ascertained first that the man's name was Gollen and that he was a doctor—the Harley Street species of doctor. Bell gave in return his own name and description. Then they enjoyed one of those unembarrassing pauses. Then Bell said, somewhat brusquely, "There's one thing we have to get straight."

"Go it," said Gollen.

"You seem to imagine you're under some sort of obligation to me."

"Well, you see, we're alive. And, before you appeared, our number was up."

"So was mine."

"Oh! everyone's is, in a sense. 'All condemned to death,' doesn't somebody say, 'with an indefinite reprieve.' But ours wasn't indefinite. We were booked to go West in five minutes."

"I was to do it in one. In less. I should have dropped off my holds in ten seconds if you people hadn't blown in."

"Hullo?"

"Sure thing. I was done. I had never known until then how far doneness could go. That's how it felt, anyhow. Then your wife's axe came along. That by itself held me on for a jiffy or two. And then you hollered—gad! you *can* holler—and everything changed. There was something new in me, or round me, at work on me somehow. Every bit of soreness and worry and funk was taken right off me—nothing was left in the world but one energy—just an enveloping, mastering sort of a push. It went up like a flame and it took me along—it made everything easy and light. And it wasn't only a thing in the mind. Old brother body himself was roped into the movement: some of the waft of this impulse seemed to get itself into my muscles. D'you follow these ravings?"

"Rather. Physicians aren't the fools that they were. We don't go on missing out what the mind—or the soul, if you like—has to say to all the dynamic affairs of the body."

Bell puffed his pipe for a while. Then he said "See? That's

how you two preserved me. So if thanking is what we're about, thanky kindly."

Gollen, too, smoked in silence for the next minute or two, before asking "The ice overhung where you were when I first caterwauled?"

"Can't tell you the angle. Hadn't got a clinometer thing. Of course it wasn't a motoring road."

Gollen laughed. Bell liked Gollen's face when he laughed, so far as it could be seen among the tangle of dry shadows thrown about the hut by a small flame that still leapt in the stove. Gollen's face made Bell think of a trade term—"good ordinary." He had blunt goodish features, strong and good-tempered. A straight, friendly man, you would say, and easily amused; a good man to be in a hole with. Bell enjoyed such men. They made the world go round. As he was thinking so, Gollen suddenly asked, "I say—why did you do it?"

As Bell did not answer at once, Gollen added, "Of course, it's cheek—asking. Tell me to go to Hell, if you like, and I'll warmly approve. Only, well—I'm a doctor."

Bell cut the thing short. He answered at once what Gollen might go on to ask in another few minutes. "Yes—the spring's running dry. The salt losing its savour, you know—the wine going flat. And worse coming."

Again Gollen did the bold thing. "Any particular evil?" he said.

Bell liked the man. And when two men would both have been dead a few hours ago if either had failed at a pinch, they may soon get on terms. Bell avowed the whole business—his symptoms, his surmises and disgusts and his specious experiment.

Gollen listened as wise doctors do. "Did that numbness cramp you to-day?" he asked at the end.

"No. But it was there all the day—except just the time—ten minutes or so, I suppose—when——" Bell hesitated for a moment.

"When you were in action?" said Gollen.

"Action?"

"Oh! I don't mean just doing violent things out of doors—pressing triggers or lassoing cows. I mean getting every Jack fibre there is in your nature alive and utterly turned on to something outside you—absorbed in it, lost in it—every bit of your consciousness taken up into some ecstasy of endeavour that's passion and peace."

Bell nodded, and Gollen went on. "I guess the great artists—all sorts of 'em—know how to bring the fit on, or it comes when they're at the top of their form—they seem to get further and further above 'emselves—hold the note out in a way that we can't—bring every tissue they have in their being to bear on the effort to get a wee touch to come right. Saints, too, I suppose—the pukka ones, like Francis, the man at Assisi: they have the knack too: they can get more alive; they've found how to exist at a sort of top pressure. I fancy all of us get just a glimpse of the thing now and then—of what living might be, you know—at a great turn in a game, or when we're in love, or if some beautiful thing in a book bowls us over. Only, we can't hold the note, or we can't do it yet: the pitch is too high for our reach; so we flop back into flatness. But we shall get there. I do believe that. What we've done since we started as jelly-fish is to get more and more of ourselves into action, and we shall go on until we are as much more in action—real true action—than now, as we are now than when we were jelly-fish. Why, in a few thousand years we may all be able to live half our time as you lived to-day for ten minutes."

"Something in that," Bell assented.

Gollen apologised meekly. "Sorry to verge upon 'uplift.' Still, one can't always bother about the convention that talk has got to be pessimist piffle."

Bell nodded. Reigning conventions had few less dutiful followers than he.

They smoked again for a while. Presently Gollen said, "How goes the weather?" He rose and opened the door of the hut very quietly. Bell followed him out to the hut's tiny terrace.

Nothing at all was wrong with that night. Beyond the queenly white shape of Mont Rose the moon rode gloriously high, burnished and flashing with frost, above sleeping Lombardy. Gowned in new snow and bejewelled with sparkles of light, the Weisshorn, the greatest great lady in Nature, looked as lovely to Bell as when the first sight of that pale supreme grace had taken his breath away in his youth. At the height where they stood the frost had silenced every trickle of water, leaving all space to be filled with subtler challenges to the ear. The air almost crackled with crispness: it was alive with the massed animation of millions of infinitesimal crystallisations. The Schalliberg Glacier, a little away to their right, had its own living whisper, the sum of the innumerable tiny creaks and fractures of its jostling molecules of ice. Up here, where the quiet of night was suffused with this audible stir of the forces fashioning the earth, it felt as if some murmurous joint voice of all existence were abroad and life itself were trying to make its high urgency felt.

"Pretty good!" Gollen said presently.

"Yes, it's all right," answered Bell.

Gollen waited a minute or two. Then he asked, "Is it all right—enough?"

"Oh! yes," said Bell. "I'm sticking on."